MW00626944

GOD, TORAH, MESSIAH

The Messianic Jewish Theology of Dr. Louis Goldberg

Edited by Dr. Richard A. Robinson

Purple Pomegranate Productions
San Francisco, CA

God, Torah, Messiah
The Messianic Jewish Theology of Dr. Louis Goldberg
Edited by Dr. Richard A. Robinson

A division of JEWS FOR JESUS™
Cover design and illustration by Steffi Ruben

For more information, including reprint permission, write to:
JEWS FOR JESUS™
60 Haight Street
San Francisco, CA 94102
USA
jewsforjesus.org
ISBN 10: 1-881022-85-5
ISBN 13: 978-1-881022-85-4

CONTENTS

FOREWORD

Richard Harvey

The contribution of Dr. Louis Goldberg to Messianic Jewish theology should not be underestimated. Whilst much of his active ministry was spent teaching Moody Bible Institute students the Old Testament, Jewish Studies and Jewish Evangelism, his contribution to Jewish missions and the Messianic movement was passionate, engaged, and scholarly. After writing a plethora of books and articles on Jewish studies, Bible commentaries, and Jewish evangelism, it was only toward the end of his life that he worked on Messianic Jewish theology in a systematic fashion.

I remember a cold February in the 1990s in Odessa, Ukraine, where I had the privilege of teaching courses alongside him at the Jews for Jesus' "School of the Prophets," a training school that would see a generation of Russian-speaking Jewish evangelists emerge in the former Soviet Union, Germany, and Israel. During breaks in our intensive teaching schedule (set by Avi Snyder, who put us to work on a full curriculum of Bible, Jewish history, religion and culture, and Jewish evangelism), we discussed the need for and possibilities of Messianic Jewish theology. Having surveyed the work of Hebrew Christian leaders like Jacob Jocz and Paul Levertoff, we regretted that no one in the contemporary Messianic movement had yet produced a work of Messianic Jewish theology that had the scholarship, authority, and relevance of these Hebrew Christian pioneers. Then Dr. Goldberg, with his curt, self-effacing, New York brand of humor, let slip "But I'm working on it, and I've got it right here"—showing me the contents of his suitcase, a manuscript of some several hundred pages. That was the beginnings of what would eventually become the present volume, now fittingly published as he would have wanted, with some further editing and redrafting from Rich Robinson and others.

Dr. Goldberg's contribution should not be assessed simply as a contribution to Messianic Jewish theology. In many respects he helped to *pioneer* the discipline. Always the man of peace in a field where controversy often raged, he was the accepted friend and advisor to many in the different streams of the movement. His contribution has always been pastoral, practical, exalting his Messiah and Lord, and building a bridge between the old-style Hebrew Christian tradition, the newer Messianic Jews of the 1970s onward, and with the ongoing priority of Jewish evangelism. His work remains an attempt to unite the Messianic movement around the core and essential beliefs, and to negotiate with alternative views wherever possible. The present volume displays both an incisive mind, a firm grasp on the essential truths of the Good News of the Messiah, combined with an open and discursive approach that deals with objections and misunderstandings to belief, and seeks to persuade by appeals to Scripture, faith, and commonsense logic.

Dr. Goldberg's writings have an apologetic edge and pastoral tone, whether he is dealing with philosophical conceptions of the nature of God, or whether he is helping the new believer understand the nature and uniqueness of Yeshua as the divine-human Messiah. He writes with the benefit of his training and background in engineering, with a clear plan, a well-constructed argument, and an economy of language to put his points across. Sections of his theology address—in a handy discipleship manual form—the theological issues from the perspectives of philosophy, Jewish interpretation, biblical exegesis, and the practical and pastoral consequences of each view. It is an ideal tool for the new or not-so-new Jewish believer in Jesus who wants to think clearly about their faith in the Messiah, or the interested Jewish or Christian reader.

In my recent defense of my PhD thesis on Messianic Jewish theology, I was asked a series of questions on my approach to the subject, on the Messianic Jewish theologians whose works I had referred to, and on my conclusions as to the nature of Messianic Jewish theology. One of the examiners specifically asked about Dr. Goldberg, whom I have been unable to categorise easily in the eight types of theology I had identified in the Messianic movement. "Where would you place him?" the senior academic asked. I admitted that I had not found it easy to locate him on the spectrum. He was more flexible than many in the dispensationalist school in seeing continuity between the Old and New Testament dispensations. His sympathy with Torah observance (in the light of Jesus' own practice and fulfillment of Torah) put him closer to the "Torah-positive" group of Messianic Jews than those who opposed such practices. But his unwillingness to compromise on the uniqueness of Christ and the priority of evangelism marked out his distinctive emphases also. My examiner agreed. "Yes, not everyone fits easily into a typology," he replied.

In my thesis I make particular reference to Dr. Goldberg's doctrine of God, and his discussions on Torah observance. I am delighted to see more of his materials on other key theological topics now made known, and am sure this edition of his work is a fitting tribute to his life and work. It is a privilege to have known him as a teacher and friend, and to see this work widely published. David Brickner, Rich Robinson, and others are to be congratulated on a fine job in assembling and editing the materials and circulating them in the present form, a fitting tribute to our friend, mentor, and teacher, and a lasting contribution to the field of Jewish mission and Messianic Jewish theology. Like the apostle Paul, Dr. Goldberg's passion and heart's desire was for his people to know his Messiah, and the work that follows will be an effective means to that end.

Richard Harvey teaches Hebrew Bible and Jewish Studies at All Nations Christian College in Ware, UK. He holds a PhD from the University of Wales where his dissertation was entitled, "Mapping Messianic Jewish Theology."

INTRODUCTION

Louis Goldberg (1923–2002) was a teacher, a scholar, an author, and "an itinerant pastor to hundreds of Messianic Jewish congregations."[1] As a Jewish follower of Yeshua the Messiah (his way of expressing the One whom most Christians called Jesus Christ), his career straddled the worlds of "Hebrew Christianity" and "Messianic Judaism," Israel and America, the academic and the practical.

The present book represents Louis Goldberg's last major contribution, though it remained uncompleted. In using this book, the reader should note that in the manuscript as it came into my hands were numerous places where footnotes were meant to be added, or sections where additional material was to be included. For the sake of providing a usable book, those missing sections are not indicated. However, I have included a few portions that remained in outline form, not yet developed.

From start to finish, this book has been through several hands. The initial preparation of the manuscript was done by Mitch Kolodin, whom I had the pleasure of meeting in the early 1990s. Mitch, a former student and assistant to Dr. Goldberg, transcribed much of the material from tapes and with his wife, Dawn, formatted the manuscript into editable form. Dr. Goldberg's daughter, Stephanie Goldberg, was of invaluable help in providing both her time as well as access to her father's files and books, which filled many filing cabinets and shelves! And I am grateful to the late Dr. Harold Hoehner who took time to check over the manuscript for format and consistency as well as for content. If the final result has any errors or has misstated anything that Dr. Goldberg intended to say, I take full responsibility.

Because of the incomplete nature of the book, as well as the fact that Dr. Goldberg was unable to approve the final result or clarify questions, it may be beneficial for those who wish to use this as a study textbook to also have an existing systematic theology alongside. Two such books are *Systematic Theology: An Introduction to Biblical Doctrine* by Wayne Grudem (1994) and *Christian Theology* by Millard J. Erickson (1983–85). This will help fill in the gaps and also lessen the possibility that Dr. Goldberg's thoughts have been mistated somewhere in the long process. Footnotes in brackets [like this—Ed.] were added by me to supplement the material by reference to other books of Dr. Goldberg or to clarify or fill in missing information.

Every effort was made to check the references against the specific editions that Dr. Goldberg indicated in his footnotes. Sometimes that was not possible and another, usually more recent, edition has been cited instead.

A word about the translation used for most of the Scripture citations. For various reasons, we were not in a position to go about securing the copyrights needed for translations such as the NIV. The public-domain King James Version (KJV), despite remaining the gold standard for a beautiful, flowing translation, would not be intelligible to many. I was happy to discover that the NET Bible was an evangelical translation that had minimal constraints and in fact was designed to be available for ministry uses. Their Bible and suite of Bible study tools is available at www.nextbible.org. I sometimes cited the NIV or NASB where it was felt those translations would more accurately reflect Dr. Goldberg's thinking. For example, in the chapter on the doctrine of the Holy Spirit, the NET often translated *ruach* as "breath," where NIV had "spirit." Both are legitimate translations, but in order for the discussion to make sense, I had to frequently note the differences between the NET and other versions. We utilized the text of the NET as found in the Accordance Bible program, "NET Bible®. First Edition. Version 3.2."

A word about the Scripture citations. It was decided to give, in the body of the text, the full text of the verses that Dr. Goldberg referenced, rather than just as a set of references to be looked up later. As a result, there are many passages that are repeated quite often throughout the book. It is hoped, though, that this will make it easier for the student to follow the discussion, and the reader is encouraged to make use of the Bible study tools available at www.nextbible.org as well as other resources.

Dr. Goldberg preferred to use the Hebrew names of New Testament writers and certain words. Throughout the book I have therefore retained this preference, including when citing Scripture references. So for example, Matthew's Hebrew name *Mattai* is used and citations such as *Mattai 4:12* are employed. In this connection, thanks are due to David Austin, the permissions director for the NET Bible, who graciously approved the various substitutions that I note below. If these substitutions make the Bible citations a bit less readable than otherwise, they allow for emphasizing the Jewishness of the New Covenant Scriptures (to use Dr. Goldberg's preferred name for the New Testament).

Names and some terms are therefore changed according to the list below. This will perhaps make it a bit more awkward for someone not used to the terminology, and is not always historically accurate (was Paul called "Paul" or "Sha'ul" when he ministered among the Gentiles?). However, again, it underscores Dr. Goldberg's preferences and his insistence on the inherent Jewishness of the New Testament writings.

The following list is a guide to this usage as well as to other abbreviations and terms used.

anti-Messiah	antichrist
ASV	American Standard Version
Bar Navah	Barnabas
Bat Sheva	Bathsheba
Kefa	Peter
KJV	King James Version
LG (in footnotes)	Louis Goldberg
Mattai	Matthew
Messiah	Christ
Messiah Yeshua	Christ Jesus
Miriam	Mary
MT	Masoretic Text (essentially, the Hebrew Bible text as we have it today)
NASB	New American Standard Bible
NIV	New International Version

NKJV	New King James Version
Qayafa	Caiaphas
qehilah	church (plural, *qehilot*)
Rav Sha'ul	an honorific for Paul, somewhat equivalent to saying "Rabbi Paul"
RSV	Revised Standard Version
shaliach (plural, *shlichim*)	apostle(s)
Sha'ul	Paul, also Saul in both Old and New Testaments—except in Acts 13:9: "Sha'ul (also known as Paul)"
Shimon	Simon
sifrim hisonim	literally, "outside books"; refers to the books of the Apocrypha and Pseudepigrapha produced during the few centuries B.C.E. and C.E., but not included in the Jewish or Protestant Bible (the Apocrypha are included, however, in Catholic Bibles)
talmid (plural, *talmidim*)	disciples
Tanach	Old Testament. It is a traditional Jewish name formed as a acronym from the three divisions of the Hebrew Bible: Torah, Nevi'im (Prophets), and Ketuvim (Writings)
tree	cross
Yaakov	James, also Old Testament Jacob
Yehudah	Jude (also Judas!)
Yeshua	Jesus
Yeshua the Messiah	Jesus Christ
Yohanan	John (usually the apostle; sometimes a different John, e.g., in Acts 4:6)

In keeping with the guidelines of the *Chicago Manual of Style* and similar reference works, punctuation in the NET citations has been minimally altered in certain cases. For example, a verse might be cited that is in the middle of someone's speech; I have added quotation marks to make that clear. Sentences that span several verses may be cited in part with a period rather than a ". . ." to improve readability, or beginning with a capital letter rather than a lowercase one. Poetry has sometimes been rendered in paragraph rather than separate verse style to save on space. Boldface italics, used in NET to represent quotations or allusions from the Hebrew Bible, have been rendered as plain text here to avoid confusion with the author's own use of italics for emphasis (indicated as "emphasis added" after the verse citation). Occasional explanatory additions not part of the NET are given in square brackets [like this]. As always, readers are encouraged to consult the complete NET translation, online or in print. Occasionally, NET, which relies on user input to catch errors (see the discussions at http://forum.bible.org) has "Lord" instead of the usual "LORD" for the four-letter name of God, YHWH. This has been corrected in the citations here.

In keeping with Dr. Goldberg's style, pronouns for deity are capitalized in the main text, though Scripture quotations follow the style of the translation used. Furthermore, his style was not gender-inclusive, reflective of the word choices of his generation. Rather than turn such terms as "man" and "men" into "people" or "humanity," I have decided to retain the original in the body text. It will be apparent where both men and women are intended, and the NET Bible will be seen to be gender-inclusive.

Richard A. Robinson, Editor
June 2009

BIOGRAPHY

Dr. Louis Goldberg

(Reprinted from the *Journal of the Evangelical Theological Society*, March 2003. Used by permission.)

Louis Goldberg was born January 28, 1923 in Los Angeles, CA, into an orthodox Jewish home, the son of Nathan and Minnie Goldberg. He met his future wife, Claire Berman, also from an Orthodox Jewish home, while at Roosevelt High School in Los Angeles. Louis was a trainer in the U.S. Army for several years while pursuing his Bachelor's in Engineering from the University of Southern California, which he received early in 1944. Still in the army, Louis and Claire were married near Newark, NJ, on July 14, 1944. After his army years, Louis began work at Automatic Electric in Chicago. Gus Graziano, a member of the Moody Memorial Church, worked with Louis and was a persistent witness to him for the Lord Jesus Christ. After six months of Gus's witness, Louis received Christ in 1948. Two months later, Claire was saved, and sometime later, Louis's brother, Daniel, also came to Christ.

The Goldbergs lived in Oaklawn and attended the Oaklawn Bible Church led by pastor Bach. Louis was also ordained in that church.

Louis obtained his theological education with a Bachelor of Divinity from Northern Baptist Theological Seminary in Chicago in 1953, and a Th.M. degree from the same institution in 1961. His Th.D. degree was earned several years later from Grace Theological Seminary, Winona Lake, IN. Louis pastored the Maranatha Baptist Church in Chicago for six years and the Dairy Dale Baptist Church of Cedar Rapids, IA, for three years.

Beginning in 1962, Louis taught at Temple Baptist Theological Seminary in Chattanooga, TN for three years, while also pastoring one of the "chapels."

He then taught at Moody Bible Institute in Chicago from 1965 until he retired in 1993. Claire, a great children's worker, always a soul-winner, and a great helper to Louis died in 1991, and is buried in Chicago.

In 1994, Louis became Scholar in Residence for Jews for Jesus, and lived at their New York City headquarters at 109 E. 31st St. He continued this work until his health began to fail in 2000, at which time he went to live with his daughter, Stephanie Anderson, in Charlotte, NC.

Louis carried on an extensive work in Israel, beginning in 1968, when the Israeli government asked him to come, tour, and write articles about the land and the people. From that time, until 2000, Louis spent every summer but one in Israel. He became an itinerant pastor to hundreds of Messianic Jewish congregations, and spoke on the same topic in a plenary session at the 52nd Annual Meeting of the ETS in Nashville. Some of Louis Goldberg's published writings were: *Our Jewish Friends* (Moody); *Leviticus* (study guide commentary, Zondervan); *Ecclesiastes* (study guide commentary, Zondervan); *Turbulence Over the Middle East* (Loizeaux); *Are There Two Ways of Atonement?* (Lederer); *Fire on the Mountain: Past Revivals, Present Revivals, and the Coming Return of Israel* (Lederer); *Counterpoints: Two Views on Messianic Movements* (Zondervan, forthcoming); as well as many chapters in symposia and dictionary articles. Louis helped translate both the NIV and the NKJV.

Louis Goldberg had been a member of the Evangelical Theological Society for forty-one years. He served as president of the society in 1983, often presented papers, and rarely ever missed an annual meeting. He died of pneumonia on Wednesday, October 23, at the home of his daughter Stephanie in Charlotte, NC. His funeral was held at Emmanuel Bible Church in Berwyn, IL, and he is buried beside his wife, Claire. He lived 79 years, 9 months, and 26 days. Left to mourn are his daughter, Stephanie Anderson, and her children, Elasheva and Aaron Arie Anderson of Charlotte; and his brother, Daniel Goldberg.

ONE

The Meaning and Validity of the Torah

Before treating biblical and rabbinical statements regarding the Torah, we need to consider the meaning of the word *Torah* as used in the Tanach and New Covenant in its many contexts. The word has various connotations for Jewish people as well as for followers of the Messiah. This author used to have a favorite question for his students in the opening session of Studies in the Pentateuch (Torah) at the Moody Bible Institute: *When you hear the word* law, *what does it communicate to you?*

My students had all kinds of responses: "law means legalism"; "we are under the law of love today, and the law on tablets of stone is no longer valid"; "we are under grace today and not under law"; or a popular response, "the Mosaic Law is no longer in existence, since Yeshua died for our sins and we now have the law on our hearts." Then there was the student who actually recited these lines from a hymn:

> Free from the Law, O happy condition,
> Yeshua has bled and there is remission,
> Cursed by the Law and bruised by the fall,
> Grace has redeemed us once for all.

This author confesses that when he heard this hymn for the first time many years ago, the words certainly sounded strange. The songwriter surely meant to say that no longer was it necessary to bring sacrifices to gain an atonement for sin, but to me as a Jewish believer, the words registered negatively. Neither do they communicate correctly to Gentile believers!

By my last years at Moody, however, students no longer offered glib statements about the Law, at least not in my presence. Perhaps the increased numbers of Jewish believers who are now found in Messianic congregations and churches has caused many non-Jewish believers to be more careful when speaking about the Law. All the responses I have heard, however, have over the years served as a motivation for me to sort out the biblical and traditional understandings of what Law really means.

In this chapter, we will consider what Torah means and in particular, how the New Covenant uses Torah to demonstrate a *continuity* with the Tanach. We will also need to indicate what *discontinuity* exists between these parts of the Scripture.

TERMS

The Hebrew Term *Torah*

The term *Torah* comes from the Hebrew verb *yarah*, meaning *throw*, *cast*, or *shoot*.[1] A noun, *moreh*, meaning *teacher*, is grammatically the *hiphil* of the same verb, while another noun derived from the *hiphil* is *torah*, defined as *instruction*.[2] So a good teacher aptly "throws," or "casts," instruction at his or her disciples. A wise mother who instructs her son from the Word actually imparts Torah, as the model of wisdom pictures:

> Listen, my child, to the instruction from your father,
> and do not forsake the teaching [*torah*] from your mother.
> (Proverbs 1:8)

As the divine Teacher or *moreh*, God has imparted His "instruction" or Word to Israel. As we will see, Torah is therefore to be regarded as "from heaven" (God-breathed) and it comes to man through the "unveiling of His presence" (revelation). This meaning of Torah, as it is understood in the Scriptures, carries no taint of legalism; though what man *does to* Torah can at times become legalistic.

In time, the word Torah also came to have several narrower meanings, referring first of all to the Torah of Moses, or the Mosaic Covenant (Constitution), which is also divine instruction. However, the wider body of Oral Law, or the traditions,[3] was also considered Torah, though it may or may not have reflected this Written Torah, the Hebrew Scriptures.

The Greek Term *Nomos*

The Greek word used in both the Septuagint and New Covenant to translate *Torah* is *nomos*. Hans-Helmut Esser provides a definition of it in its classical meaning:

> (a) The noun *nomos* is formed from the vb. *nemo*, distribute, deal out, assign, grant, especially in the sense of assigning property, apportioning pasture or agricultural land (cf. *nomē*, pasture). In other words, the reference is to those processes which are essential whenever men live together in a community, whether small or great. Relationships to earthly possessions have to be determined in a legally binding fashion, so that private and communal ownership may become a reality. Thus the basic vb. covers all shades of meaning from merely handing something over for a given period of time, right through to transferring something, once and for all, to the ownership of another person. By means of appropriate prepositions, personal or non-personal objects, and other qualifying phrases, ethical value-judgment can be expressed: to grant equally, exercise fairness, be impartial, also to favour, pass over, reject. The same vb. can also indicate the result of distributing property: to appropriate, own or possess, occupy, utilize; pass. to belong to. The communal aspect can still be seen in the mid.: to distribute (e.g. an inheritance) between one another.
>
> (b) The fig. sense covers the idea of guarding what has been entrusted: to watch over, protect; and also the way the recipient is regarded by the person who distributes: to esteem, regard as, take for, respect.[4]

While the classical meaning of Greek words makes for interesting study, we must remember that when the Hebrew Scriptures were translated into

Greek, the basic meaning of *Torah* was poured into the Greek equivalent *nomos* (and similarly for other words). In a few instances, this Greek term is used to translate Hebrew *hoq*, referring to the legal system in the covenant. But primarily, the scriptural idea remains of divine instruction, the Word given by God.

The rendering of *nomos* as *law* in English is unfortunate, because it has come to be understood in many circles as a term synonymous with legalism. But this assertion is not the biblical idea at all.

Usages of *Torah* in Scripture

Referring to the Books of Moses

As any reader of the English Bible knows, the word *law* occurs frequently and the tendency is to assume that the word means exactly the same in every context. Though *Torah* means *divine instruction*, what we will now look at are the various ways in which this term is *applied*.

No one would question that the first five books of Moses are designated *Torah*. This was true in the beginning when God gave this portion of Scripture to Moses. And particularly has this been the case since Ezra established the reading cycle of the Torah used in the synagogue for the *Shabbat* services. These weekly Scripture portions are known as *parshiyot*. Yaakov, as a Messianic Jew, made reference to this portion of Scripture when he declared at the Council in Jerusalem (about 50 C.E.),

> For Moses has had those who proclaim him in every town from ancient times, because he is read aloud in the synagogues every Sabbath. (Acts 15:21)

Referring to the Prophets

What comes as a surprise to many non-Jewish believers is that the word *Torah* is also often used to describe other portions of the Tanach. In Sha'ul's discussion in 1 Corinthians 14 concerning tongues, he cites Isaiah 28:11–12.

> It is written in the law: "By people with strange tongues and by the lips of strangers I will speak to this people, yet not even in this way will they listen to me," says the Lord. (1 Corinthians 14:21)

Note how he introduced this passage with the unusual phrase "In the Law." Sha'ul reflected the common understanding among the people of Judea that this entire section of the Hebrew Scriptures, the Prophets, are also to be understood as Torah, or Law.

Referring to the Writings

When Yeshua described the uniqueness of the sons of Israel, referring to them as gods (in the sense that they were "sons of God" through the covenants), He cited a statement from the Psalms to prove His point.

> Yeshua answered, "Is it not written in your law, 'I said, you are gods'? If those people to whom the word of God came were called 'gods' (and the scripture cannot be broken), . . ." (Yohanan 10:34–35)

Again, note that the Messiah, reflecting the common understanding of the day, referred to the Psalms as the Torah, or Law. Since the book of Psalms stands at the beginning of the third division of the Hebrew Bible, the *Ketuvim* (Writings), this entire portion is indeed Torah, or Law.

We see then that the community of Israel spoke of the Hebrew Scriptures—Moses, the Prophets, and the Writings—as the Written Law, *Torah she-bikhtav*, commonly described by non-Jewish believers as the "Old Testament." Occasionally, I have heard someone refer to this portion of the Word as the *Older Testament*, implying that since the New Testament has been revealed, the latter has somehow supplanted the "Old Testament." Judging from how much time is expended on New Testament preaching by the average pastor, one can wonder if this attitude concerning the "Old Testament" is widespread. But nothing could be further from the truth. The Hebrew Scriptures are the Written Torah, "instruction" given by God, and this portion of the Word needs to be preached and taught so that believers can be grounded in the full counsel of God.

Referring to a Covenant

Torah can also refer to the Mosaic Law as a covenant. In my teaching, I have preferred to use the phrase "Mosaic Constitution," because it usefully describes how four basic elements were put together into a unique combination, and then placed *into a package* when God concluded the covenant with His people at Sinai. This container or package is pictured as the Mosaic Covenant.

Through His Constitution, God established a pact with His people that made of them a special nation in which everyone could regard him- or herself as a free person.[5] God's desire was for each person to serve Him as the only one, living, and true God. The fact that many generations in fact did not serve God was not a fault of His in enacting this unique constitution. Rather, contained in it are the means for people to have an atonement from sin as well as for every believer to live a godly life in the power of the Holy Spirit.

While the Constitution is a *whole* and each element within it is of equal importance, a preliminary discussion is presented of each of the four elements in order to have a better understanding of this unique document, the Mosaic Constitution.[6]

The Moral Element. The moral element essentially consists of the "Ten Words," or Ten Commandments as found in Exodus 20:2–17 and Deuteronomy 5:6–21.

God's moral standard is ultimate. These Ten Words remind us that God has *an ultimate moral standard* by which He will one day judge individuals, including leaders of nations, at His bar of justice. Every unbeliever will be scrutinized, every deed and word will be tested in the light of an absolute standard. Such a statement seems phenomenal to those who share the current attitude toward morality, which is for the most part regarded as only relative. We live in a generation that resists loudly any mention of an ultimate morality given by a holy and righteous divine being; people have no fear of God or His holiness.[7]

God's moral standard informs man of his sin. These Ten Words are also a reminder that every person falls short of God's standards. Soon or later every person realizes that he or she has committed wrong, in either sins of commission or sins of omission. But a person can even sin "unintentionally," without even being aware of wrongdoing. In fact, this aspect of falling short was the very basis for the sin offering of the covenant. Moses spoke of what should be done in such a case:

> Tell the Israelites, "When a person sins by straying unintentionally from any of the Lord's commandments which must not be violated, and violates any one of them— . . ." (Leviticus 4:2)

So, these commandments were the means by which the Israelite was led to find out what the sacrificial system could offer: atonement, or the forgiveness of sin; dedication of life; and a life of fragrance reflecting the very mercies and fragrant grace of God. These three aspects are depicted in the following three verses, respectively.

> I will meet with you there, and from above the atonement lid, from between the two cherubim that are over the ark of the testimony, I will speak with you about all that I will command you for the Israelites. (Exodus 25:22)

> This will be a regular burnt offering throughout your generations at the entrance of the tent of meeting before the LORD, where I will meet with you to speak to you there. (Exodus 29:42)

> You are to beat some of it [the incense] very fine and put some of it before the ark of the testimony in the tent of meeting where I will meet with you; it is to be most holy to you. (Exodus 30:36)

God's moral standard gives guidance for a godly lifestyle. To the surprise of many, these commandments do in fact provide the possibility for the believer to live a godly lifestyle. These Words were never given by God for His followers to live the Torah legalistically; rather every possibility exists in these guidelines for learning the limitless means by which to serve God and fellow man.[8] We will discuss this further below.

The Sacrificial Element. Five basic offerings are present in this covenant, including the sin offering (Leviticus 4:1–5:13) and the trespass or guilt offering (Leviticus 5:15–6:7). These two were required of everyone when they came to worship in the sanctuary, and later, in the temple. Then there were three offerings that were completely voluntary. However, if anyone went beyond the first two to present voluntary sacrifices, he had to present these three in succession: Burnt offering (representing dedication of life, Leviticus 1); meal or grain offering (representing dedication of labor, Leviticus 2); and finally, the peace, or fellowship offering (Leviticus 3; 7:11–18, 28–34).[9]

The Juridical Element. Because Israel was constituted as a nation, special officials, both religious and civil (depending on the nature of the crime), were designated to care for the covenant's civil and criminal law codes. These judges were trained authorities, and were expected by God to dispense equitable justice whenever any of these codes were broken.

> You must appoint judges and civil servants for each tribe in all your villages that the LORD your God is giving you, and they must judge the people fairly. You must not pervert justice or show favor. Do not take a bribe, for bribes blind the eyes of the wise and distort the words of the righteous. You must pursue justice alone so that you may live and inherit the land the LORD your God is giving you. (Deuteronomy 16:18–20)

> If a matter is too difficult for you to judge—bloodshed, legal claim, or assault—matters of controversy in your villages—you must leave there and go up to the place the LORD your God chooses. You will go to the Levitical priests and the judge in office in those days and seek a solution; they will render a verdict. You must then do as they have determined at that place the LORD chooses. Be careful to do just as you are taught. You must do what you are instructed, and the verdict they pronounce to you, without fail. Do not deviate right or left from what they tell you. The person who pays no attention to the priest currently serving the LORD your God there, or to the verdict—that person must die, so that you may purge evil from Israel. Then all the people will hear and be afraid, and not be so presumptuous again. (Deuteronomy 17:8–13)

Worship and Lifestyle Elements, or Models. The covenant also had a unique element that described the religious culture of the people. For example, such practices included observance of the holidays, the specific emphasis of the seventh-day Sabbath, the dietary laws, the Levitical code of cleanliness, care for the poor, and so on.

The Four Elements as a Whole. Each of these four elements was basic to the very structure of the Mosaic Constitution. Each was parallel to the others; no one could say, "I will only observe the moral, sacrificial, and juridical elements and forget the models." Perhaps Yaakov had this in mind when he referred to the Mosaic Covenant and used the word *nomos*:

> For the one who obeys the whole law [Greek, *nomos*] but fails in one point has become guilty of all of it. (Yaakov 2:10)

Referring to the Oral Law

The Gospels, and particularly Sha'ul's letters, contain passages with the term *law* that are citing or alluding to the Oral Law, or *Torah she-be'al peh*. Sometimes these citations and allusions are found even in passages that do not use the word. Most believers will judge that the Oral Law is beyond the consideration of what constitutes the Word of God. But these traditional materials—still oral in the first century—are important for the allusions to them that occur in many New Covenant writings. This traditional body of material represents interpretations and applications of the Written Law that developed in the period between the Tanach and New Covenant, and continued to be developed by the religious leaders throughout the first century. These interpretations are reflected in what are called the *Midrash Halakhah* and *Midrash Aggadah* (respectively, commentary on legal and nonlegal portions of the Hebrew Scriptures).

By 120 C.E., Rav Akiva began to codify all this oral tradition into six major "orders" (*sedarim*). It was a massive undertaking, yet necessary to put all the various decisions and other materials into some kind of order. Others continued to work on this task throughout the second century, further subdividing the orders into tractates [*masekhtot*] and committing the materials to written form. In 200 C.E., Rav Yehudah Ha-Nasi called a halt to what had thus far been accomplished, and the resultant body of oral traditions, now written down, came to be known as the *Mishnah*.[10]

By the beginning of 500 C.E., the *Talmud*, comprised of *Mishnah* and *Gemara*[11] (commentary on *Mishnah*), was completed. But this body of material is another meaning of the word *Torah* that must be considered when it occurs, either directly or by allusion. For that reason, we will discuss further the idea of the Oral Law below.

The Validity of the Law from a New Covenant Perspective

Having already noted some of the multiple uses of the word *Torah*, or Law, in the New Covenant, consideration now needs to be given to the question: Is the Law finished, now that the New Covenant has replaced it? Or, for that matter, is it correct to even say that the Law *has* been replaced? This is a complex subject, considered further below. At the moment our concern is whether there exists a sharp dichotomy between the Tanach and the New Covenant. Let us take a closer look at the relationship between the two Testaments.

The Validity of the Hebrew Scriptures ("Old Testament")

No question exists among believers that the Written Law, commonly referred to as the Old Testament, are sacred writings for today. In these writings are the authoritative sketch of the account of creation; the account of the creation of man in his original setting; the circumstances of the fall and what ensued as to the moral nature of mankind and the presence of physical evil in the world. It further tells us of the breakdown of moral standards leading to the flood; other disasters that occurred in the course of human history; a description of the table of the nations; and then, beginning with Genesis 12, the account of Israel as a people in its faith history. This account continues in the historical and earlier prophetic books, and includes the background of the prophecy and promises regarding the Messiah that we find in the later prophetic books.[12] In addition, this sacred record proclaims prophecies awaiting further fulfillment regarding the restoration of the nation of Israel, the acceptance of its Messiah, and the inception of the fullness of the Messianic kingdom over all the earth.

As if that is not enough, the Written Law also includes the Writings, the third division of the Hebrew Bible. These consist of the Psalms (the devotional book of Israel), as well as the Wisdom literature of Job, Proverbs, and Ecclesiastes. In the Writings we also find the *Megilloth* of Ruth, Lamentations, Ecclesiastes, Song of Solomon, and Esther, all of which are read during the year at various synagogue services. And finally, there are the historical books of Ezra, Nehemiah, Daniel, and 1 and 2 Chronicles.

All these books were given for the purpose of instructing the people of Israel. That purpose remains for believers today, enabling those who follow God to cultivate an intense longing for Him and a maturing relationship.

While there were some in the early church who tried to demonstrate a discontinuity between the Hebrew Scriptures and the New Covenant, thereby insisting that the former had become obsolete, the great majority of believers accepted the Written Law as from the Lord.[13] Without question, the early Jewish believers in the Messiah Yeshua regarded the Written Law as their Scriptures, teaching new believers from it, using it for their evangelistic preaching as well as for their apologetic regarding the claims of Yeshua. To this day, even when the body of Messiah consists predominantly of Gentile believers, the Hebrew Scriptures are considered sacred writings.

The Question of the Validity of the Mosaic Covenant

With the death of Yeshua as our great sin offering, and particularly with the loss of the Second Temple in 70 C.E., a new age came into being. The people of God are now in a special sense the body of Messiah, although at the same time, Israel continues as an elect people within the purposes of God, based on the statements and promises of the other covenants, the Abrahamic, Davidic, and the New.

The religious leaders among the Pharisees also recognized that something new had transpired with the loss of the temple in 70 C.E. A major crisis presented itself for both the rabbinical leaders and the people: what now would become of the Mosaic Covenant, since it was no longer possible to offer the sacrifices?

The solution to the problem came at the Council of Yavneh[14] (70–90 C.E.), at which Israel's religious leaders structured a Judaism that made no provision for a substitute atonement, while at the same time insisting that the Mosaic Covenant was still in place, although in a modified form![15] Perhaps they thought the interval between the Second and Third Temples would be short, as it was for only fifty years between the First and Second Temples, 586 to 536 B.C.E. But the years since the Yavneh Council have stretched out to centuries, with no opportunity to build a temple,[16] and what has remained is the decision by the Yavneh Council regarding a so-called *modified Mosaic Covenant*.

For believers, there is still the question of what becomes of the Mosaic Covenant. The real crux of the issue is the relationship between the Mosaic and New Covenants. Scholars take a variety of positions on this issue, of which a few will be mentioned.

The Demise of the Mosaic Covenant. Many declare that the Mosaic Covenant is in its entirety no longer in effect. The package has in effect been broken and no elements of this covenant remain. Newell observes:

> God has repeatedly declared the day of the first Covenant is done . . . Israel then is at present out of covenant with God entirely. In the first, the legal Covenant, they continued not, and God regarded them as not. There is therefore no standing for Israel before God under the Mosaic Covenant.[17]

Newell could not see any possibility of the use of the Mosaic Covenant within the New Covenant at all, but rather, the New Covenant is something entirely different with no possible connection or continuity with the former covenant.

Possible Continuity. Chafer's comment concerning the Mosaic Law suggests a continuity; the Law of Moses is said to be

> a rule divinely given through Moses to govern Israel in the land of promise. It was commended to them because they were a covenant people. Thus it defined the manner of their daily life. It was itself a covenant of works (Exodus 19:5–6). This covenant they soon broke. It will yet be superseded by the New Covenant (Jeremiah 31:31–34; Hebrews 8:8–13). This agreement will include the former Law of Moses (Deuteronomy 30:8).[18]

Despite his statement that the Mosaic Law will be superseded, he still suggests a continuity between the two covenants, the Mosaic and the New. However, he does not spell out what this means.

Statements by the Reformers. Statements by the Reformers are particularly noteworthy with regard to the Law, especially, the Ten Words. Calvin, and to some extent Melanchthon, after Luther's death, proclaimed a "Threefold Function of the Law."

> Why should the law be taught? The law is to be taught for the sake of discipline . . . that by this pedagogy men might come to Christ . . . Secondly, the law is to be taught in order to expose sin . . . Thirdly, the law is to be retained so that the saints may know which works God requires.[19]

Here, the attempt is very definitely made to have a continuity between the moral element of the Mosaic Covenant and the New Covenant, even though the *package* of the Mosaic Covenant would be regarded as broken and therefore discontinuous, as noted below.

An Alternative Suggestion. As we compare the Mosaic and New Covenants, a *discontinuity* is apparent, especially now that the Second Temple has been lost. When the Second Temple and altar were no longer present, the Mosaic system of sacrifices was no longer possible; therefore there is no longer a covenant in the form as it was given at Sinai. Even the religious leaders at the Council of Yavneh recognized the drastic change in the Constitution with the loss of the temple when the office of sacrifices by the Levitical priests could no longer be maintained.

The Mosaic *package* is broken, signifying a discontinuity with the New Covenant. But the question now is: What happens to the *elements* that were once a part of the covenant? Are they to be scrapped as well? Or, is there an alternative way to regard them in view of the New Covenant? Our clue will focus on what did the New Covenant writers *do with these very elements*. Only as their comments are examined carefully can one come to any conclusion as to the possibility for *a continuity* between the two covenants.

The moral element and the New Covenant. With regard to the moral element, or Ten Commandments, the New Covenant contains numerous examples of how Yeshua taught and lived every one of the commandments. To the rich young ruler who wanted eternal life, He provided a lesson of what the first commandment meant.

> Now a certain ruler asked him, "Good teacher, what must I do to inherit eternal life?" Yeshua said to him, "Why do you call me good? No one is good except God alone. You know the commandments: 'Do not commit adultery, do not murder, do not steal, do not give false testimony, honor your father and mother.'" The man replied, "I have wholeheartedly obeyed all these laws since my youth." When Yeshua heard this, he said to him, "One thing you still lack. Sell all that you have and give the money to the poor, and you will have treasure in heaven. Then come, follow me." But when the man heard this he became very sad, for he was extremely wealthy. When Yeshua noticed this, he said, "How hard it is for the rich to enter the kingdom of God!" (Luke 18:18–24)

The young man was told to sell everything he had and then follow the Messiah. But is divesting oneself of all material possessions the epitome of piety? Does God ask that believers give up all they own to gain eternal life? Not at all! The young man had already announced that he not only knew but also lived the commandments. Yet he did not *really* know what he was declaring. When told to give up his possessions, it became quite clear that he knew nothing about really loving God and putting Him first—the primary objective of the first commandment. Tragically, the young man's response was to walk away from Yeshua.

Sha'ul also taught and lived the commandments. His constant exhortation for new Gentile believers was that they demonstrate their love for the Lord with a moral sense of values whose source was the word that God had given Moses. The highest love, *hesed* or *agape*, cannot be divorced from the ethics of the commandments, all of which are undergirded by the righteousness and holiness of God. And so Sha'ul wrote the Ephesians in words reflecting the Ten Commandments.

> Therefore, having laid aside falsehood, each one of you speak the truth with his neighbor, for we are members of one another. (Ephesians 4:25)

> The one who steals must steal no longer; rather he must labor, doing good with his own hands, so that he may have something to share with the one who has need. (Ephesians 4:28)

The only *apparent* loophole in Sha'ul's letters is observance of the holidays and *Shabbat*. We do note that Sha'ul himself worshipped on *Shabbat*, as in Philippi.

> On the Sabbath day we went outside the city gate to the side of the river, where we thought there would be a place of prayer, and we sat down and began to speak to the women who had assembled there. (Acts 16:13)

And he desired to be in Jerusalem for Shavuot, or Pentecost.

> For Sha'ul had decided to sail past Ephesus so as not to spend time in the province of Asia, for he was hurrying to arrive in Jerusalem, if possible, by the day of Shavuot. (Acts 20:16)

Sha'ul may have left the issue open for Gentile believers, in order to satisfy future cultural or practical needs as particular circumstances arose.

> Therefore do not let anyone judge you with respect to food or drink, or in the matter of a feast, new moon, or Sabbath days. (Colossians 2:16)

We will look at this more closely below under the fourth element, the worship and lifestyle models. And see further below when we assess the decisions of the Council of Nicea. Nevertheless, we note that Gentile believers continued to observe the Sabbath and other holidays in the first and second centuries when they lived in communities where Jewish believers were predominant.

Thus we see a continuity of the moral element between the two covenants.

The sacrificial element and the New Covenant. The issue of sacrifices certainly posed a problem after Yeshua had died and especially after the loss of the Second Temple in 70 C.E. Many confidently assert that the sacrificial element of the Mosaic Covenant has no place in the New. Once the Messiah had died for our sins, and with sacrifices no longer offered at the altar in Jerusalem, why look for this element of the Mosaic system to have any continuity with the New Covenant?

But a careful study of the New Covenant does in fact suggest the presence of the sacrificial system. The New Covenant writers demonstrate repeatedly that *all five of the Levitical sacrifices are a part of, or subsumed in, the one sacrifice of Yeshua*.

Consider, first of all, the *sin offering*. Without question, Yeshua is our sin offering. We can here briefly summarize a number of New Covenant passages that define the principles attached to the sin offering: (1) He is our *substitute*: "Therefore, since the children share in flesh and blood, he likewise shared in their humanity, so that through death he could destroy the one who holds the power of death (that is, the devil)" (Hebrews 2:14). (2) He *identified* with our sins: "He himself bore our sins in his body on the tree, that we may cease from sinning and live for righteousness. By his wounds you were healed" (1 Kefa 2:24).[20] (3) He *died for us*: "You know that from your empty way of life inherited from your ancestors you were ransomed—not by perishable things like silver or gold, but by precious blood like that of an unblemished and spotless lamb, namely Messiah" (1 Kefa 1:18–19). (4) In dying, He also *gave us His life*: "The thief comes only to steal and kill and destroy; I have come so that they may have life, and may have it abundantly" (Yohanan 10:10); "So also it is written, 'The first man, Adam, became a living person'; the last Adam became a life-giving spirit" (1 Corinthians 15:45). These are the very principles that are associated in Leviticus 4:1–5:13 with the sin offering of the Mosaic Covenant.[21] Because of this offering, David could announce that his sins were removed from him "as far as the eastern horizon is from the west" (Psalm 103:12).

Most believers probably see the death of the Messiah only in terms of the sin offering. But the Levitical system had four other sacrifices that cannot be ignored; they are also *subsumed* in the one sacrifice of the Messiah to which we must relate every day.

Yeshua is also our *trespass or guilt offering*, whereby we have forgiveness for each individual sin. Note in these verses the plural "sins" and compare with Leviticus 6:1–7.

> (My little children, I am writing these things to you so that you may not sin.) But if anyone does sin, we have an advocate with the Father, Yeshua the Messiah the righteous One, and he himself is the atoning sacrifice for our sins, and not only for our sins but also for the whole world. (1 Yohanan 2:1–2)

Yeshua is also our *burnt offering* of dedication. Compare the following verse with Leviticus 1.

> Therefore I exhort you, brothers and sisters, by the mercies of God, to present your bodies as a sacrifice—alive, holy, and pleasing to God—which is your reasonable service. (Romans 12:1)

Yeshua is also the *grain offering* representing the dedication of our work. Compare these verses with Leviticus 2.

> But in your case, dear friends, even though we speak like this, we are convinced of better things relating to salvation. For God is not unjust so as to forget your work and the love you have demonstrated for his name, in having served and continuing to serve the saints. But we passionately want each of you to demonstrate the same eagerness for the fulfillment of your hope until the end. (Hebrews 6:9–11)

Finally, Yeshua is our *thanksgiving or peace offering*. The table around which the Israelites ate the thanksgiving offering in the temple was, in a sense, the table of the Lord. Likewise, when Jewish and Gentile believers come to the *se'udat ha-Adon* (Lord's Supper), it too is the table of the Lord around which we express our thankfulness for His establishing peace in our hearts.

> For he is our peace, the one who made both groups into one and who destroyed the middle wall of partition, the hostility, when he nullified in his flesh the law of commandments in decrees. He did this to create in himself one new man out of two, thus making peace. (Ephesians 2:14–15)

To sum up this section, then, the New Covenant writers refer to the various Levitical offerings, making their application to the one sacrifice of the Messiah. Therefore a continuity can be observed between the sacrificial system of the Mosaic Covenant with its five Levitical sacrifices and the Messiah's one sacrifice.

The juridical element and the New Covenant. Regarding the juridical element with its civil and criminal law codes, there is a discontinuity in that the body of the Messiah is not a nation. Church leaders do not adjudicate at trials, commit offenders to jail, or mete out punishment to murderers. It is true that congregational elders as part of their oversight are sometimes required to exercise discipline over members who transgress spiritual or moral boundaries that can spiritually affect the body. But decisions affecting offenses against society and the state that are of a civil or criminal nature are to be left in the hands of state officials, and believers living in various societies are to be obedient to their government.

The worship and lifestyle element and the New Covenant. The element of the models of worship and lifestyle is left open for New Covenant believers. An understanding of how this element functions is based on how Yaakov interpreted the matter of holidays, dietary laws, and so on for Gentile believers. The issue was resolved to be one that rested on *freedom of choice* (see Acts 15). Gentile believers, then and now, do not have to participate in these models that existed in the Mosaic Covenant. The only exception was with the Antioch congregation, which may have had an equal number of Jewish and Gentile believers. This may be why Yaakov suggested on the occasion of Acts 15 that the non-Jewish believers not eat blood or meat where the animal had been strangled; this may have been out of consideration for the more religiously identified Jewish believers.

> . . . but that we should write them a letter telling them to abstain from things defiled by idols and from sexual immorality and from what has been strangled and from blood. . . .

> . . . that you abstain from meat that has been sacrificed to idols and from blood and from what has been strangled and from sexual

immorality. If you keep yourselves from doing these things, you will do well. Farewell. (Acts 15:20, 29)

In other words, the Gentile believers had a freedom of choice, and the counsel was that they not misuse their freedom in front of their Jewish brethren.[22] Such decisions did not apply among the congregations founded among the Gentile believers, where few Jewish believers were present. In that sense, Gentile believers exercised a greater latitude of freedom.

On the other hand, Yaakov's decision regarding the Antioch congregation does not have any impact on Jewish believers. In fact, he never said a word regarding Jewish believers, much less for those living in the land of Judea among their own brethren. And did he really have to say anything? If Jewish believers then and now live within the larger Jewish community where these models are practiced, then these believers will want to practice these models in some way as well. The only condition Scripture places on doing so is that their practice must be interpreted in light of how Yeshua lived and taught them.

There are many opinions when it comes to the practice of this fourth element. Since this is an important issue when assessing how Jewish and Gentile believers should live, this writer has thought it best to treat it further in the chapter on ecclesiology.

The Validity of the Law in Relation to the "Tragic Break"

As the body of Messiah became more and more non-Jewish in its makeup, the prevailing culture in which Gentile believers understood the Scriptures took on a Hellenistic-Roman complexion. But even with this change of culture, which affected both theology and lifestyle, the non-Jewish believers continued to consider important the application of the Hebrew Scriptures and the specifics of its moral absolutes. It is wrong to think that genuine non-Jewish believers became antinomian, meaning "opposed to the Law," as we saw already with regard to the later Reformers who in fact recognized the implications of God's holiness as shown in the moral absolutes of the Mosaic Constitution.

What *did* become a serious problem for Jewish believers and their congregations by the 500s C.E. is that the non-Jewish component of the body of Messiah came to insist that a Hellenistic-Roman cultural contextualization was the *only* acceptable way in which to express theology, preach, and live. We will discuss this further below in the topic of the decisions of the Council of Nicea in 325 C.E. For now, we will say the following.

Whereas Jewish believers had once been given latitude among their non-Jewish brethren concerning expression and lifestyle (Acts 15), decisions by the church councils stripped away any possibility of observing the Mosaic models as interpreted by Yeshua or guided by the writers of the New Covenant. Non-Jewish leaders in the body of Messiah could conveniently declare the Law was finished. In addition, because these theological decisions also took on ethical ramifications, many elements of Christendom unfortunately became anti-Jewish. By the 500s, because of the pressure of an official Christendom within the empire to enforce the decisions of the councils, Messianic Jews became fewer in number and slowly amalgamated themselves into the non-Jewish stock. Meanwhile, the larger Jewish community turned inward upon itself, and though their lives were protected by the laws of the empire, they became second or third class citizens, barred from many areas of life.[23]

To conclude this section, what can we say as to the suggestion that a continuity is present between the Mosaic Covenant and the New? As we have seen, a discontinuity does exist: the *package* of the Mosaic Covenant is broken. But certainly a case can be made for a continuity of *three of the elements* of the Mosaic Covenant and the New Covenant. This subject will continue to occupy us throughout this book.

Clearly, there are many problem passages in the New Covenant that raise questions as to the meaning of *law*. Suffice it to say, however, that the place of the Law or Torah for the New Covenant believer cannot be dismissed by a wave of the hand or by declaring we are "free of the Law" today. In the next chapter, we will set these questions in the context of the Doctrine of the Word of God (or, *Torah*).

TWO

The Doctrine of the Word of God

Revelation, Inspiration, and Illumination
—Biblical and Rabbinical Statements—

The doctrine of the Word, or Torah, of God is of key importance for us as we check the proclamation of teachers against the Torah in order that God can speak clearly to His people. We will discuss this topic under three headings: Revelation, Inspiration, and Illumination.

Revelation

The first key term in the doctrine of the Torah is *revelation*. Jewish writers have commented much on the meaning of this word, which addresses the uniqueness of the Torah, or Word, given to Israel.

Gillui HaShekinah (Unveiling of the *Shekinah*)

Revelation can be defined as "the manifestation of God in acts or appearances which overawe man,"[1] a subject that is discussed throughout the Talmud and Midrash as well. In this perspective, the "unveiling" or revelation of God is that act whereby He takes the necessary steps to bridge the gap between Himself and man. From a general perspective, God reveals Himself in nature and the universe. However, it is up to each person as to what they will do with this information. Sha'ul declared that man has been given enough information so that if he or she desires yet further information, God will provide it for them. If any person refuses this additional information, then he or she is without excuse.

> For since the creation of the world his invisible attributes—his eternal power and divine nature—have been clearly seen, because they are understood through what has been made. So people are without excuse. (Romans 1:20)

Not only is there the *general* revelation of God in nature and the universe, but in a *special* sense, the Written Law or Tanach is God's revelation through His Word (*devar Adonai*, or, "Word of God").

> Revelation in the Bible is *Mahazeh*, *hazon*, and *hizayon*, "vision"—whence *hozeh*, "seer"; or *mareh*, "sight," whence *roeh*, "*seer*."[2]

Kohler noted a twofold sense of revelation that relates to God's own self and then to God's message: "first, God's self-revelation, which the Rabbis called *Gillui HaShekinah*, 'the manifestation of the divine presence.'" [3] This self-revelation "overawes man and impresses him with what he sees, hears, or otherwise perceives of His glorious presence."[4] But another sense also attaches to the concept of revelation, namely, that it is the "manifestation of His will through oracular words, signs, statutes, or laws."[5]

As to the first sense of revelation, Kohler provides an excellent understanding of the basic biblical idea of revelation. With the second sense, he also provides the various forms that revelation takes, a topic to which we now turn.

The Forms of *Gillui HaShekinah*

As we have seen, God's message appears in words that He speaks to man, as well as through signs, visions, dreams, and other means. Revelation is both oral, whereby God speaks to man directly, but can also be written when the recipient records what he experienced.

Oral Revelation. God had various ways of speaking to man, but "He spoke with Moses 'mouth to mouth,' 'as a man would speak with his neighbor,' in clear sight"[6] of all. One could expect this preferential treatment because

Moses was preeminently used by God to deliver Israel from Egypt, and at Mount Sinai he became the channel through which Israel was committed to God in a covenant. Subsequently, in the Jewish mindset, Moses became *Moshe Rabbenu*, that is, "Moses our teacher."

Human Conscience. The Holy Spirit also communicated to man through his conscience. Sha'ul reminds us that

> what can be known about God is plain to them, because God has made it plain to them. (Romans 1:19)

That is, as we have already seen, man has a sense of "his invisible attributes—his eternal power and divine nature . . . So people are without excuse" (Romans 1:20). A person may try to deny what he or she knows of God through their conscience, but God will hold each one accountable for the decisions that are made about His being as well as for their own actions.

Dreams. Another means of revelation were dreams through which God communicated subjectively within man. Dreams have always been a source of mystery, and the attempts to interpret them have been numerous on the part of charlatans, soothsayers, and sophisticated psychologists such as Freud, who developed a body of interpretation for their meaning. While not every dream is a communication from God, He used this means of revelation with many of His servants, such as the patriarch Jacob (Genesis 40–41) and the statesman-prophet Daniel who interpreted Nebuchadnezzar's dream (Daniel 2:31–45).

Visions. The prophets also received revelation from God through a vision, a communication perceived externally to the recipient. A classic example of a vision is that of the great chariot, which Ezekiel experienced on the plains of Babylon, a vision that revealed much of the character of God. Kohler noted that this means was also provided to "non-Israelites as well as to the patriarchs and prophets of Israel,—to Abimelek and Laban, Balaam, Job, and Eliphaz."[7] He also observed the difference between the prophets of Israel and other nations in that "the Jewish genius perceived God as the moral power of life,"[8] suggesting that the prophets of Israel perceived God as maintaining a high standard of morality. However, one must not presume that pagans had no sense of morals; when their legal documents are examined with objectivity, we can clearly see that they in fact did.

Life and Experience. For the believer, experiences both good and bad can teach one something about the will of God. For the believer who walks in harmony with God's will, blessings accrue and a witness to the goodnesses of the Lord goes forth. At other times, believers may backslide, turning from the paths of righteousness, slipping into evil, darkness, and depression. But when they confess their wrongdoing, how precious is that restoration! Even David, who had walked with God and seen His great deeds, on one occasion turned away and slipped into grievous sin; but when he was recovered and restored, he could exclaim in triumph and with deep gratitude toward God,

> Let me again experience the joy of your deliverance!
> Sustain me by giving me the desire to obey!
> Then I will teach rebels your merciful ways,
> and sinners will turn to you. (Psalm 51:12–13)

History. The *Gillui HaShekinah* was also revealed through God's acts. In delivering Israel from Egypt, God first declared who He was.

> God said to Moses, "I AM that I AM." And he said, "You must say this to the Israelites, 'I AM has sent me to you.'" (Exodus 3:14)

Following this self-revelation, He then acted through Moses to guide the nation out of bondage. The revelation of God is perceived in historical events: ". . . the Lord is the God Who brought Israel out of Egypt, and Who guides them through history. The God of Israel thus reveals Himself as acting in historical events . . . history is the milieu of God's revelation."[9]

The Finger of God. One also notes the special occasion when in an awe-inspiring testimony, the finger of God appeared, inscribing His commandments on the two tablets of the Testimony, the tablets of stone.

> He gave Moses two tablets of testimony when he had finished speaking with him on Mount Sinai, tablets of stone written by the finger of God. (Exodus 31:18)

There once was an artist who attempted to portray this breathtaking experience. As Moses held up the tablets of stone, the forefinger of God appeared out of the clear blue, His finger tracing the letters from a short distance removed from the tablet, while a fire appeared from the fingertips, burning the inscription into the stone. There stood Moses, his face hidden behind the tablet, his eyes closed to avoid the fiery presence of God's righteousness, his face contorted and jaw clenched, realizing he was standing in the very sacred presence of God. Through this picture the artist tried to portray a small glimpse of the holiness of God—a holiness that reminds us that His morality is not relative but ultimate.

The Climax of *Gillui HaShekinah*

At the revelation at Mount Sinai,

> Then, when you heard the voice from the midst of the darkness while the mountain was ablaze, all your tribal leaders and elders approached me. (Deuteronomy 5:23)

This referred to God's voice from heaven, which some explain was intended to mean that all the people of Israel were present at Sinai. So at this juncture of history, at this great climax of revelation, everyone in Israel was to be bound to this revelation.[10] Kohler described the revelation of God to the people of Israel as "part of the great world-drama of history . . . we see here the dramatized form of the truth of Israel's *election* by divine Providence for its historic religious mission."[11] At Sinai, we glimpse the point in time when God opened the heavens, His presence came down on Mount Sinai, and He entered into a relationship with His people through the Mosaic Covenant.

From the New Covenant point of view, however, there was one more climax of *Gillui HaShekinah* when God again opened the heavens, as recorded in Luke.

> Now there were shepherds nearby living out in the field, keeping guard over their flock at night. An angel of the Lord appeared to them, and the glory of the Lord shone around them, and they were absolutely terrified. But the angel said to them, "Do not be afraid! Listen carefully, for I proclaim to you good news that brings great joy to all the people: Today your Savior is born in the city of David. He is Messiah the Lord. This will be a sign for you: You will find a baby wrapped in strips of cloth and lying in a manger." Suddenly a vast, heavenly army appeared with the angel, praising God and saying, "Glory to God in the highest, and on earth peace among people with whom he is pleased!" (Luke 2:8–14)

When in verse 13 the heavens opened even farther to reveal the presence of a heavenly multitude, it is possible that those present included not only angels but also departed believers from previous generations, all who joined in praise to God in the announcement of the coming of Israel's Messiah.

An Israeli once challenged me to prove that God exists. The most responsible reply was that Israel has been called as a special people and exists to this day because of a promise made to Abraham some four thousand years ago, when God said that

> I will confirm my covenant as a perpetual covenant between me and you. It will extend to your descendants after you throughout their generations. I will be your God and the God of your descendants after you. (Genesis 17:7)

Answering to this promise, there were only two major occasions at which the record shows that the heavens were opened to the people of Israel—once when God entered into the Mosaic Covenant with His people, and then again when the Messiah's entrance to earth was announced from heaven, leading to the enactment of the New Covenant.

This last *Gillui HaShekinah* is the final and greatest one, regarded as the truth once delivered to the *hasidim*, or saints.

> Dear friends, although I have been eager to write to you about our common salvation, I now feel compelled instead to write to encourage you to contend earnestly for the faith that was once for all entrusted to the saints. (Yehudah 1:3)

This is also the testimony by the writer to the Hebrews when he declared,

> The Son is the radiance of his glory and the representation of his essence, and he sustains all things by his powerful word, and so when he had accomplished cleansing for sins, he sat down at the right hand of the Majesty on high. (Hebrews 1:3)

This revelation is true and accurate.

We now turn to the idea of *inspiration*, which follows from the definition of revelation and applies to the record approved by God.

Inspiration of *Torah Min HaShamayim*

While *Gillui HaShekinah* can be described as the revelation of (1) God Himself and (2) what man must know, *Torah Min HaShamayim*—"Torah from heaven"—is the subject of *inspiration* whereby what was recorded became God-approved Scripture.

Materials Included in Inspired Scripture

Direct Revelation. The easiest situation to understand is that in which Moses, the prophets, and other Scripture writers heard direct revelation from God and then recorded what they had heard. So for instance, God provided a song to Moses that he was to write for the people of Israel.

> Then Moses recited the words of this song from start to finish in the hearing of the whole assembly of Israel. (Deuteronomy 31:30)

See further in Deuteronomy 32:1–47. Another instance is when God spoke to Jeremiah, as follows:

> The LORD spoke to Jeremiah. (Jeremiah 21:1)

Such instances can be multiplied many times over in the Word.

National Records. But we run into problems when we try to explain how the written Scripture is also inspired when the writers are using material from various sources, such as archival records, gathered by those who kept the day-to-day accounts of the nation's history. Jeremiah was reputedly the author of 1 Kings, which meant he sometimes had to access archival records in order to put together the account as it appears in the biblical record.

Genealogical records were also important to Israelite families. A Hall of Records must have existed in Jerusalem through which priests could prove the legitimacy of their family lines and whereby the people could also have an official record of their line. When Mattai and Luke needed the genealogy of Yeshua, for example, they would have gone to this Hall of Records, finding the needed information to demonstrate the lines of Yeshua: from Yosef back to David through Solomon, the line of the kings; and from Miriam to David, but through Nathan, a brother of Solomon (see Luke 3:23–31; cf. Luke 3:31 and 1 Chronicles 3:5).[12] These genealogies were then duly recorded to demonstrate the link of Yeshua to His royal heritage.

The Writings of Unbelievers. At first sight, it seems highly questionable that citations from the writings of unbelievers would appear in Scripture. Yet when Sha'ul presented his case for the claims of Yeshua to the Greek philosophers, he quoted from the Greek poets.

> For in him we live and move about and exist, as even some of your own poets have said, "For we too are his offspring." (Acts 17:28)[13]

Though this might seem surprising, one must remember the old adage, "all truth is God's truth." There are many sets of truth that can be found in the disciplines of science, mathematics, the rules of legal evidence, history, archaeology, and so on. While some people engaged in these areas are believers, many professionals who make their contributions in these specialties do not necessarily profess any faith. Not all people have gone so astray that they lack any comprehension of right or wrong, good and evil. All men are under what is known in the non-Jewish theological world as "common grace," namely, that even though man has a sin nature, he still has the fingerprints of God upon his soul. He thereby understands, for example, what it means to be honest.[14] (We will consider this further when discussing Man, Sin, and Atonement.)

Note, however, that Sha'ul did not buy into the *entire* Greek system of thought or lifestyle; he only utilized *certain* truths from the Greek cultural grid. In that endeavor he was justified, because his statements above in Acts 17:28 were supported by the biblical grid of truth that all men come from a common source, that is, from Adam and Eve. And in view of that statement of truth, the *shaliach* added that God will hold all people accountable for their deeds and be judged through the man He has appointed,

> because he has set a day on which he is going to judge the world in righteousness, by a man whom he designated, having provided proof to everyone by raising him from the dead. (Acts 17:31)

The Holy Spirit led Sha'ul to select that portion of Greek poetry, and it has now become a part of Scripture.

From a much different point of view, we have another situation whereby Satan's statements are cited. God must have provided this information for the writer, as for instance when the enemy of God tempted Eve.

> Now the serpent was more shrewd than any of the wild animals that the LORD God had made. He said to the woman, "Is it really true that God said, 'You must not eat from any tree of the orchard'?" The woman said to the serpent, "We may eat of the fruit from the trees of the orchard; but concerning the fruit of the tree that is in the middle of the orchard God said, 'You must not eat from it, and you must not touch it, or else you will die.'" The serpent said to the woman, "Surely you will not die, for God knows that when you eat from it your eyes will open and you will be like divine beings who know good and evil." (Genesis 3:1–5)

Similarly, we have a conversation between God and Satan over the ensuing temptation of Job.

> Then Satan answered the LORD, "Is it for nothing that Job fears God? Have you not made a hedge around him and his household and all that he has on every side? You have blessed the work of his hands, and his livestock have increased in the land. But extend your hand and strike everything he has, and he will no doubt curse you to your face!" So the LORD said to Satan, "All right then, everything he has is in your power. Only do not extend your hand against the man himself!" So Satan went out from the presence of the LORD. (Job 1:9–12)

> But Satan answered the LORD, "Skin for skin! Indeed, a man will give up all that he has to save his life! But extend your hand and strike his bone and his flesh, and he will no doubt curse you to your face!" So the LORD said to Satan, "All right, he is in your power; only preserve his life." (Job 2:4–6)

Satan's statements, though cited in Scripture, do not carry any weight of truth to them. Satan may speak the truth at times, but only in connection with his evil purposes so as to tempt people to sin. His statements that are found in the Written Torah and New Covenant carry with them only the assurance that he was cited accurately and for no other reason.

Traditional Jewish Writings. Another source found in the New Covenant is traditional Jewish materials, which had been passed on orally from generation to generation. Already mentioned is something surprising to many believers, namely, the possibility that the writers also cited from the *sifrim hisonim* (literally, "the Outside Books," generally known as the Apocrypha and Pseudepigrapha). In addition they may have quoted the *Midrash Halakhah* and *Midrash Aggadah*, which both comment on the Written Law and are the forerunner of what by 200 C.E. became the Mishnah. Numerous illustrations will be cited below when discussing further the materials to which the New Covenant writers referred or alluded to, and we will consider the reasons they would seek out such sources for citations. But insofar as the doctrine of inspiration is concerned, the Holy Spirit was sovereign as He led the sacred writers to select materials, enabling them to commit to writing what God actually desired, which then became Scripture. Whatever is then included in the sacred writings has God's stamp of approval.

Statements by Jewish Writers Affirming the Inspiration of Scripture

The Testimony of an Ancient *Baraita*. As early as the period preceding the *Mishnah*, the phrase *Torah Min HaShamayim* is already found. Cohen pointed out that the traditions declared that if anyone denied that the *Torah* is from heaven, he or she has no portion in the world to come.[15] Later in the *Amoraic* period of the Gemara, 200–500 C.E., we find a certain *baraita*. The word *baraita* refers to a particular statement in the Gemara that a religious leader remembered having heard from a teacher in years gone by. This *baraita* states that

> *because he hath despised the word of the Lord*—this refers to him who maintains that the Torah is not from Heaven. . . . And even if he admits that the whole Torah is from Heaven, excepting a single point, a particular *ad majus* deduction or a certain *gezerah shawah*,—he is still included in "*because he hath despised the word of the Lord*."[16]

Later Testimony to *Torah Min HaShamayim*. More recent writers have also taken a high view of the *Torah* from heaven. Jacob Joshua Ross points out that this concept is "associated primarily with the notion that every syllable of the Bible has the verity and authorship of the word of God. . . . The contents of the sacred books are to be regarded throughout as conscientious and homogeneous, with not only no contradiction in them, but also no real differences."[17] Such a view reflects a high regard for the Written Law as inspired or God-breathed.

In the 1800s, Hirsch restructured traditional Judaism along the lines of the earlier Spanish-Jewish context of 900–1450 C.E., with its philosophical undergirding. Hirsch was attempting to oppose the reformers of the *Haskalah* (Enlightenment) who were liberalizing Judaism, and he observed:

> Is the statement "And God spoke to Moses saying," with which all the laws of the Jewish Bible commence, true or not true? Do we really and truly believe that God, the Omnipotent and Holy, spoke thus to Moses? Do we speak the truth when in front of our brethren we lay our hand on the scroll containing these words and say that God has given us this Torah, that His Torah, the Torah of truth and with it of eternal life, is planted in our midst? . . . This word of God must be our eternal rule superior to all human judgment, the rule to which all our actions must at all times conform; and instead of complaining that it is no longer suitable to the times, our only complaint must be that the times are no longer suitable to it.[18]

Schechter also affirmed that

> it is the Torah as the sum total of the contents of revelation, without special regard to any particular element in it, the Torah as a faith, . . . the Torah in this abstract sense, as a revelation and a promise, the expression of the will of God, . . .[19]

Even though many other scholars of various persuasions within Judaism will disagree with these assertions, nevertheless, the point is that many Jewish thinkers, both ancient and modern, did and continue to hold to a high view of inspiration, assigning to it the greatest revelation that God could give to any nation on earth.

The Tanach's Own Testimony to Its Inspiration

We now want to note a few representative passages in which the Tanach writers themselves give testimony concerning inspiration.

The Mandate to Write. First of all, we note that the men of God involved in producing the record of the Tanach claimed to have been given a divine mandate to write, as they were led by the Spirit. So for instance we read that

> Moses wrote down all the words of the LORD. Early in the morning he built an altar at the foot of the mountain and arranged twelve standing stones—according to the twelve tribes of Israel. (Exodus 24:4)

Isaiah was told to inscribe His message on a scroll.

> Now go, write it down on a tablet in their presence,
> inscribe it on a scroll,
> so that it might be preserved for a future time
> as an enduring witness. (Isaiah 30:8)

Similarly, Jeremiah was also instructed to write in a book the word God gave him.

> The LORD God of Israel says, "Write everything that I am about to tell you in a scroll." (Jeremiah 30:2)

Other writers likewise testified to the same compulsion to write what they were given; they produced an infallible and inspired record in which every word they chose reflected that which God wanted to say.

Authentication by Fulfillment of Prophecy. Moses and the rest of the writers of the Tanach spoke of future events. Their predictions have been, or are still being, verified. Israel's lawgiver provided information as to the test of the true prophet: Did his words come to pass? If not, his message was to be rejected.

> The LORD your God will raise up for you a prophet like me from among you—from your fellow Israelites; you must listen to him. . . . I will raise up a prophet like you for them from among their fellow Israelites. I will put my words in his mouth and he will speak to them whatever I command. (Deuteronomy 18:15, 18)

An excellent short-range prophecy is provided in Jeremiah 28. Hananiah, a false prophet, challenged Jeremiah by stating that the Judean exiles in Babylon would soon be returning home. Upon God's direction, Jeremiah responded that to the contrary the exile would last far longer and that Hananiah would himself die for the sin of counseling rebellion—a prediction fulfilled within the space of two short months.

Based on the testing of short-range prophecies, the prophets' long-range messages could be accepted, some of which would not be fulfilled for hundreds of years and some of which are yet to be fulfilled. A good illustration of such a long-range prophecy is David's prediction of the death of the Messiah at the hands of the leaders of the nation, a prophecy that would not be fulfilled until about a thousand years later.

> Dogs have surrounded me;
> a band of evil men has encircled me,
> they have pierced my hands and my feet. (Psalm 22:16 NIV)[20]

Isaiah, who lived in the 700s B.C.E., also spoke of the substitutionary atoning death of the Messiah to die in our place and take away our sins.

> We all, like sheep, have gone astray,
> each of us has turned to his own way;
> and the LORD has laid on him
> the iniquity of us all. (Isaiah 53:6 NIV)[21]

This message was not fulfilled for some seven hundred years after the time of Isaiah.

What is also interesting in Isaiah 53 is the use made of the Hebrew *prophetic perfect*, that is, describing an action as though already completed.[22] The thrust of the prophet's message is obviously future from his point of view, but from God's point of view, the event is already considered to be a completed event! Isaiah had already established himself through short-range prophecies and therefore could be respected for his long-range prophecies.

In the same manner, Jeremiah predicted an exile to Babylon that would only last for seventy years.

> This whole area will become a desolate wasteland. These nations will be subject to the king of Babylon for seventy years. (Jeremiah 25:11)

> For the LORD says, "Only when the seventy years of Babylonian

> rule are over will I again take up consideration for you. Then I will fulfill my gracious promise to you and restore you to your homeland." (Jeremiah 29:10)[23]

Daniel, the statesman-prophet, was given the ability to not only know Nebuchadnezzar's dream but also to interpret it, some aspects of whose fulfillment are still future from our point of view today.

> The king told them, "I have had a dream, and I am anxious to understand the dream." . . .
>
> "You, O king, were watching as a great statue—one of impressive size and extraordinary brightness—was standing before you. Its appearance caused alarm. As for that statue, its head was of fine gold, its chest and arms were of silver, its belly and thighs were of bronze. Its legs were of iron; its feet were partly of iron and partly of clay. You were watching as a stone was cut out, but not by human hands. It struck the statue on its iron and clay feet, breaking them in pieces. Then the iron, clay, bronze, silver, and gold were broken in pieces without distinction and became like chaff from the summer threshing floors that the wind carries away. Not a trace of them could be found. But the stone that struck the statue became a large mountain that filled the entire earth. This was the dream. Now we will set forth before the king its interpretation.
>
> "You, O king, are the king of kings. The God of heaven has granted you sovereignty, power, strength, and honor. Wherever human beings, wild animals, and birds of the sky live—he has given them into your power. He has given you authority over them all. You are the head of gold. Now after you another kingdom will arise, one inferior to yours. Then a third kingdom, one of bronze, will rule in all the earth. Then there will be a fourth kingdom, one strong like iron. Just like iron breaks in pieces and shatters everything, and as iron breaks in pieces all of these metals, so it will break in pieces and crush the others. In that you were seeing feet and toes partly of wet clay and partly of iron, so this will be a divided

> kingdom. Some of the strength of iron will be in it, for you saw iron mixed with wet clay. In that the toes of the feet were partly of iron and partly of clay, the latter stages of this kingdom will be partly strong and partly fragile. And in that you saw iron mixed with wet clay, so people will be mixed with one another without adhering to one another, just as iron does not mix with clay. In the days of those kings the God of heaven will raise up an everlasting kingdom that will not be destroyed and a kingdom that will not be left to another people. It will break in pieces and bring about the demise of all these kingdoms. But it will stand forever. You saw that a stone was cut from a mountain, but not by human hands; it smashed the iron, bronze, clay, silver, and gold into pieces. The great God has made known to the king what will occur in the future. The dream is certain, and its interpretation is reliable." (Daniel 2:3, 31–45)

Authentication by Divine Power and Miracles. Moses' ministry and words were confirmed by the signs of the plagues, which even the Egyptian priests had to admit were by the finger of God.

> The magicians said to Pharaoh, "It is the finger of God!" But Pharaoh's heart remained hard, and he did not listen to them, just as the LORD had predicted. (Exodus 8:19)

In addition, God asserted His control over life through the death of the firstborn, and then afterward by the parting of the Red Sea (Sea of Reeds), and His extraordinary acts in the Sinai wilderness.

Likewise, Elijah prayed and it did not rain in Israel.

> Elijah the Tishbite, from Tishbe in Gilead, said to Ahab, "As certainly as the LORD God of Israel lives (whom I serve), there will be no dew or rain in the years ahead unless I give the command." (1 Kings 17:1)

But when he prayed again, torrents of rain came upon the land, as proof that God's power was with His prophet.

> So Ahab went on up to eat and drink, while Elijah climbed to the top of Carmel. He bent down toward the ground and put his face between his knees. He told his servant, "Go on up and look in the direction of the sea." So he went on up, looked, and reported, "There is nothing." Seven times Elijah sent him to look. The seventh time the servant said, "Look, a small cloud, the size of the palm of a man's hand, is rising up from the sea." Elijah then said, "Go and tell Ahab, 'Hitch up the chariots and go down, so that the rain won't overtake you.'" Meanwhile the sky was covered with dark clouds, the wind blew, and there was a heavy rainstorm. Ahab rode toward Jezreel. Now the LORD energized Elijah with power; he tucked his robe into his belt and ran ahead of Ahab all the way to Jezreel. (1 Kings 18:42–46)

Elisha, who followed Elijah, had a double portion of blessing and was able to do twice the signs and wonders of his mentor.

While not all who produced the divine record had the same experiences with miracles, yet all spoke with God's power and communicated His uniqueness.

Authentication by Yeshua's Testimony. Not much space will be given to Yeshua's assurance concerning the Tanach. His testimony agrees with that of the long line of writers who preceded Him. We do note, though, that in His teaching Yeshua assumed the accuracy of the record of miracles in the Tanach, as He noted eleven great miracles as facts to be accepted.

The creation of mankind. "He answered, 'Have you not read that from the beginning the Creator made them male and female?'" (Mattai 19:4).

A worldwide flood. Here the testimony of the Tanach to this flood is affirmed as well as the fact that this patriarch built a great ship. "Just as it was in the days of Noah, so too it will be in the days of the Son of Man. People were eating, they were drinking, they were marrying, they were being given in marriage—right up to the day Noah entered the ark. Then the flood came and destroyed them all" (Luke 17:26–27).

The historicity of Lot and the destruction of Sodom. "Likewise, just as it was in the days of Lot, people were eating, drinking, buying, selling, planting, building; but on the day Lot went out from Sodom, fire and sulfur rained down from heaven and destroyed them all" (Luke 17:28–29).

The historicity of Lot's wife. She is affirmed as a real person who lost her life when she looked back and lingered on the outskirts of the city. "On that day, anyone who is on the roof, with his goods in the house, must not come down to take them away, and likewise the person in the field must not turn back. Remember Lot's wife!" (Luke 17:31–32).

God's appearance in the burning bush. "But even Moses revealed that the dead are raised in the passage about the bush, where he calls the Lord the God of Abraham and the God of Isaac and the God of Jacob" (Luke 20:37).

The miracle of the manna. Yeshua affirmed that manna was a genuine food that appeared miraculously in the desert. "Your ancestors ate the manna in the wilderness, and they died" (Yohanan 6:49).

The historicity of the brass serpent incident. "Just as Moses lifted up the serpent in the wilderness, so must the Son of Man be lifted up" (Yohanan 3:14).

The lack of rain and ensuing famine in Elijah's day. "But in truth I tell you, there were many widows in Israel in Elijah's days, when the sky was shut up three and a half years, and there was a great famine over all the land" (Luke 4:25).

The healing of leprous Naaman the Syrian general. "And there were many lepers in Israel in the time of the prophet Elisha, yet none of them was cleansed except Naaman the Syrian" (Luke 4:27).

The historicity of Jonah. He is affirmed to be an actual prophet swallowed by a great sea monster. "For just as Jonah was in the belly of the huge fish for three days and three nights, so the Son of Man will be in the heart of the earth for three days and three nights" (Mattai 12:40).

The repentance of the Assyrians in Nineveh at the preaching of Jonah. "The people of Nineveh will stand up at the judgment with this generation and condemn it, because they repented when Jonah preached to them—and now, something greater than Jonah is here!" (Mattai 12:41).

Through these and other attestations, Yeshua shows that He implicitly trusted and testified to the inspiration of the *Tanach*.

Testimony by Yeshua to the Inspiration of the New Covenant

What of the inspiration of the record contained in the New Covenant? We have already seen that the writers, either through direct communication, or directed by God in choosing from among various sources, were led by the

Holy Spirit in their writing of the New Covenant. Now we want to ask how the Messiah attested to this portion of the Word of God. We will consider a number of aspects in this section.

New Covenant Revelation and the Death of Yeshua. As Yeshua was preparing to go to His death, He declared He was leaving the New Covenant revelation unfinished. On one occasion, He stated,

> I have many more things to say to you, but you cannot bear them now. (Yohanan 16:12)

The meaning of this statement will be considered below, concerning the fact that Yeshua's own disciples simply would not accept the reality of His death as the atonement for sin.[24] This was the current belief in Yeshua's day: the Messiah son of David was not expected to die for sins. We see this in the disciples' reactions to His announcement of His death.

> From that time on Yeshua began to show his disciples that he must go to Jerusalem and suffer many things at the hands of the elders, chief priests, and experts in the law, and be killed, and on the third day be raised. (Mattai 16:21)

> When they gathered together in Galilee, Yeshua told them, "The Son of Man is going to be betrayed into the hands of men. They will kill him, and on the third day he will be raised." And they became greatly distressed. (Mattai 17:22–23)

> Look, we are going up to Jerusalem, and the Son of Man will be handed over to the chief priests and the experts in the law. They will condemn him to death, and will turn him over to the Gentiles to be mocked and flogged severely and crucified. Yet on the third day, he will be raised. (Mattai 20:18–19)

Even the disciples' reaction to Yeshua's sharing of the bread and cup at the Last Passover shows that they were still not convinced of this truth. Neither has any change occurred in the views of the Jewish community to this day in this regard to the Messiah son of David. (The idea of Messiah son of Joseph, which became the way to offset the preaching of Messianic Jews, will be considered below.)

Only after Yeshua was raised from the dead was His proclamation of these truths accepted by His followers. A hint of this situation can be seen in the words of Yeshua to Kefa.

> Yeshua replied, "You do not understand what I am doing now, but you will understand after these things." (Yohanan 13:7)

When Yeshua said this, Kefa did not yet understand the reality and significance of Yeshua's impending death. Not until later did the true interpretation of the Messiah's message and His acts become clear.

New Covenant Revelation and the Promise of Yeshua. The Messiah had a plan concerning the new revelation. His promise was that

> I have told you these things in obscure figures of speech; a time is coming when I will no longer speak to you in obscure figures, but will tell you plainly about the Father. (Yohanan 16:25)

The full understanding of the reason for Yeshua's death would come with His postresurrection appearances and with the public manifestations of the Holy Spirit's coming. Only then was the mysterious connection between His suffering and the glory to come made clear. Yeshua's words and acts needed interpretation, which would ultimately be provided when this promise came to fulfillment.

> But when he, the Spirit of truth, comes, he will guide you into all truth. For he will not speak on his own authority, but will speak whatever he hears, and will tell you what is to come. (Yohanan 16:13)

New Covenant Revelation and Specially Chosen Disciples. Yeshua also explained that when the proper time would come, certain men among the disciples would be chosen to receive and write this New Covenant revelation, as shown in the same verse just quoted:

> But when he, the Spirit of truth, comes, he will guide you into all truth. For he will not speak on his own authority, but will speak whatever he hears, and will tell you what is to come. (Yohanan 16:13)

Again, the truth is emphasized that

> When the Advocate comes, whom I will send you from the Father—the Spirit of truth who goes out from the Father—he will testify about me, and you also will testify, because you have been with me from the beginning. (Yohanan 15:26–27)

New Covenant Revelation as Outlined by Yeshua. In a very general way, the Messiah outlined in advance some of the content of the New Covenant revelation.

Historical accounts of Yeshua's teaching. Yeshua may have made reference to what He had taught in the days of His flesh, as it would ultimately be contained in the four accounts that are in the New Covenant Scripture.

> But the Advocate, the Holy Spirit, whom the Father will send in my name, will teach you everything, and will cause you to remember everything I said to you. (Yohanan 14:26)

These accounts were composed by four of the disciples: Mattai (with its special emphases for Jewish people), Mark, Luke (who shared with his Greek friends his wealth of intimate knowledge of Jewish people, belief, and lifestyle), and Yohanan (with its specific testimony, following the loss of the Second Temple in 70 C.E., concerning the deity of Yeshua).

No doubt many other accounts were produced by Yeshua's disciples but only four accounts were officially selected by the Holy Spirit, although we note that the writers could well have incorporated materials from compilations made by other disciples.[25] Luke especially made reference to the accounts that had already been compiled and he could have included some of those as led by the Holy Spirit. Luke meticulously examined many of those other accounts, interviewed many people, and then sat down to put together what would become the story of Yeshua from his perspective. And what he and others wrote, as we already said, was exactly what the Holy Spirit wanted.

Other perspectives on Yeshua's teaching. New Covenant revelation also included Yeshua's teaching from the perspective of various writers. Yeshua had said concerning the Holy Spirit that

> He will glorify me, because he will receive from me what is mine and will tell it to you. Everything that the Father has is mine; that is why I said the Spirit will receive from me what is mine and will tell it to you. (Yohanan 16:14–15)

In this category are also included the letters of Sha'ul who, among other things, explained the nature of the "mystery."

> For I do not want you to be ignorant of this mystery, brothers and sisters, so that you may not be conceited: A partial hardening has happened to Israel until the full number of the Gentiles has come in. (Romans 11:25)

> Now to him who is able to strengthen you according to my gospel and the proclamation of Yeshua the Messiah, according to the revelation of the mystery that had been kept secret for long ages, . . .
> (Romans 16:25)

> . . . that is, the mystery made known to me by revelation, as I have already written briefly. (Ephesians 3:3 NIV)[26]

The question surrounding this "mystery" is: How did it come about that with the death of the Messiah, the fullness of the kingdom of peace predicted by the prophets did not come to pass? What was the nature of the "body of the Messiah," which was *not* predicted in the Tanach? The answer is that every possibility had been given to the people of Israel to receive their Messiah. Had the Sanhedrin acted on His testimony and accepted that He indeed is both man and God, then two thousand years ago Yeshua could have brought in the kingdom envisioned by the prophets, instead of our having to yet wait for it.[27]

In light of this situation, Sha'ul gave guidelines on living the new life victoriously within the body of the Messiah, always waiting for the trumpet call of God that will signal the resurrection as well as the catching away ("rapture," in theological language) of the body of Messiah into His presence.

In addition to Sha'ul's writings, much information on living the life of a believer is found in the distinctive letters of the Messianic Jews Kefa, Yaakov, and Yehudah. What they wrote spoke to the early Messianic Jews as well as to all believers.

Words of prophecy. The message of prophecy is also present in the New Covenant. Yeshua promised that

> But when he, the Spirit of truth, comes, he will guide you into all truth. For he will not speak on his own authority, but will speak whatever he hears, and will tell you what is to come. (Yohanan 16:13)

The book of Revelation is God's sure word of prophecy; while its message may baffle many, this prophetic word provides information of the first importance. Other books contain prophetic elements as well. Some passages speak of the Messiah's return.

> Now we do not want you to be uninformed, brothers and sisters, about those who are asleep, so that you will not grieve like the rest who have no hope. For if we believe that Yeshua died and rose again, so also we believe that God will bring with him those who have fallen asleep as Believers. For we tell you this by the word of the Lord, that we who are alive, who are left until the coming of the Lord, will surely not go ahead of those who have fallen asleep. For the Lord himself will come down from heaven with a shout of command, with the voice of the archangel, and with the trumpet of God, and the dead in Messiah will rise first. Then we who are alive, who are left, will be suddenly caught up together with them in the clouds to meet the Lord in the air. And so we will always be with the Lord. (1 Thessalonians 4:13–17)

Other passages have a word concerning Israel's future atonement from sin and their return to the Lord.

> And so all Israel will be saved, as it is written: "The Deliverer will come out of Zion; he will remove ungodliness from Jacob. And this is my covenant with them, when I take away their sins." (Romans 11:26–27)

A complete and final revelation. Finally, Yeshua's promise concerning the entire body of New Covenant revelation was that it would be a final and complete message on its own, in which the Holy Spirit would guide the writers into truth.

> But when he, the Spirit of truth, comes, he will guide you into all truth. For he will not speak on his own authority, but will speak whatever he hears, and will tell you what is to come. (Yohanan 16:13)

This New Covenant revelation, along with the Tanach, is the full inspired disclosure by God to Israel, to all believers, and to all people as well.

The Authority of New Covenant Revelation. Yeshua, knowing in advance what would be spoken and written under the guidance of the Holy Spirit, gave to the words of the future New Covenant the same authority as His own words. Note the last part of the next verse.

> Remember what I told you, "A slave is not greater than his master." If they persecuted me, they will also persecute you. *If they obeyed my word, they will obey yours too*. (Yohanan 15:20, emphasis added)

Furthermore, as Yeshua was sent to Israel, so His followers would be sent not only to Israel but to the entire earth.

> Just as you sent me into the world, so I sent them into the world. . . . I am not praying only on their behalf, but also on behalf of those who believe in me through their testimony. (Yohanan 17:18, 20)

God never raised up infallible *talmidim* to serve their generation only, with the Word given to them ending at their death. Rather, He intended for some parts of the Word given to them to be inscripturated so that this written Word—infallible (without error) and inspired (from God)—would serve future generations. *The distinction between revelation and inspiration must be kept in mind*; God gave Yeshua and His disciples a great deal of revealed information, but only part of that material was actually set in writing, thus becoming sacred text. Yohanan indicated this when he wrote:

> This is the disciple who testifies about these things and has written these things, and we know that his testimony is true. There are many other things that Yeshua did. If every one of them were written down, I suppose the whole world would not have room for the books that would be written. (Yohanan 21:24–25)

A proper understanding of *Torah min HaShamayim* or the inspiration of the Tanach and the New Covenant allows us to be assured of His Word and to hold it in sacred trust.

The "How" of Inspiration

Granted that with a high view of *Torah min HaShamayim*, the Torah is understood to be special, the question arises as to how God interacted with the writers of Scripture. How did it "get" from God to man? How did it end up as Holy Writ?

Kohler asserted:

> The essential feature of revelation accordingly consists . . . in the fact that it is not a merely psychological process in which the human imagination or mental faculty constitutes the main factor, but that man is but the instrument upon which a superhuman force exerts its power, . . .[28]

The point here is that God somehow gave His message to man who then wrote down His words.

But do the rabbis speak in terms of *how* it came about? Three possibilities seem to predominate among Jewish writers:

One such possibility is that through a means difficult to understand, God prompted the biblical writers to communicate His Word.[29]

A second thought is that Moses, as well as other men of God, "acted as a scribe writing from dictation, as was the case with Baruch and the prophet Jeremiah (BB 15a)."[30]

And a third possibility is that some parts of the Scripture could have been dictated, but other parts could have been by the human writer. That is, God had such confidence in His servant Moses that He knew Moses would not interject his own ideas into the Torah—but even if he did, he would reliably be conveying God's will.[31] It would appear that in later assessments of inspiration, the rabbis and Jewish scholars took a more moderate position in the view of inspiration, whereby the Lord would provide the message, allowing for the writer to reflect on it and then put it into his own words, but superintending the final product that would then have His full approval.

Because there is no single view held by Jewish writers, the "how" of inspiration seems to be left open, remaining in a sense a mystery. Some writers' statements are in fact quite puzzling, as when it is suggested that the *transmission* of the text of Scripture itself, that is, the copies of the Word, is also inspired![32]

Let us focus particularly on what Messianic Jews themselves declared in the New Covenant:

> Every scripture is inspired by God and useful for teaching, for reproof, for correction, and for training in righteousness. (2 Timothy 3:16)

The writers of Scripture are not inspired in the sense that God opened up a hole in their heads and poured in a quart of inspiration! Rather, the record is "God-breathed," that is, the final product from the hands of the writers has God's stamp of approval of what He wanted us to receive as from Him.

Kefa explained further the special ministry of the Spirit, explaining that

> no prophecy was ever borne of human impulse; rather, men carried along by the Holy Spirit spoke from God. (2 Kefa 1:21)

The *shaliach* here described the unique work of the Holy Spirit within the mind and heart of the writer, controlling him as he produced the sacred text.[33] Certainly, God did not rob the writer of his personality; all his traits, educational training, and work habits appear in the text. God did His work within the writer who was then led to provide an authoritative text. Perhaps the reason why the rabbis never sought to provide a full definition of inspiration is because of its complexity. Rather, they asserted that when "the Voice went forth" at Sinai, "coming to each Israelite with a force proportioned to his individual strength,"[34] God addressed each person with a voice he could endure.

Given the differing views among evangelicals about the method of inspiration, perhaps the more conservative Jewish scholars were wise in not saying too much about the "how" of inspiration. The final product of *Torah* as well as the New Covenant should be regarded as from the Holy One Himself, from *HaShem*.[35]

Degrees of Inspiration

In a peculiar understanding of the authority of the sacred text, Schechter pointed out that:

> It is true that in Rabbinic literature the term *Torah* is often applied to the Pentateuch to the exclusion of the Prophets and the Hagiographa. . . . It is also true that to a certain extent the Pentateuch is put on a higher level than the Prophets—the prophetic vision of Moses having been, as the Rabbis avow, much clearer than that of his successors.[36]

While this Jewish educator hastened to add that the prophets also had the scriptural authority of the Torah (Numbers 12:6–8; Deuteronomy 34:10), yet nothing is ever found in the prophets that could take away from the superior authority of Moses. The prophets certainly recognized Moses' authority. To a certain extent, Schechter's words have a measure of truth in that one of the qualifications of the prophets is that each one derived much of the content of his preaching from the writings of Moses and then applied it specifically on numerous occasions to their generations.

Nevertheless, this author finds the traditional Jewish understanding of inspiration bothersome when it is stated that the totality of the prophets' writings are less inspired and carry less weight than Moses, and that the *Ketuvim* is even less inspired than the Prophets. Yes, Moses spoke with God face to face; yes, he saw more clearly what was revealed (Exodus 33:11); yes, the prophets used Moses' lessons as preaching material for their own generations. Yet one must never deprecate the message God gave to the prophets and the other writers. Their words carry great significance for lifestyle, the future, the land, and the people of Israel. When it is stated that Scripture is *Torah Min HaShamayim*, or God-breathed, this author would never assert that God intended man to consider the writings of the prophets as any less inspired than Moses. To do so detracts from the authority of the Written Torah, which includes the Prophets and the Writings, as well as from the New Covenant, or New Torah. Sha'ul insisted that all the writings of the Written Law are "from heaven," and that no one part of Scripture is greater, or higher, than the rest. This should be our position as well. We will see later what the writers themselves had to say of what they wrote.

Proofs for Inspiration

Three points have been advanced in regard to the question as to whether there exist proofs for the inspired nature of the Bible. First, the Scriptures as a whole—the *Tanach* and the New Covenant—are a unity, and one divine Author stands behind the human writers. Second, the Author of the Scriptures is righteous in His character, and therefore, the record produced by those involved in writing the Scriptures is a truthful book. And third, the Scriptures themselves, when read and pondered by the reader, have a transforming power.

With regard to the last point, the change produced through the *Torah* and New Covenant is not merely the effect that any human author would have in challenging people's lives. Rather, when one acts on what God declares and promises in the Scriptures, the recipient receives an entirely new life, which includes a dynamic whereby the person can live a radically different life than in the past. While human authors may have challenged numerous people, yet one unique Author, God, has challenged people to make a difference within their generation, providing each recipient with peace of mind, rest in the soul, a new life, and the hope of their presence with Him for all eternity.

Illumination

What Is Illumination?

Revelation and inspiration are not enough for God's communication to fully reach man. The revealed and inspired production must be supplemented by interpretation and application, that is, by teaching. To put it another way, as many Jewish teachers have noted, the Written Law must be made livable.

To many, the last statement may sound strange indeed. The usual rejoinder is that the believer accepts only the Word of God without adding to or taking away anything. "Just the Word, please," is the usual response! But suppose for a moment that you are visiting a certain congregation. There is a special speaker who announces his topic and then, as each person present listens eagerly, gives a message consisting solely of reciting a long string of Scripture passages on the topic. Nothing else is mentioned, neither the speaker's understanding of these passages nor anyone else's views on the Scripture portion. What would you say after such a message? Would you be satisfied? Or rather, does not the topic chosen from the Torah or New Covenant need to be *interpreted* in the light of what the Scriptures teach? And would not you, the listener, also desire to know how these Scriptures could be *applied* to your daily life?

Such concerns of interpretation and application fall within the parameters of what is entailed in the *illumination* of the Torah. Illumination is enabled by the work of the Holy Spirit who teaches believers the Word of God. But this involves far more than just merely sitting in front of the Scriptures and allowing the Spirit to fill our hearts. Certainly, God enables us to learn much from devotional study. But other, more difficult aspects of study also enter illumination of the Word as the Spirit guides and teaches us. These various aspects will now be discussed.

Torah Lo BaShamayim

Before we discuss those aspects, it is instructive to consider illumination from the standpoint of the rabbinic concept of *Torah Lo BaShamayim*—"Torah that is not in heaven." This concept did not fully develop until the period of the *Amoraim* (the rabbinical teachers who formulated the Gemara 200–500 C.E.), but a commentary in the earlier Mishnah describes well what is entailed in illumination.

The issue was over a point of Torah. Some of the rabbinical leaders described how a voice from heaven confirmed a minority opinion held by Rabbi Eliezer. However, Rabbi Joshua sought to block this affirmation, stating that this Torah, this teaching, was *Lo BaShamayim*, Torah that is not in heaven. Another rabbi, Rabbi Jeremiah, declared that the Torah had already been given and it was up to the leaders to interpret it.[37] That declaration became the model for Jewish leaders by which the Written Torah is both *interpreted* by the teachers and *applied* to the particular needs of every generation.

These decisions concerning what is *Lo BaShamayim* led to the formulation of the Gemara, the commentary on the Mishnah, both of which constitute the major part of the Talmud, or what has been referred to as the Oral Law. We will consider the authority of the Oral Law as well as its usage by Messianic believers in the next chapter. The point here is that both in rabbinic Judaism and for followers of Yeshua, interpretation and application of the Scripture are necessary.

Grammar of the Biblical Languages

The first aspect of study of the Word entails a knowledge of the Hebrew and Aramaic passages in the Written Law and of the Greek of the New Covenant. Even though the average person may not know these languages, many study helps exist that enable the reader to understand the meaning of various passages.

For example, in the area of grammar, what is called the biblical Hebrew *imperfect* form of the verb emphasizes continuous action, in either the past, present, or future, depending on the context. For instance, in the period of the judges, when the clans in the middle eastern part of Israel were under heavy exploitation by the Midianites, the Scripture says that

> when they invaded with their cattle and tents, they were as thick as locusts. Neither they nor their camels could be counted. They came to devour the land. (Judges 6:5)

However, the imperfect form of the verb suggests a continuous action in the past and it should therefore be translated "used to invade with their cattle." In other words, every year at harvesttime they would come to grab everything in sight and so impoverish the people of Israel. The continuous exploitation of crops left the Israelites hungry and these were depressing slavery conditions.

Or, on another occasion, after Daniel prayed the prayer for the release of his people from Babylon after its conquest from Persia, he concluded with:

> O Lord, hear! O Lord, forgive! O Lord, pay attention, and act! Don't delay, for your own sake, O my God! For your city and your people are called by your name. (Daniel 9:19)

But the Hebrew verbs for "hear," "forgive," and "pay attention" end with *qamets he*, a grammatical form considered the strongest imperative in the language. The significance of the language is that Daniel is *commanding* God to hear, forgive, pay attention, and act to release His people from their captivity.[38]

These examples give a small glimpse of how grammar can help in preparing a message and in enabling people to understand—and therefore be encouraged—when they hear the Torah, the Word of God.

Cultural and Historical Backgrounds

Another aspect of study whereby the Spirit illumines the Word is the cultural and historical background. Why, for example, was Laban so intent on chasing Yaakov and his family, entering their encampment, and invading the women's compound—to the point that Rachel had to excuse herself because of her pregnancy? What was Laban looking for with such intent? It is true that Rachel was sitting on the saddlebags in which were the household gods of Laban's family. But even more than that, these gods were also the *title deeds to all the property Laban had*! Rachel had stolen them from her father, thinking that she could "help" Yaakov in his claim to all the family property. The possession of these gods throws a lot of light on the so-called Mizpah blessing:

> It was also called Mizpah because he said, "May the LORD watch between us when we are out of sight of one another." (Genesis 31:49)

Is this a genuine blessing of righteous hearts, or does it rather not mean something else? The understanding of cultural patterns enables the reader to better grasp the actual facts of the Scripture.

In another example, when Belshazzar offered Daniel the position of third ruler in the kingdom if he would only interpret the handwriting on the wall, critics of the Bible used to laugh at this "mistake" in Scripture:

> However, I have heard that you are able to provide interpretations and to decipher knotty problems. Now if you are able to read this writing and make known to me its interpretation, you will wear purple and have a golden collar around your neck and be third ruler in the kingdom. (Daniel 5:16)

Why the third if Belshazzar were sole ruler in the kingdom? Who then was the second? But archaeology and historical research now reveal that the father of Belshazzar was very much alive at the time but chose instead to follow his first interest of being an archaeologist and contemplator. So he proposed a division of duties: Belshazzar would actually rule while the father would still retain his portion but still be free to pursue his own interests. Belshazzar was within his legal bounds when he made the offer for Daniel to be the third ruler in the kingdom.

Similarly, historical and cultural facts help us understand what transpired when Ezra was asked by Nehemiah to read the Torah after the city walls had all been plugged up and the city gates restored:

> They read from the book of God's law, explaining it and imparting insight. Thus the people gained understanding from what was read. (Nehemiah 8:8)

I have heard numerous times that this passage refers to some kind of "spiritual" explanation, as the Levites made the Word understandable to those present. But this is not speaking of mere spiritual understanding. The first contingent of some fifty thousand people had returned to Judah from Babylon in 538 B.C.E., followed by a second group of about seven thousand who came with Ezra in 457 B.C.E. In the interim, spiritual conditions had sunk to a low; the Hebrew Bible was still in its ancient script that was used prior to the first deportation to Babylon, while all the returnees spoke Aramaic and little or no Hebrew, especially those born in the land prior to the time of Ezra's return. Bible reading was therefore impossible. What spiritual knowledge was present was because of the existence of the priests and Levites who had general knowledge of the Torah.

So one of Ezra's first tasks was to *transliterate* the Hebrew Scriptures into Aramaic; this meant that Ezra used the square characters of Aramaic to spell the Hebrew words, and these characters are the ones used in the Hebrew Bibles of today. With this arrangement, people in Ezra's day could at least *read* what the Scriptures said, although a lot would not be *understood* because of the Hebrew language. So Ezra next selected a cadre of Levites and priests and taught them the Aramaic translation of the Hebrew text by rote memory. Such translations, known as *targums*, were never written down until about 200 C.E.

Ezra could also have been the one who divided out the first five books of Moses into the weekly Sabbath readings; he would have taught this group of Levites the translation of these portions first and then possibly added other passages as needed. So when Ezra was called to read from the Torah, it was from this new transliteration that he read, while the cadre of Levites, standing at strategic places in the crowd, provided the *oral translation* so that people could understand it. This is what is meant by providing the "sense" of Scripture—not a mystical understanding, but just a good translation of the Word of God by which people could finally comprehend what was written in the Torah! Note the necessity of grasping the historical conditions along with the cultural aspects in order to understand how and why it became necessary to provide an understandable version of the Torah.

Hillel's Rules of Interpretation

In this section we also want to consider the rules of interpretation of Hillel. From early on, an attempt was made to work out the rules of interpreting the Torah, beginning with Hillel the Elder (who died 10 B.C.E.). Hillel was one of the outstanding leaders in Judea, having founded one of the main schools for study.[39] One of his formulations for hermeneutics (method of interpreting) was the seven rules,[40] although "the indications are that the rules are earlier than Hillel."[41] These were expanded a little more than a century later by Rabbi Ishmael without materially changing the substance of Hillel's work.[42] Eventually these rules became one of the standards for Talmudic rabbis engaging in exegesis.

These rules are listed below so the reader can compare them with modern rules employed by scholars today.[43] Some comments on Hillel's rules will be offered, but no exhausting analysis will be undertaken. The objective in listing these is to see if these guidelines honor the authority of the Written Law.

***A Fortiori* Inference.** This is also known in Hebrew as *qal vehomer*, "light to heavy." This refers to an inference from a premise of minor to a premise of major importance. For example, when Miriam spoke disparagingly of Moses, she was struck with leprosy by the Lord and the question arose as to how long she should be quarantined from the camp. The issued was settled on the basis of inference:

> The LORD said to Moses, "If her father had only spit in her face, would she not have been disgraced for seven days? Shut her out from the camp seven days, and afterward she can be brought back in again." (Numbers 12:14)

The Lord suggested that if her father had but spit in her face (a minor inference), she would have been in disgrace for seven days. But, since she had also fallen into God's disfavor (a major inference), she would be sent out of the camp for seven days (conclusion). The decision was to move from the father's disfavor, which was considered minor in comparison, to God's disfavor.

Bernfeld indicated that three restrictions limit the use of this inference:

> 1. The conclusion of a minor to major inference should be equivalent in quality or degree to the premise from which it is inferred. In other words, one cannot infer more than what is contained in the premise which is the basis of our inference.
> 2. A new law cannot be derived by inference from a traditional law. . . .

3. The Kal Vehomer does not apply to criminal procedure. . . . it would be unreasonable to inflict punishment on the basis of a principle which is subject to error.[44]

Analogy. This rule is called *gezerah shevah* and works like this: when two verses in the Written Law have the same key word, then those two verses are mutually interpretive. For example, note how Rav Sha'ul built his whole argument for justification in Romans 4:1–8 based on the one word common to both Genesis 15:6 ("Abram believed the LORD, and he *credited* it to him as righteousness," NIV [emphasis added])[45] and Psalm 32:2 ("Blessed is the man whose sin the LORD does not *count* [or, *impute*, *reckon*] against him," NIV [emphasis added]).[46] Abraham was counted righteous, or justified, because his sin was not reckoned, accounted, or credited to him.

Deduction from One Verse. In this rule, one generalizes with the reasoning behind a particular law to a general principle. The idea then is to take this generalization and apply it to analogous situations.

Deduction from Two Verses. One generalizes the reasoning behind two different but related laws possessing a common characteristic into a principle for application to analogous situations. For example, if one destroys his servant's eye, or destroys another's tooth, in either case, the servant can go free (Exodus 21:26–27). The conclusion is that as the eye and tooth are parts of the body, then if a servant suffers injury to any other part of his body, he can also be set free.

Inference from General and Particular and from Particular and General. When a general term is followed by a particular term, the general term is limited and speaks only for its particular. But if the reverse is true, when a particular term is followed by a general one, then the latter covers the particular as well as whatever is related to the general term. Rabbi Ishmael, in his list later on, expanded the explanation of this principle in his rules of interpretation, 4–11 in his list.

Similarity Elsewhere. This rule derives an analogy based on two similar passages. Rabbi Ishmael omits this as a separate rule of Hillel and treats it in two parts, one under his rule two and the other in his rule three.

Deduction from the Context. Understanding is derived from the context, whereby one can explain a word or passage based on contextual study.

Rabbi Ishmael added a thirteenth rule not contained in Hillel's rules, declaring that if two laws contradict each other, they can possibly be reconciled by a third passage. For example, in the first instance, God is spoken of as coming down to the top of the mountain:

> The LORD came down on Mount Sinai, on the top of the mountain, and the LORD summoned Moses to the top of the mountain, and Moses went up. (Exodus 19:20)

But in another instance, His voice was heard from heaven:

> From heaven he spoke to you in order to teach you, and on earth he showed you his great fire from which you also heard his words. (Deuteronomy 4:36)

Did He speak from the mountain or from heaven? The two can be reconciled, however, by a third passage that says that God brought the heavens down to the mount and then spoke:

> All the people were seeing the thundering and the lightning, and heard the sound of the horn, and saw the mountain smoking—and when the people saw it they trembled with fear and kept their distance. They said to Moses, "You speak to us and we will listen, but do not let God speak with us, lest we die." (Exodus 20:18–19)

In general, Hillel's rules (and the rule of Rabbi Ishmael) reflect the major ones used in contemporary evangelical hermeneutics. They reflect an honest attempt to carefully exegete the Written Law. For that reason, as the rabbis' interpretation of the Written Law is contained in the Oral Law, much of the latter represents a good exegesis of God's revelation in His Word.

To conclude this chapter, interpreting the Torah, or Word, is no easy matter. The effort to do so can exact a great toll in time and study. But proper interpretation of the Word will result in glorifying God, blessing the hearts of God's people through the pulpit ministry, and guiding students as they study the Word in the classroom. And it will result too in God using His Torah, or Word, for those seeking to know Him.

THREE

The Authority of the Torah Throughout Jewish History

This author has always been intensely interested in the subject of authority of the Written Torah and the New Covenant. Though he grew up in a traditional Jewish home, the university experience—with its antisupernatural tendencies, anti-God framework of studies, and atmosphere of unbelief—made the claim for a God-given authority in the Written Law difficult to believe. It was not a problem of identity but a problem of belief, and this writer found it exacting and troublesome. Nor was he an isolated case; other young Jewish people as well as many believers still experience the same disturbing circumstances.

Throughout the centuries, the Jewish people have been known as "The People of the Book," largely because they are the ones who have been entrusted with the very words of God (see Romans 3:2). Unfortunately, the phrase as it is used today does not necessarily refer to the Word as God gave it, but rather to the volumes of material produced by learned Jewish men and women. When it comes to the sacred God-given writings and their interpretation, a critical problem of its authority has existed ever since the *Haskalah*, or Enlightenment.

In this chapter, we will examine how the more conservative rabbis and scholars assessed the authority of the Written Torah. We will see what occurred vis-à-vis the Written Torah in light of the Oral Law, the philosophical theologies of the Middle Ages, and in the modern period of the Enlightenment—comparing all their efforts with a biblical analysis.

The Oral Law

> The story goes that when someone in eastern Europe would ask his rabbi, "Pray, tell me some Torah." The Rabbi would never answer him by reciting verses from the Bible, but would feel it incumbent on him to give him some spiritual or allegorical explanation of a verse from the Scriptures . . .[1]

This illustrates the principle that the Written Law is not sufficient in and of itself. Ancient Jewish leaders applied rules of hermeneutics quite freely, as we saw in the previous chapter, so as to provide for an interpretation and application. This body of interpretation and application was then codified into what has come to be known as the Oral Law, or the Traditions, which becomes the basis of interpreting the Written Law in such a way as to help Jewish people live piously, or to have hope for the future. This body of religious cultural literature is authoritative for Traditional and the more Conservative Jews, and especially for the former. The Oral Law is not changed so easily now as in ancient times, and if it is, there have to be strong reasons for doing so. At times, the Oral Law can be considered to be on a par with or even to take precedence over the Written Torah. Evangelicals have no such comparable procedure for their body of interpretive literature.[2]

What remains now is to examine a few instances of how the Written Law was interpreted by the ancient Jewish leaders, and also whether any use can be made of the Oral Law for believers today. Messianic Jewish believers have various ideas concerning the Oral Law, either rejecting it altogether, or using only some of it, or taking more of it than might be warranted.

I would suggest that there are three possibilities in relating to the authority of the Oral Law.

First, as already noted from Hillel's and Ishmael's rules of hermeneutics, a good part of the Oral Law reflects *sound interpretations* of the Written Law and can be used appropriately on many occasions when seeking to enhance the witness of Messianic Jews.

Second, some features of the Oral Law can be *adapted* by believers to express a scriptural faith.

And third, certain elements of the Oral Law *go far beyond and are even contrary* to the Written Law.

We will now give a few examples for each area.

The Oral Law Substantiated by the Written Law

Many rabbis had keen insight in their interpretation of the Written Law. For example, when commenting on the first part of Leviticus 19:16:

> You must not go about as a slanderer among your people. (Leviticus 19:16)

One rabbinic interpretation was that slander "kills three persons: him who tells [the slander], him who accepts it, and him about whom it is told."[3]

The rabbis once discussed the phenomenon of the red string that was fastened to the wall of the temple on the Day of Atonement. The understanding was that if God accepted the atoning sacrifice on this day, the string would turn white. If God did not accept the sacrifice, the string would remain red. After discussing the obvious curiosity of the Israelites who looked more at the string than at the sacrifice, and what eventually happened to this string, the rabbis turned to discuss other issues. However, one rabbi came back to this specific conversation and made a very pointed statement:

> For forty years before the destruction of the Temple the thread of scarlet never turned white but it remained red.[4]

The destruction of the temple took place in 70 C.E., and so the question is, what transpired forty years prior to this date that made it so important for R. Nahman b. Isaac to say that God never again accepted the atoning sacrifice? Was he a believer in Yeshua? He doesn't come out and say so but simply left us with a a cryptic remark.

Another ethical lesson is somewhat similar to what Yeshua Himself had said in warning us against judging others:

> Why do you see the speck in your brother's eye, but fail to see the beam of wood in your own? Or how can you say to your brother, "Let me remove

> the speck from your eye," while there is a beam in your own? (Mattai 7:3–4)

The rabbis also chided the faithful that if you ask your neighbor to remove the splinter from his eye, he may well retort:

> Take the beam from between your [own] eyes.[5]

In another parallel, credence and integrity should be the testimony of everyone who desires to maintain his word as honorable:

> Let your "Yes," be "Yes," and your "No," "No."[6]

Compare that with Mattai:

> Let your word be "Yes, yes" or "No, no." More than this is from the evil one. (Mattai 5:37)

The rabbis also insisted that one cannot excuse sin. Beruria, the wife of Rabbi Meir, said that we must continue to pray that sin may disappear from the earth, while interposing a kindly word for the sinner so that possibly he will repent.[7]

The Oral Law Can Be Adapted

The Holidays. Yeshua Himself demonstrated how the *seder* service of the Mishnaic observance of the *pesach* (Passover) can be adapted when He introduced the special use of *matzah* after the lamb. (No mention is made of the use of such a plate with three pieces of *matzah* in the *pesach* of that day.) Normally, the procedure was to go from the meat to the third cup, and in fact, the instructions that appear in both the Mishnah and the Gemara state that no *afikoman* must be eaten.[8] Then, when was the special use of a plate with three *matzot* admitted to the *pesach seder* after the meal?

Yeshua, however, added the *afikoman* to the *pesach* of His day, thereby providing a special illustration for His disciples of how He would bear our sins in His own body:

> While they were eating, Yeshua took bread, and after giving thanks he broke it, gave it to his disciples, and said, "Take, eat, this is my body." (Mattai 26:26)

To this day, in the *Se'udat HaAdon* (communion service), Jewish and Gentile believers remember what Yeshua said concerning the bread. The adaptation by Yeshua concerning this portion of the *seder* provides for a better understanding of the Written Law's message concerning the Messiah, son of David, and His atonement for our sins.

Yeshua also added to the meaning of the third cup; as the cup of redemption, it is a reminder for believers as well as for Israel of the deliverance from Egypt. But He also added to its significance the element of personal redemption, because He is our atonement:

> For this is my blood, the blood of the covenant, that is poured out for many for the forgiveness of sins. (Mattai 26:28)

Other holidays were also adapted to demonstrate the uniqueness of Yeshua as Messiah and Redeemer. For example, on the last day of *Sukkot* (the Feast of Tabernacles), after the priests had obtained water from the pool of Siloam, one of them mounted the altar with both wine and water, pouring it out. As he did so, everyone present began singing this passage of Scripture:

> "Look, God is my deliverer!
> I will trust in him and not fear.
> For the LORD gives me strength and protects me;
> he has become my deliverer."
> Joyfully you will draw water
> from the springs of deliverance. (Isaiah 12:2–3)

In the midst of the loud joyful singing that reverberated back and forth between the temple walls, Yeshua cried out to the crowd that they were in reality singing of Him. Now, if they would only believe in Him:

> On the last day of the feast, the greatest day, Yeshua stood up and shouted out, "If anyone is thirsty, let him come to me, and let the one who believes in me drink. Just as the scripture says, 'From within him will flow rivers of living water.'" (Yohanan 7:37–38)

With that passage, compare Isaiah 12:3 above. What a drama that must have been!

The same can be said of the great festival of Shavuot (the Feast of Weeks, or Pentecost), when the disciples were filled with the Holy Spirit and the body of the Messiah began with the salvation of three thousand Jewish people. A simple agricultural festival had been turned into a grand testimony of how the Spirit began the formation of the new body of believers. Note that the first time any mention is made of Shavuot as the time of the giving of the Torah, the traditional Jewish belief, is in the Gemara, which commenced about 200 C.E. The only explanation seems to be that the Jewish community created an alternative explanation of Shavuot; if Messianic Jews are going to remember the holiday as the beginning of a *smaller*, *select* body of believers, then the rabbis will remember Shavuot as the time when the Law was given to *all* Israel.

Other Adaptations. Adaptations other than those given in the New Covenant are also possible. The *Shabbat* liturgy can be adapted into a Messianic *siddur* in such a way as to accurately reflect the truths of both the Hebrew Scriptures and the New Covenant.[9] At a Messianic *Shabbat*[10] service, the Scripture reading of the morning can be from the *pareshah*, the particular weekly portion of the Torah, and the message can also reflect on a specific aspect of the *pareshah*.

We do, however, also see adaptations in the New Covenant writings. Sha'ul and some of the other writers adapted materials from the Mishnah; in particular, Sha'ul used a number of such passages in the book of Galatians, and this will be discussed below.[11]

Traditional materials continued to multiply down through the centuries following the close of the Talmud at about 500 C.E. Some of these can serve as further resource materials that can be adapted for use. For example, the Yom Kippur liturgy of the *Viddui* (confessions) of *Al Het* consists of a long list of sins to be confessed several times in the course of the twenty-five hour service of fasting and praying. These prayers of confession are at the very heart of repentance for wrongdoing and serve in Judaism as the means of atonement. It is supposed that through this approach to God, He will justify the truly humble penitent.

In the midst of these prayers, one line stands out very clearly: "And for the sin which only the sin offering can forgive, please forgive." The particular kind of sin mentioned here is the unintentional sin that is linked to the sin offering of Leviticus 4, the Mosaic basis for a biblical atonement. This line from the *Al Het* underscores the message of what a genuine biblical atonement means and can very well be the basis for preaching on the Day of Atonement in the Messianic congregation.

Indeed, there is a wealth of material in the Jewish literature that can be used in accordance with a biblical position: the exegesis of a Rashi; the poetry of a Gevirol and HaLevi; essays and homilies by various rabbis; short stories that have a strong moral point, all from a variety of Ashkenazi, Sephardi, and Oriental sources. It would be a pity to ignore what can provide a lifetime of supplements to biblical preaching and teaching.

Drawing the Line with the Oral Torah

However, there also exists in the Oral Law teaching that cannot be supported by the Written Law. The teacher and preacher must always remember that whatever use is made of the traditional materials must always be under the guidance of revealed truth.

The Issue of Traditions and *Shabbat*. Yeshua Himself commented on the plethora of Sabbath practices in His day:

> Then he said to them, "The Sabbath was made for people, not people for the Sabbath." (Mark 2:27)

On another occasion, Yeshua stressed that people had let go of the commands of God and were holding on to man-made traditions:

> "'They worship me in vain, teaching as doctrine the commandments of men.' Having no regard for the command of God, you hold fast to

> human tradition." He also said to them, "You neatly reject the commandment of God in order to set up your tradition. For Moses said, 'Honor your father and your mother,' and, 'Whoever insults his father or mother must be put to death.' But you say that if anyone tells his father or mother, 'Whatever help you would have received from me is corban' (that is, a gift for God), then you no longer permit him to do anything for his father or mother. Thus you nullify the word of God by your tradition that you have handed down. And you do many things like this." (Mark 7:7–13)

This observation was intended to refer to *some* and *not all* of the traditions. Yeshua Himself lived out many of the traditions. For example, He never said anything to disparage the general synagogue meetings on Mondays and Thursdays nor the *Shabbat* services with their *pareshah* and *haftorah* (prophetic portion) readings. Nor did He speak against a whole host of other practices that took place throughout each week.

What Yeshua was speaking about were the traditional concepts concerning what constituted work on *Shabbat*, as well as other observances that went far beyond what God had ever intended. His point was that mere outward observances must never minimize the right attitudes of belief, lifestyle, and worship as found in the Written Law.

As a case in point, we have this story:

> Now he was teaching in one of the synagogues on the Sabbath, and a woman was there who had been disabled by a spirit for eighteen years. She was bent over and could not straighten herself up completely. When Yeshua saw her, he called her to him and said, "Woman, you are freed from your infirmity." Then he placed his hands on her, and immediately she straightened up and praised God. But the president of the synagogue, indignant because Yeshua had healed on the Sabbath, said to the crowd, "There are six days on which work should be done! So come and be healed on those days, and not on the Sabbath day." Then the Lord answered him, "You hypocrites! Does not each of you on the Sabbath untie his ox or his donkey from its stall, and lead it to

water? Then shouldn't this woman, a daughter of Abraham whom Satan bound for eighteen long years, be released from this imprisonment on the Sabbath day?" (Luke 13:10–16)

The Messiah's answer to the hypocritical response on the part of the synagogue ruler was to challenge the Oral Law, which was so at variance with what is found in the Written Law. Is a dumb animal to be treated with greater compassion than a human being? Yeshua's point was that on this occasion the Oral Law did not do justice to the greater needs of a human being.

The Issue of Atonement. We have already looked at the decisions made by the rabbis at the Council of Yavneh (70–90 C.E.), who probably believed that their decisions concerning sacrifice would only remain in force until a new temple could be built. Perhaps, they thought, the interval would be as short as that between the First and Second Temples. Yet what they promulgated in their deliberations ended up having an emphasis other than what Moses had ever intended.

At an earlier period, about 200 B.C.E., Shimon HaZaddik (or Simon the Just) had made a profound observation: "By three things is the world sustained: by the Law, by the Temple-service, and by deeds of loving-kindness."[12] In this saying, he encapsulated the biblical message: the necessity for repentance, the need for the sin offering and other sacrifices, all followed by the living of a godly lifestyle.

At Yavneh, however, the leading rabbis faced an entirely new situation. With no temple available, trying to meet the desperate cries of other rabbis and the people, Yohanan ben Zakkai declared to Rabbi Joshua:

> My son . . . be not grieved; we have another atonement as effective as this. And what is it? It is acts of loving-kindness, as it is said, For I desire mercy and not sacrifice. (Hosea 6:6)[13]

Neusner commented concerning this view of the substitute for sacrifice:

> Yohanan likewise thought that through *hesed* the Jews might make atonement, and that the sacrifices now demanded of them were life

> and mercy . . . just as the Jews needed a redemptive act of God of compassion from God, so they must act compassionately in order to make themselves worthy of it.[14]

From the time of Yavneh, therefore, Judaism became a religion with no substitute atonement. The Oral Law thenceforth interpreted atonement in the light of Yavneh's decision. Ever afterward, when the rabbis speak of salvation, we always have to determine specifically what they have in mind, whether physical, national, spiritual, or some other kind of salvation. If it relates to one's standing before the Lord, then this Oral Law from Yavneh must be assessed in light of what Moses proclaimed as the only way to have forgiveness for sin: through the sin offering (Levitcus 4 and 16), and in light of how the New Covenant proclaims Yeshua as the only sin offering now available. The Yavneh pronouncement on this issue represents a serious break with the Written Law.

The Issue of the Greater Authority of the Oral Law. The Torah is often likened to water, to wine, to oil, to milk, to honey, and there are still other images. The term *Torah* is used to describe both the Written and the Oral Torah. Many times, however, the traditional materials convey the sense that there are a number of occasions in which the Oral Law is considered to be on a higher level than the Written Law. Perhaps ben Zakkai thought he could legitimately declare that, following the destruction of the temple, atonement could be achieved through repentance and piety until such time as the next temple could be built. But the supremacy of the Written Law is an order of authority established by God. The New Covenant never changed Moses on this issue of atonement, because the same principles that applied to the sin offering in Leviticus 4 also apply to the sacrifice of the Messiah. (See further in the chapter on biblical atonement.)

The fact is that many rabbinical authorities would declare that the Written Law *does* take precedence over any other writings. Rav Moshe ben Nachman (Nachmanides) concurred with this when he defended Judaism as a religion against Christianity,[15] stating in 1263 during his deliberation with the Dominicans before King James I that the Written Law must always take precedence over the Oral Law. The tragedy, however, is that too often this is not carried out in practice. Messianic Jews have to stand careful guard over the mandate that God gave concerning His Word. Our task is to carefully test all other materials that we might use in preaching and teaching against the Word that God gave His people.

Additional Examples of the Use of the Oral Law and Other Writings in the New Covenant

New Testament studies being done today by Messianic Jews, non-Jewish believers, and in particular, Israeli New Testament scholars have determined that, as we have already noted, Yeshua and the writers of the New Covenant dipped into sources outside of the Written Law, such as the *sifrim hisonim* (the Outside Books, known today as the Apocrypha and Pseudepigrapha), the *Pirke Avot* (*Sayings of the Fathers*), and into materials that later became known as the Mishnah. We saw above that the Holy Spirit was free to lead the writers to select materials from sources apart from direct revelation and the Written Law, and whatever was chosen was considered supportive to the writer's argument; and, since this material is now a part of the New Covenant, it too became part of God's inspired Word.

Yeshua, the Gospels, and Traditional Materials. We will now illustrate a number of examples of materials that Yeshua and the gospel writers used. On numerous occasions Mattai remembered what Yeshua said and cited His comments, also quoting from the *Midrash Halakhah* or *Midrash Aggadah*, the forerunners of the Mishnah. Or else statements from the Oral Law seem to give meaning to the discussion at hand. Only a selection of such materials will be given.

Yohanan the Immerser. When Yohanan the Immerser appeared as the forerunner of the Messiah,

> Now Yohanan wore clothing made from camel's hair with a leather belt around his waist, and his diet consisted of locusts and wild honey. (Mattai 3:4)

By today's standards, he certainly would be regarded as a strange person in polite society, but he was a choice servant of God.

Yohanan's dress, his camel-hair clothing, comes under discussion in the Oral Law, as to whether it is permissible to be worn. While camel meat was not allowable as food (Leviticus 11:4), the Mishnah states that for the purposes of the laws of *sha'atnez* (mixed materials), *Nothing is prohibited on account of [the laws of] diverse kinds except [a garment composed of a mixture of] wool and linen* (Kilayim 9:1). This observation from the Mishnah even states that *Camel's hair and sheep's wool which one hackled [combed] together—if the greater part is from the camels, it is permitted.* Because Zechariah was a priest, his son Yohanan was therefore also a priest, and so the latter would be very careful to follow the guidelines concerning what was permitted for clothing.

Yohanan's food also is mentioned in the Oral Law. Lest questions be raised as to why locusts could serve as acceptable food, Moses had already declared it permissible (Leviticus 11:21–22), and the Mishnah stipulates further instructions concerning it, even the blessing before one eats, *For all [was created at his word]* (Berakhot 6:3). While such food would assuredly not be palatable for Western tastes, yet among some Arabs today, fried locusts is a part of the accepted diet.

In a further consideration of Yohanan's meal of locusts, directives are provided as to which locusts are considered clean and acceptable for human consumption: *and among locusts: any which has (1) four legs, (2) four wings, and (3) jointed legs [Leviticus 11:21], and (4) the wings of which cover the greater part of its body* (Hullin 3:7). Locusts are considered *parve*, that is, neither milk or meat. A further instruction on how to prepare locusts, other than frying them, is that the flesh of fish and locusts can be cooked in milk (Hullin 8:1), and therefore, this might also provide for possibilities of creating a gravy with the meat of the locusts. From this instruction, we can infer that if a man took a vow not to eat meat, he could still eat locusts. Because Yohanan had been preaching in the wilderness, he probably stayed at one of the camps of the Essenes, living the life of an ascetic, and therefore, on a continual fast from eating meat. Perhaps this is the reason why locusts were a part of Yohanan's diet.

Yohanan also ate honey, but in rabbinic law, under certain circumstances, liquids can come into contact with the bees' honey and render it unclean. However, *the honey of hornets is insusceptible to uncleanliness but is permitted for eating* (Makhshirim 6:4). Wild honey could very well have been honey of hornets and that would free Yohanan from any danger of exposing himself to ritual uncleanness. One needs to highly respect Yohanan's position as a spokesman for God and a forerunner for the Messiah. As a priest, he was very careful with his activities, what he ate and wore; no one could bring any charge against him for living contrary to the given Written Torah and much of what was Oral Law at the time. No wonder Yeshua said of him, "I tell you the truth, among those born of women, no one has arisen greater than Yohanan the Immerser. Yet the one who is least in the kingdom of heaven is greater than he is" (Mattai 11:11).

The immersion that Yohanan practiced also comes under the purview of the Oral Law. Many guidelines are present in the Mishnah concerning ceremonial washings to ensure ritual cleanness. Yohanan's immersion ministry would obviously fit into the understanding of the time, although the immersion by Yohanan had a significant meaning all its own. Much of the Tractate *Mikvaot* provides instructions for the immersion pool, what would be acceptable or unacceptable for ritual use, and when it would be considered clean or unclean.

The rabbis regarded the Jordan River unacceptable for *Mikvaot* because it contained mixed water (*Parah* 8:10). But what is mixed water? The same Mishnah states that *One suitable [for mixing with ashes] and one unsuitable that were mixed together* (*Parah* 8:10).

Tractate *Mikvaot*, chapter 1, discusses the kinds of water that must be considered for a proper *mikveh*, with living or fresh water being the ideal. The one who is to be immersed is clothed in such a way so that all of the body is touched by the purifying waters (*Mikvaot* 9:1). With regard to the waters of the Jordan, although *Parah* 8:10 raises some question as to its usage for immersion purposes, it still is not clear whether its waters were unsuitable for all kinds of washings or whether it could pertain to certain of the rituals.

Did the Pharisees take Yohanan seriously because of his immersing people in the Jordan? Or would they question his efforts because it was not within the proprieties of the traditions? The people sensed that Yohanan carefully lived what was required of him as a priest; he would no doubt have been careful concerning the immersion. But even more, he had a special reason for his activities. The fact that Judea's religious leaders went out to observe what was taking place, since so many people had gone to the river for this immersion, means that they must have been curious as to Yohanan's activities and their significance. However, based on the authority that accompanied his ministry, Yohanan rebuked the Pharisees who looked on, questioning them quite sharply, "Who warned you to flee from the coming wrath?" (Mattai 3:7).

The people of Judea were accustomed to seeing *tevilah* (immersion) performed in only two situations: 1) when a person was being cleansed from ritual uncleanness; and 2) when a non-Jew wanted to enter into the commonwealth of Israel as a proselyte, as a son of Abraham, and be in a sense, *born again*, although it did not convey the spiritual sense. The immersion of Yohanan became therefore quite significant: God wanted to cleanse people from spiritual uncleanness, making them ready for the coming kingdom of God; and also, in view of the coming kingdom with Messiah's presence, it was no longer sufficient for unrepentant Judeans to be merely born as a son of Abraham to be a part of the nation. Even Judeans had to *convert*[16] to be declared righteous by God, as Ezekiel had already described it,

> I will sprinkle you with pure water and you will be clean from all your impurities. I will purify you from all your idols. I will give you a new heart, and I will put a new spirit within you. I will remove the heart of stone from your body and give you a heart of flesh.
> (Ezekiel 36:25–26)

With the preaching of Yohanan the Immerser, the call was issued to be ready for the Messiah's coming, and particularly, people had to know the Lord in order to be a part of this coming kingdom. This immersion underscored particularly the need for the decision for atonement from one's sins.

The Beatitudes. Beatitudes, as a literary form, are found in a number of places in the intertestamental literature, principally in the Psalms of Solomon 5:18; 6:1; 10:1; 14:4; and Ben Sirah 14:1; 25:8–9; 28:19. One sees them also in numerous places in the literature of the Talmud and they are usually introduced with "Blessed be," or better, "O the happinesses of."

The first beatitude. "Blessed"—we could say, "O the happinesses of"—"are the poor in spirit, for the kingdom of heaven belongs to them," says Mattai 5:3. The Mishnah poses a supposition: *Nor will an am Haretz ever be pious*, but the encouragement is that instead of belittling oneself, a person should *try to act like a man* (Avot 2:5). In other words, one is regarded as ignorant if he has no desire to be pious, or lowly and humble, and yet, such a one is invited to overcome his reluctance and be pious and humble. R. Levitas of Yavneh encouraged people to *be exceedingly humble, for the hope of humanity is the worm* (Avot 4:4). The best a man can ever achieve in business, power, and position will only leave him empty; but how much better is it for one to be humble before the Lord. A person is further encouraged by R. Meir to keep his own *business to a minimum and make* his *business Torah. And be humble before everybody* (Avot 4:10). The humble soul is regarded as a disciple of Abraham, one highly honored, and to be poor is greatly respected because such a person is teachable. The pertinent issue to be noted is that happiness is not based on how much of this world's goods a person can possess; material things in themselves do not really bring one true happiness. But if one can minimize or cease entirely from any reliance on material things, he or she will find it easier to be humble before God and have the eager anticipation of serving Him. Such people are happy because the kingdom of heaven awaits them.

The second beatitude. "Those who mourn" (Mattai 5:4) seems to draw on Isaiah's proclamation:

> to announce the year when the LORD will show his favor,
> the day when our God will seek vengeance,
> to console all who mourn,
> to strengthen those who mourn in Zion,
> by giving them a turban, instead of ashes,
> oil symbolizing joy, instead of mourning,
> a garment symbolizing praise, instead of discouragement.
> They will be called oaks of righteousness,
> trees planted by the LORD to reveal his splendor. (Isaiah 61:2–3)

At first it might sound strange to say that people who suffer degradation should rejoice, but their condition is made bearable in light of the impending deliverance from their disappointments and discouragements. And so they are comforted.

Because of who Yeshua is and what He came to do, He can be the true comforter. It is of interest to note that later rabbinic sources refer to the Messiah as Menahem, which means "comforter."[17]

The third beatitude. "Blessed are the meek, for they will inherit the earth" (Mattai 5:5). Or to paraphrase: "O the happinesses of the gentle . . ." There is a possible connection of ideas with Mattai 5:3 because there is a similarity between the words for "poor," *ani*, and "meek," *anav*. Furthermore, as Lachs points out, the phrase "they shall inherit the earth" in verse 5 is synonymous with "theirs is the kingdom of heaven" in verse 3.[18] Yeshua perhaps had in mind a statement by David, "But the humble will inherit the land [i.e., the earth)" (Psalm 37:11 NASB)[19] and used it here as a part of the third beatitude.

The hope of the humble is to one day inherit the earth, and numerous promises seem to reinforce this faith. The Mishnah encourages the righteous to be involved with Torah and *whoever does a single commandment—they do well for him and lengthen his days, and he inherits the land* (Kiddushin 1:10). The Mishnah also declares that *All Israelites have a share in the world to come, as it is said* (Sanhedrin 10:1), and there follows a prophetic announcement, "All of your people will be godly; they will possess the land permanently. I will plant them like a shoot; they will be the product of my labor, through whom I reveal my splendor" (Isaiah 60:21). Several similar statements appear in other literature, for example, *And after this all of the earth will be gathered together and they will inherit it forever* (Jubilees 32:19), and, *But to the elect there shall be light, joy, and peace, and they shall inherit the earth* (1 Enoch 5:7).

The fourth beatitude. In this beatitude, Yeshua portrays the goals of a godly lifestyle. "Blessed are those who hunger and thirst for righteousness, for they will be satisfied" (Mattai 5:6). Many examples abound where the people of God were driven by this spiritual goal (Psalms 42:3; 107:9; and so on). The longing of the man or woman of God to do His will should be comparable to the longing of a hungry and thirsty person that is so great, he or she faints for nourishment. Montefiore points out that the person who desires to do acts of kindness, *hesed*, will be enabled by God to do so.[20] In the Mishnah, *ben Azzai says, Run after the most minor religious duty as after the most important, and flee from transgression. For doing one religious duty draws in its wake doing another* (Avot 4:2). The desire to do God's will is a picture of someone hungering and thirsting after righteousness; such a person is encouraged to do deeds of kindness.

The hope for humble and righteous people is that "they shall be satisfied," a promise implying prophetic fulfillment. The Mishnah describes what happens when loans are made and when collectors come to receive payment: *The charity collectors go around everyday and collect from man whether he knows it or not. And they have grounds for what they do. And the judgment is a true judgment. And everything is ready for the meal* (Avot 2:16). The implication is that once everything is paid up by those who seek to do righteously, they can then enjoy a banquet. As Yeshua implied in His remarks, in the Beatitudes and elsewhere in the Gospels, the objective of living righteously, based on the new life made possible through the atonement, is to serve God and Him alone. Those who do so will one day enjoy God's favor at His Messianic banquet.

So far, the Beatitudes have specifically concerned the poor and humble. The next three beatitudes describe the noble ideals of those who are seekers after righteousness.

The fifth beatitude. The merciful know genuine joy because "they will be shown mercy" (Mattai 5:7). The modern Jewish understanding of the Hebrew word for righteousness, *tsedakah* (v. 6), is that it means showing mercy, or giving to charity—which could reflect acts of self-righteousness. No such sentiment appears in the Mishnah, but later statements by Jewish writers imply as much: "Whenever you show mercy to others, mercy is shown to you from heaven."[21] One must be careful that one's righteousness is not based on self-effort.

The sixth beatitude. Yeshua stated that the "pure in heart" are also filled with all happinesses because "they will see God" (Mattai 5:8). He may have had in mind the question David once asked: "Who is allowed to ascend the mountain of the LORD? Who may go up to his holy dwelling place?" (Psalm 24:3). In response to his own question, Israel's singer affirmed that only "The one whose deeds are blameless and whose motives are pure" (Psalm 24:4) may do so; these are the ones who can receive God's blessings and one day will behold His face. Because of the de-anthropomorphizing tendency in Jewish thought, already in place by Yeshua's day, the Traditions would state that to see God was to see "His Shekinah."[22]

The seventh beatitude. This beatitude states that "peacemakers" are also among the happiest of people (Mattai 5:9). A number of sources in the Mishnah address themselves to this worthy activity: *These are things the benefit of which a person enjoys in this world, while the principal remains for him in the world to come: [performance of] righteous deeds, and [acts which] bring peace between a man and his fellow* (Peah 1:1). In *Pirke Avot* are several statements portraying this ideal: 1) *Hillel says, Be disciples of Aaron, loving peace and pursuing peace, loving people and drawing them near to the Torah* (1:12); 2) *Rabban Simeon b. Gamaliel says, On three things does the world stand: on justice, on truth, and on peace* (1:18); 3) *He would say, Precious is the human being who was created in the image [of God] . . . it was an act of still greater love that they were called children to the Omnipresent* (3:18). In this last statement, the point is that because man is created in God's image, it follows that people are His children. Therefore man should know how to be a peacemaker, reflecting God's ideals of relationships between His creatures. Somewhat similar is the statement in which God is called "Peace," and therefore, His children are "Sons of peace," that is, peacemakers.[23]

A number of corresponding statements also appear in the Outside Literature: "Happy—who cultivates the love of peace" (2 Enoch 52:11) and "Happy (is he who) even though he does not speak peace with his tongue, nevertheless in his heart there is peace toward all" (2 Enoch 52:13).[24] Because God desires peace, or well-being, between His children, therefore peacemakers have a particular relationship with God, reflecting who He is: they are *sons of God*.

The eighth and ninth beatitudes. The final two beatitudes are designed to encourage believers who are under pressure and persecution by nonbelievers. Those who seek to follow the Lord and are truly happy in Him will know what it means to be persecuted for the sake of righteousness. They will understand that the gospel message will not be readily received. Yeshua encouraged His disciples to realize that they are no different than the prophets who were persecuted in previous generations. Elijah himself said that both Jezebel and many unrighteous in Israel had killed the prophets with a sword:

He answered, "I have been absolutely loyal to the LORD, the sovereign God, even though the Israelites have abandoned the agreement they made with you, torn down your altars, and killed your prophets with the sword. I alone am left and now they want to take my life." (1 Kings 19:10)

Jeremiah had been persecuted numerous times for his message:

However, Ahikam son of Shaphan used his influence to keep Jeremiah from being handed over and executed by the people. (Jeremiah 26:24)

So the officials took Jeremiah and put him in the cistern of Malkijah, one of the royal princes, that was in the courtyard of the guardhouse. There was no water in the cistern, only mud. So when they lowered Jeremiah into the cistern with ropes he sank in the mud.

An Ethiopian, Ebed Melech, a court official in the royal palace, heard that Jeremiah had been put in the cistern. While the king was holding court at the Benjamin Gate, Ebed Melech departed the palace and went to speak to the king. He said to him, "Your royal Majesty, those men have been very wicked in all that they have done to the prophet Jeremiah. They have thrown him into a cistern and he is sure to die of starvation there because there is no food left in the city." Then the king gave Ebed Melech the Ethiopian the following order: "Take thirty men with you from here and go pull the prophet Jeremiah out of the cistern before he dies." So Ebed Melech took the men with him and went to a room under the treasure room in the palace. He got some worn-out clothes and old rags from there and let them down by ropes to Jeremiah in the cistern. Ebed Melech called down to Jeremiah, "Put these rags and worn-out clothes under your armpits to pad the ropes." Jeremiah did as Ebed Melech instructed. So they pulled Jeremiah up from the cistern with ropes. Jeremiah, however, still remained confined to the courtyard of the guardhouse. (Jeremiah 38:6–13)

And Isaiah and Jeremiah were also martyrs because they held fast to the word God had given them.[25]

Yeshua prepared His disciples well for expecting similar treatment from their own people as well as from the Greeks and Romans. His disciples must not think that they would be highly esteemed for their preaching or their lifestyle. Rather, they should regard themselves as knowing the Lord's joy even when people "insult you and persecute you and say all kinds of evil things about you falsely on account of me" (Mattai 5:11).

The Mishnah also declares:

> If thou labourest in the Law [God] has abundant reward to give thee,[26]

thereby encouraging people to be faithful to Torah and righteous in their lives. Therefore, as Yeshua also said, the righteous should rejoice and be filled with happiness, not only because there will be a reward, but simply for the privilege of serving the Lord. As already noted in regard to the first beatitude, those who are persecuted have as their hope of enjoying a great reward in heaven. Furthermore, those who are faithful will receive a reward for their service, although nothing is said about receiving a reward for suffering: *Said R. Joshua b Levi, The Holy One, blessed be he, is going to give as an inheritance to every righteous man three hundred and ten worlds, as it is written, That I may cause those who love me to inherit substance and that I may fill their treasuries* (Proverbs 8:21; Uqsin 3:12). The Talmud does have a statement reflecting similar sentiments at a later date in the Gemara:

> Those who are insulted but do not insult, hear themselves reviled without answering, act through love and rejoice in suffering, of whem the Writ saith, *But they who love Him are as the sun when he goeth forth in his might* [Judges 5:31].[27]

New Covenant Writers and the *Sifrim Hisonim*. Other New Covenant writers also cited additional material from the *sifrim hisonim* ("Outside Books"), which are known today as the Apocrypha and Pseudepigrapha. Note how Kefa describes the future destiny of the fallen angels, citing 1 Enoch 11:2:

> For if God did not spare the angels who sinned, but threw them into hell and locked them up in chains in utter darkness, to be kept until the judgment, . . . (2 Kefa 2:4)

Yehudah likewise cites the *Testament of Isaiah*:

> But even when Michael the archangel was arguing with the devil and debating with him concerning Moses' body, he did not dare to bring a slanderous judgment, but said, "May the Lord rebuke you!" (Yehudah 1:9)

Some might claim that this strange piece of information was based on direct revelation from God. We do, however, note that while the *Testament of Isaiah* is not extant today, the church father Origen, about 200 C.E., testified to its existence in his day, so that from Origen's work we can observe the parallel with Yehudah's words.

Luke also dipped into the *sifrim hisonim* to portray the unparalleled chaos on earth in the period just prior to the coming of the Messiah. In this case, he cites the *Sibylline Oracles*:

> And there will be signs in the sun and moon and stars, and on the earth nations will be in distress, anxious over the roaring of the sea and the surging waves. People will be fainting from fear and from the expectation of what is coming on the world, for *the powers of the heavens will be shaken*. (Luke 21:25–26)

Though Joel has similar language, Luke is actually citing word for word from the pseudepigraphical book of the *Sibylline Oracles*.

Obviously, these Outside Books are not canonical. The rabbis at the Council of Yavneh (70–90 C.E.) proclaimed the extent of the canon of God's Word, much as Yeshua understood it in His day: "from the blood of Abel to the blood of Zechariah . . ." (Luke 11:51). It was necessary for the council to settle the question of the canon since not only were the Outside Books widely read among the Jewish people, but writers, including the New Covenant authors, were incorporating material from them. So while in their totality, these Outside Books are not considered as Scripture, when the Holy Spirit led the New Covenant writers to cite from them, they were citing true and valid material. (See above also on the topic of inspiration.)

Sha'ul and the Oral Law. At least ten references to the Oral Law, specifically to traditions current in Sha'ul's day and later incorporated in the Mishnah, are found in the book of Galatians. It is interesting that in a New Covenant book in which, in the view of several commentators, Sha'ul supposedly declared the Law finished, one should find such citations. But this *shaliach* was not totally divorced from the Written Law, the Mosaic Covenant, or even the Oral Law. Not all ten citations will be mentioned here but we will look at one of the more pertinent ones, namely, the issue of "seed" and "seeds" in order to demonstrate that Sha'ul did not hesitate to use materials from the Oral Law when it suited his purposes.

In the following verse, Sha'ul refers to the Traditions, citing them in support of his arguments. The Greek is literally "seed(s)," here translated as "descendant(s)."

> Now the promises were spoken to Abraham and to his descendant. Scripture does not say, "and to the descendants," referring to many, but "and to your descendant," referring to one, who is Messiah. (Galatians 3:16)

Compare the Mishnah:

> Because it is written, For as the earth brings forth her bud and as the garden causeth the seeds sown in it to spring forth (Isaiah 62:11). It is not written its seed, but the seeds shown in it. (Shabbat 9:2)

What is interesting is that such a discussion concerning "seed" and "seeds" was in already in existence among the traditional materials in Sha'ul's day. The distinction had specific applications, and Sha'ul was certainly aware of such deliberations about *seed* and *seeds*. Even though the context of the discussion in the Mishnah is not germane to the context of the book of Galatians, it nevertheless became the basis for Sha'ul's application to a specific interpretation, when he expanded the promise to Abraham to include an implication regarding the Messiah.

Note that a valid view of inspiration allows for such selection of materials as led by the Holy Spirit.

A Concluding Word. The New Covenant writers were careful in their assessment of the Mosaic Covenant, also in their use of the Oral Law. The early Messianic Jews generally tried to maintain a viable community until the 500s C.E. The tragedy is that because of the general church councils, this community was not permitted the freedom to retain its distinctive contextualization. Instead, the non-Jewish element of Christendom prevailed. Belief and lifestyle became Greco-Roman and anyone or anything that did not fit into this pattern was branded as heretical. Their cry was that "the Law was no more," and it therefore became acceptable to denigrate Judaism and bury the Messianic Jewish expression of faith. Anyone who tried to adhere to the latter was simply read out of the body of Messiah. Not until the nineteenth century was there an aggressive attempt to allow for various cultural expressions of the biblical faith on many mission fields of the world, and even today, resistance still prevails in many quarters to the Messianic Jewish contextualization.

This will not be the place to enter into the discussion as to how much of the Oral Law can be used in the contemporary Messianic Jewish congregations. Even among Messianic Jews, a variety of opinions exist on this subject, sometimes debated heatedly. However, we will return to this topic later when ecclesiology (the doctrine of the body of Messiah) is taken up, and especially when the special topic of a Messianic worship and lifestyle will be considered.

The Interpretations of the Middle Ages

In the late 700s and 800s, Muslim theologians began their work of what is called in the history of philosophy *Kalam*, translating the Greek classics into Arabic and contextualizing their beliefs into Aristotelian categories (that is, following the thought of the Greek philosopher Aristotle). Through this effort, the relation of revelation and reason became a pressing issue. Libraries contain a multitude of volumes in which writers of this period debated whether religious truth is a matter of revelation alone or whether it is ascertainable through the intellect. Our task is not to debate this point but to see how Jewish thinkers related these issues to the Written Law.

Saadya HaGaon (882–942)

The Muslim theologians influenced Saadya, who lived in Babylonia in the late 800s and early 900s. He adopted some of their techniques and became the father of Jewish philosophy when he formulated his *Emunot veDeot* (*Book of Beliefs and Opinions*). Much as Yohanan ben Zakkai did centuries earlier when he started the process that culminated in the Mishnah, so Saadya now felt that the traditions had become such a mass of material that it was necessary to simplify it to its essence, in the process expressing it through an Aristotelian philosophy. In this way Saadya perceived that he could demonstrate how the Jewish religion was more than adequate in responding to the test of reason.

Relation of Revelation and Reason. Saadya knew he would be opposed for his novel approach of substantiating the truths of the Written Law by means of philosophical reason. Therefore he went to great lengths to defend his position in the introduction to his *Emunot veDeot*. He told the story of a man who weighed out his money, which came to one thousand pieces.[28] He then began to distribute sums to various people. At a certain point, he declared that he had five hundred pieces left and offered to weigh it out. When he did so, he was proven right and so people trusted his word.

But on the other hand, said Saadya, suppose the man desired to calculate the remainder of his financial account in this way: He proceeded to ascertain how much money had been given to various individuals, added it up, and from the original amount subtracted what had been distributed. In this way he arrived at the precise figure of five hundred pieces.

Saadya likened the first method of determining the five hundred pieces to revelation, which provided the truth immediately through the direct means of personal testimony and correlation with personal experience. The second method, on the other hand, is what reason provides. The great sage suggested that the religious teaching of Judaism cannot be contrary to reason. Revelation functions as a means to grasp truth quickly and directly; but what is revealed will stand the test of reason and philosophical inquiry. Those who have little time or opportunity for study can quickly arrive at the truth through revelation. But also, those who search out truth through reason will come to the same conclusions.

The Balance of Revelation and Reason. Disputes arose over Saadya's position, especially by those who claimed that he had once confided that when reason and revelation conflict, then "Reason is primary, Scripture and revelation secondary in rank as sources of truth . . ." But Epstein points out that other statements by Saadya reflect the exact opposite:

> . . . in the last resort there was something inherently deficient in human reasoning so that it could not be made the final test of truth, and . . . the statements of revelation had accordingly to be accepted, even in cases where they could not be accommodated with reason.[29]

By and large, however, this Jewish philosopher reflected the Written Torah quite well in his philosophical theology.

The Rambam (Maimonides) (1135–1204)

The climax of the Rambam's philosophic work is his *Moreh Nebukhim* (*Guide of the Perplexed*), which expanded on the work of Saadya. Maimonides went to great lengths to demonstrate the limits of the human intellect to comprehend the great truths of revelation.[30] As one example of an area where reason must bow to revelation, the Rambam insisted that while Aristotelian philosophy was primarily the avenue by which to categorize the truths of Judaism, he could not hold to the Greek position that the universe is eternal. Since the opening statement in Genesis declares that the universe had a beginning, then to assert what Aristotle declared would mean that the Torah would collapse.[31] Revelation became, in this instance, the test for truth over against reason.

But also in the *Guide for the Perplexed*, other aspects of the relation of revelation vis-à-vis reason are quite disquieting. Only a few such areas will be mentioned.

The Peculiar Use of *Yachid*. For centuries, there were no articles or principles of faith to express the quintessential essence of Judaism. The rabbis felt that the Torah itself was that essence; the task of a good Jew was therefore to spend as much time as possible in study of the Torah. Beginning with the Middle Ages, the lot of Jewry was to suffer the Crusades and ferocious efforts to convert whole Jewish populations, as for example during the Spanish Catholic reconquest of the peninsula from the Muslims. It was at that time that Jewish religious leaders began to set forth articles of faith to express the simplest and most basic beliefs of Judaism to which a Jewish person needed to adhere in order to remain within the Jewish fold.

One of the earliest of these statements was the Rambam's Thirteen Principles of Faith, found in his *Commentary on the Mishnah*, introduction to Sanhedrin chapter 10, set forth to counteract any inroads of Christianity or Islam on Jewish people. They are beautifully stated, phrased in a very positive way and appear almost innocuous, yet they forcefully express the essence of what Judaism states and from which one does not depart.

In the second of the thirteen principles, Maimonides stated: "I believe with perfect faith, that God, blessed be His name, is a Unity . . ." The word here for "Unity" is *yachid*, meaning "only" one. In other words, God is one in such a way that He can never be understood as a Tri-unity, as three in one. With one neat statement, this Jewish philosopher undercut what the Council of Nicea sought to express: the Father, Son, and the Holy Spirit, each viewed as God, are one God, but in a Tri-unity. That is, God is one but in three persons. The Rambam stated clearly that such a God is clearly not the same as the God of Judaism, who is "only" one.

One can understand the theological motivation in seeking to clearly define Judaism's belief. But the disquieting feature from a biblical point of view is the announcement that God is *yachid*. *Nowhere* in Scripture is God ever referred to by this designation; rather, the word is *echad*, as in the *Shema* (Deuteronomy 6:4). While in most usages *echad* means "only one," there are a few passages in which it can also suggest "composite unity."[32] One can therefore understand the *Shema*'s declaration that "the Lord is one," to allow for a later revelation of the persons of the Godhead. To refer to God as *yachid* when the Scriptures never do only takes away from the authority of the

Written Law, which progressively unfolds the mystery of who God is. This issue concerning *'ehad* or *yachid* will be considered further at length below.

God Is Completely Separate from This World. The de-anthropomorphizing of God[33] (see also chapter seven) reached its climax with Maimonides in his doctrine of the *double negative*, which became his way of speaking of God as He relates to this world.[34] Such a position did not evolve overnight. Earlier, the rabbinical authorities following the Babylonian exile sought to "shield" the presence of God from man by using substitute words when speaking of Him. The concern was that one must be careful when using anthropomorphic terms because such usage could lead to degrading God's holiness. In one sense, this concern was good and proper, because the rabbis did not wish to see Israel ever participate again in idolatry, in which the God of Israel was brought down to the level of all the other gods. The result of this de-anthropomorphizing effort can be seen already by Yeshua's day in the creation of a library of special terms used when speaking of God, and in fact avoiding using His name altogether.

In another way, however, changing the language used to speak of God effectively created a barrier whereby God does not cross into the realm of man, neither does man cross into God's realm. This will be discussed in further detail when speaking of the Messiah's identity.

Maimonides' technique of the "double negative" was the climax of this de-anthropomorphizing process. Instead of saying that "God loves Israel," one must say: "God is in a state of non non-loving Israel"! God's oneness, *yachid*, was so wholly other that He must never be brought into any close proximity to any part of His creation, whether the natural world or man. Because of this otherness, it is not possible for God to directly teach us; rather, we are to imitate what He does as we observe Him.

In this way, Maimonides so isolated God from creation that it can be asserted that the God of Maimonides is not the God of the Bible! And while many followed him in this respect, there were other Jewish people who disagreed thoroughly with him. Nevertheless, even today many still agree with the Rambam. It is disquieting to see how the use of reason has detracted from the authority of the Written Law.

Reason Reinterprets Revelation. What can be said of other statements by the Rambam? As much as possible, he reduced the miraculous elements of Scripture to natural processes. Isidore Epstein says:

> It was the same reverence for the human intellect which led him to give allegorical explanations to the Biblical story of the Paradise, and also to identify the angels mentioned in Scripture with the forces or elements in nature or with divinely inspired men. Whilst accepting the existence of angels as the "separate intelligences" of the spheres that figure in Greek cosmology, he denied, against the traditional belief, that they ever came down on earth in human form. He likewise denied the existence of demons, and maintained that all references to them in the Talmud and Midrash were to be understood only as figurative expressions of physical plagues.
>
> For the same reason, he treats the descriptions of the idyllic conditions of the Messianic age portrayed by the Prophets as metaphorical. . . .[35]

It is no wonder that many disagreed with the Rambam, either quietly or sometimes with a great uproar, for his books were even burned in Paris soon after his death in 1204.

We conclude that the use of reason can *have a place* in the understanding of faith, but reason should *never supplant* plain literal statements of God's revelation.

Disquieting Features of the Enlightenment

Traditional Judaism maintained its testimony of faith in the Written Torah, though we may have questions concerning its doctrines of God, Messiah, sin, and atonement. In contrast, the Enlightenment period from about 1750/1800 to the present has been a destructive influence on faith in the Word. Ironically, while the Enlightenment opened the doors for Jewish people in the West to move out of the ghettos and into the mainstream of life, at the same time it also undercut the main supports for the Scriptures and the faith they offer in a living God.

Our task is not to be exhaustive but to provide the reader with a basic overview of the changes that Jewish belief and lifestyle underwent during the past 200 to 250 years. We can characterize this period as "Judaism: Questionmark!" By this we do not mean that Jews have no general concept of what they believe, but rather that there is no one group of Jewish people who can legislate what is normative Judaism for any other group. (That is the reason why it is so difficult to answer the question: Who is a Jew?)

Moses Mendelssohn (1729–1786)

One of the major emphases of the Enlightenment was education, and Moses Mendelssohn was a major player in this new emphasis among German Jews. He would never have looked upon himself as a reformer of Judaism, but he certainly was a product of the Enlightenment. Primarily, he felt his task was to introduce Jewish people, particularly the youth, to the Germanic culture. His main contribution was to open schools where Jewish young people could study not only traditional Judaism but also the full gamut of studies in German, literature, mathematics, science, music, and so on. Such studies were never permitted in the *yeshivot*, or Jewish Ashkenazi academies, where only the traditional subjects were taught. He founded several schools and his students, when they were grown, continued this effort. Mendelssohn also rendered a translation of the five books of Moses into German. In the midst of all this activity, he denied that his intention was to reform the synagogue. And yet he laid the groundwork for what was to follow in the German reform Jewish movement.

In his studies and teaching, Mendelssohn made a major decision regarding the problem of the relationship between revelation and reason. Saadya, about a thousand years earlier, had attempted to give precedence to revelation but argued that reason could arrive at many of the same truths that revelation provided. Maimonides had suggested a similar approach, and yet he had his areas of waffling, and some of his thought detracts from the authority of the Written Law.

In the case of Mendelssohn and those who followed him as leaders in the radical Reform movement, reason was given the supreme pedestal and its pronouncements were regarded as an unquestionable authority.

Mendelssohn explained, "I acknowledge no immutable truths, but such as not only may be made conceivable to the human understanding, but as also admit of being demonstrated and warranted by human faculties."[36] Epstein pointed out that

> for Mendelssohn, the only articles of religion which admit of such direct proof as should command the universal assent that is yielded to postulates of mathematics, are three: (1) The existence of God; (2) Providence; (3) Immortality. . . . Judaism . . . is not revealed religion. It is revealed law.[37]

Given these sentiments and similar ones by the reformers, what was left of the authority of the Written Law? What became paramount was not so much what a Jew believed but how he behaved! The reformers' basic presuppositions of their philosophy ran contrary to the history of Judaism and would eventually tear out its very heart.

Voices in Opposition to Radical Reform: Samson Raphael Hirsch (1808–1888)

Because of the influence of the Enlightenment on Jewish people and its encouragement for them to enter into Western society and partake of all its educational and cultural advantages, a new appeal had to be developed within traditional Ashkenazic Judaism, which accepted by faith what God revealed in His Written Law. The German Jew Samson Raphael Hirsch (1808–1888) sought for an expression of Judaism that would take advantage of all the disciplines of knowledge and still reflect the highest regard for the supremacy of the Written Law. In a sense, he did for Ashkenazic Traditional Judaism what the Jewish scholars did for a Sephardic Judaism in Spain in its golden age of literature in the Middle Ages (about 900 to the early 1400s).

Hirsch wrote several essays in response to Mendelssohn's uncritical use of knowledge gained through the rationale, one of which included sharp remarks.

> You must admit it: it is only because "religion" does not mean to you the word of God, because in your heart you deny Divine Revelation, because you believe not in Revelation given *to* man but in Revelation emanating *from* man, that you can give man the right to lay down conditions to religion.[38]

The reformers looked for acceptance from and toleration by society, and they sought to appeal to German Jews to accept Enlightenment thought. The end result was that the Jewish people were left adrift, with no compass as to where they came from, and to where they are going. Human judgment is liable to error; with no other competent guide, how could one find truth?

The Problem of the Authority of the Torah Today

The Enlightenment had devastating effects on Jewish people even to this day. The movement spawned an apostasy the result of which is that today, most do not believe in any authoritative Word, or Written Torah. The majority of Jewish people in America and Europe have no working knowledge of the Scriptures, and very few Jewish teachers impart a high view of the authority of the Written Law. The result is that there has been a heartfelt void of meaning in life, and young people have turned elsewhere for answers. Some listen to the testimony of Messianic Jews. Others, trying to find peace and answers, turn to the occult, some form of the New Age movement, or even go fully into Eastern religions.

In Israel, while children and young people are taught the Written Torah in both the state secular and religious schools, the secular system—which has the largest attendance—does not generally assign any binding authority to the Torah for everyday personal life. No wonder that in the last few years, some young Israelis have been turning back to Traditional Judaism, trying to find an anchor for their souls in which credence is given to the validity of the Written Law. But a good number of Jewish people are also listening to the proclamation of Messianic Jews and finding in Yeshua and the Scriptures the answers for which their souls desperately seek.

There is great heat being generated today between the Traditional religious establishment in Israel and the Conservative and Reform movements. This only points up how wide is the gulf between those who wish to hold on to a Written Law given by God, and those who hold positions that detract from a high view of the Word of God. The fight between these branches of Judaism is far more than just an acrimonious battle over how whether non-Jews who convert to Judaism need to undergo an Orthodox conversion or not. The issue really is whether we take the view that there is a revelation given by God or whether we place primary emphasis on human reason.

Long ago, the prophet Isaiah declared:

> To the law and to the testimony! If they do not speak according to this word, they have no light of dawn. (Isaiah 8:20 NIV)[39]

Isaiah's proclamation recognized the Written Law as authoritative and puts a stamp of approval on how we proclaim our faith and live our lives. We would not want to hold to any interpretation that demeans or limits the authority of the Written Law. This is our task as believers today: to proclaim the Written Torah and the New Covenant as authoritative truth—the guide for belief, the means for godly living, and the hope for the future.

FOUR

The Relationship of the Torah to the New Covenant

In this chapter, the discussion will center on the relationship of the Torah to the New Covenant. We will be dealing with the problem of structuring a contemporary theology in which we can utilize the Torah in various areas of doctrine without being called a legalist. We will need to explore the basis for such a theology, and address objections as well. Such objections may be raised by the rest of the body of Messiah in regard to our purpose in relating to Torah, since many believers may support that "the Law is finished."

We will not retrace what has already been presented regarding the Torah. Instead we will focus on how Yeshua, Sha'ul, and other New Covenant writers related to the Torah and what their statements have meant for the New Covenant in which both Messianic Jews and non-Jewish believers participate, each within their particular culture.

Yeshua and the Law

Some of Yeshua's statements with regard to the Law can be baffling. One such statement was,

> Do not think that I have come to abolish the law or the prophets. I have not come to abolish these things but to fulfill them. (Mattai 5:17)

Some might take this to mean that because Yeshua fulfilled all that the prophets had said concerning the coming Messiah, therefore the Law was rendered invalid. But is that what it means?

The Meaning of "Fulfill"

To determine what this verse means, it is necessary to settle the meaning of *fulfill*, behind which is the Greek verb *pleroo*. The word suggests "fill, complete, accomplish, carry out," and is "virtually a technical term used in connection with the fulfillment of scripture . . ."[1]

In his commentary on Mattai, Ulrich Luz discusses this passage at length and gives us several possibilities as to what Mattai had in mind, summarized as follows.

First, the "fulfillment" to which Yeshua refers may refer to His *teachings*. Then we have two possibilities. If Yeshua *did not* change anything concerning the Law, then "to fulfill" would mean "to bring out in its true meaning," or "to bring to full expression." If, however, Yeshua *did* change the Law, then it would mean "to add," "complete."

Alternately, the "fulfillment" can refer to Yeshua's *ministry*. This could mean that Yeshua "fulfills" salvation history as seen in the promises of the Law and prophets, or else it could mean that in His life, Yeshua by His obedience "fulfills" what the Law and the prophets require.[2]

Besides these possibilities, Luz discusses various interpretations of the passage that have been offered across the centuries.[3]

The Meaning of "Law"

"Law" Refers to the Written Law. From the discussion of Torah in previous chapters, we can state that because Yeshua mentions the Law *and the Prophets*, the entire Written Scripture appears to be in view. As Luz suggests, if "fulfillment" relates to Yeshua's ministry, then He appears to have offered Israel the Messianic kingdom as promised by the many writers of the Written Law, that is, the Scripture. He demonstrated by both word and deed that He could initiate this kingdom, making quite clear that "until heaven and earth disappear, not the smallest letter, not the least stroke of a pen, will be any means disappear from the law until everything is accomplished" (Mattai 5:18). But this does *not* mean that the Written Law is finished, or is meaningless for today.

"Law" Can Also Refer to the Moral Element. Likewise, in a number of passages in Mattai 5, Yeshua had something to say regarding the *moral element* of the Mosaic Covenant[4] *as a part of the New Covenant*. In other words, He added to the meaning of the moral element to convey more than just the letter of the moral element. Yeshua wanted believers to develop a greater sensitivity that would lead to a godly lifestyle, such as, "Do not resist the evildoer" (Mattai 5:39), "Love your enemy" (Mattai 5:44), and so on. There were always believers in Israel whose lives reflected the true spirit of the moral element; Yeshua, however, brought out a deeper meaning, a fullness of expression, and moreover lived every facet of this moral element of the Mosaic Covenant, *which is now a part of the New Covenant*. He is now the living Torah, and His lifestyle is the model for the New Covenant believers who now also have the indwelling ministry of the Holy Spirit.

Unlike in Israel of the Tanach, in the body of the Messiah *everyone* is a believer and each one is to demonstrate an ethic of unselfish love. G. Campbell Morgan may have said it best: "For the moment love is the law, the rule, the regulation, the principle of life that crowns everything."[5] According to Morgan, love is the major guiding principle of this entire chapter of Mattai. But while many believers today insist we are under the love of the Messiah today, true love is meaningless without a strong moral undergirding. Without a heightened sense of morality, love becomes meaningless.

Sha'ul and the Law

Sha'ul's statements about the Law occur in a new context that is different from that of Yeshua. Yeshua's concerns with the Law were entirely in a Jewish context; He often answered questions and addressed problems in the typical rabbinic fashion of the day. Because of this, Jewish people find it easy to consider Him as a typical product of His people in His day. He is a Jew and is accepted as one.

Sha'ul, on the other hand, has for centuries been regarded by the Jewish community as an opposer of the Torah, the founder of a new religion, and therefore not a Jew. Many of his pronouncements appear to be removed from the lifestyle of Judea; most of his remarks are directed to non-Jewish believers. In short, the apostle is criticized for departing from the norms of the Law.

But is he so far removed from his Jewish roots? That is what we must explore. It is noteworthy that many contemporary Jewish scholars are now taking a closer look at Sha'ul, in the process clearly linking his life and writings with his Jewish background.

"We Have Died to the Law" (Romans 7:4)

The verse under discussion comes as part of an illustration of Sha'ul's: a woman is married to her husband; as long as he lives, she is bound by the law of marriage to him. But when the husband dies, the wife is released from her marriage vows, and if she wishes, she can then remarry.

> Or do you not know, brothers and sisters (for I am speaking to those who know the law), that the law is lord over a person as long as he lives? For a married woman is bound by law to her husband as long as he lives, but if her husband dies, she is released from the law of the marriage. So then, if she is joined to another man while her husband is alive, she will be called an adulteress. But if her husband dies, she is free from that law, and if she is joined to another man, she is not an adulteress. (Romans 7:1–3)

The apostle now draws a parallel. The key parts of his argument have been put in italics.

> So, my brothers and sisters, *you also died to the law through the body of Messiah*, so that you could be joined to another, to the one who was raised from the dead, to bear fruit to God. For when we were in the flesh, the sinful desires, aroused by the law, were active in the members of our body to bear fruit for death. *But now we have been released from the law, because we have died to what controlled us, so that we may serve in the new life of the Spirit and not under the old written code*. (Romans 7:4–6, emphasis added)

What exactly does this mean? Did Sha'ul actually proclaim that the Law is finished, now that the Messiah has come and died for our sins? Many would say as much and explain the passage in just that way.

However, based on what we have seen about the Torah in previous chapters, we need to look more closely at Sha'ul's statement.

The Entire Hebrew Scriptures? Does Sha'ul mean that the Written Law—understood, as we have seen, to mean the Hebrew Scriptures *in their entirety*—is no longer in effect? Hardly! Believers will continue to be instructed from this portion of the Scriptures for all eternity; there is much we have to learn from what Moses wrote, what the prophets proclaimed, and what the wisdom and other types of literature teach.

The Entire Mosaic Covenant? Is Sha'ul then referring to the Mosaic Covenant? When the entire chapter of Romans 7 is examined, we note Sha'ul's statement that he would not have known what sin was except through the Mosaic Covenant. Specifically, he admits, "For indeed I would not have known what it means to desire something belonging to someone else if the law had not said, 'Do not covet'" (Romans 7:7). Clearly the apostle is referring to the Mosaic Covenant, and in particular, the moral element with its commandments.

In regard to Romans 7:4, one major dimension needs to be considered: How did Sha'ul relate to the Mosaic Covenant before becoming a believer? From what we can tell of his lifestyle as a loyal Jew and servant of the high priest, he related to this portion of the Word with a legalistic mindset. Sha'ul knew the Mosaic Covenant and many of the rabbinical interpretations, but he never realized the possibility of an atonement by the grace of God as shown by Moses in the sin offering (Leviticus 4 and 16). What righteousness he thought he had with God was achieved through many of the deeds he performed, including arresting his own people who had become Messianic believers and putting them into prison. That is why he wrote afterward that his people were "zealous for God, but their zeal is not in line with the truth" (Romans 10:2). Furthermore, he asserted that after he became a believer, he was not justified by legalistic works of the Law but by faith in what the Messiah had accomplished for him—a truth based on what Moses had already declared. But at the same time, Sha'ul insisted that the Law, that is, the Mosaic Covenant, is "holy, and the commandment is holy, righteous, and good" (Romans 7:12); the Mosaic Covenant is *not* a legalistic document.

Elements of the Mosaic Covenant. What, therefore, is the meaning of "we have been released from the law . . . so that we may serve in the new life of the Spirit" (Romans 7:6)? The only reply is what we said above: once the New Covenant was in place, the *package* containing the Mosaic Covenant was broken. *Something* of the Mosaic Covenant is no more; but the *moral and sacrificial elements* of the Mosaic Covenant remain *as a part of the New Covenant*. This conclusion arises out of a perusal of Sha'ul's letters. We can avoid taking a legalistic approach to the Mosaic Covenant by accepting instead the guidelines of the New Covenant. The apostle knew what it meant to "serve in the new life of the Spirit" (Romans 7:6); it was new because the Holy Spirit now indwells every believer in the body of Messiah, in contrast to the Mosaic Covenant under which the Spirit either indwelt or enveloped only a remnant of believers while the rest of the nation still remained in unbelief.

In this discussion we again see that we need to address these passages with care; we need to note that there are various usages of the word *Torah*. And we need to recognize that the Written Law (entire Hebrew Scriptures) and elements of the Mosaic Covenant remain very much a part of the New Covenant itself.

"The 'End' of the Law for Righteousness" (Romans 10:4)

Here is another passage that supposedly proves the Law is finished.

> For Messiah is the end of the law, with the result that there is righteousness for everyone who believes. (Romans 10:4)

A number of commentators suggest that the Law could not accomplish righteousness, or that God declares the believer justified upon his receiving the Messiah.

But does Sha'ul's statement mean that "The law could not accomplish righteousness"? In another passage it is supposed that he suggests the same idea even more sharply.

> Know that a man is not justified by observing the law, but by faith in Yeshua the Messiah. So we, too, have put our faith in Messiah Yeshua that we may be justified by faith in Messiah and not by observing the law, because by observing the law no one will be justified.
> (Galatians 2:16 NIV)[6]

With this verse, too, the commentaries seem to suggest that the Law is finished.

But once more, the question can be raised, "Was anyone *ever* justified by works under the Law?"

"End" as a Goal Within the Mosaic Covenant. Taking up the Romans 10:4 passage first, the word *end* needs special scrutiny. The Greek word behind *end* is *telos*, which actually refers to a "goal" to be realized.

Did the Law then have a goal? Of course it did! We can enumerate several of them. One such goal was *justification*. Through the sacrificial system, and the sin offering in particular, it was possible for individuals to know the Lord. The sin offering was an offer of atonement by God's grace, accepted only by faith, for the purpose of removing the sin barrier between man and God. This was the offering for "people as they are," human beings with a sin nature. Through this offering one could realize the goal of justification, whereby God declares the believer justified when he or she has come to faith. From that point on, such a person knew his sins were taken away.[7]

But did everyone in Israel avail him- or herself of that possibility? Unfortunately the answer is no. In any generation of Israel, even during times of great spiritual renewals, there were numerous unbelievers as well as believers. And for the unbelievers, the goal of justification was never realized. Israel, though set apart by God for specific purposes, existed as a nation comprised of both believers and unbelievers with "hardness of heart."

A second goal of the Law was *sanctification*. At any given time, under the Mosaic Covenant in all its aspects, the believer could avail him- or herself of a multitude of opportunities for spiritual growth. Opportunities also arose at various times during the history of Israel.

Sanctification has three stages.

At the time of initially coming to faith. At that point, the believer is declared justified. From that point on, God undertakes a special care for that person. He or she has become separated from their past as an unbeliever.

On the spiritual journey. The believer is in the process of spiritual growth, of being made more righteous. This is not a matter of self-effort or works-righteousness. Rather, there is a pattern of spiritual development: going forward, at times falling back, being restored, and then going forward again. Spiritual growth can even encompass times when a believer backslides. At such times, the Lord has to work in a special way to restore them, sometimes through a painful process that leads to their confession of sin and a "getting back on track" with their walk with God. We can see this pattern of spiritual struggle many times in the Psalms as David went through times of growth, then failure (as in the incident with Bat Sheva), then restoration, and finally going forward again. Note that *santification was a goal perfectly possible within the Mosaic Covenant and also guided by the entire Written Law.*

At the time of death. This is when the believer joins with all believers of ages past to await the day of resurrection, followed by service to the Lord Messiah.

Yeshua as the Goal of the Mosaic Covenant. Just as Yeshua is the "fulfillment" of the Mosaic Covenant, so likewise, He is the only one who can fulfill all the "goals" of this covenant. Obviously, He did not need to be justified, because He had no sin nature. But in the days of His flesh, Yeshua lived the fully sanctified life. Even so, growth was still involved: Yeshua grew first as a baby; then as a boy, attending school and learning as any other young man in Nazareth; then finally maturing into manhood.

> And Yeshua increased in wisdom and in stature, and in favor with God and with people. (Luke 2:52)

The fact that Yeshua had to develop and grow might sound strange to some. If He was already deity, what could it mean for Him to mature? Here is where we face the mysterious subtlety of the relationship between the deity and humanity of the Messiah.

Not only Luke but also the writer to the Hebrews speaks of this mystery of Yeshua's growth.

> During his earthly life Messiah offered both requests and supplications, with loud cries and tears, to the one who was able to save him from death and he was heard because of his devotion. Although he was a son, he learned obedience through the things he suffered. And by being perfected in this way, he became the source of eternal salvation to all who obey him. (Hebrews 5:7–9)

While Yeshua was the perfect man because He had no sin nature, yet He had to learn obedience by choosing to live out the purposes of God for His life within the guidelines of the Torah. The path God wanted Him to follow meant disappointment, rebuff, and rejection—even to the point where some accused Him of performing His works by the power of Satan (Mattai 12:24). No doubt these negative responses cut Him deeply in His heart. And He felt these responses far more than we can, precisely because He had no sin nature. At the same time, He spent much time in prayer, sometimes entire nights, so as to be fortified in His spirit to face His challenges. Ultimately, He was confronted with the most difficult of choices: choosing to drink the cup of mankind's sins. This decision did not spring from Him ready and tailor-made but was instead accompanied with prayer, crying, and tears. He suffered physically and in His soul in His last hours before He died.

Yeshua lived out the perfect goal of the Mosaic Covenant in the days of His flesh. He was and remains the perfect example for every one of His followers.

In conclusion, then, we want to ask: Because the Messiah is the goal of the Law (or, in this context, the Mosaic Covenant), does it follow that the Mosaic Covenant has come to an end? We have to conclude as we previously did, that the *package* of the Mosaic Covenant is no longer in force, but two of the elements (moral and sacrificial) are present in the New Covenant, while the third (ceremonial) is also a possibility, based on freedom of choice. The Messiah is the goal of *all* the Torah, the Written Law, as well as the goal of the Mosaic Covenant. Since the New Covenant has come into force, He remains our example. About this passage, Stern says,

> The normal meaning of *telos* in Greek—which is also its meaning here—is "goal, purpose, consummation," not "termination." The

> Messiah did not and does not bring the *Torah* to an end. Rather, attention to and faith in the Messiah is the goal and purpose toward which the *Torah* aims, the logical consequence, result and consummation of observing the *Torah* out of genuine faith, as opposed to trying to observe it out of legalism.[8]

Contrasting Positions over the Issue of Righteousness

Sha'ul next takes up an issue presented in the passage: "The righteousness that is by the law . . . the righteousness that is by faith . . ."

> For Moses writes about the righteousness that is by the law: "The one who does these things will live by them." But the righteousness that is by faith says: "Do not say in your heart, 'Who will ascend into heaven?'" (that is, to bring Messiah down) or "Who will descend into the abyss?" (that is, to bring Messiah up from the dead). But what does it say? "The word is near you, in your mouth and in your heart" (that is, the word of faith that we preach), because if you confess with your mouth that Yeshua is Lord and believe in your heart that God raised him from the dead, you will be saved. For with the heart one believes and thus has righteousness and with the mouth one confesses and thus has salvation. (Romans 10:5–10)

The problem is to understand the seeming opposites in this passage (and in Galatians 2:16 already cited). Does it mean that righteousness is unattainable through the Law but can be appropriated by what grace has to offer in the gospel of the New Covenant? This is what one hears so often from many pulpits in the church.

The Argument from the Adversative. The difficulty would appear to begin with the understanding of what the word *but* conveys in Romans 10:6. Is this a sharp adversative, asserting, "No, righteousness cannot be had by the Law; instead, it comes only through faith in what the Messiah accomplished for us through His death." But, is this Greek word *de* really the strong word some commentators make it out to be?

Actually, the stronger adversative in Greek is *alla*, meaning, "on the contrary," but this is not the word that appears in the text. The word *de* is a weaker word by contrast, "and," "also." Why then do the commentators insist on making the weaker Greek word carry the brunt of the argument for a supposedly exclusion of righteousness by the Law?

The Written Law and Mosaic Covenant Were Not Legalistic. Let us hold that observation aside for the moment. Note how Sha'ul proceeds to build the case for his point in verses 6–8. He referred to the Written Law in Romans 10:5 (citing Leviticus 18:5) and in Romans 10:6–8 (referring to Deuteronomy 30:1–14). He saw no contradiction when he used passages from the Written Law in his gospel message, declaring in Romans 10:5 (Leviticus 18:5) that when one follows the Written Law and Mosaic Covenant, and does what God asks him to do, he will attain life. But one most important matter must be kept in mind, however: one should never follow the Written Law, or Mosaic Covenant, in any legalistic way!

Yeshua told of how two men who had gone up to the temple to pray, one a certain Pharisee, a seemingly good religious leader, and the other a tax collector, one of a people who were notorious for gouging the poor (Luke 18:9–14). The religious man began to tell God of his own righteousness, of his difference from those who fell short in their spiritual responsibilities, of his care to tithe everything he received and to fast twice a week. Meanwhile the tax collector, knowing how far short he had come of God's righteousness, kept his head toward the ground, beat his breast, and called out to the God of mercy to forgive his needy, empty soul. Yeshua declared this tax collector justified because he had confessed his sin and humbled himself in the presence of the Almighty God; the Pharisee, a good representative of self-justification, still had to learn to humble himself and confess his need. Legalism was a perversion of the grace that was possible within the Mosaic Covenant.

Righteousness Must Be on the Basis of Faith. After the Messiah had died for our sins, and with the formation of a new body of the Messiah, the same righteousness is available by faith. Believers acknowledge that Yeshua is Lord and that He has been raised from the dead (Romans 10:9–10). Righteousness is not attained today by legalistic efforts—that is, trying to bring Messiah down from heaven (Romans 10:6), or going on a long journey to try and find what the Messiah offers through some empty self-effort (Romans 10:7). Instead, the word of faith is near one's mouth and heart (Romans 10:8) and righteousness is possible, *as it always had been*, through faith.

The point Sha'ul is making in these passages, as well as in Galatians 2:16, is not to set up a contrast between what was not possible under the Mosaic Covenant and what can be had within the New Covenant. Nevertheless, in the course of church history, many, including the reformers of both Lutheran and Reformed theology, expressed their theology in terms of this contrast.

The same contrast is also expressed today by many Bible teachers who falsely conceive that no believers existed in Israel prior to the Messiah's coming, or that Israelites had no concept of grace within the Mosaic Covenant. Some teach that all Jewish people sinned against God through their disobedience, or that no one could even be born again prior to the coming of the Messiah! In one case, a professor actually lectured his students that in the days of the Tanach, people could be justified, but not regenerated! As to how this pronouncement can be established in any biblical manner is beyond this writer's understanding.

And yet, the question arises: If atonement for sin was possible within the Mosaic Constitution, why then was it necessary for the Messiah to die for our sins on the tree? This question is a legitimate one; we will address some aspects below and some in a later chapter on the subject of atonement.

Addressing Again the Issue of Righteousness (Philippians 3:29)

> Watch out for those dogs, those men who do evil, those mutilators of the flesh. For it is we who are the circumcision, we who worship by the Spirit of God, who glory in Messiah Yeshua, and who put no confidence in the flesh—though I myself have reasons for such confidence. If anyone else thinks he has reasons to put confidence in the flesh, I have more: circumcised on the eighth day, of the people of Israel, of the tribe of Benjamin, a Hebrew of Hebrews; in regard to the law, a Pharisee; as for zeal, persecuting the church; as for legalistic righteousness, faultless. But whatever was to my profit I now consider

> loss for the sake of Messiah. What is more, I consider everything a loss compared to the surpassing greatness of knowing Messiah Yeshua my Lord, for whose sake I have lost all things. I consider them rubbish, that I may gain Messiah and be found in him, not having a righteousness of my own that comes from the law, but that which is through faith in Messiah—the righteousness that comes from God and is by faith. (Philippians 3:2–9 NIV)[9]

Returning again to the passage in Philippians 3:2–3, Sha'ul expressed his deep concern over the "false circumcision," which was characteristic of those who opposed him. Rather, this *shaliach* spoke of the possibility of "the true circumcision" of genuine Messianic Jews and Gentile believers who now had the privilege to worship God because of the Spirit's indwelling presence. He declared that he would not place any confidence in the flesh in order to gain favor with God, for his trying experiences showed him that he must trust the Lord and have faith in His provision through His Word.

However, the issue of righteousness, "works of the Law," "good deeds," "works given to believers by the Messiah," all can be confusing if one is not "teaching the message of truth accurately" (2 Timothy 2:15).

Justification by the "Works of the Law"?—the Experience of Sha'ul. Was it possible that anyone living the elements of the Mosaic Covenant could be justified by his good deeds alone? As already noted, this covenant does not sanction any such notion. The sacrificial element with its sin offering would preclude any righteousness gained through self-effort. God did not give His Constitution to His people for this purpose; rather, some had added to the elements of the Mosaic Covenant and thereby created a works-righteousness in which Sha'ul became engaged.

This *shaliach* grew up in a home where his father and others of the family line were Pharisees, and so Sha'ul also walked in the footsteps of his fathers (Acts 23:6). He had been sent to study under Gamaliel (Acts 22:3) who was the leading moderate of the Pharisee party. But something must have gnawed at Sha'ul's soul, and he is perhaps a good study in human psychology. He seemed to be driven, thinking perhaps that he was not doing enough to satisfy God's righteousness. At some point in his training, therefore, he moved over to the stricter side of the Pharisee movement, the Beth Midrash Shammai, or the house of study of Shammai. The only clue that might suggest such a move is found in his words immediately after his mention of Gamaliel: "educated with strictness under Gamaliel according to the law of our ancestors,"[10] thereby claiming that he was as zealous for God according to the house of Shammai as many in his audience. Later, when he defended himself before King Agrippa, he explained more explicitly that he lived as a Pharisee, "according to the strictest party of our religion," hence, according to the house of Shammai (Acts 26:5).

His lifestyle of following the strictest interpretation of the Written Law, as a way of finding satisfaction, led him into a violent clash with the Messianic Jews of his day. Sha'ul thus became responsible for the death of Stephen; when his clothes were laid at the feet of Sha'ul, the latter was marked as the perpetrator (Acts 7:58; 8:1). But he proceeded still further, seeking out believers and putting them into prison (Acts 8:3). Finally, he asked for permission from the high priest to go to Damascus to apprehend those he thought to be apostates, and to bring them in chains to Jerusalem (Acts 9:1–2). By seeking to stamp out the presence of these believers, Sha'ul thought that he was serving God, believing that such a commendable goal would earn for him God's righteousness.

But when the radiant holiness of God knocked him to the ground on the Damascus road and laid him out helpless and blinded, he knew that he had been confronted by the mysterious presence of the eternal, infinite God. Bewildered, he cried out, "Who are you, Lord?" The reply that came left Sha'ul in utter shock: "I am Yeshua whom you are persecuting!" (Acts 9:5). Later, before King Agrippa, he remembered an additional statement of Yeshua: "You are hurting yourself by kicking against the goads" (Acts 26:14), a reference to an everyday event as a farmer would guide his oxen as he plowed his field. At times, the ox would kick backward; to discourage this habit, the farmer would attach a crossbar with sharp spikes placed behind the animal. Every time the ox kicked, its leg hit the spike and it suffered excruciating pain. Likewise, all of Sha'ul's churning around in an attempt to perform the deeds of the Law, and thereby please God, would only bring him dissatisfaction, unfulfillment, emptiness, and no righteousness or justification to satisfy his soul. That is why he could say that all his advantages (Philippians 3:4–8) and his deeds, while good in themselves as he lived as a Jewish person, would never earn him the possibility of ever being justified.

Justification by Faith Within the Mosaic Covenant. The Mosaic Covenant, in itself—apart from any legalistic additions to the text—taught a different view of righteousness. Moses had confronted his people with the question, "Now, Israel, what does the LORD your God require of you?" (Deuteronomy 10:12). He then enumerated several desirable goals: "revere him," "obey all his commandments," "love him," "serve him with all your mind and being," and so on. These are all beautiful objectives that exemplify a godly life in the Lord's service. But how is one to attain these goals? And if one does all of them, are they by themselves sufficient for justification? If one fails in any area, hasn't he or she forfeited the right to be righteous? The only response to these questions was offered by Moses when he asked each Israelite to "circumcise your hearts" (Deuteronomy 10:16 NIV)[11]—not merely the flesh but the heart as well, by which a person is justified. The heart must be changed. Circumcision is one of the Tanach's equivalents to the New Covenant message of being "born again." Can anyone change the heart by his or her own efforts? No, but rather, one needs a new life, as a study of the sin offering demonstrates (see below).

What was stated by Moses was also echoed by the prophets. Thus, Jeremiah told his generation that in circumcision, the foreskins of the heart must be removed. The goal of the covenant was not circumcision of the flesh but rather the heart.

> Circumcise yourselves to the LORD, circumcise your hearts, you men of Judah and people of Jerusalem, or my wrath will break out and burn like fire because of the evil you have done—burn with no one to quench it. (Jeremiah 4:4 NIV)[12]

The prophet pleaded with his people to return to the Lord, to be forgiven for their sins and justified by faith. Tragically, though circumcised in the flesh, they are regarded as uncircumcised, as unjustified as the nations around them. This could only lead to the Lord's discipline for both Judah and the nations, as they failed to avail themselves of what He offered in His Torah.

> The LORD says, "Watch out! The time is soon coming when I will punish all those who are circumcised only in the flesh. That is, I will punish the Egyptians, the Judeans, the Edomites, the Ammonites, the Moabites, and all the desert people who cut their hair short at the temples. I will do so because none of the people of those nations are really circumcised in the LORD's sight. Moreover, none of the people of Israel are circumcised when it comes to their hearts."
> (Jeremiah 9:25–26)

On the other hand, those who responded to the grace of God, accepting by faith the lessons of the sin offering, knew what it meant to have their sins forgiven. Such persons knew the ministry of the Spirit in their heart; they experienced the work of justification and enjoyed the presence of the Holy Spirit, enabling them to live a godly life. This was not justification by self-effort, by the deeds of the Mosaic Covenant, although living the lifestyle of that covenant was the necessary outworking of a sanctified life.

Of course, not everyone in Israel was a believer. Only a remnant availed themselves of the atonement that was made possible, a fact that was a matter of genuine concern for God. With the advent of the message concerning the New Covenant, a new day has dawned with the formation of the body of Messiah, in which all people, Jewish and non-Jewish, will know the Lord. In the long-range proclamation of Jeremiah, we also see that one day all Israel will know the Lord, when the kingdom of peace will come in its fullness.

> "Indeed, a time is coming," says the LORD, "when I will make a new covenant with the people of Israel and Judah. It will not be like the old covenant that I made with their ancestors when I delivered them from Egypt. For they violated that covenant, even though I was like a faithful husband to them," says the LORD. "But I will make a new covenant with the whole nation of Israel after I plant them back in the land," says the LORD. "I will put my law within them and write it on

> their hearts and minds. I will be their God and they will be my people.
>
> "People will no longer need to teach their neighbors and relatives to know me. For all of them, from the least important to the most important, will know me," says the LORD. "For I will forgive their sin and will no longer call to mind the wrong they have done."
> (Jeremiah 31:31–34)

Justification by Faith Within the New Covenant. In Philippians 3:2–9 quoted above, Sha'ul spoke of his advantages prior to becoming a believer. Now that he knew God in a personal way, however, he no longer placed his trust in his privileges, as great as they were, nor did he have confidence in the legalistic deeds he used to do in the flesh.

Sha'ul does not rule out that Jewish believers will continue to be physically circumcised in accordance with the Abrahamic Covenant to maintain an identity with their kinsmen. But even as Moses, Jeremiah, and others called for the circumcision of the heart within the Mosaic Covenant, so this message remains the same in the New Covenant: circumcision of the heart is a condition of the born again experience.

> For a person is not a Jew who is one outwardly, nor is circumcision something that is outward in the flesh, but someone is a Jew who is one inwardly, and circumcision is of the heart by the Spirit and not by the written code. This person's praise is not from people but from God.
> (Romans 2:28–29)

One must place his or her faith in the message of Yeshua as our great sin offering.

The Messiah's death, burial, and resurrection indicated that something had occurred to the Mosaic Covenant, which became quite apparent with the loss of the temple. The *package* of the covenant no longer exists but *elements* do exist in the New Covenant. Righteousness was and is now available in a new body in which all are believers. What is important to note is that Sha'ul did not say that the Written Law is over, but rather, it remains in place; the Mosaic Covenant, however, has been modified.

The Works of the New Covenant. The New Covenant, of course, does not speak of a works-righteousness for the believer. However, God asks believers to live a godly lifestyle and to produce works that reflect the love and graciousness of God. Sha'ul declared,

> For we are his workmanship, having been created in Messiah Yeshua for good works that God prepared beforehand so we may do them. (Ephesians 2:10)

> He gave himself for us to set us free from every kind of lawlessness and to purify for himself a people who are truly his, who are eager to do good. (Titus 2:14)

Kefa also maintained,

> Live such good lives among the pagans that, though they accuse you of doing wrong, they may see your good deeds and glorify God on the day he visits us. (1 Kefa 2:12 NIV)[13]

In the one sense, the phrase "works of the law" is used by Sha'ul to say that as an unbeliever, these were his works of legalism. But in the biblical context of genuine godly living, good works are what attracted unbelievers under the Mosaic Covenant to come to faith as part of the remnant. In the context of the New Covenant, the very same lifestyle is the means by which unbelievers can consider the claims of the Messiah who stands ready to give people a new and godly life.

Under the Law

The Greek phrase *upo nomon*, rendered "under the law," occurs eleven times in the books of Romans, 1 Corinthians, and Galatians. This writer has heard the charge many times, sometimes directed to him personally, that Messianic Jews, by not walking after the Spirit, are placing themselves again "under the law." But is this the case?

So what Sha'ul speaks of as a questionable kind of law-lifestyle has been turned by some into a description of the Law as undesirable. But again, is this the assertion Sha'ul is making?

Sha'ul's phrase "under the law" needs to be regarded in a different light. From the point of this *shaliach*, it refers to something undesirable, namely, a lifestyle within a legalistic framework. Cranfield suggests,

> . . . we should always, we think, be ready to reckon with the possibility that Pauline statements, which at first sight seem to disparage the law, were really directed not against the law itself but against that misunderstanding and misuse of it for which we now have a convenient terminology. In this very difficult terrain Paul was pioneering.[14]

Therefore, it is *not the Law itself* that is heresy for the believer today. Sha'ul himself emphasized that "the law is holy, and the commandment is holy, righteous and good" (Romans 7:12) but rather, it was the *misuse of the Law* in which it becomes a system of legalistic observances that is not desirable. Because of this misunderstanding of the phrase "under the law," it is necessary to realize that believers in the days of the Tanach did not experience the Law as a burden to them. Nor did the Law represent an unattainable lifestyle.

The Apostle's Difficulty with Those Who Opposed Him

At times Sha'ul appeared to use harsh words concerning some of his own countrymen, and it is not easy to determine exactly who these opponents were. In fact, some of Sha'ul's statements sound shocking by today's standards of what constitutes speech becoming to believers. For instance, he wrote,

> Beware of the dogs, beware of the evil workers, beware of those who mutilate the flesh! For we are the circumcision, the ones who worship by the Spirit of God, exult in Messiah Yeshua, and do not rely on human credentials. (Philippians 3:2–3)

Many times, non-Jewish believers have described these people as "Judaizers," a word synonymous with "legalists." Yet the term "Judaizer" does not appear in Scripture. Too often the understanding of some Bible scholars is that these opponents were not even believers, their sole purpose being to place people "under the law" when, supposedly, the Law had already ceased.

Who then were these people who have been described as "Judaizers"? More importantly, why did Sha'ul take such a hard line with them? To answer these questions, we need to understand God's purposes for Israel before the coming of the Messiah, and also what changes took place after He came, especially following the loss of the temple.

God's Purpose for Israel Prior to the Coming of the Messiah. God had called Israel into existence at Sinai, as the nation entered into the Mosaic Covenant with God. He created a people who were to serve Him, including being a presence witness to other peoples in the Middle East. Israel and Judah, during their centuries of existence in the homeland, in fact experienced some seven or eight spiritual renewals, with the result that not only were believers spiritually revived, but the Spirit also worked among unbelievers within the nation, enabling many of them to come to faith as well.

And the outreach also spread beyond Israel. The testimony of believers had a great appeal for non-Jewish people who came to the temple in Jerusalem from throughout the then-known world. As a result, a good number became a part of the commonwealth of Israel and lived as full proselytes under the Mosaic Constitution. Even within the line of the Messiah, three non-Jewish women came from pagan backgrounds to become one with Israel (Tamar, Rahab, and Ruth). In the first century B.C.E., with Jewish centers all over the Roman Empire, many non-Jewish people left their paganism behind, preferring to be in the synagogues. Some went all the way, converting to be a part of Israel, taking on the responsibility of living in accordance with the covenant. These were known at times as God-fearing proselytes, although they had become Jews ("devout converts to Judaism," Acts 13:43 NIV).[15] Others held back from going all the way and were known as "proselytes at the gate," not fully entering into the covenant. These people the New Covenant refers to as "God-fearers" ("God-fearing Greeks," Acts 17:4; "God-fearing Gentiles," Acts 17:17).

Jewish Believers and God's Goal. When the message of Yeshua burst upon Israel after the great Shavuot (Pentecost) of Acts 2, as it was then carried to Gentile peoples, a crisis arose as to how the Messianic Jews were to relate to the Gentile believers and integrate them into the body of the Messiah. Today, the question is often in the minds of non-Jewish believers: What shall we do with the new Jewish believers in the body of Messiah?

In the first century, Kefa had to justify to the Jerusalem congregation his visit to the home of Cornelius the Gentile (Acts 10–11). Only the account of how the Holy Spirit had fallen upon Cornelius and his household, along with others, was able to convince the Jewish believers that God was doing something new and unexpected. A short while later, a further crisis among the believers in Antioch made it pressing to have the Acts 15 council called, and a decision made by the Jerusalem leaders as to how to handle the new Gentile believers within the body of Messiah.

The majority view. The decision by Yaakov that concluded the Jerusalem conference revealed a major disagreement among the Jewish believers. The majority of the group realized that a new age was dawning; their views were reflected by Kefa, Bar Navah, and Sha'ul in the debate at the council, and also by Yaakov's conclusion: Each of the peoples, Jewish and non-Jewish, had the privilege of freedom of choice to choose their specific lifestyle. If Gentile believers did not want to follow the element of the models or worship and lifestyle of the Mosaic Constitution, they had the privilege to not do so. If Jewish believers desired to live within the Jewish community in Israel, they had the freedom to also choose to live the element of the models within the New Covenant, as long as no basic Bible doctrine was compromised, especially in the area of the basis for atonement.

The minority view. But a smaller group of believers disagreed, expressing their opinion at the council.

> But some from the religious party of the Pharisees who had believed stood up and said, "It is necessary to circumcise the Gentiles and to order them to observe the law of Moses." (Acts 15:5)

Perhaps in the period between 30 and 70 C.E., this faction never realized that the temple would be lost; thus, they would have felt that Messianic

Jews must continue their distinctive witness in the same way as prior to the first century. Israel was the witness nation under the Mosaic Covenant; the new non-Jewish believers in the Messiah, they felt, had to take their place among Israel and live under this Constitution, *as always had been* the case in the past. This smaller group was comprised of genuine believers; they were not legalists, the so-called Judaizers. One would hardly imagine that Sha'ul would address these brethren in the harsh language he used in some of his letters.

The only problem was that they were badly mistaken as to God's purposes within the New Covenant. Once the temple was lost, this group must have then realized that a drastic change had occurred, and one does not hear of their efforts anymore after 70 C.E. But until that date, they caused Sha'ul some difficulty. Note for instance Galatians 2:12, concerning the delegation from Yaakov before whom Kefa had misgivings about eating with non-Jewish believers. The point here is that these men from Yaakov were of the more religiously identified Jewish believers who preferred to see non-Jewish believers come under the Mosaic Covenant.

Note also that no harsh word from Sha'ul appears in reference to these Messianic Jews; rather, the council of Acts 15 was called in Jerusalem at which an attempt would be made to settle the issue of freedom for believers in choosing the element of a lifestyle.

The non-Messianic Jew. Another factor also enters the picture. As Sha'ul's ministry became more widely known among religious Jewish people in the cities of the Roman Empire, many of these non-Messianic Jews would have taken issue with Sha'ul's message. They would not have agreed that a new day had dawned in God's purposes, nor would they have accepted in any way congregations of Gentile believers who acknowledged Yeshua as Israel's Messiah. Nor would they have acceded to Sha'ul's recommendation that they could choose to not accept the models of worship and lifestyle of the Mosaic Covenant.

In other words, non-Messianic Jews wanted to keep on accepting Gentiles if they became Jews, as had always been the practice. However, that entire approach seemed to follow a religious path of self-effort, just as Sha'ul had lived before he became a believer. These seem to have been the people who earned the *shaliach*'s ire to the point of harshness, because they were confusing the new Gentile believers.

Note how in turn these non-Messianic Jewish people were blunt with Sha'ul when he was in the temple worshipping the Lord.

> When the seven days were almost over, the Jews from the province of Asia who had seen him in the temple area stirred up the whole crowd and seized him, shouting, "Men of Israel, help! This is the man who teaches everyone everywhere against our people, our law, and this sanctuary! Furthermore he has brought Greeks into the inner courts of the temple and made this holy place ritually unclean!" (Acts 21:27–28)

For these Jewish people, the *shaliach* was out of control, in the process of wrecking the Mosaic Law and initiating an entirely new religion. They completely disagreed that the Messianic kingdom was beginning, and that they were seeing the fulfillment of what the prophets had predicted.

This has also been the attitude of many within Israel vis-à-vis the Messianic Jew throughout the centuries. Only in recent days have a number of Jewish scholars begun to reclaim Sha'ul as a Jew in the recognition that his writings include much of what is found in Judaism. We shall note this background below.

The New Covenant as Torah?

David Stern, author of the *Jewish New Testament*, brought attention to the Greek word found in Hebrews 8:6, *nenomothetetai*, translated in the NET as "enacted" and in the NIV as "founded":

> But now Yeshua has obtained a superior ministry, since the covenant that he mediates is also better and is enacted [NIV: founded] on better promises. (Hebrews 8:6)

One of the words that make up this compound word is *nomos*, or law. The verb *tithemi* means "to put, place." Stern points out that if this word had reference to Greek or Roman law, it could properly be translated "legislated," or "put or placed as law."

Other usages of the verb *nenomothetetai* appear. In the following verse, it obviously describes the giving of the Mosaic Law at Sinai.

> So if perfection had in fact been possible through the Levitical priesthood—for on that basis the people received the law [NIV: the law was given to the people]—what further need would there have been for another priest to arise, said to be in the order of Melchizedek and not in Aaron's order? (Hebrews 7:11)

In this next verse in Romans, a related word appears, *nomothesia*, again referring to Mount Sinai.

> . . . who are Israelites. To them belong the adoption as sons, the glory, the covenants, the giving [NIV: receiving] of the law, the temple worship, and the promises. (Romans 9:4)

Accordingly, the word *nomos* is translated as "law" the fourteen times it appears in the book to the Hebrews. Therefore, Stern suggests a translation of Hebrews 8:6 as follows.

> But now the work Yeshua has been given to do is far superior to theirs, just as the covenant he mediates is better. For this covenant has been given as Torah on the basis of better promises.[16]

Stern divides the sentence into two, slips the extra word *covenant* into the passage, and then strongly suggests that this second use of *covenant* is given as *Torah*.

No doubt, Stern's understanding of the second use of *covenant* is an attempt to bring out the meaning of the passage that the New Covenant can be regarded as a new Torah, given to believing Jewish people and non-Jews as well. Stern has proceeded to develop this concept in another reference.

This writer consulted a number of New Covenant scholars knowledgeable in Greek studies and noted their observations.

It can certainly be agreed that the New Covenant can be regarded as the "New Torah," provided that there is no suggestion of legalism and no suggestion that the Oral Law is to be followed; both these would undermine the major thrust of the New Covenant message. For clarity, until the discussion on ecclesiology in a later chapter, the term *New Covenant* will continue to be used since it is a more easily understood designation when trying to define a theology for the Messianic Jew. When treating how Messianic congregations should be structured and what their lifestyle should be, then the phrase *New Torah* might be useful in speaking of God's intention for this new document.

By way of summary, in considering the relationship between the Torah and the New Covenant, we need to emphasize three things. First, we must always ask ourselves to what is the term *Torah* referring when it appears in the New Covenant Scriptures. Second, in considering the Mosaic Covenant vis-à-vis the New Covenant, we need to think in terms of the former's total "package," and which models within that package are present in the New Covenant. Third, we must understand that the Written Law is never "scrapped." If we keep these factors in mind, the nature of the New Covenant will be clearer, both for the Messianic Jew as well as for the non-Jewish believer.

The Unfortunate Collision Between Jewish and Non-Jewish Believers

There is one reason why it is difficult to evaluate the entire argument as to whether "the Law is finished." Namely, the early Jewish believers did not have the time to develop a full-blown theology concerning the righteousness of faith, comparing it with what the Mosaic and New Covenants taught. They were busy with the ministry of evangelism, and had to also deal with persecutions by their own non-Messianic brethren, especially after the Council of Yavneh (70–90 C.E.). Most of the Messianic Jews saw their world through a Jewish perspective and culture, although there were those like Sha'ul who were well equipped to transfer the truths of these two covenants into the Hellenistic and Roman cultural contexts.

On the other hand, non-Jewish believers had the time to write extensively, eventually producing, by the time of Augustine in the early

400s C.E., a theology based on a Greco-Roman contextualization. For the most part, the theology that was hammered out in such a cultural context was sound. Unfortunately, no provision was allowed for *alternate contextualizations* whereby Jewish believers could express their views and live their lifestyles from within a Jewish context. The non-Jewish believers felt that their expression of theology and lifestyle had to be *the only way* to live as a believer. Furthermore, they had difficulty distinguishing between what was indeed sound belief and godly living within the Mosaic Covenant, and what was simply a legalistic attempt to earn a righteousness based on self-effort.

Tragically, some of the more prominent non-Jewish leaders also displayed an anti-Jewish bias. They were more than ready to declare that the expressions "works of the law" and living "under the law" demonstrated that the Law was hopeless, and that "grace" was the only way by which to understand a righteousness provided by God—as if people under the Mosaic Covenant could have come to faith any other way than by grace! Setting law and grace in opposition produced a misunderstanding that is still with us to this day. As a result, Jewish people have a difficult time understanding the message of Yeshua when presented in a Hellenistic mindset, with a lack of understanding of the Jewish backgrounds of the New Covenant, as well as of the relationship between the Mosaic and New Covenants.

FIVE

Recontextualization of the Doctrine of the Trinity as Formulated by the Council of Nicea

THE TRINITY THROUGH JEWISH EYES: A STORY

This author once encountered a young *hasid* whose piercing black eyes looked me over suspiciously. He knew of my faith as a Messianic Jew, and thinking perhaps he could lead a "misguided" Jew back to his roots, he took the time to talk with me.

"How can you believe in three gods?" he asked, and before this writer could reply, he added, "I know what you are going to say: 'We don't believe in three gods, but one God in three persons,'" he told me in a singsong voice. "But what does that mean?" he demanded.

I responded to him, "Is the very being of God so easy to understand? You would declare Him to be only one, but there are statements in the Hebrew Scriptures in which it is difficult to grasp who He is."

But my *hasid* friend cut me off, as if anticipating which passages I wanted to discuss. He declared sarcastically, "The Gentiles created this concept of the Trinity at the Council of Nicea. But you do not find that in the Torah, do you?"

His mention of Nicea intrigued me and I knew that he had done his homework. "No, the actual word is not present in the Torah," I replied, "but there are statements by Moses and the prophets that do appear to suggest some kind of mystery in God's nature, and I think you ought to consider them."

As I began to state the passages, the *hasid* threw his hands up in the air and walked off, not wanting to get into a serious discussion with someone he sensed would not change his views.

The Decisions of the Council of Nicea

Since that encounter with the *hasid*, this writer has thought long and hard about his mention of Nicea and his problem with the triune formulation of who God is. When this author first became a believer in 1948, and later on during seminary, he struggled with the best way to express his faith in God from the perspective of a Jew who believed in Yeshua. Now, from the vantage point of many years of faith, he understands that it was necessary for Gentile believers to contextualize their faith in a cultural setting familiar to *them*, which in the 300s C.E. was a world of Greek philosophy. However, in the first century, we also see that the writers of the New Covenant sought to communicate the concept of God's being from within a Jewish mindset.

The Council of Nicea, to which the *hasidic* man was referring, took place in 325 C.E. Already by the third century C.E., a number of problems had arisen among non-Jewish believers as how to understand the mystery of God's being. Ultimately, the bishops of the churches were convened in a council by Emperor Constantine in order to formulate a specific statement concerning who God is, and to delineate the respective positions of the Son and the Holy Spirit in relation to the Father.

The Deity of Yeshua in a Hellenistic Culture

The statements of the first major decision made by this council are presented here only in their bare outline form, one familiar to many Christians today who recite them in their worship services as the Nicene Creed, which states,

> I believe in one God the Father Almighty; Maker of heaven and earth and of all things visible and invisible.
>
> And in one Lord Jesus Christ, the only-begotten Son of God, begotten of the Father before all worlds, God of God, Light of Light, very God of very God, begotten, not made, being of one substance with the Father; by whom all things were made; who, for us men and for our salvation, came down from heaven, and was incarnate by the Holy Spirit of the Virgin Mary, . . .[1]

The original statement of 325 C.E. had been further revised by the Constantinople conclave in 381 C.E., reflecting what most conservative bishops considered necessary to protect the deity of Yeshua. In particular, the phrase "being of one substance"—in Greek, *homoousia*—insists that the Messiah is of the same substance as the Father. This word was deliberately selected to allay any suspicion that at a certain time in the past, the Messiah was not, and that He was not equal to God in His very being.

The Arians, who opposed the statement of the council and declared it to be unscriptural, proclaimed that at a certain time in the past, Yeshua had been brought into existence. The choice of the word *homoousia* was, in contrast, intended to "establish the doctrine of the true deity of the Son."[2]

It was certainly within the prerogative of the bishops to formulate a biblically based belief system that would reflect the culture of most non-Jewish believers of the period. Within that system, this formulation of the tri-unity of God was adopted by the church. But does this formulation of who God is really communicate when attempting to present it to Jewish people? Certainly, the Jewish community would not accept the Nicene Creed: The rabbis have insisted, in their pronouncements from the first century on, that God is only one, not three-in-one. For that reason, many Jewish people who express interest in Yeshua have problems when considering the triune nature of God.

The Separation of Jewish and Non-Jewish Believers

However, there was more involved in the Nicene statements than just matters of *belief*. There were also statements put forth bearing on *practice*, and these in turn shaped a particular attitude toward Jewish people.

Specifically, three statements came out of the Nicene conclave that created an ever-widening breach between the Jewish community and Christendom.

***Pesach* (Passover) or Easter.** The council decreed that no church should henceforth celebrate the Passover, which had furnished a vehicle for proclaiming the death, burial, and resurrection ofYeshua. Rather, from now on the churches must recognize Easter, to be celebrated on the first day of the week in commemoration ofYeshua's resurrection on that day. It was still allowed that on the previous Friday His death could be commemorated, but the bottom line was that the non-Jewish bishops wanted a calendar year that served their interests rather than following the Jewish calendar. Therefore, a totally different means was enacted for calculating the date of Easter separate from Passover.

Therefore, for no reason other that the church must now have a calendar all her own, a division was created between believers. From now on, no matter what the origins of believers, whether Jewish or not, they would have to conform to this new practice of calendar setting.

***Shabbat* (Saturday) or Sunday.** The council further insisted that no church should meet on the Jewish Sabbath so as to avoid any confusion with synagogue worship. The bishops of the conference insisted that henceforth, all worship would have to be on the first day of the week. Again, the idea was to commemorate the day on whichYeshua was resurrected from the dead; but it meant that worship was to be unified throughout all the empire; all churches, no matter the ethnic origins, had to conform to this new calendar.

These two practices of Easter and Sunday worship established a particular lifestyle in which to rememberYeshua as the object of faith. But it occurred in a context apart from the original culture of the gospel message. A good number of churches had still recognized the Jewish roots of their faith; they had celebrated the Passover and met on *Shabbat*. But from Nicea on, no freedom was permitted to utilize any truths from the Jewish community. The net result of this new cultural expression of faith was to completely separate the church from the Jewish community, *including the communities of Messianic Jews*. The latter particularly found themselves caught in the middle; they either had to submit to the practices of the non-Jewish community of believers, or else be considered outsiders and, therefore, heretics. Bagatti comments on this lack of freedom of choice:[3] ". . . this divergence generally did not touch the substantial doctrines of Christianity, but it did have enough influence to bring about a great division of souls."[4] Bagatti puts it mildly indeed, especially when we remember the latitude provided by Yaakov to the non-Jewish believers in the Antioch congregation.

An Anti-Jewish Emperor. When the Council of Nicea had ended, Constantine wrote a letter to those who were unable to be present. Unfortunately, his epistle expressed a virulent anti-Jewishness, in which his statements revealed the intensity of his anti-Jewishness. Coming from the most prominent leader of the empire, his epistle only served to breed hatred for Jews by so-called Christians; it left a debilitating legacy within professing Christendom, affecting theology and behavior vis-à-vis Jewish people. And in the 300s through to the 500s C.E., *the effect was devastating for Messianic Jews* who were caught in the crossfire. While they continued to witness to their Jewish brethren, their influence was waning. Eventually they became separated from the official church. Increasingly so as well, the Jewish community regarded them as traitors.

Subsequent Developments

At its best, the formulation of Nicea properly served the interests of non-Jewish believers. The downside was that the church after Constantine created its own religious culture to which everyone had to conform. Not until the early twentieth century was there an understanding that as long as basic biblical theology was not violated, the gospel allowed for a multiplicity of cultural expressions. It is a good thing when people of various backgrounds can express their beliefs and lifestyle best suited to their interests and culture. Therefore, Messianic Jews should also be given the privilege to do so.

Indeed, the possibility exists today for Messianic Jews to distinctively express their faith and practice from within a biblically undergirded Jewish expression. However, doing this has not been easy, because there are many leaders who move within a Hellenistic-Roman cultural context, who raise questions about a contextualization of belief and lifestyle that sounds Jewish. In the past several chapters we considered just such a contextualization of Torah. Now we want to undertake a recontextualization of the pronouncements of the Council of Nicea regarding the doctrine of God. For the purposes of this chapter, our attention will focus on the texts of the Written Law as well as what the Jewish writers of the New Covenant had to say. This will help in producing a definitive statement concerning the unique nature of God.

The Mosaic Affirmation of God as *Echad*

Israel's confession in Deuteronomy 6:4 is an affirmation that God is one (*echad*, אחד). Is there a possibility that the word *echad* suggests something other than an absolute one, or as we might put it, "only one"? The Tanach is not a "happy hunting ground" for finding many passages in which God is portrayed as "three-in-one." But if words have any meaning, can it be determined from the usage of *echad* that there exists a possibility that would lend itself to a recontextualization of who God is from within the Tanach? Our search, then, is to see how the word *echad* is used.

While there are hundreds of times in the Torah where it means "only one," there are also a good number of passages that suggest something other than "just one." A few of them will be considered here, with the word "one" highlighted in italics:

> And the LORD said, "If as *one* people all sharing a common language they have begun to do this, then nothing they plan to do will be beyond them." (Genesis 11:6)

Here "one" is used collectively, referring to all the people involved in building the Tower of Babel; and yet, they are considered as one.

> "If Esau attacks *one* camp," he thought, "then the other camp will be able to escape." (Genesis 32:8)

The reference to "one group" refers again, collectively, to an unspecified number of people.

> Then Joseph said to Pharaoh, "The dreams of Pharaoh are *one* and the same. God has revealed to Pharaoh what he is about to do. The seven good cows are seven years, and the seven good ears of corn are seven years; it is *one* and the same dream." (Genesis 41:25–26 NIV)[5]

Once more, "one" actually refers to two dreams that Pharaoh had, but the word "one" is used in a collective sense.

> Its length is to be a foot and a half and its width a foot and a half; it will be square. Its height is to be three feet, with its horns of *one* piece with it. (Exodus 30:2)

The use of "one" describes the altar made of one material, acacia wood, but actually the text speaks of two horns made of the one material. The possibility is again of a collective use of "one."

> When they came to the valley of Eshcol, they cut down from there a branch with *one* cluster of grapes, and they carried it on a staff between two men, as well as some of the pomegranates and the figs. (Numbers 13:23)

Every translated text adds the word "cluster," so that the Hebrew word *echad* can make sense. Otherwise it makes no sense to say that two men were carrying "one grape" slung on a line connecting two poles; no, they were carrying a cluster of many grapes. And once again, the word "one" is used in a collective sense.

> For this reason a man will leave his father and mother and be united to his wife, and they will become *one* flesh. (Genesis 2:24 NIV)[6]

"One," as it refers to the flesh, suggests that it takes both a father and a mother together in the marriage relationship to produce a child. The child is then one flesh, stating that the two were involved in its creation.

What Can Be Affirmed Regarding the Word *Echad*?

We have seen that in a number of occurrences of *echad*, "one" is used in a collective sense. But does that enable us to confidently assert that in Israel's great confession "The LORD is our God, the LORD is one!" (Deuteronomy 6:4), the word *echad* also represents a collective reference to the very being of God? This writer would hesitate to affirm such a statement based on a few usages of *echad*. Recall his *hasid* friend. He, and the rabbis, will insist that, from their system of hermeneutics, the confession proclaims that God is only one and that *echad* means just that!

However, what can we say *against* the possibility of *echad* referring to God in a collective sense? Here, we are on firmer ground because even in the Tanach, some Scriptures are present that point to a profound mystery concerning who God is. This is exactly what this author had tried to point out to his friend. At least three passages warrant serious consideration.

The Mysterious Angel Who Led Israel in the Desert. Even from the Jewish point of view, this passage has always been a mystery:

> I am going to send an angel before you to protect you as you journey and to bring you into the place that I have prepared. Take heed because of him, and obey his voice; do not rebel against him, for he will not pardon your transgressions, for my name is in him. (Exodus 23:20–21)

Rashi suggests, "Our Rabbis said that he (the angel) is Mattatron (מטטרון) whose name is even as the name of His Master, for מטטרון has the numerical value (314) of שדי, 'the Almighty' (Sanh. 38b),"[7] an astounding statement.

But what further information can be gleaned as to the nature of this mysterious Metatron? An interesting discussion in tractate Sanhedrin occurs where a *min* (that is, a Messianic Jew) witnessed to a prominent leader in the Jewish community:

> Once a *Min* said to R. Idith, It is written, *And unto Moses He said, Come up to the Lord*. But surely it should have stated, *Come up unto* me!—It was Metatron [who said that], he replied, whose name is similar to that of his Master, for it is written, *For my name is in him*. But if so, [he

retorted,] we should worship him! The same passage, however,—replied R. Idith—says: *Be not rebellious against him*, i.e., exchange Me not for him. But if so, why is it stated: *He will not pardon your transgression?* He answered: By our troth we would not accept him even as a messenger, for it is written, *and he said to him, If Thy* [personal] *presence go not* etc.[8]

The Soncino footnote explains:

The *Min* was a believer in the doctrine of two rulers and he sought support for this belief from Ex. XXIV, 1. R. Idith met his argument by showing that even Metatron was accepted by Jews only as guide, and in no sense a second god.[9]

But if words mean anything, does the written Torah declare this mysterious being to be *only a guide* who cannot forgive transgression? Or, are there other reasons why, from a traditional Jewish point of view, Metatron is not perceived as engaging in the task the Written Torah declares to be his right?

Scholem provides a further discussion on this mysterious word, Metatron, indicating that various ideas appear in the Talmud and Karaite literature in which a number of mysterious assertions are made about him. He is said to be the only one who can sit in the presence of God; he is a kind of a heavenly scribe, recording the good deeds of Israel. But a further question remains as to why the special name of God, YHWH, is in him. In the Karaite literature, specifically by Kirkisana, he is regarded as the lesser YHWH, but this view has been rejected by Israel's teachers. The major traditional opinion against considering him deity in any way is that no one wanted to assert this mysterious person is *another* deity. The engagement in the task of the de-anthropomorphization of God would not permit the worship of any other deity, even though a lesser YHWH.[10] And yet, the Karaites appeared to recognize this "angel" as someone special, "another lesser deity," which would reflect their interest in commenting on Scripture without any distracting Oral Law. Exodus 23:20–21 remains an enigma for the Jewish community to this day.[11]

The Meaning of God Who Has a Son. In a chapter replete with riddles, Agur comes up with one of the most mysterious enigmas of all:

> Who has ascended into heaven, and then descended?
> Who has gathered up the winds in his fists?
> Who has bound up the waters in his cloak?
> Who has established all the ends of the earth?
> What is his name, and what is his son's name?—if you know!
> (Proverbs 30:4)

The questions he raises reach a climax, with the strong implication that no one could perform these deeds except God Himself. The last question, "What is his son's name?" is the peak of the enigma. What do the Jewish commentators have to say regarding this passage?

One response has been to interpret the parts of this verse as follows:

> Who has ascended heaven and come down?—Moses.
> Who has gathered up the wind in the hollow of his hand?—Aaron.
> Who has wrapped the waters in his garment?—Elijah.
> Who has established all the extremities of the earth?—Our father Abraham.
> What is his name?—His name is the Lord, as it is said, The Lord, the Warrior—Lord is His name (Exodus 15:3).
> Or his son's name?—Israel, as it is said, Israel is My firstborn son (Exodus 4:22).[12]

Rosenberg follows Rashi in his interpretation,[13] who suggested that Proverbs 30:4 referred to Moses, while Rashi explains the last two lines as a poetic device, "If there was anyone like him, tell me his name, or, if you have forgotten his name, tell me his son's name, if you know there was ever one like him." But again, because of the increasing strong rabbinical emphasis that God is "only one," the interpretation of the Proverbs passage could not be allowed to yield to the mysterious enigma within it.

The Mysterious Person Born in Bethlehem. Consider this verse:

As for you, Bethlehem Ephrathah,
seemingly insignificant among the clans of Judah—
from you a king will emerge who will rule over Israel on my behalf,
one whose origins are in the distant past.
(Micah 5:2 NIV [5:1 Tanach])

The word "origins" is literally in Hebrew "goings out" or "existence," while the literal words behind "distant past" are "day of eternity." Here indeed is a mystery: Someone born in Bethlehem, the Messiah, who will come to rule Israel, but who has always existed from eternity. Again, we note a serious question as how to properly understand the nature of God. Only God exists from eternity, but now the suggestion by the prophet is that the Messiah, though born in Bethlehem as a human being, in a mysterious way has yet existed from eternity. What does this do to the concept that God is one?

Not many other passages are present in the Tanach that raise the question of the mysterious nature of God. One needs to be careful not to read New Covenant theology back into the Hebrew Scriptures if it is not readily apparent from the latter texts themselves. For example, one cannot turn to Genesis 1:1 and claim that the term *Elohim* (with its plural ending) is an obvious reference to the three persons in the one God in the Hebrew Bible. Such an understanding is only readily apparent from the revelation of the Messiah in the New Covenant. On the other hand, we can learn from what the rabbis asserted, that *Elohim* as a plural term accentuates the majesty of God. Even Girdlestone admits that the plurality of *Elohim* can also express the majesty and power of God.[14]

One must, therefore, be careful when exegeting Scripture, that we do not make the Hebrew Scriptures say more than what they actually say. With the New Covenant revelation, however, we do have a fuller description of who God is.

The Alternate Word for "One": *Yachid*

The Hebrew word *yachid* (יחיד) means absolutely one, only one. It is illustrated by God's use of the word when He called upon Abraham:

God said, "Take your son—your *only* son, whom you love, Isaac—and go to the land of Moriah! Offer him up there as a burnt offering on

one of the mountains which I will indicate to you."
(Genesis 22:2, emphasis added)

When God said, "your only son," the word *yachid* is used to describe Isaac, for he was in reality the only covenant son of Abraham.

Maimonides had used this very word in the second of his Thirteen Principles of Faith to describe the nature of God as *only one*, with no possibility of what *echad* might suggest, namely, a composite unity. By establishing this principle of the oneness of God, he could at the same time deny any claim for Yeshua's deity; no Jewish person could rightfully accept it, a conclusion that was already drawn from centuries of de-anthropomorphizing God.

However, nowhere in the Tanach is God ever referred to as *yachid*. In particular, the Rambam, or Maimonides, had declared that God cannot be in direct contact with this world at all. To undergird his assertion, he formulated what he called the doctrine of the double negative, whereby, instead of being able to say, "God loves any person," the statement must be: "God is in a state of non non-loving someone." The Rambam had put such an emphasis on the oneness of God, that it was therefore impossible for Him to be in direct contact with anything or anyone in this world.[15] One of the aspects by which Maimonides could say men can know Him is to "imitate His ways in the pursuit of loving-kindness and justice" on earth.[16]

What can we therefore conclude? It appears that the word *echad*, in its collective sense seen in a number of significant passages from the Tanach, suggests the concept of God as a composite being: one God, but mysteriously, with more than one person within the Godhead.

The Messianic Jewish Position as Expressed in the New Covenant

Another source exists that our Jewish friends could take into account concerning the unique nature of God. If one would consider carefully the data of this source, in its original cultural setting, the conclusion will shed further light on the meaning of the passages already considered, such as, Exodus 23:20–21; Proverbs 30:4; and Micah 5:2 (5:1 Tanach).

The Messianic Jews who wrote the New Testament did not set forth a theological-philosophical understanding of who God is. Rather, they began with the proclamation that God is one, as we shall soon see. But, in addition, once they became apprised of the claims of Yeshua, they asserted in simple statements their testimony of involvement with Him, as exemplified by Kefa, "You are the Messiah, the Son of the living God" (Mattai 16:16), which was an astounding statement indeed by a religious Jew.[17]

Some Jewish scholars respond by declaring that only a handful of people in Judah would have believed such stories. But the fact of the matter is that Yeshua had a following in the thousands. Once Kefa offered this assessment of the Messiah's very being, no rebuke was forthcoming. Indeed, as a religious Jew in His humanity, which few in the Jewish community would deny, Yeshua made an astounding announcement as He commended Kefa, "You are blessed, Simon son of Jonah, because flesh and blood did not reveal this to you, but my Father in heaven!" (Mattai 16:17).

What becomes interesting now is how each of the Jewish writers of the New Covenant considered the basic doctrine of God in the Hebrew Scriptures through the use of simple, succinct, but profound statements. They also had to evaluate this doctrine in the light of significant statements by Yeshua concerning Himself as well as in light of His ministry and the unique events that occurred in His life. The theological convictions by these writers are presented as follows.

Based on the Torah

Every one of the writers of the New Covenant affirmed the basic premise of the Torah that God is indeed one:

> One of the teachers of the law came and heard them debating. Noticing that Yeshua had given them a good answer, he asked him, "Of all the commandments, which is the most important?" "The most important one," answered Yeshua, "is this: 'Hear, O Israel, the Lord our God, the Lord is one.'" (Mark 12:28–29 NIV)[18]

The starting point of the proclamation of the doctrine of God by the Messianic Jewish writers of the New Covenant was the unity of God, not the unique nature of the

Godhead. The unity of God was the "fixed star" in their theology. In the midst of a sea of polytheism of the surrounding nations, Israel had had a revelation that God is one. This then was the Jewish environment in which Messianic Jews reflected theologically.

However, as these Messianic Jews reflected further on their experiences with Yeshua, they *also* became a witness to the unique nature of the Godhead.

Three Persons, yet Still One God

When speaking of God, three persons are mentioned, but each one is recognized as deity by the Jewish writers. Note each person in turn:

> Do not work for the food that disappears, but for the food that remains to eternal life—the food which the Son of Man will give to you. For God the Father has put his seal of approval on him. (Yohanan 6:27)

One person, God, is called "the Father." This was hardly an unknown concept among the people of first-century Judea, as we see when Yeshua taught His disciples how to pray, "Our Father in heaven" (Mattai 6:9).

Concerning the second person, the record states,

> but of the Son he says, "Your throne, O God, is forever and ever, and a righteous scepter is the scepter of your kingdom." (Hebrews 1:8)

Note how the second person, "the Son," is addressed as "God," and that His throne will endure forever and ever.

Passages in the New Covenant also highlight how the third person should be addressed:

> But Kefa said, "Ananias, why has Satan filled your heart to lie to the Holy Spirit and keep back for yourself part of the proceeds from the sale of the land? Before it was sold, did it not belong to you? And when it was sold, was the money not at your disposal? How have you thought up this deed in your heart? You have not lied to people but to God!" (Acts 5:3–4)

The third person is called "the Holy Spirit," but Kefa also refers to Him as God. Jewish thinkers would not have a problem regarding the "Spirit" or the "Holy Spirit" as God because He is considered to be God. The real problem begins with how to assess Yeshua, as both deity and humanity. In this chapter, the primary concern is how the Jewish writers of the New Covenant addressed Yeshua. A full consideration of His dual nature will be treated in later chapters.

Each Person Clearly Distinguished from the Other Two

Some will argue that the references to three persons are actually referring to only one person with three names. In the Jewish sources, for example, the "Father" and the "Spirit" are actually designations of only one person. But in their encounter with Yeshua's ministry, the New Covenant writers were confronted with an alternative concept. Consider passages where these three distinct persons are mentioned together.

The angel Gabriel announces to Miriam an event of astounding importance, which information Luke probably obtained from an interview with Miriam.

> The angel replied, "The Holy Spirit will come upon you, and the power of the Most High will overshadow you. Therefore the child to be born will be holy; he will be called the Son of God." (Luke 1:35)

Three persons are mentioned, but each is distinct from the other: The Holy Spirit; the Most High one; and the Holy One, or the "Son of God." Luke was undergirding profound aspects of God's nature that were difficult to understand.

Still another passage declares:

> Then I will ask the Father, and he will give you another Advocate to be with you forever. (Yohanan 14:16)

The word "Advocate," in some other translations "Counselor," is *paraklete* ("one who comes alongside"). A few verses later we find the designation "Holy Spirit":

> But the Advocate, the Holy Spirit, whom the Father will send in my name, will teach you everything, and will cause you to remember everything I said to you. (Yohanan 14:26)

At the very least, the Father and Holy Spirit are considered separate persons, but each exercises the function of deity. So, the Spirit will actually remind the writers of the New Covenant of what Yeshua had taught the disciples. And keeping in mind that Kefa had already addressed Yeshua as deity, three distinct persons are recognized in the passage, where each is one is God.

Again, the truth that there are three distinct persons, yet each is God, can be seen here:

> When the Advocate comes, whom I will send you from the Father—the Spirit of truth who goes out from the Father—he will testify about me. (Yohanan 15:26)

> After Yeshua was baptized, just as he was coming up out of the water, the heavens opened and he saw the Spirit of God descending like a dove and coming on him. And a voice from heaven said, "This is my one dear Son; in him I take great delight." (Mattai 3:16–17)

Mattai's intent was to specify not only that there are three distinct persons but that each one is also God.

In these selected passages, all three persons appear together, and this by the intention of each of the writers.

The Three Persons Set Forth as One God, Not Three Gods

Yeshua and the Father as One. An assertion appears in Yohanan's gospel that has perplexed some:

> The Father and I are one. (Yohanan 10:30)

Some claim that this statement only expresses the oneness of purpose of the Father and the Messiah as they work together. However, much more was intended by Yohanan's statement that was not lost on Yeshua's listeners. Immediately following this announcement, some of the Jewish people picked up stones to hurl at Him (Yohanan 10:31–32), precisely because they perceived that Yeshua was claiming equality with God! To the people of that day, these words were tantamount to blasphemy, just as they would be today if someone made this announcement in a religious Jewish community.

The Father and the Spirit as One. In another statement, we read:

> Do you not know that you are God's temple and that God's Spirit lives in you? (1 Corinthians 3:16)

Sha'ul did not arrive at the viewpoint represented in this verse on his own. Before coming to faith in Yeshua, he was a representative of a strict group of religiously identified Jews who believed in the oneness of God. Such Jews were utterly opposed to the beliefs of the Messianic Jews who believed in Yeshua's deity as well as a separate personhood of the Holy Spirit from that of God. Sha'ul later in the same letter commented that, "For I passed on to you as of first importance what I also received" (1 Corinthians 15:3). Elsewhere he remarks about the good news he preached, that "For I did not receive it or learn it from any human source; instead I received it by a revelation of Yeshua the Messiah" (Galatians 1:12). In other words, his statements of the deity of persons who are a part of the very being of God was what the Lord Himself revealed to him.

So then, Sha'ul affirmed in the 1 Corinthians 3:16 passage that, without any doubt, two persons are in view, namely, the Father and the Spirit. And yet, Sha'ul was still speaking of one God.

The Son and the Spirit as One. In support of the peculiar relation within the oneness of God, Sha'ul affirms another truth:

> You, however, are not in the flesh but in the Spirit, if indeed the Spirit of God lives in you. Now if anyone does not have the Spirit of Messiah, this person does not belong to him. (Romans 8:9)

That Messiah is deity is certainly implied in this passage. The Messiah and the Holy Spirit are each separate persons and yet, in a mysterious way, it is the one God who is being spoken of.

All Three as One. Once more, three persons are viewed as God, yet only one God is present:

> Then I will ask the Father, and he will give you another Advocate to be with you forever— . . . I will not abandon you as orphans, I will come to you. . . . If anyone loves me, he will obey my word, and my Father will love him, and we will come to him and take up residence with him. (Yohanan 14:16, 18, 23)

Of all the claims, these statements appear to be the most confusing of all. How can we speak of the Father, Son, and Holy Spirit, each of whom is God, and not avoid speaking of three gods? The latter is what the Jewish community seemed to understand about the faith of the Messianic Jews in Yeshua's day, as it still does to this day. But strange as it may seem, Yeshua Himself *as a religious Jew* uttered these statements. Nor did His disciples, once they had become convinced of His deity, protest these statements. Nor did Yeshua stop His disciples from teaching these things; to the contrary, He wanted them to proclaim these truths! But in all their proclamations, Messianic Jews were very careful to assert that while each of the persons are God as part of His very being, *only one God is proclaimed*.

All Three Persons Equal in Being, Power, and Glory. Each of these three persons are supremely unique. As already noted, each of these persons is called "God." In addition:

Their association not consistent with inequality. In a final proclamation to His messengers of the New Covenant, Yeshua's declaration underscored the equality of these persons:

> Therefore go and make disciples of all nations, baptizing them in the name of the Father and the Son and the Holy Spirit. (Mattai 28:19)

Likewise Sha'ul also proclaimed the same truth:

> The grace of the Lord Yeshua the Messiah and the love of God and the fellowship of the Holy Spirit be with you all. (2 Corinthians 13:14)

No fixed numerical order. Neither Sha'ul, nor Kefa, nor Yehudah ever sought to establish an order among the persons:

But we ought to thank God always for you, brothers and sisters loved by the Lord, because God chose you from the beginning for salvation through sanctification by the Spirit and faith in the truth. He called you to this salvation through our gospel, so that you may possess the glory of our Lord Yeshua the Messiah. (2 Thessalonians 2:13–14)

There is one body and one Spirit, just as you too were called to the one hope of your calling, one Lord, one faith, one baptism, one God and Father of all, who is over all and through all and in all. (Ephesians 4:4–6)

Note the same message in the following passages:

Now there are different gifts, but the same Spirit. And there are different ministries, but the same Lord. And there are different results, but the same God who produces all of them in everyone.
(1 Corinthians 12:4–6)

And do not get drunk with wine, which is debauchery, but be filled by the Spirit, speaking to one another in psalms, hymns, and spiritual songs, singing and making music in your hearts to the Lord, always giving thanks to God the Father for each other in the name of our Lord Yeshua the Messiah. (Ephesians 5:18–20)

. . . according to the foreknowledge of God the Father by being set apart by the Spirit for obedience and for sprinkling with Yeshua the Messiah's blood. May grace and peace be yours in full measure! Blessed be the God and Father of our Lord Yeshua the Messiah! By his great mercy he gave us new birth into a living hope through the resurrection of Yeshua the Messiah from the dead. (1 Kefa 1:2–3)

But you, dear friends, by building yourselves up in your most holy faith, by praying in the Holy Spirit, maintain yourselves in the love of God, while anticipating the mercy of our Lord Yeshua the Messiah that brings eternal life. (Yehudah 1:20–21)

In the above passages, each of the names of the three persons appears in varying orders. In one passage, believers are encouraged to pray to God the Father, in the name of Yeshua the Messiah, through the Holy Spirit. Normally, this can be the general pattern, in a kind of fixed order of persons, but lest we think this is the only pattern, Scripture demonstrates otherwise: as Stephen lay dying as the stones thrown at him took their toll, he cried out, "Lord Yeshua, receive my spirit!" (Acts 7:59).

No inequality between "Son of God" and "Spirit of God." These two designations might suggest an inequality to the superficial reader where there actually is none. The Son is not derived from the Father in the sense that somehow God created Him at some time in the distant past; we may see Him as the Son of Man in His humanity, living as a Jew among His people in Judea, but in His designation as "Son of God," there is no inequality with the Father. In a mystery, Yeshua has two natures, human and divine, but He is one person. As will be noted below, it may be that His special function was to carry out the wishes of the Father, but in His very deity, there is equality with God. We will consider this under the doctrine of the Messiah in a later chapter. The reference again to what Sha'ul made regarding these two, Son of God and Spirit of God, seems appropriate: The Spirit of God lives in the believer, but in a manner of equation, if one does not have the Spirit of the Messiah, he does not belong to the Messiah, Son of God.

> You, however, are not in the flesh but in the Spirit, if indeed the Spirit of God lives in you. Now if anyone does not have the Spirit of Messiah, this person does not belong to him. (Romans 8:9)

The Son and the Father of equal power and deserving of equal honor. The *shaliach* Yohanan recorded this statement relating the Son and the Father, which has occasioned difficulty to some:

> For this reason the Jewish leaders were trying even harder to kill him, because not only was he breaking the Sabbath, but he was also calling God his own Father, thus making himself equal with God. (Yohanan 5:18)

The affirmation behind Yohanan's statement was certainly not the commonly held view of God. The Jewish position in the first century was that God is the "only God." Yet Yohanan had full support in light of what Yeshua Himself had claimed. We note the tension, then as well as now, between Jewish belief and a distinctively Messianic Jewish one.

Again in Yohanan's gospel we read:

> For just as the Father raises the dead and gives them life, so also the Son gives life to whomever he wishes. Furthermore, the Father does not judge anyone, but has assigned all judgment to the Son, so that all people will honor the Son just as they honor the Father. The one who does not honor the Son does not honor the Father who sent him. (Yohanan 5:21–23)

The very clear implication from this passage, as well as from others, is that each person has equal power and must therefore be recognized for who they are.

Distinctions of priority and subordination. As one reads the texts of the writers of the New Covenant, we notice that there are distinctions of priority and subordination among the three persons, which concern their respective *functions*. This concerns what these three persons *do*, not *who they are*. Some observations are in order:

First, in the *work* of the three persons, the Father is mentioned first, the Son second, and the Spirit third. Note the various Greek prepositions that are used to explain these *functions*:

> Yet for us there is one God, the Father, from [*ek*, referring to the source] whom are all things and for whom we live, and one Lord, Yeshua the Messiah, through [*dia*, referring to the channel] whom are all things and through whom we live. (1 Corinthians 8:6)

Note also:

> . . . so that through him we both have access in [*en*, referring to the agent] one Spirit to [*pros*, referring to the goal] the Father. (Ephesians 2:18)

While these prepositions point out the various *functions* of the three persons, yet Sha'ul is still speaking of only one God.

Secondly, in the work among the persons of the Godhead, the peculiar being who is God the Son is subordinate in His *work* to the Father, while the Spirit is subordinate to the Father and the Son. Note:

> In this is love: not that we have loved God, but that he loved us and sent his Son to be the atoning sacrifice for our sins. (1 Yohanan 4:10)

> But the Advocate, the Holy Spirit, whom the Father will send in my name, will teach you everything, and will cause you to remember everything I said to you. (Yohanan 14:26)

> When the Advocate comes, whom I will send you from the Father—the Spirit of truth who goes out from the Father—he will testify about me. (Yohanan 15:26)

We see how Sha'ul indicates the function of the Father who sent His Son to be our sacrifice, while Yohanan states that the Father sent the Holy Spirit for the function of teaching the disciples. Again, Yohanan says that Yeshua will send the Holy Spirit to testify of Him. Even here, the subordination is voluntary and not necessary in the sense that each one was commanded to serve. We think of the well-known passage describing the *kenosis* or the "emptying" of the Son, describing how He divested Himself of so much of what He had in glory in order to be born as a human being (Philippians 2:5–8; see further below). As the Son of Man, a human being (though without sin), Yeshua was subordinate to the Father and to the Holy Spirit, living under the direction of God and the Holy Spirit.

God is a God of order and each specific function is correlated with the different persons. And once again it must be emphasized that the Jewish writers of the New Covenant never intended to imply that the Son and the Spirit were subordinate in their *being*; rather, while there is a oneness in the peculiar being of God, yet each person had His function to accomplish. We will take this up further in a later chapter.

Conclusion

All of these statements are proclamations of the infinite mystery of God. After hearing Yeshua's teaching about Himself and His relationship to the Father, and after observing His deeds, the Jewish New Covenant writers concluded that in a mystery, God is more than merely one, more than the only God of religious Judaism, and, we might add, of Islam as well.

These authors were not inclined to enter into rationalistic explanations of this mystery or to provide a philosophic understanding of how God can be one and yet three. That became the work of the non-Jewish believers, who being trained in Greek philosophy, Plato and Aristotle among others, proceeded to outline their beliefs in their particular contextualization.

Confronted by all the statements on this subject made by Yeshua and by the New Covenant writers, we might conclude either that they were out of their minds; or that they were completely misguided and gullible; or that every one of them spoke the truth. The third is the only obvious conclusion: Yeshua and the writers were rational beings; they were not incoherent in what they said nor did anyone ever conclude that they were void of their faculties.

Some Messianic Jews have sought to ingratiate themselves with the Jewish community and are speaking of God as simply a unity. However, I believe this statement accommodates too much to the Jewish position on God as interpreted by the rabbis and to say this therefore gives away what the Scriptures assert. We must have a strong positive witness that God is considered as a *composite* unity, thereby allowing for the possibility of persons within the Godhead. At the same time, we must insist that God is one. Our only guide is to see what the Hebrew texts have to say, along with considering what the Messianic Jews of the first century asserted regarding God.

Others of our fellow Messianic Jewish brethren, in order to emphasize the Jewishness of Yeshua, have accommodated themselves to thinking that Yeshua is a created being; God in some special sense, but yet a created man who was thoroughly Jewish in his context of ethnicity and culture. This discussion will be continued later, when we consider the Messiah in His deity and humanity, and also when we consider Yeshua's preexistence (that is, prior to His birth as a human being). But we can make one observation now: If

Yeshua is only a being who was created at some time in the past, there is then no possibility of asserting that He has a divine nature.

Every Jewish person has the challenge to examine carefully the claims concerning the nature of God: Is He merely one, or, is He one God, but in a mystery, three persons who comprise the one Godhead? A person's future destiny is at stake, depending on the final decision.

SIX

The Doctrine of God

The Existence of God

The question of whether God exists or does not will not be a major element of this book. A few comments will be offered but the main concern will be how God has communicated to mankind through His revelation and what we may know about Him, especially as the God who has entered into a number of covenants with Israel and made promises to them.

In a brief discussion of God's existence, we may frame the following questions: 1) Is there a God? 2) If so, has He revealed Himself? 3) Who is God like? and 4) What does God do?

The first question does not belong to theology proper but rather to the philosophy of religion. Hopefully, those engaged in the pursuit of whether God exists or not will choose the presuppositions that lead them to assert that He does.

The answer to the second question lies in the field of Christian evidences within apologetics. Once again, the idea is to choose the set of presuppositions that best answers the problems, which means asserting that He does exist and has revealed Himself.

It is important to note that the Torah and New Covenant, being concerned primarily with practical rather than philosophical matters, *begin* with God. Since man who is a sinner cannot wait for the settlement of all the intellectual problems of theism, and since the Bible was written for sinful men, it brings the reader without delay into the presence of

God—"In the beginning God" (Genesis 1:1). In fact, God will hold man responsible to accept His existence.

In answer to the first question "Is there a God?" there are four answers.

Atheism: There Is No God

The atheist finds fault with the Christian for being dogmatic. Yet the atheist is also dogmatic, declaring, "I know there is no God!" If one sets out to prove that there is no God, then one faces the problem of explaining all past generations, all future generations, all corners of the universe—explaining mankind and the physical world—and also explaining the experience of everyone who says that they believe in God.

Agnosticism: We Do Not Know if There Is a God

For the honest agnostic who admits that he or she is in the dark, there is help. On the other hand, there is a form of agnosticism that deserves no sympathy, in which someone not only admits they are in the dark but denies the possibility of light. This is self-defeating and dogmatic as well. The very assertion of denial assumes the possibility that one *can* know.

Possible replies to agnosticism: Man is ignorant of what others know and has experienced; no one has the right to adopt this position until they find God and know God; many times people are unwilling to give time and effort to try and find out.

Materialism: There Is No Need for a God in Order to Explain the Universe

The materialist faces the problem of explaining force and matter in the universe. Even if we can explain matter, we still need to explain force: Why did force operate on matter to produce an orderly universe? There must have been a mind behind the processes.

Biblical Faith: Acceptance of the Presupposition That God Exists

If no God exists, we cannot explain the great facts of the universe: its existence, its origin, the moral and intellectual nature of man. Nor can we explain the fact that the idea of God is universal, nor the Bible, nor Messiah, nor the Christian experience of individuals. This does not mean that the Bible presents no proofs for the existence of God, for it does. But the primary method is direct and practical rather than argumentative. A rose, for example, needs no philosophical arguments to prove its existence. Its beauty and fragrance are immediate channels of revelation, entirely sufficient for those whose minds are unspoiled by agnostic speculation. So also there are channels of revelation concerning God that are immediate. "God hath spoken"—concerning Himself, His nature, and His work—in ways that are more universally accessible and convincing than in the case of any other fact of human experience.

Of course, the agnostic question can always be raised, about anything and everything—even about the existence of a rose. But we must observe that people go on enjoying roses nevertheless, including the agnostics themselves. And we further observe that no skeptic ever acts in complete consistency with his doubts. He may indeed doubt the actual existence of bread, but he goes on eating bread nevertheless. As a matter of fact, he must have bread to sustain the intellectual energy he needs to argue against the existence of bread. Thus also the skeptic draws from God the very energy that sustains him as he reasons against the divine existence.

The Personality of God

A Definition of "Personality"

Before one can even speak of God having a distinct personality, a definition of the term is vital. While personality is perhaps the most important fact in the world as far as living beings are concerned, yet, in spite of its certainty and effects, nothing is more elusive as to its definition.

An Older Philosophic Definition. According to an older psychology, personality consists of three components: knowledge, emotion, and will. But recent psychological theories dispute even the existence of personality as a specific possession by man, unique and different from any so-called lower animal. Even the brute, they argue, has intelligence, emotion, and will, to a degree. But is man the same as any other animal? Obviously not, because the Torah, or Word, defines man otherwise, as we will see.

Modern Definitions. Modern psychologists dispute the separate existence of the mind, soul, or any other intangible entity. The scientific method is the sole means for investigation and therefore so-called intangibles are demonstrated to not exist; they are either denied or reduced to what can be tested. In other words, whereas older theologians spoke of the mind, soul, or heart as the seat of emotions, these terms are reinterpreted to mean the brain and so on. They are treated as phenomena that can be tested by scientific means.

A Biblical Definition. Such theories compel us to seek a closer analysis of what personality entails. The following may be offered as a tentative and rather abstract definition: "Personality is a name given to the nucleus of a definite group of functions or characteristics."

When considering the personality of God as the Torah or Word declares, He may be regarded as living, intelligent, purposive, active, free, self-conscious, and with emotional capacity. (The category of God as a Spirit, having spirituality as an intangible entity, will be treated later when considering the doctrine of the Spirit.) As we consider the personality of God, note the predicate, which refers to God, and the adjective, which relates to an activity that characterizes His personality. As each characteristic is treated, note that some are not peculiar to the concept of personality. Even an animal has life and intelligence of a sort, but the combination of these personality characteristics in a common center is peculiar to a special person, God. There can be no personality without their presence.

We will now examine specific personality characteristics of God.

God Is Living

The biblical testimony concerning God as living was shared by Moses:

> Who is there from the entire human race who has heard the voice of the living God speaking from the middle of the fire as we have, and has lived? (Deuteronomy 5:26)

This refers to the major occasion when the heavens were rent and God's presence came down on Mount Sinai.

The Biblical Meaning of "Living." Strong has suggested a tentative meaning, namely, that life in the Bible refers to potential energy or activity. When the Bible speaks of the "the living God," it means that He is able to reveal Himself and accomplish specific acts which the non-person cannot do, as in the example just noted when God appeared on Mount Sinai to face His people.[1]

Scripture further defines it:

> Joshua continued, "This is how you will know the living God is among you and that he will truly drive out before you the Canaanites, Hittites, Hivites, Perizzites, Girgashites, Amorites, and Jebusites. Look! The ark of the covenant of the Ruler of the whole earth is ready to enter the Jordan ahead of you. Now select for yourselves twelve men from the tribes of Israel, one per tribe. When the feet of the priests carrying the ark of the LORD, the Ruler of the whole earth, touch the water of the Jordan, the water coming downstream toward you will stop flowing and pile up."
>
> So when the people left their tents to cross the Jordan, the priests carrying the ark of the covenant went ahead of them. When the ones carrying the ark reached the Jordan and the feet of the priests carrying the ark touched the surface of the water—(the Jordan is at flood stage all during harvest time)—the water coming downstream toward them stopped flowing. It piled up far upstream at Adam (the city near Zarethan); there was no water at all flowing to the sea of the Arabah (the Salt Sea). The people crossed the river opposite Jericho. The priests carrying the ark of the covenant of the LORD stood firmly on dry ground in the middle of the Jordan. All Israel crossed over on dry ground until the entire nation was on the other side. (Joshua 3:10–17)

As a sign of His living presence, the waters of the Jordan would be held back—at spring flood time, no less—until all the people of Israel could cross over into the land.

Ample revelation in the Scripture affirms that God is living, for example, when the armies of Israel are referred to as "the armies of the living God" who will give victory to His people over the Philistines through David:

> David asked the men who were standing near him, "What will be done for the man who strikes down this Philistine and frees Israel from this humiliation? For who is this uncircumcised Philistine, that he defies the armies of the living God?" (1 Samuel 17:26)

The prophet Jeremiah was in a constant altercation with his people, demonstrating that the "living God" is greater in all His power and glory than the despicable idols of the gods Judah was worshipping:

> The LORD is the only true God.
> He is the living God and the everlasting King.
> When he shows his anger the earth shakes.
> None of the nations can stand up to his fury.
> You people of Israel should tell those nations this:
> "These gods did not make heaven and earth.
> They will disappear from the earth and from under the heavens."
> The LORD is the one who by his power made the earth.
> He is the one who by his wisdom established the world.
> And by his understanding he spread out the skies.
> When his voice thunders, the heavenly ocean roars.
> He makes the clouds rise from the far-off horizons.
> He makes the lightning flash out in the midst of the rain.
> He unleashes the wind from the places where he stores it.
> (Jeremiah 10:10–13)

It was even possible for an unbelieving ruler as King Darius of Persia to recognize that the God of Daniel is the "living God and enduring forever," because He was able to deliver His servant from the hungry lions:

> I have issued an edict that throughout all the dominion of my kingdom people are to revere and fear the God of Daniel. For he is the living

God; he endures forever. His kingdom will not be destroyed; his authority is forever. He rescues and delivers and performs signs and wonders in the heavens and on the earth. He has rescued Daniel from the power of the lions! (Daniel 6:26–27)

Contrasted with Lifeless Idols. Tragically, Israel and Judah during the First Temple period had to learn the hard way that false gods were utterly impotent in contrast to the true living God. Isaiah was the classic prophet who with biting sarcasm confirmed how useless these dead objects of worship really were. In one instance, God challenged their devotees in this way:

"Present your argument," says the LORD.
"Produce your evidence," says Jacob's king.
Let them produce evidence! Let them tell us what will happen!
Tell us about your earlier predictive oracles,
so we may examine them and see how they were fulfilled.
Or decree for us some future events!
Predict how future events will turn out,
so we might know you are gods.
Yes, do something good or bad,
so we might be frightened and in awe.
Look, you are nothing, and your accomplishments are nonexistent;
the one who chooses to worship you is disgusting. (Isaiah 41:21–24)

Isaiah also scathingly mocked idol makers in this poetic passage:

All who form idols are nothing;
the things in which they delight are worthless.
Their witnesses cannot see;
they recognize nothing, so they are put to shame.
Who forms a god and casts an idol
that will prove worthless?
Look, all his associates will be put to shame;
the craftsmen are mere humans.
Let them all assemble and take their stand!

They will panic and be put to shame.
A blacksmith works with his tool
and forges metal over the coals.
He forms it with hammers;
he makes it with his strong arm.
He gets hungry and loses his energy;
he drinks no water and gets tired.
A carpenter takes measurements;
he marks out an outline of its form;
he scrapes it with chisels,
and marks it with a compass.
He patterns it after the human form,
like a well-built human being,
and puts it in a shrine.
He cuts down cedars
and acquires a cypress or an oak.
He gets trees from the forest;
he plants a cedar and the rain makes it grow.
A man uses it to make a fire;
he takes some of it and warms himself.
Yes, he kindles a fire and bakes bread.
Then he makes a god and worships it;
he makes an idol and bows down to it.
Half of it he burns in the fire–
over that half he cooks meat;
he roasts a meal and fills himself.
Yes, he warms himself and says,
"Ah! I am warm as I look at the fire."
With the rest of it he makes a god, his idol;
he bows down to it and worships it.
He prays to it, saying,
"Rescue me, for you are my god!"
They do not comprehend or understand,
for their eyes are blind and cannot see;

their minds do not discern.
No one thinks to himself,
nor do they comprehend or understand and say to themselves:
"I burned half of it in the fire—
yes, I baked bread over the coals;
I roasted meat and ate it.
With the rest of it should I make a disgusting idol?
Should I bow down to dry wood?"
He feeds on ashes;
his deceived mind misleads him.
He cannot rescue himself,
nor does he say, "Is this not a false god I hold in my right hand?"
(Isaiah 44:9–20)

Finally, the same prophet sarcastically portrays the foolishness of Judah in comparing the pagan gods with the living God:

Bel kneels down,
Nebo bends low.
Their images weigh down animals and beasts.
Your heavy images are burdensome to tired animals. . . .
To whom can you compare and liken me?
Tell me whom you think I resemble, so we can be compared!
Those who empty out gold from a purse
and weigh out silver on the scale
hire a metalsmith, who makes it into a god.
They then bow down and worship it.
They put it on their shoulder and carry it;
they put it in its place and it just stands there;
it does not move from its place.
Even when someone cries out to it, it does not reply;
it does not deliver him from his distress. (Isaiah 46:1, 5–7)

How could anyone be so foolish!

Practical Value. The truth that God is living is a strong antidote for all idolatry. Israel and Judah's pursuit of idols had only led to a dead end. While in Babylon, exposed to the 7,500 or so gods and goddesses of the Babylonian pantheon, our ancestors learned firsthand how barren and vain was their trust in dead graven images.

This great truth is also a good antidote for pantheism, according to which God is in everything and everything is God. Can material things be God? Or can everything lose its own identity in the being of God? A positive answer to the second question would mean the end of all created beings as separate entities, a total reversal of the plan and purpose of the living God in creation, including the creation of human beings who were supposed to be His companions. It is exactly in the fact that we were created to serve the living God and love Him forever that we see the full meaning of David's cry, when his heart cried out for "the living God":

> I desperately want to be
> in the courts of the Lord's temple.
> My heart and my entire being shout for joy
> to the living God. (Psalm 84:2)

God Is Intelligent

The biblical testimony describes God as astute, keen, thoughtful, shrewd in the best sense of the word, and wise. There is a whole host of similar terms: He is the "God who knows" such that we need to thoughtfully analyze our actions:

> Don't keep speaking so arrogantly,
> letting proud talk come out of your mouth!
> For the LORD is a God who knows;
> he evaluates what people do. (1 Samuel 2:3)

In the following statement, the reference is to what God knew of the great fountains of the deep, huge subterranean bodies of water that were burst open, contributing to the great flood of the earth:

> By wisdom the LORD laid the foundation of the earth;
> he established the heavens by understanding.
> By his knowledge the primordial sea was broken open,
> and the clouds drip down dew. (Proverbs 3:19–20)

Isaiah also taunts the idolaters of his day regarding God's knowledge:

> Your thinking is perverse!
> Should the potter be regarded as clay?
> Should the thing made say about its maker, "He didn't make me"?
> Or should the pottery say about the potter, "He doesn't understand"?
> (Isaiah 29:16)

These are only a few examples where we see the attribute of God's intelligence.

Terms Indicative of Intelligence. One term that can describe God is that He is *intuitive*, that is, He has the ability to see things clearly as they are. Another term that describes God is *reflective*. He is quite capable of gathering all the facts of intelligence, think them through, and then come to a conclusion for a course of action. Furthermore, God is *creative*. He has the ability of taking the facts of knowledge and creating new forms. God is also *ethical* because He can use something known to Him, although often unknown to people, in order to bring about good results.

With God, morals and ethics are never divorced from intelligence and knowledge. He is holy and righteous; the Ten Words (or Commandments) represent an ultimate morality. Because God is cognizant of the multitude of situations in which believers can find themselves, therefore He can work all things for the good on behalf of those who love Him (Romans 8:28). The Hebrew words for wisdom, which relates to the fact that God is intelligent, are helpful regarding understanding this ethical good. God has *knowledge*; He can perceive facts as they are. He has *understanding*; He has insight into the meaning of the facts perceived, including discriminating between good and evil. He has *wisdom*—the ability to place facts in proper relation to other facts and use them for good ends.

This connection between morality and ethics was recognized by Job. No matter where one searches, wisdom is not to be found in the things of this world but only in God:

> But wisdom—where can it be found?
> Where is the place of understanding?
> Mankind does not know its place;
> it cannot be found in the land of the living.
> The deep says, "It is not with me."
> And the sea says, "It is not with me."
> Fine gold cannot be given in exchange for it,
> nor can its price be weighed out in silver.
> It cannot be measured out for purchase with the gold of Ophir,
> with precious onyx or sapphires.
> Neither gold nor crystal can be compared with it,
> nor can a vase of gold match its worth.
> Of coral and jasper no mention will be made;
> the price of wisdom is more than pearls.
> The topaz of Cush cannot be compared with it;
> it cannot be purchased with pure gold.
> But wisdom—where does it come from?
> Where is the place of understanding? (Job 28:12–20)

Therefore God said:

> And he said to mankind,
> "The fear of the LORD—that is wisdom,
> and to turn away from evil is understanding." (Job 28:28)

Intelligence without morality is very dangerous, as was forcefully demonstrated by the (intelligent!) men who ran the Gestapo, searching for Jewish people to fulfill Hitler's goal of making Europe *Judenrein*.

Practical Value. First, the truth that God is intelligent serves as a warning to the arrogance of evildoers who loudly boast of themselves and their actions. The Scripture warns:

Don't keep speaking so arrogantly,
letting proud talk come out of your mouth!
For the Lord is a God who knows;
he evaluates what people do. (1 Samuel 2:3)

Here we see how Scripture makes the connection between God's intelligence, wisdom, knowledge, and the execution of His moral will against evil.

The second value is that of comfort to the godly. Here Job's testimony is very much a consolation:

But he knows the pathway that I take;
if he tested me, I would come forth like gold. (Job 23:10)

No matter what we may suffer in this vale of tears, God is entirely cognizant of where we are and what we are going through, and He encourages us along the way. With this grand truth, believers can take heart!

God Is Purposeful

Human personality includes the aspect of purpose, which is to say, a reason is present for what one does. God is no different, sharing some of His purposes with His prophet:

"This is the plan I have devised for the whole earth;
my hand is ready to strike all the nations."
Indeed, the LORD who commands armies has a plan,
and who can possibly frustrate it?
His hand is ready to strike, and who can possibly stop it?
(Isaiah 14:26–27)

From this biblical evidence, we may define God's purposefulness in this way: "God, as a person, acts in regard to some future goal, which exists first only in His mind, but as if the goal were already present." The goal is already set in His mind, even though the completion is not as yet present. For example, He sees believers from the vantage point of today, but He purposes us to be something very different in the future, toward which goal He will guide each one.

God Is Active

Regarding the truth that God is active, the biblical testimony asserts,

> I am speaking to you because you are the ones who saw all the great deeds of the LORD! (Deuteronomy 11:7)

and

> For you, O LORD, have made me happy by your work.
> I will sing for joy because of what you have done.
> How great are your works, O LORD!
> Your plans are very intricate! (Psalm 92:4–5)

God is not only living, but He is active and therefore able to perform great works: in creation when bringing it into existence; in His relation to the universe and the earth, in sustaining them; in providing for every living creature, including man. Activity is a mark and sign of life. In the case of God, He is able to act beyond what anyone can ask or even think.

God Is Free

The nature of God's freedom as well as the freedom of His creatures is a concept that demands careful consideration. Biblical testimony gives ample proof as to His freedom when He acts in the hearts of people. For example, regarding those who have backslidden, this verse speaks of what God can freely do:

> Let me again experience the joy of your deliverance!
> Sustain me by giving me the desire to obey! (Psalm 51:12)

In another illustration, God brought Nebuchadnezzar, an unbeliever, low for his pride over the greatness of Babylon. After seven years, the king recovered his senses, after which God worked in his heart such that he became a believer. At that time Nebuchadnezzar proclaimed:

> All the inhabitants of the earth are regarded as nothing.
> He does as he wishes with the army of heaven
> and with those who inhabit the earth.
> No one slaps his hand
> and says to him, "What have you done?" (Daniel 4:35)

God was able to work freely in the heart of a foreigner such that he was able to praise the God of Israel.

The Meaning of God's Freedom. The concept of freedom needs to be explored further. Does it mean God can do anything? In what sense is He free? God's freedom is determined by His will. He can never do anything contrary to His will or to His very being. For example, He can never lie, or lead anyone to do likewise because that would go against His righteousness and, that which underlies it all, His holiness, which is the essence of His very being.

However, He can impose a self-limitation on Himself in order to allow people to make their moral decisions whether for good or ill. When Adam and Eve sinned, moral evil settled upon the human race. The line of Cain demonstrated repeatedly that they were governed by their sin nature. The line of Seth, though they at first followed God's directives in their lives, finally gave in to wrongdoing as they were led by their sin nature. Then, just prior to the flood, the entire human race became embroiled in evil. In all this time, God did not stand by helpless, but rather in His mercy He allowed people to make their moral decisions. Nevertheless, one day there came a reckoning. God went into action and brought about the judgment of the flood, as in other ways He judged people many times in the course of history. When it becomes necessary, God knows how to "stick His finger" into the course of human events in order to reestablish righteousness.

God's self-limitation has an ethical goal, that of righteousness. Some philosophers have thought that other goals were ultimate; a number of Greek philosophers considered happiness to be the most desirable aim. Such a goal is not necessarily ancient; the modern version goes "Why worry? Be happy!"

Mistaken Ideas of Freedom. An example of a mistaken kind of self-limitation was articulated by Diogenes, who defined happiness as being comfortable. In other words, if any idea or action makes one uncomfortable, then logic demands that the idea or action must be eliminated from one's life. For example, let's say that a man marries and that for some reason the wife is not happy. That possibility suggests that marriage should never be contemplated. Or a marriage might occur, but one of the children might die. Again, the conclusion is that one should never even think of getting married. As Diogenes thought of all the possibilities of what would make a person unhappy or uncomfortable, he concluded that he or she must not engage in any of them. In the end, Diogenes reduced all his possessions down to a cup that he used to dip into the fountain for a drink of water. However, one day he saw someone drink from the fountain without any cup, and *that* made him unhappy and very uncomfortable. So he threw away his cup!

The difference between the ancient and modern versions of unhappiness is that for Diogenes, it was a matter of getting along with the least of material items. Today it really is the complete opposite, a misuse of freedom in the hedonistic philosophy of "eat, drink, be merry, for tomorrow we die."

For the believer, happiness is not the *summum bonum*, or supreme ethical good. Rather, God wishes for us to live righteously and serve Him in such a way that others will also find Him as their ultimate Friend.

When people seek for happiness, or for any other goal, are they wholly free? The only reply is: Not entirely, because man is finite, living in an environment that is finite, with very definite boundaries. While we may be able to escape from the earth in a rocket, we still have to bring along earth's atmosphere and material goods and eventually return to the home base. What about being totally free in ethical choices? Not entirely either. If a person wishes to live a profligate life, sexually transmitted diseases will soon remind him or her that God has set certain barriers in place that man cannot trespass. In spite of the boundaries, though, earth is still the place where a human being can learn to mature and make the choices that will prepare him or her for eternity. Even in eternity, where we will have an even greater amount of freedom, God's redeemed people will still be in the process of learning and exercising choices. We will never be as totally free as God is.

Practical Value. One value of the truth that God is free is its opposition to fatalism, a philosophy we meet in pantheism, whereby the belief is that God is locked into this universe. That is, He is a part of His universe. Therefore, what the universe does, God does; what God does, the universe does. God's activity is determined by fate. Everything is fixed and nothing can be done about it. If this is the case, how can there be any answer to prayer?

The Tanach testifies to the fact that God is free because He is transcendent:

> Yes, I know the LORD is great,
> and our Lord is superior to all gods.
> He does whatever he pleases
> in heaven and on earth,
> in the seas and all the ocean depths. (Psalm 135:5–6)

For this exact reason, He is free to do miracles. The firstborn of the Egyptians did not die from natural causes; the death angel, sent by God, intervened to release Israel from their bondage and started them on their journey to freedom. God is not bound by fatalism, unable to do anything. He can intervene, doing miracles and answering prayer.

From God's freedom also comes consolation and hope:

> Why should the nations say,
> "Where is their God?"
> Our God is in heaven!
> He does whatever he pleases! . . .
> O Israel, trust in the LORD!
> He is their deliverer and protector. (Psalm 115:2–3, 9)

Israel learned firsthand through their exodus that God is free and therefore able to answer prayer and to give His people consolation. Pharaoh and his leaders may have asked where the God of this slave people was; the answer is, that He is in heaven, not locked up helplessly in nature.

Similarly, Yeshua's instructions to the disciples on how to pray began with, "Our Father in heaven." Because He is God in heaven, He is free to do for us beyond what we can ask or think. Hope and consolation are thereby held out to each believer as he or she calls upon the Lord.

God Is Self-Conscious

Self-consciousness is a fundamental aspect of human personality. When a child comes to the point where he or she is able to say, "I," a personality is being asserted. Animals, on the other hand, are conscious, but not self-conscious. Strong observes, "If a pig could say, 'I am a pig,' he would no longer be a pig." The Scriptures are clear that man has been created in the image of God, therefore, and since God is self-conscious, man is likewise, in contrast to the animal kingdom.

The best testimony to God as a self-conscious being is when He declared to Moses,

> God said to Moses, "I AM THAT I AM." And he said, "You must say this to the Israelites, 'I AM has sent me to you.'" (Exodus 3:14)

This statement showed Moses that God is self-conscious and therefore able, when He desired, to call Israel out of Egypt, bring His people to Sinai, conclude a covenant with them, and make Israel a distinct people out of all nations. He is aware of what He wishes to accomplish; when He spoke to Moses, the deliverance was as good as already accomplished.

Furthermore, God is completely self-conscious of Himself. While man is made in His image, yet he finds out to his chagrin many times that his own self-consciousness is incomplete:

> Examine me, and probe my thoughts!
> Test me, and know my concerns!
> See if there is any idolatrous tendency in me,
> and lead me in the reliable ancient path! (Psalm 139:23–24)

We can ask God to search us because He knows us, and all things, perfectly. He also knows Himself completely. In contrast, while people may be conscious of self, they are never completely so. As David declared:

> Who can know all his errors?
> Please do not punish me for sins I am unaware of.
> Moreover, keep me from committing flagrant sins;
> do not allow such sins to control me.
> Then I will be blameless,
> and innocent of blatant rebellion. (Psalm 19:12–13)

Exactly because we are not aware of hidden faults, we have to confess we do not know ourselves in every aspect. We do not know how far we may fall, as David himself found out only too painfully. Therefore, we need to pray as the psalmist did that unforeseen evils do not get the upper hand.

This truth that God is entirely self-conscious of Himself has a practical value because it answers pantheism. If God were locked into His creation as a part of it, He could not be self-conscious. Inasmuch as He is both self-conscious and free, as we saw in the previous section, He is not a dumb brute force. As a person, He is entirely separate from His creation, and because He is self-conscious, He knows why He acts as He does.

God Is Emotional

The Torah testimony abounds in testimony that God is an emotional being:

> You must not worship or serve them, for I, the LORD your God, *am a jealous God.* I punish the sons, grandsons, and great-grandsons for the sin of the fathers who reject me. (Deuteronomy 5:9, emphasis added)

God's jealousy is not like that of human beings that can be tainted by self-interest. Rather, God's jealousy is for His very being, which must not be lowered to the same level as that of man-made gods.

He is also a person who can be grieved:

> They threw away the foreign gods they owned and worshiped the Lord. Finally the Lord grew tired of seeing Israel suffer so much. (Judges 10:16)

The period of the judges was a trying time, as the members of one tribe after another apostatized. Though knowing the God of Israel, they went astray after other gods. For their infidelity, they suffered untold misery as they were overrun by pagan peoples. Finally each clan, one after another, returned to the Lord, confessing their sin and lostness. As God reasoned with them, pointing out their failure, He also grieved for them. It was because of their suffering and pain that He sent judges to deliver them from oppression. God can be touched with the feeling of our infirmities and with our pain even when brought about because of our stubbornness.

The Psalms reflect this, as the psalmist's personal needs bring to mind God's various emotions:

> Arrogant people cannot stand in your presence;
> you hate all who behave wickedly. (Psalm 5:5)

> As a father has compassion on his children,
> so the Lord has compassion on his faithful followers. (Psalm 103:13)

In the first example above, the idea of a God who can hate is baffling to many people. After all, He is supposed to be a God of love. Yet hate and love are actually personality expressions on opposite sides of the same coin. God does love, but anyone who spites or provokes that love will also know His displeasure and hate. Thus, the people of Israel as God's people experienced His love on many occasions, but when they turned their backs on Him, or despised His many tokens of love, they discovered that He despised their ways, their sins, and their obstinacy. God can hate *what a person does*, but He loves *the person*.

As we see in the second example above, God also has compassion for those who fear or reverence Him. The tenderness of a father toward his children is just a fraction of what the Lord feels toward those who have humbled themselves before Him and who trust Him wholly. He cares for those who have made Him their all in all.

Two additional aspects of God's emotion are articulated by the prophet:

As a young man marries a young woman,
so your sons will marry you.
As a bridegroom rejoices over a bride,
so your God will rejoice over you. (Isaiah 62:5)

and

Through all that they suffered, he suffered too.
The messenger sent from his very presence delivered them.
In his love and mercy he protected them;
he lifted them up and carried them throughout ancient times.
(Isaiah 63:9)

Imagine the depth of emotion a bridegroom feels over his bride: love, kindness, exultation. God feels the same for those who honor Him, and the prophet tells us that He will one day feel this way toward a redeemed Israel, when the Messianic kingdom is established and all His people are back in the land and in favor with their Benefactor.

Likewise with a redeemed Israel, God will have sympathy for His people who, after going through the horror of Jacob's trouble, are once more in favor with Him and planted on their land. The picture of being lifted and carried as a child is by its mother and father is a special endearing touch.

And finally, one notes the highest of all God's emotions:

In a far-off land the LORD will manifest himself to them.
He will say to them, "I have loved you with an everlasting love.
That is why I have continued to be faithful to you." (Jeremiah 31:3)

The special word *hesed*, translated as *loving-kindness*, expresses the depth of God's love that cannot be plumbed or measured in any way. By redeeming Israel out of Jacob's trouble, from an experience that will draw all the surviving families of Israel back to God, He expresses His everlasting depth of love. Thereby He will fulfill the covenant promises He had made with Abraham and David to establish Israel on their land in a kingdom of peace presided over by Messiah.

All these emotional expressions are not mere anthropomorphisms, that is, merely attributed emotion based on human experience. To the contrary, *we* are made in the image of *God*. If we have emotions, it is because God has all these emotions *beyond* mere human feeling. His emotions are absolute. It is a poor God who does not feel and cannot express emotion.

Furthermore, God's emotions are not mixed with human imperfection and weakness. They are all balanced and pure. His jealousy is pure; His wrath is righteous; His love is deep, beyond what a human being can even begin to fathom.[2]

God as Communicator

Introduction

We have already seen some of the ways in which God has revealed Himself and the content of that revelation. Now we will take a closer look at revelation.

The central affirmation of Scripture is not that "There is a God" but rather that "God has spoken." Of course, if God has spoken, He must exist and His revelation may properly be used as an argument for His existence. But in the Bible, the emphasis is always on the fact of revelation, not on the rational uses to which it may be put.

Primary Ideas in the Biblical Revelation of God

The Torah and New Covenant demonstrate the various ways that God reveals Himself.

In the Material and Animal Creation. The Scripture frequently testifies to the revelation of God in the material creation as well as in animal life.

All the beasts, birds, and fish are a testimony that:

> Which of all these does not know
> that the hand of the LORD has done this,
> in whose hand is the life of every creature
> and the breath of all the human race. (Job 12:9–10)

More broadly, God has revealed Himself in creation and is also continually involved in sustaining it:

> The heavens declare the glory of God;
> the sky displays his handiwork.
> Day after day it speaks out;
> night after night it reveals his greatness.
> There is no actual speech or word,
> nor is its voice literally heard.
> Yet its voice echoes throughout the earth;
> its words carry to the distant horizon.
> In the sky he has pitched a tent for the sun. (Psalm 19:1–4)

Sha'ul also adds,

> Yet he did not leave himself without a witness by doing good, by giving you rain from heaven and fruitful seasons, satisfying you with food and your hearts with joy. (Acts 14:17)

And in Romans, he says:

> . . . because what can be known about God is plain to them, because God has made it plain to them. For since the creation of the world his invisible attributes—his eternal power and divine nature—have been clearly seen, because they are understood through what has been made. So people are without excuse. (Romans 1:19–20)

From these and similar passages, we learn that the revelation of God reminds us that God does indeed exist. Given the presence of creation, there must of necessity be a Creator, as also seen in the medieval arguments regarding the proofs for God's existence. Furthermore, when we realize that all the many parts of the universe are connected in intricate relationships on both the microscopic and macroscopic levels, when we consider all the laws that govern its operation, we can surmise that this God is intelligent and omniscient. Moreover we understand that He is also omnipotent—all-powerful—since He simply spoke the Word and the cosmos came into existence. He also continues to keep it in operation, and His care is also seen in that He has planned all things necessary for man and animals to live in a suitable environment.

The Scriptures we have looked at, especially Romans 1:19–20, are reminders that regardless of the angle from which we observe the cosmos, the presence of the Creator can be detected. All that is necessary to sense God's presence is already there for man to know, "because what can be known about God is plain to them, because God has made it plain to them" (Romans 1:19). From the normal powers of human observation and intelligence, we can make the necessary rational inference there is a God who wishes to communicate with man.

The problem with affirming His presence and existence lies in man's heart. Jeremiah once asked:

> The human mind is more deceitful than anything else.
> It is incurably bad. Who can understand it? (Jeremiah 17:9)

God's reply is that He alone can fully understand the vagaries of the human heart. Though God gives to every person enough light to know that He exists, most of the time people turn away from this knowledge:

> For although they knew God, they did not glorify him as God or give him thanks, but they became futile in their thoughts and their senseless hearts were darkened. (Romans 1:21)

The information God provides through the creation is not a full one, but it is enough for a person to be guided by if there is the desire. If one responds, more light will be given in time for that person to know the Lord in salvation and have enough guidance to worship and serve Him.

In the Nature and Constitution of Man. God also reveals Himself specifically in humanity, as the Torah and New Covenant testify. In the beginning, the Scripture says:

> Then God said, "Let us make humankind in our image, after our likeness, so they may rule over the fish of the sea and the birds of the air, over the cattle, and over all the earth, and over all the creatures that move on the earth."
>
> God created humankind in his own image,
> in the image of God he created them,
> male and female he created them. (Genesis 1:26–27)

Isaiah also comments on this creation in the context of the stubbornness of the human heart,

> Your thinking is perverse!
> Should the potter be regarded as clay?
> Should the thing made say about its maker, "He didn't make me"?
> Or should the pottery say about the potter, "He doesn't understand"?
> (Isaiah 29:16)

As he cited the Greek poets, Sha'ul also commented:

> For in him we live and move about and exist, as even some of your own poets have said, "For we too are his offspring." So since we are God's offspring, we should not think the deity is like gold or silver or stone, an image made by human skill and imagination. (Acts 17:28–29)

Human beings are different from animals in their total being; each person is a self-conscious, rational, moral, and spiritual being with the capacity to be God-conscious. Being created in God's image, people should be aware of God's existence and have the opportunity to respond to God's revelation through the God-image in them.

This revelation is only partial, not as full as the Torah itself. Nevertheless, this limited revelation cannot be set aside as though it were as nothing. Primarily, the limitations of this revelation have to do with who man is. The human heart has a barrier that can block any work of the Spirit. God can provide information by the Spirit, but we can very easily turn away from it as Romans 1:18, 23 so eloquently declares:

> For the wrath of God is revealed from heaven against all ungodliness and unrighteousness of people who suppress the truth by their unrighteousness, . . . and exchanged the glory of the immortal God for an image resembling mortal human beings or birds or four-footed animals or reptiles. (Romans 1:18, 23)

In Primitive and Direct Revelation. Scripture emphasizes how God spoke directly to man prior to the presence of a written revelation in the Torah. We learn that He communicated with Noah concerning the destruction of the human race prior to the flood:

> So God said to Noah, "I have decided that all living creatures must die, for the earth is filled with violence because of them. Now I am about to destroy them and the earth." (Genesis 6:13)

This communication was God's promise to spare the patriarch, his immediate family, and select animals through the means of an ark. It also included such matters as when to enter the ark, and on their departure from the ark, the commandment to replenish the earth. It further included the conclusion of a covenant with Noah promising that the earth would not again be destroyed with a flood:

> So God said to Noah, "I have decided that all living creatures must die, for the earth is filled with violence because of them. Now I am about to destroy them and the earth. . . . Then God blessed Noah and his sons and said to them, "Be fruitful and multiply and fill the earth. . . . then I will remember my covenant with you and with all living creatures of all kinds. Never again will the waters become a flood and destroy all living things." (Genesis 6:13; 9:1, 15)

God also communicated directly with Abraham in a well-known promise:

> The LORD had said to Abram,
> "Leave your country, your people and your father's household
> and go to the land I will show you.
> I will make you into a great nation
> and I will bless you;
> I will make your name great,
> and you will be a blessing.
> I will bless those who bless you,
> and whoever curses you I will curse;
> and all peoples on earth
> will be blessed through you." (Genesis 12:1–3 NIV)[3]

Concerning the content of this direct revelation, the communication was very full and rich. Much of what we know about God can be gleaned from what was revealed to these men of old. Abraham learned that El Shaddai not only means "the Almighty One":

> When Abram was 99 years old, the LORD appeared to him and said, "I am the sovereign God. Walk before me and be blameless." (Genesis 17:1)

But as he and his wife became parents at ninety-nine and ninety years of age respectively, they came to know Him as the one who can do beyond what anyone can even ask or think:

> The Lord visited Sarah just as he had said he would and did for Sarah what he had promised. So Sarah became pregnant and bore Abraham a son in his old age at the appointed time that God had told him. Abraham named his son—whom Sarah bore to him—Isaac. When his son Isaac was eight days old, Abraham circumcised him just as God had commanded him to do. (Now Abraham was a hundred years old when his son Isaac was born to him.)
>
> Sarah said, "God has made me laugh. Everyone who hears about this will laugh with me." She went on to say, "Who would have said

> to Abraham that Sarah would nurse children? Yet I have given birth to a son for him in his old age!" (Genesis 21:1–7)

These and similar early communications from God are considered "primitive revelation" in the sense that they came prior to the selection of Israel as a nation at Mount Sinai and prior to the written Torah and New Covenant. However, even later in the era of the writing prophets, there are many examples of how God communicated directly with His servants. He gave them information that became part of the sacred record; in the instance of Jeremiah the prophet, when God called him He communicated to him that he had been specially prepared for his task:

> The LORD said to me,
> "Before I formed you in your mother's womb I chose you.
> Before you were born I set you apart.
> I appointed you to be a prophet to the nations."
>
> I answered, "Oh, Lord GOD, I really do not know how to speak well enough for that, for I am too young."The LORD said to me, "Do not say, 'I am too young.' But go to whomever I send you and say whatever I tell you. Do not be afraid of those to whom I send you, for I will be with you to protect you," says the LORD. Then the LORD reached out his hand and touched my mouth and said to me, "I will most assuredly give you the words you are to speak for me. Know for certain that I hereby give you the authority to announce to nations and kingdoms that they will be uprooted and torn down, destroyed and demolished, rebuilt and firmly planted." (Jeremiah 1:4–10)

Who had access to this knowledge of God? At that time, only those to whom God revealed Himself. That revelation was given only to selected individuals, not to all men, in order to guide them to accomplish His purposes.

Today, of course, God's revelation is available to anyone now that the biblical record is completed. Can we say that God speaks directly today apart from the Written Torah and New Covenant? In general, the answer is no; and though no doubt God could do so if He desired, for the most part this is an age of silence in which the Spirit of God addresses believers in Scripture and thereby leads them to do His good will. While not all will agree with this viewpoint, the position of this writer is that with the completed Word of God in our possession, we have all the information needed for God to speak and lead people to serve Him.

In Miraculous and Providential Works. God also revealed Himself through His miracles and the providential upholding of His creation. Only a few out of the wealth of biblical passages will be considered.

First, let us look at the story of the exodus. Through the tedious process of managing a relationship with Pharaoh, Moses' task was to persuade him to let Israel depart from Egypt, as we first see in Exodus 5:1–2:

> Afterward Moses and Aaron went to Pharaoh and said, "Thus says the LORD, the God of Israel, 'Release my people so that they may hold a pilgrim feast to me in the desert.'" But Pharaoh said, "Who is the LORD that I should obey him by releasing Israel? I do not know the LORD, and I will not release Israel!" (Exodus 5:1–2)

The Egyptian leader responded with stubbornness, imagining that the God of Israel was of no consequence, since He allowed His people to endure slavery. In response, God sent plagues on Egypt, each one actually being an attack on the gods and goddesses of the nation. The plagues increased in severity on the people as well as on the leaders, demonstrating that the God of Israel was the Lord:

> Then the Egyptians will know that I am the LORD, when I extend my hand over Egypt and bring the Israelites out from among them. . . . Thus says the LORD: "By this you will know that I am the LORD: I am going to strike the water of the Nile with the staff that is in my hand, and it will be turned into blood." (Exodus 7:5, 17)

with no one to compare with Him:

> For this time I will send all my plagues on your very self and on your servants and your people, so that you may know that there is no one like me in all the earth. (Exodus 9:14)

As Pharaoh hardened his heart, refusing to listen to the warnings through the plagues, he became the "vessel of wrath" through whom Israel would be delivered. Finally, God's greatest judgment on Egypt came with the death of the firstborn of all the Egyptians, including Pharaoh's own son. At first, under the duress of this loss, he allowed Israel to go, but soon after changed his mind. As the Egyptian army pursued Israel, chasing them into the bed of the Sea of Reeds (Red Sea), they were subsequently drowned when the waters closed in on them. In the future, God promised, Moses and the people of Israel would be able to tell their descendants of how their God made a mockery of the Egyptians:

> . . . and in order that in the hearing of your son and your grandson you may tell how I made fools of the Egyptians and about my signs that I displayed among them, so that you may know that I am the LORD. (Exodus 10:2)

This revelation through miracle and providential works was reiterated when through Moses, God reasoned with His people in retrospect:

> Indeed, ask about the distant past, starting from the day God created humankind on the earth, and ask from one end of heaven to the other, whether there has ever been such a great thing as this, or even a rumor of it. Have a people ever heard the voice of God speaking from the middle of fire, as you yourselves have, and lived to tell about it? Or has God ever before tried to deliver a nation from the middle of another nation, accompanied by judgments, signs, wonders, war, strength, power, and other very terrifying things like the Lord your God did for you in Egypt before your very eyes?You have been taught that the LORD alone is God—there is no other besides him. (Deuteronomy 4:32–35)[4]

After the time of Moses, God restrained the waters of the Jordan River as Israel crossed—during the springtime of flooding!—in order to show the nations, particularly those in Canaan, that the hand of the Lord was powerful:

> For the LORD your God dried up the water of the Jordan before you while you crossed over. It was just like when the Lord your God dried up the Red Sea before us while we crossed it. He has done this so all the nations of the earth might recognize the Lord's power and so you might always obey the LORD your God. (Joshua 4:23–24)

The prophet Isaiah also spoke of miraculous works: the naming of Cyrus long before he was ever born; the conquering of Babylon by the Persian Cyrus, thereby enabling Judah and other refugee nations to return to the countries of their origins. In accomplishing such a great event, the nations would learn that besides the God of Israel, there is no other living God:

> This is what the LORD says to his chosen one,
> to Cyrus, whose right hand I hold
> in order to subdue nations before him,
> and disarm kings,
> to open doors before him,
> so gates remain unclosed:
> "I will go before you
> and level mountains.
> Bronze doors I will shatter
> and iron bars I will hack through.
> I will give you hidden treasures,
> riches stashed away in secret places,
> so you may recognize that I am the LORD,
> the one who calls you by name, the God of Israel.
> For the sake of my servant Jacob,
> Israel, my chosen one,
> I call you by name
> and give you a title of respect, even though you do not recognize me.
> I am the Lord, I have no peer,
> there is no God but me.
> I arm you for battle, even though you do not recognize me.
> I do this so people will recognize from east to west

> that there is no God but me;
> I am the LORD, I have no peer." (Isaiah 45:1–6)

A different kind of providential working is seen when a generation arose in which most did not listen to God. At those times, God would bring pagan nations to discipline His people so that they would know there is a God who really cared for them. Sometimes God had to work in such drastic circumstances so as to accomplish a positive purpose. Out of the pressure cooker of death at home and exile abroad would come a remnant:

> But I will take you out of the city. And I will hand you over to foreigners. I will execute judgments on you. You will die by the sword; I will judge you at the border of Israel. Then you will know that I am the LORD. (Ezekiel 11:9–10)

In turning to the New Covenant, we note that Yeshua did many great works and miracles by which people could recognize who He was, for His works many times reflected not only His humanity but also His deity:

> But if I do them, even if you do not believe me, believe the deeds, so that you may come to know and understand that I am in the Father and the Father is in me. (Yohanan 10:38)

And Sha'ul refered to the unfaithfulness of Israel when through the intervening hand of God, a plague struck Israel leading to the death of some twenty-three thousand people in one day. In this way the nation would learn to recognize His holiness and act accordingly. Sha'ul alludes to other similar circumstances as examples for believers today:

> So do not be idolaters, as some of them were. As it is written, "The people sat down to eat and drink and rose up to play." And let us not be immoral, as some of them were, and twenty-three thousand died in a single day. And let us not put Messiah to the test, as some of them did, and were destroyed by snakes. And do not complain, as some of

> them did, and were killed by the destroying angel. These things happened to them as examples and were written for our instruction, on whom the ends of the ages have come. (1 Corinthians 10:7–11)

These are only a few of the miraculous and providential circumstances recorded in the Torah and New Covenant. They reveal God as a special person, who with power directs not only Israel but the nations as well.

When considering all these acts of God, we face the question as to who had access to these experiences and were therefore able to recount them. First and foremost, the miracles and providential deeds were available to those who actually saw or took part in the divine acts. They were eyewitnesses to the actual events. Some of these eyewitnesses recorded what took place, as in the examples from Scripture we have just seen. Present-day readers can then read the accounts and consider what lessons can be derived for today.

What are the limitations to the revelation of God through miracles and providential acts? At best, they are most meaningful to those who actually experienced them. Yet even then, the totality of meaning was not always grasped. Israel experienced an abundance of miracles from the time Moses interceded with Pharaoh, through the release from Egypt, to the arrival at Mount Sinai. Yet many Israelites ended up engaging in a synthesized worship of the Egyptian bull and the God of Israel. Did they not understand what God was doing for them? To that generation, the revelation became only partial or was misinterpreted by them; they did not perceive what God was accomplishing for them.

Another danger with revelation through providential acts has do with preserving the account of what God did. Some believers, for instance, preserved the records of the temptation of Eve or the flood in the time of Noah. Others also recorded these events in a form that became garbled, distorted, and corrupted, as for example in the Babylonian account of the garden, or in the Gilgamash Epic.

Finally, the biggest problem with revelation through the miraculous and providential acts of God is that they do not compel belief. This was true of the generation who left Egypt; because of their lack of faith in what God had accomplished for them, all the first generation who left Egypt, twenty years and above, died in the wilderness with the exception of Moses, Joshua, and Caleb. Today, while God can still do miracles as well and we can see His providential works in salvation and healing, yet these same acts of God cannot make people believe His message. God's directives must be accepted by faith. Miracles can touch hearts that are open to receive truth, but by themselves they are not a substitute for faith in God's Torah.

In the Life and Experiences of His People. One of most helpful ways we learn about God is as He reveals Himself through personal experiences. A classic illustration is the account of David's sin in violating Bat Sheva and then murdering her husband (see 2 Samuel 11). Having followed that with taking Bat Sheva as his wife, he thought to cover up his deeds—but God never gave him a moment's rest. David described his inner state as the Spirit of God ravaged him for the evil he had committed. Finally, in his confession, he cried out,

> Let me again experience the joy of your deliverance!
> Sustain me by giving me the desire to obey!
> Then I will teach rebels your merciful ways,
> and sinners will turn to you. (Psalm 51:12–13)

David recognized that through his experiences, he would be able to share meaningfully with others in similar circumstances.

Yeshua spoke much on God's revelation in personal experiences. According to Him, as His followers walk with the Lord and learn from Him, each one is the salt of the earth (and cautioned to not lose his saltiness through a lax lifestyle or because of sin, thereby rendering his testimony ineffective). Likewise, believers are to be light for this world as a testimony; the light is not to be hidden. As one walks with God in these two aspects as salt and light, their life and experience with God will teach others about Him:

> You are the salt of the earth. But if salt loses its flavor, how can it be made salty again? It is no longer good for anything except to be

> thrown out and trampled on by people. You are the light of the world. A city located on a hill cannot be hidden. People do not light a lamp and put it under a basket but on a lampstand, and it gives light to all in the house. In the same way, let your light shine before people, so that they can see your good deeds and give honor to your Father in heaven. (Mattai 5:13–16)

Yohanan reminds believers to keep the commandments of God, which then becomes a sign of love for God. As believers do what the commandments ask out of a willing heart, Yeshua will disclose even greater precious truths concerning Himself:

> The person who has my commandments and obeys them is the one who loves me. The one who loves me will be loved by my Father, and I will love him and will reveal myself to him. (Yohanan 14:21)

Sha'ul likewise spoke of what God can reveal through personal experience. He reminded the Corinthians:

> You yourselves are our letter, written on our hearts, known and read by everyone, revealing that you are a letter of Messiah, delivered by us, written not with ink but by the Spirit of the living God, not on stone tablets but on tablets of human hearts. (2 Corinthians 3:2–3)

Likewise, Sha'ul speaks of the revelatory light that comes from God that is present even in affliction:

> For God, who said "Let light shine out of darkness," is the one who shined in our hearts to give us the light of the glorious knowledge of God in the face of Messiah. But we have this treasure in clay jars, so that the extraordinary power belongs to God and does not come from us. We are experiencing trouble on every side, but are not crushed; we are perplexed, but not driven to despair; we are persecuted, but not abandoned; we are knocked down, but not

> destroyed, always carrying around in our body the death of Yeshua, so that the life of Yeshua may also be made visible in our body. For we who are alive are constantly being handed over to death for Yeshua's sake, so that the life of Yeshua may also be made visible in our mortal body. (2 Corinthians 4:6–11)

Similarly:

> Do not lie to one another since you have put off the old man with its practices and have been clothed with the new man that is being renewed in knowledge according to the image of the one who created it. (Colossians 3:9–10)

and:

> Because of this, in fact, I suffer as I do. But I am not ashamed, because I know the one in whom my faith is set and I am convinced that he is able to protect what has been entrusted to me until that day. (2 Timothy 1:12)

Kefa likewise could say that believers are part of a royal priesthood, a royal nation, with great privileges, and for a purpose of a lifestyle:

> But you are a chosen race, a royal priesthood, a holy nation, a people of his own, so that you may proclaim the virtues of the one who called you out of darkness into his marvelous light. (1 Kefa 2:9)

What a wonderful revelation each one has within His body to share with others, but the significance is clear: no believer has the right to walk away from his or her responsibilities, once having received His mercy and having been placed within the family of God.

In all of these examples, one can learn the great lessons about God through personal experience, hopefully through obedience, but also through the bitterness of wrong choices. Believers also find great examples in observing and learning from other older *hasidim*, or saints, as they live out their lives in obedience to God's call and Word, thereby glorifying Him. As believers live what God expects of them, they exhibit His moral character and goodness.

Who has access to this revelation through experience? Primarily, it is limited to those who have come to faith either in the days of the Tanach or under the New Covenant. As one lives out the presence of Yeshua in his or her life, the knowledge of God is exhibited to both believers and to other people. The glory of God, His light and power, and His undeniable presence, when seen in the lives of believers, impact all kinds of people, some of whom come to faith in the Lord. Revelation through experience is limited, however, by the willingness of believers to live according to the resources God has provided. The message has all too often been marred by an uncontrolled sinful nature, thereby misrepresenting God and occasioning lost opportunities to reach the unregenerate.

In the Revelation of the Torah and New Covenant. A full discussion of the doctrine of the Torah and New Covenant was the subject of an earlier discussion. Only a few comments will be offered here so as to complete our observations concerning the revelation of God.

While God's Word does not contain all knowledge, yet it has all that we need to begin a relationship with God through atonement and to walk with Him throughout our lives. The culmination of that revelation is the Messiah Yeshua Himself:

> For in him all the fullness of deity lives in bodily form. (Colossians 2:9)

Of Him, Hebrews tells us that

> in these last days he has spoken to us in a son, whom he appointed heir of all things, and through whom he created the world. The Son is the radiance of his glory and the representation of his essence, and he sustains all things by his powerful word, and so when he had accomplished cleansing for sins, he sat down at the right hand of the Majesty on high. (Hebrews 1:2–3)

In response to Philip's request "Show us the Father,"

> Yeshua replied, "Have I been with you for so long, and you have not known me, Philip? The person who has seen me has seen the Father! How can you say, 'Show us the Father'?" (Yohanan 14:9)

Though the Written Torah is sacred and supreme, Yeshua represents the highest revelation of God, the living Torah or Word,

> in whom are hidden all the treasures of wisdom and knowledge. (Colossians 2:3)

We cannot afford to ignore Yeshua!

The Written Torah, or Word, is accessible to all who hear and receive the message of atonement. Only one limitation exists regarding this knowledge of the Lord, namely, our finite capacity to know an infinite God. Solomon struggled with this very limitation when he realized that the more he sought to know, the more the vistas of knowledge extended further and further, causing him much pain:

> For with great wisdom comes great frustration;
> whoever increases his knowledge merely increases his heartache.
> (Ecclesiastes 1:18)

Solomon had to reconcile himself to the fact that ultimate knowledge will never be attained, or else we would be God; but we *can* know practical knowledge based on the Torah and New Covenant.

In the future, we will have greater knowledge of God. Sha'ul declared:

> For now we see in a mirror indirectly, but then we will see face to face. Now I know in part, but then I will know fully, just as I have been fully known. (1 Corinthians 13:12)

Kefa also alludes to this further knowledge:

> Therefore, get your minds ready for action by being fully sober, and set your hope completely on the grace that will be brought to you when Yeshua the Messiah is revealed. (1 Kefa 1:13)

One day every believer will see the face of God and there will no longer be a barrier. At that time, learning will be sheer joy!

In concluding this section on revelation, we can note the value of each aspect:

The material universe
The nature of man
Direct revelation: partial, can be distorted
Miracles and providence: inadequate
Experience and life
But the Torah and New Covenant are perfect in original form.
And the Messiah is complete, perfect, final.

The Unity of God

This topic was previously discussed under the descriptions of *echad* and *yachid* where we showed that the latter word is never a biblically tenable description of God's oneness. At this point we will revisit the subject, examining the Torah and New Covenant material at hand.

Meaning and Content of the Unity of God

The great confession of Israel, the *Shema*, acknowledges the oneness of God. Moses proclaims to the people:

> Hear, O Israel: The LORD our God, the LORD is one. (Deuteronomy 6:4 NIV)

In light of what we have already seen, we note once more the composite nature of this God who yet is one. The New Covenant also testifies to this truth, as for instance when Yeshua said:

> How can you believe, if you accept praise from one another and don't seek the praise that comes from the only God? (Yohanan 5:44)

To a hostile audience, Yeshua had announced:

> The Father and I are one. (Yohanan 10:30)

The word *one* is here grammatically neuter, with the meaning of "a unity, one essence." Some have tried to get around this strange statement, whereby Yeshua made Himself equal with God, and have sought instead to explain that the Father and Yeshua are one in *purpose* in their desire to teach the people. However, the neuter of the noun suggests otherwise. But more importantly, how did Yeshua's listeners understand His statement? The following verses make it quite plain:

> The Jewish leaders picked up rocks again to stone him to death. Yeshua said to them, "I have shown you many good deeds from the Father. For which one of them are you going to stone me?" The Jewish leaders replied, "We are not going to stone you for a good deed but for blasphemy, because you, a man, are claiming to be God." (Yohanan 10:31–33)

Sha'ul declared God to be one in a setting where he rejected the pagan notion that animals sacrificed to idols should not become everyday food:

> Yet for us there is one God, the Father, from whom are all things and for whom we live, and one Lord, Yeshua the Messiah, through whom are all things and through whom we live. But this knowledge is not shared by all. And some, by being accustomed to idols in former times, eat this food as an idol sacrifice, and their conscience, because it is weak, is defiled. Now food will not bring us close to God. We are no worse if we do not eat and no better if we do. (1 Corinthians 8:6–8)

As far as Sha'ul was concerned, only one God exists, "from whom are all things," and one Lord, Yeshua HaMashiach, "through whom are all things."

Sha'ul also declared God to be one because He is the God of all peoples:

> Or is God the God of the Jews only? Is he not the God of the Gentiles too? Yes, of the Gentiles too! Since God is one, he will justify the circumcised by faith and the uncircumcised through faith. (Romans 3:29–30)

Supporting Evidence for God's Unity

Many examples abound regarding God's miraculous works that mark His unity. The classic example is seen when Israel stood before Mount Sinai:

> Indeed, ask about the distant past, starting from the day God created humankind on the earth, and ask from one end of heaven to the other, whether there has ever been such a great thing as this, or even a rumor of it. Have a people ever heard the voice of God speaking from the middle of fire, as you yourselves have, and lived to tell about it? Or has God ever before tried to deliver a nation from the middle of another nation, accompanied by judgments, signs, wonders, war, strength, power, and other very terrifying things like the LORD your God did for you in Egypt before your very eyes? You have been taught that the LORD alone is God—*there is no other besides him*. From heaven he spoke to you in order to teach you, and on earth he showed you his great fire from which you also heard his words. Moreover, because he loved your ancestors, he chose their descendants who followed them and personally brought you out of Egypt with his great power to dispossess nations greater and stronger than you and brought you here this day to give you their land as your property. Today realize and carefully consider that the LORD is God in heaven above and on earth below—*there is no other!* (Deuteronomy 4:32–39, emphasis added)

Predictive prophecy also relies on the special nature of the oneness of God, specifically, that He is *unique* in who He is. The prince of the prophets, Isaiah, underscored this aspect of God's unity. He testified that since God is first and the last, there is no God like Him. God Himself raises the question:

Don't panic! Don't be afraid!
Did I not tell you beforehand and decree it?
You are my witnesses! Is there any God but me?
There is no other sheltering rock; I know of none. (Isaiah 44:8)

I am the LORD, I have no peer,
there is no God but me.
I arm you for battle, even though you do not recognize me.
I do this so people will recognize from east to west
that there is no God but me;
I am the LORD, I have no peer. (Isaiah 45:5–6)

Remember what I accomplished in antiquity!
Truly I am God, I have no peer;
I am God, and there is none like me,
who announces the end from the beginning
and reveals beforehand what has not yet occurred,
who says, "My plan will be realized,
I will accomplish what I desire." (Isaiah 46:9–10)

The emphasis is clear; as we "remember the former things, those of long ago," we should conclude that God is unique. Indeed, He is God who can declare the end from the beginning long before events actually take place. Therefore, no one like Him exists. In no uncertain terms, Judah is reminded that their God is unique.

One needs to also note that the evidence for the composite nature of God's unity. The prophet Isaiah offered specific promises that in the coming kingdom,

Then blind eyes will open,
deaf ears will hear.
Then the lame will leap like a deer,
the mute tongue will shout for joy;
for water will flow in the desert,
streams in the wilderness. (Isaiah 35:5–6)

Furthermore, in the kingdom, the afflicted will one day rejoice in the good news specifically offered to them:

> The spirit of the sovereign LORD is upon me,
> because the LORD has chosen me.
> He has commissioned me to encourage the poor,
> to help the brokenhearted,
> to decree the release of captives,
> and the freeing of prisoners. (Isaiah 61:1)

We note that Yeshua offered the same promises as a testimony to Yohanan the Immerser:

> Now when Yohanan heard in prison about the deeds Messiah had done, he sent his disciples to ask a question: "Are you the one who is to come, or should we look for another?" Yeshua answered them, "Go tell Yohanan what you hear and see: The blind see, the lame walk, lepers are cleansed, the deaf hear, the dead are raised, and the poor have good news proclaimed to them. Blessed is anyone who takes no offense at me." (Mattai 11:2–6)

What we see in all this is that Yeshua does exactly what God does, demonstrating that there is a composite nature to the unity of God.

Note Yeshua's reply when a scribe asked Him which were the foremost of the commandments:

> "The most important one," answered Yeshua, "is this: 'Hear, O Israel, the LORD our God, the LORD is one. Love the LORD your God with all your heart and with all your soul and with all your mind and with all your strength.' The second is this: 'Love your neighbor as yourself.' There is no commandment greater than these." (Mark 12:29–31 NIV)

Yeshua replied by quoting the two specific commandments of Deuteronomy 4:4–5 and Leviticus 19:18: to love God and to love one's neighbor as oneself. Yeshua sought to emphasize the unity of God, albeit a composite unity!

Yaakov also asserts that God is one:

> You believe that God is one; well and good. Even the demons believe that—and tremble with fear. (Yaakov 2:19)

And Yehudah links the Father and the Messiah into one, once more a composite unity:

> For certain men have secretly slipped in among you—men who long ago were marked out for the condemnation I am about to describe—ungodly men who have turned the grace of our God into a license for evil and who deny our only Master and Lord Yeshua the Messiah. (Yehudah 1:4)

The Messianic Jewish writers of the New Covenant never denied the unity of God. They were just as emphatic on this as the writers of the Tanach. But they were a testimony to the unique kind of divine unity that Yeshua continually demonstrated.

The Greatness of God

There are many aspects to the greatness of God, and we will need to be selective.

God Is Self-Existent

When Moses asked how to respond to those who asked him the name of the God who sent him, the Lord announced:

> God said to Moses, "I AM THAT I AM." And he said, "You must say this to the Israelites, 'I AM has sent me to you.'" (Exodus 3:14)

It is noteworthy that this word is related to YHWH, the name for God, usually rendered in English as LORD. Jewish people, including Messianic Jews, do not generally pronounce this name and instead read it as *Adonai*. The name is derived from *hayah*, *to be*, and therefore it forms the basis of speaking of God as *ever continuing*, inherently self-existing in His very being.

Yeshua Himself touched on this issue in speaking to an audience of Jewish people:

> For just as the Father has life in himself, thus he has granted the Son to have life in himself. (Yohanan 5:26)

One can never imagine a time when the Father was dependent on life from any source outside of Himself; by the very definition of who God is, we would expect Him to be self-existent. And from what has already been noted concerning the concept of the composite nature of God, Yeshua likewise is also self-existent.

The Nature of God's Self-Existence. The source of God's existence lies wholly within Himself. God does not depend on anything external to Himself. Philosophically, this is referred to as His being an "absolute existing being," while human beings are "contingent" beings. God's existence is in His very being, while mankind is dependent on God for life itself.

As a Philosophical Problem. Numerous thinkers and philosophers ever since the age of the philosophic Enlightenment began, about the nineteenth century, have wrestled with this question. Jewish thinkers also had their Enlightenment, called the *Haskalah*, and discussed similar questions. The problem is that many thinkers of the Enlightenment did not want to consider a concept such as the self-existence of God but rather asked whether the *universe* was self-existent.

Practical Value. God's self-existence is a comfort and encouragement to the believer. Since the Father has life in Himself (see Yohanan 5:26 above), we have the assurance that our lives are not simply streams that will be cut off when we die physically. Yeshua promised:

> I tell you the solemn truth, a time is coming—and is now here—when the dead will hear the voice of the Son of God, and those who hear will live. (Yohanan 5:25)

Therefore, we will never more be separated from Him. In a sense, we are "tied to" this God who is self-existent.

God Is Eternal

A corollary to self-existence is the fact that God is also eternal. A wealth of biblical material attests to this.

The Biblical Material. Just prior to Abraham's supreme test of his life when he was asked to offer up Isaac as a burnt offering on Mount Moriah, God had revealed Himself to the patriarch as "Everlasting" or "Eternal":

> Abraham planted a tamarisk tree in Beer Sheba. There he worshiped the LORD, the eternal God. (Genesis 21:33)

Evidently, Abraham must have understood something about the eternality of God, because he called on Him by that name. That is why he was able to offer up Isaac, believing that God is the God of the living. Indeed, the book of Hebrews suggests as much:

> And he [Abraham] reasoned that God could even raise him [Isaac] from the dead, and in a sense he received him back from there. (Hebrews 11:19)

Moses too proclaimed this aspect of God's nature:

> O Lord, you have been our protector through all generations!
> Even before the mountains came into existence,
> or you brought the world into being,
> you were the eternal God. (Psalm 90:1–2)

Thus the God of Israel is not like the gods of the nations in whom is no breath and are nothing more than figments of the imagination.

The psalmist also says:

> But you, O LORD, rule forever,
> and your reputation endures. (Psalm 102:12)

while Isaiah speaks of God in these terms:

> For this is what the high and exalted one says,
> the one who rules forever, whose name is holy:
> "I dwell in an exalted and holy place,
> but also with the discouraged and humiliated,
> in order to cheer up the humiliated
> and to encourage the discouraged." (Isaiah 57:15)

Encouraging believers, Isaiah reminds them that while God is in one sense inaccessible, dwelling in eternity, yet He also dwells with the lowly in spirit.

Consider also the words of Habakkuk, as the nation was faced with the invasion of the Babylonian armed forces, ready to tear them apart:

> LORD, you have been active from ancient times;
> my sovereign God, you are immortal.
> LORD, you have made them your instrument of judgment.
> Protector, you have appointed them as your instrument of punishment.
> (Habakkuk 1:12)

Though many individuals did in fact die when Jerusalem was sacked and the First Temple lost, the prophet was correct to link the God who is eternal to His people Israel, who will exist as long as there is a history of mankind!

The Messianic Jews of the New Covenant also had a good grasp of God's eternal nature, as seen in these verses:

> For since the creation of the world his invisible attributes—his eternal power and divine nature—have been clearly seen, because they are understood through what has been made. So people are without excuse. (Romans 1:20)

> Now to the eternal king, immortal, invisible, the only God, be honor and glory forever and ever! Amen. (1 Timothy 1:17)

> In these last days he has spoken to us in a son, whom he appointed heir of all things, and through whom he created the world [literally, "the ages"]. (Hebrews 1:2)

> The twenty-four elders throw themselves to the ground before the one who sits on the throne and worship the one who lives forever and ever, and they offer their crowns before his throne. (Revelation 4:10)

The Nature of God's Eternality. Having considered some of the Scripture in connection with this doctrine, we can now state something about this doctrine. From what Moses had declared in his prayer, long before this world and universe existed, God is already from everlasting to everlasting (see Psalm 90:1–2 above). That means that His existence cannot be measured by a human way of counting, that is, by time. While God created time and seasons for the benefit of all living creatures, including man, He is not bound by it. Time is a relationship of things in a finite, changing world. But God *started* our universe of finitely changing things. God dwells (in the wording of the King James Version) in "eternity" (see Isaiah 57:15 above),[5] and is therefore above and beyond time. He fills everything within the universe in the sense that He is immanent, but He sees all, not only within time, but also beyond time as well.

Furthermore, as Sha'ul had stated, because God is King of the ages and since all honor and glory are to be His to the ages of the ages, it is appropriate to say that God is the Author and Ruler of time. And going a step further, Yeshua Himself shares in this distinction, when it is asserted that God worked through Him when He made the ages (see Hebrews 1:2 above). Yeshua is also eternal, because He both preexisted (see below in a later chapter) and exists throughout eternity:

> Then I saw a new heaven and a new earth, for the first heaven and earth had ceased to exist, and the sea existed no more. . . . And there will no longer be any curse, and the throne of God and the Lamb will be in the city. His servants will worship him. (Revelation 21:1; 22:3)

Practical Value. One major practical value regarding the eternality of God was uttered by Moses in his farewell speech after blessing the clans:

> The everlasting God is a refuge,
> and underneath you are his eternal arms;
> he has driven out enemies before you,
> and has said, "Destroy!" (Deuteronomy 33:27)

We can trust Him because He is ever present while we are here on earth, and certainly when we will be in a special relationship with Him in the next world. This and other promises can assure us, no matter what our experiences may be in this life.

God Is Omnipresent

The Biblical Material. In the Tanach, consider these verses:

> God does not really live on the earth! Look, if the sky and the highest heaven cannot contain you, how much less this temple I have built! (1 Kings 8:27)

> Where can I go to escape your spirit?
> Where can I flee to escape your presence?
> If I were to ascend to heaven, you would be there.
> If I were to sprawl out in Sheol, there you would be.
> If I were to fly away on the wings of the dawn,
> and settle down on the other side of the sea,
> even there your hand would guide me,
> your right hand would grab hold of me. (Psalm 139:7–10)

> In the year of King Uzziah's death, I saw the sovereign master seated on a high, elevated throne. The hem of his robe filled the temple. Seraphs stood over him; each one had six wings. With two wings they covered their faces, with two they covered their feet, and they used the remaining two to fly. They called out to one another,

> "Holy, holy, holy is the Lord who commands armies! His majestic splendor fills the entire earth!"The sound of their voices shook the door frames, and the temple was filled with smoke. (Isaiah 6:1–4)

> "Do you people think that I am some local deity
> and not the transcendent God?" the LORD asks.
> "Do you really think anyone can hide himself
> where I cannot see him?" the LORD asks.
> "Do you not know that I am everywhere?"
> the LORD asks. (Jeremiah 23:23–24)

In the New Covenant, Sha'ul spoke to the pagan philosophers of God's omnipresence: we live, move, and are in Him, which is to say, that He is everywhere we are.

> . . . so that they would search for God and perhaps grope around for him and find him, though he is not far from each one of us. For in him we live and move about and exist, as even some of your own poets have said, "For we too are his offspring." (Acts 17:27–28)

The Nature of God's Omnipresence. On the one hand, God is immanent, in the midst of His creation. He is everywhere present in the universe at the same time. Yet He is not corporeal, that is, not locked in or tied to any object in the universe; He is free to be anywhere.

On the other hand, God is also transcendent, above and beyond creation as well. The universe proceeded from Him when He spoke it into existence. Therefore, in making any theological statement concerning His presence, one must always remember to start with God, since He preceded the existence of the universe.

Some Problems. If God is omnipresent, how do we explain texts such as:

> But the LORD came down to see the city and the tower that the people had started building. (Genesis 11:5)

And how do we relate that verse to the fact that Yeshua taught His disciples:

> So pray this way: Our Father in heaven, may your name be honored. (Mattai 6:9)

Is this pair of verses an example of a contradiction in concepts?

Yet if we carefully consider the concept of omnipresence, God can be spoken of being in both places, using what is called the "language of appearance." Obviously, this aspect of God as both immanent and transcendent is difficult to grasp, yet for God it is no problem to be in both places at the same time. *We* are the ones who have the problem visualizing His omnipresence.

Practical Value. One value is that the great truth of God's omnipresence is a warning to the ungodly. When the day of reckoning comes, they will find no place in which to hide from the wrath of God:

> I saw the sovereign One standing by the altar and he said, "Strike the tops of the support pillars, so the thresholds shake!
> Knock them down on the heads of all the people,
> and I will kill the survivors with the sword.
> No one will be able to run away;
> no one will be able to escape.
> Even if they could dig down into the netherworld,
> my hand would pull them up from there.
> Even if they could climb up to heaven,
> I would drag them down from there.
> Even if they were to hide on the top of Mount Carmel,
> I would hunt them down and take them from there.
> Even if they tried to hide from me at the bottom of the sea,
> from there I would command the Sea Serpent to bite them.
> Even when their enemies drive them into captivity,
> from there I will command the sword to kill them.
> I will not let them out of my sight;
> they will experience disaster, not prosperity." (Amos 9:1–4)

Neither can believers escape His presence, try as they might. Jonah found out the hard way that no ship on the high seas was "safe" from the presence and commission of God (see Jonah 1).

On the other hand, this truth of God is a consolation for believers who walk in the will of God, no matter what trials they undergo. As each one loves and keeps the words of Yeshua, no matter where he or she might be on the face of this earth, each one will be the object of the Father's love, and both the Father and Yeshua will come and make their home with either him or her. His omnipresence is an encouragement by which to live with complete confidence and assurance.

God Is Omniscient

All-Inclusive. God's knowledge includes all things that have occurred in the past, that are now occurring in the present, and that will happen in the future. The Torah and New Covenant has such a wealth of material on this subject that we can only look at a few verses; it is left to the reader to discover other passages.

> For he looks to the ends of the earth
> and observes everything under the heavens. (Job 28:24)

> He counts the number of the stars;
> he names all of them. (Psalm 147:4)

> Aren't two sparrows sold for a penny? Yet not one of them falls to the ground apart from your Father's will. (Mattai 10:29)

> The underworld is naked before God;
> the place of destruction lies uncovered. (Job 26:6)

That is, God has knowledge of those who are already in the next world, on either the side of the redeemed or the unredeemed.

> The LORD watches from heaven;
> he sees all people.

> From the place where he lives he looks carefully
> at all the earth's inhabitants.
> He is the one who forms every human heart,
> and takes note of all their actions. (Psalm 33:13–15)

That is, He determines what people are thinking, understanding their motives and priorities.

Then, in connection with the disciples who asked God's guidance for the one who would replace Yehudah:

> Then they prayed, "Lord, you know the hearts of all. Show us which one of these two you have chosen." (Acts 1:24)

> O LORD, you examine me and know.
> You know when I sit down and when I get up;
> even from far away you understand my motives.
> You carefully observe me when I travel or when I lie down to rest;
> you are aware of everything I do.
> Certainly my tongue does not frame a word
> without you, O LORD, being thoroughly aware of it. (Psalm 139:1–4)

What a sobering thought indeed! God knows all the minute details of one's personal life. What if more people realized this truth before they decided on their actions?

While all past events are known to God, the future also stands before Him as if it has already occurred:

> Remember what I accomplished in antiquity!
> Truly I am God, I have no peer;
> I am God, and there is none like me,
> who announces the end from the beginning
> and reveals beforehand what has not yet occurred,
> who says, "My plan will be realized,
> I will accomplish what I desire,"

> who summons an eagle from the east,
> from a distant land, one who carries out my plan.
> Yes, I have decreed,
> yes, I will bring it to pass;
> I have formulated a plan,
> yes, I will carry it out. (Isaiah 46:9–11)

In the light of this vast mass of information, God is able to know all possible events under all possible combinations of circumstances. That is why He is able to pinpoint things accurately in the Messianic prophecies, because He knows the multitude of the historical "bites" of information in which prophetic fulfillment occurs (for just one instance, see Luke 2:1–7).

Eternal, Perfect, and Complete. Elihu, the youngest of the friends confronting Job, asked Job concerning the limitations of his knowledge:

> Do you know how God commands them,
> how he makes lightning flash in his storm cloud?
> Do you know about the balancing of the clouds,
> that wondrous activity of him who is perfect in knowledge?
> (Job 37:15–16)

Later in the same book, God asked Job forty questions concerning the creation of which Job could not answer a single one (see Job 38).

In contrast, the writer of Hebrews asserted:

> And no creature is hidden from God, but everything is naked and exposed to the eyes of him to whom we must render an account. (Hebrews 4:13)

The point of these passages as well as many similar ones is to remind us that unlike ours, God's knowledge is perfect and complete, known to Him from the beginning. Such fullness of knowledge is awesome indeed.

This knowledge that God possesses is not for the purpose of self-gratification. Rather, His knowledge involves a moral purpose. He always tests the purpose of having knowledge; He is concerned with what motivates people with the knowledge they possess and the ends to which they put their knowledge:

> The eyes of the LORD are in every place,
> keeping watch on those who are evil and those who are good.
> (Proverbs 15:3)

Some Problems. The Torah states:

> Remember how the LORD your God led you all the way in the desert these forty years, to humble you and to test you in order to know what was in your heart, whether or not you would keep his commands.
> (Deuteronomy 8:2 NIV, emphasis added)

Does this mean that God did not know what would occur, that He did not know what decisions Israel would make during their march in the wilderness?

Consider also the passage in which God is portrayed as coming down to Sodom and Gomorrah:

> So the LORD said, "The outcry against Sodom and Gomorrah is so great and their sin so blatant that I must go down *and see if they are as wicked as the outcry suggests.* If not, I want to know."
> (Genesis 18:20–21, emphasis added)

Again, does that imply that He was unaware of what was occurring in these ancient twin cities?

The point is that He knows exactly what is going on, what people will decide, and what actions they will commit. However, we can suggest that these are more anthropomorphic expressions. Testing is for the people involved. What decisions will they make? God certainly foreknows what man will do; He does not predetermine their actions.

Another question is whether God is not too great to notice every trivial event that happens. But this is exactly the point of His greatness. Though He is on high, and nothing escapes His notice, yet He can intervene to aid the lowliest of people:

> Who can compare to the LORD our God,
> who sits on a high throne?
> He bends down to look
> at the sky and the earth.
> He raises the poor from the dirt,
> and lifts up the needy from the garbage pile,
> that he might seat him with princes,
> with the princes of his people.
> He makes the barren woman of the family
> a happy mother of children.
> Praise the LORD! (Psalm 113:5–9)

Yet another question is this: If God knows everything about a person, does it mean that He can make someone do what He wants him to do? The response is that while He knows what man will do beforehand, it does not mean He can predetermine what a person will do. This issue is one of the most baffling problems in philosophy (freedom vs. determinism) as well as in theology (free will and God's sovereignty).

Another way of stating the question is, If God knows all future events, are they certain to occur, regardless of what anyone does? For example, Daniel had read the prophecies of Jeremiah 25:12 and 29:10, which foretold that Judah would be released from exile after seventy years of captivity. The prophet had lived to see the end of the Babylonian reign of almost seventy years, and in fact became part of the Persian leadership that then came into power. Did he wait to see how God would accomplish what He said? No, but rather, Daniel began to pray for the release of his people. Here one learns a valuable lesson. While God's prophetic Word will take place as predicted, in His plan He has given it to human beings to pray for that fulfillment. Prayer is a part of the plan of God so that His Word can be accomplished. If Daniel had not prayed, the Spirit of God would have burdened someone else to pray that the Word would be fulfilled. So prayer has its part in God's program for His purposes to take place.

On another occasion, however, God had predicted that Judah would fall to enemy invaders who would destroy Jerusalem and the temple, killing many and taking thousands more into exile:

> Look at the nations and pay attention!
> You will be shocked and amazed!
> For I will do something in your lifetime
> that you will not believe even though you are forewarned.
> Look, I am about to empower the Babylonians,
> that ruthless and greedy nation.
> They sweep across the surface of the earth,
> seizing dwelling places that do not belong to them.
> They are frightening and terrifying;
> they decide for themselves what is right.
> Their horses are faster than leopards
> and more alert than wolves in the desert.
> Their horses gallop, their horses come a great distance;
> like a vulture they swoop down quickly to devour their prey.
> All of them intend to do violence;
> every face is determined.
> They take prisoners as easily as one scoops up sand.
> They mock kings and laugh at rulers.
> They laugh at every fortified city;
> they build siege ramps and capture them.
> They sweep by like the wind and pass on.
> But the one who considers himself a god will be held guilty.
> (Habakkuk 1:5–11)

> This is what the LORD says: "I am about to bring disaster on this place and its residents, the details of which are recorded in the scroll which they read before the king of Judah. This will happen because they have abandoned me and offered sacrifices to other gods, angering me with all the idols they have made. My anger will ignite against this place and will not be extinguished!" (2 Chronicles 34:24–25)

Nevertheless, the prophetess Huldah declared that because King Josiah had greatly humbled himself before the Lord, tearing his clothes and weeping, he would not see the evil that would come upon Judah. What did that mean?

Simply, that God gave Josiah time to bring about a spiritual renewal in the nation. And so believers were revived by the Spirit of God, while unbelievers also came to Jerusalem to hear the Word and partake in a Passover unlike any since the days of Samuel. One man, standing in the gap, brought about a delay in God's purposes for the purpose of turning the nation back to Him for a season:

> Say this to the king of Judah, who sent you to seek an oracle from the LORD: "This is what the LORD God of Israel says concerning the words you have heard: 'You displayed a sensitive spirit and humbled yourself before God when you heard his words concerning this place and its residents. You humbled yourself before me, tore your clothes and wept before me, and I have heard you,' says the LORD. 'Therefore I will allow you to die and be buried in peace. You will not have to witness all the disaster I will bring on this place and its residents.'" Then they reported back to the king.
>
> The king summoned all the leaders of Judah and Jerusalem. The king went up to the LORD's temple, accompanied by all the people of Judah, the residents of Jerusalem, the priests, and the Levites. All the people were there, from the oldest to the youngest. He read aloud all the words of the scroll of the covenant that had been discovered in the LORD's temple. The king stood by his pillar and renewed the covenant before the LORD, agreeing to follow the LORD and to obey his commandments, laws, and rules with all his heart and being, by carrying out the terms of this covenant recorded on this scroll. He made all who were in Jerusalem and Benjamin agree to it. The residents of Jerusalem acted in accordance with the covenant of God, the God of their ancestors. (2 Chronicles 34:26–32; see also 35:1–18)

Practical Value. The omniscience of God is a great consolation to God's people. Sarah wreaked vengeance on Hagar after she gave birth to Ishmael, totally contrary to the customs and culture of the day. Yet God afterward met Hagar in the desert:

> So Hagar named the LORD who spoke to her, "You are the God who sees me," for she said, "Here I have seen one who sees me!" (Genesis 16:13)

Similarly, after being attacked by his enemies, David could affirm that God knew all about it and would care for His servant (see Psalm 56).

Likewise, Yeshua encouraged His disciples to not be like the pagans, who pray multitudes of words to their gods. His own should recognize that God knows our needs even before we articulate them in words:

> Do not be like them, for your Father knows what you need before you ask him. (Mattai 6:8)

The omniscience of God also serves as a warning to the wicked:

> O LORD, how long will the wicked,
> how long will the wicked celebrate?
> They spew out threats and speak defiantly; all the evildoers boast.
> O LORD, they crush your people;
> they oppress the nation that belongs to you.
> They kill the widow and the one residing outside his native land,
> and they murder the fatherless.
> Then they say, "The LORD does not see this;
> the God of Jacob does not take notice of it."
> Take notice of this, you ignorant people!
> You fools, when will you ever understand?
> Does the one who makes the human ear not hear?
> Does the one who forms the human eye not see? (Psalm 94:3–9)

As Scripture says, no one can escape His scrutiny and assessment of every thought, word, and deed—whether good or evil:

> The eyes of the LORD are in every place, keeping watch on those who are evil and those who are good. (Proverbs 15:3)

God Is Omnipotent

The Biblical Material. God's omnipotence was announced to Abraham and Sarah:

> When Abram was 99 years old, the LORD appeared to him and said, "I am the sovereign God [Hebrew, El Shaddai]. Walk before me and be blameless." (Genesis 17:1)

> God said, "No, Sarah your wife is going to bear you a son, and you will name him Isaac. I will confirm my covenant with him as a perpetual covenant for his descendants after him." (Genesis 17:19)

> Is anything impossible for the LORD? I will return to you when the season comes round again and Sarah will have a son. (Genesis 18:14)

Indeed, about a year later this couple had a son, Yitzhak or Isaac, who was truly the son of promise. From then on, Abraham and Sarah knew the real meaning of *El Shaddai*: all-powerful. And this power had been exerted on behalf of God's friend whom He loved.

Near the end of Job's suffering and misery, he was confronted by God as to His vast knowledge of the universe and this earth. At that point we read:

> Then Job answered the LORD:
> "I know that you can do all things;
> no purpose of yours can be thwarted." (Job 42:1–2)

With this admission of God's omnipotence and other statements of his faith, Job was released from his burden and restored to complete health, once again able to serve the Lord.

Isaiah, the prince of the prophets, asserted God's omnipotence:

> Do you not know?
> Have you not heard?
> The LORD is an eternal God,
> the creator of the whole earth.
> He does not get tired or weary;
> there is no limit to his wisdom. (Isaiah 40:28)

So did Jeremiah, who had weighed out silver for the purchase of his cousin's field as a way to assure the nation that, though they were in the throes of being conquered and humiliated, yet once again houses would be sold and lands would be paid for:

> After I had given the copies of the deed of purchase to Baruch son of Neriah, I prayed to the LORD, "Oh, Lord GOD, you did indeed make heaven and earth by your mighty power and great strength. Nothing is too hard for you!" (Jeremiah 32:16–17)

Jeremiah's hope was that, though it now seemed impossible, God would one day restore Judah to its land.

Yeshua also spoke of the omnipotence of God:

> Then Yeshua said to his disciples, "I tell you the truth, it will be hard for a rich person to enter the kingdom of heaven! Again I say, it is easier for a camel to go through the eye of a needle than for a rich person to enter into the kingdom of God." The disciples were greatly astonished when they heard this and said, "Then who can be saved?" Yeshua looked at them and replied, "This is impossible for mere humans, but for God all things are possible." (Mattai 19:23–26)

Finally, in the book of Revelation the curtain rolls back and the reader gets a glimpse of heaven in all its glory and splendor:

> Then I heard what sounded like the voice of a vast throng, like the roar of many waters and like loud crashes of thunder. They were shouting:
>
> "Hallelujah! For the Lord our God, the All-powerful, reigns!" (Revelation 19:6)

What a fitting testimony to the omnipotence of God!

The Nature of God's Omnipotence. From these and other passages, God is portrayed as able to do all things that are consistent with His nature and character. There are things He cannot do:

> If we are unfaithful, he remains faithful, since he cannot deny himself. (2 Timothy 2:13)

> . . . in hope of eternal life, which God, who does not lie [NASB, KJV: cannot lie], promised before the ages began. (Titus 1:2)

> Let no one say when he is tempted, "I am tempted by God," for God cannot be tempted by evil, and he himself tempts no one. (Yaakov 1:13)

There is an old conundrum as to whether God can create a huge rock that He Himself can never lift. But this is totally inconsistent with His character; if He brought the universe into existence, He also is entirely capable of running it.

Another question is whether God is ever exhausted by the exercise of His power. After the creation, the Torah says God "rested" from all His work. Does this suggest that He grew weary in the exercise of His power in the creation? Hardly! The word in the text is *shavat*, which does not mean that He was tired but that He *completed* the work He set out to do. The Scripture specifically notes that the Creator does not become weary or tired:

> He does not get tired or weary;
> there is no limit to his wisdom. (Isaiah 40:28)

Manifestations of God's Omnipotence. God's omnipotence can be seen:

In creation. "The LORD is the one who by his power made the earth. He is the one who by his wisdom established the world. And by his understanding he spread out the skies" (Jeremiah 10:12).

In nature. "When his voice thunders, the heavenly ocean roars. He makes the clouds rise from the far-off horizons. He makes the lightning flash out in the midst of the rain. He unleashes the wind from the places where he stores it" (Jeremiah 10:13).

In history. "This announcement is by the decree of the sentinels; this decision is by the pronouncement of the holy ones, so that those who are alive may understand that the Most High has authority over human kingdoms, and he bestows them on whomever he wishes. He establishes over them even the lowliest of human beings" (Daniel 4:17). That is, He gives leadership to the ones He chooses, and sometimes gives people the kind of leaders they deserve.

In the heavenly realms. "All the inhabitants of the earth are regarded as nothing. He does as he wishes with the army of heaven and with those who inhabit the earth. No one slaps his hand and says to him, 'What have you done?'" (Daniel 4:35).

In redemption. ". . . —since the eyes of your heart have been enlightened—so that you may know what is the hope of his calling, what is the wealth of his glorious inheritance in the saints, and what is the incomparable greatness of his power toward us who believe, as displayed in the exercise of his immense strength. This power he exercised in Messiah when he raised him from the dead and seated him at his right hand in the heavenly realms far above every rule and authority and power and dominion and every name that is named, not only in this age but also in the one to come. And God *put all things under* Messiah's *feet*, and he gave him to the *qehilah* as head over all things" (Ephesians 1:18–22). Here, Sha'ul prayed that the *hasidim*, or saints, would know something of the greatness of the Messiah and His subjection of all things to Himself.

Practical Value. God's omnipotence, as seen in the passages we have looked at, means that the believer can take heart and be encouraged as he or she lives for Yeshua every day along with the hope of eternal glory to come.

God Is Perfect

Of all God's attributes, this one leads some people to despair, since they can never be as perfect as is God. Before addressing that problem, we will look at some aspects of God's perfection.

The Biblical Material. In one of the greatest songs in the Torah, Moses ascribed greatness and perfection to the God of Israel, in contrast to the character of Israel who often acted exactly the opposite of what is ascribed to the perfect God.

> For I will proclaim the name of the LORD;
> you must acknowledge the greatness of our God.
> As for the Rock, his work is perfect,
> for all his ways are just.
> He is a reliable God who is never unjust,
> he is fair and upright. (Deuteronomy 32:3–4)

Elihu, when he quizzed Job, referred to God's perfection in knowledge as He provided for the wonders of nature:

> Do you know about the balancing of the clouds,
> that wondrous activity of him who is perfect in knowledge?
> (Job 37:16)

Similarly David often spoke of the God who is perfect, whose ways are blameless, or complete:

> The one true God acts in a faithful manner;
> the LORD's promise is reliable;
> he is a shield to all who take shelter in him. (Psalm 18:30)

Furthermore, the Torah also is perfect, that is, complete, or whole:

> The law of the LORD is perfect
> and preserves one's life.
> The rules set down by the LORD are reliable
> and impart wisdom to the inexperienced. (Psalm 19:7)

That is what one would expect from the Word that God spoke, a word that represents who He is. Furthermore, only this kind of perfect Word, spoken by a perfect God, can be the means by which the soul can be restored.

In the New Covenant, Yeshua called on His followers to be perfect:

> So then, be perfect, as your heavenly Father is perfect. (Mattai 5:48)

We will discuss below how we, imperfect as we are, can live the life that Yeshua asks us to.

In Yaakov, the good things we receive from God—all His perfect gifts showered upon us in abundance—come from Him who is perfect, that is without peer:

> All generous giving and every perfect gift is from above, coming down from the Father of lights, with whom there is no variation or the slightest hint of change. (Yaakov 1:17)

The Hebrew and Greek Terms. Before we discuss the meaning of perfection, it is necessary to know the meaning of the Hebrew and Greek words used to describe this quality. The Hebrew word *tamim* means "perfect, complete, full, whole, without blemish." The Greek term is similar: *teleios*, which has the idea of "perfect" in the sense of "complete, finished."

Therefore in understanding the definition of divine perfection, the meaning is that He is complete, nothing lacking. He is all that God ought to be and He falls short in nothing.

Some Problems. The Torah ascribes perfection to created beings:

> This is the account of Noah. Noah was a godly man; he was blameless among his contemporaries. He walked with God. (Genesis 6:9)

> There was a man in the land of Uz whose name was Job. And that man was pure and upright, one who feared God and turned away from evil. (Job 1:1)

> Son of man, sing a lament for the king of Tyre, and say to him,
> "This is what the sovereign LORD says:

'You were the sealer of perfection,
full of wisdom, and perfect in beauty.'" (Ezekiel 28:12)

This last passage describes Lucifer before he became *Ha-Satan*, or God's opposer.

But the meaning of the Hebrew word explains what is in mind; these were people (or with Lucifer, a being) who were perfect as a creature is perfect: whole, complete, and without blemish. As one saw them, they were a complete person. It does not suggest that they were perfect as God is perfect in His being and knowledge. Noah and Job had a great deal of maturing to do in order to continue in the completeness they had, and in fact they did so. With Lucifer, however, when the test came in his experience, he made the wrong decisions, and therefore did not go on to further maturing, but rather fell to a state from which there was no redemption, as there was with Adam and Eve.

Another problem arises from Yeshua's command that we be perfect as God is perfect (Mattai 5:48, cited above). Two possibilities are suggested by way of understanding this: either Yeshua held forth the perfection of God for which we strive as our ideal, or else, we strive but are limited by our failures and we so we continue to strive.

Wesley had what this writer feels to be the solution. Obviously, neither in this life nor in the next will any believer be perfect as God is perfect. If we were, we would then be God, which obviously is not possible. But as we mature in the Lord, we seek to live in accordance with what we know. At times, some of us will fail to do so, and we will need to find our way back and live by what we know. When we do so, however, God will provide further knowledge by which to live. It is this incremental doing of His will day by day, ever learning more about Him, whereby believers mature in Him. This is the objective of "being perfect."

Practical Value. This attribute qualifies all other attributes of God. Believers can be assured that God's love, mercy, all-power, all-knowledge, and so on are perfect, complete in every way. Nothing needs to be added to them. This attribute of perfection is also a reminder that all we will ever need is found in God who is perfect in all ways. That is comforting, an assurance to us as we look to Him for all that we need.

God Is Infinite

This attribute also falls under the category of God's greatness, although the English word occurs only once in the Torah:

> Our LORD is great and has awesome power;
> there is no limit to his wisdom. [NASB, "his understanding is infinite"]. (Psalm 147:5)

The Hebrew phrase is *en mispar*, meaning, literally, *without an end*, or, *without any limits*. In this sense, the word is an apt term, highly suggestive of what "infinite" really means.

The Biblical Material. An abundance of material appears in the Psalms, for instance:

> O LORD, my God, you have accomplished many things;
> you have done amazing things and carried out your purposes for us.
> No one can thwart you!
> I want to declare them and talk about them,
> but they are too numerous to recount! (Psalm 40:5)

> I will sing continually about the LORD'S faithful deeds;
> to future generations I will proclaim your faithfulness.
> For I say, "Loyal love is permanently [Hebrew, *olam*, that is, without end] established;
> in the skies you set up your faithfulness." (Psalm 89:1–2)

> As far as the eastern horizon is from the west,
> so he removes the guilt of our rebellious actions from us.
> (Psalm 103:12)

In this last verse, one of the grandest testimonies to God's forgiveness that comes from the heart of David, the point of the simile is that just as distant as the east is from the west, so in coming to faith one's sins are taken an infinite distance away.

Some Problems. A number of problems arise as to how to understand this attribute of God as infinite. Is not God limited in some ways? So some philosophers have stated with regard to the presence of evil in this world. How can we understand a God who is loving and kind and yet who does not control evil? A supposed solution is that inasmuch as evil is present, it appears that God is not able to control it entirely and must somehow work His way around it. In this way, say some of these philosophers, we can at least preserve the goodness of God.

But nothing could be further from the truth. If we regard God as limited because He cannot control evil, just so that we can be assured of His goodness, then what kind of God do we have left? This would be no God at all. Rather, what we should recognize is that ever since the fall of Adam and Eve, God has temporarily self-limited Himself to allow man to make his choices for evil or good. When man corrupts himself to such an extent that it appears that his situation is beyond redemption, then God knows how to "stick His finger" in the course of human events and rearrange them. He did exactly that in the flood, and twice in the history of Judah, with the loss of two temples as well as life.

There will come a time when God will ultimately control evil, particularly in the Messianic kingdom:

> Then blind eyes will open,
> deaf ears will hear.
> Then the lame will leap like a deer,
> the mute tongue will shout for joy;
> for water will flow in the desert,
> streams in the wilderness. (Isaiah 35:5–6)

> He will judge disputes between nations;
> he will settle cases for many peoples.
> They will beat their swords into plowshares,
> and their spears into pruning hooks.
> Nations will not take up the sword against other nations,
> and they will no longer train for war. (Isaiah 2:4)

In other words, no diseases will ever again be present, death will no longer occur, evil will be controlled, and war will be eradicated. This period will end in a separation between believers and unbelievers, and the latter will be eliminated from any presence on the new earth:

> Now when the thousand years are finished, Satan will be released from his prison and will go out to deceive the nations at the four corners of the earth, Gog and Magog, to bring them together for the battle. They are as numerous as the grains of sand in the sea. They went up on the broad plain of the earth and encircled the camp of the saints and the beloved city, but fire came down from heaven and devoured them completely. (Revelation 20:7–9)

Then one day in the eternal state, God will once again resume complete control and the redeemed will willingly do His good, acceptable, and perfect will.

Asaph raises another problem when he describes Israel as putting God to the test and paining the Holy One of Israel:

> They again challenged God,
> and offended the Holy One of Israel. (Psalm 78:41)

Does this not suggest a God who is limited? However, the answer again must be seen in the light of what has already been suggested: God has self-limited Himself to allow man to exercise his freedom of choice; thus He allowed Israel to do just that. His self-limitation is self-imposed. When He desires, at the right moment, He can act decisively to clean up evil. In contrast to the solution mentioned by the philosophers above, God's self-imposition is temporary. One day, He will assert Himself and completely remove evil from the new heavens and new earth.

Still another problem is this: How can a finite mind think of infinity? While at first the question may seem insurmountable, yet one must recognize the distinctiveness of man in God's creation. God has created man such that eternity is in his heart:

> He has made everything beautiful in its time. He has also set eternity in the hearts of men; yet they cannot fathom what God has done from beginning to end. (Ecclesiastes 3:11 NIV)[6]

There is a two-pronged view of man in this assertion: First, man does have the concept of certain intangibles in his understanding—eternity, infinity—so that those concepts do have meaning. And second, yet man does not in this world ever attain to ultimate knowledge. Solomon sought to attain it, but realized that he never would. What he and we *can* have is practical knowledge in this world. But just as clearly, man certainly understands what infinite or ultimate knowledge means. However, God is the only one who *has* that capacity.

An additional problem is the question how, if infinity puts God so far above mankind, finite beings can ever reach Him. This is is a problem that we already considered under the omnipresence of God. Yes, God is transcendent, above all the creation and everything it contains. In that sense, there is a parallel between His transcendence and His infinity. Yet, God does move in His universe and is present on earth as well. We are finite and God knows that. Therefore He has taken the steps to make Himself present so that finite man can reach out to Him.

Practical Value. As before, there are twin practical values. On the one hand, this attribute is a comfort to God's people. Only a personal being who is infinite can relate to a man who is finite exactly because He can enter man's world and relate to his needs. On the other hand, this attribute is also a warning to the wicked because God takes note of who they are and what they have done. Because He is infinite, He can superintend their eventual judgment after this life. Furthermore, a punishment that calls for a suffering that is infinite takes on new meaning since God Himself is also infinite. How terrible indeed will it be for those assigned to an infinity of suffering!

God Is Incomprehensible

The Biblical Material. Eliphaz reminded Job concerning God that:

> He does great and unsearchable things,
> marvelous things without number. (Job 5:9)

One of the other friends asked Job:

Can you discover the essence of God?
Can you find out
the perfection of the Almighty? (Job 11:7)

In the Psalms, David commented:

The LORD is great and certainly worthy of praise!
No one can fathom his greatness! (Psalm 145:3)

So too Isaiah:
Look up at the sky!
Who created all these heavenly lights?
He is the one who leads out their ranks;
he calls them all by name.
Because of his absolute power and awesome strength,
not one of them is missing. (Isaiah 40:26)

And Sha'ul broke out in a paean of praise, exclaiming,

Oh, the depth of the riches and wisdom and knowledge of God! How unsearchable are his judgments and how fathomless his ways!
For who has known the mind of the Lord,
or who has been his counselor?
Or who has first given to God,
that God needs to repay him?
(Romans 11:33–35)

The Nature of God's Incomprehensibility. From what these Scriptures teach, we learn that God is unfathomable in His totality, that is, He cannot be completely comprehended by the finite mind.

Does this mean, therefore, that God is unknowable? What then does Yohanan mean when he says:

> The person who does not love does not know God, because God is love. (1 Yohanan 4:8)

The answer lies in what we have already emphasized: since God has set eternity in man's heart, people can comprehend a great deal about the eternity, infinity, and many other things about the incomprehensible God. Sha'ul writes that:

> For since the creation of the world his invisible attributes—his eternal power and divine nature—have been clearly seen, because they are understood through what has been made. So people are without excuse. (Romans 1:20)

Even when one becomes a believer, we still have not plumbed the depths of God's incomprehensibility. Yet, we know much more of Him than does an unbeliever. And as believers, we will be learning more and more of Him through all eternity, with still always more to know. How exciting is this prospect of ever knowing more of the God we adore!

Some Problems. Again, problems surface with regard to this attribute. For example, what is the meaning of:

> As the heaven is high and the earth is deep
> so the hearts of kings are unsearchable. (Proverbs 25:3)

For that matter, how often can we know what is in the hearts of any people? In reply, there is a qualitative difference between man and God. A person may indeed hold much within his heart that is inaccessible to others. But the difference is that while no person will ever discover all that God holds within Himself, God knows exactly what is in every person's heart. Jeremiah raised the question as to who can understand the human heart, and in reply God asserted,

> I, the LORD, probe into people's minds.
> I examine people's hearts.
> I deal with each person according to how he has behaved.

I give them what they deserve based on what they have done.
(Jeremiah 17:10)

Practical Value. One value is the intellectual one that assures the believer of an inexhaustible fund of knowledge. Man was made to discover and understand his universe. While a tremendous amount is already known, it is also apparent that the current level of studies is not even at the kindergarten stage. The amount of knowledge yet to be acquired is staggering, as are the experiences in areas of achievement and leadership.

Another value lies in the spiritual dimension. When the veil of heaven was briefly stripped away at the announcement of the Messiah's birth, there was an infinitesimal glimpse of the worship of heaven:

"Glory to God in the highest,
and on earth peace among people with whom he is pleased!"
When the angels left them and went back to heaven, the shepherds said to one another, "Let us go over to Bethlehem and see this thing that has taken place, that the Lord has made known to us."
(Luke 2:14–15)

It is glimpsed yet again in Revelation:

The twenty-four elders and the four living creatures threw themselves to the ground and worshiped God, who was seated on the throne, saying: "Amen! Hallelujah!"
Then a voice came from the throne, saying:
"Praise our God all you his servants,
and all you who fear Him,
both the small and the great!"
Then I heard what sounded like the voice of a vast throng,
like the roar of many waters and like loud crashes of thunder.
They were shouting:
"Hallelujah!
For the Lord our God, the All-powerful, reigns!" (Revelation 19:4–6)

We have yet to be introduced to the highest level of ecstasy in worship. Eventually we will be mastered and overwhelmed by a reality that is incomprehensible—the reality of the infinite God.

God Is Unchangeable

One great truth of the greatness of our God is His nature, which is unchangeable and forms the basis by which we can trust Him implicitly.

The Goodness of God

So far we have considered the arguments for the existence of God, along with His unity and the attributes of His greatness. These considerations speak to us of His metaphysical vastness and lead us to think with awe of how God would deign to reveal Himself to us. But considering the goodness of God is what will pluck a person's emotional heartstrings and evoke a response to Him and His love for us. In fact, the consideration of the attribute of perfection leads us into the moral realm. The perfect God must also be a good God. And such is what the Bible affirms Him to be, in verses such as these:

> The LORD is both kind and fair;
> that is why he teaches sinners the right way to live. (Psalm 25:8)

> The LORD promotes equity and justice;
> the LORD'S faithfulness extends throughout the earth. (Psalm 33:5)

> Why do you boast about your evil plans, O powerful man?
> God's loyal love protects me all day long!
> Your tongue carries out your destructive plans;
> it is as effective as a sharp razor, O deceiver. (Psalm 52:1–2)

> Praise the LORD, O my soul!
> Do not forget all his kind deeds!
> He is the one who forgives all your sins,

who heals all your diseases,
who delivers your life from the Pit,
who crowns you with his loyal love and compassion,
who satisfies your life with good things,
so your youth is renewed like an eagle's.
(Psalm 103:2–5; see the entire psalm)

Yeshua said to him, "Why do you call me good?
No one is good except God alone." (Mark 10:18)

Or do you have contempt for the wealth of his kindness, forbearance, and patience, and yet do not know that God's kindness leads you to repentance? (Romans 2:4)

Notice therefore the kindness and harshness of God—harshness toward those who have fallen, but God's kindness toward you, provided you continue in his kindness; otherwise you also will be cut off. (Romans 11:22)

When using the term "goodness" in its broadest moral sense, as applied to God, His goodness as set forth in the Bible includes two classes of attributes: first, attributes that describe who God is in Himself, and second, attributes that describe who God is in relation to others. These are attributes of character, and the expression of His character.

In describing the goodness of God, the Bible uses a great many terms, which are easiest to grasp as a part of an economy of ideas, as follows:

In Himself, God is holy, true, and loving.

In relation to others, God is righteous, faithful, and merciful, with various ideas being encompassed under that term.

It is helpful to note Strong's classification. He puts all the divine attributes under two heads: (1) Absolute or Immanent; and (2) Relative or Transitive.[7] This classification is especially useful for the moral attributes.

With this introduction, we begin our discussion of God's goodness. Under that category fall several aspects of God's nature.

God Is Holy

As we will see, God's holiness is not really an attribute of God, but rather, it is actually His essence. That is, it describes *who God fundamentally is*. From this center point flow all the attributes. While we can understand some aspects of holiness, it is quite difficult to describe this essence from a positive stance.

The Biblical Material. In the Mosaic Covenant that God made with Israel, He wanted to impress on His people that He is indeed holy. Even what we place in the mouth for food should be judged as clean or unclean, thereby affecting one's relationship with the holy God. Thus, the people of Israel were not to eat of any animal that swarmed on the earth, but only of specified creatures that were herbivorous. Animals that fed on their prey as well as the flesh with the blood were forbidden. This call to holiness was not merely for hygiene, but in order that people should have respect for the blood, which is synonymous with life. By thus respecting life, people would respect the holiness of God:

> Every swarming thing that swarms on the land is detestable; it must not be eaten. You must not eat anything that crawls on its belly or anything that walks on all fours or on any number of legs of all the swarming things that swarm on the land, because they are detestable. Do not make yourselves detestable by any of the swarming things. You must not defile yourselves by them and become unclean by them, for I am the LORD your God and you are to sanctify yourselves and be holy because I am holy. You must not defile yourselves by any of the swarming things that creep on the ground, for I am the LORD who brought you up from the land of Egypt to be your God, and you are to be holy because I am holy. (Leviticus 11:41–45)

Another aspect of holiness consisted of how people regarded what is proscribed and set apart to the Lord: tithes, the firstborn of clean and unclean animals, fields that were consecrated until the following jubilee, or whatever else was supposed to be dedicated to the Lord. It was all "most holy to the Lord":

> Surely anything which a man permanently dedicates to the LORD from all that belongs to him, whether from people, animals, or his landed property, must be neither sold nor redeemed; anything permanently dedicated is most holy to the LORD. (Leviticus 27:28)

As people followed the details of the Mosaic Covenant with a willing heart, they could expect God to look down from His holy place, from heaven, and bless His people in the land He had given to them:

> Look down from your holy dwelling place in heaven and bless your people Israel and the land you have given us, just as you promised our ancestors—a land flowing with milk and honey.
> (Deuteronomy 26:15)

The psalmists were God-intoxicated people and therefore had a keen awareness of the holiness of God. These writers saw God as ruling in holiness:

> God reigns over the nations!
> God sits on his holy throne! (Psalm 47:8)

When David prayed for forgiveness after the Bat Sheva affair, he dearly desired that the Holy Spirit not be taken from him:

> Do not reject me!
> Do not take your Holy Spirit away from me! (Psalm 51:11)

And in fact God did not remove His Spirit from David, for when he had been anointed, the Spirit rushed upon him and was with him from that day on:

> So Samuel took the horn full of olive oil and anointed him in the presence of his brothers. The Spirit of the LORD rushed upon David from that day onward. Then Samuel got up and went to Ramah.
> (1 Samuel 16:13)

Had he had not confessed his sin, the departure of the Spirit would have been obvious. And when God enacted the Davidic Covenant with His servant, God invoked His own holiness, as we see in comparing these two passages speaking of the same thing:

> When the time comes for you to die, I will raise up your descendant, one of your own sons, to succeed you, and I will establish his kingdom. He will build a house for my name, and I will make his dynasty permanent. I will become his father and he will become my son. When he sins, I will correct him with the rod of men and with wounds inflicted by human beings. But my loyal love will not be removed from him as I removed it from Sha'ul, whom I removed from before you. Your house and your kingdom will stand before me permanently; your dynasty will be permanent. (2 Samuel 7:12–16)

> Once and for all I have vowed by my own holiness,
> I will never deceive David.
> His dynasty will last forever.
> His throne will endure before me, like the sun. (Psalm 89:35–36)

In a group of Psalms exalting the Lord (Psalms 96–100), two are especially significant. The psalmist praises the Lord for His victories, for His right hand and holy arm that give His followers cause to rejoice:

> Sing to the LORD a new song,
> for he performs amazing deeds!
> His right hand and his mighty arm
> accomplish deliverance. (Psalm 98:1)

And then, the entirety of Psalm 99 emphasizes various aspects of God's holiness:

> Let them praise your great and awesome name!
> He is holy! . . .

> Praise the LORD our God!
> Worship before his footstool!
> He is holy! . . .
> Praise the LORD our God!
> Worship on his holy hill,
> for the LORD our God is holy! (Psalm 99:3, 5, 9)

The word that the Lord had spoken with Abraham His servant, the promise of caring for his descendants, is designated as holy (Psalm 105:42).

> Yes, he remembered the sacred promise
> he made to Abraham his servant. (Psalm 105:42)

However, the classic exposition of the holy presence of God is when Isaiah the prophet was privileged to see the Lord sitting on His lofty and exalted throne:

> In the year of King Uzziah's death, I saw the sovereign master seated on a high, elevated throne. The hem of his robe filled the temple. Seraphs stood over him; each one had six wings. With two wings they covered their faces, with two they covered their feet, and they used the remaining two to fly. They called out to one another, "Holy, holy, holy is the Lord who commands armies! His majestic splendor fills the entire earth!" The sound of their voices shook the door frames, and the temple was filled with smoke. (Isaiah 6:1–4)

The sight sent shock waves through the prophet's being, as he cried out concerning how sinful he felt, a man with unclean lips who lived in the midst of people with unclean lips!

And again, coming back to an oft-cited passage, the prophet again reminds us that the high and exalted One has a name that is holy:

> For this is what the high and exalted one says,
> the one who rules forever, whose name is holy:
> "I dwell in an exalted and holy place,

> but also with the discouraged and humiliated,
> in order to cheer up the humiliated
> and to encourage the discouraged." (Isaiah 57:15)

Kefa called on his fellow believers, then as well as now, to be like the Holy One in their behavior:

> Like the Holy One who called you, become holy yourselves in all of your conduct, for it is written, "You shall be holy, because I am holy." (1 Kefa 1:15–16)

Some aspects of this call have already been discussed in the topic on perfection, but we will examine it again below.

The Terms Used for "Holy." Etymologically, the English word "holy" means "whole." In usage, however, it refers to being wholly pure in a moral sense. The word often translated as *saint* refers to a person wholly devoted to a sacred purpose.

The Hebrew and Greek terms are, respectively, 1) *kadesh*, or *separateness*; and 2) *hagios*, or *set apart*.

In its root meaning, the term may have had no original reference to *moral* purity, so that for example it could be said that a piece of furniture was set apart. Even a prostitute could be designated a *qedoshah*, or a *set apart one* for what she did. But by an easy transition, these words came to express the idea of moral purity, as when Sha'ul told the Thessalonian believers they were not called for the purpose of impurity but for sanctification:

> For God did not call us to impurity but in holiness. (1 Thessalonians 4:7)

The Nature of God's Holines. Generally, God's holiness tends to be defined in terms of separateness, whereby God is separate from all that is earthly or created. Psalm 99, verses of which were cited above, asserts the holiness of God. David described the hill of the Lord as a "holy place" (Psalm 24:3), while the person who receives a blessing from the holy God is the one who has acted accordingly:

> Who is allowed to ascend the mountain of the LORD?
> Who may go up to his holy dwelling place?
> The one whose deeds are blameless
> and whose motives are pure,
> who does not lie,
> or make promises with no intention of keeping them. (Psalm 24:3–4)

In other words, holiness is defined as God's absolute separation from all that is unclean. One can say then that this is a holiness of *moral purity*.

But holiness can also be seen as *divine majesty*. From what is already noted above in Psalm 99:1–3 and Isaiah 57:15, one senses a holiness of divine majesty. He is enthroned above the cherubim; He is great and exalted; His name is great and awesome. We will see Him in all His glory when we are gathered to Him in His presence. Neither the sin nature nor any acts of sin will be present. All that we will know is His high and lofty majesty.

Of these two aspects of God's holiness, in the New Covenant, the emphasis falls almost exclusively on moral purity. The call is for the people of God to separate themselves from sinful practices. But the idea of divine majesty is not completely lost. It is seen in Miriam's paean of praise, as she exclaimed her devotion at being chosen to be the mother of the Messiah:

> ... because he who is mighty has done great things for me, and holy is his name. (Luke 1:49)

The Fundamental Moral Attribute. This is a topic much discussed among theologians. Some want to make love the essence of God because of the statement of Yohanan:

> The person who does not love does not know God, because God is love. (1 Yohanan 4:8)

But by far, most theologians insist that the essence of God is holiness because He is holy. From what has been observed from the Scripture already, holiness seems to be the dominant theme when speaking of God's very being, as in Isaiah 6:1–3; 57:15 (cited above); and other passages.

In considering these verses further, it can be said that *all God's acts are acts of holiness; but not all are acts of love*. Theologians have spoken of holiness as God's self-affirmation, and love as His self-giving. However, before God can give, there must be something *to* give. God is not holy because He loves. He loves because He is holy.[8]

Some Problems. One major problem regarding the holiness of God, in both His moral purity as well as His divine majesty, is how He can permit the presence of sin. Amos described the downfall of the nation:

> This is what the LORD says:
> "Because Israel has committed three covenant transgressions—
> make that four!—I will not revoke my decree of judgment.
> They sold the innocent for silver,
> the needy for a pair of sandals.
> They trample on the dirt-covered heads of the poor;
> they push the destitute away.
> A man and his father go to the same girl;
> in this way they show disrespect for my moral purity." (Amos 2:6–7)

Habakkuk likewise complained to God concerning Judah:

> Why do you force me to witness injustice?
> Why do you put up with wrongdoing?
> Destruction and violence confront me;
> conflict is present and one must endure strife. (Habakkuk 1:3)

In Habakkuk's day, God answered him by announcing that He would eventually bring the Babylonians down on the nation. They would proceed to tear apart the nation, finally sacking Jerusalem and destroying the temple. Compounding the problem in the modern world, what does one say concerning the designs of a man like Hitler who was responsible for the death of six million Jewish people in the last century alone?

These and similar questions torment many people who ask why, if God is holy and righteous, does He allow these things to happen?

In the first instance, we spoke above of the self-limitation by God, whereby He allows people to make their good or evil choices. Only when the cultural, human, or historical context comes to the point where fewer and fewer people care to listen to God does He intervene. At that point, He destroys the wicked people and curbs the evil so that the community can be restored to a semblance of righteousness. Then the process starts all over again. Ultimately, as we saw, one day God will separate out all evil people and create a new earth and heavens.

Habakkuk struggled with this question in his own day. He asked God how He could use a wicked nation such as the Babylonians as a means to correct Judah. His second objection was even more difficult: How could God use such evil people as the Babylonians when He Himself is holy, with eyes too pure to look at the evil they will commit?

> You are too just to tolerate evil;
> you are unable to condone wrongdoing.
> So why do you put up with such treacherous people?
> Why do you say nothing when the wicked devour those more righteous than they are? (Habakkuk 1:13)

God never fully answered the second question but instead told His servant that the righteous should live by their faith in His promises:

> See, he is puffed up;
> his desires are not upright—
> but the righteous will live by his faith. (Habakkuk 2:4 NIV)[9]

Is this a full answer? No. Answers are not easy to come by in this world when we do not have all the facts in the case of Judah, nor do we have the full picture as God sees it.

Are there answers to the Hitler problem? Yes, God gave him time to make his evil decisions and he will pay for his crimes for all eternity. But what about the people who suffered? This again is a question to which no person has all the answers to a difficult problem, only bits and pieces. One such notable piece is that three years after Hitler's suicide, the state of Israel came into existence, which in one way was God's answer to the madman's idea that he could rid Europe of all its Jewish people.

Another piece of an answer is that God led some of His choice believers into the camps. Because of the testimony of these special servants of God, many a Jewish person came to faith, either in the camps, or after being delivered.

Another part of the bits and pieces of an answer is that we can say that Hitler functioned much in the same way as did the pharaoh of the exodus. The more Pharaoh hardened his heart, the more he became the vessel of wrath by which many Jewish people afterward would be able to escape out of Egypt. In the same way, Hitler was also the vessel of wrath by which many of those who remained after the war would go to Israel. The ancient pharaoh and the modern Hitler were tools in God's hands to accomplish His purposes. He thoroughly despised them for their wicked deeds, but by their intransigence, Jewish people were led on to where God wanted them to go.

Do these bits and pieces fully satisfy the problem? No! We live in an imperfect world. Like the believers in the time of Habakkuk, we need again to realize that often all we can do is live by our faith in God's promises and seek to be used of Him as He leads us.

Practical Value. First, God's holiness reveals our own uncleanness and how far short we come of His standards. It also calls us to a life of holiness of our own. Recall again when Isaiah was granted the high privilege of seeing the throne room of God, with the Lord seated on His throne, high and exalted. The seraphim called to one another.

> They called out to one another, "Holy, holy, holy is the LORD who commands armies! His majestic splendor fills the entire earth!" (Isaiah 6:3)

When the prophet viewed this sight, he also saw his own sin and cried out:

> I said, "Too bad for me! I am destroyed, for my lips are contaminated by

> sin, and I live among people whose lips are contaminated by sin. My eyes have seen the king, the LORD who commands armies." (Isaiah 6:5)

The only remedy for his impurity came when a seraph flew to him, holding with tongs a hot coal from the altar, which he then placed on the prophet's lips. If the seraph could not directly hold the hot coal and had to use tongs, why then did not Isaiah cry out in pain, as his lips would surely have suffered second or third degree burns? The point is that the coal burned, or atoned for his sin, and did no harm to Isaiah. The lesson is clear: God's holiness will always cause people to realize that they do not measure up to His holiness. People need to be cleansed of their sins if they wish to stand in the presence of God, the Holy One.

The holiness of God demands a corresponding life of holiness among His people. From the Hebrew Scriptures, God reminded Israel He is a forgiving God although He had to punish them for their misdeeds:

> O LORD our God, you answered them.
> They found you to be a forgiving God,
> but also one who punished their sinful deeds. (Psalm 99:8)

As a people who had been set apart to Him, they were encouraged to

> Praise the LORD our God!
> Worship on his holy hill,
> for the LORD our God is holy! (Psalm 99:9)

The message of the New Covenant likewise reminds the believers within the body that they are to make every effort to live in peace with all men and to be holy:

> Pursue peace with everyone, and holiness, for without it no one will see the Lord. (Hebrews 12:14)

Kefa also writes:

> Like the Holy One who called you, become holy yourselves in all of

> your conduct, for it is written, "You shall be holy, because I am holy." (1 Kefa 1:15–16)

Such is the norm: God is holy and the people of God are bound to Him in a special way. Therefore, they also need to reflect His holiness among all peoples.

God's holiness also offers us assurance regarding His promises. When God concluded His covenant with David, He said that He would not alter what His lips have uttered. Whatever He had promised David, He had sworn by His holiness and would not lie to David:

> I will not break my covenant
> or go back on what I promised.
> Once and for all I have vowed by my own holiness,
> I will never deceive David.
> His dynasty will last forever.
> His throne will endure before me, like the sun. (Psalm 89:34–36)

The covenant spelled out promises regarding a future kingdom of peace on earth, in which the Messiah would sit upon the throne of David, ruling as the Messianic king. We find the same thing with regard to the promise God made to Abraham concerning his descendants as well as those of Isaac and Jacob:

> Yes, he remembered the sacred promise
> he made to Abraham his servant. (Psalm 105:42)

which refers to the day when He would bring His people back to their homeland.

God's agreements extend even to the body of Messiah. On the occasion of Messiah's leaving this world to return to the Father, He asked this of the "Holy Father":

> I am no longer in the world, but they are in the world, and I am coming to you. Holy Father, keep them safe in your name that you have given me, so that they may be one just as we are one. (Yohanan 17:11)

His holiness reveals the character of the coming kingdom of peace on earth. No one will contest His authority because God reigns over the nations as He sits upon His holy throne:

> God reigns over the nations!
> God sits on his holy throne! (Psalm 47:8)

Furthermore, His promise is changeless. Consider God's declaration:

> They will no longer injure or destroy
> on my entire royal mountain.
> For there will be universal submission to the LORD's sovereignty,
> just as the waters completely cover the sea. (Isaiah 11:9)

His holiness guarantees the day will come when the knowledge of the Lord will be recognized by all who live on earth. No one will ever again be hurt because the curse will be removed from the earth. His promise is fixed and guarantees this kingdom yet to come, offering us a great assurance that He will fulfill all His promises.

Finally, the holiness of God serves as a warning for the unbeliever and encouragement for the believer. It provides the dire background of divine judgment. Scripture gives us the picture of the Great White Throne judgment at which the unsaved of all the ages will stand and be evaluated as to their lack of any decision regarding the Messiah. They will then be judged according to the deeds recorded in the heavenly books. Each person standing at this judgment will be sentenced in accordance to the deeds that he had committed. It is a dreadful and solemn scene:

> Then I saw a large white throne and the one who was seated on it; the earth and the heaven fled from his presence, and no place was found for them. And I saw the dead, the great and the small, standing before the throne. Then books were opened, and another book was opened—the book of life. So the dead were judged by what was written in the books, according to their deeds. The sea gave up the

> dead that were in it, and Death and Hades gave up the dead that were in them, and each one was judged according to his deeds. (Revelation 20:11–13)

The Great White Throne will be a frightful experience for those who have totally ignored God's grace and love, despite every attempt on His part to reach out and bring them among the people of God. Because they had turned away, we are told, their names were not found written in the Book of Life; they then face an unending future, suffering the penalty of their deeds, and filled with a never-ending remorse because they did not decide to respond to the love and mercy of God. In contrast, the believer can be encouraged by God's holiness because though God is high and lofty, over and above and beyond this universe, yet at the same time He is also at home among believers who have humble and contrite hearts:

> For this is what the high and exalted one says,
> the one who rules forever, whose name is holy:
> "I dwell in an exalted and holy place,
> but also with the discouraged and humiliated,
> in order to cheer up the humiliated
> and to encourage the discouraged." (Isaiah 57:15)

God Is Truth, and True

Truth and being truthful are precious commodities these days. Everyone seems to establish their own standards for what is true. Aristotle, from a rational point of view, established the law of noncontradiction. But from a biblical perspective, what is true or what is truth is grounded in the very being of God. The fact that we have a sense of truth and of being truthful is ultimately a reflection of the integrity of God Himself.[10]

The Biblical Material. There are three aspects to the dimension of the nature of God as "true."

Concerning God Himself. In the great "psalm of the heart," Yeshua declared:

Now this is eternal life—that they know you, the only true God, and Yeshua the Messiah, whom you sent. (Yohanan 17:3)

Similarly Sha'ul noted about the congregation in Thessalonica:

For people everywhere report how you welcomed us and how you turned to God from idols to serve the living and true God. (1 Thessalonians 1:9)

Concerning God's Word. Reflecting this, Yeshua prayed that God would:

Set them apart in the truth; your word is truth. (Yohanan 17:17)

The psalmist also gives his testimony:

All your words are true; all your righteous laws are eternal. (Psalm 119:160 NIV)[11]

The "God of truth." This is seen in David's plea to be redeemed:

Into your hands I commit my spirit;
redeem me, O LORD, the God of truth. (Psalm 31:5 NIV)[12]

And Isaiah states,

Whoever invokes a blessing in the land
will do so by the God of truth;
he who takes an oath in the land
will swear by the God of truth.
For the past troubles will be forgotten
and hidden from my eyes. (Isaiah 65:16 NIV)[13]

Thus, truth or "true-ness" can be seen in the God who is true, where His Word is true, and where He Himself is the God of truth.

The Meaning of Truth. We can suggest a preliminary definition of what is meant by "trueness": When something is said to be true, this necessarily implies conformity to a standard. The question then is, who or what is the standard? After all, it is possible to have false standards. The twentieth century alone has demonstrated the falseness of leaders' ideologies, such as Marxism or Hitler's National Socialism. Both ideologies could not stand the test of time and experience. Their flaws were revealed under the pressure of circumstances at a time when men needed "true-ness" most desperately.

What is "true" can be demonstrated in two ways.

First, it can be applied to a person, as for example, a true man. In that case, who can serve as the standard? Who is the genuinely "true man"? From the biblical point of view, the only true man who ever walked the face of this earth was Yeshua in the days of His flesh. A number of statements affirm that He indeed was the true man because

> He did not need anyone to testify about man, for he knew what was in man. (Yohanan 2:25)

Furthermore, He Himself declared:

> Who among you can prove me guilty of any sin? If I am telling you the truth, why don't you believe me? (Yohanan 8:46)

In other words, Yeshua saw the flaws in every person while He Himself was flawless. Therefore He can serve as the model of the "true man."

A second application of what is "true" is seen when the term is applied to knowledge or to statements about an object. For example, we ask whether an ideology is true or not. We inquire as to true knowledge about man himself. What then is the standard we use in order to learn if the object is true or not? From a biblical point of view, it would appear that the only ultimate standard is the Word of God itself. Because it is the Word of truth, it can point to flaws in man's ideologies, for instance Marx's insistence that materialism is the only reality of this world. Of course, the Word of God tells us that man is more than just a material thing. Not only that, but it tells us that God exists above and beyond this universe and that He Himself brought this universe with its material things into existence. And we can also ask, who is to be the judge of who man is? Man is a fallen creature, flawed in his character, with a barrier in his heart between himself and God. Jeremiah raised the question:

> The human mind is more deceitful than anything else.
> It is incurably bad. Who can understand it? (Jeremiah 17:9)

The prophet points to the true standard here, namely, God Himself, who has the ultimate right to say:

> I, the LORD, probe into people's minds.
> I examine people's hearts.
> I deal with each person according to how he has behaved.
> I give them what they deserve based on what they have done.
> (Jeremiah 17:10)

Many dispute this standard of the true man and of God Himself. But then the question comes quickly: "What other true standard do we have?"

The Nature of God's True-ness. We can now give a working definition that corresponds to the three aspects of truth noted above: God is the "*true God*" in that His very being conforms exactly to the highest possible ideal of what He ought to be:

> Now this is eternal life—that they know you, the only true God, and Yeshua the Messiah, whom you sent. (Yohanan 17:3)

Furthermore, God is the *truthful God* in that His knowledge and His words conform exactly to reality, that is, the things as they are:

> The commands to fear the LORD are right
> and endure forever.
> The judgments given by the LORD are trustworthy [NASB, KJV: "true"]
> and absolutely just. (Psalm 19:9)

> Set them apart in the truth; your word is truth. (Yohanan 17:17)

Yet again, He is the "*the God of truth*" in that all truth is grounded in His own being and nature:

> Into your hands I commit my spirit; redeem me, O LORD, the God of truth. (Psalm 31:5 NIV)[14]

Relation of God's True-ness to Other Attributes. This threefold aspect of God as "true," "truthful," and "the God of truth" can be applied to His other attributes, further enlightening us on the ways of God.

When Moses went up to Mount Sinai the second time, after the restoration of Israel from its apostasy, God passed in front of Moses. The Lord spoke of several of His attributes:

> The LORD passed by before him and proclaimed: "The LORD, the LORD, the compassionate and gracious God, slow to anger, and abounding in loyal love and faithfulness." (Exodus 34:6)

"Love and faithfulness" can be thought of as "love and what is true." The terms "faithful" and "true" come from the basic verb *aman*, meaning to confirm or to support.[15]

When the men of Jabesh Gilead gave Sha'ul an honorable burial following the Philistines' humiliation of his corpse, David proclaimed:

> Now may the LORD show you true kindness [NIV: kindness and faithfulness]! I also will reward you, because you have done this deed. (2 Samuel 2:6)

Once again faithfulness is conformity to a standard of what is true. The psalmist cried out to God:

> Send forth your light and your truth, let them guide me;
> let them bring me to your holy mountain,

> to the place where you dwell. (Psalm 43:3 NIV)

Here light and truth appear together. Only the God who is true, or faithful, can provide the kind of moral light that leads a person on his way in serving the Lord.

Elsewhere, the psalmist reflects on the deeds and works of the Lord, declaring,

> They are steadfast for ever and ever,
> done in faithfulness and uprightness. (Psalm 111:8 NIV)

In other words, God Himself provides the standard for all that He does, performing them in truth and straightness. That is what one would expect from the God who in Himself is the ultimate standard.

The prophet Jeremiah frequently remonstrated with his generation, people who by any God-revealed, objective standard were far removed from the truth:

> You must be truthful, honest and upright
> when you take an oath saying, "As surely as the LORD lives!"
> If you do, the nations will pray to be as blessed by him as you are
> and will make him the object of their boasting. (Jeremiah 4:2)

Note how the standard of truthfulness is applied along with the other attributes of God as just and righteous. Similarly the prophet described the day when real peace would be restored in Jerusalem:

> But I will most surely heal the wounds of this city and restore it and its people to health. I will show them abundant peace and security [NASB, KJV: "peace and truth"]. (Jeremiah 33:6)

This choice of terms is quite apropos because the popular idea of peace was far from what God had in mind. While they thought they were enjoying *shalom*, they were in reality worshipping false gods and going their own way. In contrast, when the Messianic kingdom of peace will be established, the

Lord will bring to pass everything He has promised, and thereby demonstrate that His standard of truth never fails.

One cannot help but note that in every scriptural illustration, the idea of a standard of truth runs through all of God's attributes. Nothing that He ever says of His personality characteristics can be misconstrued as conforming to man's standards; rather, all who God is, is measured by His own standard of truth, which defines exactly His person, deeds, and speech. Sha'ul pointed out that when people followed their own standards:

> They exchanged the truth of God for a lie and worshiped and served the creation rather than the Creator, who is blessed forever! Amen. (Romans 1:25)

In becoming his own standard, man ends up straying far from the true standard. When, however, people respond to the only true standard in the universe, they then experience all that God's other attributes can mean for them.

Practical Value. The truth of God guarantees that the material and moral universe conforms to truth, that is, to the laws governing the material universe:

> The works of his hands are faithful [NASB, "truth"] and just;
> all his precepts are trustworthy.
> They are steadfast for ever and ever,
> done in faithfulness [NASB, "truth"] and uprightness.
> (Psalm 111:7–8 NIV)

Not only are the laws governing the universe true but so are God's moral precepts. Because He is holy, this alone guarantees the standard of His "true-ness" as a moral being. The doctrine is an assurance that God, being true, will respond to worshippers who honestly desire to have a relationship with Him. David asserted that:

> The LORD is near to all who call on him,
> to all who call on him in truth [NET: "sincerely"]. (Psalm 145:18 NIV)

And Yeshua also echoed this in saying:

> But a time is coming—and now is here—when the true worshipers will worship the Father in spirit and truth, for the Father seeks such people to be his worshipers. (Yohanan 4:23)

The chief ingredient in establishing a relationship with God is that someone be honest in what they want from God; then, He will remove all obstacles in order to relate to such a seeker.

The fact that He is the God of truth and true in every way is also an affirmation that He will make good on every promise:

> You must be truthful, honest and upright
> when you take an oath saying, "As surely as the LORD lives!"
> If you do, the nations will pray to be as blessed by him as you are
> and will make him the object of their boasting. (Jeremiah 4:2)

This doctrine also guarantees the justice of final judgment on those who follow evil. David declared,

> May those who wait to ambush me be repaid for their evil!
> As a demonstration of your faithfulness, destroy them!
> (Psalm 54:5; verse 7 MT)

God will not allow evil to go unpunished. He will sometimes exact justice on sinners while they are still living, but His "true-ness" will also see that justice is done on evil people who live the good life, dying in prosperity. Sha'ul reminds us that:

> The sins of some people are obvious, going before them into judgment, but for others, they show up later. Similarly good works are also obvious, and the ones that are not cannot remain hidden. (1 Timothy 5:24–25)

Their misdeeds will not remain secret. Those who escape judgment in this world will be confronted by them afterward in the final judgment of the next world.

God's true-ness is likewise a reminder that the Lord will never prove unworthy of trust. David committed his spirit into God's hands, recognizing that his redemption would be an ultimate reality. Why? Because the Lord Himself as the God of truth was David's guarantor:

> Into your hands I commit my spirit;
> redeem me, O LORD, the God of truth.[16]
> (Psalm 31:5 NIV; verse 6 MT)

And this faithfulness or true-ness will protect every person who trusts in Him:

> He will shelter you with his wings;
> you will find safety under his wings.
> His faithfulness [KJV: "truth"] is like a shield or a protective wall.
> (Psalm 91:4)

Because God is faithful to every believer, we can always count on Him for protection and support, for He is "true."

God Is Loving

There may be no other doctrine that plucks the strings of the human heart more than that of God's love. As we consider the love of God, we note that "it is not classed as primarily emotional. Love is a settled purpose of will involving the whole person in seeking the well-being of others."[17] What then is this love that lies within the very nature of God?

The Biblical Material. To begin with, we note that the doctrine of the love of God is the same in the Tanach as well as in the New Covenant. Some wrongly think that the God of the Tanach is stern and unforgiving, while in the New Covenant we find a God whose love is extended to everyone. Nothing could be further from the truth. There is as much of the love of God in the Tanach as in the New Covenant, just as in the latter there as much emphasis on lifestyle and following the commandments as in the Tanach.

A sample of scriptural verses shows this to be the case. Because of His love, God chose Israel and promised to never give them up entirely. Therefore when it came time to execute judgment on the northern kingdom of Israel, the great heart cry of God was that He found it hard to give them up and hand them over:

> It is not because you were more numerous than all the other peoples that the LORD favored [NIV: "set his affection on"] and chose you—for in fact you were the least numerous of all peoples. (Deuteronomy 7:7)

> How can I give you up, O Ephraim?
> How can I surrender you, O Israel?
> How can I treat you like Admah?
> How can I make you like Zeboiim?
> I have had a change of heart!
> All my tender compassions are aroused! (Hosea 11:8)

> Through all that they suffered, he suffered too.
> The messenger sent from his very presence delivered them.
> In his love and mercy he protected them;
> he lifted them up and carried them throughout ancient times.
> (Isaiah 63:9)

In the New Covenant, the classic passage is Yohanan 3:16. And in his epistle, Yohanan shows that not only *does* God love but He Himself *is* love.

> For this is the way God loved the world: He gave his one and only Son, so that everyone who believes in him will not perish but have eternal life. (Yohanan 3:16)

> The person who does not love does not know God, because God is love. By this the love of God is revealed in us: that God has sent his one and only Son into the world so that we may live through him. (1 Yohanan 4:8–9)

The Meaning of Love. There are various meanings encompassed by the word *love*. 1) Love may be considered in its physical connotation of erotic expression, the satisfying of sensual desire; 2) It can also be the expression of natural affection, as between family members such as parents and children, or siblings; 3) Love can be used in an aesthetic context, as when even unbelievers care for the aged, oppressed, poor, orphans, and anyone in need; and finally, 4) Love has a moral dimension. In the highest form of love, there is the undergirding element in which an "unwavering determination to do good is present, reflecting God's determination to do the greatest possible good, to all."[18] Love, as a divine attribute, is that which moves God to give Himself and His gifts voluntarily, righteously, and eternally, for the good of personal beings, regardless of their merit of response. We will explore this below.

The Nature of God's Love. Here we take note of several aspects of what it means to say that God is love.

Unselfish. God extended His love to Israel because He had made a promise to Abraham, Isaac, and Jacob to sustain their descendents and keep them. Therefore, in redeeming them from Egypt, He was completely unselfish, even in spite of the fact that many did not respond to His love.

> It is not because you were more numerous than all the other peoples that the LORD favored and chose you—for in fact you were the least numerous of all peoples. Rather it is because of his love for you and his faithfulness to the promise he solemnly vowed to your ancestors that the LORD brought you out with great power, redeeming you from the place of slavery, from the power of Pharaoh king of Egypt. (Deuteronomy 7:7–8)

Voluntary. God extends His love in spite of how people may act. He instructed Hosea to show love again for his wife, even though she may have served as a temple prostitute in the pagan fertility cult. Despite her behavior, Hosea went again and again to his wife in an attempt to bring her back into his home. In the same way, God loved the people of the northern kingdom of Israel, in spite of their involvement with pagan idolatry that was tearing the heart out of the nation.

> The LORD said to me, "Go, show love to your wife again, even though she loves another man and continually commits adultery. Likewise, the LORD loves the Israelites although they turn to other gods and love to offer raisin cakes to idols." (Hosea 3:1)

One day, God promised, after disciplining His people severely, He would extend His love for His people Israel, restoring them to divine favor:

> I will heal their waywardness
> and love them freely,
> for my anger will turn away from them. (Hosea 14:4)

By far, the most telling expression of God's love is expressed by Sha'ul:

> But God demonstrates his own love for us, in that while we were still sinners, Messiah died for us. (Romans 5:8)

And when mankind showed no love for God at all, He nevertheless loved people, demonstrated by sending His Son:

> In this is love: not that we have loved God, but that he loved us and sent his Son to be the atoning sacrifice for our sins. (1 Yohanan 4:10)

Righteous. Even while God loves human beings as sinners, He does not lower His moral standards in any way. The psalmist puts love and standards together when he declares,

> The LORD loves righteousness and justice;
> the earth is full of his unfailing love. (Psalm 33:5 NIV)

Some imagine God as a kindly figure far removed from the realities of this world, one who loves to the point of foregoing His standards. Yet how can we speak of God's highest love without a moral undergirding? If we could, His love would be meaningless.

Everlasting. This is in contrast to someone who is fickle and changes from day to day. In spite of how Judah had treated their Benefactor when they trafficked with the idol systems of the nations, still the time will come when He will be able to say to His people,

> In a far-off land the LORD will manifest himself to them.
> He will say to them, "I have loved you with an everlasting love.
> That is why I have continued to be faithful to you." (Jeremiah 31:3)

Sha'ul echoed this viewpoint when he declared that, though prophecies, tongues, and knowledge will disappear:

> Love never ends. But if there are prophecies, they will be set aside; if there are tongues, they will cease; if there is knowledge, it will be set aside. (1 Corinthians 13:8)

Expressive of His kindness toward everyone. This is seen in the life of Israel and in Yohanan:

> In a far-off land the LORD will manifest himself to them.
> He will say to them, "I have loved you with an everlasting love.
> That is why I have continued to be faithful to you." (Jeremiah 31:3)

> For this is the way God loved the world: He gave his one and only Son, so that everyone who believes in him will not perish but have eternal life. (Yohanan 3:16)

It is further illustrated regarding the body of Messiah:

> Husbands, love your wives just as Messiah loved the *qehilah* and gave himself for her to sanctify her by cleansing her with the washing of the water by the word. (Ephesians 5:25–26)

Some theologians consider God's love to be the very essence of His being, as mentioned above (see 1 Yohanan 4:7–8 previously cited), but we will leave that discussion until the topic of the righteousness of God is considered below.

Satisfying to the inner core of a person's being. This writer has a personal note to give here. Whenever someone is close to realizing the claims of Yeshua the Messiah, he asks them to read Yohanan 3:16. As they read, "For this is the way God loved the world . . ." He then asks them to apply the passage personally using their own name, as for example, "For this is the way God loved Yaakov . . ." This writer has shared the Messiah with many people over the years, and the usual response when someone personalizes the verse in this way is that it brings tears to the eyes of the reader. Why is this? For most of these people, it is the first time they have begun to realize the possibility of having a personal relationship with God. Indeed, He is concerned for each and every human being. He desires to "pluck the strings" of a needy heart and bring music into their life.

God's desire is ever to have fellowship with each object of His human creation. Such is His desire regarding the Jewish people:

> The LORD your God is in your midst;
> he is a warrior who can deliver.
> He takes great delight in you;
> he renews you by his love;
> he shouts for joy over you. (Zephaniah 3:17)

But this message is not confined only to the people of Israel. God wishes to touch the hearts of Gentiles as well. Yeshua's prayer was that as all believers work together, serving God in harmony, the world will know that God loves them and that He sent Yeshua so that they might have fellowship with Him:

> I in them and you in me—that they may be completely one, so that the world will know that you sent me, and you have loved them just as you have loved me. (Yohanan 17:23)

Only God has a heart to care for and love all people.

The Objects of God's Love. As we consider God's love, we note that His love requires an object that to some extent resembles Himself. Though He cares for all living creatures (see Psalm 104:10–23), He can extend His love to mankind in a special way because we have been created in His image. Because of that, people exhibit God's attributes to a limited degree (in contrast to God Himself, in whom we see His attributes to the infinite degree).

For this reason, God loves sinners—because they are persons, even while He dislikes intensely their evil deeds. God loves believers in Him in a special sense—because they are persons in whom God's own character is being reproduced:

> Yeshua replied, "If anyone loves me, he will obey my word, and my Father will love him, and we will come to him and take up residence with him." (Yohanan 14:23)

And God has a special love for the Messiah Yeshua—because His character is perfectly manifested in Him as a person:

> This is why the Father loves me—because I lay down my life, so that I may take it back again. (Yohanan 10:17)

Special Manifestation of God's Love. God suffers with and for the objects of His love. He is the one who daily bears our burdens, our griefs, and our sorrows. During the trying period of the judges when at various times the clans of Israel were under one dominating power or another, God saw their anguish. On one occasion, when He delivered them through Jephthah,

> They threw away the foreign gods they owned and worshiped the LORD. Finally the LORD grew tired of seeing Israel suffer so much. (Judges 10:16)

> Daily He bears the burdens of believers:
> The Lord deserves praise!

> Day after day he carries our burden,
> the God who delivers us. (Selah) (Psalm 68:19; verse 20 MT)

Isaiah likewise reflects:

> Through all that they suffered, he suffered too.
> The messenger sent from his very presence delivered them.
> In his love and mercy he protected them;
> he lifted them up and carried them throughout ancient times.
> (Isaiah 63:9)

And this is a New Covenant truth as well. Because God loves all mankind, Yeshua willingly died for all our sins:

> But God demonstrates his own love for us, in that while we were still sinners, Messiah died for us. (Romans 5:8)

Note that God's love does not negate His dislike for wrongdoing and evil.

Nor does His care cease when people accept Yeshua's sacrifice for sin and so become believers. Yeshua walks with believers through every sorrow and carries them in their trials. We see this concern and love as He disciplines His own children:

> For the LORD disciplines those he loves,
> just as a father disciplines the son in whom he delights.
> (Proverbs 3:12)

> And have you forgotten the exhortation addressed to you as sons?
> "My son, do not scorn the Lord's discipline
> or give up when he corrects you.
> For the Lord disciplines the one he loves and chastises every son he accepts."
> Endure your suffering as discipline; God is treating you as sons.

> For what son is there that a father does not discipline? But if you do not experience discipline, something all sons have shared in, then you are illegitimate and are not sons. (Hebrews 12:5–8)

Exactly because He is a Father in the ultimate sense of the word, He is also responsible for the training of His children, as an expression of His great love.

Practical Value. The love of God guarantees the eternal safety of all who come to Him through the Messiah. Yeshua declared in His "Psalm of the Heart":

> . . . I in them and you in me—that they may be completely one, so that the world will know that you sent me, and you have loved them just as you have loved me.
>
> Father, I want those you have given me to be with me where I am, so that they can see my glory that you gave me because you loved me before the creation of the world. Righteous Father, even if the world does not know you, I know you, and these men know that you sent me. I made known your name to them, and I will continue to make it known, so that the love you have loved me with may be in them, and I may be in them. (Yohanan 17:23–26)

This love of God also guarantees the righteous nature of final judgment (see the section below on God's righteousness). The world needs to know that even though God is a God of love, there will be a judgment for who do not fear God and refuse to humble themselves. Therefore,

> he has set a day on which he is going to judge the world in righteousness, by a man whom he designated [Yeshua], having provided proof to everyone by raising him from the dead. (Acts 17:31)

In the final judgment, those who have refused to acknowledge the sovereignty of this God of love will realize then how righteous and just is this judgment.

Finally, the love of God also guarantees the righteous character of His Messianic kingdom. David declared that the throne on which the Messiah will sit will be forever and ever. A scepter of uprightness, or moral "straightness," will be the means by which this kingdom will be ruled:

> Your throne, O God, is permanent.
> The scepter of your kingdom is a scepter of justice.
> (Psalm 45:6; verse 7 MT)

The Righteousness of God

A number of English words encompass the concept of righteousness: *just*, *justice*, *right*, *righteous*, and *righteousness*. The Hebrew root *ts-d-q* means *just*, *true*, *clear*, or *righteous*. The noun *tsedeq* can be translated *what is right*, *just*, *normal*, or as *rightness*, *justness*. Another noun is *tsedaqah*, *righteousness*, with the same connotations. The person who is *just* and *righteous* is called a *tsaddiq*, one who is *just in one's cause*, *righteous in conduct and character*, *right* and *correct*.[19]

The corresponding Greek verb is *dikaioo* with roughly the same meaning as the Hebrew: "*to deem right . . . to do one justice . . . to be treated rightly*."[20] All the various usages of the noun *dikaiosune* correspond to the Hebrew usage: "*righteousness*, conformity to the Divine will in purpose, thought and action."[21]

The Biblical Material. Several passages concerning righteousness can be found in the book of Psalms.[22] David declares:

> For the LORD is righteous,
> he loves justice;
> upright men will see his face. (Psalm 11:7 NIV)

In the following verse, the word for *justice* reflects the Hebrew *mishpat* rather than *tsedeq*:

> Righteousness and justice are the foundation of your throne;
> love and faithfulness go before you. (Psalm 89:14 NIV; verse 15 MT)

In Psalm 119, the extended psalm of 176 verses that describes God's Word in a multitude of ways, God is addressed in this way:

Righteous are you, O LORD,
and your laws are right. (Psalm 119:137 NIV)

Again:

The LORD is righteous in all his ways
and loving towards all he has made. (Psalm 145:17 NIV)

Jeremiah declared the reason for the captivity of Judah:

All who came upon them have devoured them; And their adversaries have said, "We are not guilty, Inasmuch as they have sinned against the LORD who is the habitation of righteousness, Even the LORD, the hope of their fathers." (Jeremiah 50:7 NASB)

Here NASB translates so as to show the underlying Hebrew word *tsedeq*: "the habitation of righteousness."[23]

Jeremiah also speaks of a time in the future, describing the character of the Messiah:

"The days are coming," declares the LORD, "when I will raise up to David a righteous Branch, a King who will reign wisely and do what is just and right in the land. In his days Judah will be saved and Israel will live in safety. This is the name by which he will be called: The LORD Our Righteousness." (Jeremiah 23:5–6 NIV)

In the New Testament, the word is used in several verses, such as the following (for NET's rendering "faithfulness of Yeshua" vs. the more usual "faith in Yeshua," see note 20).

But now apart from the law the righteousness of God (which is attested by the law and the prophets) has been disclosed—namely, the righteousness of God through the faithfulness of Yeshua the Messiah for all who believe. For there is no distinction, for all have sinned and

> fall short of the glory of God. But they are justified freely by his grace through the redemption that is in Messiah Yeshua. God publicly displayed him at his death as the mercy seat accessible through faith. This was to demonstrate his righteousness, because God in his forbearance had passed over the sins previously committed. This was also to demonstrate his righteousness in the present time, so that he would be just and the justifier of the one who lives because of Yeshua's faithfulness.[24] (Romans 3:21–26)

Two Kinds of Divine Righteousness. Both in the Tanach as well as the New Covenant, we need to carefully distinguish two kinds of divine righteousness. First, there is the righteousness of God accomplished for everyone at Golgotha (Calvary) by the death of the Messiah. This righteousness can then be claimed by those who believe in His atoning work.

Second, there is the righteousness of God that is an attribute of His character, and this kind of righteousness is not "transferable." It is this latter kind of righteousness that is seen in Jeremiah 23:6 as well as in Romans 3:26, cited above.

The Nature of God's Righteousness. The basic idea of the verb *tsadaq* is that which is perfect or straight. God is righteous because He is free from any taint of unrighteousness, because He is upright, that is, "straight."

God's righteousness far exceeds any righteousness on the part of man. For example, while Kefa asserted about Lot that:

> (for while he lived among them day after day, that righteous man was tormented in his righteous soul by the lawless deeds he saw and heard). (2 Kefa 2:8)

Sha'ul affirmed that:

> just as it is written:
> "There is no one righteous, not even one." (Romans 3:10)

Sha'ul surely had in mind Solomon's prayer at the dedication of the temple, when he emphasized:

> The time will come when your people will sin against you (for there is no one who is sinless!) and you will be angry at them and deliver them over to their enemies, who will take them as prisoners to their land, whether far away or close by. (2 Chronicles 6:36)

Man has a certain sense of righteousness, but it is tainted and marred by sin. In order to know ultimate righteousness, possessed by God alone, God must reveal Himself. In the "Psalm of the Heart," Yeshua prayed:

> Righteous Father, even if the world does not know you, I know you, and these men know that you sent me. I made known your name to them, and I will continue to make it known, so that the love you have loved me with may be in them, and I may be in them. (Yohanan 17:25–26)

Manifestations of God's Righteousness. As God disclosed His righteousness to Israel, He expected the people of Israel to also manifest righteousness.

> You must not do injustice in the regulation of measures, whether of length, weight, or volume. You must have honest balances, honest weights, an honest ephah, and an honest hin. I am the LORD your God who brought you out from the land of Egypt. (Leviticus 19:35–36)

The people of Israel were to reflect a divine righteousness as God revealed it to His people. Thus they would display not only a righteousness of their own but a righteousness that had been disclosed by God in the Torah.

God also brings judgment on the unrighteous, that is, those who ignore His righteousness. Numerous passages concerning this are to be found in the Torah. But a very pointed example of how God will one day judge the unrighteous is found in the New Covenant, describing the day just before the coming of the Messiah to establish His kingdom. At that time, we read:

> Then the third angel poured out his bowl on the rivers and the springs of water, and they turned into blood. Now I heard the angel of the waters saying:
>
> "You are just—the one who is and who was,
> the Holy One—because you have passed these judgments,
> because they poured out the blood of your saints and prophets,
> so you have given them blood to drink. They got what they deserved!"
>
> Then I heard the altar reply, "Yes, Lord God, the All-powerful, your judgments are true and just!" (Revelation 16:4–7)

The fate of people on this earth during the tribulation period is one of terrible judgments. These righteous judgments are not frivolous; they are deserved. Yet when they come, we read, the people facing judgment will only curse God, rather than repent and ask for forgiveness.

For believers, God's righteousness means that He will keep His promises that were given in His covenants with Israel; His righteousness will not allow Him to act otherwise:

> "Gather to me my consecrated ones,
> who made a covenant with me by sacrifice."
> And the heavens proclaim his righteousness,
> for God himself is judge. (Psalm 50:5–6 NIV)

On another occasion, Israel bemoaned the fact that after a remnant returned to the land from the Babylonian captivity, they entered into the very same sinful practices that had caused their exile in the first place, such as giving their sons and daughters in marriage to pagans. Ezra confessed that God is righteous and but for His grace, His righteousness would fall such that no survivor would remain:

> O LORD God of Israel, you are righteous, for we are left as a remnant this day. Indeed, we stand before you in our guilt. However, because of this guilt no one can really stand before you. (Ezra 9:15)

By God's grace, however, judgment was averted when Ezra led the people to rectify their misdeeds.

When necessary, God knows how to discipline His people. Daniel's confession was that the exile took place because of the sins of the people:

> The LORD did not hesitate to bring the disaster upon us, for the LORD our God is righteous in everything he does; yet we have not obeyed him. (Daniel 9:14 NIV)

God's discipline likewise extends to believers in the body of Messiah who, if they persist in sin, will also feel God's hand of correction—exactly because He is righteous and it is necessary that we conform to His righteousness. And then, when we confess our wrongdoing, God is faithful and just to forgive our sins, purifying us from all unrighteousness:

> But if we confess our sins, he is faithful and righteous, forgiving us our sins and cleansing us from all unrighteousness. (1 Yohanan 1:9)

Finally, God's righteousness was manifested at the tree where Yeshua died for our sins. The very basis for forgiving sins is at the place where He became our propitiatory sacrifice, in His blood through faith. This, Sha'ul tells us, was to demonstrate His righteousness:

> God publicly displayed him at his death as the mercy seat accessible through faith. This was to demonstrate his righteousness, because God in his forbearance had passed over the sins previously committed. This was also to demonstrate his righteousness in the present time, so that he would be just and the justifier of the one who lives because of Yeshua's faithfulness.[25] (Romans 3:25–26)

Some Problems. One major problem was addressed above under the topic of holiness, but it comes to the fore again as we speak of God's righteousness. Namely, how can we reconcile the doctrine of a righteous God with the existence of a world filled with evil? The presence of this contrast is a major ethical dilemma: how can God permit a Hitler to exist, someone responsible for the death of six million Jewish people as well millions of others? For discussion, see above under the topic of holiness.

Practical Value. God's righteousness is an assurance to believers that no good ever done in His name will ever be forgotten. God reminds the believers in the Jerusalem congregation:

> For God is not unjust so as to forget your work and the love you have demonstrated for his name, in having served and continuing to serve the saints. (Hebrews 6:10)

Note that in context the writer calls the congregants "Dear friends" (verse 9) and expresses his confidence toward them, encouraging them to be diligent to the very end in order to make their hope sure.

The Faithfulness of God

One dimension of God's faithfulness as *true* or *truth* has already been considered. Now we will turn to the wider meaning of the concept.

The Biblical Material. Moses marveled at God's choice of Israel:

> So realize that the LORD your God is the true God, the faithful God who keeps covenant faithfully with those who love him and keep his commandments, to a thousand generations. (Deuteronomy 7:9)

David described the greatness of God's faithfulness:

> Your love, O LORD, reaches to the heavens,
> your faithfulness to the skies. (Psalm 36:5 NIV; verse 6 MT)

The lengthy wisdom psalm, Psalm 119, offers this reflection:

> You demonstrate your faithfulness to all generations.
> You established the earth and it stood firm. (Psalm 119:90)

Concerning the message of the Messianic kingdom of peace, Isaiah's description of the coming ruler is that:

> Righteousness will be his belt and faithfulness the sash round his waist. (Isaiah 11:5 NIV)

Though Jeremiah lamented the loss of the First Temple and the death of so many of his fellow countrymen, yet he could declare:

> The LORD's loyal kindness never ceases;
> his compassions never end.
> They are fresh every morning;
> your faithfulness is abundant! (Lamentations 3:22–23)

In the New Covenant, the words *faithful* and *faithfulness* appear many times. Specifically with regard to the Messiah, the assertion that God is faithful occurs some eleven times, for example:

> But as God is faithful, our message to you is not "Yes" and "No." (2 Corinthians 1:18)

Hebrew and Greek Terms. The Hebrew term *aman* has the basic idea of *confirm*, *support*, and in another form of the verb, *sure*, *established*. The picture is essentially that of "being firm."[26] The basic Greek verb is *pisteuo*, meaning *to have faith*, *to believe*, *to rely on*, *to be firm and confident*. Both the Hebrew and Greek terms have roughly the same meaning.

Note that the English word *amen* comes directly from the Hebrew and it appears in English simply as a transliteration from the Hebrew. When we say *amen*, we are affirming that God is the "Amen" God, the God who is faithful and the One in whom we have the utmost trust. This is well illustrated in Yeshua's statement:

> To the angel of the *qehilah* in Laodicea write the following:
> "This is the solemn pronouncement of the Amen, the faithful and true witness, the originator of God's creation." (Revelation 3:14)

Practical Value. God's faithfulness guarantees the stability of the material universe. Ethan declares God established His faithfulness in heaven itself:

> For I say, "Loyal love is permanently established;
> in the skies you set up your faithfulness." (Psalm 89:2)

Compare:

> You demonstrate your faithfulness to all generations.
> You established the earth and it stood firm. (Psalm 119:90)

He will also make good on all of His promises and warnings:

> If we are unfaithful, he remains faithful, since he cannot deny himself. (2 Timothy 2:13)

Furthermore, we are encouraged to persevere in our hope:

> Let us hold unswervingly to the hope we profess, for he who promised is faithful. (Hebrews 10:23 NIV)

This faithfulness of God assures us as we go about serving Him. Because He is faithful, He has made possible our participation in fellowship with the Messiah.

> God is faithful, by whom you were called into fellowship with his son, Yeshua the Messiah our Lord. (1 Corinthians 1:9)

We are assured of victory in all of our temptations:

> No trial has overtaken you that is not faced by others. And God is faithful: He will not let you be tried beyond what you are able to bear, but with the trial will also provide a way out so that you may be able to endure it. (1 Corinthians 10:13)

His faithfulness guarantees forgiveness and cleansing for all believers:

> But if we confess our sins, he is faithful and righteous, forgiving us our sins and cleansing us from all unrighteousness. (1 Yohanan 1:9)

The One who calls us also guarantees our preservation:

> Now may the God of peace himself make you completely holy and may your spirit and soul and body be kept entirely blameless at the coming of our Lord Yeshua the Messiah. He who calls you is trustworthy [NIV: "faithful"], and he will in fact do this. (1 Thessalonians 5:23–24)

Finally, He enables us to trust Him as we submit to Him, even in the most difficult of experiences. Curiously, the wisdom psalm reminds us that:

> I know, LORD, that your regulations are just.
> You disciplined me because of your faithful devotion to me. (Psalm 119:75)

While this may sound strange, we also recognize that difficult times do come in the life of every believer. It is His faithfulness to us that will enable us to triumph in the end.

The Mercy of God

The last of the attributes of God that falls under the larger category of "the goodness of God" is that of His mercy. The term "mercy" can be applied to both God and to man, for we have been created in God's image, and thus we have a sense of what mercy entails. About 75 to 80 percent of the occurrences of the word as applied to God are found in the Tanach, the remainder in the New Covenant.

The Biblical Material. Moses reminded Israel:

> (for he is a merciful God), he will not let you down or destroy you, for he cannot forget the covenant with your ancestors that he confirmed by oath to them. (Deuteronomy 4:31)

Micah, too, wrote that though God may be angry with His people, He does not remain so forever:

> There is no other God like you!
> You forgive sin
> and pardon the rebellion
> of those who remain among your people.
> You do not remain angry forever,
> but delight in showing loyal love [NIV: "mercy"].
> You will once again have mercy on us;
> you will conquer our evil deeds;
> you will hurl our sins into the depths of the sea. (Micah 7:18–19)

The New Covenant likewise describes God:

> Blessed is the God and Father of our Lord Yeshua the Messiah, the Father of mercies and God of all comfort. (2 Corinthians 1:3)

Hebrew and Greek Terms. Two basic verbs are used in describing mercy. One has the sense of *compassion*, the other of *lovingkindness*.

The first of these verbs is the Hebrew term *racham*. The concept here is *to be compassionate*, and at times there is also the concept of *being soft*. Since one of the related nouns is *rechem* or *womb*, some older versions used the word "bowels" when translating words in this group. The thought is that of the inner emotions of a person as they reflect softness and gentleness, which are the basic ideas behind being compassionate.

Another Hebrew verb, *chasad*, means *to be good* or *kind*, and has come to be used to express the highest form of God's love, God's lovingkindness.

The Greek verbs for these two words are respectively *oikteiro*, meaning *to pity*, *to have compassion*, and *eleeo*, also meaning *to have pity or mercy*, *to show mercy*. Also relevant is the basic verb for love in Greek, *agapao*, which describes not only human affection toward others but functions as the Greek equivalent of the Hebrew *hasad* in order to express both the highest love of God toward man, and also the highest form of love between human beings.

The Distinction Between Mercy and Love. In general, love describes God's character defining who He *is*, while mercy pictures God's actions, that is, what He *does*. The mercy of God is spoken of differently from the love of God and a number of passages seem to suggest the difference.

In the following verse, the first word translated "love" is *chesed* or lovingkindness; the second word translated "love" indicates a filial love (as in the love between a man and woman, the love between friends, and so on).

> . . . but showing love to a thousand generations of those who love me and keep my commandments. (Deuteronomy 5:10 NIV)

Nehemiah's recorded prayer indicates that he sought God's blessings and, in particular, that He grant him "favor," which is Hebrew *rachamim* (a form of *rechem*) or compassion. The NET Bible captures this:

> "Please, O Lord, listen attentively to the prayer of your servant and to the prayer of your servants who take pleasure in showing respect to your name. Grant your servant success today and show compassion [NIV, "favor"] to me in the presence of this man." Now I was cupbearer for the king. (Nehemiah 1:11)

The New Covenant has numerous references that show the differences between the terms used for compassion and lovingkindness. Sha'ul described how the believers at Rome have "received mercy" (a word related to *eleeo*, indicating God's compassion, corresponding more to *rechem* in the Hebrew Scriptures):

> Just as you were formerly disobedient to God, but have now received mercy due to their disobedience, . . . (Romans 11:30)

Two verses later, "mercy" comes from the same word *eleeo*.

> For God has consigned all people to disobedience so that he may show mercy to them all. (Romans 11:32)

Similarly in this verse:

> Therefore, since we have this ministry, just as God has shown us mercy, we do not become discouraged. (2 Corinthians 4:1)

A good example of where both terms appear together is when Sha'ul expressed his deepest gratitude. Here the term "mercy" is again from *eleeo*, while "love" comes from *agapao*, referring to God's deepest love.

> But God, being rich in mercy, because of his great love with which he loved us, even though we were dead in transgressions, made us alive together with Messiah—by grace you are saved! (Ephesians 2:4–5)

A Remark on God's Mercy in the Tanach. While many believers might think that there is more of the love of God in the New Covenant and more of the harsh justice of God in the Tanach, nothing could be further from the truth. Let us look at a selection of passages from the Tanach. After David had taken a census of his fighting men, he was stricken in his conscience and declared his sin to God. Confronted with the possibility of judgment, David could only respond by saying:

> David said to Gad, "I am very upset! I prefer to be attacked by the LORD, for his mercy [from *rechem*, or compassion] is very great; I do not want to be attacked by men!" (1 Chronicles 21:13)

The remainder of our Tanach passages come from the Psalms where the psalmists praised God for His mercy and love because of God's marvelous care:

> For your loyal love [*chesed*, or great lovingkindness] extends
> beyond the sky, and your faithfulness reaches the clouds.
> (Psalm 57:10; verse 11 MT)

> Certainly O Lord, you are kind and forgiving,
> and show great faithfulness [*chesed*; NIV, "love"]

to all who cry out to you. (Psalm 86:5)

For I say, "Loyal love [*chesed*] is permanently established;
in the skies you set up your faithfulness." (Psalm 89:2; verse 3 MT)

For your loyal love extends beyond the sky,
and your faithfulness reaches the clouds. (Psalm 108:4)

O LORD, your loyal love [*chesed*] fills the earth.
Teach me your statutes! (Psalm 119:64)

Finally, in Psalm 136, every verse gives glory to God with the phrase "*ki le'olam chasdo*," "for his loyal love endures [forever]," again using a form of the word *chesed*.

Manifestations of God's Mercy. When in the days of Nehemiah, the walls around Jerusalem were completed, there followed a great spiritual revival during the month of Tishrei. The people took the occasion to recount the spiritual rebellion of their ancestors, particularly the generation that came out of Egypt. They recalled the making of the image of the calf (really a replica of the bull worshipped by Egypt) and the attempt to make that into a means of worshipping God. Yet despite this recitation of Israel's sins, there was also the realization that it was only because of God's great "compassion" (from *rechem*) that He did not abandon that generation. Here is the text from Nehemiah:

> They refused to obey and did not recall your miracles that you had performed among them. Instead, they rebelled and appointed a leader to return to their bondage in Egypt. But you are a God of forgiveness, merciful and compassionate, slow to get angry and unfailing in your loyal love. You did not abandon them, even when they made a cast image of a calf for themselves and said, "This is your God who brought you up from Egypt," or when they committed atrocious blasphemies.
>
> Due to your great compassion you did not abandon them in the

> desert. The pillar of cloud did not stop guiding them in the path by day, nor did the pillar of fire stop illuminating for them by night the path on which they should travel. You imparted your good Spirit to instruct them. You did not withhold your manna from their mouths; you provided water for their thirst. For forty years you sustained them. Even in the desert they never lacked anything. Their clothes did not wear out and their feet did not swell. (Nehemiah 9:17–21)

The text continues to recall succeeding generations too, in the period of the judges, and how God had great compassion (*rehem*) on them despite their rebellion against God at that time:

> Nonetheless they grew disobedient and rebelled against you; they disregarded your law. They killed your prophets who had solemnly admonished them in order to cause them to return to you. They committed atrocious blasphemies. Therefore you delivered them into the hand of their adversaries, who oppressed them. But in the time of their distress they called to you, and you heard from heaven. In your abundant compassion [from rechem, and also in the following verses] you provided them with deliverers to rescue them from their adversaries.
>
> Then, when they were at rest again, they went back to doing evil before you. Then you abandoned them to their enemies, and they gained dominion over them. When they again cried out to you, in your compassion you heard from heaven and rescued them time and again. And you solemnly admonished them in order to return them to your law, but they behaved presumptuously and did not obey your commandments. They sinned against your ordinances—those by which an individual, if he obeys them, will live. They boldly turned from you; they rebelled and did not obey. You prolonged your kindness with them for many years, and you solemnly admonished them by your Spirit through your prophets. Still they paid no attention, so you delivered them into the hands of the neighboring peoples. However, due to your abundant mercy you did not do away with them altogether;

> you did not abandon them. For you are a merciful and compassionate God.
>
> So now, our God—the great, powerful, and awesome God, who keeps covenant fidelity—do not regard as inconsequential all the hardship that has befallen us—our kings, our leaders, our priests, our prophets, our ancestors, and all your people—from the days of the kings of Assyria until this very day! (Nehemiah 9:26–32)

Yes, in spite of this litany of treachery and evil, the great, mighty, and awesome God kept His covenant fidelity (or NIV, "covenant of love"; the Hebrew is *ha-brit ve-ha-chesed*) (Nehemiah 9:32).

David, too, in recounting greatness and goodness of Israel's true king, the Lord, declared that:

> The LORD is merciful and compassionate;
> he is patient and demonstrates great loyal love [*chesed*].
> The LORD is good to all,
> and has compassion [from *rechem*] on all he has made. (Psalm 145:8–9)

We have already noted above Sha'ul's statement in Ephesians 2:4–5 that utilizes the two different verbs for mercy and love.

Precious then are these truths regarding the two different usages of the verbs that tell us something about how God many times took the initiative to express His care, concern, compassion, and deepest love for His people.

Some Problems. Sometimes Sha'ul talks in assured terms about how God extends His love to people, particularly to believers. How then does one explain other passages where he states that God will have mercy on whomever He wishes, and that He can also harden whom He wishes to harden?

> For he says to Moses: "I will have mercy on whom I have mercy, and I will have compassion on whom I have compassion." So then, it does not depend on human desire or exertion, but on God who shows mercy. For the scripture says to Pharaoh: "For this very purpose I have

> raised you up, that I may demonstrate my power in you, and that my name may be proclaimed in all the earth." So then, God has mercy on whom he chooses to have mercy, and he hardens whom he chooses to harden. (Romans 9:15–18)

Is this not a contradiction?

The problem may seem difficult to resolve, but in one way it is similar to the problem of why God loved Jacob and hated Esau. Because God is omniscient, He knows people's decisions before they are made. He knew beforehand that Jacob would eventually respond to the pressures placed on him by turning to God. On the other hand, He also knew what kind of decisions Esau would make, leading to his becoming an idolater, marrying the women of the land, causing thereby much grief to his parents, and eventually becoming a father of a nation that held hatred toward their half brothers, the Judeans.

In the same way, God knew exactly what Pharaoh would do. Yet God gave him every opportunity to respond favorably to all of the plagues; He desired to help Pharaoh come to terms with the sovereignty of the true God. Nevertheless, Pharaoh refused and hardened his heart (see Exodus 8:15–32).

Therefore, when someone spurns God's gracious attempts to extend mercy and love, God must then relate differently to such a rebel. In the end, Pharaoh became a testimony to God's goodness as well as to His justice.

Therefore, there does not seem to be any contradiction between the biblical passages concerning the mercy and love of God.

Practical Value. How can knowledge of God's love and mercy be a source of comfort and help for us, His people? As one example, David directed praise to God because of His great blessings; the Psalms show how God extended Himself on David's behalf and express this thought exquisitely:

> But I am like a flourishing olive tree in the house of God;
> I continually trust in God's loyal love [chesed]. (Psalm 52:8; verse 10 MT)

When David cried for protection from his enemies, he called on God:

> As a demonstration of your loyal love [chesed],
> destroy my enemies!
> Annihilate all who threaten my life,
> for I am your servant. (Psalm 143:12)

David always expected God to intervene on his behalf when the difficulties became great; as a result, God delivered him out of all his predicaments.

In Daniel's great prayer beseeching the deliverance of his people from Babylon, he implored God:

> Listen attentively, my God, and hear! Open your eyes and look on our desolated ruins and the city called by your name. For it is not because of our own righteous deeds that we are praying to you, but because your compassion [from rechem] is abundant. (Daniel 9:18)

The New Covenant also uses these twin concepts of love and compassion to express how God cares for His people. Yeshua reminded His disciples that they were not only to love those who loved them, but were also to demonstrate love to those who would despitefully use them. That is, they were to demonstrate a tender mercy:

> Be merciful, just as your Father is merciful. (Luke 6:36)

Sha'ul called for believers to yield their lives to God in view of God's mercy (or "mercies"; *oiktirmos*, usually used as the Greek equivalent of *rechem*, or compassion):

> Therefore I exhort you, brothers and sisters, by the mercies of God, to present your bodies as a sacrifice—alive, holy, and pleasing to God—which is your reasonable service. (Romans 12:1)

A combination of terms appears when Sha'ul exhorts the believers at Philippi:

> Therefore, if there is any encouragement in Messiah, any comfort provided by love [agape, corresponding to hesed], any fellowship in the Spirit, any affection or mercy [*oiktirmos*, corresponding to rechem], complete my joy and be of the same mind, by having the same love [*agape*], being united in spirit, and having one purpose. (Philippians 2:1–2)

Sha'ul skillfully combines both words in expressing the greatest and highest concern that God has for His people. Therefore, every believer ought to readily respond to what God asks of us, knowing where they came from, and realizing that we have been bought with a price.

SEVEN

A Major Watershed of Thought at the End of the Second Temple Period

PART ONE

How Can the Messiah be Both Human and Divine?

Among the various issues raised by the claims of Yeshua, two are especially noteworthy:

1) How can the Messiah be both human and divine?
2) How is it possible for the Messiah son of David both to die as an atonement for sin and be resurrected, and to also sit upon His throne, ruling a kingdom of peace?

The resolution of these two issues created a division in the first century between the followers of Yeshua and the rest of the Jewish people. Even Yeshua's own followers, though they initially accepted both His humanity and deity, could not at first accept His death as the atonement for sin. That is why after His death some of His followers began to disperse homeward, while those who remained in Jerusalem were deeply disillusioned. Nevertheless, as this second issue was resolved, it too proved to be a dividing point.

To this day, these two "watershed questions" continue to be the major issues that separate Messianic Jews from the rest of the Jewish community. *To reiterate: the two issues are the dual nature of Messiah (both human and divine); and His atonement for the sins of mankind.*

In this and succeeding chapters, we will examine 1) the thinking of the rabbinical authorities at the end of the Second Temple period regarding the nature of God and Messiah, and 2) what Yeshua said and did that countered the mindset of the religious leaders of His day. We will try to understand the dynamics with which the disciples themselves had to wrestle, and we will look at the conclusions to which the early Messianic Jews came.

The "De-Anthropomorphizing" of God: Why the Messiah Was Understood to Be Only Human

During the Second Commonwealth[1] of Judea—from about 400 B.C.E. on—the religious leaders of Israel sought for ways to protect the high and lofty character of Israel's divine calling from being degraded. What this meant was that the leaders intended that the people of Judea should never again confuse their God with the gods of the pagan nations of the Middle East. Recall that this was in fact what did happen during the First Commonwealth. The Babylonian exile was a national trauma; one of its main purposes, in God's providence, was to purify Israel by creating a remnant among the people who would never again place their God on the same level with pagan deities:

> Jerusalem, why are you now shouting so loudly?
> Has your king disappeared?
> Has your wise leader been destroyed?
> Is this why pain grips you as if you were a woman in labor?
> Twist and strain, Daughter Zion, as if you were in labor!
> For you will leave the city
> and live in the open field.
> You will go to Babylon,
> but there you will be rescued.

> There the LORD will deliver you
> from the power of your enemies. (Micah 4:9–10)

Therefore, the postexilic leaders and as well as postexilic writers wanted to impress on the people of Israel that their God is indeed holy and transcendent, and far above all pagan deities. For that reason Jewish literature of the centuries following the exile—from the close of the Tanach at about 400 B.C.E. up to the first century C.E.—is the source of a number of ideas that are particularly relevant for our discussion concerning the concept of Messiah.

Sometimes these centuries are referred to as the "silent years," coming as they did between the close of the Tanach and the writing of the New Covenant documents. But in fact they were *not* silent. This period is one of the golden ages of Jewish literature, showing the literary genius of the people of Israel through the production of a large corpus of noncanonical (that is, not included in the Bible) writings. We will now examine some of this literature to see what light it sheds on the issues we are considering.

The Targumim

The interpretation of Scripture had already began in the days of Ezra and Nehemiah:

> They read from the book of God's law, explaining it and imparting insight. Thus the people gained understanding from what was read. (Nehemiah 8:8)

By this point in time, the people no longer understood Hebrew as a daily language but only Aramaic. Thus there was a need for interpretation. The phrase "explaining it" refers to the fact that Ezra and the cadre of Levites gathered around him had begun a system of oral interpretation and paraphrasing of Scripture. Through succeeding generations of *sopherim*, *hasidim*, and *parushim*, the interpretation and paraphrasing of the Tanach continued to develop. Eventually, this body of originally oral material came to be compiled in writing and became known as the *Targumim* (singular, *Targum*).[2]

We will look now at the Targumim to see what the religious leaders of

Israel did with the concept of God in those writings.

The Term *Memra*. In the Targumim, there is a prominent term *memra*, translated as "word," which is frequently used in place of the name of God. The meaning of the word is given by Jastrow under *memar* as "1) *word, command*. . . . 2) (hypostatized) . . . the Word, i.e., *the Lord* (used in the Targum to obviate anthropomorphism . . ."[3] Examples include:

Exodus 16:8

Bible: "Your murmurings are not against us, but against the LORD."

Targum: "Your grumblings should not be directed against us but against the Memra of the Lord."[4]

Exodus 32:35

Bible: "And the LORD sent a plague on the people because they had made the calf—the one Aaron made."

Targum: The *memra* "plagued the people."[5]

Exodus 33:22

Bible: "I will . . . cover you with my hand . . ."

Targum: "I . . . will shield you with My Memra . . ."[6]

Deuteronomy 1:32

Bible: ". . . you did not have confidence in the LORD your God . . ."

Targum: ". . . you did not trust the Memra of the Lord your God . . ."[7]

Isaiah 45:2

Bible: "I will go before you . . ."

Targum: "My Memra will go before you, . . ."[8]

The *memra* refers to the manifestation of divine power, and is also the messenger of God on His behalf. In early Jewish thought, *memra* refers to an intermediate agency between God and man, and a means of revelation of God to man. A few examples of the use of *memra* will help make this clearer:

The *memra* is regarded as the manifestation of God. Targum Yerushalmi for

Deuteronomy 4:7 says that "The Memra brings Israel nigh unto God and sits on His throne receiving the prayers of Israel."[9] The *memra* is the one who guards Jacob (Genesis 28:20–21; 35:3) and Israel (Exodus 12:28–29). The *memra* is also regarded as the agent of God, for example, in the creation of the earth (Isaiah 45:12).[10] The *memra* is the one who executes justice (Targum Yerushalmi for Numbers 33:4).[11] The *memra* is even regarded as the comforter in the future: ". . . so my Memra will comfort you; . . ." (Targum Isaiah 66:13).[12]

Texts like these could be multiplied over and over.

The problem before us is just how did the Jewish scholars use and appropriate this term *memra* by the first century C.E. George Foot Moore comments on this understanding: ". . . nowhere in the Targums is *memra* a 'being' of any kind or in any sense, much less a personal being. The appearance of personality which in some places attaches to the word is due solely to the fact the *memra* of the Lord and similar phrases are reverent circumlocutions for 'God,' introduced precisely where in the original God is personally active in the affairs of men; . . ."[13] In addition, Moore states that "*memra* is purely a phenomenon of translation, not a figment of speculation; it never gets outside the Targums."[14] Referring to the *memra*, Wolfson echoes the same sentiments: "No scholar nowadays will entertain the view that it is either a real being or an intermediary."[15]

In the first century, then, as modern commentators have noted, the use of *memra* was intended as a means to *de-anthropomorphize* the manner in which people understood and talked about God. This was the means Israel's religious leaders chose so as to *protect the transcendency of the God of Israel* so that He would not be brought down to the level of the deities of other nations.

The Term *Shekinah*. Another means to obviate anthropomorphic expressions was the use of the term *Shekinah* as a way to describe the immanence of God, or His presence among people. This word appears many times in the Targumim as well as in other Jewish literature.

The Targum Onkelos[16] uses this expression in interesting ways: For example, the biblical verse "The LORD is not among you" (Numbers 14:42) is rendered in the Targum as "The *Shekinah* is not in your midst." The verse "You cannot see my face, for no one can see me and live" (Exodus 33:20) is given as "You cannot see the face of my *Shekinah*." In Deuteronomy 12:5, where one reads, "To put his Name there [NIV]," Onkelos renders it as "To rest his *Shekinah* there."

Other Ways to Speak About God. The Targumim paraphrasers (called *meturgemanim*) had additional ways to speak reverently about God and His activities. For example, when describing God's relationship with the world, He is never made the direct subject or object of an action. *Active* words in the biblical text were handled in the *passive* so as to avoid undue anthropomorphic expressions. We see this technique used in a number of examples from the Targum known as Targum Neofiti:[17]

1) Genesis 1:4 is rendered in this Targum as "and it was manifest before the Lord that the light was good";

2) Instead of "God heard their groaning" (Exodus 2:24), the Targum reads, "and their complaint was heard before the Lord";

3) In Exodus 2:25, "God looked on the Israelites and was concerned about them [NIV]," the paraphrasers rendered it as "the servants of the sons of Israel were manifest before the Lord."

Many more examples could be provided. These paraphrases avoid suggesting that God comes into any direct contact with man. The phrase "before the LORD" was chosen to avoid false impressions of God among the unlearned. Every care was exercised to render biblical materials so as to preclude any reader from identifying the God of Israel with pagan deities.

The "Outside Literature"

The "Outside Literature" of Israel refers to writings of the first few centuries B.C.E. and also continuing into the early C.E. era that were not included in the canon of the Bible. Such writings would include what is called the Apocrypha as well as the Pseudepigrapha. These writings can reflect quite accurately what the Hebrew Scriptures say when speaking about God. On the other hand, some of the de-anthropomorphizing process that we saw in the

Targumim is also present in this literature:

1) "Thy all-powerful *word* leaped from heaven, from the royal throne, into the midst of the land that was doomed, a stern warrior carrying the sharp sword of thy authentic command" (*Wisdom of Solomon* 18:15–16). Written in Greek, the term here for *word* is *logos*. Though the language is Greek, the passage is not to be understood through the framework of Greek philosophy. Rather, it is Hebraic in its worldview and appears to mirror the imagery of 1 Chronicles 21:16 where the angel of the Lord drew out his sword over Jerusalem for destruction.[18]

2) "By the words (*memra*) of the Lord His works are done" (Ecclesiasticus 42:15);

3) "Thy word (*memra*), O LORD, which heals all men" (Wisdom 16:12);

4) "Thy word (*memra*) preserves those who trust in Thee" (Wisdom 16:26), and so on.

The Septuagint

The Septuagint (often abreviated LXX) is the first Greek translation of the Hebrew Scriptures (made about 250–100 B.C.E.). It represents a further step along the way in the de-anthropomorphizing process. A few examples will show the distinction between the Hebrew Masoretic text and the Septuagint's translation. For instance, the word "likeness" as used of God is rendered as follows in the Septuagint:

1) "Likeness" (*temunah*) is rendered as "glory" when referring to God. "I shall be satisfied when thy glory (*doxa*, for *temunah*, likeness) appears."

2) In Numbers 12:8, "He [Moses] will see the form (*temunah*) of the Lord" is rendered, "He (Moses) had the glory (*doxa*) of the Lord."

"The mouth of the LORD" is also a phrase that is handled circumspectly at times. Examples include:

1) In Isaiah 40:5, "For the mouth of the LORD has spoken." (NIV)

2) In Isaiah 45:23, "My mouth has uttered in all integrity a word." (NIV)

These are rendered in the Greek translation as "Righteousness shall surely proceed out of my mouth; my words shall not be frustrated."

There were also later Greek translations, such as *Symmachus*, which even more consistently engaged in de-anthropomorphizing. At that point, however, we are already post-first century, after the Council of Yavneh,[19] at a time when the original Greek translation (the LXX) was suspect in Jewish eyes because of the way the Messianic Jews were using it to proclaim the uniqueness of Yeshua. Despite a heightening of such concerns after the proclamation of the Messianic Jews, the pattern had already been set before that time as to the way one talked about God. A genuine reluctance existed to in any way bring God down to the level of mankind.

Was this de-anthropomorphizing process in the Septuagint due to the influence of Greek philosophy, which had an aversion to speaking of God in human terms and attributing to God anything corporeal? Philo, the first-century Jewish philosopher, recognized this philosophic distaste for speaking of God in humanlike terms, and so he allegorized the Old Testament Scriptures with Greek sensibilities in mind. However, some have argued that there are no traces of an influence of Greek philosophy on Jewish "mainstream" thinkers and religious leaders.[20] The de-anthropomorphizing by the Jewish translators of the Hebrew Scriptures reflected an activity that had *already* taken place on Jewish soil and reflected the intense interest in keeping the being of God as lofty as possible.

When the project to translate the Scriptures into Greek was first broached in Egypt at about 250 B.C.E., the Jerusalem authorities were reluctant to produce one. However, when permission was finally given, the Jewish translators in Egypt reflected the concern of the religious leaders back in Judea as to a proper understanding of anthropomorphisms. The translation of the LXX in the Prophets and the Writings was not as adequate as that of the Torah of Moses. However, in all three sections of the Hebrew Bible, anthropomorphisms of the more glaring kind were toned down—not because of the aversion of Greek thinking but from the common understanding of the Jewish scholars in the land of Israel and elsewhere.

Special Names for God

Jewish literature after the first century abounded with a vareity of names for God. In particular, by the first century specific names were being used so as to carefully protect the being of God from contact with His creation, including man.[21]

One such prominent name is *heaven*. We find it used quite often in a number of compound expressions, such as *fear of heaven*, which approximates the biblical *fear of the LORD*. Besides the numerous places where this word appears in traditional Jewish literature, we may also note its presence in the gospels:

> "Where did Yohanan's baptism come from? From heaven or from people?" They discussed this among themselves, saying, "If we say, 'From heaven,' he will say, 'Then why did you not believe him?'" (Mattai 21:25)

> Yohanan's baptism—was it from heaven or from people? Answer me. (Mark 11:30)

> I will get up and go to my father and say to him, "Father, I have sinned against heaven and against you." . . . Then his son said to him, "Father, I have sinned against heaven and against you; I am no longer worthy to be called your son." (Luke 15:18, 21)

Also, Mattai often uses the phrase *kingdom of heaven*, which is a periphrastic or roundabout way of saying *kingdom of God*.

Another substitute name for God is *power*, often found in the rabbinic literature. We also note its use when Yeshua described His uniqueness. When asked by the high priest if He was the son of the Blessed One, He replied:

> Yeshua said to him, "You have said it yourself. But I tell you, from now on you will see the Son of Man sitting at the right hand of the Power and coming on the clouds of heaven." (Mattai 26:64; NASB likewise renders "Power" while NIV has "Mighty One")

The term *power* is a circumlocution for *God*.

The Implications of De-Anthropomorphizing God

What does all this de-anthropomorphizing activity mean for first-century Judaism's view of God?

First, while God could certainly be regarded as personal, at the same time He became far removed from the average Jewish person. A warm, loving, vital relationship was lost, in comparison with how the prophets of the Hebrew Bible, for example, spoke of God. God had become "wholly other."

Second, this trend was to have a devastating influence on the understanding of the person of the Messiah. The de-anthropomorphizing process created a great gulf between God and man, with the result that it became impossible to think in terms of a human Messiah who would at the same time be divine. Deity could not be entangled with humanity; Israel's God was not an idol like that of any other nation. To first-century Jews, Yeshua might be considered a Messiah, even superhuman, but *not* divine. The development of a Jewish religious tradition of speaking about God had schooled the nation to the concept of Messiah as only human.

Yeshua's Proclamation About Himself

In the course of His ministry, Yeshua did not proclaim to one and all that He is the Son of God. Neither did He constantly speak about His Messiahship. In fact, there seemed to be a reticence about it all. Wrede spoke of a doctrine of "veiled glory" and the "Messianic secret."[22] David Flusser, professor of comparative religion at the Hebrew University, connected Yeshua's reticence about His Messiahship with the parallel reticence displayed at Qumran by the Teacher of Righteousness and by Simon of Kosebah (Bar Kochba) of Murabba'at.[23]

Flusser's conviction was that "from the strictly theological point of view no man can be defined as a messiah before he has accomplished the task of the anointed."[24] In other words, before the title can begin to have any true meaning, the Messiah's real mission must be realized. Although Yeshua, the Teacher of Righteousness, and Simon of Kosebah had totally different goals, Yeshua's reticence is more readily understood in light of these parallels. So the Messiah Yeshua took the title "Son of Man," and set out to demonstrate who He is, through first, His teaching and testimony about Himself, and second, the works that He accomplished. Sadly, while Yeshua could be regarded as a great teacher and even a prophet, both in His day as well as today, His own message concerning Himself has gone unheeded.

The Teaching of Yeshua

Yeshua presented His teaching and preaching in unique ways. At the very beginning of his ministry, in the Sermon on the Mount, which comprised six major lessons, we find Him stating over and over, "I say to you" (see Mattai 5:22, 28, 32, 34, 39, 44). No religious leader of that day would dare to utter such a statement. Teaching was understood to be a compendium of what other sages and rabbis had taught. Yeshua, however, dared to violate that methodology and say, "I." No wonder people exclaimed that He taught as "like one who had authority, not like their experts in the law" (Mattai 7:29). But then again, He was no mere man.

Yeshua's teaching was both sublime and down to earth. Much of His imagery was taken from simple home life: the farm, the carpenter's bench, the fishing at Yam Kinneret (the Sea of Galilee). His words spoke to the depths of hardship, suffering, and pain that the common people experienced. Yeshua Himself knew that kind of life: born in a cave where the animals were kept, He grew up also in a cave in Nazareth. He spoke of a woman who carefully swept the floor, looking for a lost coin that would possibly be the difference whether the family ate that night or not (see Luke 15:8–10). Could this have been His own mother? Was His own family poor? Somewhere between the time Yeshua was twelve and thirty years of age, Joseph must have died; since Yeshua was the oldest, He had to assume the headship of the family and be the main supporter of the family, working as a carpenter. The hands that fashioned the worlds were also the roughened hands that shaped the implements at the carpenter's bench where He worked. No wonder He could speak the heart language of the poor, downtrodden, homeless, and sick.

But Yeshua's teaching did not speak only to the average person. Yeshua could also relate to the religious leaders as well, for example, to a *baal torah*, an expert in the Law, who had asked Him how he might inherit eternal life. Yeshua replied with a counterquestion—the typical repartee of teaching—"What is written in the Torah? . . . How do you read it?" To this, the *baal torah* answered by citing Deuteronomy 6:5 as well as Leviticus 19:18. Yeshua's response to the expert in the Law was that he had responded well; now, if he would live it out in his life, he would find the answer to his question. Merely citing the Scripture, however, did not satisfy this expert; he wanted an explanation as to who indeed was his neighbor. Yeshua then *applied* the Torah and reminded His questioner that his neighbor was not merely one he admired and loved but the Samaritan as well, the one who had put his love into action and cared for the Jewish man who had been attacked and left for dead. And so, if the expert would really love his neighbor, it made no difference as to what was the nationality or race. He was to do as the Samaritan did: he was to *live* what the Torah asked him to do, not merely *cite* one Scripture after another.

The Deeds of Yeshua

A quick perusal of how Mattai related the claims of Yeshua's works is interesting (in Mattai 8:1–9:8; 9:23–26). Since this *shaliach* presented Yeshua's testimony of teaching and deeds to the people of Israel, he therefore had a strategy in his exposition that needs careful attention.

Yeshua as Healer. Yeshua is the healer, caring for all who came to Him: The leper who desired to be cleansed; the Roman officer who asked the Messiah to only give the word and fully expected his servant to be healed from his paralysis; Kefa's mother-in-law healed with merely a touch on her hand; and finally, the account of how He healed the multitudes, exactly as the prophet had predicted:

> But he lifted up our illnesses,
> he carried our pain;

even though we thought he was being punished,
attacked by God, and afflicted for something he had done. (Isaiah 53:4)

After he came down from the mountain, large crowds followed him. And a leper approached, and bowed low before him, saying, "Lord, if you are willing, you can make me clean." He stretched out his hand and touched him saying, "I am willing. Be clean!" Immediately his leprosy was cleansed. Then Yeshua said to him, "See that you do not speak to anyone, but go, show yourself to a priest, and bring the offering that Moses commanded, as a testimony to them."

When he entered Capernaum, a centurion came to him asking for help: "Lord, my servant is lying at home paralyzed, in terrible anguish." Yeshua said to him, "I will come and heal him." But the centurion replied, "Lord, I am not worthy to have you come under my roof. Instead, just say the word and my servant will be healed. For I too am a man under authority, with soldiers under me. I say to this one, 'Go' and he goes, and to another 'Come' and he comes, and to my slave 'Do this' and he does it." When Yeshua heard this he was amazed and said to those who followed him, "I tell you the truth, I have not found such faith in anyone in Israel! I tell you, many will come from the east and west to share the banquet with Abraham, Isaac, and Jacob in the kingdom of heaven, but the sons of the kingdom will be thrown out into the outer darkness, where there will be weeping and gnashing of teeth." Then Yeshua said to the centurion, "Go; just as you believed, it will be done for you." And the servant was healed at that hour.

Now when Yeshua entered Kefa's house, he saw his mother-in-law lying down, sick with a fever. He touched her hand, and the fever left her. Then she got up and began to serve them. When it was evening, many demon-possessed people were brought to him. He drove out the spirits with a word, and healed all who were sick. In this way what was spoken by Isaiah the prophet was fulfilled:

"He took our weaknesses and carried our diseases." (Mattai 8:1–17)

In all these instances, Yeshua in His healings exhibited the power entrusted to Him by God as the Son of Man.

Yeshua as Teacher. Yeshua is the superb teacher and one can learn much by reading and re-creating the accounts of how He related to people. One of the Jewish teachers, perhaps one of His disciples, declared his readiness to follow no matter where that might lead. But then Yeshua made a strange observation:

> Now when Yeshua saw a large crowd around him, he gave orders to go to the other side of the lake. Then an expert in the law came to him and said, "Teacher, I will follow you wherever you go." Yeshua said to him, "Foxes have dens, and the birds in the sky have nests, but the Son of Man has no place to lay his head." (Mattai 8:18–20)

While the animals and birds had their places of refuge, no promise of material comfort, lodging, or food was guaranteed for Yeshua or His disciples. Why did the Messiah offer such a bleak prospect to this teacher? The challenge was directed to his motives: he already had prestige, a home, and sufficient food but by following Yeshua, did he think he would have greater influence and authority? No, if he would come after the Messiah, he must count the cost and not be impetuous.

Another disciple meekly announced his intention to follow Yeshua but he wanted to first bury his father:

> Another of the disciples said to him, "Lord, let me first go and bury my father." But Yeshua said to him, "Follow me, and let the dead bury their own dead." (Mattai 8:21–22)

On the surface, the request sounds reasonable to Western ears, but the cultural scene must be understood if the Messiah's remarks are to be understood. Had this young man's father just died? If so, he certainly would not be roaming around in the marketplace following the other disciples. His place would have been at home with his family. Was his father *about to* die? Again, the son would not have been with the Messiah; he would be home instead with his family. Yeshua's implied question was: When would this disciple's father die?

And so, issuing a command with the force, "Follow me, *now*," He intimated that this man must not shrink back from doing the will of God, not even because of such an important matter as the death of a close family member. Certainly, living in that culture, one would not ignore the death of a father, but the will of God must ever be important, even prior to that of caring for the family. In these examples of Yeshua the teacher, as the Son of Man, everyone who heard Him sensed the hand of God on Him.

The Mysterious Nature of His Deeds. After the disciples and Yeshua entered a boat, they set out to cross Yam Kinneret (the Sea of Galilee) to the other side:

> As he got into the boat, his disciples followed him. And a great storm developed on the sea so that the waves began to swamp the boat. But he was asleep. So they came and woke him up saying, "Lord, save us! We are about to die!" But he said to them, "Why are you cowardly, you people of little faith?" Then he got up and rebuked the winds and the sea, and it was dead calm. And the men were amazed and said, "What sort of person is this? Even the winds and the sea obey him!" (Mattai 8:23–27)

Windstorms such as these do occur at times when the wind whistles through the valleys between the hills surrounding the sea, and the waves can be stirred to such heights that boats can easily swamp and sink.

When Yeshua was awakened, His response was to rebuke His disciples because of their fear, but then He faced the winds and raging waves:

> So he got up and rebuked the wind, and said to the sea, "Be quiet! Calm down!" Then the wind stopped, and it was dead calm. (Mark 4:39)

Almost instantly, the winds died down, the sea became calm, and the ride appeared so serene compared to just a few moments previously. No wonder the disciples were amazed, recognizing His *control over nature*.

On the other side of the Kinneret lake, almost immediately two demon-possessed men ran to Yeshua and His disciples:

> When he came to the other side, to the region of the Gadarenes, two demon-possessed men coming from the tombs met him. They were extremely violent, so that no one was able to pass by that way. They cried out, "Son of God, leave us alone! Have you come here to torment us before the time?" A large herd of pigs was feeding some distance from them. Then the demons begged him, "If you drive us out, send us into the herd of pigs." And he said, "Go!" So they came out and went into the pigs, and the herd rushed down the steep slope into the lake and drowned in the water. The herdsmen ran off, went into the town, and told everything that had happened to the demon-possessed men. Then the entire town came out to meet Yeshua. And when they saw him, they begged him to leave their region. (Mattai 8:28–34)

Interestingly, the demons, using the vocal chords of the two unfortunate men, addressed Him as the Son of God, instinctively recognizing His supreme uniqueness. The Messiah made no pretense of answering them, even though they inquired concerning torturing them before the appointed time of judgment. His only comment was when they asked to be sent into the herd of pigs, telling them, "Go!" and the two men were delivered from their nightmare. Through this act, the Messiah exhibited His authority and *control over the unseen world*, certainly the world of Satan and his powers, but also that of the good side, where God and the angels are. All this underscores the real presence of an unseen world, but also another mysterious side of Yeshua.

On still another occasion, after returning to Tiberia (Tiberius), Yeshua was preaching in a house when four men brought a paralytic to Him:

> After getting into a boat he crossed to the other side and came to his own town. Just then some people brought to him a paralytic lying on a stretcher. When Yeshua saw their faith, he said to the paralytic, "Have courage, son! Your sins are forgiven." Then some of the experts in the

> law said to themselves, "This man is blaspheming!" When Yeshua saw their reaction he said, "Why do you respond with evil in your hearts? Which is easier, to say, 'Your sins are forgiven' or to say, 'Stand up and walk'? But so that you may know that the Son of Man has authority on earth to forgive sins"—then he said to the paralytic—"Stand up, take your stretcher, and go home." And he stood up and went home. When the crowd saw this, they were afraid and honored God who had given such authority to men. (Mattai 9:1–8)

Yeshua's challenge here was, in so many words, "Whoever has the ultimate authority to heal also has the ultimate authority to forgive sins!" And with the pronouncement, "Stand up, take your stretcher, and go home," following by the man's arising, the people realized another aspect of this Messiah's mystery: He has authority to forgive sins, even as the Father does!

Finally, Mattai recounts how a ruler (actually a synagogue ruler, possibly the president; compare Mark 5:22) came to Yeshua asking for Him to come and raise his daughter to life again:

> As he was saying these things, a ruler came, bowed low before him, and said, "My daughter has just died, but come and lay your hand on her and she will live." Yeshua and his disciples got up and followed him. . . .
>
> When Yeshua entered the ruler's house and saw the flute players and the disorderly crowd, he said, "Go away, for the girl is not dead but asleep." And they began making fun of him. But when the crowd had been put outside, he went in and gently took her by the hand, and the girl got up. And the news of this spread throughout that region. (Mattai 9:18, 19, 23–26)

This account reveals how well known the Messiah was and that He had a following of a vast multitude, rather than the handful of people some of the Jewish religious leaders would have us believe. He put out everyone after they had laughed Him to scorn when He said the girl had not died but had actually fallen asleep. Yeshua entered the room where the dead girl's body lay on a cot,[25] took her by the hand, and according to the account in Mark 5:41, said in Aramaic, *Taleyeta' kumi*, "Little girl, get up!" The news of this event spread everywhere and once more, the mystery of Yeshua is that He has *control over life*. In the first Passover, God sent His death angel throughout the land of Egypt and the life of the firstborn of man and animals was taken; in this account, Yeshua the Messiah is the one who can give life, even as He had announced:

> The thief comes only to steal and kill and destroy; I have come so that they may have life, and may have it abundantly. (Yohanan 10:10)

A Call for a Decision About Yeshua's Identity. At the midpoint of His ministry, after the disciples had heard Yeshua's teaching and saw His many deeds for about a year and a half, He asked them a question:

> When Yeshua came to the area of Caesarea Philippi, he asked his disciples, "Who do people say that the Son of Man is?" They answered, "Some say Yohanan the Immerser, others Elijah, and others Jeremiah or one of the prophets." He said to them, "But who do you say that I am?" Shimon Kefa answered, "You are the Messiah, the Son of the living God." And Yeshua answered him, "You are blessed, Shimon son of Jonah, because flesh and blood did not reveal this to you, but my Father in heaven!" (Mattai 16:13–17)

His challenge, "Who do you say I am?" was a searching question that called for a statement of faith. And in fact Kefa replied with conviction, after which Yeshua affirmed that no mere man could convince anyone of this mysterious connection within Himself, namely, His humanity (as "the Messiah" in verse 16) and His deity (as "the Son of the living God" in the same verse). Only God could have revealed this to open hearts ready to consider seriously the claims of Yeshua because of His teaching and deeds. It was evident that the disciples agreed with Kefa's proclamation.

Yeshua's Open Confession of His Humanity and Deity. At various points in His ministry, Yeshua's claims concerning His identity did not go unnoticed.

The Pharisees. At the end of His ministry when Yeshua was confronted by some of the Pharisees, He openly challenged their thinking concerning Messiah. To the Pharisees who questioned Him as to the greatest commandment of the Law, He gave the standard response of the day and appeared they were satisfied. But, as these spiritual leaders were present, Yeshua then put forth a seemingly innocent question:

> While the Pharisees were assembled, Yeshua asked them a question: "What do you think about the Messiah? Whose son is he?" They said, "The son of David." He said to them, "How then does David by the Spirit call him 'Lord,' saying,
> 'The Lord said to my lord,
> "Sit at my right hand,
> until I put your enemies under your feet'"?
> If David then calls him 'Lord,' how can he be his son?" No one was able to answer him a word, and from that day on no one dared to question him any longer. (Mattai 22:41–46)

The response "the son of David" was a calculated one. But then came the second provocative question. The crux of the argument centered on the interpretation of Psalm 110:1, and in pressing the point, Yeshua queried further, "If David then calls him 'Lord,' how can he be his son?" To this challenge, the Pharisees had no reply. But what was Yeshua doing? He had cut across the tradition of de-anthropomorphizing the deity and demonstrated the distinct mysterious possibility: He is the son of David, that is, referring to His humanity, but when David alluded to Him as "my Lord," the mystery characteristic of the Messiah is disclosed, that is, His deity.

At Yeshua's trial. Yeshua faced the Sanhedrin at His trial. False witness after false witness was rejected as the court rightfully tested their claims and judged them to be admissible. Finally, Qayafa accepted the witness of two who made the claim they heard Yeshua say He could destroy the temple and then rebuild it in three days:

> Yeshua replied, "Destroy this temple and in three days I will raise it up again." (Yohanan 2:19)

Their testimony was obviously a matter of exactly what these witnesses actually heard Yeshua say. But what Yeshua had claimed was the kind of evidence that could be used to test either the truth claims of the witnesses, or, if Yeshua would really respond and reveal His true identity, would confirm His words.

And so, the high priest then asked Yeshua to respond to the charge by the witnesses, yet He kept quiet. The reason is that He did not feel it necessary to respond to the misconstrued charge by these two men. Finally, Qayafa, the high priest, put Yeshua under the Oath of Testimony,[26] which meant that any Jewish person on trial had to respond with the truth. And so then came the most significant question:

> But Yeshua was silent. The high priest said to him, "I charge you under oath by the living God, tell us if you are the Messiah, the Son of God." (Mattai 26:63)

Actually, there are two questions: 1) Is Yeshua the Messiah? and 2) Is Yeshua the Son of God, or, the Son of the Blessed One? Note that the high priest was well aware of His claims as a result of His witness through His teaching as well as His deeds.

To the first question, Yeshua had no difficulty confirming His Messiahship:

> Yeshua said to him, "You have said it yourself. But I tell you, from now on you will see the Son of Man sitting at the right hand of the Power and coming on the clouds of heaven." (Mattai 26:64)

To which Qayafa and the Sanhedrin made no comment, for they were quite willing to accept Him as a man, maybe a superhuman being, but still a man. To this day, there are many traditional Jewish authorities who could agree to acknowledge Yeshua in a Messiahship role, if it is viewed solely through His humanity.

But the second question is what produced the watershed, and in response to it, Yeshua did not answer on His own but replied by paraphrasing Daniel 7:13, and then applying it to Himself,

I was watching in the night visions,
And with the clouds of the sky
one like a son of man was approaching.
He went up to the Ancient of Days
and was escorted before him. (Daniel 7:13)

Yeshua said to him, "You have said it yourself. But I tell you, from now on you will see the Son of Man sitting at the right hand of the Power and coming on the clouds of heaven." (Mattai 26:64)

No doubt was left in the mind of Qayafa as to the implications of the proclamation. Not only was Yeshua human, but He actually had the nerve in that society to claim to have the right to cross the barrier between God and man, to come directly into God's presence and even to sit at His right hand—as deity, again in a mystery. Yeshua claimed a unique relationship with His Father.

And that is where the matter rests to this day. While Yeshua can be accepted by the Jewish community as a great teacher and even a prophet, and to some extent as a Messiah, His claims as to the mystery of His deity are ignored or misconstrued, and still bring a denial of who Him really is.

Some Responses to Yeshua's Claims

Response by the Jewish Community in the Second Century

When Messianic Jews gave witness to Yeshua as Messiah following the destruction of the temple, the rabbis of the Tannaitic period drew sharp lines as to what passages formerly understood as messianic could still be employed as such and which ones had to be reinterpreted. As a case in point, on one occasion Rabbi Akiva was reprimanded of his interpretation of the plural word "thrones" in Daniel 7:9. In explaining the plural, Akiva gave the traditional answer based on the Written Torah: "One [throne] was for Himself and one for David," i.e., one for God and one for Messiah the son of David. Rabbi Yose severely criticized him: "Akiba, how long wilt thou profane the *Shechinah*? Rather, one [throne] for justice, and the other for mercy."[27]

Testimony of Messianic Jews Through the Second Century

Daniélou considered how Messianic Jews proclaimed the uniqueness of Yeshua, with the term *the Name*:

> The beginnings of this Christology of the Name are already to be found in the New Testament. On the one hand Old Testament texts mentioning the Name are frequently quoted in the New Testament. Thus *Acts* 15:17, quoting *Amos*. 9:12, reads: 'All the Gentiles, upon whom my Name is called . . .' Paul (*Rom*. 2:24) mentions *Is*. 52:5: 'The Name of God is blasphemed among the Gentiles because of you.' The same Epistle quotes *Ex*. 9:16: 'that my Name might be published abroad in all the earth' (*Rom*. 9:17) . . . In these various quotations the Name can in fact only mean Yahweh, but it is hard to see why these texts should have been collected in messianic dossiers unless the Name had appeared to have some relation to Christ. There are, moreover, some passages in which this relationship is explicitly stated. Thus *Joel* 3:5: 'Whosoever shall call upon the Name of the Lord shall be saved' is quoted in *Acts* 2:21 and 4:12 in a somewhat indeterminate sense. But the same text is repeated in *Rom*. 10:12, as follows: '(Christ) is the same Lord (*Kurios*) of all, and is rich unto all that call upon him: for, Whosoever shall call upon the Name of the Lord shall be saved.' Here the Name is clearly that of Christ; . . .[28]

What can we then conclude? Instead of using the title *Son of God*, Jewish believers spoke of Yeshua as *the Name*, an unquestionably Jewish term that would emphasize His uniqueness.

Daniélou also points out the peculiar use of the words *law* and *covenant*. The Greek *nomos* (or, Hebrew *Torah*) was used in such a way as to emphasize the uniqueness of Yeshua. Exactly because the Torah is somehow regarded as the presence of the divine Word, this designation becomes a very appropriate means of describing Yeshua as the living Torah:

> One of the first passages to be considered occurs in Hermas and treats of the vision of an immense willow-tree: 'This great tree which

> over-shadows plains and mountains and all the earth is the Law of God (*nomos theou*) which was given to the whole world; and this Law is the Son of God preached unto the ends of the earth' (Sim. VIII, 3:2). The text could hardly be more explicit. The Law is the name of the Son of God. This is clearly an archaic expression in which *nomos* takes the place of *logos*, which never occurs in the Shepherd . . .
>
> . . . Quoting the Preaching of Peter Clement of Alexandria writes: 'In the Preaching of Peter you will find the Lord called *Law* and *Word* (*nomos kai logos*)' (Strom. I, 182:3) . . .
>
> . . . In Justin . . . in the *Dial.* XXIV, 1 he writes 'There is now another Covenant; another Law has gone forth from Sion, Yeshua the Messiah.' Justin again refers to Isaiah . . . a little further on: 'The Son of God . . . Christ . . . was proclaimed as about to come as an everlasting Law (*nomos*) and new Covenant for the whole world' (*Dial.* XLIII, 1). It will be noticed that Christ is here called at the same time both Law and Covenant (*diatheke*). . . .
>
> . . . This conception of Christ as the Covenant is found several times in Justin: 'The new Covenant (*kaine diatheke*) which had long since been proclaimed by God was now already present, that is to say, the Christ himself' (*Dial.* LI, 3). It is interesting to note that the expression had already been applied to the person of Christ by the Epistle of Barnabas, which quotes Is. 42:6: 'I have given thee to be a covenant of the peoples' (XIV, 7). The text of Isaiah applying the word Covenant to the Servant justified its application to Christ. In connection with this same text of Isaiah, Justin writes: 'What is the covenant of God? Is it not Christ?' (*Dial.* CXXII, 5; cf. also CXVIII, 3; CXII, 4).[29]

Therefore, because of Jewish comprehension of the uniqueness of Yeshua, Messianic Jews dared to equate Him with the *Living Torah* and the *New Covenant*, terms that certainly underscored His deity.

Also relevant to this are the terms *arche* and *hemera* (*day*), two additional terms that were used in reference to Yeshua. This is fully described by Daniélou.[30]

These designations cited by the early ante-Nicene Fathers, although they do not furnish us with a full theology, nevertheless provide ample information concerning the understanding of Yeshua by Messianic Jews. We get a glimpse of how rich their testimony must have been in the Jewish community.

The tragedy is that the Messianic Jewish presence disappeared after the total Arabization of the land in the 600s. There remained isolated instances of Jewish believers over the centuries bearing testimony to the uniqueness of Yeshua among their brethren. But the task facing us today is much the same as it was in the first century at the end of the Second Temple period. We still wrestle with the Jewish community over the major watershed of how to conceive of the Messiah who is both human and divine.

In conclusion, Yeshua's affirmations of His humanity and His deity are based on a literal understanding of the Hebrew Scriptures, rather than being an interpretation made through the tinted sunglasses of tradition, which sometimes does not accurately reflect what the Written Law declares. That Yeshua is both human and divine also became the emphasis of Sha'ul in his "Messiahology" when sharing the gospel with non-Jewish people. What has to be underscored is: our people need to listen and assess carefully what Yeshua said concerning Himself, and not simply explain away His full-orbed identity.

EIGHT

A Major Watershed of Thought at the End of the Second Temple Period

PART TWO

How Can the Messiah Both Initiate the Kingdom and Yet Also Die for Our Sins?

THE TESTIMONY OF THE ISAIAH TARGUM AND ISAIAH 52:13–53:12

In the previous chapter, we saw the development of the concept that the Messiah would be only human. There is however no evidence of a Jewish understanding that the Messiah son of David would suffer and die for our sins. This writer suggests that when dealing with the key passages that believers associate with Messiah's death (Psalm 22; Isaiah 53), the Jewish mindset simply could not conceive of a suffering Messiah son of David. Instead, the suffering was transferred to the nation while the concept of the Messiah was restricted to the one who comes in triumph to establish the Messianic kingdom. Therefore, to think in terms of a Messiah who died was seen as completely inconsistent with His ministry of establishing world peace and restoring Israel to the head of the nations.

A case in point is found in one of the earliest testimonies to how Messiah's ministry was thought of in the later intertestamental period, namely, in the Targum on Isaiah,[1] part of the Targum Yonatan on the Prophets. Much of the Isaiah Targum was already in oral form by Yeshua's day. This makes it a valuable tool in determining the understanding of Isaiah 53 by the Jewish community of that time. For the purpose of comparing the biblical text with the Targum text, the two are set out below side by side, for easy comparison. The biblical text on Isaiah appears on the left side while Targum Isaiah is matched as best as possible on the right side.[2]

Bible (RSV)	**Targum**
Isaiah 52:13 Behold, my servant shall prosper, he shall be exalted and lifted up, and shall be very high.	Behold, my servant, the Messiah, shall prosper, he shall be exalted and increase, and shall be very strong.
Isaiah 52:14 As many were astonished at him—his appearance was so marred, beyond human semblance, and his form beyond that of the sons of men—	Just as the house of Israel hoped for him many days—their appearances were so dark among the peoples, and their aspect beyond that of the sons of men—
Isaiah 52:15 so shall he startle many nations; kings shall shut their mouths because of him; for that which has not been told them they shall see, and that which they have not heard they shall understand.	so he shall scatter many peoples; kings shall be silent because of him, they shall place their hands upon their mouth; for things which have not been told to them they have seen, and that which they have not heard they have understood.
Isaiah 53:1 Who has believed what we have heard? And to whom has the arm of the LORD been revealed?	Who has believed this our report? And to whom has the strength of the mighty arm of the LORD been so revealed?
Isaiah 53:2 For he grew up before him like a young plant, and like a root out of dry ground; he had no form or comeliness that we should look at him, and no beauty that we should desire him.	And the righteous shall be exalted before him, behold, like tufts which sprout, and like a tree which sends its roots by streams of waters, so holy generations will increase on the land which was needing him; his appearance is not a common appearance and his fearfulness is not an ordinary fearfulness, and his brilliance will be holy

Bible (RSV)	Targum
	brilliance, that everyone who looks at him will consider him.
Isaiah 53:3 He was despised and rejected by men; a man of sorrows, and acquainted with grief; and as one from whom men hide their faces he was despised, and we esteemed him not.	Then the glory of all the kingdoms will be for contempt and cease; they will be faint and mournful, behold, as a man of sorrows and appointed for sicknesses; and as when the face of the Shekhinah was taken up from us, they are despised and not esteemed.
Isaiah 53:4 Surely he has borne our griefs and carried our sorrows; yet we esteemed him stricken, smitten by God, and afflicted.	Then he will beseech concerning our sins and our iniquities for his sake will be forgiven; yet we were esteemed wounded, smitten before the LORD and afflicted.
Isaiah 53:5 But he was wounded for our transgressions, he was bruised for our iniquities; upon him was the chastisement that made us whole, and with his stripes we are healed.	And he will build the sanctuary which was profaned for our sins, handed over for our iniquities; and by his teaching his peace will increase upon us, and in that we attach ourselves to his words our sins will be forgiven us.
Isaiah 53:6 All we like sheep have gone astray; we have turned every one to his own way; and the LORD has laid on him the iniquity of us all.	All we like sheep have been scattered; we have gone into exile, every one his own way; and before the LORD it was a pleasure to forgive the sins of us all for his sake.
Isaiah 53:7 He was oppressed, and he was afflicted, yet he opened not his mouth; like a lamb that is led to the slaughter, and like a sheep that before its shearers is dumb, so he opened not his mouth.	He beseeches, and he is answered, and before he opens his mouth he is accepted; the strong ones of the peoples he will hand over like a lamb to the sacrifice, and like a ewe which before its shearers is dumb, so there is not before him one who opens his mouth or speaks a saying.
Isaiah 53:8 By oppression and judgment he was taken away; and as for his generation, who considered that he was cut off out of the land of the living,	From bonds and retribution he will bring our exiles near; the wonders which will be done for us in his days, who will be able to recount? For he will take away

Bible (RSV)	Targum
stricken for the transgression of my people?	the rule of the Gentiles from the land of Israel; the sins which my people sinned he will cast on to them.
Isaiah 53:9 And they made his grave with the wicked, and with a rich man in his death, although he had done no violence, and there was no deceit in his mouth.	And he will hand over the wicked to Gehenna and those rich in possessions which they robbed to the death of the corruption, lest those who commit sin be established, and speak of possessions with their mouth.
Isaiah 53:10 Yet it was the will of the LORD to bruise him; he has put him to grief; when he makes himself an offering for sin, he shall see his offspring, he shall prolong his days; the will of the LORD shall prosper in his hand;	Yet before the LORD it was a pleasure to refine and to cleanse the remnant of his people, in order to purify their soul from sins; they shall see the kingdom of their Messiah, they shall increase sons and daughters, they shall prolong days; those who perform the law of the LORD shall prosper in his pleasure;
Isaiah 53:11 he shall see the fruit of the travail of his soul and be satsified; by his knowledge shall the righteous one, my servant, make many to be accounted righteous; and he shall bear their iniquities.	from the slavery of the Gentiles he shall deliver their soul, they shall see the retribution of their adversaries. They shall be satisfied with the plunder of their kings; by his wisdom shall he make innocents to be accounted innocent, to subject many to the law; and he shall beseech concerning their sins.
Isaiah 53:12 Therefore I will divide him a portion with the great, and he shall divide the spoil with the strong; because he poured out his soul to death, and was numbered with the transgressors; yet he bore the sin of many, and made intercession for the transgressors.	Then I will divide him the plunder of many peoples, and he shall divide the spoil, the possessions of strong fortresses; because he handed over his soul to the death, and subjected the rebels to the law; yet he will beseech concerning the sins of many, and to the rebels it shall be forgiven for him.

The Isaiah Targum's View of the Messiah

This well-known portion of the Tanach, Isaiah 52:13–53:12, has two emphases: First, the Messiah is personal, the Servant and Anointed One; second, the future kingdom of peace is designated as the kingdom of the Anointed One.[3] The people of Judea at the end of the Second Temple period had not given up on a concept of a personal Messiah at whose appearance the kingdom of peace would commence, with Israel again be at the head of the nations.

But the Targum treats this passage in an unusual manner. The nation Israel is described as suffering for its *own* sins.[4] Note particularly how this contrasts markedly with modern Jewish thought in which Israel suffers for the sins of the entire world and no belief exists in a personal Messiah.[5] But in Yeshua's day, the mentions of suffering in this chapter is relegated to the nation who will lament and agonize in pain; while all references to exaltation are applied to the Messiah as a human being. It seemed unthinkable that the promised Messiah should suffer at all.

What Does the Text of Isaiah Say?

Such treatment in the Isaiah Targum text does not square with the plain sense of the biblical text where sufferings and glories are ascribed to *one and the same person*.[6] The text of Isaiah very clearly indicates: ". . . though the LORD makes his life a guilt offering," or, alternatively translated, "You shall make of his soul an offering from sin" (Isaiah 53:10). Both renderings are possible. Either way, the subject in this chapter is the one whose soul is made an offering for sin. But suppose it is granted that the one mentioned in this verse is the nation. Sacrifices, however, must be perfect, without spot or blemish. Yet the same prophet who is supposed to be describing the suffering of the nation confesses that Israel is sick:

> From the soles of your feet to your head,
> there is no spot that is unharmed.
> There are only bruises, cuts,
> and open wounds.
> They have not been cleansed or bandaged,
> nor have they been treated with olive oil. (Isaiah 1:6)

It is true that the nation did suffer for its own sins, and the reason for that suffering was that they were far from God in the prophet's day. In the text of Isaiah 52:13–53:12, however, Israel cannot be the means of suffering as an atonement for its own sins. The subject of the chapter is other than the nation; it is a *person* on whom the Lord has laid all our sins:

> We all, like sheep, have gone astray, each of us has turned to his own way; and the LORD has *laid on him* the iniquity of us all. (Isaiah 53:6 NIV, emphasis added)

A Mediatorial Ministry

The Messiah also has a mediatorial ministry as he prays on behalf of Israel's sins and iniquities. He prays on behalf of Israel's transgressions and the nation is pardoned for his sake; he also prays for Israel before the Almighty and is answered before he even opens his mouth; and finally, he makes intercession and the rebellious shall be forgiven for his sake.[7] But a serious question remains; while the Messiah may be described in terms of suffering vicariously, this is not sufficient in itself to accomplish an atonement for sin. If the passage calls for one to make of his soul an offering for sin (Isaiah 53:10), then the mediator must actually die in the place of the one he represents. Another aspect of mediation describes him as actually delivering his soul unto death,[8] but this is the only reference in the Targum Isaiah referring to a mediator's supposed death. However, does it mean the Messiah actually died as an atonement for sin? It would seem that what is described here in the Targum still does not include what an atoning sacrifice would mean where the Messiah makes expatiation, that is, he dies on behalf of Israel and for the sins of mankind.[9]

The Testimony of the Outside Books

The only other body of literature that has much to say about the Messiah son of David is in the *sifrim hisonim* (Outside Books), that is, the Apocrypha and the Pseudepigrapha.

Many of the Apocryphal books depict the Messiah as the Anointed One who reigns over a delivered Israel and a rebuilt Jerusalem.

The *Testament of Judah* (2nd c. B.C.E.) says that the Messiah is the "Shoot of God" (i.e., the Branch), as well as the "fountain for the life of all humanity"; the scepter of his kingdom will shine and he will be a "rod of righteousness for the nations, to judge and to save all that call on the Lord" (24:4–6; "nations" referring to the Gentiles; Charlesworth, 801, see footnote).[10]

The *Testament of Naphtali* (2nd c. B.C.E.) states that after a second defection of the children of Israel, the Messiah will come who "effects righteousness, and he will work mercy on all who are far and near" (4:4–5; Charlesworth, 812).

The *Testament of Levi* (2nd c. B.C.E.) asserts that the Lord will raise up a new priest who will reign on the earth righteously and "effect the judgment of truth over the earth for many days"; during his ministry, "the knowledge of the Lord will be poured out on the earth like the water of the seas," and this priest "will open the gates of paradise" (ch. 18; Charlesworth, 794–95. "Poured out on the earth" means "among the Gentiles").

1 Enoch (2nd c. B.C.E.–1st c C.E.) refers to the Messiah as "the Righteous One" (38:2); he is "the Elect One" (40:5); he is "chosen" by God, the one who "will open all the hidden storerooms" (46:3). He is called the "Messiah" (Anointed One) standing before the "Lord of the Spirits" (48:10). In him "dwells the spirit of wisdom" (49:3). All wealth is created to serve the dominion of God's Anointed (ch. 52). The Messiah is "the Righteous and Elect One" at the head of "the house of his congregation"; the time is coming when this congregation "shall not be hindered" by wicked people (53:6). He is also to reign over his dominion when Jerusalem is rebuilt after a great judgment (90:30–38) (Charlesworth, 30, 32, 34, 36, 37, 38, 71).

The *Psalms of Solomon* (1st c. B.C.E.) picture all that people have ever hoped for concerning Messiah's reign over Israel: "he will gather a holy people" (17:26); "he will purge Jerusalem" (17:30); "he will strike the earth with the word of his mouth forever" (17:35) and purify it from sin. The Lord himself is king and people will "see the good things of the Lord which he will do for the coming generation; . . ." (18:6) (Charlesworth, 2: 667, 668, 669).

The *Sibylline Oracles* (2nd–1st c. B.C.E. for the portions of Book 3 quoted here[11]) states there is a time coming when "a holy prince will come to gain sway over the scepters of the earth forever"; he will bring judgment on the wicked in general, and in particular, Rome (3:49–56). The *Oracles* state furthermore that there will come "a King from the sun who will stop the entire earth from evil war"; he will rule "in obedience to the noble teachings of the great God" (3:652–56) and he will "shield" the righteous in the kingdom and encircle them as "as if he had a wall of blazing fire round about" (3:705–6). The Messiah will bring upon evil men a great judgment; and in the rule of the Messianic empire, "from every land they will bring incense and gifts to the house of the great God" (3:772–73) (Charlesworth, 363, 376, 377, 379).

The *Assumption of Moses*, otherwise known as the *Testament of Moses* (1st c. C.E.), describes how the Messiah as the "Heavenly One" will "arise from his kingly throne" and "go forth from his holy habitation with indignation and wrath on behalf of his sons," in other words, to fight on behalf of the righteous (10:3; Charlesworth, 932).

2 Baruch (2nd c. C.E.) speaks of "the Anointed One" (that is, the Messiah) who "will begin to be revealed" at the beginning of the kingdom (29:3); and "when the time of the appearance of the Anointed One has been fulfilled and he returns with glory," "then all who sleep in hope of him will rise" (30:1; that is, be resurrected, a reference to believers in the days of the Tanach); and there will be "bright waters which come at the end after these black ones" (72:1), that is, after a tribulation of darkened days the principate of the Messiah will be revealed (Charlesworth, 630, 631, 645).

The Testimony of the Dead Sea Scrolls: A "Slain Messiah"?

One of the most recently published fragments from the *War Scroll* of the Qumran literature supposedly depicts a Messiah figure who is slain. Such at least is the contention of Professor Robert Eisenman of Long Beach,

California. He had long taught that there were close links between Qumran and the early believers in Yeshua, both communities sharing a belief in a Messiah who was to die.

In this discussion, we cannot adequately cover all the details because of all the technicalities involved in an examination of this particular fragment. This writer commented in an editorial article in the *Moody Student* newspaper of Moody Bible Institute as follows:

> . . . this interpretation [of Eisenman] is now being challenged by numerous reputable scholars. Everyone agrees that the specific source under investigation is indeed a "mutilated fragment . . . suitable as a basis for a revolutionary thesis" according to the noted Qumran scholar Geza Vermes (*British Jewish Chronicle*, 10 January 1992). He had convened an Oxford seminar to study the fragment in question, and three different possibilities seem apparent, including the killing of the Messianic figure. The other two suggestions, however, are equally valid!
>
> Stephen Read of the Ancient Biblical Center study group in Claremont, Calif. calls Eisenman's view a "major interpretative jump," saying that it is impossible to clearly conclude from the fragment construction the death of a Messiah. Eugene Ullrich of the Notre Dame center for the study of the Scrolls declares that Eisman's [sic] suggestion is not explosive or revolutionary but after all is said and done, there is nothing conclusive.[12]

Since then, most scholars who have examined the fragment under consideration agree with the majority considered opinion that the people of Qumran do not appear to refer to a "slain Messiah" in their documents.

Having studied the literature of the intertestamental period, including Qumran, this writer feels it is best to conclude that this community did believe their priestly leader to be Messiah, but they also believed in the coming of the Messiah son of David. But apart from this controversial passage, nowhere else in the actual Qumran literature has any reference been found to the notion of a dying Messiah.

THE TESTIMONY OF THE NEW COVENANT

Let us now look at the various passages in which the disciples consider the concept of the death of the Messiah son of David.

Yeshua's First Announcement of His Death

After Kefa's great confession that Yeshua is the Messiah, the Son of the living God in Mattai 16:16, we read that:

> From that time on Yeshua began to show his disciples that he must go to Jerusalem and suffer many things at the hands of the elders, chief priests, and experts in the law, and be killed, and on the third day be raised. (Mattai 16:21; compare Mark 8:31; Luke 9:22)

How did Kefa respond to this announcement? Surprisingly, after being commended so favorably by Yeshua for his observations concerning His deity, Kefa practically took Yeshua by the hand, dragged Him across the road, and reacted vocally with a blunt, "God forbid, Lord!" The Messiah then turned on him and proclaimed:

> But he turned and said to Kefa, "Get behind me, Satan! You are a stumbling block to me, because you are not setting your mind on God's interests, but on man's." (Mattai 16:23)

Mark also relates this reaction by Kefa.

While Yeshua in His response was certainly addressing Satan, who had suggested to Kefa's mind the absolute unthinkability of Yeshua's death, the plain sense of Kefa's response is that he and the other disciples *were never schooled in the belief* that a Messiah son of David was supposed to die for our sins, be raised from the dead, and yet still be Israel's deliverer and inaugurator of the Messianic kingdom. When most evangelicals read this account in Mattai, they do not usually ask *why* Kefa responded so violently to Yeshua's statement of His death, except only to say that Satan spoke through him in order to, if possible, thwart the necessity for an atoning death.

Jewish believers, including this writer, understand exactly Kefa's sentiments on this occasion.

Yeshua's Second Announcement of His Death

The next time a disclosure of His death occurred was at this scene with Yeshua and His disciples:

> When they gathered together in Galilee, Yeshua told them, "The Son of Man is going to be betrayed into the hands of men. They will kill him, and on the third day he will be raised." And they became greatly distressed. (Mattai 17:22–23)

Mark also mentions this statement (9:31) and Luke provides a more "bare bones" description (9:44). What should be noted again is the response by the disciples: they "became greatly distressed" (Mattai 17:23). Why should they have such a reaction? Simply, because their concept of a Messiah excluded any notion of His death. Rather, they followed Him because they believed He was the true Messiah who would soon initiate the kingdom of peace.

Yeshua's Third Announcement of His Death

The next occasion when Yeshua announced concerning His impending death was when He and the disciples were on their way to Jerusalem:

> As Yeshua was going up to Jerusalem, he took the twelve aside privately and said to them on the way, "Look, we are going up to Jerusalem, and the Son of Man will be handed over to the chief priests and the experts in the law. They will condemn him to death, and will turn him over to the Gentiles to be mocked and flogged severely and crucified. Yet on the third day, he will be raised." (Mattai 20:17–19)

Mark 10:32–34 and Luke 18:31–33 parallel this passage. One significant difference from Mattai is that Luke has, "We are going up to Jerusalem, and everything that is written about the Son of Man by the prophets will be accomplished." Luke, however, is the only one who adds by way of interpretating the disciples' response:

> But the twelve understood none of these things. This saying was hidden from them, and they did not grasp what Yeshua meant. (Luke 18:34)

By the time Luke wrote those words, the disciples had already gone through the experience of the resurrection. They had already been taught the meaning of the death, burial, and resurrection of Yeshua by the Messiah Himself in His postresurrection ministry, and also had viewed His ascension. Luke's comment is based on what the disciples had already come to realize by the time the gospel was written; by then, the disciples recognized that the Messiah *both* suffers/dies/is resurrected, *and also* in the future will deliver Israel and bring in the kingdom of peace. It is the final event in this sequence that matches what the rabbis indicated regarding Messiah son of David.

Yeshua's Announcement of His Death to Greek Jews

The next mention of Messiah's death is found in Yohanan:

> Now some Greeks were among those who had gone up to worship at the feast. So these approached Philip, who was from Bethsaida in Galilee, and requested, "Sir, we would like to see Yeshua." Philip went and told Andrew, and they both went and told Yeshua. Yeshua replied, "The time has come for the Son of Man to be glorified. I tell you the solemn truth, unless a kernel of wheat falls into the ground and dies, it remains by itself alone. But if it dies, it produces much grain." (Yohanan 12:20–24)

Yohanan penned these words after the loss of the Second Temple. At the time he wrote, he already knew of the necessity for the Messiah to die and be raised from the dead. He understood that the same Messiah would one day come to establish the kingdom of peace on earth. The statement by Yeshua could be construed as cryptic; it would only have made sense to the disciples if they had remembered and believed what He had already announced. Nevertheless, His words do indicate that through His death He would be glorified. When any good kernel is planted in the earth, the outer protective shell dies, but the life remains in the seed inside. Then, when given the opportunity, it brings forth its stem of wheat with many seeds. Similarly, when Yeshua died, His atonement was enacted at a certain point in history. Ever since, when people believe in Him, not only does His vicarious death take sin away, but His life is given to every believer who then in turn can share with others who will also believe. In that way, the Messiah is glorified.

Yeshua's Announcement of His Death Before Passover

The Messiah yet again predicted to His disciples that He would be put to death:

> When Yeshua had finished saying all these things, he told his disciples, "You know that after two days the Passover is coming, and the Son of Man will be handed over to be crucified." (Mattai 26:1–2)

Mattai is the only one of the gospel writers who makes this comment. This time, the disciples make no response. By this point in Yeshua's ministry, they knew perfectly well what He had been saying all along, but for good reason, they did not want to relate to it or consider the possibility in their thinking. They were so under the impression of what mainstream Judaism had been teaching—that no bona fide Messiah son of David was ever to die—that they were not ready to consider any alternative to the idea that the Messiah would appear in glory to initiate the kingdom. This is the same picture that we saw above in the *sifrim hisonim*, the Outside Books.

Both Mark and Luke also remark that the chief priests and scribes were looking for a way to seize Yeshua, arrest Him, and hand Him over to the Romans to be killed (see Mark 14:1–2; Luke 22:2). Since both writers were writing from the vantage point of time years after Yeshua's death, they presented their case as those who were already convinced of the meaning of Yeshua's death.

Yeshua's Announcement of His Death at the Passover Table

The next occasion where the Messiah graphically described His coming death was at the Passover table. Yeshua participated in the Jewish Passover of His day, many details of which are provided in the Mishnah tractate *Pesahim*.[13] In the Passover of that time, after partaking of the roast lamb, the next step was to take the third cup, called the cup of redemption. But Yeshua introduced a new concept into the course of the Passover; after the meat, He reached for the unleavened bread on the table,[14] broke it into pieces, and gave it to everyone present to eat. As He did so He said:

> Then he took bread, and after giving thanks he broke it and gave it to them, saying, "This is my body which is given for you. Do this in remembrance of me." (Luke 22:19)

Following the bread, Yeshua then took the third cup, the cup after supper, the cup of redemption. This cup signified the divine deliverance of Israel from Egypt. Yeshua, however, now added a new meaning, declaring:

> And in the same way he took the cup after they had eaten, saying, "This cup that is poured out for you is the new covenant in my blood." (Luke 22:20)

What did the disciples understand about these two elements? We have no evidence that they comprehended what Yeshua was doing when He made special use of the bread and offered His comments concerning the wine. Similarly, neither did the disciples grasp the full significance of the Messiah dying as our substitute, nor that His blood would be the means to cleanse our sins.

On the Road to Emmaus

On the first day of the week, possibly late afternoon, two of Yeshua's disciples were walking on the road to Emmaus. Frustrated with their lost hope of the commencement of the kingdom, they had been discussing all that had occurred since the Messiah's body was nailed to the tree and He had been buried. As they conversed, Yeshua—in a glorified body—joined them. The full passage in Luke reads as follows:

> Now that very day two of them were on their way to a village called Emmaus, about seven miles from Jerusalem. They were talking to each other about all the things that had happened. While they were talking and debating these things, Yeshua himself approached and began to accompany them (but their eyes were kept from recognizing him). Then he said to them, "What are these matters you are discussing so intently as you walk along?" And they stood still, looking sad. Then one of them, named Cleopas, answered him, "Are you the only visitor to Jerusalem who doesn't know the things that have happened there in these days?" He said to them, "What things?" "The things concerning Yeshua the Nazarene," they replied, "a man who, with his powerful deeds and words, proved to be a prophet before God and all the people; and how our chief priests and rulers handed him over to be condemned to death, and crucified him. But we had hoped that he was the one who was going to redeem Israel. Not only this, but it is now the third day since these things happened. Furthermore, some women of our group amazed us. They were at the tomb early this morning, and when they did not find his body, they came back and said they had seen a vision of angels, who said he was alive. Then some of those who were with us went to the tomb, and found it just as the women had said, but they did not see him." (Luke 24:13–24)

Notice how Cleopas expressed succintly the hopes that all the disciples had had. He described Yeshua as "a man who, with his powerful deeds and words, proved to be a prophet before God and all the people." Cleopas also reflected on the longed-for hope of the people: "But we had hoped that he was the one who was going to redeem Israel."

But then it turns out that Cleopas knew of the reports of the resurrection. In light of that startling information, which confirmed what the Messiah had said all along, we wonder why these two did not remain in Jerusalem to investigate further this strange turn of events. But instead, they returned to Emmaus when they were encountered en route by the Messiah, who sharply reprimanded them for not understanding what Moses and the prophets had predicted: The Messiah son of David was indeed to first suffer and then enter into His glory.

In Connection with the Resurrection

After the death and burial of Yeshua, many other disciples besides Cleopas and his friend left town, while those who remained became greatly disillusioned. If we again ask why, the answer is that their entire focus was on the Messiah's function of redeeming Israel, bringing in the kingdom of peace, rectifying all unrighteousness, and restoring the earth to the idyllic conditions of the garden of Eden.

But they had never been schooled in the fact that the Messiah son of David was to come as the atonement for our sins. Yeshua's attempts to prepare His disciples for His death and resurrection was met with an inability to comprehend and even with repugnance.

When the women reported that the tomb was empty, Kefa and Yohanan ran to see for themselves. The younger disciple, Yohanan, offered in his gospel a penetrating statement concerning his entrance into the empty tomb:

> Then the other disciple, who had reached the tomb first, came in, and he saw and believed. (Yohanan 20:8)

And what did he see? The only articles on the floor of the now-empty tomb were the burial cloth for the head along with the strips of cloth used to wrap the body. Since the latter were left unwrapped, as a kind of shell, Yohanan noted their highly unusual appearance. The significance was that when Yeshua came forth, His body came directly through the cloth strips. Yohanan now realized the truth of what the Messiah had said all along: He was to be raised from the dead. Therefore, "he believed," that is, he now finally accepted all that the Messiah had told His disciples. It is no wonder that, from the perspective of writing some sixty years after the event,[15] Yohanan added:

> (For they did not yet understand the scripture that Yeshua must rise from the dead.) (Yohanan 20:9)

We can say, however, that Yohanan, as he saw the unwrapped grave clothes left on the floor and no body present, finally understood that the Messiah son of David would both die as our atonement and would also be resurrected.

This is a problem that remains for the Jewish community to this day. Yeshua was crucified and buried, and therefore He cannot be the Messiah. He simply does not match what the traditions have declared the Messiah should be. But that is where the testimony must rest: Yeshua said that Moses and the Prophets had described the Messiah as one who must first suffer and then enter into His glory. The challenge remains the same today: we must listen to what Yeshua—and Moses and the Prophets—have to say!

Changes in Teaching Concerning Atonement

The Teaching About Atonement in the Written and Oral Law

The question that now must be raised is if there was any concept of redemption at all in the Jewish thinking at the end of the Second Temple period. Certainly, when one examines the tractate *Yoma*[16] in the Mishnah, such an emphasis certainly existed. Building on what Leviticus 4 and 16 taught, *Yoma* is very precise in its message for the Day of Atonement: The bull was a sin offering for the priest and then two goats were offered on behalf of the people. One of the goats became the goat of sacrifice whose blood was taken into the Holy of Holies, while the second goat was the scapegoat and, with the sins of the nation laid upon it, was taken outside the city with enough distance from it before it was pushed over a cliff and killed.[17]

The prayer that the high priest offered over this scapegoat leaves no question as to the meaning of a sacrifice, in connection not only with the altar but also with sin being taken away:

> Oh God, thy people, the House of Israel, have committed iniquity, transgressed, and sinned before thee. O God, forgive, I pray, the iniquities and transgressions and sins which thy people, the House of Israel, have committed and transgressed and sinned before thee; as it is written

> in the law of thy servant Moses, *For on this day atonement shall be made for you to cleanse you: from all your sins shall ye be clean before the Lord.* And when the priests and the people which stood in the Temple Court heard the Expressed Name come forth from the mouth of the High Priest, they used to kneel and bow themselves and fall down on their faces and say, "Blessed be the name of the glory of his kingdom forever and ever!"[18]

Many of the priests and people within the nation had indeed grasped the significance of atonement in connection with the altar, and knew what it was to have a new life within them. Why then was it so difficult to make the connection between the meaning of the sin offering at the altar and what the Messiah Yeshua did on His altar—on the tree—where He died as the sin offering? Nevertheless, as already pointed out, the disciples and others found it hard to make this transfer.

For that reason, after the resurrection, Yeshua severely scolded the disciples on their way to Emmaus for not understanding what He had been telling them all along:

> Then he said to them, "These are my words that I spoke to you while I was still with you, that everything written about me in the law of Moses and the prophets and the psalms must be fulfilled." Then he opened their minds so they could understand the scriptures, and said to them, "Thus it stands written that the Messiah would suffer and would rise from the dead on the third day, and repentance for the forgiveness of sins would be proclaimed in his name to all nations, beginning from Jerusalem." (Luke 24:44–47)

What the Messiah tried to get people to realize is that once the resurrection had occurred, they should have then been able to "cut through" the Oral Law, which taught that the Messiah would only come with great glory to bring in the kingdom. Ultimately, the point underscored by the writers of the New Covenant was that the resurrection was the great keynote of God's approval of Yeshua's ministry. Without that event, He would have been no different than any other religious leader. The fact that the Messiah

Yeshua is a living person, sitting at God's right hand today, is proof positive that whatever Yeshua said and did had God's stamp of endorsement on Him. Therefore everyone ought to listen all the more carefully to how He interpreted Moses, the Prophets, and the Psalms or Writings: namely, concerning a suffering Messiah who also will one day have the power to initiate the kingdom of peace.

Israel's Response

The loss of the Second Temple in 70 C.E. was a crisis within Israel and everyone recognized the catastrophe. George Foot Moore explains,

> The loss was keenly felt. It is narrated that R. Johanan ben Zakkai was one day going out of Jerusalem accompanied by his disciple, R. Joshua (ben Hananiah). At the site of the temple in ruins, Joshua exclaimed, "Woe to us, for the place where the iniquities of Israel were atoned for is destroyed!"[19]

Two major responses are noted regarding this tragedy of loss of the temple, and a third response appears later on.

First Response: Changes in Scriptural Interpretation. After the loss of the temple and the end of the war with Rome, Messianic Jews used the tragedy as the means to again point out the importance of Yeshua's claims. They reminded their listeners that the fall of Jerusalem had been predicted:

> For the days will come upon you when your enemies will build an embankment against you and surround you and close in on you from every side. They will demolish you—you and your children within your walls—and they will not leave within you one stone on top of another, because you did not recognize the time of your visitation from God. (Luke 19:43–44)

Many listened to the prophecy, realized the truth of what Yeshua had foreseen, and they responded to the atoning work of Israel's Messiah. The result was that a great window of opportunity opened up such that the number of believers in Israel grew; by the end of the first century *perhaps*—and this writer emphasizes *perhaps*—as many as twenty percent of the nation could have acknowledged Yeshua as the Messiah. A good measure of the strength of the witness can be gauged by the reaction of the religious leaders who changed many of the interpretations that Messianic Jews used; the Jewish leaders reinterpreted many of the important portions of the Scriptures as a counteraction to the testimony of genuine believers.[20]

Second Response: The Council of Yavneh and a Religion Without Substitute Atonement. After the temple was lost in 70 C.E., a council of many of the religious leaders, called by Yohanan ben Zakkai, met in Yavneh between 70 and 90 C.E. to make a number of decisions affecting mainline Judaism and primarily to determine the nature of the worship experience of Judea without its main sanctuary. Of course, synagogues already existed in every town and city for Sabbath worship when it was not possible to go to the Jerusalem temple. At this meeting of leading rabbis, Yohanan ben Zakkai became the leading architect of restructuring Judaism into a religion with no substitute atonement. Judaism was now on a course whereby one was made righteous by means of self-effort, which became the basis of traditional belief and practice concerning atonement. This decision also became a direct challenge against the testimony that Yeshua's death is the basis for an atonement for sin.[21]

We have subsequent statements concerning this self-realization. Already by the time of the Talmud, we note that atonement is now made possible by the study of Torah. There, we read that while the descendants of Eli could find no atonement by sacrifice and meat offering, they might receive pardon through the occupation with the study of Torah:

> Therefore I have sworn unto the house of Eli that the iniquity of Eli's house shall not be expiated with sacrifice nor offering. Raba said: With sacrifice and offering it cannot be expiated, but it can be expiated with Torah. Abaye said: With sacrifice and offering it cannot be expiated, but it can be expiated with Torah and charitable deeds.[22]

Also:

> But the study of Torah is more beloved by God than burnt offerings.[23]

In quick succession across the centuries, rabbis have pointed out that prayer, repentance, and the service of "doing charity" become the means of atonement—a far cry from what Yeshua said, that He Himself is the atonement for our sins through His suffering and death.

Third Response: The Concept of Two Messiahs. Another response by the rabbis appears by at least 200 C.E., the proclamation of two Messiahs. First, there is Messiah ben Yosef, who in fighting Israel's enemies, suffers and dies. Then, there is the second Messiah, Messiah ben David, the one who will bring in the Messianic kingdom envisioned by the prophets.

Moore suggests:

> The earliest mention of this Messiah is a report of a difference between a certain R. Dosa and the prevailing opinion of scholars on the question what the mourning in Zechariah 12, 10 . . . is about. One—it is not clear which—said that it was for the Messiah ben Joseph who was killed, the other that it was for the 'evil impulse' which was slain.[24]

But Moore also indicates that "it does not appear how commonly it was accepted among the authorities of the time."[25]

The point is, however, that by the early 200s C.E. a certain rabbi, R. Samuel ben Nahman, declared that "Esau's seed"—meaning Rome—"would be delivered only into the hand of Joseph's seed. . . ."[26] From a passage in Sukkah 52a[27] "it appears that the career of the Josephite Messiah and his death was imagined to precede the coming of the Messiah son of David; but no other particulars are forthcoming."[28]

Subsequently, across the years, the rabbis have used this as an argument against the one Messiah who both suffers, dies, and is resurrected and yet also acts in the role of Messiah ben David. The rabbis now propounded two Messiahs, one who suffers and dies, and the second one who will deliver Israel. It would seem this two-Messiah position became the apologetic against the witness by Messianic Jews as late as the end of 300s, and is still used to this day by the more religious Jew.

Conclusion

Today, most Jewish people no longer believe in a personal Messiah, but rather, in a Messianic kingdom in which all good people work together to create a kingdom of peace.

Concerning the two watershed questions discussed in this and the previous chapters, religious Judaism answers with an emphatic, *No!* The view is that the Messiah is human and perhaps even superhuman, but never divine. This usually becomes a test question regarding the identity of the Messianic Jew when he is confronted by a religious Jewish leader. Does he believe in the deity of Yeshua? If so, then the Jewish community will read this person out of the "family," and declare that the Messianic Jew is no longer a Jew.

Regarding the second issue, the religious Jewish community will again respond, *No!* The Messiah does not suffer and die in the way that is understood when Yeshua is proclaimed. If such is the case, then *He cannot be the Messiah son of David*. For the exact reason that He did not bring in the Messianic kingdom, Yeshua's claims have been compromised. The religious Jew will, however, affirm the concept of two Messiahs, whereby Messiah son of Yosef is the one who suffers and dies fighting Israel's enemies, while the Messiah son of David will yet bring in the Messianic kingdom.

To conclude, we are still faced with the Gordian knot of trying to assert the claims of Yeshua. Believers must have a vested interest in sharing these two major watershed concepts with the Jewish community. When that happens, however, we can expect reactions by the religious Jew. Only the Spirit of God can open the mind and heart of a Jewish person to enable him or her to realize the biblical claims concerning Yeshua the Messiah ben David.

NINE

The Doctrine of the Messiah

With an Emphasis on the Difficult Concepts

In the doctrine of God, we noted that a mystery exists as to His personality. While we may speak of God as a composite unity—Father, Son, and Holy Spirit—we possess only a limited understanding.

We should now turn in our discussion to each of the three persons. It would be logical to begin with a consideration of the Father. However, much of what was discussed under the doctrine of God can be regarded as the doctrine of the Father. Therefore we may proceed to give attention to the doctrines of the Son and Holy Spirit.

We will spend a good deal of time considering what Scripture says concerning the Son as well as the Holy Spirit. The subject of the Son or Messiah entails a number of subtopics, beginning with His preexistence and finishing with His return. In between these two, we will consider such topics as His deity, incarnation, virgin birth, humanity, person, and others.

The doctrines of the Messiah as well as of the Holy Spirit are also important for this reason. The Messiah and the Holy Spirit reveal the Father in unique ways. In the historical manifestation of the Son, the Father is revealed, while one special function of the Holy Spirit is to make this revelation clear.

The Preexistence of the Messiah

We begin with the Messiah's existence before His sojourn on earth. While His preexistence will be considered separately from His deity, the latter is affirmed by a study of this topic. Some in the past have asserted His preexistence but have denied His deity, as for example Arius in the 300s. However, viewed in its fullness, His preexistence actually provides a complete picture of the identity and ministry of the Messiah who was already at work, even before the days of His flesh.

The Messiah's Preexistence in the New Covenant

We begin first with the testimony by Jewish believers as well as by the Messiah Himself:

Testimony of the Messiah. Note the peculiar usage of "I am," which God used of Himself as He revealed Himself to Moses:

> God said to Moses, "I AM THAT I AM." And he said, "You must say this to the Israelites, 'I AM has sent me to you.'" (Exodus 3:14)

Yet note how Yeshua uses this expression of Himself:

> Yeshua said to them, "I tell you the solemn truth, before Abraham came into existence, I am!" (Yohanan 8:58)

In addition we have the following testimony from Yeshua.

> And now, Father, glorify me at your side with the glory I had with you before the world was created. . . . Father, I want those you have given me to be with me where I am, so that they can see my glory that you gave me because you loved me before the creation of the world. (Yohanan 17:5, 24)

Testimony of Yohanan the Immerser. As forerunner of the Messiah, Yohanan also gave a word of testimony.

> Yohanan testified about him and shouted out, "This one was the one about whom I said, 'He who comes after me is greater than I am, because he existed before me.'" (Yohanan 1:15)

Note that the above passages from the Gospel of Yohanan were written after the temple had been destroyed. At that point, Yohanan's strategy was to openly proclaim both the preexistence and the deity of the Messiah. Prior to that time, especially in the first half of Yeshua's ministry, these particular emphases were veiled.

Testimony of the Apostles. We have testimony from Yohanan and Sha'ul.

> In the beginning was the Word, and the Word was with God, and the Word was fully God. The Word was with God in the beginning. (Yohanan 1:1–2)

> And all drank the same spiritual drink. For they were all drinking from the spiritual rock that followed them, and the rock was Messiah. But God was not pleased with most of them, for they were cut down in the wilderness. These things happened as examples for us, so that we will not crave evil things as they did. So do not be idolaters, as some of them were. As it is written, "The people sat down to eat and drink and rose up to play." And let us not be immoral, as some of them were, and twenty-three thousand died in a single day. And let us not put Messiah to the test, as some of them did, and were destroyed by snakes. (1 Corinthians 10:4–9)

The background for this last passage is found in Numbers 21.

> And the people spoke against God and against Moses, "Why have you brought us up out of Egypt to die in the wilderness, for there is no bread or water, and we detest this worthless food." So the LORD sent poisonous snakes among the people, and they bit the people; many people of Israel died. (Numbers 21:5–6)

Sha'ul gives further testimony in the following verses.

> . . . who though he existed in the form of God
> did not regard equality with God
> as something to be grasped,
> but emptied himself
> by taking on the form of a slave,
> by looking like other men,
> and by sharing in human nature. (Philippians 2:6–7)

> He himself is before all things and all things are held together in him. (Colossians 1:17)

These passages should not be taken to suggest that Yeshua had a beginning before all beings were created and before the universe was brought into existence. Such was the position of Arius: He was "made out of nothing by God, first in the created order certainly, but of it."[1] However, the statement of Yohanan 1:1–2 is quite clear: While Yeshua was with God in the beginning, He was also God, *the* God, and not a created being of God.

The Preexistence of the Messiah in the Tanach: the "Angel of the LORD"

Some of the New Covenant passages above refer back to the period of the Tanach. Now we will look at selected passages specifically from there. Some of these verses raise difficulties as to the identity of the person under consideration:

Passages That Mention "the Angel of the LORD." Three passages in particular deserve our attention.

> But God heard the boy's voice. The angel of God called to Hagar from heaven and asked her, "What is the matter, Hagar? Don't be afraid, for God has heard the boy's voice right where he is crying." (Genesis 21:17)

> Now Moses was shepherding the flock of his father-in-law Jethro, the priest of Midian, and he led the flock to the far side of the

> desert and came to the mountain of God, to Horeb. The angel of the LORD appeared to him in a flame of fire from within a bush. He looked—and the bush was ablaze with fire, but it was not being consumed! (Exodus 3:1–2)

> There was a man named Manoah from Zorah, from the Danite tribe. His wife was infertile and childless. The LORD's angelic messenger appeared to the woman and said to her, "You are infertile and childless, but you will conceive and have a son." (Judges 13:2–3)

Suggestions That the Messiah Can Be Identified as "the Angel of the LORD." Sometimes the same word is used in two passages, applied to the angel of the Lord in one, and to the Messiah in the other. In the NET translation of Judges 13:15–18 below, the Hebrew is *mal'ach*, meaning both "angel" and "messenger." NIV translates as "angel of the LORD."

> Manoah said to the LORD's messenger, "Please stay here awhile, so we can prepare a young goat for you to eat." The LORD's messenger said to Manoah, "If I stay, I will not eat your food. But if you want to make a burnt sacrifice to the LORD, you should offer it." (He said this because Manoah did not know that he was the LORD's messenger.) Manoah said to the LORD's messenger, "Tell us your name, so we can honor you when your announcement comes true." The LORD's messenger said to him, "You should not ask me my name, because you cannot comprehend it." (Judges 13:15–18)

> For to us a child is born, to us a son is given, and the government will be on his shoulders. And he will be called Wonderful Counsellor, Mighty God, Everlasting Father, Prince of Peace. (Isaiah 9:6 NIV)[2]

In both passages, the same Hebrew root *pele'* is used for both "beyond understanding" and "Wonderful."

The Term "the Angel of the LORD" Never Used After Yeshua's Birth. Professor Alva McClain of Grace Theological Seminary had observed:

> Matt. 1:20: ". . . an Angel of the Lord appeared to him in a dream, . . ." that is, to Joseph, but here it is an indefinite article, referring to any angel, in a supporting capacity of the Messiah, but not to the specific Angel of the LORD. However, in Matt. 1:24, the phrase, the Angel of the LORD is used, but this would be for contextual purposes, providing information from the Hebrew Scriptures concerning Jesus's birth *yet* to come. On this one occasion, Matthew still referred to *the* Angel from an Old Testament point of view when he cited Isaiah 7:14, and spoke of how Joseph was obedient when the Angel directed Joseph to take Mary as his wife.[3]

After the birth of the Messiah, note how the phrase "*an* angel of the Lord" appears only on three occasions, Mattai 2:19 and Acts 12:7, 23, and in each instance, some angelic being in the service of Yeshua appears, doing some specific task. The designation "*the* Angel of the Lord" in the New Covenant is ever afterward conspicuously absent.

Note that in the discussion so far, no attempt has been made to identify the Messiah with God or the Lord. That observation will be made below when the deity of the Messiah is considered.

The Deity of the Messiah

By way of introduction, several preliminary points can be made.

First, when discussing the deity of the Messiah from the theological literature, our starting point will be to assume that the Scriptures are "from God," and inerrant in every respect. We will not attempt to demonstrate that here; that is the realm of apologetics, which has the responsibility to demonstrate the truthfulness of the Word of God.

Second, in discussing the deity of the Messiah, the theological task is to search the Scriptures, both the Tanach and the New Covenant. It is not the task of theology, however, to delve into the reasons why the people of Israel could not conceive of the Messiah as God. Certainly there are reasons why the people of Yeshua's day thought of the Messiah as only human, or perhaps as superhuman, but never as divine. Nevertheless, before the subject of Messiah's deity is taken up, we will review some of our observations made above as to why the Messiah, in the Jewish context of His day, was regarded as only human, and how Yeshua introduced His corrective to this belief.

So, then, here we reiterate some of the reasons why the Messiah could not be recognized as divine.

First, there had been underway a process of de-anthropomorphizing God. This was initially an attempt to protect the concept of Deuteronomy 6:4, so that Israel would never again fall into idolatry. As time went on, the Targums and the Septuagint show a substantial process of de-anthropomorphizing that was in place by the end of the Second Temple period, that is, by the end of the first century.

Second, Yeshua provided a biblical alternative to the current way of thinking, intended to show that He indeed has a divine nature. We see this in His teaching whereby He would say, "*I* tell you" (see Mattai 5:18, 22, 28, 34, 39, 44). The people understood the import of this way of speaking:

> When Yeshua finished saying these things, the crowds were amazed by his teaching, because he taught them like one who had authority, not like their experts in the law. (Mattai 7:28–29)

Besides His teaching, His works indicate His deity. Mattai, as we saw above, had a strategy in presenting Yeshua's divine nature. Mattai showed His control over nature (Mattai 8:23–27); His control over the unseen world (Mattai 8:28–34); His right to forgive sin (Mattai 9:1–8); His ability to do what God does, such as giving life to the dead and raising them up (Mattai 9:18, 23–26).

This biblical alternative to the teaching of de-anthropomorphism, namely, proclaiming that the Messiah has a divine nature, continues to be the strategy to this day with Jewish people. Yeshua never argued with Jewish people about His claims to have a divine nature; rather, He left it for them to think through the implications of His teaching and deeds and then believe them.

Now we will consider other evidences for the deity of Yeshua.

The Names of God Applied to Yeshua

The Messiah is called by a number of names indicative of deity.

God. A key passage is found at the very beginning of Yohanan:

> In the beginning was the Word, and the Word was with God, and the Word was fully God. (Yohanan 1:1)

Some, such as the Jehovah's Witnesses, have attempted to take away from the deity of the Messiah and insist that the phrase must be translated, "The Word was *a* god" because no definite article appears in the Greek text. But any good Greek grammatical consideration of the use of the definite article will state that this position is unacceptable, and that cases do exist where the lack of the definite article only points out a specific aspect of deity.[4]

> No one has ever seen God. The only one, himself God, who is in closest fellowship with the Father, has made God known. (Yohanan 1:18) [NASB: "only begotten God"; NKJV: "only begotten Son"]

The NET translates the Greek word *monogenes* as *only one*, but the older versions have *only begotten*. The idea behind the Greek word refers to one who is uniquely brought forth, but no idea of "begetting," or human procreation, should be implied. While both redeemed people and angels are called "sons of God," the Messiah is in a unique relationship with God the Father in His preexistent state as well as through the incarnation when Yeshua the Messiah took on human flesh. He remains the same today, after His resurrection, and Sha'ul alluded to the act of "begotten," as implying the resurrection. Compare Psalm 2:7 and Acts 13:33:

> The king says, "I will announce the LORD's decree. He said to me: 'You are my son! This very day I have become your father!'" (Psalm 2:7)
> . . . that this promise God has fulfilled to us, their children, by raising Yeshua, as also it is written in the second psalm, "You are my Son; today I have fathered you." (Acts 13:33)

In addition, see:

Thomas replied to him, “My Lord and my God!” (Yohanan 20:28)

. . . as we wait for the happy fulfillment of our hope in the glorious appearing of our great God and Savior, Yeshua the Messiah. (Titus 2:13)

To them belong the patriarchs, and from them, by human descent, came the Messiah, who is God over all, blessed forever! Amen. (Romans 9:5)

And we know that the Son of God has come and has given us insight to know him who is true, and we are in him who is true, in his Son Yeshua the Messiah. This one is the true God and eternal life. (1 Yohanan 5:20)

What must be carefully noted is that the writers of the New Covenant were themselves Jewish. They lived in a period where the de-anthropomorphization of God had reached the point where He was considered “wholly other,” where He supposedly did not enter directly into the human realm nor does man enter into God’s realm. Only as the New Covenant writers were carefully apprised as to the true identity of Yeshua did they refer to Him as *God*. They had become convinced of His identity through His teaching and deeds that could lead to no other conclusion.

Finally, note that Yeshua Himself, as a Jew in His flesh, never rebuked anyone when they addressed Him as God, as in the case with Thomas:

Thomas replied to him, “My Lord and my God!” (Yohanan 20:28)

The Lord. A number of examples have already been noted but the following verses can also be examined (and there are others). Many Jewish believers in Yeshua’s day used the Septuagint, the Greek Old Testament, which translated “the LORD” as *kurios*, the same word used for “Lord” in the verses below.

> Today your Savior is born in the city of David. He is Messiah the Lord. (Luke 2:11)

> You call me "Teacher" and "Lord," and do so correctly, for that is what I am. (Yohanan 13:13)

> . . . because if you confess with your mouth that Yeshua is Lord and believe in your heart that God raised him from the dead, you will be saved. (Romans 10:9)

The Lord of Glory. Sha'ul's use of Psalm 24:8–10 to designate Yeshua as "the Lord of glory" is revealing:

> None of the rulers of this age understood it. If they had known it, they would not have crucified the Lord of glory. (1 Corinthians 2:8)

> Who is this majestic king?
> The LORD who is strong and mighty!
> The LORD who is mighty in battle!
> Look up, you gates!
> Rise up, you eternal doors!
> Then the majestic king will enter!
> Who is this majestic king?
> The LORD who commands armies!
> He is the majestic king! (Selah) (Psalm 24:8–10)

The Holy One. Kefa likewise described Yeshua the Messiah as "the Holy One," using a very specific title of God:

> But you rejected the Holy and Righteous One and asked that a man who was a murderer be released to you. (Acts 3:14)

> I cannot carry out my fierce anger!
> I cannot totally destroy Ephraim!

> Because I am God, and not man—the Holy One among you—
> I will not come in wrath! (Hosea 11:9)

The First and the Last. Yohanan, likewise, using the language of Isaiah, described Yeshua as "the First and the Last."

> When I saw him I fell down at his feet as though I were dead, but he placed his right hand on me and said: "Do not be afraid! I am the first and the last, and the one who lives! I was dead, but look, now I am alive—forever and ever—and I hold the keys of death and of Hades!" (Revelation 1:17–18)

> To the angel of the *qehilah* in Smyrna write the following:
> "This is the solemn pronouncement of the one who is the first and the last, the one who was dead, but came to life." (Revelation 2:8)

> This is what the LORD, Israel's king, says,
> their protector, the LORD who commands armies:
> "I am the first and I am the last,
> there is no God but me." (Isaiah 44:6)

> Listen to me, O Jacob,
> Israel, whom I have called:
> I am he;
> I am the first and I am the last. (Isaiah 48:12 NIV)[5]

The Son of God. We have saved this term for last. When Messiah is called "the Son of God," the question arises immediately as to what this term means. The phrase occurs in a number of passages: Kefa identified Yeshua as such and the Messiah acknowledged the designation:

> Shimon Kefa answered, "You are the Messiah, the Son of the living God." And Yeshua answered him, "You are blessed, Shimon son of Jonah, because flesh and blood did not reveal this to you, but my Father in heaven!" (Mattai 16:16–17)

Does the term point to an origin, whereby Yeshua had a beginning at some point in time? We pointed to this interpretation when considering the preexistence of the Messiah and possible meanings of "the one and only Son," or, "only begotten Son." But no evidence is apparent that it refers to an origin in time.

The Greek words used of the Messiah are also helpful: *teknon* (child, infant), referring to natural descent, that is, origin,

> When his parents saw him, they were overwhelmed. His mother said to him, "Child [teknon], why have you treated us like this? Look, your father and I have been looking for you anxiously." (Luke 2:48)

and *pais*, or, boy or girl, which also at times describes a child or servant in a legal relation, such as in Acts 4:30, which is why some translations such as NET and NIV translate as "servant":

> . . . while you extend your hand to heal, and to bring about miraculous signs and wonders through the name of your holy servant [*pais*, literally *child*] Yeshua. (Acts 4:30)

The passages that speak of Yeshua as the Son of God use a different Greek word, *huios*.

The term "Son of God" refers to a special relationship that the Messiah holds to God. One specific example from Scripture is where the phrase is understood as "equal with God":

> For this reason the Jewish leaders were trying even harder to kill him, because not only was he breaking the Sabbath, but he was also calling God his own Father, thus making himself equal with God. (Yohanan 5:18)

> The Jewish leaders replied, "We are not going to stone you for a good deed but for blasphemy, because you, a man, are claiming to be God." . . .
>
> . . . do you say about the one whom the Father set apart and sent

> into the world, "You are blaspheming," because I said, "I am the Son of God"? (Yohanan 10:33, 36)

See also:

> The Jewish leaders replied, "We have a law, and according to our law he ought to die, because he claimed to be the Son of God!" (Yohanan 19:7)

Only after about the midpoint of Yeshua's ministry do the Synoptic Gospels begin to emphasize His deity, while Yohanan's references came after the Second Temple was lost in 70 C.E. Yeshua was quite reticent about proclaiming His deity at the beginning, because of the specific view of Messiah held by Jewish people in the first century. As time went on, however, the implications as to His deity became plainer. This, by far, was the chief reason for the decision by the Sanhedrin to turn Him over to the Romans for execution: the leaders felt He was guilty of heresy.

The phrase "Son of God" was the description chosen by Yeshua to define His deity. "Son of Man" became the designation of His humanity, as noted already at the beginning of this discussion.

God's Attributes Applied to Yeshua

Yeshua had made an all-encompassing statement that suggested that He had God's attributes:

> Everything that the Father has is mine; that is why I said the Spirit will receive from me what is mine and will tell it to you. (Yohanan 16:15)

With such an amazing claim, it is instructive to see what the New Covenant writers had to say concerning Yeshua.

When we discussed the doctrine of God, three major categories had been used to describe who God is: His personality, His greatness, and His goodness. When demonstrating that the Messiah Yeshua is deity, implied already is His personality. What remains to be discussed are His attributes of greatness and goodness.

The Messiah's Greatness. Here we can compare these attributes with what was said above in the chapter, "The Doctrine of God."

He is eternal. A number of passages suggest this attribute.

> For a child has been born to us,
> a son has been given to us.
> He shoulders responsibility
> and is called:
> Extraordinary Strategist,
> Mighty God,
> Everlasting Father,
> Prince of Peace. (Isaiah 9:6 NIV; verse 5 MT)

One of the child's titles is "Everlasting Father."

> As for you, Bethlehem Ephrathah,
> seemingly insignificant among the clans of Judah—
> from you a king will emerge who will rule over Israel on my behalf,
> one whose origins are in the distant past. (Micah 5:2; verse 1 MT)

Note the phrasing *whose origins* are *in the distant past* (NIV: *from of old, from ancient times*; literally, *from days of eternity*).

> And the life was revealed, and we have seen and testify and announce to you the eternal life that was with the Father and was revealed to us. (1 Yohanan 1:2)

Other passages appear at first glance to raise questions as to Yeshua's eternality, by employing the term "firstborn."

> He is the image of the invisible God, the firstborn over all creation. (Colossians 1:15)

> But when he again brings his firstborn into the world, he says, "Let all

> the angels of God worship him!" (Hebrews 1:6)

However, Yohanan declares of Him:

> All things were created by him, and apart from him not one thing was created that has been created. (Yohanan 1:3)

Therefore, the point is that if the Messiah were a created being, how could He make Himself? Obviously, He did not!

In these passages, we have to make a distinction between *first in position*, and *first in time*. There is a difference between implying that the Messiah was first in time, with an origin, and saying that He was first in position, for instance, first in the resurrection, or "firstborn among many brothers," that is, preeminent in *position* in the body of Messiah:

> . . . and from Yeshua the Messiah—the faithful witness, the firstborn from among the dead, the ruler over the kings of the earth. To the one who loves us and has set us free from our sins at the cost of his own blood . . . (Revelation 1:5)

> . . . because those whom he foreknew he also predestined to be conformed to the image of his Son, that his Son would be the firstborn among many brothers and sisters. (Romans 8:29)

This distinction should be considered carefully, otherwise grave error can result.

He is immutable. An equivalent way of saying this would be to state that He is unchangeable.

And,

> You founded the earth in the beginning, Lord,
> and the heavens are the works of your hands.
> They will perish, but you continue.

And they will all grow old like a garment,
and like a robe you will fold them up
and like a garment they will be changed,
but you are the same and your years will never run out.
(Hebrews 1:10–12)

Yeshua the Messiah is the same yesterday and today and forever!
(Hebrews 13:8)

Even though Yeshua at a specific point in time became a man in the incarnation, His personhood never changes. His *position* changed when He passed from glory to dwell with man as a human being, and again, when He returned to glory, some of that position changed again. But in His *person*, He is always the same.

He is omnipotent. When we consider this dimension as well as His omniscience and omnipresence, the Messiah certainly had unlimited power, knowledge, and presence prior to His incarnation. After He returned to glory, He still retained all these qualities, as we see from Scripture. Some aspects of these attributes, however, were withheld in the days of His flesh, as a result of His emptying Himself:

. . . but emptied himself
by taking on the form of a slave,
by looking like other men,
and by sharing in human nature.
He humbled himself,
by becoming obedient to the point of death
—even death on a tree! (Philippians 2:7–8)

His omnipotence is shown is such verses as:

But our citizenship is in heaven—and we also await a savior from there, the Lord Yeshua the Messiah, who will transform these humble bodies of ours into the likeness of his glorious body by means of that power by which he is able to subject all things to himself. (Philippians 3:20–21)

The meaning of "everything under his control" is illustrated in the same verses we considered when examining Yeshua's divine nature.

He has control over nature:

But he said to them, "Why are you cowardly, you people of little faith?" Then he got up and rebuked the winds and the sea, and it was dead calm. And the men were amazed and said, "What sort of person is this? Even the winds and the sea obey him!" (Mattai 8:26–27)

He has the ability to heal:

So he stood over her, commanded the fever, and it left her. Immediately she got up and began to serve them. (Luke 4:39)

He has the ability to raise to life:

Then he came up and touched the bier, and those who carried it stood still. He said, "Young man, I say to you, get up!" So the dead man sat up and began to speak, and Yeshua gave him back to his mother. (Luke 7:14–15)

Besides the examples above, we further note:

For all things in heaven and on earth were created by him—all things, whether visible or invisible, whether thrones or dominions, whether principalities or powers—all things were created through him and for him. (Colossians 1:16)

He himself is before all things and all things are held together in him. (Colossians 1:17)

He receives and answers prayer:

If you ask me anything in my name, I will do it. (Yohanan 14:14)

He is the agent of the resurrection:

Martha said, "I know that he will come back to life again in the resurrection at the last day." Yeshua said to her, "I am the resurrection and the life. The one who believes in me will live even if he dies." (Yohanan 11:24–25)

Further verses could be cited.

He is omnipresent. Some statements seem to limit His omnipresence in the days of His flesh. The Scripture declares:

. . . but emptied himself
by taking on the form of a slave,
by looking like other men,
and by sharing in human nature.
He humbled himself, by becoming obedient to the point of death
—even death on a tree! (Philippians 2:7–8)

Now, He is in heaven, still in a body in which He will return to receive us; He will also be here in His resurrected body when He reigns on earth as God's Messiah.

But in addition, note these other statements:

For where two or three are assembled in my name, I am there among them. (Mattai 18:20)

. . . teaching them to obey everything I have commanded you. And remember, I am with you always, to the end of the age. (Mattai 28:20)

He is omniscient. That is, He knows all things. Compare what is said of God in the Tanach, that

> The human mind is more deceitful than anything else.
> It is incurably bad. Who can understand it?
> I, the LORD, probe into people's minds.
> I examine people's hearts.
> I deal with each person according to how he has behaved.
> I give them what they deserve based on what they have done.
> (Jeremiah 17:9–10)

In the New Covenant,

> But Yeshua would not entrust himself to them, because he knew all people. He did not need anyone to testify about man, for he knew what was in man. (Yohanan 2:24–25)

> "But there are some of you who do not believe." (For Yeshua had already known from the beginning who those were who did not believe, and who it was who would betray him.) (Yohanan 6:64)

That is, some of what Yeshua knew reflected knowledge that He had prior to His incarnation.

> "Now we know that you know everything and do not need anyone to ask you anything. Because of this we believe that you have come from God." Yeshua replied, "Do you now believe?" (Yohanan 16:30–31)

> . . . in whom are hidden all the treasures of wisdom and knowledge. (Colossians 2:3)

There are difficulties, however. In the following verses, are we to understand that Yeshua really did not know the time of His return?

> But as for that day and hour no one knows it—not even the angels in heaven—except the Father alone. (Mattai 24:36)

We will discuss this issue under the topic of the incarnation, but for now, let us suggest that a wrong response is to say that He did in fact know *in His divine nature* while *in His human nature*, He did not know. The problem here is that of splitting the unity of His personality. However we answer, we must avoid error by all means possible.

The Messiah's Goodness. This brings us to our second main category of attributes.

He is holy.

> The angel replied, "The Holy Spirit will come upon you, and the power of the Most High will overshadow you. Therefore the child to be born will be holy; he will be called the Son of God." (Luke 1:35)

Compare:

> But you rejected the Holy and Righteous One and asked that a man who was a murderer be released to you. (Acts 3:14)

He is righteous.

> Finally the crown of righteousness is reserved for me. The Lord, the righteous Judge, will award it to me in that day—and not to me only, but also to all who have set their affection on his appearing. (2 Timothy 4:8)

Who is this "Lord"? We can answer by comparing:

> For we must all appear before the judgment seat of Messiah, so that each one may be paid back according to what he has done while in the body, whether good or evil. (2 Corinthians 5:10)

> (My little children, I am writing these things to you so that you may not sin.) But if anyone does sin, we have an advocate with the Father, Yeshua the Messiah the righteous One. (1 Yohanan 2:1)

He is merciful.

Two blind men were sitting by the road. When they heard that Yeshua was passing by, they shouted, "Have mercy on us, Lord, Son of David!" The crowd scolded them to get them to be quiet. But they shouted even more loudly, "Lord, have mercy on us, Son of David!" Yeshua stopped, called them, and said, "What do you want me to do for you?" They said to him, "Lord, let our eyes be opened." Moved with compassion, Yeshua touched their eyes. Immediately they received their sight and followed him. (Mattai 20:30–34)

Maintain yourselves in the love of God, while anticipating the mercy of our Lord Yeshua the Messiah that brings eternal life. (Yehudah 1:21)

He is love.

Just before the Passover feast, Yeshua knew that his time had come to depart from this world to the Father. Having loved his own who were in the world, he now loved them to the very end. (Yohanan 13:1)

Who will separate us from the love of Messiah? Will trouble, or distress, or persecution, or famine, or nakedness, or danger, or sword? As it is written, "For your sake we encounter death all day long; we were considered as sheep to be slaughtered." No, in all these things we have complete victory through him who loved us! For I am convinced that neither death, nor life, nor angels, nor heavenly rulers, nor things that are present, nor things to come, nor powers, . . . (Romans 8:35–38)

. . . you may be able to comprehend with all the saints what is the breadth and length and height and depth, and thus to know the love of Messiah that surpasses knowledge, so that you may be filled up to all the fullness of God. (Ephesians 3:18–19)

We have come to know love by this: that Yeshua laid down his life for us; thus we ought to lay down our lives for our fellow believers. (1 Yohanan 3:16)

He is faithful.

To the angel of the *qehilah* in Laodicea write the following:
This is the solemn pronouncement of the Amen, the faithful and true witness, the originator of God's creation. (Revelation 3:14)

Then I saw heaven opened and here came a white horse! The one riding it was called "Faithful" and "True," and with justice he judges and goes to war. (Revelation 19:11)

A Major Difficulty

Earlier we spoke of the teaching of de-anthropomorphizing as an impediment to understanding the mystery of Yeshua's deity. Now let us approach the problem from another direction by means of this question: Was Yeshua made into a god, by either Sha'ul, or by those present at the Council of Nicea in 325 C.E.?

There are two major reasons that argue against the idea that a divine Messiah was only a later formulation.

First, there is the argument from the dating of the New Covenant writings. Every book of the New Covenant, with the exception of the writings of Yohanan, appeared before the loss of the Second Temple. Therefore, any proclamation that Yeshua is both human and divine could not have come after 70 C.E.

Second, there is the internal evidence of the books of the New Covenant. Those books, especially Mattai, show that Yeshua had a strategy to present Himself to Israel, first, as the Son of Man (humanity) but then, both by His teaching and His works, as also deity.

Therefore, we have to insist that Sha'ul was convinced of the deity of Yeshua, especially if we take at face value his experience on the Damascus Road. Imagine his shock on asking "Who are you, Lord?" when the answer came back, "I am Yeshua." Without a doubt, he was convinced of the divine nature of the Messiah.

Again, from the internal evidence of the gospels, we see that when Yeshua stood on trial before the Sanhedrin, it was exactly because He had made the claim to be not only human but also deity. Most members of the Sanhedrin did not believe His claim, though there were exceptions such as Joseph and Nicodemus.

Sometimes our Gentile believing friends wonder why it was so difficult for many in Judea to recognize His deity. But we have to recognize that the Tanach does not explicitly declare the deity of the Messiah. There was good reason for this lack of explicit testimony. Preexilic Israel had enough difficulty understanding the oneness of God as delineated in Deuteronomy 6:4, that to introduce a concept such as the composite unity of God would only have compounded the problem of idolatry. As it was, because of idolatry, Israel of the north ceased as a political unit in 721 B.C.E., while a good many of Judah were taken to Babylon.

Implicit in the Tanach, however, are several statements concerning the Messiah. Those truths, however, did not become explicit until the New Covenant proclamation. Some of these implicit statements include:

> As for you, Bethlehem Ephrathah,
> seemingly insignificant among the clans of Judah–
> from you a king will emerge who will rule over Israel on my behalf,
> one whose origins are in the distant past. (Micah 5:2; verse 1 MT)

> Who has ascended into heaven, and then descended?
> Who has gathered up the winds in his fists?
> Who has bound up the waters in his cloak?
> Who has established all the ends of the earth?
> What is his name, and what is his son's name?—if you know!
> (Proverbs 30:4)

> I am going to send an angel before you to protect you as you journey and to bring you into the place that I have prepared. Take heed because of him, and obey his voice; do not rebel against him, for he will not pardon your transgressions, for my name is in him. (Exodus 23:20–21)

Implications of the Deity of the Messiah

A True Revelation of God. If the Messiah is God, then He truly reveals God to man; furthermore, if the Messiah is God, then what He says becomes of utmost importance to us. His words are not merely to be copied on paper and then forgotten. The Word of God has an assurance concerning Messiah's deity that not only changes our lives but gives meaning when we proclaim Him to unbelievers.

An Assurance to Believers. Note in this passage the various words of assurance regarding our future:

> "Do not let your hearts be distressed. You believe in God; believe also in me. There are many dwelling places in my Father's house. Otherwise, I would have told you, because I am going away to make ready a place for you. And if I go and make ready a place for you, I will come again and take you to be with me, so that where I am you may be too. And you know the way where I am going."
>
> Thomas said, "Lord, we don't know where you are going. How can we know the way?" Yeshua replied, "I am the way, and the truth, and the life. No one comes to the Father except through me. If you have known me, you will know my Father too. And from now on you do know him and have seen him."
>
> Philip said, "Lord, show us the Father, and we will be content." Yeshua replied, "Have I been with you for so long, and you have not known me, Philip? The person who has seen me has seen the Father! How can you say, 'Show us the Father'?" (Yohanan 14:1–9)

Some Theories Opposing the Deity of the Messiah

Arianism. The position developed by Arius (250–336 C.E.) was that Messiah is the highest preexistent created being. He called Messiah a "God" who created all things, and most gladly worshipped Him. Yet Arius held Him to be a created being (with Colossians 1:15 as a proof text, "the firstborn over all creation"). In other words, "there was a time when he was not."

Socinianism. The position taken by Soncinus (a leader in the movement from 1579–1604 C.E.) was that Messiah is the best of all men, who was exalted to share the divine nature and so be worshipped. But He was born as a man.

Unitarianism. This position was held by a number of people after the Reformation in Europe. Many also picked up on this heresy in the United

States in the 1800s. Yeshua is considered to be a great and good man who lived in communion with God. He is to be honored and imitated, but must never be worshiped.

All the modern cults deny the deity of Yeshua and merely repeat the above three errors with different embellishments. In this respect, Satan does not do anything new.

THE INCARNATION OF THE MESSIAH

The Term

Incarnation comes from the Latin *en carno*, that is, *in flesh*. It can therefore be described as an *enfleshment*.

Introduction to the Concept of the Incarnation

If we say that someone was conceived in his mother's womb or that a baby has just been born, everyone can understand that a new life has commenced.

But how does one describe the process whereby Yeshua the Messiah entered into the human experience? The writers of the New Covenant had to find the terms to depict, not the beginning of existence in the human sphere, but the process by which the always-existing Messiah entered into this world. This makes Yeshua different from all other human beings. Hardly ever do the writers of the New Covenant speak of Yeshua being "conceived," or "born," in the ordinary sense, because they had always to think of His uniqueness as a person.

What is provided below are specific terms used by the New Covenant writers to describe how the Messiah entered into this world. No one writer, however, presents the entire picture. Together the writers somehow communicate the great truth of the incarnation, and yet the process still holds an element of awe and mystery.

Relevant Passages

This writer is indebted to Professor Alva McClain for the following list of passages that speak of Yeshua's coming into this sphere of human experience.

. . . just as the Son of Man did not come to be served but to serve, and to give his life as a ransom for many. (Mattai 20:28)

Now the Word became flesh and took up residence among us. We saw his glory—the glory of the one and only, full of grace and truth, who came from the Father. (Yohanan 1:14)

No one has ascended into heaven except the one who descended from heaven—the Son of Man. (Yohanan 3:13)

For God did not send his Son into the world to condemn the world, but that the world should be saved through him. (Yohanan 3:17)

I am the living bread that came down from heaven. If anyone eats from this bread he will live forever. The bread that I will give for the life of the world is my flesh. (Yohanan 6:51)

. . . concerning his Son who was a descendant of David with reference to the flesh, . . . (Romans 1:3)

For God achieved what the law could not do because it was weakened through the flesh. By sending his own Son in the likeness of sinful flesh and concerning sin, he condemned sin in the flesh. (Romans 8:3)

The first man is from the earth, made of dust; the second man is from heaven. (1 Corinthians 15:47)

For you know the grace of our Lord Yeshua the Messiah, that although he was rich, he became poor for your sakes, so that you by his poverty could become rich. (2 Corinthians 8:9)

But when the appropriate time had come, God sent out his Son, born of a woman, born under the law. (Galatians 4:4)

. . . but emptied himself
by taking on the form of a slave,
by looking like other men,
and by sharing in human nature. (Philippians 2:7)

He humbled himself,
by becoming obedient to the point of death
—even death on a tree! (Philippians 2:8)

This saying is trustworthy and deserves full acceptance: "Messiah Yeshua came into the world to save sinners"—and I am the worst of them! (1 Timothy 1:15)

And we all agree, our religion contains amazing revelation:
He was revealed in the flesh,
vindicated by the Spirit,
seen by angels,
proclaimed among Gentiles,
believed on in the world,
taken up in glory. (1 Timothy 3:16)

But we see Yeshua, who was made lower than the angels for a little while, now crowned with glory and honor because he suffered death, so that by God's grace he would experience death on behalf of everyone. (Hebrews 2:9)

Therefore, since the children share in flesh and blood, he likewise shared in their humanity, so that through death he could destroy the one who holds the power of death (that is, the devil). (Hebrews 2:14)

Therefore he had to be made like his brothers and sisters in every respect, so that he could become a merciful and faithful high priest in things relating to God, to make atonement for the sins of the people. (Hebrews 2:17)

> So when he came into the world, he said,
> "Sacrifice and offering you did not desire, but a body you prepared for me. . . .
> . . . "Then I said, 'Here I am: I have come—it is written of me in the scroll of the book—to do your will, O God.'" (Hebrews 10:5, 7)

> And you know that Yeshua was revealed to take away sins, and in him there is no sin. (1 Yohanan 3:5)

Changes in Yeshua Occasioned by the Incarnation

A Change in His Glory. In His former presence with the Father, He had an unspeakable glory, but in His human nature, He appeared as any other Israelite.

> And now, Father, glorify me at your side with the glory I had with you before the world was created. (Yohanan 17:5)

A Change in His Form. The Greek word for "form" is *morphe*.

> . . . who though he existed in the form [Greek, *morphe*; NIV has "nature"] of God
> did not regard equality with God
> as something to be grasped,
> but emptied himself
> by taking on the form [*morphe*, and "nature" in NIV] of a slave,
> by looking like other men,
> and by sharing in human nature. (Philippians 2:6–7)

A Change in His Position. Philippians 2:6–7, just cited, illustrates this as well. From being equal with God, He went in His humanity to being a servant.

A Change in His Economic Status. He became poor for our sakes.

> For you know the grace of our Lord Yeshua the Messiah, that although he was rich, he became poor for your sakes, so that you by his poverty could become rich. (2 Corinthians 8:9)

On one occasion, He described His status as even less than that of birds and animals:

> Yeshua said to him, "Foxes have dens and the birds in the sky have nests, but the Son of Man has no place to lay his head." (Luke 9:58)

Yeshua After His Return to Heaven

As to His Human Nature. The question arises as to what was temporary and what was permanent regarding the Messiah in the days of His flesh, in His humanity.

Every aspect of Yeshua reverted to what they had been prior to His incarnation, except for His form:

> The Son is the radiance of his glory and the representation of his essence, and he sustains all things by his powerful word, and so when he had accomplished cleansing for sins, he sat down at the right hand of the Majesty on high. (Hebrews 1:3)

But He remains in His human form. In His incarnation, He took this form and with it He sits on His appointed throne until He one day returns, and will accomplish the following:

Make war on His enemies on earth.

> Then I saw heaven opened and here came a white horse! The one riding it was called "Faithful" and "True," and with justice he judges and goes to war. His eyes are like a fiery flame and there are many diadem crowns on his head. He has a name written that no one knows except himself. He is dressed in clothing dipped in blood, and he is called the Word of God. The armies that are in heaven, dressed in white, clean, fine linen, were following him on white horses. From his mouth extends a sharp sword, so that with it he can strike the nations. He will rule them with an iron rod, and he stomps the winepress of the furious wrath of God, the All-powerful. He has a name written on his clothing and on his thigh: "King of kings and Lord of lords." (Revelation 19:11–16)

Be recognized by Israel as their deliverer.

> I will pour out on the kingship of David and the population of Jerusalem a spirit of grace and supplication so that they will look to me, the one they have pierced. They will lament for him as one laments for an only son, and there will be a bitter cry for him like the bitter cry for a firstborn. (Zechariah 12:10)

Rule over Israel as God's servant David.

> My servant David will be king over them; there will be one shepherd for all of them. They will follow my regulations and carefully observe my statutes. (Ezekiel 37:24)

It is noteworthy that both Stephen and Yohanan saw Yeshua in that very human form:

> When they heard these things, they became furious and ground their teeth at him. But Stephen, full of the Holy Spirit, looked intently toward heaven and saw the glory of God, and Yeshua standing at the right hand of God. "Look!" he said. "I see the heavens opened, and the Son of Man standing at the right hand of God!" (Acts 7:54–56)

> When I saw him I fell down at his feet as though I were dead, but he placed his right hand on me and said: "Do not be afraid! I am the first and the last, and the one who lives! I was dead, but look, now I am alive—forever and ever—and I hold the keys of death and of Hades! (Revelation 1:17–18)

As to His Divine Nature. Yeshua always remained God while He had His human nature, and He retained His divine nature when He returned to glory.

While the above truths are difficult to grasp, they are basic to understanding who Yeshua is. Tampering with them will result in a seriously damaged view of Messiah and serious error.

The Necessity for the Incarnation

The question "Where can man find God?" has always been a most vexing one. Job echoed this continual human cry of frustration:

> For he is not a human being like I am,
> that I might answer him,
> that we might come together in judgment.
> Nor is there an arbiter between us,
> who might lay his hand on us both. (Job 9:32–33)

Sha'ul also must have cried out this question on the Damascus Road:

> So he said, "Who are you, Lord?" He replied, "I am Yeshua whom you are persecuting!" (Acts 9:5)

The purpose of Messiah's incarnation was to provide an answer to this age-old question. God desired to communicate with man, not only indirectly through the authors of the Tanach, but directly in the presence of Yeshua through the virgin birth (discussed below). Yohanan declared:

> Now the Word became flesh and took up residence among us. We saw his glory—the glory of the one and only, full of grace and truth, who came from the Father. (Yohanan 1:14)

The answer to Job is that, in a mystery, God has taken on humanity. Our involvement with God is more focused because Yeshua is that "arbitrator" between man and God whom Job sought for.

One can never lose sight of the fact that Yeshua is *both* human and divine. In the first few centuries, many Jewish and Gentile believers began to enter into error on this one major theological consideration. Jewish believers, who once clearly held to this doctrine, began to falter on it. Perhaps it was because the Council of Yavneh had already decided that as part of the *Shemoneh Esre*, or *Amidah*, one had to recite, "I thank God I am not a *min*," that is, not an apostate—referring primarily to one who believes Yeshua is human as well as divine.

Such an addition to the prayers made for a massive problem for Messianic Jews attending the synagogues: how could they recite such lines in the liturgy? Either they had to leave the synagogues, or else give up sound doctrine. In the latter case, Messianic Jews became actual apostates.

The same was true for Gentile believers. For the most part they did not attend the synagogues, but many were already being influenced by Gnosticism near the end of the first century. Primarily, Gnosticism taught that Messiah was a divine being who never assumed a human body, nor did He ever die. Perhaps, it was taught, Messiah somehow "inhabited" the human being Yeshua, or assumed a kind of phantom human appearance. This may be why Yohanan wrote:

> By this you know the Spirit of God: Every spirit that confesses Yeshua as the Messiah who has come in the flesh is from God, but every spirit that does not confess Yeshua is not from God, and this is the spirit of the anti-Messiah, which you have heard is coming, and now is already in the world. (1 Yohanan 4:2–3)

The message is quite plain: Anyone who affirms that Yeshua is the Messiah but cannot affirm that He also has a human nature is a heretic.

Granted the centrality of the doctrine of Yeshua's humanity, we now need to consider *why* the New Covenant writers considered it to be of such importance. The basic answer, to be elaborated below, is that *Yeshua became human so that He could be our representative.*

He had to take on a human form whereby He could represent us in our humanity. Merely for God to sit in heaven would never do; the incarnation provided for God, in the person of the Son, to be born as a human being and grow through the stages of babyhood, boy, teenager, and man. In that way, He tasted life as a human being from the inside, knowing the joys and struggles of life: He earned a living, He managed the family into which He was born after Joseph's death, He ministered to people in their needs, He experienced the meaning of rejection, and finally He died for us on the tree. Because of having experienced everything any human being will ever face, Yeshua as the Son of Man can be our representative in the following ways:

As Our Ideal Example. When He came in the days of His flesh, Yeshua became the ideal representative man. He was and remains the ideal of human life for us as believers. Adam, prior to the fall, had this unique position in his perfect fellowship with God, so that the psalmist exclaimed:

> Of what importance is the human race, that you should notice them?
> Of what importance is mankind, that you should pay attention to them,
> and make them a little less than the heavenly beings?
> You grant mankind honor and majesty. (Psalm 8:4–5)

Adam and Eve both made the wrong choice when they ignored God's descriptive knowledge concerning the tree of the knowledge of good and evil and consequently removed themselves from the circle of God's will. While God shared with them how they could be restored to fellowship again, the effects of the fall are seen in every descendant of our first parents: in our souls and spirits, in our minds, and even in our physical bodies. But the fingerprints of God are still on the human soul. Therefore, when Yeshua died, God made it possible that as we accept Him, we can have His life in us (see further under man, sin, and atonement) for the purpose of reflecting the life of Yeshua.

In this present life. The New Covenant writers are quite insistent that Yeshua's life can be replicated in the life of every believer:

> For to this you were called, since Messiah also suffered for you, leaving an example for you to follow in his steps. (1 Kefa 2:21)

> The one who says he resides in God ought himself to walk just as Yeshua walked. (1 Yohanan 2:6)

While many believers would say that such a goal is an impossible one, we are reminded that when we were born again, we became *hasidim*, or, saints. God sees us in the Messiah, justified, "just as if we had never sinned." With the new birth, God begins the task of progressive sanctification in each of us. Some respond rapidly while others are slower in grasping just what God wants in each of our lives. The ultimate goal, however, is to conform us to the image of the Messiah:

> . . . because those whom he foreknew he also predestined to be conformed to the image of his Son, that his Son would be the firstborn among many brothers and sisters. (Romans 8:29)

What is impossible with men is possible with God; our part is to cooperate with His purposes for our lives.

In the world to come. Many times the lessons of sanctification are difficult to learn, and in a world of sin and imperfection all around us, believers tend to become discouraged. But we have a promise:

> Dear friends, we are God's children now, and what we will be has not yet been revealed. We know that whenever it is revealed we will be like him, because we will see him just as he is. (1 Yohanan 3:2)

In the world to come, we will be delivered from the *presence* of sin and ultimately, we shall no longer be tempted by the *power* of sin. So, the encouragement is to keep on and not grow weary and fainthearted. One day we shall be like Him; as He was separated from the presence of sin, so will we likewise. With this goal, we should submit to God's work in our lives in the here and now, looking more and more like Him even in this world.

As Providing an Everlasting Revelation. I am indebted to Alva McClain for the following observation, namely, that while Yeshua reverted back to His original state in glory, one aspect did not change: He still remained in the body He received in the incarnation, except that in His resurrection, He acquired a glorified body. He ascended into the glory in that body and He sits today at the right hand of the Majesty on high.

The writers of Scripture seek to remind us of this fact. When following His resurrection, Yeshua revealed Himself to the *shlichim* (the apostles), He particularly singled out Thomas.

> Then he said to Thomas, "Put your finger here, and examine my hands. Extend your hand and put it into my side. Do not continue in your unbelief, but believe." (Yohanan 20:27)

The obvious implication was that Yeshua had the same body He had before His death, although it was now a glorified body.

Furthermore, at the end of the book of Revelation, Yeshua spoke to Yohanan, saying,

> I, Yeshua, have sent my angel to testify to you about these things for the *qehilot*. I am the root and the descendant of David, the bright morning star! (Revelation 22:16)

His name, given when He entered into the stream of humanity, remained the same, reflecting the fact that He was in a body as He was when on earth.

Furthermore, one day Israel will recognize Yeshua when He comes to deliver her in her most trying hour; at that time He will be in a body, riding the white horse.

> Then I saw heaven opened and here came a white horse! The one riding it was called "Faithful" and "True," and with justice he judges and goes to war. His eyes are like a fiery flame and there are many diadem crowns on his head. He has a name written that no one knows except himself. He is dressed in clothing dipped in blood, and he is called the Word of God. The armies that are in heaven, dressed in white, clean, fine linen, were following him on white horses. From his mouth extends a sharp sword, so that with it he can strike the nations. He will rule them with an iron rod, and he stomps the winepress of the furious wrath of God, the All-powerful. He has a name written on his clothing and on his thigh: "King of kings and Lord of lords." (Revelation 19:11–16)

In that body too, He will make Himself known to His brethren.

> I will pour out on the kingship of David and the population of Jerusalem a spirit of grace and supplication so that they will look to me, the one they have pierced. They will lament for him as one laments for an only son, and there will be a bitter cry for him like the bitter cry for a firstborn. (Zechariah 12:10)

As Our Substitute Through His Death. God as a pure spirit could not die, but Yeshua, in His humanity, could in fact die. Yeshua was both human and divine; God does not die, but the God incarnate in Yeshua could do so. And as our representative He could take our place in that death. This a mystery, yet with God all things are possible.

The writer to the Hebrews makes this startling announcement. First, in a doxology to the Messiah, the second person within the composite unity of God, he proclaims,

> In these last days he has spoken to us in a son, whom he appointed heir of all things, and through whom he created the world. The Son is the radiance of his glory and the representation of his essence, and he sustains all things by his powerful word, and so when he had accomplished cleansing for sins, he sat down at the right hand of the Majesty on high. (Hebrews 1:2–3)

Of this person it is also said,

> But we see Yeshua, who was made lower than the angels for a little while, now crowned with glory and honor because he suffered death, so that by God's grace he would experience death on behalf of everyone. (Hebrews 2:9)

and

> Therefore, since the children share in flesh and blood, he likewise shared in their humanity, so that through death he could destroy the one who holds the power of death (that is, the devil). (Hebrews 2:14)

When the God incarnate in Yeshua as the Son of Man came into this world, He demonstrated that He was our true representative, and that He came to die on behalf of each one of us. This He could do in His representative humanity. Merely living a good life that we might imitate was not enough. He had to die as our representative, and *only through His death* can we ever receive His life, enabling us to live as He lived while on earth. We will discuss this further below when considering His death as the atonement for our sins, but it is enough for now to indicate that He is our representative in His death. We can never forget one of the basic reasons why He came: He came to die on our behalf.

As Our Advocate and High Priest. Because Yeshua died on our behalf, He can also serve as our Advocate when we sin, and represent us before God. Since He Himself was our guilt offering—the sacrifice for every individual sin—He can then plead on our behalf before God, having already died for every specific sin.

> (My little children, I am writing these things to you so that you may not sin.) But if anyone does sin, we have an advocate with the Father, Yeshua the Messiah the righteous One, and he himself is the atoning sacrifice for our sins, and not only for our sins but also for the whole world. (1 Yohanan 2:1–2)

And He can interpose Himself between us and God because He is our high priest.

> Therefore he had to be made like his brothers and sisters in every respect, so that he could become a merciful and faithful high priest in things relating to God, to make atonement for the sins of the people. For since he himself suffered when he was tempted, he is able to help those who are tempted. (Hebrews 2:17–18)

In the Mosaic system, the high priest represented every person in the nation before God, and on the Day of Atonement he went into the Holy of Holies with the appropriate sacrifices. Everyone then felt that the priest was doing something for him that he could not do for himself. In the same way, Yeshua as our representative does something for us that we ourselves cannot do; He speaks to God on our behalf and also, because of His sacrificial death for us, He enables us to be free of sin.

The Virgin Birth of the Messiah

By way of introduction, we note the distinction between the virgin birth (that Yeshua was born without a human father) and the immaculate conception (the Roman Catholic doctrine that Miriam was also without sin).

The Virgin Birth and the Tanach

Genesis 3:15. God's message to the snake, and to Satan indirectly, carries an intimation of this truth.

> And I will put hostility between you and the woman
> and between your offspring and her offspring;
> her offspring will attack your head,
> and you will attack her offspring's heel.[6] (Genesis 3:15)

Through the seed of the man, sin entered the world; through the seed of the woman, salvation will come. The intimation is that a man will not produce the redeeming seed.

Isaiah 7:14. This is the well-known passage that speaks of a virgin birth.

> Therefore the Lord himself will give you a sign: The virgin will be with child and will give birth to a son, and will call him Immanuel. (Isaiah 7:14 NIV)[7]

We need to be careful how we interpret this passage, which has both a historical meaning, as well as a connection to what Mattai says concerning the virgin birth.

Historical connection. In fear of King Ahaz, with Judah under attack, Isaiah's promises concerning this child that

> He will eat sour milk and honey, which will help him know how to reject evil and choose what is right. Here is why this will be so: Before the child knows how to reject evil and choose what is right, the land whose two kings you fear will be desolate. (Isaiah 7:14–16)

The Hebrew word* almah *in other contexts. Most of the seven occurrences of *almah* in the Tanach demand the meaning of virgin.

> Here I am, standing by the spring. When the young woman [NIV: "maiden"] goes out to draw water, I'll say, "Give me a little water to drink from your jug." (Genesis 24:43)

> Pharaoh's daughter said to her, "Yes, do so." So the young girl went and got the child's mother. (Exodus 2:8)

> Singers walk in front;
> musicians follow playing their stringed instruments,
> in the midst of young women [NIV: "maidens"] playing tambourines.
> (Psalm 68:25; verse 26 MT)

> The fragrance of your colognes is delightful;
> your name is like the finest perfume.
> No wonder the young women [NIV: "maidens"] adore you!
> (Song of Solomon 1:3)

> There may be sixty queens,
> and eighty concubines,
> and young women [NIV: "virgins"] without number.
> Sixty queens there may be, and eighty concubines, and virgins beyond number. (Song of Solomon 6:8)

> . . . the way of an eagle in the sky,
> the way of a snake on a rock,
> the way of a ship in the sea,
> and the way of a man with a woman [NIV: "maiden"]. (Proverbs 30:19)

Mattai's use of Isaiah 7:14. When Mattai in 1:23 translated *almah* from Isaiah 7:14, he used *parthenos*, which is the Greek word meaning *virgin*. On this basis, he understood the meaning of the word in Isaiah 7:14.

But the point to make is that even though the Isaiah 7:14 passage is a prophecy that relates to a certain point in history, a divine design exists that connects the Isaiah 7:14 passage and the way Mattai used it in application to the birth of the Messiah. Isaiah may only have seen the perspective of his own day—though perhaps he saw a future connotation—but the Holy Spirit led Mattai to the full meaning of Isaiah 7:14.

The Virgin Birth in Mattai and Luke

The Two Accounts of Mattai 1:18–2:1 and Luke 1:26–38, 2:1–11, 21. Both accounts agree as to the main facts surrounding the birth of Yeshua.

Main Facts	Scripture References
The mother of Yeshua was called Miriam.	His mother **Miriam**. (Mattai 1:18) The virgin's name was Miriam. (Luke 1:27)
Miriam was a virgin (in Greek, *parthenos*).	While his mother **Miriam** was engaged to Joseph, but **before they came together,** she was found to be pregnant through the Holy Spirit. (Mattai 1:18) The virgin will conceive . . . (Mattai 1:23) . . . a **virgin** engaged to a man whose name was Joseph, a descendant of David, and the virgin's name was Miriam. (Luke 1:27) Miriam said to the angel, "How will this be, since **I have not had sexual relations with a man**?" (Luke 1:34)
Miriam was pledged to be married to a man named Joseph. Note that she became pregnant *after* she was pledged to be married and *before* the actual consummation of the marriage.	Now the birth of Yeshua the Messiah happened this way. While his mother Miriam was engaged to Joseph, but **before they came together, she was found to be pregnant through the Holy Spirit.** . . . When he had contemplated this, an angel of the Lord appeared to him in a dream and said,

Main Facts	Scripture References
	"Joseph, son of David, do not be afraid to take Miriam as your wife, because the child conceived in her is from the Holy Spirit." (Mattai 1:18, 20). . . . his mother Miriam **was engaged to Joseph**, . . . (Mattai 1:18) . . . a virgin **engaged to a man whose name was Joseph**, a descendant of David, . . . (Luke 1:27)
Angels explained to Joseph and Miriam the unusual circumstances of birth.	. . . an **angel of the Lord** appeared to him in a dream and said, "Joseph, son of David, do not be afraid to take Miriam as your wife, because the child conceived in her is from the Holy Spirit." (Mattai 1:20) In the sixth month of Elizabeth's pregnancy, **the angel Gabriel was sent by God** to a town of Galilee called Nazareth, to a virgin engaged to a man whose name was Joseph . . . **The angel** came to her and said, "Greetings, . . ." (Luke 1:26–28)
Joseph never broke the pledge of marriage with Miriam; they were married before the birth of Yeshua.	When Joseph awoke from sleep he did what the angel of the Lord told him. **He took his wife**, . . . (Mattai 1:24) He went to be registered with **Miriam, who was promised in marriage to him**, and who was expecting a child. (Luke 2:5)
The child to be born was to be named Yeshua.	She will give birth to a son and **you will name him Yeshua**, because he will save his people from their sins. (Mattai 1:21)

Main Facts	Scripture References
The child was born in order to be the Savior who would save his people from their sins.	Listen: You will become pregnant and give birth to a son, and **you will name him Yeshua**. (Luke 1:31) She will give birth to a son and you will name him Yeshua, **because he will save his people from their sins**. (Mattai 1:21) Today your Savior is born in the city of David. He is Messiah the Lord. (Luke 2:11)
Yeshua was born in Bethlehem and Joseph and Miriam named him Yeshua.	After Yeshua was **born in Bethlehem** in Judea, . . . (Mattai 2:1) a son, **whom he named Yeshua**. (Mattai 1:25) So Joseph also went up from the town of Nazareth in Galilee to Judea, **to the city of David called Bethlehem**, because he was of the house and family line of David. He went to be registered with Miriam, who was promised in marriage to him, and who was expecting a child. While they were there, the time came for her to deliver her child. And **she gave birth to her firstborn son** . . . (Luke 2:4–7) At the end of eight days, when he was circumcised, **he was named Yeshua**, . . . (Luke 2:21)

Why Two Accounts? In the wisdom of God, two accounts were provided for the following reasons.

Mattai: Yeshua's lineage through Joseph back to Solomon. This confers on Yeshua the right to sit on the throne of David through the line of

Solomon. However, the prophet Jeremiah had placed a curse on Jehoiachin, also known as Jeconiah, who was a descendant in the line of Solomon.

> This man, Jeconiah, will be like a broken pot someone threw away.
> He will be like a clay vessel that no one wants.
> Why will he and his children be forced into exile?
> Why will they be thrown out into a country they know nothing about?
> O land of Judah, land of Judah, land of Judah!
> Listen to what the LORD has to say!
> The LORD says,
> "Enroll this man in the register as though he were childless.
> Enroll him as a man who will not enjoy success during his lifetime.
> For none of his sons will succeed in occupying the throne of David
> or ever succeed in ruling over Judah." (Jeremiah 22:28–30)

Because of this curse, it was not possible for Joseph to be biologically related to Yeshua. Another way would have to be demonstrated that Yeshua is linked to David.

Luke: Yeshua's lineage through Nathan, Solomon's brother, back to David.

> These were the sons born to him in Jerusalem: Shimea, Shobab, Nathan, and Solomon—the mother of these four was Bat Sheva the daughter of Ammiel. (1 Chronicles 3:5)

In that way, Yeshua's lineage is related to David through Miriam, who conferred on Yeshua His identity, and so Yeshua was not involved in a line with a curse on it. Furthermore, the line in Luke goes back even further, all the way to Adam. Thus, even though Yeshua had no earthly father, He still had a link to humanity.

A criticism has been put forth by Jewish scholars who have questioned this understanding of Luke's genealogy, for the genealogy seems to establish a link with Joseph when it says,

> So Yeshua, when he began his ministry, was about thirty years old. He was the son (as was supposed) of Joseph, the son of Heli, . . . (Luke 3:23)

If this is the case, the criticism is that the validity of the line is compromised. But is this what the text says? Literally, the text in Luke 3:23 reads, "being *as it was thought* the son of Joseph . . ." Luke's position is quite clear.[8] Therefore, Joseph is not to be considered as part of the genealogy. The name next mentioned is Heli, the father or ancestor of Miriam. Yeshua is then the grandson of Heli. The fact that Miriam's name is omitted is not so unusual; note how in Mattai 1:8, three generations are omitted: Ahaziah, Joash, and Amaziah.

> Asa the father of Jehoshaphat, Jehoshaphat the father of Joram, Joram the father of Uzziah, . . . (Mattai 1:8)

Note also that none of the opponents of the early Jewish believers ever tried to disprove the genealogies. After all, all records were open to the public.

The Virgin Birth and Other New Covenant Writers

Some have felt since the virgin birth is such a significant event, other New Covenant writers should have recorded it. For example, Mark and Yohanan seem silent on the subject. But silence does not disprove the fact. One mention of such a doctrine would be adequate enough to prove it. Furthermore, the purposes of Mark and Yohanan did not include discussing the virgin birth. In addition, this doctrine was universally accepted by genuine believers in the early church.

However, let us consider the words Yohanan used of the coming of Yeshua into this world. Two words for the idea of "birth" appear in Greek: *gennao* and *ginomai*. As the Holy Spirit led Yohanan in describing how the Messiah entered the stream of the human race, the choice was for *ginomai*.

> Now the Word became [Greek: *egeneto*, a form of ginomai] flesh and took up residence among us. We saw his glory—the glory of the one and only, full of grace and truth, who came from the Father. (Yohanan 1:14)

The point is that the birth of Yeshua was not like the birth of any other baby.

When Yeshua was dying on the tree, He directed His mother Miriam's attention to Yohanan, and likewise pointed Yohanan to His mother. Yohanan then took Miriam from the scene, sparing her the anguish of seeing Him die. Across the years as the two spent time together, Miriam must have shared the particulars of the virgin birth with Yohanan. For that and for other reasons, Yohanan's choice of word was made carefully.

The *shaliach* Sha'ul also made mention of the unique birth.

> But when the appropriate time had come, God sent out his Son, born of a woman, born under the law. (Galatians 4:4)

The specific Greek word behind "born" is again *ginomai* rather than *gennao*. On the other hand, when Sha'ul spoke of the two sons, one born of the slave woman and the other born of the free woman, the word is *gennao* (Galatians 4:23), as other children are born.

> But one, the son by the slave woman, was born by natural descent, while the other, the son by the free woman, was born through the promise. (Galatians 4:23)

The words used are precise; Sha'ul knew of the circumstances of the virgin birth.

Yeshua's Knowledge of His Own Background; the Community's Knowledge of His Family

The Discussion in Luke 2. Note the discussion between Miriam, Joseph, and Yeshua after they found Him in the temple.

> When his parents saw him, they were overwhelmed. His mother said to him, "Child, why have you treated us like this? Look, your father and I have been looking for you anxiously." But he replied, "Why were you looking for me? Didn't you know that I must be in my Father's house?" (Luke 2:48–49)

Note the play on words: "Your father . . . my Father." We may wonder how much Yeshua already understood of the circumstances under which He had been born. As Yeshua "increased in wisdom" (Luke 2:52) at home, Miriam and Joseph must have said *something* to Him. It was very possible also that others in the community knew of His background; no doubt Yeshua could have been the target of hostility on the part of some of His neighbors.

The Charges in Yohanan 8. In Yohanan 8 we encounter three major charges against Yeshua questioning His origin. The first charge, phrased as an insinuation, is "Who is the father of Yeshua?"

> "I testify about myself and the Father who sent me testifies about me." Then they began asking him, "Who is your father?" Yeshua answered, "You do not know either me or my Father. If you knew me you would know my Father too." (Yohanan 8:18–19)

The cry that arose from the crowd—"Where is your father?" in the NIV—in effect was saying, "You cannot even point to a human father."

Yeshua's reply, "You do not know either me or my Father," implies that they did not even know His *real* father; all they knew was that Joseph had married Miriam knowing full well she was already pregnant.

The second charge is even more pointed.

> "You people are doing the deeds of your father." Then they said to Yeshua, "We were not born as a result of immorality! We have only one Father, God himself." (Yohanan 8:41)

Some in the crowd accused Yeshua of being illegitimate. This was a serious charge, as we see in the Torah.

> A person of illegitimate birth may not enter the assembly of the Lord; to the tenth generation no one related to him may do so. (Deuteronomy 23:2)

But note His response.

> Yeshua replied, "If God were your Father, you would love me, for I have come from God and am now here. I have not come on my own initiative,

> but he sent me. Why don't you understand what I am saying? It is because you cannot accept my teaching. You people are from your father the devil, and you want to do what your father desires. He was a murderer from the beginning, and does not uphold the truth, because there is no truth in him. Whenever he lies, he speaks according to his own nature, because he is a liar and the father of lies. But because I am telling you the truth, you do not believe me. Who among you can prove me guilty of any sin? If I am telling you the truth, why don't you believe me? The one who belongs to God listens and responds to God's words. You don't listen and respond, because you don't belong to God." (Yohanan 8:42–47)

His claim was that He truly came from God. If God were the Father of each one in the crowd facing Him, they would all love one another and love Yeshua. But sadly, Yeshua had to accuse some of His opponents that they were only doing the deeds of their father, Satan, the one who opposes God.

Finally, a third charge is again made as to Yeshua's origin.

> The Judeans replied, "Aren't we correct in saying that you are a Samaritan and are possessed by a demon?" (Yohanan 8:48)

The charge is brutal. Even if Miriam and Joseph were Jews, if Joseph was not the father, who then was? The implication here is that Yeshua's father could have been an unknown Samaritan.

How did Yeshua respond to this charge? He said,

> Yeshua answered, "I am not possessed by a demon, but I honor my Father—and yet you dishonor me." (Yohanan 8:49)

Yeshua's charge is serious: Anyone who denies the virgin birth, casting aspersion on His origin from God above, dishonors God, and furthermore, that person will die in his or her sins.

> Yeshua replied, "You people are from below; I am from above. You

> people are from this world; I am not from this world. Thus I told you that you will die in your sins. For unless you believe that I am he, you will die in your sins." (Yohanan 8:23–24)

The Importance of the Virgin Birth

Guards the Doctrine of the Messiah's Sinlessness. It could be argued that even if Yeshua were the physical son of Joseph and Miriam, still God could surely perform a miracle to preserve Him from any taint of sin from His earthly father and mother.

But David had already stated what we find in the normal scheme of things, namely, that one generation passes on its sin nature to the next one.

> Look, I was guilty of sin [NIV: "sinful"] from birth, a sinner [NIV: "sinful"] the moment my mother conceived me. (Psalm 51:5)

There is therefore no need to doubt the scriptural record of how Miriam was able to conceive Yeshua with the partnership of the Holy Spirit. The record seems to suggest a distinct relationship of some kind between Yeshua's conception and His sinlessness.

Explains How Yeshua Could Be Clothed with Human Nature. It was not necessary to have the union of two human beings (Joseph and Miriam) in order for their offspring, Yeshua, to be a human personality. He did not *receive* His personality in the ordinary process of procreation; He was *already* a person from all eternity before He was brought forth to enter the stream of humanity. The virgin birth, as it appears in the sacred record, accounts for the only way Yeshua could be clothed with human nature and form. In fact, if it be insisted that a normal human birth was the only way Yeshua could have a human personality, then it implies doubt as to His preexistence and deity.

The Humanity of the Messiah

We discussed some aspects of the humanity of the Messiah under the topic of His deity. Because the Jewish religious leaders of the first century had no conception of a Messiah who is both human and divine, Yeshua began His ministry by calling Himself the Son of Man. Then, through what He said as well as what He did, people came to realize that the Messiah is indeed both human and divine.

Beginning with Kefa's confession of Mattai 16:16, the disciples became aware of the deity of the Messiah. The New Covenant Scriptures all declare that Yeshua is not only truly God but *God incarnate in human nature*. That is, the Messiah has both human as well as divine natures. Only as a truly *human* being, yet without sin, was it possible for Him to take our place. We thereby see how the doctrine of the Messiah's humanity is as important as the doctrine of His deity.

The Testimony of the New Covenant Writers

The New Covenant writers use a variety of terms and descriptions that point out the human nature of the Messiah Yeshua.

> This is the record of the genealogy of Yeshua the Messiah, the son of David, the son of Abraham. (Mattai 1:1)

> "Isn't this the carpenter, the son of Miriam and brother of Yaakov, Joses, Yehudah, and Shimon? And aren't his sisters here with us?" And so they took offense at him. (Mark 6:3)

> This will be a sign for you: You will find a baby wrapped in strips of cloth and lying in a manger. (Luke 2:12)

> But when the feast was over, as they were returning home, the boy Yeshua stayed behind in Jerusalem. His parents did not know it. (Luke 2:43)

> And he has granted the Son authority to execute judgment, because he is the Son of Man. (Yohanan 5:27)

> But now you are trying to kill me, a man who has told you the truth I heard from God. Abraham did not do this! (Yohanan 8:40)

For since death came through a man, the resurrection of the dead also came through a man. . . . The first man is from the earth, made of dust; the second man is from heaven. (1 Corinthians 15:21, 47)

For there is one God and one intermediary between God and humanity, Messiah Yeshua, himself human. (1 Timothy 2:5)

Some verses are even clearer in this regard.

Men of Israel, listen to these words: Yeshua the Nazarene, a man clearly attested to you by God with powerful deeds, wonders, and miraculous signs that God performed among you through him, just as you yourselves know— . . . (Acts 2:22)

. . . concerning his Son who was a descendant of David with reference to the flesh [NIV: "as to his human nature"], . . . (Romans 1:3)

To them belong the patriarchs, and from them, by human descent, came the Messiah, who is God over all, blessed forever! Amen. (Romans 9:5)

Therefore, since the children share in flesh and blood, he likewise shared in their humanity, so that through death he could destroy the one who holds the power of death (that is, the devil). (Hebrews 2:14)

There is no question, therefore, as to what the Jewish New Covenant writers had in mind. They had no hesitation in demonstrating that Yeshua is both divine and also a true human being. They knew full well what a proclamation concerning the Messiah as both human and divine would mean in the Jewish community. Nevertheless, they proclaimed the truth as they had seen and heard it from the lips of Yeshua Himself.

The "Components" of a Genuine Human Being

Every human being has certain "components," which Sha'ul describes.

> Now may the God of peace himself make you completely holy and may your *spirit* and *soul* and *body* be kept entirely blameless at the coming of our Lord Yeshua the Messiah. (1 Thessalonians 5:23, emphasis added, as also in the following verses)

The description of man as composed of body, soul, and spirit suggests a trichotomy. Yeshua also shared in all of these three dimensions.

> But Yeshua was speaking about the temple of his *body*. (Yohanan 2:21)

> Now my *soul* [Greek: *pseuche*; NIV: "heart"] is greatly distressed. And what should I say? "Father, deliver me from this hour"? No, but for this very reason I have come to this hour. (Yohanan 12:27)

> Then Yeshua, calling out with a loud voice, said, "Father, into your hands I commit my spirit!" And after he said this he breathed his last. (Luke 23:46)

Some texts may appear to contradict the notion that Yeshua is truly human with the three basic components of humanity. As we will see, some have insisted that Yeshua only *took* a body, but that His soul and spirit were *eternal*. For example, the following verse might be taken to suggest that Yeshua only took on a body.

> Now the Word became flesh and took up residence among us. We saw his glory—the glory of the one and only, full of grace and truth, who came from the Father. (Yohanan 1:14)

However, the word *flesh* means more than just merely a body. *Flesh* refers to a total humanity, soul and spirit, in addition to a body. After all, a body by itself has no will of its own. A human being must have a soul and spirit in order to exhibit the characteristics of will.

> Therefore, since the children share in flesh and blood, he likewise shared in their humanity, so that through death he could destroy the one who holds the power of death (that is, the devil). (Hebrews 2:14)

Likewise, the designation *flesh and blood* suggests a genuine human nature of body, soul, and spirit. Similarly, for Kefa to have made his confession that Yeshua is both human (the Messiah) and divine (Son of the Living God), there had to have been an understanding of the totality of body, mind, and spirit.

The Marks of a Genuine Human Being

Prenatal and Infant Experiences. Luke describes these stages of Yeshua's life.

> He went to be registered with Miriam, who was promised in marriage to him, and who was expecting a child. . . . "This will be a sign for you: You will find a baby wrapped in strips of cloth and lying in a manger." (Luke 2:5, 12)

Boyhood and Teenage Experiences. Luke similarly recounts these ages of His life.

> And the child grew and became strong, filled with wisdom, and the favor of God was upon him. . . . And Yeshua increased in wisdom and in stature, and in favor with God and with people. (Luke 2:40, 52)

What one must recognize is that at every stage in Yeshua's development, He was perfect for that particular stage: as a baby, He was perfect, and as a teenager, He was also perfect. Therefore, one cannot say that He was not fully developed at any particular stage.

Human Appearance. We see this in, for instance, the encounter with the Samaritan woman.

> So the Samaritan woman said to him, "How can you—a Jew—ask me, a Samaritan woman, for water to drink?" (For Jews use nothing in common with Samaritans.) (Yohanan 4:9)

If a Samaritan woman could recognize Yeshua through His facial expressions as well as His clothing, then surely Yeshua appeared as a normal being to those who saw and heard Him.

Human Appetites. These include being hungry and thirsty.

> After he fasted forty days and forty nights he was famished. (Mattai 4:2)

> After this Yeshua, realizing that by this time everything was completed, said (in order to fulfill the scripture), "I am thirsty!" (Yohanan 19:28)

Human Emotions. His emotions included anger and love.

> After looking around at them in anger, grieved by the hardness of their hearts, he said to the man, "Stretch out your hand." He stretched it out, and his hand was restored. (Mark 3:5)

> As Yeshua looked at him, he felt love for him and said, "You lack one thing. Go, sell whatever you have and give the money to the poor, and you will have treasure in heaven. Then come, follow me." (Mark 10:21)

Note that even though He knew that the rich young man would walk away, refusing Yeshua's advice, the Messiah still loved him!

> Yeshua wept. (Yohanan 11:35)

Here, His weeping was a soft one, grieving because of the death of Lazarus.

> And in his anguish he prayed more earnestly, and his sweat was like drops of blood falling to the ground. (Luke 22:44)

> He took with him Kefa and the two sons of Zebedee, and became anguished and distressed. Then he said to them, "My soul is deeply grieved, even to the point of death. Remain here and stay awake with me." (Mattai 26:37–38)

In fact, it is precisely because Yeshua had no sin nature that He could feel these emotions to the core of His being.

Certain Human Limitations. These included tiredness, the need to sleep, and so on.

> And a great storm developed on the sea so that the waves began to swamp the boat. But he was asleep. (Mattai 8:24)

Just as we would do in similar circumstances, Yeshua fell asleep because He was tired.

> Jacob's well was there, so Yeshua, since he was tired from the journey, sat right down beside the well. It was about noon. (Yohanan 4:6)

> During his earthly life Messiah offered both requests and supplications, with loud cries and tears, to the one who was able to save him from death and he was heard because of his devotion. Although he was a son, he learned obedience through the things he suffered. (Hebrews 5:7–8)

We can understand why Yeshua could grow weary and fall asleep; we can grasp why, facing the cup that He had to drink, as it were, before He suffered and died for our sins, He would pray with crying and tears. Far more difficult to understand is the statement that He had to learn obedience from what He suffered. In His humanity, He exhibited genuine limitations; and this experience was *real* as He represented us as a human being. Again, it is because He was without sin that He could feel His limitations all the more keenly.

Demonstrated in His Suffering and Death. Note these verses from Yohanan.

> When he had received the sour wine, Yeshua said, "It is completed!" Then he bowed his head and gave up his spirit. Then, because it was the day of preparation, so that the bodies should not stay on the trees

> on the Sabbath (for that Sabbath was an especially important one), the Jewish leaders asked Pilate to have the victims' legs broken and the bodies taken down. So the soldiers came and broke the legs of the two men who had been crucified with Yeshua, first the one and then the other. But when they came to Yeshua and saw that he was already dead, they did not break his legs. But one of the soldiers pierced his side with a spear, and blood and water flowed out immediately. (Yohanan 19:30–34)

In His death, He exhibited every essential aspect of true human nature, yet He was without sin. Sin is an abnormality, not an essential component of human nature. The poet may have said, "To err is human," but that is an error! In the entire record we have of Yeshua, never once through word or deed did He sin. He was without sin, yet He was also truly human.

Theories Reflecting Error Concerning Messiah's True Humanity

Heresies Reflecting an Incomplete Humanity. *Apollinarianism* was an ancient heresy that suggested that Yeshua had a human body and soul, but that His own eternal spirit took the place of the human spirit. Since a human being has a body, soul, and spirit, if any one of the three is omitted, there is no complete humanity in the Messiah. The objection to this view, then, is that if true, Yeshua could not redeem the whole of human nature but only its spiritual elements.

H. W. Beecher and others offered a modern form of the ancient heresy. Beecher taught that the Messiah had a human body, but no human spirit or soul. This is essentially a dichotomist position once again, which leaves Yeshua with an incomplete humanity.

Heresies Reflecting an Unreal Humanity. An ancient form of this view was *Docetism*. In this view, the humanity and suffering of the earthly Messiah is only apparent rather than real. Adherents of this view believe that matter was evil, and God infinite. Therefore, He could not truly become man. From birth to death, Messiah's presentation is only an appearance of humanity. Among some evangelicals, the deity of Yeshua is so overemphasized that there can be a danger in coming close to this ancient position, whereby His humanity is hardly considered.

The position was assumed by Mary Baker Eddy, who held that since matter is not real, then flesh is only a delusion of the "mortal mind." This position would also assert that the humanity of Yeshua was unreal.

Practical Value

The greatest value of recognizing the humanity of the Messiah is that it enables us to to realize that He indeed knew what it meant to suffer, to be hungry and grow tired, to suffer denial and rejection. It enables us to understand that in His act of redemption He took our place as a human being, dying in our stead, and that even today, He sits at the right hand of God interceding for us.

The Person of the Messiah

We have already seen that the Messiah is both God and man in the truest sense. Having noted the Scriptures regarding the two natures, we hasten to add this doctrine raises, from the standpoint of rationalism, some of the most difficult questions one could ever consider, such as:

- If Yeshua had two natures, how could they be joined together into one Savior?
- How can the Messiah be God and man without having two personalities?
- How can Yeshua have two natures and not have two minds, two consciences, and two wills?
- If there is one personality, in which of the two natures is the personality to be "found"?
- What is the relationship of human to divine in the present situation whereby Yeshua has a glorified body, which He did not have prior to His incarnation?

Such questions have never been answered to everyone's satisfaction, and no attempt will be made to resolve them here. Our main concern is what the Scripture says about them, in order that we might understand the doctrine as far as it is possible. One must always remember that going beyond what is written in the Word will lead one into serious error, something that occurred only too frequently in the early days of the body of the Messiah.

The Person of the Messiah as a Mystery

Any number of passages in the New Covenant depict this mystery.

> All things have been handed over to me by my Father. No one knows the Son except the Father, and no one knows the Father except the Son and anyone to whom the Son decides to reveal him. (Mattai 11:27)

> And we all agree, our religion contains amazing revelation:[9]
> He was revealed in the flesh,
> vindicated by the Spirit,
> seen by angels,
> proclaimed among Gentiles,
> believed on in the world,
> taken up in glory. (1 Timothy 3:16)

These Scriptures remind us to seek to examine the mystery even though a rationalistic explanation is not possible.

> Then he said to Thomas, "Put your finger here, and examine my hands. Extend your hand and put it into my side. Do not continue in your unbelief, but believe." (Yohanan 20:27)

Yeshua presented Himself to Thomas, asking him to believe that He indeed is divine, as well as human. Yet He commended others who would not see in the flesh but also would believe.

The Person of the Messiah as an Indivisible Unity

Yeshua's References to Himself. He spoke of Himself as one personality, distinguishing Himself from other men.

> Yeshua replied, "You people are from below; I am from above. You people are from this world; I am not from this world." (Yohanan 8:23)

He distinguished Himself from the Father.

> I testify about myself and the Father who sent me testifies about me. (Yohanan 8:18)

He distinguished Himself from the Holy Spirit.

> But I tell you the truth, it is to your advantage that I am going away. For if I do not go away, the Advocate will not come to you, but if I go, I will send him to you. (Yohanan 16:7)

But Yeshua never distinguished Himself as a divine person apart from a human person. He declared that "I am," that is, one person.

> Yeshua said to them, "I tell you the solemn truth, before Abraham came into existence, I am!" (Yohanan 8:58)

He had a divine nature but He was also human, therefore, one person.

Human and Divine Aspects Applied to Yeshua as One Person. The various acts, powers, and attributes of the two natures are applied without any distinction to one person, not to two persons.

> "Look! The virgin will conceive and bear a son, and they will call him Emmanuel," which means "God with us." (Mattai 1:23)

> Yeshua the Messiah is the same yesterday and today and forever! (Hebrews 13:8)

Sha'ul speaks of the incarnate God, describing Him as human and emphasizing that He, through His death and shed blood, made it possible for a new body of believers, wherein all know Him.

> Watch out for yourselves and for all the flock of which the Holy Spirit has made you overseers, to shepherd the *qehilah* of God that he obtained with the blood of his own Son. (Acts 20:28)

> None of the rulers of this age understood it. If they had known it, they would not have crucified the Lord of glory. (1 Corinthians 2:8)

In Revelation, the Messiah, who in His human body is now in glory, receives worship and praise.

> Then I looked and heard the voice of many angels in a circle around the throne, as well as the living creatures and the elders. Their number was ten thousand times ten thousand—thousands times thousands—all of whom were singing in a loud voice:
>
> "Worthy is the lamb who was killed
> to receive power and wealth
> and wisdom and might
> and honor and glory and praise!"
>
> Then I heard every creature—in heaven, on earth, under the earth, in the sea, and all that is in them—singing:
> "To the one seated on the throne and to the Lamb
> be praise, honor, glory, and ruling power forever and ever!"
>
> And the four living creatures were saying "Amen," and the elders threw themselves to the ground and worshiped. (Revelation 5:11–14)

While it is the Messiah in His humanity who sits upon the throne, yet at the same time His deity is apparent to everyone in heaven who worships Him.

Two natures are definitely visible, yet we are only dealing with one person.

Many times the Scripture describes the Messiah's two natures side by side, yet every such statement is ascribed to one person and not two.

> And a great storm developed on the sea so that the waves began to swamp the boat. But he was asleep. So they came and woke him up saying, "Lord, save us! We are about to die!" But he said to them, "Why are you cowardly, you people of little faith?" Then he got up and rebuked the winds and the sea, and it was dead calm. (Mattai 8:24–26)

Note how Yeshua the man was sleeping. When He arose and rebuked the wind and the waves, He expressed His deity in that He had control over nature.

In the case of Lazarus, Yeshua wept as any of the people of Bethany would have done because of the departure of Lazarus. He had an empathy with the mourners and expressed His feelings as any other human would do. On the other hand, He demonstrated His divine nature by raising Lazarus from the dead, giving him life, which only God can do.

> Yeshua wept. . . . When he had said this, he shouted in a loud voice, "Lazarus, come out!" The one who had died came out, his feet and hands tied up with strips of cloth, and a cloth wrapped around his face. Yeshua said to them, "Unwrap him and let him go." (Yohanan 11:35, 43–44)

However, even though we see both natures, we are still speaking of only one person.

It is wrong to divide out words and acts that we then ascribe to separate natures. In some ways, Yeshua acts as a human being, while in other ways, He demonstrates the power of God through His divine nature. Nevertheless, one person is involved in all of these activities. Below, we will note a number of heresies in which the two natures are considered separately.

Passages Speaking of the Divine Nature and Silent on the Human Nature, but Referring to the Same One Personality.

> Yeshua the Messiah is the same yesterday and today and forever! (Hebrews 13:8)

While this passage is obviously referring to His divine nature, nevertheless the implication is that the entire person of the Messiah lives forever. This also includes the glorified body in which He was raised, in which are also the wounds He suffered in His death for us. Note that the writer reached back into the Hebrew Scriptures; statements that are there applied to God are applied to Yeshua in Hebrews 13:8. For example,

> The Levites—Jeshua, Kadmiel, Bani, Hashabneiah, Sherebiah, Hodiah, Shebaniah, and Pethahiah—said, "Stand up and bless the LORD your God!
>
> "May you be blessed, O LORD our God, from age to age. May your glorious name be blessed; may it be lifted up above all blessing and praise." (Nehemiah 9:5)
>
> For God, our God, is our defender forever!
> He guides us! (Psalm 48:14)

These truths are also applied to the Messiah. His person exists for all eternity.

Scriptural Testimony to the Union of the Two Natures in the Messiah

The attempt to explain the union of the two natures in the Messiah in a rationalistic manner has baffled the best of all human minds. However, while one may have difficulty in understanding how such a person can be, nevertheless we continue to observe what Scripture itself has to say about this union. Below, we shall attempt to demonstrate it in a more theological and philosophical manner.

Two Natures United in One Person. We see this for instance in Sha'ul's writings.

> . . . concerning his Son who was a descendant of David with reference to the flesh, who was appointed the Son-of-god-in-power according to the Holy Spirit by the resurrection from the dead, Yeshua the Messiah our Lord. (Romans 1:3–4)

> To them belong the patriarchs, and from them, by human descent, came the Messiah, who is God over all, blessed forever! Amen. (Romans 9:5)

We note from Sha'ul's writings that the Messiah is one person, but there is no question that there is both a human and a divine nature. Each of the natures is distinct. Yet the *shaliach* Sha'ul thought of Yeshua as only one person. We need to remember that all during the days of his training under the leading rabbis in Jerusalem, Sha'ul had no question about the God who is only one (Deuteronomy 6:4)—not a composite unity but one. It took the drastic confrontation between Yeshua and Sha'ul on the Damascus highway to change Sha'ul's thinking. He thought he knew who the God of Israel was, but when confronted by the shining brightness of God's brightness, he cried out, "Who are you, Lord?" (Acts 9: 5). Did he not know who Israel's God was according to Moses? But this was something different. Sha'ul instinctively knew he had been confronted by God and that is why he called out to the Lord. Imagine his shock when the answer came back, "I am Yeshua whom you are persecuting!"

The Human Nature Empowered. In this union, the divine nature, in a mystery, imparts power to the human nature.

> I am the living bread that came down from heaven. If anyone eats from this bread he will live forever. The bread that I will give for the life of the world is my flesh. (Yohanan 6:51)

The flesh about which the Messiah spoke was explained by Him:

> The Spirit is the one who gives life; human nature is of no help! The words that I have spoken to you are spirit and are life. (Yohanan 6:63)

It was words imparted by the divine nature that were supposed to have lent meaning to the notion of eating the flesh of the Messiah, that is, what would be His humanity. Obviously, if people misunderstood and thought they were actually required to eat the living flesh of the Messiah, they were seriously mistaken and Yeshua corrected them. But the point is that it was a message from the divine nature that lent graphic meaning to what it would mean for people to partake of the truth of the words as if eating the flesh of the Messiah, without, of course, literally doing so.

Human Experiences for the Divine Nature. Because of this union, certain human experiences are made possible for the divine nature.

> Therefore, since the children share in flesh and blood, he likewise shared in their humanity, so that through death he could destroy the one who holds the power of death (that is, the devil), . . . Therefore he had to be made like his brothers and sisters in every respect, so that he could become a merciful and faithful high priest in things relating to God, to make atonement for the sins of the people. For since he himself suffered when he was tempted, he is able to help those who are tempted. (Hebrews 2:14, 17–18)

The incarnation made it possible to suffer death, for though God Himself could not die, God incarnate in human flesh was enabled to make an atonement, suffering in the body. Experiential knowledge was necessary in the plan of redemption.

One Person as the Mediator. The union in one person of the two natures thereby made it possible for one person to be the mediator between God and man.

> Therefore since we have a great high priest who has passed through the heavens, Yeshua the Son of God, let us hold fast to our confession. For we do not have a high priest incapable of sympathizing with our weaknesses, but one who has been tempted in every way just as we are, yet without sin. Therefore let us confidently approach the throne of grace to receive mercy and find grace whenever we need help. (Hebrews 4:14–16)

Already noted was the necessity for the incarnation whereby the Messiah takes our place by dying in our stead. In that capacity, He is the mediator between God and man, taking our place in dying for us, at the same time satisfying the righteousness of God that will enable us who believe in Him to be justified.

A Theological and Philosophical Attempt to Understand the Person of the Messiah with His Two Natures

The Hypostatic Union. The doctrine that is known by the term *hypostatic union* teaches that the two natures of Messiah, divine and human, are united in one person forever. As already stated, the union entails a complete separate identity of natures and no transfer of attributes from one nature to the other.

The Statement of the Chalcedonian Creed. This creed states that

> He is one Messiah existing in two natures without mixture, without division, without separation; the diversity of the natures not being destroyed by their union in the one person; but the peculiar properties of each nature being preserved and concurring to the One Person.

In the technical language of the creed, this is defined as:

> one and the same Messiah . . . to be acknowledged in two natures, *inconfusedly, unchangeably, indivisibly and inseparably,* the distinction of natures being in no means taken away by the union, but rather the property of each nature being preserved, and concurring in one Person and one substance not parted or divided into two persons, but one and the same Son . . .

These basic facts of the creed are summarized as follows: There is one person; there are two natures (divine and human); the two natures have a unique relationship.

In this unique relationship, the two natures do not fuse (*inconfusedly*); do not change (*unchangeably*); do not divide (*indivisibly*); and do not separate (*inseparably*).

The term "nature" has been defined by Berkhof as "the sum-total of all the essential qualities of a thing, that which makes it what it is."[10] Paul Nevin, professor at Moody Bible Institute, states that a person is not the same thing as a nature but is a nature with personality or individuality added. A person is a complete nature, substance, or essence, endowed with reason, emotion, and will. And nature may exist without a person, but not a person without a nature. The Messiah has two natures but as pointed out already, His personality is not split. The believer today has two natures (the old and the new), but they are of a different sort than the Messiah's two natures (the divine and the human). Note again, the Christian's two natures do not split his personality.

Philippians 2:6–11, a Key Passage. This is the primary passage that depicts the hypostatic union. Verse numbers are given so as to follow the discussion below.

> [6] . . . who though he existed in the form of God
> did not regard equality with God
> as something to be grasped,
> [7] but *emptied himself*
> by taking on the form of a slave,
> by looking like other men,
> and by sharing in human nature.
> [8] He humbled himself,
> by becoming obedient to the point of death
> —even death on a tree!
> [9] As a result God exalted him
> and gave him the name
> that is above every name,

[10] so that at the name of Yeshua
every knee will bow
—in heaven and on earth and under the earth—
[11] and every tongue confess
that Yeshua the Messiah is Lord
to the glory of God the Father. (Philippians 2:6–11)

First, a definition: the doctrine of the limitation of the divine attributes of Yeshua the Messiah during His earthly life is known as the *kenosis*, from verse 7 of the above passage.

> . . . but *emptied himself* [as also in NASB; NIV: "made himself nothing"] by taking on the form of a slave, by looking like other men. (Philippians 2:7, emphasis added)

In this verse, the Greek for *emptied Himself* or *made Himself nothing* is *ekenosen*, from which comes the word *kenosis*.

A few remarks can be made on this passage:

In verse 6, the word *form* means the outward expression of the inner nature or being. The word does not refer only to the outer shape but to the inner substance as well. Furthermore, He had equality with God but in the emptying He did not cling to it. This equality, however, was the glory of the outward expressions of His deity.

In verse 7, when Yeshua *emptied Himself* or *made Himself nothing*, this meant that He set aside the outward expression of deity or His glory but not the divine nature itself. The limitation would also mean laying aside many of the privileges of His omnipresence, omnipotence, and omniscience. When we go to verse 7, the statement is also made that He was made in human likeness (NET has "looking like other men"; NIV has "made in human likeness"); it meant that His humanity was genuine. To conclude, it may be stated that the Messiah, who is God, exchanged His divine splendor for human nature, took on the appearance of mere man, and submitted Himself to death in its most degraded form, the death on the tree!

As a final statement, the attributes of both of the natures of the Messiah apply to the same person, yet without confusing them. His eternity, for example, applies only to His divine nature; His physical thirst, weakness, and so on apply only to His human nature. Nevertheless, as a person, He exists for all eternity with both natures.

Four Erroneous Views of the *Kenosis*[11]

To review, the word *kenosis* comes from Philippians 2:7, where the Greek word *ekenosen* is translated as "emptied Himself" (NET and NASB) or "made himself nothing" (NIV). It refers to the idea that Yeshua in some way divested Himself of or limited His divine attributes, but the problem is knowing exactly what is meant in Philippians 2:7.

Four Views. There are essentially four views on what the *kenosis* actually entailed. (1) The Messiah gave up *all* His divine attributes; (2) The Messiah gave up the *use* of all divine attributes; (3) the Messiah *pretended* not to possess the divine attributes; and (4) the Messiah *gave up (no longer had) the three privileges* of omnipresence, omniscience, and omnipotence.

Responses to the Views. Each of these views compromises the divine nature in the Messiah. But the last one is probably the most well known of the incorrect views. In regard to this fourth view, it would not be possible for the Messiah to surrender any divine attribute without changing His divine essence. Moreover, this view contradicts Scriptures that the Messiah *did* exercise these attributes.

For example, we see Yeshua's omnipresence in a situation where He was already resurrected and in glory.

> For where two or three are assembled in my name, I am there among them. (Mattai 18:20)

The Scripture also shows Him to have been omniscient.

> But Yeshua would not entrust himself to them, because he knew all people. He did not need anyone to testify about man, for he knew what was in man. (Yohanan 2:24–25)

> Yeshua said a third time, "Shimon, son of Yohanan, do you love me?" Kefa was distressed that Yeshua asked him a third time, "Do you love me?" and said, "Lord, you know everything. You know that I love you." Yeshua replied, "Feed my sheep." (Yohanan 21:17)

However, there were occasions where Yeshua limited the knowledge that He retained in His human nature, as when He said:

> But as for that day or hour no one knows it—neither the angels in heaven, nor the Son—except the Father. (Mark 13:32)

Finally, omnipotence is seen in most of His miracles, which demonstrated that He had a divine nature.

Therefore the fourth view above is not the teaching of Scripture.

There are further wrong theories of the Messiah's person. There is the notion whereby *the person is divided*, as for example in the fifth-century heresy of *Nestorianism*. In this view, the two natures are so sharply separated that one can only see the Messiah as two persons. With this heresy, in the Messiah is both God and man, but the Messiah is not the God-man.

There are heresies that confuse the two natures, such as *Eutychianism*, also from the fifth century. This view is the opposite of Nestoriansim. In Nestorianism, one loses sight of the one person, while in Eutychianism, the one person is so emphasized that the two distinct natures become almost irrelevant, with an insistance that the human nature was completely absorbed into the divine nature.

A Correct View of the *Kenosis*. We can summarize a correct idea of the *kenosis* in three points:

First, Yeshua *veiled* His divine glory. On one occasion, however, in the transfiguration, some of that glory did shine through:

> And he was transfigured before them. His face shone like the sun, and his clothes became white as light. (Mattai 17:2)

Second, Yeshua's divine nature was *joined* to an unglorified humanity in the days of His flesh.

And third, Yeshua voluntarily *restricted* His use of omniscience, omnipresence, and omnipotence while on earth. One can never say, however, that He no longer *possessed* them, for He still had them within Himself.

Concluding Reflections and Practical Values

As we conclude this discussion, we note that there is no antagonism between the two natures of the Messiah. Both dwell together in perfect harmony. There is, however, a real tension between God and man with his sinful human nature.

The mystery of two natures in the Messiah has intrigued the minds of many believers down through the centuries. While we may have continual progress in the attempt to understand the relationship, it is doubtful that we can ever reach the end of the mystery in this life. It remains a doctrine that offers a fruitful field for reverent study and contemplation.

Finally, the doctrine of Messiah's person and natures should humble us before God. When it is all said and done, there are limits to our understanding concerning the Messiah. He remains a mystery to the people of Israel. When Jewish people have insisted to me that Yeshua was only a human being, I have responded, "Are you satisfied that this is the end of the question?" And often, some have admitted to me that there is something about Yeshua that demands further study. We should always be humble before this mystery, realizing that while we cannot fully explain who He is, we certainly can know Him by personal experience.

THE DEATH OF THE MESSIAH

Normally, the topic of the death of the Messiah would be handled under the major doctrinal topic of soteriology, or the doctrine of salvation. We include it here, however, because it has a very direct bearing on the doctrine of the Messiah, or Christology.

Before investigating this topic as expounded primarily in the New Covenant, we need to understand the concept of the death of a substitute on our behalf.

An Atonement According to Moses

The Sin Offering of the Mosaic Sacrificial System. The major offering of atonement under the sacrificial Mosaic Covenant was the sin offering as described in Leviticus 4. The chapter itself is a narrative of which offerings were brought by various people as well as how each person handled the particular offering. Running through the particular variations is an overall pattern in which we find four major principles in connection with the atonement for sin.

The Four Principles. We have mentioned these in previous chapters, and it will be helpful to reiterate them here.

Substitution. Every individual in Leviticus 4 brought his specific animal substitute. For example, a priest was to bring a bull.

Identification. As each person brought his sin offering, he put his hand on the head of the animal and confessed his sins. The offerer's sin then was considered as being transferred to the animal and the animal was now identified with the sin of the offerer.

The death of the substitute. Note who it is that kills the animal: it is the offerer himself.

The exchange of life. When the animal died, it gave its life to the offerer.

Possible Responses to Moses' Lesson of Atonement. The Scriptures do not presume that atonement for sin was secured by merely bringing an offering. A proper response was necessary. Below we note four responses to the sacrificial system.

No regard for the Mosaic system. Particularly this was so in the period before the exile to Babylon. Many people went off to the pagan shrines to offer the sacrifices there and become a part of the cult worship as well as adultery associated with the cult.

A ritualistic observance. Most people knew that they needed to bring their specific sacrifice, but they did so in a ritualistic manner. Perhaps a father came with his son, or two brothers came together. While they offered their sacrifices, imagine that they were talking to each other about family business, or the weather. In such cases, the sacrifice was to no avail because the person's heart was not in it. If there ever was an attitude that the prophets excoriated, it was this one: a mere ritual response (see Isaiah 1 and Amos 5).

A legalistic presentation. Some who offered their sacrifice said in effect to God, "I brought what I owed You, and now *You* owe *me*." In this case also, the sacrifice was of no avail, because God is not a debtor to anybody. In this instance, the offerer was punctilious in bringing his sacrifice, but it became a mere religious exercise.

A response of faith. The last type of response is seen whereby the offerer, in presenting his sacrifice, seemed to understand the four major principles outlined above. Then, through the ministry of the Holy Spirit, these principles were internalized. The Spirit worked in his heart, changing a hard heart to a heart of flesh, and the heart was circumcised:

> Circumcise your hearts, therefore, and do not be stiff-necked any longer. (Deuteronomy 10:16 NIV)

Those who accepted in faith the principles of the sin offering had the knowledge that their sins had been forgiven:

> As far as the eastern horizon is from the west,
> so he removes the guilt of our rebellious actions from us. (Psalm 103:12)

> You will once again have mercy on us;
> you will conquer our evil deeds;
> you will hurl our sins into the depths of the sea. (Micah 7:19)

In particular, the Day of Atonement had a special meaning for the believer. When he saw the scapegoat being led out of the temple area, he could think to himself, "There go my sins. I don't have to face them again."

The Meaning of the Death of the Messiah

The Foundation and Source of a Genuine Biblical Lifestyle.

> What shall we say then? Are we to remain in sin so that grace may increase? Absolutely not! How can we who died to sin still live in it? Or do you not know that as many as were baptized into Messiah

> Yeshua were baptized into his death? Therefore we have been buried with him through baptism into death, in order that just as Messiah was raised from the dead through the glory of the Father, so we too may live a new life.
>
> For if we have become united with him in the likeness of his death, we will certainly also be united in the likeness of his resurrection. We know that our old man was crucified with him so that the body of sin would no longer dominate us, so that we would no longer be enslaved to sin. (For someone who has died has been freed from sin.)
>
> Now if we died with Messiah, we believe that we will also live with him. We know that since Messiah has been raised from the dead, he is never going to die again; death no longer has mastery over him. For the death he died, he died to sin once for all, but the life he lives, he lives to God. So you too consider yourselves dead to sin, but alive to God in Messiah Yeshua. (Romans 6:1–11)

> For God achieved what the law could not do because it was weakened through the flesh. By sending his own Son in the likeness of sinful flesh and concerning sin, he condemned sin in the flesh, so that the righteous requirement of the law may be fulfilled in us, who do not walk according to the flesh but according to the Spirit. (Romans 8:3–4)

We must not assume that what Sha'ul says in Romans 8:3–4 applied to *Israelites who were genuine believers*. Such Jewish people had the Torah, and through the power of the Holy Spirit, *they could and did* live genuine biblical lives. The problem was rather that, within the community of Israel, there was an unbelieving element. If such unbelieving people offered their sacrifices through ritual or legalism (see above on the responses to the sacrificial system), then the sacrifice never availed for the offerer. In such cases, he or she therefore did not fulfill "the righteous requirements of the law."

In contrast, in the body of the Messiah, all are believers. Therefore, all within this body have the means to live a genuine biblical lifestyle.

Of Great Interest to the Heavenly World.
To righteous men.

Then two men, Moses and Elijah, began talking with him [Yeshua]. They appeared in glorious splendor and spoke about his departure that he was about to carry out at Jerusalem. (Luke 9:30–31)

To angels.

They probed into what person or time the Spirit of Messiah within them was indicating when he testified beforehand about the sufferings appointed for Messiah and his subsequent glory. They were shown that they were serving not themselves but you, in regard to the things now announced to you through those who proclaimed the gospel to you by the Holy Spirit sent from heaven—things angels long to catch a glimpse of. (1 Kefa 1:11–12)

As the song of the redeemed in heaven.

And when he had taken the scroll, the four living creatures and the twenty-four elders threw themselves to the ground before the Lamb. Each of them had a harp and golden bowls full of incense (which are the prayers of the saints). They were singing a new song:

> "You are worthy to take the scroll
> and to open its seals
> because you were killed,
> and at the cost of your own blood you have purchased for God
> persons from every tribe, language, people, and nation.

You have appointed them as a kingdom and priests to serve our God, and they will reign on the earth." (Revelation 5:8–10)

As an everlasting monument of God's love and grace. This is depicted in the scenes of the eternal state portrayed in Revelation 21 and 22. The prominent figure in these chapters is the Messiah Himself, called "the Lamb."

This name, given to the Messiah, is forever a reminder of what He accomplished for us when He died on the tree.

> Then one of the seven angels who had the seven bowls full of the seven final plagues came and spoke to me, saying, "Come, I will show you the bride, the wife of the Lamb!" (Revelation 21:9)

> The wall of the city has twelve foundations, and on them are the twelve names of the twelve apostles of the Lamb. (Revelation 21:14)

> Now I saw no temple in the city, because the Lord God—the All-powerful—and the Lamb are its temple. (Revelation 21:22)

> The city does not need the sun or the moon to shine on it, because the glory of God lights it up, and its lamp is the Lamb. (Revelation 21:23)

> But nothing ritually unclean will ever enter into it, nor anyone who does what is detestable or practices falsehood, but only those whose names are written in the Lamb's book of life. (Revelation 21:27)

> Then the angel showed me the river of the water of life—water as clear as crystal—pouring out from the throne of God and of the Lamb. (Revelation 22:1)

> And there will no longer be any curse, and the throne of God and the Lamb will be in the city. His servants will worship him. (Revelation 22:3)

The Necessity for the Death of the Messiah

Yeshua's Declaration. Yeshua declared that He "must" die. The word *must* translates the Greek word *dei*, which is the strongest possible Greek term to express a necessity.

> From that time on Yeshua began to show his disciples that he must go to Jerusalem and suffer many things at the hands of the elders, chief

> priests, and experts in the law, and be killed, and on the third day be raised. (Mattai 16:21)

In the days of Yeshua, Jewish people had no concept of a Messiah who had to die. Instead, so ran the usual conception, when the Messiah would come, He would bring in the kingdom and sit on the throne of David.

The passage above, Mattai 16:21, was Yeshua's first announcement to His disciples of His impending death. Clearly, it greatly startled them. Kefa's reaction was to take Yeshua by the arm, draw Him away across the road, and rebuke Him: "God forbid, Lord!" The six or seven times that Yeshua made this same announcement, the disciples for the most part paid no attention. Only when Kefa and Yohanan went to the tomb to examine it, as Yohanan wrote many years later, "he [Yohanan] saw and believed" (Yohanan 20:8). What did he believe? When he saw the empty grave clothes, he remembered what Yeshua had taught His disciples all along. It is likely that most of Yeshua's resurrection ministry had to do with the concept that the Messiah, son of David, had to die as the atonement for our sins.

Voluntary and Self-Imposed. This "necessity," as rendered by the word "must," was not imposed on Yeshua by anyone or anything, nor was it fate or circumstance:

> I am the good shepherd. I know my own and my own know me—just as the Father knows me and I know the Father—and I lay down my life for the sheep. I have other sheep that do not come from this sheepfold. I must bring them too, and they will listen to my voice, so that there will be one flock and one shepherd. This is why the Father loves me—because I lay down my life, so that I may take it back again. No one takes it away from me, but I lay it down of my own free will. I have the authority to lay it down, and I have the authority to take it back again. This commandment I received from my Father. (Yohanan 10:14–18)

> And live in love, just as Messiah also loved us and gave himself for us, a sacrificial and fragrant offering to God. (Ephesians 5:2)

He humbled himself,
by becoming obedient to the point of death
—even death on a tree! (Philippians 2:8)

The Means of Accomplishing God's Own Eternal Purpose.

Now my soul is greatly distressed. And what should I say? "Father, deliver me from this hour"? No, but for this very reason I have come to this hour. (Yohanan 12:27)

. . . but by precious blood like that of an unblemished and spotless lamb, namely Messiah. He was foreknown before the foundation of the world but was manifested in these last times for your sake. (1 Kefa 1:19–20)

In Obedience to the Will of His Father.

Then he said to them, "My soul is deeply grieved, even to the point of death. Remain here and stay awake with me." Going a little farther, he threw himself down with his face to the ground and prayed, "My Father, if possible, let this cup pass from me! Yet not what I will, but what you will." (Mattai 26:38–39)

He went away a second time and prayed, "My Father, if this cup cannot be taken away unless I drink it, your will must be done." (Mattai 26:42)

So leaving them again, he went away and prayed for the third time, saying the same thing once more. (Mattai 26:44)

Furthermore:

So when he came into the world, he said,

"Sacrifice and offering you did not desire, but a body you prepared for me.

"Whole burnt offerings and sin-offerings you took no delight in.

"Then I said, 'Here I am: I have come—it is written of me in the scroll of the book—to do your will, O God.'" . . .

By his will we have been made holy through the offering of the body of Yeshua the Messiah once for all. (Hebrews 10:5–7, 10)

To Fulfill Prophecy.

Then Yeshua said to him, "Put your sword back in its place! For all who take hold of the sword will die by the sword. Or do you think that I cannot call on my Father, and that he would send me more than twelve legions of angels right now? How then would the scriptures that say it must happen this way be fulfilled?" (Mattai 26:52–54)

Then he said to them, "These are my words that I spoke to you while I was still with you, that everything written about me in the law of Moses and the prophets and the psalms must be fulfilled." Then he opened their minds so they could understand the scriptures, and said to them, "Thus it stands written that the Messiah would suffer and would rise from the dead on the third day." (Luke 24:44–46)

To Share His Own Eternal Life with Sinful Men.

Just as Moses lifted up the serpent in the wilderness, so must the Son of Man be lifted up, so that everyone who believes in him may have eternal life. (Yohanan 3:14–15)

Now some Greeks were among those who had gone up to worship at the feast. So these approached Philip, who was from Bethsaida in Galilee, and requested, "Sir, we would like to see Yeshua." Philip went and told Andrew, and they both went and told Yeshua. Yeshua replied, "The time has come for the Son of Man to be glorified. I tell you the solemn truth, unless a kernel of wheat falls into the ground and dies, it remains by itself alone. But if it dies, it produces much grain." (Yohanan 12:20–24)

Note in this last passage how Yeshua likened Himself to a kernel of wheat that falls to the ground and dies. Only in that way can it produce many seeds. The implication is that He came in order to die so that others may have life.

At times, some have noted that we are saved by the *life* of the Messiah. There is an element of truth in that, since Yeshua gave His life. On the other hand, one must always remember that it was the *death* of the Messiah that made His life available to sinners.

The Nature of Messiah's Death

The Meaning of the Term *Death*. The word *death*, when applied to human beings in the Scriptures, pictures the idea of *separation*. Note the warning by God to Adam and Eve concerning not eating from the tree of the knowledge of good and evil:

> But you must not eat from the tree of the knowledge of good and evil, for when you eat from it you will surely die. (Genesis 2:17)

The first aspect of death, as seen with Adam and Eve, was their separation from God following their eating from the tree of the knowledge of good and evil. One of the results was that as God walked in the garden, expecting fellowship with Adam and Eve, they instead hid from Him because of fear:

> When the woman saw that the tree produced fruit that was good for food, was attractive to the eye, and was desirable for making one wise, she took some of its fruit and ate it. She also gave some of it to her husband who was with her, and he ate it. . . .
>
> Then the man and his wife heard the sound of the LORD God moving about in the orchard at the breezy time of the day, and they hid from the LORD God among the trees of the orchard. But the LORD God called to the man and said to him, "Where are you?" The man replied, "I heard you moving about in the orchard, and I was afraid because I was naked, so I hid." (Genesis 3:6, 8–10)

Ever since, the descendants of Adam and Eve have borne the characteristic known as the *sin nature*, which exists as a barrier between God and man.

This was not the end of the matter, however. Some nine hundred years later, Adam died; that is, his spirit was separated from his body and the body then was laid to rest in the ground from which it came. Physical death entails the separation from the spirit and the body; without the spirit's presence, the body dies.

In the death of the Messiah, we see both aspects involved in His experience, as described next.

Separation from God.

> At about three o'clock Yeshua shouted with a loud voice, "Eli, Eli, lema sabachthani?" that is, "My God, my God, why have you forsaken me?" (Mattai 27:46)

There is a mystery in exactly what was happening when Yeshua cried out, "Why have you forsaken me?" How could the Son, who is one with the Father, be forsaken by Him? This is an area beyond human understanding. What we can know, though, is the reason He put Himself into this situation: He has taken our place and borne our sins.

In attempting to understand the meaning of Mattai 27:46, we must guard against certain errors:

First, what occurred when Yeshua died was not some metaphysical *separation of two persons* in the Godhead. Such a possibility is impossible because God is of one essence.

Nor was there a *separation of the two natures* of the Messiah, the divine and the human. Such a possibility would destroy the incarnation. In that case personal suffering would be impossible, for the human nature was not a personality apart from the divine nature, as we have already seen.

Finally, we are not to understand a *moral separation* between the Father and the Son. The Scripture plainly declares:

> This is why the Father loves me—because I lay down my life, so that I may take it back again. (Yohanan 10:17)

The scriptural statement is that some separation indeed took place, but we are left with a genuine mystery as to the nature of this separation. Perhaps it is best just simply to recognize the truth without attempting a rationalistic explanation.

Separation of Spirit and Body.

> Then Yeshua cried out again with a loud voice and gave up his spirit. (Mattai 27:50)

The Messiah's death was accompanied by the pouring out of His blood, representative of a life given up. When the soldiers came to Yeshua and determined that He had already died, they did not break His legs but instead "confirmed" that He was dead:

> But when they came to Yeshua and saw that he was already dead, they did not break his legs. But one of the soldiers pierced his side with a spear, and blood and water flowed out immediately. (Yohanan 19:33–34)

Note the order of Messiah's experiences: First, He was forsaken of God. Then came physical death. Whatever occurred in the issue of being forsaken, when He had assumed the burden of human sin, physical death followed very quickly.

Some argue that the physical cause of Messiah's death had to do with the rupture of His heart because of the soldier's spear. While there may be an element of truth to this, behind the physical death was the spiritual cause, namely, being forsaken by God.

Interpreting the Death of the Messiah

The Scriptures interpret the meaning of Messiah's death by referring to it by various terms and concepts. It thereby gives us a number of ways to understand His death.

Ransom (Greek, *Lutron*).

> . . . just as the Son of Man did not come to be served but to serve, and to give his life as a ransom for many. (Mattai 20:28)

As a ransom, Yeshua's death represented a purchase price paid to redeem the person. The price is understood in the light of the penalty that was required because of man's offenses against God. Man broke God's standard of behavior, the Law, but by dying, Messiah paid the penalty.

Redemption (Greek, *Apolutrosis*).

> In him we have redemption through his blood, the forgiveness of our trespasses, according to the riches of his grace. (Ephesians 1:7)

Here, the picture is that of the release of an offender because of the payment of a price. The price here is Messiah's blood, that is, His life given up.

A Passover Sacrifice or Passing Over (Greek, *Pascha*).

> Clean out the old yeast so that you may be a new batch of dough—you are, in fact, without yeast. For Messiah, our Passover lamb, has been sacrificed. (1 Corinthians 5:7)

The images reflect the original Passover setting. As the death angel crossed Egypt on that fateful night, the blood on the doorpost protected the firstborn in the Jewish families. Homes that did not have the blood invited judgment; the firstborn of the Egyptians died:

> Then Moses summoned all the elders of Israel, and told them, "Go and select for yourselves a lamb or young goat for your families, and kill the Passover animals. Take a branch of hyssop, dip it in the blood that is in the basin, and apply to the top of the doorframe and the two side posts some of the blood that is in the basin. Not one of you is to go out the door of his house until morning. For the LORD will pass through to strike Egypt, and when he sees the blood on the top of the doorframe and the two side posts, then the LORD will pass over the door, and he will not permit the destroyer to enter your houses to strike you." (Exodus 12:21–23)

In the same way, the Messiah became our Passover sacrifice. Because of His blood, we are no longer under condemnation.

Propitiation (Greek, *Hilasterion*). The NASB translation reflects the Greek more closely than the NIV here:

> . . . whom God displayed publicly as a propitiation [NIV: sacrifice of atonement] in His blood through faith. This was to demonstrate His righteousness, because in the forbearance of God He passed over the sins previously committed. (Romans 3:25 NASB)[12]

> In this is love, not that we loved God, but that He loved us and sent His Son to be the propitiation [NIV and NET: atoning sacrifice] for our sins. (1 Yohanan 4:10 NASB)

The picture is that of the high priest entering the Holy of Holies on the Day of Atonement. On that day he sprinkled the "mercy seat," as it is translated in KVJ (Hebrew, *kapporet*), the place where God met and communed with man. (Note the NET translation of either "atonement lid" or "atonement plate.")

> You are to put the atonement lid on top of the ark, and in the ark you are to put the testimony I am giving you. I will meet with you there, and from above the atonement lid, from between the two cherubim that are over the ark of the testimony, I will speak with you about all that I will command you for the Israelites. (Exodus 25:21–22)

> He must then slaughter the sin offering goat which is for the people. He is to bring its blood inside the veil-canopy, and he is to do with its blood just as he did to the blood of the bull: He is to sprinkle it on the atonement plate and in front of the atonement plate. (Leviticus 16:15)

In the same way God gave His Son, Yeshua the Messiah, to die on the tree—which is the mercy seat.

Reconciliation (Greek, *Katallage*).

> For if while we were enemies we were reconciled to God through the death of his Son, how much more, since we have been reconciled,

> will we be saved by his life? Not only this, but we also rejoice in God through our Lord Yeshua the Messiah, through whom we have now received this reconciliation. (Romans 5:10–11)

The concept of "reconciliation" is that of "thorough change." But this raises a theological problem: who was changed?

According to Shedd, God is reconciled to man, which would imply that God changed. According to Hodge, both man and God are reconciled to each other, while Strong's view is that man is reconciled to God.

Scripture tells us:

> And all these things are from God who reconciled us to himself through Messiah, and who has given us the ministry of reconciliation. (2 Corinthians 5:18)

Morever, according to Yaakov, God does *not* change:

> All generous giving and every perfect gift is from above, coming down from the Father of lights, with whom there is no variation or the slightest hint of change. (Yaakov 1:17)

This appears to be the biblical position. Yeshua the Messiah died in our place and on our behalf. *We* are the ones who need to be reconciled to God.

Substitution.

Two Greek prepositions. The first preposition is *huper*, which means "on behalf of" and can also mean "instead of" when the context suggests it. It appears some twenty times in reference to the Messiah's substitutionary death (Luke 22:19; 22:20; Yohanan 6:51; 10:11, 15; 11:50–52; 18:14; Romans 5:6, 8; 9:3 [here it is used of Sha'ul's desire to be cut off from Messiah for—*huper*—his brethren]; 2 Corinthians 5:14–15, 20–21; Galatians 3:13; Titus 2:14; 1 Kefa 3:18).

The second preposition is *anti*, meaning "instead of" and used of the Messiah's atonement in these verses:

> . . . just as the Son of Man did not come to be served but to serve, and to give his life as a ransom for [*anti*] many. (Mattai 20:28)

For even the Son of Man did not come to be served but to serve, and to give his life as a ransom for [*anti*] many. (Mark 10:45)

Giving His body and blood for us.

Then he took bread, and after giving thanks he broke it and gave it to them, saying, "This is my body which is given for you. Do this in remembrance of me." And in the same way he took the cup after they had eaten, saying, "This cup that is poured out for you is the new covenant in my blood." (Luke 22:19–20)

Giving His life for us.

I am the good shepherd. The good shepherd lays down his life for the sheep. . . .

. . . just as the Father knows me and I know the Father—and I lay down my life for the sheep. (Yohanan 10:11, 15)

. . . just as the Son of Man did not come to be served but to serve, and to give his life as a ransom for many. (Mattai 20:28)

A death of one person for all.

For the love of Messiah controls us, since we have concluded this, that Messiah died for all; therefore all have died. And he died for all so that those who live should no longer live for themselves but for him who died for them and was raised. (2 Corinthians 5:14–15)

Because we were sinners.

For while we were still helpless, at the right time Messiah died for the ungodly. (For rarely will anyone die for a righteous person, though for a good person perhaps someone might possibly dare to die.) But God demonstrates his own love for us, in that while we were still sinners, Messiah died for us. (Romans 5:6–8)

Our sins exchanged for His righteousness. We already saw these same principles with regard to the sacrifices of the Mosaic system.

He took our sins away:

> On the next day Yohanan saw Yeshua coming toward him and said, "Look, the Lamb of God who takes away the sin of the world!" (Yohanan 1:29)

> For then he would have had to suffer again and again since the foundation of the world. But now he has appeared once for all at the consummation of the ages to put away sin by his sacrifice. (Hebrews 9:26)

He exchanged our sins for His righteousness:

> Therefore we are ambassadors for Messiah, as though God were making His plea through us. We plead with you on Messiah's behalf, "Be reconciled to God!" God made the one who did not know sin to be sin for us, so that in him we would become the righteousness of God. (2 Corinthians 5:20–21)

Our sins taken upon Himself and cursed for us because of our sins.

> On the next day Yohanan saw Yeshua coming toward him and said, "Look, the Lamb of God who takes away the sin of the world!" (Yohanan 1:29)

> Messiah redeemed us from the curse of the law by becoming a curse for us (because it is written, "Cursed is everyone who hangs on a tree.") (Galatians 3:13)

The Results of Messiah's Death

In Relation to Believers.

Redeemed from the curse of the Law.

> Messiah redeemed us from the curse of the law by becoming a curse for us (because it is written, "Cursed is everyone who hangs on a tree.") (Galatians 3:13)

You know that from your empty way of life inherited from your ancestors you were ransomed—not by perishable things like silver or gold, but by precious blood like that of an unblemished and spotless lamb, namely Messiah. (1 Kefa 1:18–19)

Loosed from our sins.

. . . and from Yeshua the Messiah —the faithful witness, the firstborn from among the dead, the ruler over the kings of the earth. To the one who loves us and has set us free from our sins at the cost of his own blood . . . (Revelation 1:5)

Purchased for God.

They were singing a new song:
"You are worthy to take the scroll
and to open its seals
because you were killed,
and at the cost of your own blood you have purchased for God
persons from every tribe, language, people, and nation." (Revelation 5:9)

Brought near to God.

But now in Messiah Yeshua you who used to be far away have been brought near by the blood of Messiah. (Ephesians 2:13)

Have eternal life secured.

Just as Moses lifted up the serpent in the wilderness, so must the Son of Man be lifted up, so that everyone who believes in him may have eternal life. (Yohanan 3:14–15)

He died for us so that whether we are alert or asleep we will come to life together with him. (1 Thessalonians 5:10)

Justified when we appropriated His death on our behalf.

> Much more then, because we have now been declared righteous [NIV: "justified"] by his blood, we will be saved through him from God's wrath. (Romans 5:9)

Sanctified.

> By his will we have been made holy [NASB, KJV: "sanctified"] through the offering of the body of Yeshua the Messiah once for all. (Hebrews 10:10)

Made perfect in God's sight.

> For by one offering he has perfected for all time those who are made holy. (Hebrews 10:14)

Cleanses us constantly from all sin.

> But if we walk in the light as he himself is in the light, we have fellowship with one another and the blood of Yeshua his Son cleanses us from all sin. (1 Yohanan 1:7)

Here it is good to be reminded that in our day-to-day walk with the Messiah, we need to confess our sins daily.

Opened a way into the presence of God.

> Therefore, brothers and sisters, since we have confidence to enter the sanctuary by the blood of Yeshua, by the fresh and living way that he inaugurated for us through the curtain, that is, through his flesh. (Hebrews 10:19–20)

Made it impossible to condemn us.

> Who will bring any charge against God's elect? It is God who justifies. Who is the one who will condemn? Messiah is the one who died (and

more than that, he was raised), who is at the right hand of God, and who also is interceding for us. (Romans 8:33–34)

Able to dwell with God in heaven.

And I heard a loud voice from the throne saying: "Look! The residence of God is among human beings. He will live among them, and they will be his people, and God himself will be with them." (Revelation 21:3)

We can summarize all the above by saying that the death of the Messiah secured salvation and all of its blessing for us forever.

In Relation to the Entire Human Race.

Reconciled the world to God.

In other words, in Messiah God was reconciling the world to himself, not counting people's trespasses against them, and he has given us the message of reconciliation. (2 Corinthians 5:19)

On the next day Yohanan saw Yeshua coming toward him and said, "Look, the Lamb of God who takes away the sin of the world!" (Yohanan 1:29)

For the love of Messiah controls us, since we have concluded this, that Messiah died for all; therefore all have died. (2 Corinthians 5:14)

. . . who gave himself as a ransom for all, revealing God's purpose at his appointed time. (1 Timothy 2:6)

But we see Yeshua, who was made lower than the angels for a little while, now crowned with glory and honor because he suffered death, so that by God's grace he would experience death on behalf of everyone. (Hebrews 2:9)

The death of the Messiah took away the barrier of sin that separates a lost world from a God who is holy. God was in the Messiah reconciling the world to Himself. Because of the death of the Messiah on the tree, the door is open to everyone who wishes to enter into the family of God. Our task as believers is therefore to share this good news, the message that the door is open to everyone.

Has a "magnetism" that draws all men to Himself.

> And I, when I am lifted up from the earth, will draw all people to myself. (Yohanan 12:32)

The tree on which the Messiah died holds an attraction to all people. Every year on the date of Messiah's death, newspapers will for instance make mention of the event and describe the visits by pilgrims to the associated sites in the land of Israel.

The Results of Messiah's Death in Relation to Satan and His Followers. There is a certain mystery in the attempt to understand how the death of the Messiah relates to Satan. The Scriptures do speak of this, however, as delineated below:

Satan rendered powerless over believers in the experience of death.

> Therefore, since the children share in flesh and blood, he likewise shared in their humanity, so that through death he could destroy the one who holds the power of death (that is, the devil), and set free those who were held in slavery all their lives by their fear of death. (Hebrews 2:14–15)

Satan and his followers shorn of their power to use the Word against us.

> He has destroyed what was against us, a certificate of indebtedness expressed in decrees opposed to us. He has taken it away by nailing it to the tree. Disarming the rulers and authorities, he has made a public disgrace of them, triumphing over them by the tree. (Colossians 2:14–15)

Sha'ul's note here concerns our daily walk and the victory we can have over sin.

Then I heard a loud voice in heaven saying,
"The salvation and the power
and the kingdom of our God,
and the ruling authority of his Messiah, have now come,
because the accuser of our brothers and sisters,
the one who accuses them day and night before our God,
has been thrown down.
But they overcame him
by the blood of the Lamb
and by the word of their testimony,
and they did not love their lives so much that they were afraid to die."
(Revelation 12:10–11)

In Relation to Himself as the Mediator.
Fulfilled His part in the eternal covenant with God the Father.

Now may the God of peace who by the blood of the eternal covenant brought back from the dead the great shepherd of the sheep, our Lord Yeshua the Messiah, . . . (Hebrews 13:20)

Made it possible for there to be an entirely new covenant people.

For it was fitting for him, for whom and through whom all things exist, in bringing many sons to glory, to make the pioneer of their salvation perfect through sufferings. (Hebrews 2:10)

Laid the foundation of His priestly work for us.

But now Messiah has come as the high priest of the good things to come. He passed through the greater and more perfect tent not made with hands, that is, not of this creation, and he entered once for all into the most holy place not by the blood of goats and calves but by his own blood, and so he himself secured eternal redemption. (Hebrews 9:11–12)

Secured His exaltation above all things.

He humbled himself, by becoming obedient to the point of death
—even death on a tree!
As a result God exalted him and gave him the name
that is above every name, . . . (Philippians 2:8–9)

Received the "crown of glory and honor."

. . . but we see Yeshua, who was made lower than the angels for a little while, now crowned with glory and honor because he suffered death, so that by God's grace he would experience death on behalf of everyone. (Hebrews 2:9)

Was ushered into a great experience of joy.

. . . keeping our eyes fixed on Yeshua, the pioneer and perfecter of our faith. For the joy set out for him he endured the tree, disregarding its shame, and has taken his seat at the right hand of the throne of God. (Hebrews 12:2)

In Relation to God

Revealed the love of God for sinners.

But God demonstrates his own love for us, in that while we were still sinners, Messiah died for us. (Romans 5:8)

Revealed the righteousness of God in forgiving sin.

God publicly displayed him at his death as the mercy seat accessible through faith. This was to demonstrate his righteousness, because God in his forbearance had passed over the sins previously committed. (Romans 3:25)

> ***Revealed the wrath of God against sin.***
>
> At about three o'clock Yeshua shouted with a loud voice, "Eli, Eli, lema sabachthani?" that is, "My God, my God, why have you forsaken me?" (Mattai 27:46)
>
> ***Revealed the wisdom of God whereby a way was found to save sinners.***
>
> This was also to demonstrate his righteousness in the present time, so that he would be just and the justifier of the one who lives because of Yeshua's faithfulness. (Romans 3:26)

The Finality of the Death of the Messiah

Final for Himself. His death was an experience that was accomplished once for all. No repetition is possible concerning any future death on the tree.

> He has no need to do every day what those priests do, to offer sacrifices first for their own sins and then for the sins of the people, since he did this in offering himself once for all. (Hebrews 7:27)
>
> And he did not enter to offer himself again and again, the way the high priest enters the sanctuary year after year with blood that is not his own, for then he would have had to suffer again and again since the foundation of the world. But now he has appeared once for all at the consummation of the ages to put away sin by his sacrifice. And just as people are appointed to die once, and then to face judgment, . . . (Hebrews 9:25–27)
>
> And every priest stands day after day serving and offering the same sacrifices again and again—sacrifices that can never take away sins. But when this priest had offered one sacrifice for sins for all time, he sat down at the right hand of God. (Hebrews 10:11–12)

Final for Those Who Are Redeemed. The death of the Messiah will stand forever as a finished and complete redemption. Nothing more should or can be ever added to the work performed on the tree.

> But now Messiah has come as the high priest of the good things to come. He passed through the greater and more perfect tent not made with hands, that is, not of this creation, and he entered once for all into the most holy place not by the blood of goats and calves but by his own blood, and so he himself secured eternal redemption. (Hebrews 9:11–12)

It is true that God has not yet performed everything He will do for us, because He is infinite and eternal. However, whatever God will do for us in the future flows from what occurred on the tree on which the Messiah died.

> By his will we have been made holy through the offering of the body of Yeshua the Messiah once for all. . . .
>
> For by one offering he has perfected for all time those who are made holy. (Hebrews 10:10, 14)

From this we determine that nothing more is ever needed to add to what the Messiah performed on the tree of suffering and death.

Final for a Lost World. The death of the Messiah is the final act of God's redeeming love for a lost world. If people do not avail themselves of this love, then they can expect nothing less than God's wrath and judgment.

> But when this priest had offered one sacrifice for sins for all time, he sat down at the right hand of God, where he is now waiting until his enemies are made a footstool for his feet. (Hebrews 10:12–13)

Does Messiah wait to die again? Could He ever do anything better or more by which sinners could come to know a loving God? The answer is no.

The Death of the Messiah and the Life of the Believer

The death of the Messiah is not merely a theological pronouncement without practical ramifications. His death has a necessary connection with the kind of lives that believers live.

Enables Us to Enter into a Godly Lifestyle. The Messiah died in order that we might live a godly life:

A life of righteousness.

> For God achieved what the law could not do because it was weakened through the flesh. By sending his own Son in the likeness of sinful flesh and concerning sin, he condemned sin in the flesh, so that the righteous requirement of the law may be fulfilled in us, who do not walk according to the flesh but according to the Spirit. (Romans 8:3–4)

> He himself bore our sins in his body on the tree, that we may cease from sinning and live for righteousness. By his wounds you were healed. (1 Kefa 2:24)

A life of holiness.

> But now he has reconciled you by his physical body through death to present you holy, without blemish, and blameless before him. (Colossians 1:22)

A life of unselfishness.

> For the love of Messiah controls us, since we have concluded this, that Messiah died for all; therefore all have died. And he died for all so that those who live should no longer live for themselves but for him who died for them and was raised. (2 Corinthians 5:14–15)

A life of unworldliness.

> But may I never boast except in the tree of our Lord Yeshua the Messiah, through which the world has been crucified to me, and I to the world. (Galatians 6:14)

A life of victory.

> Therefore, since we are surrounded by such a great cloud of witnesses, we must get rid of every weight and the sin that clings so closely, and run with endurance the race set out for us, keeping our eyes fixed on Yeshua, the pioneer and perfecter of our faith. For the joy set out for him he endured the tree, disregarding its shame, and has taken his seat at the right hand of the throne of God. Think of him who endured such opposition against himself by sinners, so that you may not grow weary in your souls and give up. (Hebrews 12:1–3)

> . . . because everyone who has been fathered by God conquers the world. This is the conquering power that has conquered the world: our faith. Now who is the person who has conquered the world except the one who believes that Yeshua is the Son of God? (1 Yohanan 5:4–5)

A life of service.

> How much more will the blood of Messiah, who through the eternal Spirit offered himself without blemish to God, purify our consciences from dead works to worship the living God. (Hebrews 9:14)

Translating the Death of the Messiah into Living a Godly Lifestyle. Many books have been written on how to live the godly life. All of these books are profitable, but nevertheless each one of us must personally learn how to appropriate the means of living a godly life. The death of the Messiah on the tree helps us in these ways:

Separating us from the world.

> But may I never boast except in the tree of our Lord Yeshua the Messiah, through which the world has been crucified to me, and I to the world. (Galatians 6:14)

We need to look at Yeshua's tree of suffering and death as Sha'ul did, as enabling us to be separated from the world. For Sha'ul, the separation was so complete that he could say that the world was dead to him and he to the world. This did not mean that Sha'ul could not relate to people; he recognized the necessity of sharing the gospel message with them. But he very clearly emphasizes the fact that he will not be tempted into the ways of the world and away from the love of God.

Setting our conscience free from dead works.

> How much more will the blood of Messiah, who through the eternal Spirit offered himself without blemish to God, purify our consciences from dead works to worship the living God. (Hebrews 9:14)

> Let us draw near with a sincere heart in the assurance that faith brings, because we have had our hearts sprinkled clean from an evil conscience and our bodies washed in pure water. (Hebrews 10:22)

The conscience will never be set free if we attempt to appropriate redemption and the grace of God by means of our efforts. When we fail, every wrong deed will only increase the burden of guilt. A good illustration is that of a man who is trying to pay off a debt. The debt only keeps increasing so that in the end, the man is greatly discouraged. However, when we receive the Messiah and recognize that His death is for us personally, He clears away the burden. And furthermore, He keeps it cleared. We may fail, but at every moment He is ready to pray for us and help us to start each day with a clean slate.

Uniting us with His own omnipotent life.

> What shall we say then? Are we to remain in sin so that grace may increase? Absolutely not! How can we who died to sin still live in it? Or do you not know that as many as were baptized into Messiah Yeshua were baptized into his death? Therefore we have been buried with him through baptism into death, in order that just as Messiah was raised from the dead through the glory of the Father, so we too may live a new life.
>
> For if we have become united with him in the likeness of his death, we will certainly also be united in the likeness of his

> resurrection. We know that our old man was crucified with him so that the body of sin would no longer dominate us, so that we would no longer be enslaved to sin. (For someone who has died has been freed from sin.)
>
> Now if we died with Messiah, we believe that we will also live with him. We know that since Messiah has been raised from the dead, he is never going to die again; death no longer has mastery over him. For the death he died, he died to sin once for all, but the life he lives, he lives to God. So you too consider yourselves dead to sin, but alive to God in Messiah Yeshua. (Romans 6:1–11)

Through the atonement that paid our debt, we are also united with the eternal and omnipotent life of God. We are conscious of another presence in our lives through the Holy Spirit.

Setting before us a supreme example of unselfish obedience and godly suffering.

> You should have the same attitude toward one another that Messiah Yeshua had,
> who though he existed in the form of God
> did not regard equality with God
> as something to be grasped,
> but emptied himself by taking on the form of a slave,
> by looking like other men,
> and by sharing in human nature. (Philippians 2:5–7)

> For what credit is it if you sin and are mistreated and endure it? But if you do good and suffer and so endure, this finds favor with God. For to this you were called, since Messiah also suffered for you, leaving an example for you to follow in his steps. He committed no sin nor was deceit found in his mouth. When he was maligned, he did not answer back; when he suffered, he threatened no retaliation, but committed himself to God who judges justly. (1 Kefa 2:20–23)

Opening the door into the presence of an infinite God.

> Therefore, brothers and sisters, since we have confidence to enter the sanctuary by the blood of Yeshua, . . . (Hebrews 10:19)

We can come for pardon and help, both morally and spiritually. Furthermore, we can enter into the presence of God boldly.

Putting us under the infinite debt of gratitude to Yeshua the Messiah.

> For you were bought at a price. Therefore glorify God with your body. (1 Corinthians 6:20)

> And he died for all so that those who live should no longer live for themselves but for him who died for them and was raised. (2 Corinthians 5:15)

One of the most powerful motives in any experience with God is that of gratitude. In view of the fact that the Messiah loved me and gave Himself for me, how can I go out among unbelievers in this world joining them in a life of sin? The only answer is that we cannot if we are truly born of God.

The Resurrection of the Messiah

The Key Passage: 1 Corinthians 15

> And if Messiah has not been raised, then our preaching is futile and your faith is empty. Also, we are found to be false witnesses about God, because we have testified against God that he raised Messiah from the dead, when in reality he did not raise him, if indeed the dead are not raised. For if the dead are not raised, then not even Messiah has been raised. And if Messiah has not been raised, your faith is useless; you are still in your sins. Furthermore, those who have fallen asleep in Messiah have also perished. For if only in this life we have hope in Messiah, we should be pitied more than anyone. (1 Corinthians 15:14–19)

In this passage, the *shaliach* Sha'ul notes six tragic results if the Messiah has not risen from the dead. (1) The preaching of the gospel is then useless (verse 14); (2) the faith of the believer is then futile (verse 14); (3) those who preach the good news concerning the Messiah then all become liars (verse 15); (4) no forgiveness of sins is then possible (verse 17); (5) no immortality is possible (verse 18); (6) believers then become the greatest fools on earth (verse 19).

Proofs of Messiah's Resurrection[13]

The Seventeen Appearances of the Risen Messiah. In one case He appeared to over five hundred people.

The Empty Tomb. Based on the valid testimony of the witnesses, the disciples examined the tomb carefully. Had it not been empty, the Jewish leaders and the people would have found Yeshua's body. Either the Messiah arose, or else the body was disposed of in another way. A relevant question here is: How could the disciples steal the body when soldiers were guarding it? And if the enemies of the Messiah had stolen it, they would surely have produced it when the disciples claimed the resurrection of the Messiah had occurred.

The Competency of the Witnesses to the Resurrection. We might note that the disciples would never have been fooled by the wrong body; they knew Yeshua intimately. The fact of the matter is that the disciples did not even expect Yeshua to rise; therefore, there is an unlikelihood that the resurrection was merely a hallucination.

The Subsequent Change in the Disciples. Prior to the knowledge of the resurrection, the disciples were discouraged skeptics. Afterward, by contrast, they became joyous and fearless witnesses.

The Miracles Confirming the Disciples' Testimony. Scripture records that people were raised from the dead, as well as examples of miraculous protection and numerous healings in the name of the risen Messiah.

The Denials of the Resurrection

We will only mention the various theories by name. We will not here enter into a further discussion of them. Six such theories are: (1) the Swoon Theory; (2) the Hallucination Theory; (3) the Mythical Theories; (4) the Stolen Body Theory; (5) the Wrong Tomb Theory; (6) the False Testimony Theory.[14]

The Nature of the Resurrection Body

A Real Human Body. Yeshua had a body with which He could eat. He could also display the wounds in His body.

> So they gave him a piece of broiled fish, and he took it and ate it in front of them. (Luke 24:42–43)

> Then he said to Thomas, "Put your finger here, and examine my hands. Extend your hand and put it into my side. Do not continue in your unbelief, but believe."Thomas replied to him, "My Lord and my God!" (Yohanan 20:27–28)

A Glorified Body. His body was different from the one that had been buried. He now had a body that could, for example, go through closed doors.

> On the evening of that day, the first day of the week, the disciples had gathered together and locked the doors of the place because they were afraid of the Jewish leaders. Yeshua came and stood among them and said to them, "Peace be with you." . . .
>
> Eight days later the disciples were again together in the house, and Thomas was with them. Although the doors were locked, Yeshua came and stood among them and said, "Peace be with you!" (Yohanan 20:19, 26)

A "Model" or Prototypical Body. Yeshua's resurrection body is the prototype of what we as believers will one day have. It will be suited to the heavenly sphere as well as for living on a renovated earth on which the curse is removed. Our bodies will then be incorruptible.

Like the one made of dust, so too are those made of dust, and like the one from heaven, so too those who are heavenly. And just as we have borne the image of the man of dust, let us also bear the image of the man of heaven.

Now this is what I am saying, brothers and sisters: Flesh and blood cannot inherit the kingdom of God, nor does the perishable inherit the imperishable. Listen, I will tell you a mystery: We will not all sleep, but we will all be changed—in a moment, in the blinking of an eye, at the last trumpet. For the trumpet will sound, and the dead will be raised imperishable, and we will be changed. For this perishable body must put on the imperishable, and this mortal body must put on immortality. (1 Corinthians 15:48–53)

The Results and Importance of the Resurrection

Authenticates His Deity. Otherwise, His deity could have remained in grave doubt.

Authenticates the Scriptures. Since the Scriptures predicted His resurrection, it was important for them to be authenticated by this fulfillment.

Vindicates His Vicarious Death and the Plan of Redemption.

. . . because if you confess with your mouth that Yeshua is Lord and believe in your heart that God raised him from the dead, you will be saved. (Romans 10:9)

He was given over because of our transgressions and was raised for the sake of our justification. (Romans 4:25)

Guarantees Our Own Resurrection. Because Yeshua rose from the grave, believers are assured that we too will one day be resurrected.

Makes Possible the Messiah's Present Ministries. These ministries consist of being the head of the body, the church; being our High Priest; and having the right to bestow eternal life.

Authenticates His Future Return to Earth. At that time, He will judge people who had never accepted Him, and will reign as the King over the kingdom.

THE ASCENSION OF THE MESSIAH

We will only offer here a basic outline concerning the ascension.

The Fact of the Ascension

Foretold by the Messiah.

> Then Yeshua said, "I will be with you for only a little while longer, and then I am going to the one who sent me. You will look for me but will not find me, and where I am you cannot come."
>
> Then the Jewish leaders said to one another, "Where is he going to go that we cannot find him? He is not going to go to the Jewish people dispersed among the Greeks and teach the Greeks, is he? What did he mean by saying, 'You will look for me but will not find me, and where I am you cannot come'?" (Yohanan 7:33–36)

> Then Yeshua said to them again, "I am going away, and you will look for me but will die in your sin. Where I am going you cannot come." (Yohanan 8:21)

> You heard me say to you, "I am going away and I am coming back to you." If you loved me, you would be glad that I am going to the Father, because the Father is greater than I am. I have told you now before it happens, so that when it happens you may believe. (Yohanan 14:28–29)

> But now I am going to the one who sent me, and not one of you is asking me, "Where are you going?" (Yohanan 16:5)

> For it is like a man going on a journey, who summoned his slaves and entrusted his property to them. (Mattai 25:14)

Took Place Within History.

> After the Lord Yeshua had spoken to them, he was taken up into heaven and sat down at the right hand of God. They went out and proclaimed everywhere, while the Lord worked with them and confirmed the word through the accompanying signs. (Mark 16:19–20)

> Then Yeshua led them out as far as Bethany, and lifting up his hands, he blessed them. Now during the blessing he departed and was taken up into heaven. (Luke 24:50–51)

> After he had said this, while they were watching, he was lifted up and a cloud hid him from their sight. (Acts 1:9)

Was Confirmed Through the Experiences of Stephen, Sha'ul, and Yohanan.

Stephen.

> But Stephen, full of the Holy Spirit, looked intently toward heaven and saw the glory of God, and Yeshua standing at the right hand of God. "Look!" he said. "I see the heavens opened, and the Son of Man standing at the right hand of God!" (Acts 7:55–56)

Sha'ul. So indelible was the impression on Sha'ul concerning the ascension that he relates the story twice, in addition to the initial account:

> As he was going along, approaching Damascus, suddenly a light from heaven flashed around him. He fell to the ground and heard a voice saying to him, "Saul, Saul, why are you persecuting me?" So he said, "Who are you, Lord?" He replied, "I am Yeshua whom you are persecuting!" (Acts 9:3–5)

> As I was en route and near Damascus, about noon a very bright light from heaven suddenly flashed around me. Then I fell to the ground

> and heard a voice saying to me, "Saul, Saul, why are you persecuting me?" I answered, "Who are you, Lord?" He said to me, "I am Yeshua the Nazarene, whom you are persecuting." (Acts 22:6–8)

> About noon along the road, Your Majesty, I saw a light from heaven, brighter than the sun, shining everywhere around me and those traveling with me. When we had all fallen to the ground, I heard a voice saying to me in Aramaic, "Saul, Saul, why are you persecuting me? You are hurting yourself by kicking against the goads." So I said, "Who are you, Lord?" And the Lord replied, "I am Yeshua whom you are persecuting." (Acts 26:13–15)

Yohanan.

> After these things I looked, and there was a door standing open in heaven! And the first voice I had heard speaking to me like a trumpet said: "Come up here so that I can show you what must happen after these things." (Revelation 4:1)

> Then I saw standing in the middle of the throne and of the four living creatures, and in the middle of the elders, a Lamb that appeared to have been killed. He had seven horns and seven eyes, which are the seven spirits of God sent out into all the earth. (Revelation 5:6)

Is Assumed by the Entire Doctrine of the Second Coming. In the following passage, note that if the Messiah comes from heaven for the body of Messiah, then He must have already gone there!

> For people everywhere report how you welcomed us and how you turned to God from idols to serve the living and true God and to wait for his Son from heaven, whom he raised from the dead, Yeshua our deliverer from the coming wrath. (1 Thessalonians 1:9–10)

Is Assumed by Faith in Historical Events Reported Through Legitimate Witnesses. As believers, our faith is in a living Savior who today is at the right hand of God.

The Nature of the Ascension

Apparent to the Physical Senses. The disciples both heard and saw what occurred:

> After he had said this, while they were watching, he was lifted up and a cloud hid him from their sight. (Acts 1:9)

Mysterious in Nature. There is no hint that Luke was writing fiction when he described the ascension. Though it actually occurred, as with other doctrines, a mystery remains. There are questions: did Messiah's ascension override the weight of His body? Then too we notice how quickly a veil or curtain was drawn: "a cloud hid him from their sight." The nature of the ascension is simply not described in human language in the Scripture. Someday we shall know more of Messiah's ascension when we ascend to go with Him.

> And we all agree, our religion contains amazing revelation:
> He was revealed in the flesh,
> vindicated by the Spirit, seen by angels,
> proclaimed among Gentiles,
> believed on in the world,
> taken up in glory. (1 Timothy 3:16)

> Then we who are alive, who are left, will be suddenly caught up together with them in the clouds to meet the Lord in the air. And so we will always be with the Lord. (1 Thessalonians 4:17)

The Ascension and the Messiah's Present Work

Closed His Redemptive Work on Earth.

> The Son is the radiance of his glory and the representation of his essence, and he sustains all things by his powerful word, and so when

he had accomplished cleansing for sins, he sat down at the right hand of the Majesty on high. (Hebrews 1:3)

Exalted Him as Head over All Things.

This power he exercised in Messiah when he raised him from the dead and seated him at his right hand in the heavenly realms far above every rule and authority and power and dominion and every name that is named, not only in this age but also in the one to come. And God put all things under Messiah's feet, and he gave him to the *qehilah* as head over all things. Now the *qehilah* is his body, the fullness of him who fills all in all. (Ephesians 1:20–23)

Inaugurated Him into His High Priestly Work.

Now the main point of what we are saying is this: We have such a high priest, one who sat down at the right hand of the throne of the Majesty in heaven, a minister in the sanctuary and the true tabernacle that the Lord, not man, set up. For every high priest is appointed to offer both gifts and sacrifices. So this one too had to have something to offer. Now if he were on earth, he would not be a priest, since there are already priests who offer the gifts prescribed by the law. (Hebrews 8:1–4)

For it is indeed fitting for us to have such a high priest: holy, innocent, undefiled, separate from sinners, and exalted above the heavens. (Hebrews 7:26)

Made Possible the Messiah's Present Work Through the Holy Spirit.

But now I am going to the one who sent me, and not one of you is asking me, "Where are you going?" Instead your hearts are filled with sadness because I have said these things to you. But I tell you the truth, it is

> to your advantage that I am going away. For if I do not go away, the Advocate will not come to you, but if I go, I will send him to you. (Yohanan 16:5–7)

> So then, exalted to the right hand of God, and having received the promise of the Holy Spirit from the Father, he has poured out what you both see and hear. (Acts 2:33)

The Guarantees of the Ascension

Concerning Yeshua.

A guarantee of the truths of His claims. His ascension makes real the claims He made on earth. The fact that He said that He would ascend was verified by God.

> But Yeshua was silent. The high priest said to him, "I charge you under oath by the living God, tell us if you are the Messiah, the Son of God." Yeshua said to him, "You have said it yourself. But I tell you, from now on you will see the Son of Man sitting at the right hand of the Power and coming on the clouds of heaven." (Mattai 26:63–64)

A guarantee that He is righteous. If the ascension had not occurred, then the witness of Yeshua Himself would have been false.

> . . . concerning righteousness, because I am going to the Father and you will see me no longer. (Yohanan 16:10)

A guarantee of His final triumph over all His enemies.

> So then, exalted to the right hand of God, and having received the promise of the Holy Spirit from the Father, he has poured out what you both see and hear. For David did not ascend into heaven, but he himself says,
>
> "The Lord said to my lord,
> 'Sit at my right hand

until I make your enemies a footstool for your feet.'" (Acts 2:33–35)

Those who listened to Kefa certainly understood the meaning of the apostle's claim:

Now when they heard this, they were acutely distressed and said to Kefa and the rest of the apostles, "What should we do, brothers?" (Acts 2:37)

Concerning Believers.
A guarantee that we have an advocate at the right hand of God.

Therefore since we have a great high priest who has passed through the heavens, Yeshua the Son of God, let us hold fast to our confession. For we do not have a high priest incapable of sympathizing with our weaknesses, but one who has been tempted in every way just as we are, yet without sin. Therefore let us confidently approach the throne of grace to receive mercy and find grace whenever we need help. (Hebrews 4:14–16)

For Messiah did not enter a sanctuary made with hands—the representation of the true sanctuary—but into heaven itself, and he appears now in God's presence for us. (Hebrews 9:24)

A guarantee of a greater ministry for us in the world.

I tell you the solemn truth, the person who believes in me will perform the miraculous deeds that I am doing, and will perform greater deeds than these, because I am going to the Father. (Yohanan 14:12)

A guarantee of our entrance into heaven.

. . . where Yeshua our forerunner entered on our behalf, since he became a priest forever in the order of Melchizedek. (Hebrews 6:20)

We have an anchor within the curtain in God's tabernacle that will not leave us here any longer than God intends.

Practical Values

Brings Joy.

> You heard me say to you, "I am going away and I am coming back to you." If you loved me, you would be glad that I am going to the Father, because the Father is greater than I am. I have told you now before it happens, so that when it happens you may believe. (Yohanan 14:28–29)

Produces Steadfastness.

> Therefore since we have a great high priest who has passed through the heavens, Yeshua the Son of God, let us hold fast to our confession. (Hebrews 4:14)

In other words, the ascension is a call for us to hold fast the profession of our faith.

Gives Assurance.

> In the same way God wanted to demonstrate more clearly to the heirs of the promise that his purpose was unchangeable, and so he intervened with an oath, so that we who have found refuge in him may find strong encouragement to hold fast to the hope set before us through two unchangeable things, since it is impossible for God to lie. We have this hope as an anchor for the soul, sure and steadfast, which reaches inside behind the curtain, where Yeshua our forerunner entered on our behalf, since he became a priest forever in the order of Melchizedek. (Hebrews 6:17–20)

Makes Us Heavenly Minded. In so doing, it shows us that heaven is a real location.

> But now I am going to the one who sent me, and not one of you is asking me, "Where are you going?" Instead your hearts are filled with sadness because I have said these things to you. (Yohanan 16:5–6)

Demonstrates the Possibilities for a Glorified Body. We will heave the same kind of glorified body as Yeshua had when He was raised to heaven.

TEN

The Person and Work of the Spirit in the Household of Israel

A number of passages directly relate to the person and work of God the Spirit in the Old Testament.[1] Our task in this chapter is not to examine every such passage but, first, to note some of the usages that particularly describe the Spirit's task among the people of Israel, and to ascertain what it meant for the Holy Spirit to come upon certain individuals to be with them and empower them for their ministry.

Second, we want to ascertain whether the Spirit convicted people of sin in a work of pre-evangelism, and regenerated them when they came to faith.

And third, we want to ask if, aside from the permanent presence of the Holy Spirit in believers within the body of the Messiah after the great Shavuot of Acts 2, the ministry of the Holy Spirit was any different in the days of the Tanach than in the New Testament.

The Spirit and God's Being

The writers of the Hebrew Scriptures refrained from a discussion as to the *being* of God (as a Godhead with persons), and underscored rather His *activity* among the people of Israel. They spoke of the working of God, or the Spirit, in specific operations. Nevertheless, several passages imply that the Spirit of God is identical with the being of God.

> The Egyptians are mere humans, not God;
> their horses are made of flesh, not spirit. (Isaiah 31:3)

Here the prophet Isaiah contrasts what is "flesh," that is, something that is part of the thinking of this world, with "spirit." From the parallelism, God and spirit, or Spirit, appear to be aligned.

> Carefully read the scroll of the LORD!
> Not one of these creatures will be missing, none will lack a mate.
> For the LORD has issued the decree,
> and his own spirit gathers them. (Isaiah 34:16)

In Isaiah 34:16, where NET has "For the LORD has issued the decree," NIV reads "For it is his mouth that has given the order," reflecting the literal Hebrew *pi*, "mouth." We then have a parallelism between the "mouth" of the Lord and the Spirit of the Lord, or the Spirit, where in a statement depicts the divine work, the Spirit is as God's mouth, bringing to man what he so desperately needs.

> Who comprehends the mind [Hebrew, *ruach* or spirit] of the LORD,
> or gives him instruction as his counselor? (Isaiah 40:13)

Again, the prophet identifies the Spirit with the mind of the Lord.

Good reasons exist why the writers of the Hebrew Scriptures were reticent to discuss the very *being* of God and focused instead on His *activity* through the Spirit. The primary emphasis on God's being in the Hebrew Scriptures is on His oneness:

> Hear, O Israel: The LORD our God, the LORD is one.
> (Deuteronomy 6:4 NIV)

God had a hard time, so to speak, teaching this lesson to His people, and it took the Babylonian exile for Judah to finally affirm that God is one.

Therefore, the Hebrew Scriptures could not introduce a full-blown concept of the composite unity of God; such a declaration could only be more clearly seen in the ultimate revelation of the Messiah, Son of God (see Hebrews 1:1–3). Even so, we already saw that some Scriptures do depict a mystery of His composite nature (see above).

The *Shekinah*

This is a term used in the rabbinic literature to refer to God's presence, and it has affinities with the idea of God's Spirit. In discussing the Shekinah (which literally means "dwelling" or "resting," related to the verb *shakhen*[2]), Alan Unterman suggests that the term refers to the divine presence; he says that it "refers most often in rabbinic literature to the numinous immanence of God in the world . . . particularly in a this-worldly context: when He sanctifies a place, an object, an individual, or a whole people . . ."[3] Payne tells us that Shekinah refers to God's glory,[4] but a case can also be made for the identification of this term, and His glory, with that of the Spirit's work among Israel as a nation, and individuals within the people of Israel.

So sensitive were the rabbis within Israel as to the danger of equating the "Spirit," "the Holy One," or "the *Shekinah*" with God Himself, thereby creating a *hypostasis*, that they insisted that any mention of any three of these designations must be viewed purely figuratively and not as representing a separable aspect of God or as being in any sense a part of the Godhead. "The latter notion is totally alien to the strict monotheism of rabbinic Judaism for which the unity of the divine Essence is a basic premise."[5]

However, for intimations in the Hebrew Scriptures concerning the mystery of God's composite unity, see above in an earlier chapter.

The Work of the Spirit Within the Nation of Israel

In numerous ways, the Spirit revealed Himself at work within Israel. He set the nation apart to the Lord under the Mosaic Covenant. His presence with leaders, warriors, and builders gave these individuals a distinctive status, which did not go unnoticed by other nations in the Middle East. While other peoples had their worship systems and manifestations of spirits, yet when Israel was obedient to the Lord God and the leadership of His Spirit, most among the nations recognized that a power was at work among them far greater than the powers found within their own belief system. Here we will discuss some of these unique factors.

Among the Nation as a Whole

David frequently speaks in the Psalms about his personal relationship with God.

> Teach me to do what pleases you,
> for you are my God.
> May your kind presence
> lead me into a level land. (Psalm 143:10)

As David is also the teacher in Israel, he declares that the Spirit of God is the real teacher of the nation, and prays that God's "good Spirit" would lead both him and the nation on a "level ground," that is, in the good way of life.

Isaiah declares:

> At that time the sovereign master will wash the excrement from Zion's women,
> he will rinse the bloodstains from Jerusalem's midst,
> as he comes to judge
> and to bring devastation. (Isaiah 4:4)

The Spirit worked in a unique way in the midst of Israel as a nation, for guidance and, if necessary, for judgment as well. Although this passage from Isaiah has an eschatological orientation, the prophet Isaiah also faced severe difficulties in his own day. Thus he announced that the people of Jerusalem had to be cleansed. The Spirit of God, reflecting the mind of God, reminded the people that He would take action and discipline His people so as to preserve a faithful remnant.

This "prince of the prophets" also described how God cared for His people when He delivered them from Egypt:

> But they rebelled and offended his holy Spirit,
> so he turned into an enemy
> and fought against them.
> His people remembered the ancient times.
> Where is the one who brought them up out of the sea,
> along with the shepherd of his flock?
> Where is the one who placed his holy Spirit among them,
> the one who made his majestic power [Hebrew, *z'roah*, "arm"; NIV: "glorious arm of power] available to Moses,
> who divided the water before them,
> gaining for himself a lasting reputation,
> who led them through the deep water?
> Like a horse running on flat land they did not stumble.
> Like an animal that goes down into a valley to graze,
> so the Spirit of the LORD granted them rest.
> In this way you guided your people,
> gaining for yourself an honored reputation. (Isaiah 63:10–14)

Note that in a Hebrew poetic parallelism, Isaiah equated the "arm of power" of the Lord and "his Holy Spirit." Through this unique manifestation of the presence of God, Israel was protected from her enemies and eventually the covenant was made with them, marking the nation distinctively as the Lord's. Note also, in Isaiah 63:10, how Isaiah describes someone can do violence against the personality of the Spirit. From this passage, it is very evident that Isaiah did not understand the Spirit as some kind of superpower or influence but rather as a person who can be grieved, as someone who can even turn and become an enemy to the nation. On the other hand, as the Spirit of the Lord guided Israel through the wilderness, He also was the one who gave them rest (verse 14).

The prophet Ezekiel also added some important details regarding the ministry of the Spirit of God:

> Throw away all your sins you have committed and fashion yourselves a new heart and a new spirit! Why should you die, O house of Israel? (Ezekiel 18:31)

Taken away in the second exile from Jerusalem (597 B.C.E.), he was given the task of ministering to his fellow captives in exile. In this capacity, he had to prepare them for the greater conflagration to come, with the destruction of the Solomonic temple (586 B.C.E.), the loss of many lives, and with still more Judeans going into exile. In pleading with his fellow countrymen to "get a new heart and a new spirit," the prophet held out to his countrymen the distinctive possibility for a complete change of spirit within each person. Later, he added an even more distinctive message when he announced God's program for the nation:

> I will give you a new heart, and I will put a new spirit within you. I will remove the heart of stone from your body and give you a heart of flesh. I will put my Spirit within you; I will take the initiative and you will obey my statutes and carefully observe my regulations. (Ezekiel 36:26–27)

In the first passage, from chapter 18, Ezekiel addresses his fellow captives in a chapter emphasizing personal responsibility. In the second passage, from chapter 36, Ezekiel delivers an eschatological message concerning the future restored Israel. The fact that he speaks of believers possessing a new spirit shows that Ezekiel had no doubt of what the new birth entailed and what happens when any individual within the nation turns to God and becomes a believer. Below we discuss the issue of regeneration, but at this point note that believers within the nation did understand that something took place within each of them when they came to faith. Through the ministry of the Spirit, a transformation of the human character occurs, and believers within the nation appeared to understand the meaning of an atonement.

The Spirit of God had a very definite influence on the nation, working in their midst through His chosen vessels, reminding the people of their necessity to follow the Lord, warning them of what would happen if they turned away from Him, but also holding out the possibility that He could have a very definite influence on the hearts of individuals.

Among the Leaders of Israel

When the Spirit came upon individuals, He became the source of mental and spiritual guidance, providing the power to accomplish various tasks. He bestowed on these various leaders qualities so that they could fulfill their calling in a way pleasing to God. The Spirit provided the gifts necessary for leadership for kings and rulers.

Beginning with the judges, individuals were gifted with qualities that enabled them to provide leadership for the nation and deliver them from their oppressors. Concerning Othniel:

> The LORD's spirit empowered him and he led Israel. When he went to do battle, the LORD handed over to him King Cushan-rishathaim of Aram and he overpowered him. (Judges 3:10)

With the power given him, he led the people in overcoming the king of Aram, repelling his troops. In the same way the Spirit of the Lord came upon Gideon:

> The LORD's spirit took control of Gideon. He blew a trumpet, summoning the Abiezrites to follow him. (Judges 6:34)

whereupon he called for soldiers from his own family as well as from Manasseh, Asher, Zebulun, and Naphthali to join with him in overpowering the Midianite invaders. Likewise, the Spirit of the Lord came upon Jephthah:

> The LORD's spirit empowered Jephthah. He passed through Gilead and Manasseh and went to Mizpah in Gilead. From there he approached the Ammonites. (Judges 11:29)

In still another example, the Spirit of God came upon Sha'ul:

> The Spirit of God rushed upon Sha'ul when he heard these words, and he became very angry. (1 Samuel 11:6)

He then led Israel in fighting against the Ammonites and so rescued the people of Jabesh Gilead.

In a special sense, the Spirit of the Lord came upon David in power after his anointing by Samuel:

> So Samuel took the horn full of olive oil and anointed him in the presence of his brothers. The Spirit of the LORD rushed upon David from that day onward. Then Samuel got up and went to Ramah. Now the Spirit of the LORD had turned away from Saul, and an evil spirit from the LORD tormented him. (1 Samuel 16:13–14)

This reflected God's choice, and as Israel's king David became a Spirit-led ruler. Significantly, the Scripture records that right after the anointing of David with the Spirit, the Spirit of the Lord departed from Sha'ul.

For some of Israel's other servants, the Scripture provides descriptions too. Of Joseph:

> So Pharaoh asked his officials, "Can we find a man like Joseph, one in whom the Spirit of God is present?" (Genesis 41:38)

Here we have Pharaoh's assessment of Joseph as (literally) "a man where the Spirit of God is in him." Then, of Daniel:

> Later Daniel entered (whose name is Belteshazzar after the name of my god, and in whom there is a spirit of the holy gods). I recounted the dream for him as well. (Daniel 4:8; verse 5 MT)

Nebuchadnezzar literally said, "In him is a spirit (or, the Spirit) of the holy gods (God)." Also, we read of Bezalel:

> And I have filled him with the Spirit of God in skill, in understanding, in knowledge, and in all kinds of craftsmanship. (Exodus 31:3)

The Nature of the Spirit's Presence in Israel

The Terms "Coming Upon" and "Dwelling In." This brings up the important question as to what is meant when the Spirit of the Lord "comes upon" an individual, particularly, David. Does it mean that the Spirit *rests only for a time* on the ruler, giving him wisdom and qualities whereby people will instinctively sense that God's hand is on them in a special way? Or does it mean that the Spirit of God *indwelt* the ruler?

Let us review some of the verses considered above:

> The LORD's spirit empowered him and he led Israel. When he went to do battle, the LORD handed over to him King Cushan-rishathaim of Aram and he overpowered him. (Judges 3:10)

In the case of Othniel, the Scripture pictures the Spirit's contact with him as *wattehi alaw* ("came upon him").

> The LORD'S spirit took control of Gideon. He blew a trumpet, summoning the Abiezrites to follow him. (Judges 6:34)

With Gideon the terminology is, in the Hebrew, *labeshaw* ("clothed").

> The LORD'S spirit empowered Jephthah. He passed through Gilead and Manasseh and went to Mizpah in Gilead. From there he approached the Ammonites. (Judges 11:29)

For Jephthah, the word is the same as with Othniel: *wattehi al* ("came upon").

> The Spirit of God rushed upon Sha'ul when he heard these words, and he became very angry. (1 Samuel 11:6)

With Sha'ul, the description is *wattitselach* with *al* pointing to Sha'ul as the direct object ("the Spirit rushed upon Sha'ul").[6]

> So Pharaoh asked his officials, "Can we find a man like Joseph, one in whom the Spirit of God is present?" (Genesis 41:38)

> Later Daniel entered (whose name is Belteshazzar after the name of my god, and in whom there is a spirit of the holy gods). I recounted the dream for him as well. (Daniel 4:8; verse 5 MT)

In the cases of Joseph and Daniel, we read of the Spirit actually *dwelling in* them, and the question is raised as to what this might mean. The answer may lie in how pagan kings spoke of the Spirit; in their understanding it would be a way to contrast these individuals with other wise men who did not have the same communication with divine beings.

Turning to commentators for insight, in the case of Joseph, Keil and Delitzsch translate: "in whom the Spirit of God is." They explain: "*'The Spirit of Elohim;' i.e.* the spirit of supernatural insight and wisdom."[7] The only discussion they offer is the comparison with other wise men and an assessment by a pagan ruler who recognized a distinction between Joseph and other wise men who sought to interpret dreams. But nothing is offered as to whether the Spirit indwelt Joseph in a biblical sense.

In the same way, Gleason Archer suggested concerning the similar observation made by Nebuchadnezzar regarding Daniel:

> He then added that in contrast to the other soothsayers in his court, Daniel was truly inspired by God (or the gods): "The spirit of the holy gods is in him." (That this *ᵓᵉlāhîn*, ["gods"] is meant as a true plural—rather than a plural of majesty—is shown by the plural form of the adjective *qaddîšîn* accompanying it.) Daniel had demonstrated real communication with the high God in transcending the merely human wisdom of the rest of the diviners (ch. 2).[8]

Given that there are special instances concerning Joseph, Daniel, and David, can we understand this special ministry of the Spirit more generally? Ryrie suggests:

> . . . although the Spirit did indwell men in Old Testament times, it was a selective ministry, both in regard to whom He indwelt and for how long. Can this relationship be summarized in any simple way? Yes, for the Lord summarized it by telling His disciples that up to that time the Spirit had been abiding with them, though on and after the day of Pentecost He would be in them (Yohanan 14:17).[9]

Ryrie is certainly correct regarding the New Testament. There we have specific statements that the Spirit indwells every believer. Once a person is born again, the Spirit never leaves, even though He can be grieved or His fire can be put out through immoral and rebellious actions of believers (see Ephesians 4:30; 1 Thessalonians 4:19).

But is it that simple regarding believers within Israel under the Mosaic Constitution? While only selected leaders and persons are mentioned upon whom the Spirit came, are they not models of what was taking place among *all* believers as they sought to serve God? Even as it takes the ministry of the Spirit with believers today to do the tasks He asks us to do, so it would also seem to be true for believers in Israel; it would appear that the Spirit of God came upon many more people than what is recorded.

The Continual Presence of the Spirit. Let us explore further the ministry of the Spirit among a few of Israel's leaders.

> So Samuel took the horn full of olive oil and anointed him in the presence of his brothers. The Spirit of the LORD rushed upon David from that day onward. Then Samuel got up and went to Ramah. (1 Samuel 16:13)

David's experience with the Spirit is described initially the same way as is Sha'ul's. As soon as David is anointed, the Spirit of the Lord *watteselah el* ("rushed upon David" or, "came mightily upon David"). But the comment that follows marks David as someone different than Sha'ul. "The Spirit was with David," we read, "from that day on."

Does this mean that the Spirit of the Lord "indwelt" David permanently? He was very sensitive to the Spirit's presence and after his moral and spiritual lapse with Bat Sheva, he himself cried out in despair:

> Do not reject me!
> Do not take your Holy Spirit away from me!
> (Psalm 51:11; verse 13 MT)

One thing we can say is that in some way the Spirit was with David throughout most of his ministry, though on this one occasion there was the possibility that He would take leave of David. The text does not say that He actually did so, however. The best that we can say about most of Israel's leaders and people who served God is that somehow the Spirit clothed or enveloped the person. The Spirit gave him or her powers that were recognized by the people. Isarel instinctively followed these leaders going into battle and gaining a victory over their enemies. They recognized them as leaders who possessed divinely given wisdom to guide their people. It would seem that on occasion, the Spirit of God could leave. But even on such occasions, the question remains as to whether it actually happened for those rulers specially selected by God.

In David's case, he represented the house from which the Messiah would eventually come, and it would appear that the Spirit of God had a specialized ministry with this house that did not pertain to the house of Sha'ul. David was a divinely chosen king of Israel and in a very special sense, the Spirit was present with him, a fact that everyone recognized instinctively.

The same could be said of Joseph, Daniel, and others like them. Of Daniel, nothing is ever said of any moral or spiritual lapse in his life. Therefore, we can say that the Spirit continued to envelop him as he performed the duties of a statesman, as he stood before kings, as he shared a God-given wisdom, as he maintained a prayer life even at the cost of his own safety, and as he proclaimed prophecies pertaining to his people Israel as well as to the nations. This would seem to surely demonstrate that certain men enjoyed a continual presence of the Spirit, even though we may ask whether the Spirit indwelt or only enveloped these very people.

Transfer of the Spirit from One Ruler to Another

On a number of occasions, a ruler of the people of Israel sought to transfer power to another qualified and designated person to either be his representative or to succeed him in office. In particular, note what occurred regarding Joshua:

> The LORD replied to Moses, "Take Joshua son of Nun, a man in whom is such a spirit, and lay your hand on him; set him before Eleazar the priest and before the whole community, and commission him publicly. Then you must delegate some of your authority to him, so that the whole community of the Israelites will be obedient. And he will stand

> before Eleazar the priest, who will seek counsel for him before the LORD by the decision of the Urim. At his command they will go out, and at his command they will come in, he and all the Israelites with him, the whole community."
>
> So Moses did as the LORD commanded him; he took Joshua and set him before Eleazar the priest and before the whole community. He laid his hands on him and commissioned him, just as the LORD commanded, by the authority of Moses. (Numbers 27:18–23)

> Now Joshua son of Nun was full of the spirit of wisdom, for Moses had placed his hands on him; and the Israelites listened to him and did just what the LORD had commanded Moses. (Deuteronomy 34:9)

Everyone had already recognized that the Spirit of God rested on Joshua. Now, however, in a special sense, Joshua is singled out and with the approval of Eleazar, the priest, the new ruler is commissioned in the presence of all the people. The Deuteronomy passage recognizes this transfer of power after the departure of Moses. The passing of power was demonstrated through the transfer of the Spirit who now rested on the new leader. Everyone recognized the wisdom, power, and guidance he now possessed, similar to that of the prior leader.

The same occurred when seventy specially selected men were called to serve as leaders under Moses:

> And the LORD came down in the cloud and spoke to them, and he took some of the Spirit that was on Moses and put it on the seventy elders. When the Spirit rested on them, they prophesied, but did not do so again. (Numbers 11:25)

One of the signs of the Spirit upon them was their gift to prophesy; in addition, they had wisdom from God by which to aid Moses in dispensing justice for the people.

The Spirit and God's Special Servants

God's Spirit—rendered by the Hebrew word *ruach*—means *breath*, *wind*, or *spirit*.[10] In addition, in the context in which the Spirit or Spirit of God appears, "Spirit stands for invisible entity or power. The Spirit of God is the outgoing energy or power of God working in the world, and in particular to especially selected people."[11] This power is not thought of as separate from God; rather, the Spirit makes God's presence very apparent among people He uses.

Israel's special people were endowed with extraordinary physical strength. Samson is an example in these two verses:

> The LORD's spirit empowered him and he tore the lion in two with his bare hands as easily as one would tear a young goat. But he did not tell his father or mother what he had done. (Judges 14:6)

> The LORD's spirit empowered him. He went down to Ashkelon and murdered thirty men. He took their clothes and gave them to the men who had solved the riddle. He was furious as he went back home. (Judges 14:19)

The Spirit worked on Samson with tremendous force. Says Lampe:

> The Spirit of the Lord is regarded as the source of the endowment of Israel's heroes with extraordinary physical strength (Judges 14:6, 19; 15:14). It is a supernatural and unpredictable power, which takes possession of a man, and controls his actions like a tremendous inner force. In such contexts "spirit" retains something of its original meaning of "wind." As the wind seizes upon the dust of the ground and animates it, blowing it where it will, like a live object, so the divine Spirit animates the human personality.[12]

So too with Ezekiel, where the Spirit is a force physically taking hold of him:

> As he spoke, the Spirit came into me and raised me to my feet, and I heard him speaking to me. (Ezekiel 2:2 NIV)[13]

> Then the Spirit lifted me up, and I heard behind me a loud rumbling

> sound—May the glory of the LORD be praised in his dwelling-place! (Ezekiel 3:12 NIV)

> Then the Spirit lifted me up and brought me to the gate of the house of the LORD that faces east. (Ezekiel 11:1 NIV)

> The Spirit lifted me up and brought me to the exiles in Babylonia in the vision given by the Spirit of God. Then the vision I had seen went up from me. (Ezekiel 11:24 NIV)

As to Gideon:

> The LORD's spirit took control of Gideon. He blew a trumpet, summoning the Abiezrites to follow him. (Judges 6:34)

We have already looked at this verse, seeing how the Spirit of the Lord clothed Gideon. It was as if he had donned an outward garment, but because this judge was under God's complete control, he had an unmistakable dynamic. The picture is an interesting one; when God wanted His servant to minister, he or she was so under His perfect control, that each one did what He wanted—sometimes willingly (as with Gideon after he was thoroughly convinced in the fleece affair) and sometimes struggling with God's commission (as Ezekiel did in the beginning). Nevertheless, the prophet was obedient and this power of the Spirit enabled him to minister effectively to his people.

Therefore, in many ways the Spirit came upon various individuals, enabling them to serve in a number of capacities, such as rulers and leaders in battle; to succeed previous rulers; and, in several particular cases such as those of Joshua, David, and Daniel, to apparently be continually under the guidance of the Spirit.

The Spirit and the Prophets

One of the primary ministries of the Spirit was in communicating the Word of God, and in particular the material that had to do with prophecy.

In one regard, especially in the early days of the nation, prophecy was not on an "elevated" level. At times these early prophets appeared to be almost irresponsible, acting in a very peculiar manner, and appeared among communities of ecstatics. Sha'ul encountered such a band of prophets coming down from the high place, playing lyres, tambourines, flutes, and harps, who then prophesied. The Spirit of the Lord also came upon Sha'ul and he also joined the prophets, prophesying with them. As he did so, he was "changed" into a different person:

> Afterward you will go to Gibeah of God, where there are Philistine officials. When you enter the town, you will meet a company of prophets coming down from the high place. They will have harps, tambourines, flutes, and lyres, and they will be prophesying. Then the spirit of the LORD will rush upon you and you will prophesy with them. You will be changed into a different person. (1 Samuel 10:5–6)

On another occasion at Gibeah, Sha'ul was found in company with a similar group of prophets as they prophesied.

> As Sha'ul turned to leave Samuel, God changed his inmost person. All these signs happened on that very day. When Sha'ul and his servant arrived at Gibeah, a company of prophets was coming out to meet him. Then the spirit of God rushed upon Sha'ul and he prophesied among them. (1 Samuel 10:9–10)

In an even stranger context, as a company of prophets was prophesying, with Samuel presiding over them, King Sha'ul sent his soldiers to capture David:

> So Sha'ul sent messengers to capture David. When they saw a company of prophets prophesying with Samuel standing there as their leader, the spirit of God came upon Saul's messengers, and they also prophesied. When it was reported to Sha'ul, he sent more messengers, but they prophesied too. So Sha'ul sent messengers a third time, but they also prophesied. Finally Sha'ul himself went to Ramah. When

> he arrived at the large cistern that is in Secu, he asked, "Where are Samuel and David?" They said, "At Naioth in Ramah."
>
> So Sha'ul went to Naioth in Ramah. The Spirit of God came upon him as well, and he walked along prophesying until he came to Naioth in Ramah. He even stripped off his clothes and prophesied before Samuel. He lay there naked all that day and night. (For that reason it is asked, "Is Sha'ul also among the prophets?") (1 Samuel 19:20–24)

However, as time went by, the entire experience of prophecy became more and more elevated and complicated, and one sees less and less of these ecstatic experiences. Some have questioned whether these early ecstatic prophets were genuine, and have suggested a number of means to interpret this phenomenon: According to some, ecstatic prophecy is associated with a psychological state: "All prophecy, at least until a comparatively late post-exilic period, was based on a peculiar psychological condition to which the name ecstasy is often given. It was characteristic of the false prophet as well as of the true, . . ."[14] Others find affinities with the phenomena of Acts; Scott, for instance, says that these "dervish 'prophets'" did not prophesy "in intelligible speech, but resembled rather the 'speaking with tongues' in the Acts of the Apostles."[15] Mowinckel made a distinction between the ecstatic prophets who had a "Spirit" ministry while the later canonical prophets (that is, those whose books became part of the Bible, such as Isaiah) claimed to be the recipients of the Word of the Lord.[16]

However, while the behavior of these early prophets appear odd, they were genuine, as Freeman reminds us:

> . . . the distinction between the precanonical prophets and the canonical prophets, . . . is both arbitrary and artificial. The true prophets of Israel, whether precanonical or canonical, possessed *both* the word and the *Spirit* of the Lord.[17]

With Elijah and Elisha, a more elevated ministry of prophecy took place, guided by the Spirit. It was less ecstatic, more measured and more under control. When Elijah ran from Jezebel in Samaria to Mount Horeb (1 Kings 19:1–2), God did not rebuke His servant but instead sent him back to pursue the ministry God had given him in the Israel of the north, but with Elisha as an assistant.

> When they had crossed over, Elijah said to Elisha, "What can I do for you, before I am taken away from you?" Elisha answered, "May I receive a double portion of the prophetic spirit that energizes you." (2 Kings 2:9)

> When the members of the prophetic guild in Jericho, who were standing at a distance, saw him do this, they said, "The spirit that energized Elijah rests upon Elisha." They went to meet him and bowed down to the ground before him. (2 Kings 2:15)

When Elijah was caught up to heaven, Elisha was also privileged to witness his master's glorious ascension in the chariot; a double portion of the divine Spirit was transferred to Elisha whereby he could perform twice the number of miracles than that of his master, and so his possession of the Spirit became all the more significant.

David, although a general and a king-statesman, also had the gift of prophecy, and was recognized as a prophet when he declared:

> The LORD's spirit spoke through me;
> his word was on my tongue. (2 Samuel 23:2)

The Spirit enabled David to deliver the inspired prophecies of God.

In the postexilic period, after a spiritual renewal of Judah (see Nehemiah 8:9–10), the priests and Levites acknowledged the history of Israel as unique in a long passage. Among many statements, they confessed their sins as well as those of the nation:

> You prolonged your kindness with them for many years, and you solemnly admonished them by your Spirit through your prophets.

> Still they paid no attention, so you delivered them into the hands of the neighboring peoples. (Nehemiah 9:30)

This followed the pattern whereby Israel had always been warned by the prophets that, failing to listen to His word, disaster would befall them.

With the major and minor canonical prophets, the Spirit of God played a major role in the prophetic messages regarding the nation and its people. In Isaiah we read that in a peculiar sense, the message came from the Lord God and His Spirit as He spoke in power:

> "Approach me! Listen to this!
> From the very first I have not spoken in secret;
> when it happens, I am there."
> So now, the sovereign Lord has sent me, accompanied by his spirit.
> (Isaiah 48:16)

The Spirit is also recognized as synonymous with the presence of God in ministry:

> The spirit of the sovereign LORD is upon me,
> because the LORD has chosen me.
> He has commissioned me to encourage the poor,
> to help the brokenhearted,
> to decree the release of captives,
> and the freeing of prisoners. (Isaiah 61:1)

In this capacity the Spirit directs the people to do in accordance with the prophetic word. In the above passage, Isaiah on one unusual occasion declared that his mission was not something personal but that from "the Spirit of the Lord God." And yet, while this passage has a prophetic Messianic significance, Isaiah's personal ministry was also unique and emphatic because of the Spirit's inspiration and authentication.

Ezekiel likewise, ministering to his fellow countrymen who had already gone into exile and also to those who would yet come after the third deportation in 586 B.C.E., declared:

> Then the Spirit of the LORD came upon me and said to me, "Say: This is what the LORD says: 'This is what you are thinking, O house of Israel; I know what goes through your minds.'" (Ezekiel 11:5)

In this way God gave him an authentic message to deliver to his people, reflecting a word that was one of doom. Later on, toward the end of his ministry and when most of his fellow exiles acknowledged him as a true prophet, he was then brought to the site of the new temple to receive a vision of how the new sanctuary will be filled with the glory of God. He was to then take this message back to his people of that day so as to encourage them:

> Then the Spirit lifted me up and brought me into the inner court, and the glory of the LORD filled the temple. (Ezekiel 43:5 NIV)

The position of the prophet within the nation was extremely important. Sometimes these prophets had to deliver undesirable and unwanted messages. But they were faithful nevertheless to share the prophetic word, reminding their people that judgment would come if they were not obedient. So with Hosea:

> The time of judgment is about to arrive!
> The time of retribution is imminent!
> Let Israel know!
> The prophet is considered a fool—
> the inspired man is viewed as a madman—
> because of the multitude of your sins
> and your intense animosity. (Hosea 9:7)

Hosea announced to his own shame that people thought of him in a derogatory way; he described himself as a man of the Spirit, but the people only referred to him as a maniac. Likewise Micah:

> But I am full of the courage that the LORD's Spirit gives,

and have a strong commitment to justice.
This enables me to confront Jacob with its rebellion,
and Israel with its sin. (Micah 3:8)

Micah's task was not a pleasant one, but his message was one of authentication, even though he was not comfortable with such a word. And similarly we read in Zechariah, referring to the reason for the Babylonian exile:

> Indeed, they made their heart as hard as diamond, so that they could not obey the Torah and the other words the LORD who rules over all had sent by his Spirit through the former prophets. Therefore, the LORD who rules over all had poured out great wrath. (Zechariah 7:12)

In many ways, therefore, the prophets had a function to fulfill, as preachers to their day, but also prophesying in a sure sense through the work of the Spirit of what would happen to people who either listened to His word and therefore could receive His blessing, or if not, face dire consequences for their disobedience.

The Spirit's Ministry and Its Eschatological Significance

The Spirit and the Coming Messiah. We have already looked at the anointing of David by Samuel. At that time, the Spirit rushed on David in power:

> So Samuel took the horn full of olive oil and anointed him in the presence of his brothers. The Spirit of the LORD rushed upon David from that day onward. Then Samuel got up and went to Ramah. (1 Samuel 16:13)

Similarly, the psalmist Ethan explained:

I have discovered David, my servant.
With my holy oil I have anointed him as king.
My hand will support him,

and my arm will strengthen him. (Psalm 89:20–21)

Here God's "arm" can be paralleled to the peculiar work of the Spirit as He came upon David, clothing him and giving him a power only He can provide.

In a similar way, the prophet Isaiah described the ideal figure of an inspired king of the future, on whom God's Spirit would rest, providing him with a sevenfold abundance of gifts that would make him a wise and just ruler:

A shoot will grow out of Jesse's root stock,
a bud will sprout from his roots.
The LORD's spirit will rest on him—
a spirit that gives extraordinary wisdom,
a spirit that provides the ability to execute plans,
a spirit that produces absolute loyalty to the LORD. (Isaiah 11:1–2)

This is a description of a Messiah who was yet to appear. This link between anointing and the special work of the Spirit is further described by Isaiah:

Here is my servant whom I support,
my chosen one in whom I take pleasure.
I have placed my spirit on him;
he will make just decrees for the nations. (Isaiah 42:1)

And here, Isaiah indicates that the Messiah will have a number of assigned functions:

The spirit of the sovereign LORD is upon me,
because the LORD has chosen me.
He has commissioned me to encourage the poor,
to help the brokenhearted,
to decree the release of captives,
and the freeing of prisoners,
to announce the year when the LORD will show his favor,
the day when our God will seek vengeance,

to console all who mourn. (Isaiah 61:1–2)

When the Messiah Yeshua read from this passage on that particular day in the synagogue, no doubt the Haftorah for that particular *Shabbat*, He quite naturally made the application apply to Himself:[18]

The Spirit of the Lord is upon me,
because he has anointed me to proclaim good news to the poor.
He has sent me to proclaim release to the captives
and the regaining of sight to the blind,
to set free those who are oppressed. (Luke 4:18)

When Yeshua stopped where He did, not even finishing Isaiah 61:2, much less the rest of the passage, He folded up the scroll, returned to His seat, and then announced this passage was being fulfilled in His day! Luke evidently took special care to include this passage in his version of Yeshua's life as a way to emphasize his special claims of Yeshua as prophesied by Isaiah.

Every gospel writer announced this hope of a Spirit-possessed Messiah in the coming of the Spirit at His baptism:

After Yeshua was baptized, just as he was coming up out of the water, the heavens opened and he saw the Spirit of God descending like a dove and coming on him. (Mattai 3:16)

And just as Yeshua was coming up out of the water, he saw the heavens splitting apart and the Spirit descending on him like a dove. (Mark 1:10)

Now when all the people were baptized, Yeshua also was baptized. And while he was praying, the heavens opened. (Luke 3:21)

And I did not recognize him, but the one who sent me to baptize with water said to me, "The one on whom you see the Spirit descending and remaining—this is the one who baptizes with the Holy Spirit." (Yohanan 1:33)

Kefa also used the same idea:

> . . . with respect to Yeshua from Nazareth, that God anointed him with the Holy Spirit and with power. He went around doing good and healing all who were oppressed by the devil, because God was with him. (Acts 10:38)

Just as God anointed David so that the Spirit of God came on him, so now the same idea is transferred to Yeshua.

But not only are messages present that speak of the long-range prophecies regarding the Messiah; the words of the prophets also speak of the last days, describing the renewal of Israel as well as the nation's repentance. In a very specific manner, the Spirit of God came on the prophets and provided them with these eschatological messages.

The Spirit and the National Renewal of Israel. Some of these prophecies for the future describe the renewal of Israel:

> Look, a king will promote fairness;
> officials will promote justice. (Isaiah 32:1)

> till the Spirit is poured upon us from on high, and the desert becomes a fertile field, and the fertile field seems like a forest. (Isaiah 32:15 NIV)[19]
> I will give them one heart and I will put a new spirit within them; I will remove the hearts of stone from their bodies and I will give them tender hearts. (Ezekiel 11:19)

> I will give you a new heart, and I will put a new spirit within you. I will remove the heart of stone from your body and give you a heart of flesh. I will put my Spirit within you; I will take the initiative and you will obey my statutes and carefully observe my regulations. (Ezekiel 36:26–27)

Furthermore, the nation will in the last days repent and turn to the Messiah:

> I will pour out on the kingship of David and the population of Jerusalem a spirit of grace and supplication so that they will look to

> me, the one they have pierced. They will lament for him as one laments for an only son, and there will be a bitter cry for him like the bitter cry for a firstborn. (Zechariah 12:10)

Isaiah also announced that changes will occur in the entire land in the day when Israel repents:

> For I will pour water on the parched ground
> and cause streams to flow on the dry land.
> I will pour my spirit on your offspring
> and my blessing on your children. (Isaiah 44:3)

In every case, the Scripture indicates how new life will occur because of the Spirit who has been poured out so as to exert an influence on the nation.

The Spirit and Personal Renewal. Here we can make some observations about the work of the Spirit in pre-evangelism and in regeneration during the period of the Tanach.

Much has already been said about how the Spirit came on various individuals, aiding them in God's tasks. Yet the Hebrew Scriptures seem silent on how the Spirit works in the individual heart, how He brings about a sensitivity to what God desires from His people, how a person can be regenerated through the Spirit to be born again. Many scholars have various ideas on this subject and some have even suggested that salvation was not even possible until the appearance of the Messiah Yeshua.

Certainly, the New Testament provides an abundance of description of how the Spirit works beforehand to create the interest in a person's heart for spiritual things, as Yohanan describes:

> And when he comes, he will prove the world wrong concerning sin and righteousness and judgment—concerning sin, because they do not believe in me; concerning righteousness, because I am going to the Father and you will see me no longer; and concerning judgment, because the ruler of this world has been condemned. (Yohanan 16:8–11)

But the question is, did the Spirit work in such a way among the people of Israel under the Mosaic Constitution? There must in fact have been some work of the Spirit, judging by various statements by Israel's leaders and prophets. For example, on the occasion of the great prayer of confession of Nehemiah 9, following the revival under Ezra and Nehemiah, one of the Levites prayed this prayer:

> You imparted your good Spirit to instruct them. You did not withhold your manna from their mouths; you provided water for their thirst. (Nehemiah 9:20)

In doing so, he was referring to how the Spirit taught Israel through Moses, showing the possibility of God's presence in the lives of individuals.

Then, we have the account of Israel's apostasy in Exodus:

> Go up to a land flowing with milk and honey. But I will not go up among you, for you are a stiff-necked people, and I might destroy you on the way. (Exodus 33:3)

The background to this verse is that Israel had sinned miserably at the base of Mount Sinai, worshipping a synthesis of Israel's God with one of Egypt's gods. The Lord's rejoinder was that while Israel could proceed on their way to the Promised Land, His presence would not go with them. In response, the people began to mourn and stripped off the ornaments they had worn in their debauchery. It appears that many genuinely turned to the Lord on that occasion. It may be that the Spirit did a "pre-evangelistic" work in the hearts of people, causing many of them to mourn and become believers as a result of His special work.

In times of great spiritual renewal, the Spirit of God came on people. This example is taken from the height of the renewal in the days of King Asa:

> He assembled all Judah and Benjamin, as well as the settlers from Ephraim, Manasseh, and Simeon who had come to live with them. Many people from Israel had come there to live when they saw that the LORD

> his God was with him. They assembled in Jerusalem in the third month of the fifteenth year of Asa's reign. At that time they sacrificed to the LORD some of the plunder they had brought back, including 700 head of cattle and 7,000 sheep. They solemnly agreed to seek the LORD God of their ancestors with their whole heart and being. (2 Chronicles 15:9–12)

The result was a revival of the believers; the response and their changed lives deeply moved the hearts of many unbelievers who were also present in Jerusalem at the temple services.

A second example comes from the renewal in Hezekiah's day:

> But some men from Asher, Manasseh, and Zebulun humbled themselves and came to Jerusalem. (2 Chronicles 30:11)

> The majority of the many people from Ephraim, Manasseh, Issachar, and Zebulun were ceremonially unclean, yet they ate the Passover in violation of what is prescribed in the law. For Hezekiah prayed for them, saying: "May the LORD, who is good, forgive everyone who has determined to follow God, the LORD God of his ancestors, even if he is not ceremonially clean according to the standards of the temple." (2 Chronicles 30:18–19)

> Hezekiah and all the people were happy about what God had done for them, for it had been done quickly. (2 Chronicles 29:36)

> The LORD responded favorably to Hezekiah and forgave the people. (2 Chronicles 30:20)

> There was a great celebration in Jerusalem, unlike anything that had occurred in Jerusalem since the time of King Solomon son of David of Israel. (2 Chronicles 30:26)

Great numbers of people were present at the rededication of the temple, as well as at the observance of the Passover shortly thereafter. On this occasion the Spirit worked in great power: "it was done so quickly." Could it not be that many believers were revived and a good number of unbelievers came to the Lord as the Spirit worked in hearts and "He healed the people"?

The third example comes from the days of Nehemiah:

> Then Nehemiah the governor, Ezra the priestly scribe, and the Levites who were imparting understanding to the people said to all of them, "This day is holy to the LORD your God. Do not mourn or weep." For all the people had been weeping when they heard the words of the law. He said to them, "Go and eat delicacies and drink sweet drinks and send portions to those for whom nothing is prepared. For this day is holy to our Lord. Do not grieve, for the joy of the LORD is your strength." (Nehemiah 8:9–10)

In Nehemiah's time another spiritual renewal came upon the people; Ezra publicly read the Torah of God, and by the end of the reading on the first day, believers began to cry as they heard the Word. This may well have been a work of the Spirit of God in the hearts of people. No doubt the occasion also spoke to the hearts of unbelievers, when we read that "all the people had been weeping as they listened to the words of the Law."

And yet, the Scripture does not specifically say how the Spirit of God was at work; we are left to re-create the situation, reading between the lines of Scripture, imagining ourselves present, and sensing His special ministry as He strove with the hearts of the people.

Did the Spirit regenerate people, so that they repented as they turned to the Lord, and did the Spirit definitely change people's hearts? Again, Scripture does not specifically say so as it does in numerous places in the New Testament.

We do know that the lessons concerning the atonement are already present in the Mosaic Covenant through the sin offering. There, as each one brought his particular animal, four major principles are seen.[20] (1) Each worshipper, as he brought his particular animal, had to regard it as his particular *substitute*; (2) the offerer's sins became *identified* with the animal substitute, making it thereby sin; (3) the substitute underwent *death*, because it had become sin and it died in place of the offerer; and finally, (4) there was an *exchange of life* that, while not spelled out clearly in the book of Leviticus, is described by later prophets, namely, that as the animal died, it gave its life to the offerer.

In order for these principles to be effective, the individual had to respond by faith and accept them, and then the Spirit would work in his heart and change him. But once more, the Hebrew Scriptures do not discuss how it was done.

Several passages seem to imply some particular work of the Spirit in regeneration.

Circumcision. In a pointed remark, Moses called on Israel in these verses:

> Now, Israel, what does the LORD your God require of you except to revere him, to obey all his commandments, to love him, to serve him with all your mind and being, and to keep the LORD's commandments and statutes that I am giving you today for your own good? (Deuteronomy 10:12–13)

> Circumcise your hearts, therefore, and do not be stiff-necked any longer. (Deuteronomy 10:16 NIV)

But how was one to live this lifestyle? We have already seen that Israel consisted of two classes of people: on the one hand, the remnant who were believers, seeking to serve God, and on the other hand the hardhearted, the unregenerate. But how could the "hard hearts" be changed? Moses' answer was interesting: "Circumcise your hearts, and do not be stiff-necked any longer." But how was this to be performed by each Israelite who took the message to heart? Was this not the particular work of the Spirit who touched the heart of the individual, and changed him or her?

So too with Jeremiah:

> Circumcise yourselves to the LORD, circumcise your hearts, you men of Judah and people of Jerusalem, or my wrath will break out and

> burn like fire because of the evil you have done—burn with no one to quench it. (Jeremiah 4:4 NIV)

In Jeremiah's day, the prophet faced a nation on the skids, following the spiritual renewal that had occurred in the days of Josiah (see 2 Chronicles 35:18). The course for Judah continued to spiral downward until ultimately the temple was destroyed and many were killed or went into exile. What was Jeremiah's message in the midst of such dire circumstances? The only fitting reply was, "Circumcise yourselves to the LORD . . ."

The literal circumcision of cutting away the foreskin becomes the metaphor of what is necessary for a person's heart. Thompson explains regarding the passage in Deuteronomy:

> If that which hinders is cut away (the parallel with physical circumcision is obvious), then the circumcised heart becomes open and, being freed from hindering obstructions, it can become pliable and amenable to the direction of God. . . . Indeed, without circumcision of the heart true fear of God and true love of God are both impossible.[21]

Keil observed concerning the Jeremiah passage:

> In the flesh all Jews were circumcised. If they then are called to circumcise themselves to the Lord, this must be meant spiritually, of the putting away of the spiritual impurity of the heart, i.e. of all that hinders the sanctifying of the heart; . . . The foreskins are the evil lusts and longings of the heart . . .[22]

From the comments by these two sources, it appears that circumcision reflects the change of heart possible by the individual; he or she must make the decision to change their hearts, turning away from sin and impurity. In other words, the person must have a repentant attitude. A. B. Davidson reflects on this view of God's message to Jeremiah, that people must circumcise their hearts, but then questions whether this was possible, because " . . . appeals to men to regenerate themselves are vain."[23] In support of his position, he asked if the Ethiopian could change his skin, or the leopard his spots (see Jeremiah 13:23). In the light of this "impossibility" for change, Davidson declared that it would have to take the New Covenant as enunciated by God to Jeremiah to provide for this circumcision of heart: "The ethical unit becomes the individual mind, and sin and righteousness become matters of the relation of the personal mind to God."[24]

But does this mean that no Israelite ever became a believer? Was circumcision and regeneration only a New Covenant phenomenon? Obviously not. Could the people themselves, living in the evil they had chosen, ever circumcise their own hearts? For a person to know the Lord, a work of repentance and regeneration is implied. No other course can be entertained but that the Spirit must enable a person to repent, turn to Him, and experience the change only God can perform. Moses and Jeremiah called on the people to circumcise themselves, obviously not in their flesh, but as a reminder that a supernatural work of God had to be performed to enable the person to turn away from sin and turn toward God. We are left with no word describing such an action, but if the New Covenant is any guide, there must have been some special work of the Spirit in changing the individual.

A New Heart and a New Spirit. A second message is the statement by the prophet Ezekiel, already alluded to in the above discussions:

> I will give you a new heart, and I will put a new spirit within you. I will remove the heart of stone from your body and give you a heart of flesh. (Ezekiel 36:26)

In a day yet to come, a restored Israel will know what it means to have a new heart and a new spirit within them, for God the Spirit will take from them their heart of stone and instead provide them with a heart of flesh. But is this a message only for the future, a New Covenant message, with regard to Israel at the time when it will be restored? Could not this message also be the way the Spirit worked in the days of the Hebrew Scriptures within Israel? Was it not possible that when a person was born again, the heart of stone was removed and the Spirit provided the heart of flesh in the work of regeneration?

Yeshua seemed to allude to Ezekiel in His discussion with Nicodemus when He said that for a person to be born again, he must be born "of the Spirit":

> Yeshua replied, "I tell you the solemn truth, unless a person is born from above, he cannot see the kingdom of God." . . .
>
> Yeshua answered, "I tell you the solemn truth, unless a person is born of water and spirit, he cannot enter the kingdom of God."
>
> The wind blows wherever it will, and you hear the sound it makes, but do not know where it comes from and where it is going. So it is with everyone who is born of the Spirit. (Yohanan 3:3, 5, 8)

Kaiser points out that Yeshua was amazed by the fact that Nicodemus did not understand this message, essentially asking, How could this man be a teacher of the Jews and not know either about being born again or being born of the Spirit? Where must this man have gone to yeshivah or seminary? Had he never read Ezekiel 36:25–32 with its teaching about the "new heart" and the "new Spirit"? The point must be faced: Yeshua expected Nicodemus (and all subsequent interpreters) to understand that no one (in any period of time) is ever converted into the kingdom of God without experiencing the new birth and the regenerating work of the Holy Spirit. Says Kaiser, "If the God of the New Testament is the God of the Old Testament, then the Holy Spirit of the New Testament is the Holy Spirit of the Old Testament. He is one, not several divided deities."[25]

Concerning the message of Ezekiel, Montague states that it

> is unprecedented in the pneumatology of the Old Testament. The need for a washing clean had of course already been stressed by the prophets (cf. Is 4:4) but the *rûaḥ* or "spirit" there was the agent of the cleansing itself. Here the new spirit appears as the positive life which *follows* the cleansing. The "new spirit" (vs. 26) is the Lord's own spirit (vs. 27) and that is why it manifests itself in a willing observance of the Lord's mind for his people, the law (36:27).[26]

Kaiser adds:

> . . . Ezekiel, like Jeremiah, has a form of inaugurated eschatology which embodies a "now" and a "not yet" aspect of the Spirit's work . . . the new heart and the new spirit are likewise correctly connected to the Spirit's work in regeneration and the new birth.[27]

Kaiser does affirm the full aspect of Ezekiel's prophecy will not be fulfilled until that "final eschaton," but again, if the prophet Ezekiel could speak of a regeneration brought about by the peculiar work of the Spirit in his day, then he and others knew something of His distinctive work in the lives of believers.

Something of this message and experience must have been known by Israel's leaders and prophets but unfortunately, until Ezekiel actually mentions this type of ministry, we can only read between the lines and surmise of what did take place among unbelievers at various times and when great spiritual revivals occurred.

Conclusion

The burden of this chapter was not to discuss the work of the Spirit in creation, nor His specific work in inspiration and the producing of Scripture. The concern was to treat selected passages with regard to the nation and people of Israel and to note how the Spirit came upon various individuals to perform their God-given tasks under His guidance. We also saw how the Spirit came upon rulers of the nation and also certified the passing of power from one ruler to the next. And we have observed how the Spirit of God worked within the nation itself, in first establishing the covenant, and then in guiding the people in their life under that covenant.

Noted also was how the Spirit strove in the lives of the prophets, the preachers of their day, providing both the short-term prophecies that related to the nation as well as providing the long-range prophecies that spoke of the coming Messiah and the last days of the nation.

In conclusion, we can say that in a very special way, the Holy Spirit clothed various individuals on whom He came, empowering them, giving them wisdom, and providing them an unction from on high to serve the living God. Can we say that the Spirit ministered *continually* in certain individuals? For some individuals, the answer is apparently no, while for certain other individuals, the Spirit evidently enveloped the person and never left—except when specific violations of the covenant occurred, as for example, with King Sha'ul. In regard to King David, the Spirit of God was with him, as well as with other prophets as they served Him.

One major difference between the Tanach and the New Covenant is that in the latter the Holy Spirit *indwells* the person when he makes a confession of faith, sealing him or her with the promised Spirit as a deposit, guaranteeing her or her inheritance:

> And when you heard the word of truth (the gospel of your salvation)–when you believed in Messiah—you were marked with the seal of the promised Holy Spirit, who is the down payment of our inheritance, until the redemption of God's own possession, to the praise of his glory. (Ephesians 1:13–14)

But in all other aspects, there does not seem to be any difference between the way the Spirit worked in the Tanach and the way He does so within the body of the Messiah. While the Scriptures specifically note particular individuals in whom we see the work of the Spirit, who is to say that He did not also work in countless other believers who also served Him, not as a king or prophet, but just in their day-to-day walk with the Lord?

We also noted the work of the Spirit in pre-evangelism as well as in that of regeneration. Nothing seems to be mentioned in the Old Testament of the specific work of the Spirit in these respects. In contrast, in the New Testament a number of passages can be adduced to demonstrate His involvement with individuals as well as with those who specifically make decisions concerning their faith. I would suggest the possibility that the Spirit worked in the same way in the Old Testament. Otherwise, we cannot satisfactorily explain what is meant for the heart to be circumcised, or for the heart of stone to be removed and a heart of flesh implanted. These are pictures in the Hebrew

Scriptures of what takes place with someone who becomes a believer. No doubt, many among the remnant in Israel could testify to this particular work of the Spirit in their lives.

ELEVEN

The Doctrine of the Holy Spirit

The subject of the Holy Spirit is an extensive one, as we can gauge from the number of texts that are available to us from both the Hebrew Scriptures and the New Covenant. The Holy Spirit witnesses not to Himself but to the Word and to the testimony of Yeshua. Nevertheless, Scripture does tell us much concerning the person of the Holy Spirit as well as His work and the way in which He empowers believers to serve God.

Since there is much possibility of error regarding the identity and work of the Holy Spirit, in this chapter we will examine the Scripture carefully so that we can have a proper knowledge of the Holy Spirit's ministry. To know the Lord means involving us in an experience of delight as we work in harmony with the Holy Spirit, whose desire is to serve us and enable us to work with power the mighty deeds of God.

Our approach to the study of the Holy Spirit will lead us into three major areas: the personality of the Holy Spirit, His deity, and His work.

The Personality of the Holy Spirit

One characteristic of many cults is that they deny the personality of the Holy Spirit. Instead, they equate Him instead with a vague power that operates in the universe. Even many genuine believers may think of the Holy Spirit in this way, not yet having grasped the great truth that *the Holy Spirit is a person* with whom we need to become acquainted and to seek in order that He may empower us to serve the living God. But we cannot neglect the personal presence of the Holy Spirit in our lives.

The Holy Spirit has all the distinguishing marks of personality, which we already covered when discussing the distinguishing marks of who God is. The Holy Spirit is indeed a person with all the distinguishing marks of a personality.

Life

Like any other person, the Holy Spirit has life.

> On the last day of the feast, the greatest day, Yeshua stood up and shouted out, "If anyone is thirsty, let him come to me, and let the one who believes in me drink. Just as the scripture says, 'From within him will flow rivers of living water.'" (Now he said this about the Spirit, whom those who believed in him were going to receive, for the Spirit had not yet been given, because Yeshua was not yet glorified.) (Yohanan 7:37–39)

> For the law of the life-giving Spirit in Messiah Yeshua has set you free from the law of sin and death. (Romans 8:2)

> . . . revealing that you are a letter of Messiah, delivered by us, written not with ink but by the Spirit of the living God, not on stone tablets but on tablets of human hearts. (2 Corinthians 3:3)

Intelligence

> In the same way, the Spirit helps us in our weakness, for we do not know how we should pray, but the Spirit himself intercedes for us with inexpressible groanings. And he who searches our hearts knows the mind of the Spirit, because the Spirit intercedes on behalf of the saints according to God's will. (Romans 8:26–27)

> For who among men knows the things of a man except the man's spirit within him? So too, no one knows the things of God except the Spirit of God. (1 Corinthians 2:11)

Purpose

> The LORD's spirit will rest on him—
> a spirit that gives extraordinary wisdom,
> a spirit that provides the ability to execute plans,
> a spirit that produces absolute loyalty to the LORD. (Isaiah 11:2)

> It is one and the same Spirit, distributing as he decides to each person, who produces all these things. (1 Corinthians 12:11)

Activity

The activity of the Holy Spirit is described in numerous passages. Though there is no area of the universe in which the Spirit is not active, He is particularly active in the spiritual sphere.

> When the Advocate comes, whom I will send you from the Father—the Spirit of truth who goes out from the Father—he will testify about me. (Yohanan 15:26)

> And when he comes, he will prove the world wrong concerning sin and righteousness and judgment. (Yohanan 16:8)

> Then the Spirit said to Philip, "Go over and join this chariot." (Acts 8:29)

> While they were serving the Lord and fasting, the Holy Spirit said, "Set apart for me Bar Navah and Saul for the work to which I have called them." (Acts 13:2)

> In the same way, the Spirit helps us in our weakness, for we do not know how we should pray, but the Spirit himself intercedes for us with inexpressible groanings. (Romans 8:26)

> And we speak about these things, not with words taught us by human wisdom, but with those taught by the Spirit, explaining spiritual things to spiritual people. (1 Corinthians 2:13)

Freedom

> It is one and the same Spirit, distributing as he decides to each person, who produces all these things. (1 Corinthians 12:11)

> Now the Lord is the Spirit, and where the Spirit of the Lord is present, there is freedom. (2 Corinthians 3:17)

Self-Consciousness

> For who among men knows the things of a man except the man's spirit within him? So too, no one knows the things of God except the Spirit of God. (1 Corinthians 2:11)

Emotional Feeling

> Now I urge you, brothers and sisters, through our Lord Yeshua the Messiah and through the love of the Spirit, to join fervently with me in prayer to God on my behalf. (Romans 15:30)

> And do not grieve the Holy Spirit of God, by whom you were sealed for the day of redemption. (Ephesians 4:30)

From these passages, then, we can see that the Holy Spirit represents the very essence of personality. His very name trumpets this truth loudly, and it reflects what we have already said concerning the personality of God.

Designated as a Person by Yeshua

The Designation "Comforter," "Counselor," "Advocate," or "Helper." The Greek word is *parakletos*, meaning "one called alongside" to be a helper or an advocate. The KVJ translates *parakletos* as "Comforter" while the NIV has "Counselor," the NET, "Advocate," and the NASB, "Helper." Sometimes the word is rendered in English as *Paraclete*. The Messiah Himself had been the *Paraclete* when He lived among His disciples; now, He promised that as He went away, He would send another *Paraclete*.

> Then I will ask the Father, and he will give you another Advocate to be with you forever—the Spirit of truth, whom the world cannot accept, because it does not see him or know him. But you know him, because he resides with you and will be in you. (Yohanan 14:16–17)

The use of this particular word strongly suggests that the Holy Spirit is not merely a power or influence sent to take the place of the Messiah. Rather, the *Paracletos* is a living person.

Use of Personal Pronouns. Note the number of times the Messiah uses either "Him" or "He" when speaking of the Holy Spirit: for example, (in the Greek) *auton* in Yohanan 16:7; *ekeinos* in Yohanan 16:8. In such verses the Greek pronouns referring to the Holy Spirit are masculine in gender.

> But I tell you the truth, it is to your advantage that I am going away. For if I do not go away, the Advocate will not come to you, but if I go, I will send him to you. And when he comes, he will prove the world wrong concerning sin and righteousness and judgment. . . .
>
> . . . I have many more things to say to you, but you cannot bear them now. But when he, the Spirit of truth, comes, he will guide you into all truth. For he will not speak on his own authority, but will speak whatever he hears, and will tell you what is to come. He will glorify me, because he will receive from me what is mine and will tell it to you. Everything that the Father has is mine; that is why I said the Spirit will receive from me what is mine and will tell it to you. (Yohanan 16:7–8, 12–15)

Associated as a Person with the Father and the Son

God's statement is that the Holy Spirit is not some mere power or influence but rather a very distinct personality associated with the Lord of Hosts:

> Therefore he told me, "These signify the word of the LORD to Zerubbabel: 'Not by strength and not by power, but by my Spirit,' says the LORD who rules over all." (Zechariah 4:6)

Here the Holy Spirit appears on the same level of personhood as the Father and the Son:

> Therefore go and make disciples of all nations, baptizing them in the name of the Father and the Son and the Holy Spirit. (Mattai 28:19)

Again, the Holy Spirit is not some power but rather stands on the same level as the Messiah and God and is therefore a person:

> The grace of the Lord Yeshua the Messiah and the love of God and the fellowship of the Holy Spirit be with you all. (2 Corinthians 13:14)

The Deity of the Holy Spirit

Called "God"

> But Kefa said, "Ananias, why has Satan filled your heart to lie to the Holy Spirit and keep back for yourself part of the proceeds from the sale of the land? Before it was sold, did it not belong to you? And when it was sold, was the money not at your disposal? How have you thought up this deed in your heart? You have not lied to people but to God!" (Acts 5:3–4)

Described with God's Attributes

Omnipresent. No matter where David tries to run or hide, the Holy Spirit is present. He is omnipresent just as God is described in Scripture as being omnipresent.

> Where can I go to escape your spirit?
> Where can I flee to escape your presence?

> If I were to ascend to heaven, you would be there.
> If I were to sprawl out in Sheol, there you would be.
> If I were to fly away on the wings of the dawn,
> and settle down on the other side of the sea,
> even there your hand would guide me,
> your right hand would grab hold of me. (Psalm 139:7–10)

Eternal. The Holy Spirit is described as being eternal, just as God is eternal.

> How much more will the blood of Messiah, who through the eternal Spirit offered himself without blemish to God, purify our consciences from dead works to worship the living God. (Hebrews 9:14)

Omnipotent. The Holy Spirit is here regarded as omnipotent, again, just as God is omnipotent:

> The angel replied, "The Holy Spirit will come upon you, and the power of the Most High will overshadow you. Therefore the child to be born will be holy; he will be called the Son of God." (Luke 1:35)

Omniscient. After Sha'ul tells us that it is inconceivable that we could have any real idea of what God has prepared for those who love Him, he then adds the words of these two verses:

> God has revealed these to us by the Spirit. For the Spirit searches all things, even the deep things of God. For who among men knows the things of a man except the man's spirit within him? So too, no one knows the things of God except the Spirit of God. (1 Corinthians 2:10–11)

The Holy Spirit is omniscient just as God is omniscient. He, the Holy Spirit, knows perfectly the thoughts of the Messiah as well as the thoughts, the "deep things," of God.

Performs God's Works

Creation. The Holy Spirit is involved in creation as well as in the constant renewal of creation:

> When you send your Spirit, they are created, and you renew the face of the earth. (Psalm 104:30 NIV)[1]

Regeneration. The Holy Spirit is involved with the regeneration of a person, in the act known as justification. This is what occurs when a person is born again:

> Do not be amazed that I said to you, "You must all be born from above." The wind blows wherever it will, and you hear the sound it makes, but do not know where it comes from and where it is going. So it is with everyone who is born of the Spirit. (Yohanan 3:7–8)

Resurrection. The Holy Spirit is involved in the resurrection. He was present and involved in Yeshua's resurrection and will likewise be involved with our own:

> Moreover if the Spirit of the one who raised Yeshua from the dead lives in you, the one who raised Messiah from the dead will also make your mortal bodies alive through his Spirit who lives in you. (Romans 8:11)

Denials of the Deity of the Holy Spirit

Paul of Samasota, deposed from his church in Antioch for heretical views, in 268 C.E. put forth a peculiar teaching concerning the Godhead. He thought of it as a closely knit tri-unity of Father, Wisdom, and Word. Paul of Samasota held that in the incarnation, the Word rested upon the human Yeshua as one person upon another. Thus, the incarnate Messiah differed from the prophets only in degree. No mention is made by him of the Holy Spirit, and therefore there appears to be a denial of the Holy Spirit as a person.

The earliest heretic, Arius, formulated a belief that the Son of God was not eternal but was created by the Father from nothing, in order to be an instrument for the creation of the world. This entailed a denial of the deity of the Holy Spirit as well.

In the Middle Ages, Socinus initiated a heresy, later described as Unitarianism, which was not only a denial of the deity of the Messiah but also of the Holy Spirit. In the modern period, Unitarianism radically departs from Scripture in rejecting the doctrines of the tri-unity of God as well as the deity of the Messiah and the deity of the Holy Spirit. The belief is rather in what is called the "uni-personality" of God, "the lone" God.

Russellism and the movement of the Jehovah's Witnesses is best desribed as Socinian with reference to the Holy Spirit and Arian with reference to the Son. In this system there is no deity of either the Holy Spirit or of Yeshua. Personal, yes; but not divine nor eternal.

The Work of the Holy Spirit

The Spirit's Work and the Material Universe

As we consider the unique *work* of the Holy Spirit, we will incidentally also find further confirmation about His *person*, in Scriptures that describe the Holy Spirit as not only a co-worker of God but also as deity, equal to God.

Creation of the Universe. The Hebrew word *ruach*, here translated as "breath," is also equivalent to "Spirit." We might have at least a suggestion of the persons of the Godhead: the Word or the Messiah; Lord or the Father; and breath or the Spirit. In this verse all are equivalent, implying, therefore, that the Spirit is deity. Here we can also note that the word *ruach* is translated in some versions as "breath," whereas in another translation it is rendered as "spirit" or "Spirit." We will generally note the differences when citing the verses in question.

> By the word of the LORD were the heavens made,
> their starry host by the breath [*ruach*] of his mouth. (Psalm 33:6 NIV)[2]

Source of Energy and Order Within Nature. The terms "formless" (NET: "without shape") and "empty" suggest a chaos or orderlessness that somehow came into existence. The Hebrew behind these English words, *tohu ve-vohu*, is always used in connection with some form of destruction elsewhere in the Hebrew Scriptures, for example, Isaiah 34:11; Jeremiah 4:23. In this same verse, the action of the Spirit is described as "hovering" (NET: "moving over"), the same word used for the eagle that "hovers" over its young before breaking up the nest (Deuteronomy 32:11).

> In the beginning God created the heavens and the earth. Now the earth was without shape and empty, and darkness was over the surface of the watery deep, but the Spirit of God was moving over the surface of the water. (Genesis 1:1–2)

Furthermore, after Genesis 1:2 the Spirit works with God, first bringing about light (Genesis 1:3), which involves energy, and then in the ensuing verses, reestablishing order on the earth.

Active in Natural Processes. The breath, or Spirit, of the Lord that blows on both grass and flowers reflects some of the destructive processes that take place within nature. Some of this action surely must reflect the results of the curse on creation that followed the fall of Adam and Eve, and that eventually brings death on the created order.

> The grass dries up,
> the flowers wither,
> when the wind sent by the LORD [NIV: "breath of the LORD," Hebrew *ruach YHWH*] blows on them.
> Surely humanity is like grass. (Isaiah 40:7)

In the next passage, the animals are dependent on God for their very well-being.

> How many living things you have made, O LORD!
> You have exhibited great skill in making all of them;

the earth is full of the living things you have made.
Over here is the deep, wide sea,
which teems with innumerable swimming creatures,
living things both small and large.
The ships travel there,
and over here swims the whale you made to play in it.
All of your creatures wait for you
to provide them with food on a regular basis.
You give food to them and they receive it;
you open your hand and they are filled with food.
When you ignore them, they panic.
When you take away their life's breath, they die
and return to dust.
When you send your life-giving breath [NIV: "your Spirit,"
Hebrew *ruach*], they are created,
and you replenish the surface of the ground. (Psalm 104:24–30)

Though when God hides His face, the animals die, yet with the coming of the Spirit, life is renewed. This reflects the cycle of death and birth among animals as well as plants. The Spirit of God is the one involved in these renewing processes. Furthermore, one day when the curse is removed from the earth and the kingdom is established, this unique work of the Holy Spirit will be apparent as He replenishes the earth. In particular, death will no longer exist within the kingdom, as Isaiah says.

This desolation will continue until new life [NIV: "the Spirit,"
Hebrew *ruach*] is poured out on us from heaven.
Then the desert will become an orchard
and the orchard will be considered a forest. (Isaiah 32:15)

The Artist in Nature. The Spirit's artistry reflects a God-ordained beauty.

By his breath the skies became fair;
his hand pierced the fleeing serpent. (Job 26:13)

The word "fair" indicates beauty; compare the New King James Version rendering of "by His Spirit He adorned the heavens." The beauty of this world, whether it be the variety of colors in a sunset or the beauty of a landscape with its multihued mountains and valleys, is the work of the Holy Spirit. He is greater than any human artist who depicts these same things.

The Spirit's Work and the Word of God

The Author of Scripture. Consider these verses:

> These are the final words of David:
> "The oracle of David son of Jesse,
> the oracle of the man raised up as
> the ruler chosen by the God of Jacob,
> Israel's beloved singer of songs:
> The LORD's spirit spoke through me;
> his word was on my tongue." (2 Samuel 23:1–2)

> I have many more things to say to you, but you cannot bear them now. But when he, the Spirit of truth, comes, he will guide you into all truth. For he will not speak on his own authority, but will speak whatever he hears, and will tell you what is to come. (Yohanan 16:12–13)

> And we speak about these things, not with words taught us by human wisdom, but with those taught by the Spirit, explaining spiritual things to spiritual people. (1 Corinthians 2:13)

> Every scripture is inspired by God [NIV: "God-breathed"] and useful for teaching, for reproof, for correction, and for training in righteousness. (2 Timothy 3:16)

Note that although God used people to write the Scripture, He allowed them to express their personality in words of their choosing. Yet the Scripture passages as we have them today have God's stamp of approval. This is no "dictation theory" of writing Scripture, for God does allow for the background, training, education, and personality of the writers. Nevertheless the final copy of what the writer produced is said to be "God-breathed." So we also see in 2 Kefa:

> For no prophecy was ever borne of human impulse; rather, men carried along by the Holy Spirit spoke from God. (2 Kefa 1:21)

Here we gain insight into how God worked in the production of Scripture: men, though under the control of the Holy Spirit, were not robbed of their personality. And in the end, the product was exactly what God wanted.

The Interpreter of Scripture. One of the functions of the Holy Spirit is to give us wisdom in interpreting God's Word:

> God has revealed these to us by the Spirit. For the Spirit searches all things, even the deep things of God. For who among men knows the things of a man except the man's spirit within him? So too, no one knows the things of God except the Spirit of God. Now we have not received the spirit of the world, but the Spirit who is from God, so that we may know the things that are freely given to us by God. (1 Corinthians 2:10–12)

> I pray that the God of our Lord Yeshua the Messiah, the Father of glory, may give you spiritual wisdom [NIV: "the Spirit of wisdom"] and revelation in your growing knowledge of him. (Ephesians 1:17)

This does not preclude our own study; the Spirit may lead us to learn something of the cultural background of a passage, or to examine grammatical structures in order to ascertain meaning.

The Spirit's Work in the Tanach

In the Tanach, we find many references as to the unique work of the Holy Spirit among people, both prior to Israel's establishment as well as with the history of Israel and Judah. There are in fact some eighty-eight specific references in the Tanach that relate to the ministry of the Holy Spirit.

"Contending" About Sin. Consider the following verse.

> So the LORD said, "My spirit will not remain in humankind indefinitely, since they are mortal. They will remain for 120 more years." (Genesis 6:3)

Compare NIV, "My Spirit will not contend with man" and NASB, "My Spirit will not strive with man." How did the Spirit of God "contend with man" or "remain in humankind"? No doubt part of the answer is that the Holy Spirit worked within people's consciences. While the conscience can be seared and marred, it is never made completely insensitive. Even those who live on the lowest possible moral plane will under certain circumstances reveal that they still have a conscience, knowing something of the difference between good and evil.

Another part of the answer is that the Holy Spirit preached to mankind. One example is during the building of the ark. Noah no doubt warned mankind of the impending disaster, as the Spirit spoke through him.

"Coming Upon" and Equipping Certain Individuals for Service. We can comment on seven aspects of this equipping where it is said that the Spirit "came upon" certain individuals.

For the task of government. Note the description of Joshua as (in NIV's translation) "a man in whom is the spirit." The priests, too, were to also have the same authority as Joshua.

> Then Moses spoke to the LORD: "Let the LORD, the God of the spirits of all humankind, appoint a man over the community, who will go out before them, and who will come in before them, and who will lead them out, and who will bring them in, so that the community of the LORD may not be like sheep that have no shepherd." The LORD replied to Moses, "Take Joshua son of Nun, a man in whom is such a spirit [NIV: "in whom is the spirit"], and lay your hand on him; set him before Eleazar the priest and before the whole community, and commission him publicly. Then you must delegate some of your authority to him, so that the whole community of the Israelites will be obedient. (Numbers 27:15–20)

For military leadership. This was the case for Gideon, whereby after the Spirit came upon him, he called together the men of war and became their leader. Gideon had a unique ministry for which the Spirit of God empowered him.

> The LORD's spirit took control of Gideon. He blew a trumpet, summoning the Abiezrites to follow him. He sent messengers throughout Manasseh and summoned them to follow him as well. He also sent messengers throughout Asher, Zebulun, and Naphtali, and they came up to meet him.
>
> Gideon said to God, "If you really intend to use me to deliver Israel, as you promised, then give me a sign as proof." (Judges 6:34–36)

Note that later on he became involved in making an ephod before which the people of Israel prostrated themselves and prostituted themselves in idolatry. From this we learn that the Spirit of the Lord did not come upon Gideon because he was necessarily better morally than others in Israel. Rather, it was in order to provide military leadership to deliver Israel.

For great physical strength. This is seen in the story of Samson.

> Samson went down to Timnah. When he approached the vineyards of Timnah, he saw a roaring young lion attacking him. The LORD's spirit empowered him and he tore the lion in two with his bare hands as easily as one would tear a young goat. But he did not tell his father or mother what he had done. . . .
>
> When he arrived in Lehi, the Philistines shouted as they approached him. But the LORD's spirit empowered him. The ropes around his arms were like flax dissolving in fire, and they melted away from his hands. He happened to see a solid jawbone of a donkey. He grabbed it and struck down a thousand men. (Judges 14:5–6; 15:14–15)

Samson was able to slay a thousand Philistines with the fresh jawbone of a donkey. As with Gideon, we note that Samson was not empowered because of some great moral character, but simply because God wanted to use him to deliver Israel from the power of the Philistines.

For artistic workmanship. We notice this in the account of the tabernacle's construction.

> And I have filled him with the Spirit of God in skill, in understanding, in knowledge, and in all kinds of craftsmanship, to make artistic designs for work with gold, with silver, and with bronze, and with cutting and setting stone, and with cutting wood, to work in all kinds of craftsmanship. (Exodus 31:3–5)

Other men were appointed to help Bezalel and they too were given skill. The Holy Spirit was involved in producing the beautiful designs of the tabernacle furniture. His enabling of someone to be an artistic genius again reflects that the Holy Spirit is the Creator of the universe and can impart His craft and aesthetic to whomever He wishes.

For literary and musical expression. The Spirit enabled David to write poetry and also to set some of it to music.

> These are the final words of David:
> "The oracle of David son of Jesse,
> the oracle of the man raised up as
> the ruler chosen by the God of Jacob,
> Israel's beloved singer of songs:
> The LORD's spirit spoke through me;
> his word was on my tongue." (2 Samuel 23:1–2)

Through the unique work of the Holy Spirit came the creation of poetry to uplift the spirit and music to speak to the soul.

For moral and spiritual courage. When King Joash gave orders to kill the high priest, Zechariah was given the courage in his dying moments to face his executioners and to cry out his rebuke to the king.

> God's Spirit energized Zechariah son of Jehoiada the priest. He stood up before the people and said to them, "This is what God says: 'Why are you violating the commands of the LORD? You will not be prosperous! Because

> you have rejected the LORD, he has rejected you!'" They plotted against him and by royal decree stoned him to death in the courtyard of the LORD's temple. King Joash disregarded the loyalty his father Jehoiada had shown him and killed Jehoiada's son. As Zechariah was dying, he said, "May the LORD take notice and seek vengeance!" (2 Chronicles 24:20–22)

Later, his word would in fact come back to trouble Joash.

For prophetic ministry. Two diverse examples come from Balaam and from Ezekiel.

> When Balaam lifted up his eyes, he saw Israel camped tribe by tribe; and the Spirit of God came upon him. Then he uttered this oracle:
> "The oracle of Balaam son of Beor;
> the oracle of the man whose eyes are open." (Numbers 24:2–3)

What Balaam prophesied was contrary to what Balak had hired him to say. The latter understood that he could never face Israel on a field of battle until he could get the gods to curse the nation of Israel. But God had already established both the Abrahamic Covenant, which guaranteed Israel's existence throughout the course of human history (see Genesis 17:7), and also the Mosaic Covenant. Once the words establishing those covenants had gone forth from God's mouth as prophecy, they could never be changed. No one could thereafter curse Israel with effect. As divine intervention changed Balaam's message from curse to blessing several times, Balak felt he was dealing with a stubborn prophet!

Another example under the Spirit's empowerment of prophetic ministry comes from Ezekiel:

> Then the Spirit lifted me up and brought me to the gate of the house of the LORD that faces east. There at the entrance to the gate were twenty-five men, and I saw among them Jaazaniah son of Azzur and Pelatiah son of Benaiah, leaders of the people.
>
> Then the Spirit of the LORD came upon me, and he told me to say: "This is what the LORD says: That is what you are saying, O house of Israel, but I know what is going through your mind."

> The Spirit lifted me up and brought me to the exiles in Babylonia in the vision given by the Spirit of God. Then the vision I had seen went up from me, and I told the exiles everything the LORD had shown me. (Ezekiel 11:1, 5, 24–25 NIV)

Ezekiel had been transported to the temple where he saw men plotting evil, giving wicked advice to both leaders and people. In contrast to their message of peace and deliverance, Ezekiel was given a message of impending destruction. In the end, it would take the destruction of the temple and the arrival of refugees from Israel to the Babylonian settlements where Ezekiel lived to vindicate Ezekiel's words. In all this, note the work of the Holy Spirit in providing God's prophetic message.

Summary of the Work of the Holy Spirit in the Tanach. Above we noted a number of ways in which the Holy Spirit worked among individuals in the history of Israel and Judah. We could further explore other aspects of His distinctive work. For instance, we could examine passages showing that no one is ever born again apart from the Holy Spirit: a remnant existed in every generation in Israel because of the unique work of the Holy Spirit in conviction of sin and in the regenerative process that enables people to know the living God.

Did the Holy Spirit come upon men in a permanent way? David's prayer to God that the Holy Spirit not be taken from him (see Psalm 51:11) suggests otherwise. While the Holy Spirit "enveloped" believers, enabling them to do the work of God, it did not mean that the Holy Spirit in every instance remained with them. On occasion the Spirit could leave, especially if there was a moral lack exhibited by the person, or even if no necessity existed at a particular moment for that person to be empowered. When the Spirit left people as they strayed from the Lord, they were certainly made aware of the fact, especially as they realized their powerlessness.

The message is different for the believers in the body of Messiah, where the Holy Spirit continually indwells everyone:

> And when you heard the word of truth (the gospel of your salvation)—when you believed in Messiah—you were marked with the seal of the promised Holy Spirit. (Ephesians 1:13)

Though believers may backslide, grieving and quenching the Holy Spirit, nevertheless He does not leave. But He will certainly make the believer unhappy. This author has said on a number of occasions that he has yet to meet a "happy backslider"!

The Spirit's Work and Yeshua the Messiah

The Miraculous Birth of the Messiah. The unique nature of the Messiah's birth was due to the work of the Holy Spirit.

> The angel replied, "The Holy Spirit will come upon you, and the power of the Most High will overshadow you. Therefore the child to be born will be holy; he will be called the Son of God." (Luke 1:35)

Provision of Remarkable Wisdom. From the prophecy of Isaiah 11:1–4, we know that the Messiah's remarkable wisdom comes from the Holy Spirit. In the New Covenant Scripture, we also see some examples of this wisdom.

> Then the Jewish leaders were astonished and said, "How does this man know so much when he has never had formal instruction?" (Yohanan 7:15)

Yeshua's Powerful Preaching. The Holy Spirit gave Yeshua the ability to proclaim powerfully. His hearers found it difficult to resist His words.

> The Spirit of the Lord is upon me,
> because he has anointed me to proclaim good news to the poor.
> He has sent me to proclaim release to the captives
> and the regaining of sight to the blind,
> to set free those who are oppressed. (Luke 4:18)

Even the guards sent by the chief priests and Pharisees came back empty-handed after hearing Him.

> Then the officers returned to the chief priests and Pharisees, who said to them, "Why didn't you bring him back with you?" The officers replied, "No one ever spoke like this man!" (Yohanan 7:45–46)

Yeshua's Mighty Works. This included driving out demons as well as His acts of healing.

> But if I cast out demons by the Spirit of God, then the kingdom of God has already overtaken you. (Mattai 12:28)

> You know what happened throughout Judea, beginning from Galilee after the baptism that Yohanan announced: with respect to Yeshua from Nazareth, that God anointed him with the Holy Spirit and with power. He went around doing good and healing all who were oppressed by the devil, because God was with him. (Acts 10:37–38)

Yeshua's Victorious Life. The victorious life was not something that came automatically for Yeshua in the days of His flesh. Even He had to suffer and learn how to be obedient. But through temptation and learning how to lean wholly on God, He was able to live a victorious life and demonstrate to us how we can do likewise as we are empowered by the Holy Spirit.

> Then Yeshua, full of the Holy Spirit, returned from the Jordan River and was led by the Spirit in the wilderness, where for forty days he endured temptations from the devil. He ate nothing during those days, and when they were completed, he was famished. (Luke 4:1–2)

> During his earthly life Messiah offered both requests and supplications, with loud cries and tears, to the one who was able to save him from death and he was heard because of his devotion. Although he was a son, he learned obedience through the things he suffered. (Hebrews 5:7–8)

Yeshua's Atoning Death. Even His death relates to the work of the Holy Spirit.

> How much more will the blood of Messiah, who through the eternal Spirit offered himself without blemish to God, purify our consciences from dead works to worship the living God. (Hebrews 9:14)

In Relation to His Glorious Resurrection. As already noted, the Holy Spirit is involved in our resurrection, enabling our soul and spirit to be reunited with a new body. Likewise He was instrumental in raising Yeshua from the dead with a glorified body, so that we too may one day have a glorified body animated not by blood but by the Spirit.

> Moreover if the Spirit of the one who raised Yeshua from the dead lives in you, the one who raised Messiah from the dead will also make your mortal bodies alive through his Spirit who lives in you. (Romans 8:11)

All the seven examples just given of how the Spirit of God related to Yeshua was done with respect to Yeshua as a *human being*, during the days of His humiliation. Everything He said and did was under the guidance and power of the Holy Spirit. What was true in His case can also be true in our case, as we will explore in the following sections.

The Spirit's Work and the Body of the Messiah

Creating the Body of the Messiah. The book of Acts recounts the beginning of the new body in visible form; people saw as well as heard something unusual taking place.

> Now when the day of Shavuot had come, they were all together in one place. Suddenly a sound like a violent wind blowing came from heaven and filled the entire house where they were sitting. And tongues spreading out like a fire appeared to them and came to rest on each one of them. All of them were filled with the Holy Spirit, and they began to speak in other languages as the Spirit enabled them. (Acts 2:1–4)

Sha'ul later elaborates on this activity of the Holy Spirit.

> For in one Spirit we were all baptized into one body. Whether Jews or Greeks or slaves or free, we were all made to drink of the one Spirit. (1 Corinthians 12:13)

Indwelling the Body of the Messiah. Through another figure, Sha'ul likens the new body to a building joined together as a holy temple of the Lord.

> Do you not know that you are God's temple and that God's Spirit lives in you? If someone destroys God's temple, God will destroy him. For God's temple is holy, which is what you are. (1 Corinthians 3:16–17)

> In him the whole building, being joined together, grows into a holy temple in the Lord, in whom you also are being built together into a dwelling place of God in the Spirit. (Ephesians 2:21–22)

Presiding over the Body of the Messiah. This is seen in four ways. ***In preaching.*** Consider the bold preaching of Kefa in the book of Acts.

> Then Kefa, filled with the Holy Spirit, replied, "Rulers of the people and elders, if we are being examined today for a good deed done to a sick man—by what means this man was healed—let it be known to all of you and to all the people of Israel that by the name of Yeshua the Messiah the Nazarene whom you crucified, whom God raised from the dead, this man stands before you healthy. This Yeshua is the stone that was rejected by you, the builders, that has become the cornerstone. And there is salvation in no one else, for there is no other name under heaven given among people by which we must be saved." (Acts 4:8–12)

In government of the* qehilah*, or church. Here the Holy Spirit empowers the leaders—the elders and overseers—to guard and guide the new body. People are therefore to respect and listen to their leadership.

> Watch out for yourselves and for all the flock of which the Holy Spirit

has made you overseers, to shepherd the *qehilah* of God that he obtained with the blood of his own Son. (Acts 20:28)

In worship. The Holy Spirit leads in worship so that all glory is given to God the Father, who has given us so much that we might know Him, serve Him, worship Him, and proclaim His Word.

And do not get drunk with wine, which is debauchery, but be filled by the Spirit, speaking to one another in psalms, hymns, and spiritual songs, singing and making music in your hearts to the Lord, always giving thanks to God the Father for each other in the name of our Lord Yeshua the Messiah. (Ephesians 5:18–20)

In prayer.

With every prayer and petition, pray at all times in the Spirit, and to this end be alert, with all perseverance and requests for all the saints. (Ephesians 6:18)

Uniting the Body of the Messiah. Without the Holy Spirit, there could be no unity among believers.

. . . making every effort to keep the unity of the Spirit in the bond of peace. (Ephesians 4:3)

Keeping the unity of the Spirit does not mean having to agree on all minor points and nonessentials. It does mean finding agreement on major issues and doctrines, as well as on the main means by which we can live sanctified lives. Beyond that, there is allowance for nonessential differences, for example different expressions among various ethnic groups. These matters do not need to affect the unity of the body.

Equipping the Body of the Messiah for Ministry. This is seen in five areas.

Selecting the messengers of the gospel.

> While they were serving the Lord and fasting, the Holy Spirit said, "Set apart for me Bar Navah and Sha'ul for the work to which I have called them." (Acts 13:2)

Sending forth the messengers of the gospel.

> So Bar Navah and Sha'ul, sent out by the Holy Spirit, went down to Seleucia, and from there they sailed to Cyprus. (Acts 13:4)

Choosing the fields in which the messengers of the gospel will work.

> They went through the region of Phrygia and Galatia, having been prevented by the Holy Spirit from speaking the message in the province of Asia. When they came to Mysia, they attempted to go into Bithynia, but the Spirit of Yeshua did not allow them to do this. (Acts 16:6–7)

Following this incident, Sha'ul had a vision of a man of Macedonia who requested help in proclaiming the message. As they traveled to Macedonia, they were also guided by the Holy Spirit. Believers today should likewise be sensitive to the Holy Spirit as to where the message should be preached.

Sustaining His messengers under persecution.

> But the Jews incited the God-fearing women of high social standing and the prominent men of the city, stirred up persecution against Sha'ul and Bar Navah, and threw them out of their region. So after they shook the dust off their feet in protest against them, they went to Iconium. And the disciples were filled with joy and with the Holy Spirit. (Acts 13:50–52)

In the face of persecution from Sha'ul's kinsmen and others, he and Bar Navah took courage from the Holy Spirit. They simply turned away, realizing that a door had been closed for the moment, and continued on to a place of greater receptivity.

Guiding in resolving problems between believers. Note these three examples in the New Covenant.

> For it seemed best to the Holy Spirit and to us not to place any greater burden on you than these necessary rules. (Acts 15:28)

While the problem of Jewish-Gentile relationships in the congregation in Antioch seemed to be insurmountable, nevertheless Yaakov and the rest of the Jerusalem elders came to an agreement through the Holy Spirit. With men, what may seem impossible to resolve can find resolution with God, for whom all things are possible.

A second instance is the fight that broke out between Sha'ul and Bar Navah over the issue of Mark's presence on the team:

> After some days Sha'ul said to Bar Navah, "Let's return and visit the brothers in every town where we proclaimed the word of the Lord to see how they are doing." Bar Navah wanted to bring Yohanan called Mark along with them too, but Sha'ul insisted that they should not take along this one who had left them in Pamphylia and had not accompanied them in the work. They had a sharp disagreement, so that they parted company. Bar Navah took along Mark and sailed away to Cyprus, but Sha'ul chose Silas and set out, commended to the grace of the Lord by the brothers and sisters. (Acts 15:36–40)

Bar Navah was minded to restore Mark and be a blessing to him, but Sha'ul thought otherwise. Though unable to resolve their differences at this time, the work did not cease. There is a valuable lesson in this, namely, that many times God will use us in spite of who we are. As it turned out, Mark went with Bar Navah to Cyprus and over a period of time he was restored in service to God. And by the end of Sha'ul's life, that *shaliach* too had come to recognize God's work in Mark and even requested his presence:

> Only Luke is with me. Get Mark and bring him with you, because he is a great help to me in ministry. (2 Timothy 4:11)

So, not only did the work proceed through the conflict by the fact that two teams were sent to different places, but healing also did later take place between Sha'ul and Mark.

The Spirit's Work in Individual Believers

In the Past. In a believer's coming to faith, we see the following aspects of the work of the Spirit.

Regenerating the heart.

> Yeshua answered, "I tell you the solemn truth, unless a person is born of water and spirit, he cannot enter the kingdom of God." (Yohanan 3:5)

Note also,

> He saved us not by works of righteousness that we have done but on the basis of his mercy, through the washing of the new birth and the renewing of the Holy Spirit. (Titus 3:5)

Sealing the believer.

> And do not grieve the Holy Spirit of God, by whom you were sealed for the day of redemption. (Ephesians 4:30)

Also,

> And when you heard the word of truth (the gospel of your salvation)—when you believed in Messiah—you were marked with the seal of the promised Holy Spirit. (Ephesians 1:13)

This passage indicates what this sealing consists of, namely, the Holy Spirit.

Indwelling the believer.

> Or do you not know that your body is the temple of the Holy Spirit who is in you, whom you have from God, and you are not your own? For you were bought at a price. Therefore glorify God with your body. (1 Corinthians 6:19–20)

Furthermore,

> You, however, are not in the flesh but in the Spirit, if indeed the Spirit of God lives in you. Now if anyone does not have the Spirit of Messiah, this person does not belong to him. (Romans 8:9)

These two statements echo each other. Because the Spirit indwells us, we are to show evidence of a different kind of lifestyle.

Baptizing the believer in the body of the Messiah.

> For in one Spirit we were all baptized into one body. Whether Jews or Greeks or slaves or free, we were all made to drink of the one Spirit. (1 Corinthians 12:13)

We will consider this work of the Holy Spirit in more detail below.

In the Present. In the ongoing daily life of believers, the Spirit's work encompasses the following.

Infilling the believer.

> And do not get drunk with wine, which is debauchery, but be filled by the Spirit. (Ephesians 5:18)

We will have more to say about this below.

Imparting spiritual gifts to the believer. From Sha'ul comes this well-known passage about spiritual gifts.

> With regard to spiritual gifts, brothers and sisters, I do not want you to be uninformed. You know that when you were pagans you were often led astray by speechless idols, however you were led. So I want you to understand that no one speaking by the Spirit of God says, "Yeshua is cursed," and no one can say, "Yeshua is Lord," except by the Holy Spirit.
>
> Now there are different gifts, but the same Spirit. And there are different ministries, but the same Lord. And there are different results, but the same God who produces all of them in everyone. To each person the manifestation of the Spirit is given for the benefit of all. For one person is given through the Spirit the message of wisdom, and another the message of knowledge according to the same Spirit, to another faith by the same Spirit, and to another gifts of healing by the one Spirit, to another performance of miracles, to another prophecy, and to another discernment of spirits, to another different kinds of tongues, and to another the interpretation of tongues. It is one and the same Spirit, distributing as he decides to each person, who produces all these things. (1 Corinthians 12:1–11)

Leading the believer.

> . . . (for if you live according to the flesh, you will die), but if by the Spirit you put to death the deeds of the body you will live. For all who are led by the Spirit of God are the sons of God. (Romans 8:13–14)

Teaching the believer.

> But the Advocate, the Holy Spirit, whom the Father will send in my name, will teach you everything, and will cause you to remember everything I said to you. (Yohanan 14:26)

There is a general sense in which the Holy Spirit teaches, but specifically this saying may allude to the Holy Spirit's leading in the writing of Scripture, particularly of the Gospels.

Sanctifying, or setting apart, the believer.

But we ought to thank God always for you, brothers and sisters loved by the Lord, because God chose you from the beginning for salvation through sanctification by the Spirit and faith in the truth. (2 Thessalonians 2:13)

Note also,

From Kefa, an apostle of Yeshua the Messiah, to those temporarily residing abroad (in Pontus, Galatia, Cappadocia, the province of Asia, and Bithynia) who are chosen according to the foreknowledge of God the Father by being set apart by the Spirit for obedience and for sprinkling with Yeshua the Messiah's blood. May grace and peace be yours in full measure! (1 Kefa 1:1–2)

Witnessing to believers of their spiritual sonship.

For you did not receive the spirit of slavery leading again to fear, but you received the Spirit of adoption, by whom we cry, "Abba, Father." (Romans 8:15)

Interceding for believers.

In the same way, the Spirit helps us in our weakness, for we do not know how we should pray, but the Spirit himself intercedes for us with inexpressible groanings. (Romans 8:26)

Producing truth in the lives of believers.

But the fruit of the Spirit is love, joy, peace, patience, kindness, goodness, faithfulness, . . . If we live by the Spirit, let us also behave in accordance with the Spirit. (Galatians 5:22, 25)

In the Future. The promise we have is that one day in the resurrection, our souls and spirits will be reunited in our new, glorified bodies, and we will experience a newness of life.

> Moreover if the Spirit of the one who raised Yeshua from the dead lives in you, the one who raised Messiah from the dead will also make your mortal bodies alive through his Spirit who lives in you. (Romans 8:11)

Special Topics Concerning the Holy Spirit

Several topics concerning the work of the Holy Spirit we have only touched on briefly. The following sections will expand on the indwelling, the baptism, and the infilling of the Holy Spirit. In addition, we will treat the question of the gift of tongues, and finally the kinds of sins that are possible to be committed against the Holy Spirit.

Special Topic 1: The Indwelling of the Holy Spirit

The indwelling of the Holy Spirit, the baptism of the Holy Spirit, and the infilling of the Holy Spirit—these three doctrines have been controversial among believers, even to the point where once someone adopts a particular position, they may become completely closed to considering other views. Our task will be to present the three topics in as positive a manner as possible, seeking to find what the Word of God speaks on these subjects.

There is another aspect to our discussion. We can find statements about the Holy Spirit in the gospels and in Acts, prior to the coming of the Holy Spirit on the day of Pentecost. The tendency may be to take materials *prior to* Pentecost and make them be the norm for what happened *after* Pentecost. In particular, the work of the Spirit in the gospels may not be the norm for after His coming on the day of Pentecost, as we will see below in looking at Sha'ul's writings.

Several questions arise for our consideration regarding the indwelling of the Holy Spirit.

Meaning of the Indwelling. First, the Spirit is said to indwell the church collectively.

> Do you not know that you are God's temple and that God's Spirit lives in you? If someone destroys God's temple, God will destroy him. For

> God's temple is holy, which is what you are. (1 Corinthians 3:16–17)
> In him the whole building, being joined together, grows into a holy temple in the Lord, in whom you also are being built together into a dwelling place of God in the Spirit. (Ephesians 2:21–22)

In these passages, Sha'ul's reference to the temple is focused on the church as a whole, not on individual believers. All believers are being built *together* in a temple that comprises the body of the Messiah. The indwelling is a reference to the *collective* body.

Second, the Spirit indwells each member of the body individually.

> Or do you not know that your body is the temple of the Holy Spirit who is in you, whom you have from God, and you are not your own? (1 Corinthians 6:19)

In contrast to the previous passages, here each believer is considered as a temple. Each needs to keep himself or herself unspotted from the world.[3]

For All Believers. To answer this question, we need to look at statements made *after* the Holy Spirit had come at Pentecost. Therefore, we will look at Sha'ul's letters, which, obviously, were written after the Pentecost experience.

> . . . to the *qehilah* of God that is in Corinth, to those who are sanctified in Messiah Yeshua, and called to be saints, with all those in every place who call on the name of our Lord Yeshua the Messiah, their Lord and ours. (1 Corinthians 1:2)

Compare this with:

> For everyone who calls on the name of the Lord will be saved. (Romans 10:13)

and,

> Or do you not know that your body is the temple of the Holy Spirit who is in you, whom you have from God, and you are not your own? (1 Corinthians 6:19)

Sha'ul declares that when we call on the Lord, we become believers. Then the Holy Spirit indwells us. Consider also:

> And when you heard the word of truth (the gospel of your salvation)—when you believed in Messiah—you were marked with the seal of the promised Holy Spirit, who is the down payment of our inheritance, until the redemption of God's own possession, to the praise of his glory. (Ephesians 1:13–14)

> And because you are sons, God sent the Spirit of his Son into our hearts, who calls "Abba! Father!" (Galatians 4:6)

And note these three passages:

> . . . who also sealed us and gave us the Spirit in our hearts as a down payment. (2 Corinthians 1:22)

> Now the one who prepared us for this very purpose is God, who gave us the Spirit as a down payment. (2 Corinthians 5:5)

> You, however, are not in the flesh but in the Spirit, if indeed the Spirit of God lives in you. Now if anyone does not have the Spirit of Messiah, this person does not belong to him. (Romans 8:9)

From what Sha'ul says, we learn that when believers come to know the Lord—when they accept Yeshua into their hearts, or whatever language is used to describe being born again—he or she is indwelt by the Holy Spirit.

Note that *the infilling is not true of mere professing believers*. It may be that unbelievers enter a local church, either out of ignorance or deliberately falsifying information. The person is taken into the church, although he or she has never been born again. The task of the elders is then to discern whether the person has truly accepted the Messiah. It is possible for such an individual to become a member of a congregation because he or she knows all the "God-talk," though they were never really born again. In time, however, their fruits will sooner or later betray them. In the context of this discussion, the point is that professing believers who have not actually been born again do not experience the infilling of the Spirit.

The First Disciples. Note that Yeshua's first disciples did *not* receive the indwelling when they first believed. It is a fact that they did not have the Spirit within them.

> Then I will ask the Father, and he will give you another Advocate to be with you forever—the Spirit of truth, whom the world cannot accept, because it does not see him or know him. But you know him, because he resides with you and will be in you. (Yohanan 14:16–17)

The promise from verse 16 is that the Counselor, or Comforter, will come and be with each believer forever. But Yeshua promised that after the coming of the Holy Spirit on the day of Pentecost, He will *indwell* each believer. Prior to Pentecost, the Holy Spirit only *enveloped* the believer.

The Holy Spirit was not present at all in unbelievers, and never "enveloped" such people. Though they may have been conversant with Scripture, and surely were in the days when the temple still stood, nevertheless, because they had not been born again, there was no presence of the Spirit at all.

We get further insight from the following passage in Yohanan.

> On the last day of the feast, the greatest day, Yeshua stood up and shouted out, "If anyone is thirsty, let him come to me, and let the one who believes in me drink. Just as the scripture says, 'From within him will flow rivers of living water.'" (Now he said this about the Spirit, whom those who believed in him were going to receive, for the Spirit had not yet been given, because Yeshua was not yet glorified.) (Yohanan 7:37–39)

Again, we emphasize that throughout the period of the Tanach and on into the period of the Gospels and Acts, up until the day of Pentecost the Spirit of God never *indwelt* believers; He *enveloped* them, and sometimes would leave because of sin, or simply because of inactivity (as, for example, when the person was sleeping!). The time had not yet come for the Holy

Spirit to actually live *within* each individual. That appears to be the meaning of the statement of Yohanan 7:39.

However, now the time *has* come. At Pentecost, the Spirit came, as Kefa declared that since Yeshua was

> So then, exalted to the right hand of God, and having received the promise of the Holy Spirit from the Father, he has poured out what you both see and hear. (Acts 2:33)

Therefore, the present experience of believers with the Messiah since Pentecost is *not* the same as in the period of the gospels and Acts 1. The distinction is apparent between what occurred prior to Pentecost and what took place afterward. A new way had opened up and the Holy Spirit lives in our hearts today, based on the prayer of the Messiah for the new day to come after Pentecost.

In Order to Have the Indwelling. First, a person needs to become a believer. What is necessary is "to believe"; all believers have the Spirit. Note again Yohanan 7:39:

> (Now he said this about the Spirit, whom those who believed in him were going to receive, for the Spirit had not yet been given, because Yeshua was not yet glorified.) (Yohanan 7:39)

Note too Kefa's explanation of what happened in the house of Cornelius:

> Therefore if God gave them the same gift as he also gave us after believing in the Lord Yeshua the Messiah, who was I to hinder God? (Acts 11:17)

Even non-Jews, when they believed Kefa's message, were also indwelt by the Holy Spirit.

However, a person does not need to agonize in prayer to have the Holy Spirit, as shown in Luke.

> If you then, although you are evil, know how to give good gifts to your children, how much more will the heavenly Father give the Holy Spirit to those who ask him! (Luke 11:13)

Nor does a person need to obey in order to have the Spirit. But what about this verse:

> And we are witnesses of these events, and so is the Holy Spirit whom God has given to those who obey him. (Acts 5:32)

The question is what is meant by *obedience*. Here it can only be in the sense of believing the gospel and accepting Yeshua as their Savior. When that occurs—obedience to the proclamation of the Messiah Himself—then the Holy Spirit will live in us.

A distinction, however, must be made between the actual indwelling and the filling of the Holy Spirit. At this point, we are only speaking of when the Spirit of God comes to dwell in us. The filling of the Holy Spirit is another dimension of His work, which will be discussed below.

Cessation of the Indwelling. In the Old Testament, the presence of the Spirit was withdrawn from individuals in certain situations. Such a situation might be the case of disobedience, as in Psalm 51, or when the believer did not particularly need the power of the Holy Spirit, if, for instance, he was sleeping.

But these situations do not exist in the present age.

> Then I will ask the Father, and he will give you another Advocate to be with you forever—the Spirit of truth, whom the world cannot accept, because it does not see him or know him. But you know him, because he resides with you and will be in you. (Yohanan 14:16–17)

Note the word "forever." One of the signs of the ministry of the Holy Spirit since Pentecost is that He indwells His body, which is to say He indwells every believer.

Special Topic 2: The Baptism of the Holy Spirit

The Biblical Material. Some passages use the words "baptize" and "Spirit" together.

> And I remembered the word of the Lord, as he used to say, "Yohanan baptized with water, but you will be baptized with the Holy Spirit." (Acts 11:16)

> For in one Spirit we were all baptized into one body. Whether Jews or Greeks or slaves or free, we were all made to drink of the one Spirit. (1 Corinthians 12:13)

Other passages use only the word "baptize." In these instances, the context must determine whether it describes water baptism or Spirit baptism.

> What shall we say then? Are we to remain in sin so that grace may increase? Absolutely not! How can we who died to sin still live in it? Or do you not know that as many as were baptized into Messiah Yeshua were baptized into his death? Therefore we have been buried with him through baptism into death, in order that just as Messiah was raised from the dead through the glory of the Father, so we too may live a new life. (Romans 6:1–4)

> For all of you who were baptized into Messiah have clothed yourselves with Messiah. (Galatians 3:27)

> . . . one Lord, one faith, one baptism, . . . (Ephesians 4:5)

> In him you also were circumcised—not, however, with a circumcision performed by human hands, but by the removal of the fleshly body, that is, through the circumcision done by Messiah. Having been buried with him in baptism, you also have been raised with him through your faith in the power of God who raised him from the dead. (Colossians 2:11–12)

> And this prefigured baptism, which now saves you—not the washing off of physical dirt but the pledge of a good conscience to God—through the resurrection of Yeshua the Messiah, . . . (1 Kefa 3:21)

Water baptism is a symbol for spiritual baptism.

Finally, the next passage uses only the word "Spirit." This is the description of the experience of Pentecost.

> Now when the day of Shavuot had come, they were all together in one place. Suddenly a sound like a violent wind blowing came from heaven and filled the entire house where they were sitting. And tongues spreading out like a fire appeared to them and came to rest on each one of them. All of them were filled with the Holy Spirit, and they began to speak in other languages as the Spirit enabled them. (Acts 2:1–4)

The Six Factors in Water and Spirit Baptism. The background of Spirit baptism is the experience of water baptism. Water baptism, conceptually speaking, comes first. The chart on the next page compares the six factors of each. Below we will enlarge on these six elements in relation to Spirit baptism.

Spirit baptism: the baptizer. The Messiah, not the Holy Spirit, is the one who baptizes.

> I baptize you with water, for repentance, but the one coming after me is more powerful than I am—I am not worthy to carry his sandals. He will baptize you with the Holy Spirit and fire. (Mattai 3:11)

Note how the Messiah states that He is the one who will baptize with the Holy Spirit. Note also:

> I baptize you with water, but he will baptize you with the Holy Spirit. (Mark 1:8)

> Yohanan answered them all, "I baptize you with water, but one more powerful than I am is coming—I am not worthy to untie the strap of his sandals. He will baptize you with the Holy Spirit and fire." (Luke 3:16)

> And I did not recognize him, but the one who sent me to baptize with water said to me, "The one on whom you see the Spirit descending

and remaining—this is the one who baptizes with the Holy Spirit." (Yohanan 1:33)

From these passages, we see that the Messiah is the one who does the baptizing.

Kefa understood that the Messiah is the one who sends the Holy Spirit:

So then, exalted to the right hand of God, and having received the promise of the Holy Spirit from the Father, he has poured out what you both see and hear. (Acts 2:33)

This might explain why the Messiah Himself never baptized anyone in water. Though this is only a conjecture, this writer would suggest that His ministry was to baptize with the Holy Spirit and, therefore, not with water:

Now when Yeshua knew that the Pharisees had heard that he was

	Water Baptism	**Spirit Baptism**
The baptizer	The minister	The Messiah (not the Holy Spirit)
The element	Water	The Holy Spirit
The one baptized	The believer	All believers since Pentecost
The condition for being baptized	One must believe	One must believe
The mode	Immersion (following the meaning of the Greek word baptizo)	Immersion
The results	Entrance into the local congregation	Entrance into the body of the Messiah, bringing us into God

> winning and baptizing more disciples than Yohanan (although Yeshua himself was not baptizing, but his disciples were), . . . (Yohanan 4:1–2)

Spirit baptism: the element. Note how the work of the Holy Spirit is mentioned.

> For Yohanan baptized with water, but you will be baptized with the Holy Spirit not many days from now. (Acts 1:5)

> The Spirit told me to accompany them without hesitation. These six brothers also went with me, and we entered the man's house. (Acts 11:12)

> For in one Spirit we were all baptized into one body. Whether Jews or Greeks or slaves or free, we were all made to drink of the one Spirit. (1 Corinthians 12:13)

The Scriptures emphasize how the Holy Spirit was sent to do particular tasks.

Note the Greek preposition *en*. It is the same in each case: *en hudati* (in water), *en pneumati* (in the Holy Spirit), for example, in Mattai 3:11:

> I baptize you with water, for repentance, but the one coming after me is more powerful than I am—I am not worthy to carry his sandals. He will baptize you with the Holy Spirit and fire. (Mattai 3:11)

However, since the Holy Spirit is a person, it is better to refer to Him as the agent. The Messiah is the sender, while the Spirit is the one sent to actually do the work.

Spirit baptism: the one is baptized. First, note the situation prior to Pentecost in Acts 2. No person in the Tanach was ever baptized with water as a symbol of being baptized with the Holy Spirit. Neither is anyone baptized with water as a symbol of the Holy Spirit in the gospel records. Prior to Pentecost, every reference to the baptism as a symbol of Holy Spirit is put into the future. This is even so in Acts 1:5 as well:

> For Yohanan baptized with water, but you will be baptized with the Holy Spirit not many days from now. (Acts 1:5)

However, the situation changes after the Pentecost experience in Acts 2. Note that the word "baptize" does not occur in Acts 2:1–4. Later, when Kefa speaks, he mentions the prophetic passage in Joel that describes an event yet to happen in the future:

> "And in the last days it will be," God says,
> "that I will pour out my Spirit on all people,
> and your sons and your daughters will prophesy,
> and your young men will see visions,
> and your old men will dream dreams." (Acts 2:17)

When the three thousand are baptized in water, this is said of the Holy Spirit:

> Kefa said to them, "Repent, and each one of you be baptized in the name of Yeshua the Messiah for the forgiveness of your sins, and you will receive the gift of the Holy Spirit." (Acts 2:38)

> So those who accepted his message were baptized, and that day about three thousand people were added. (Acts 2:41)

Since that day, all true believers have been baptized in the Spirit:

> For in one Spirit we were all baptized into one body. Whether Jews or Greeks or slaves or free, we were all made to drink of the one Spirit. (1 Corinthians 12:13)

This was not just simply a promise to the Corinthians but rather it applies to all believers in Yeshua the Messiah, Jewish as well as Gentile.

Spirit baptism: the condition for receiving the Holy Spirit. There are differences of opinion among believers as to what one must do to receive the Holy Spirit. Some suggest that we need to agonize, to completely surrender ourselves, to "pray through," and/or enter into some other spiritual engagements. While the disciples were certainly praying on the day of Pentecost, nowhere does it say that they were praying to receive the Holy Spirit. When He came, it was simply God's appointed time in fulfillment of His promise. It was not based on people having to do something in order to receive Him. The Bible is very clear on this matter:

> For Yohanan baptized with water, but you will be baptized with the Holy Spirit not many days from now. (Acts 1:5)

The men to whom the message of Acts 1:5 was addressed were believers; but no condition is mentioned for them to receive Him.

> Therefore if God gave them the same gift as he also gave us after believing in the Lord Yeshua the Messiah, who was I to hinder God? (Acts 11:17)

Note the condition for receiving the Holy Spirit: it is "after believing" (compare NIV: "who believed")! Nothing else is mentioned.

> For in one Spirit we were all baptized into one body. Whether Jews or Greeks or slaves or free, we were all made to drink of the one Spirit. (1 Corinthians 12:13)

With the above verse see also:

> . . . to the *qehilah* of God that is in Corinth, to those who are sanctified in Messiah Yeshua, and called to be saints, with all those in every place who call on the name of our Lord Yeshua the Messiah, their Lord and ours. (1 Corinthians 1:2)

> For everyone who calls on the name of the Lord will be saved. (Romans 10:13)

Once a person becomes a believer, he is baptized by the Spirit.

Some might ask why we don't *feel* the experience of being baptized in the Spirit today? Yet nowhere in Scripture does God say that we are to feel the work of being baptized with the Holy Spirit. Some might experience such a feeling if they have a particular psychological "bent"; on the other hand, neither does Scripture tell us that we *must* feel something in order to become a believer. In order to be baptized in the Spirit, the only condition is that we need to be a believer. Our part is to believe what God says. When we believe and are baptized, feelings may come later.

Spirit baptism: the mode. The Greek word *baptizo* means "to immerse." Believers have been immersed in the Holy Spirit. Certainly, it is difficult to picture the Holy Spirit as a mere element like water. Yet, the Greek word indicating immersion suggests a very precious idea. Because we have been immersed in the Holy Spirit, we can say that we are "in the Spirit." We are surrounded by the very life and power of the Holy Spirit. Furthermore, since the Holy Spirit is God, to be baptized in the Spirit means to be "in God."

Spirit baptism: the results. The agent is the Holy Spirit who, when we are baptized by Him, brings us into the one body of the Messiah.

> For in one Spirit we were all baptized into one body. Whether Jews or Greeks or slaves or free, we were all made to drink of the one Spirit. (1 Corinthians 12:13)

The result is that we are also brought into the Messiah Himself:

> For all of you who were baptized into Messiah have clothed yourselves with Messiah. (Galatians 3:27)

The Spirit's indwelling in us brings God into us, and baptism brings us into God. Water baptism is a suggestion, a crude picture, of these truths.

Finally a result is that we are brought into identification with the Messiah into His death and resurrection:

> Absolutely not! How can we who died to sin still live in it? Or do you not know that as many as were baptized into Messiah Yeshua were

> baptized into his death? Therefore we have been buried with him through baptism into death, in order that just as Messiah was raised from the dead through the glory of the Father, so we too may live a new life. (Romans 6:2–4)

No Repetition of the Baptism of the Holy Spirit. If a person could backslide and lose his or her salvation, would that mean that if such a person came back to faith in the Messiah, he or she would then be rebaptized into the body? This can hardly be true. When we became believers, we were called to

> . . . one Lord, one faith, one baptism, . . . (Ephesians 4:5)

The word "baptism" in this verse does not refer to water baptism. The encouragement is that if we believe that God is our eternal Keeper, then we trust Him that *one baptism is sufficient* to place us within the body. It then becomes His responsibility to keep us.

Special Topic 3: The Infilling of the Holy Spirit

This topic is the third special topic concerning the work of the Holy Spirit. The infilling of the Spirit is not to be confused with the indwelling or the baptism. There are numerous passages in the period prior to Shavuot (Pentecost) of the infilling work of the Holy Spirit, in the Tanach, in the Gospels, and in Acts both prior to and following Pentecost.

> The LORD spoke to Moses: "See, I have chosen Bezalel son of Uri, the son of Hur, of the tribe of Judah, and I have filled him with the Spirit of God in skill, in understanding, in knowledge, and in all kinds of craftsmanship, to make artistic designs for work with gold, with silver, and with bronze, and with cutting and setting stone, and with cutting wood, to work in all kinds of craftsmanship." (Exodus 31:1–5)

> But the angel said to him, "Do not be afraid, Zechariah, for your prayer has been heard, and your wife Elizabeth will bear you a son; you will

name him Yohanan. Joy and gladness will come to you, and many will rejoice at his birth, for he will be great in the sight of the Lord. He must never drink wine or strong drink, and he will be filled with the Holy Spirit, even before his birth. He will turn many of the people of Israel to the Lord their God. And he will go as forerunner before the Lord in the spirit and power of Elijah, to turn the hearts of the fathers back to their children and the disobedient to the wisdom of the just, to make ready for the Lord a people prepared for him." (Luke 1:13–17)

In those days Miriam got up and went hurriedly into the hill country, to a town of Judah, and entered Zechariah's house and greeted Elizabeth. When Elizabeth heard Miriam's greeting, the baby leaped in her womb, and Elizabeth was filled with the Holy Spirit. She exclaimed with a loud voice, "Blessed are you among women, and blessed is the child in your womb! And who am I that the mother of my Lord should come and visit me?" (Luke 1:39–43)

Then his father Zechariah was filled with the Holy Spirit and prophesied. (Luke 1:67)

Then Yeshua, full of the Holy Spirit, returned from the Jordan River and was led by the Spirit in the wilderness, where for forty days he endured temptations from the devil. He ate nothing during those days, and when they were completed, he was famished. (Luke 4:1–2)

Now when the day of Shavuot had come, they were all together in one place. Suddenly a sound like a violent wind blowing came from heaven and filled the entire house where they were sitting. And tongues spreading out like a fire appeared to them and came to rest on each one of them. All of them were filled with the Holy Spirit, and they began to speak in other languages as the Spirit enabled them. (Acts 2:1–4)

After making Kefa and Yohanan stand in their midst, they began to inquire, "By what power or by what name did you do this?" Then Kefa, filled with the Holy Spirit, replied, "Rulers of the people and elders, if we are being examined today for a good deed done to a sick man—by what means this man was healed—let it be known to all of you and to all the people of Israel that by the name of Yeshua the Messiah the Nazarene whom you crucified, whom God raised from the dead, this man stands before you healthy. This Yeshua is the stone that was rejected by you, the builders, that has become the cornerstone. And there is salvation in no one else, for there is no other name under heaven given among people by which we must be saved." (Acts 4:7–12)

When they had prayed, the place where they were assembled together was shaken, and they were all filled with the Holy Spirit and began to speak the word of God courageously. (Acts 4:31)

Now in those days, when the disciples were growing in number, a complaint arose on the part of the Greek-speaking Jews against the native Hebraic Jews, because their widows were being overlooked in the daily distribution of food. So the twelve called the whole group of the disciples together and said, "It is not right for us to neglect the word of God to wait on tables. But carefully select from among you, brothers, seven men who are well-attested, full of the Spirit and of wisdom, whom we may put in charge of this necessary task. But we will devote ourselves to prayer and to the ministry of the word." The proposal pleased the entire group, so they chose Stephen, a man full of faith and of the Holy Spirit, with Philip, Prochorus, Nicanor, Timon, Parmenas, and Nicolas, a Gentile convert to Judaism from Antioch. They stood these men before the apostles, who prayed and placed their hands on them. (Acts 6:1–6) For this reason I kneel before the Father, from whom every family in heaven and on the earth is named. I pray that according to the wealth of his glory he may grant you to be strengthened with power through his Spirit in the inner person, that Messiah may dwell in your hearts through faith, so that, because you have been rooted and grounded in love, you may be able to comprehend with all the saints what is the breadth and length and height and depth, and thus to know the love

> of Messiah that surpasses knowledge, so that you may be filled up to all the fullness of God. (Ephesians 3:14–19)

> And do not get drunk with wine, which is debauchery, but be filled by the Spirit. (Ephesians 5:18)

The Biblical Command. The command is found in Ephesians, and there are six point to be made about it.

> And do not get drunk with wine, which is debauchery, but be filled by the Spirit. (Ephesians 5:18)

First, the instruction implies that *not all believers* are "filled" with the Holy Spirit. Therefore, we conclude that the filling is different from the indwelling or baptism of the Spirit.

Second, the believers in Ephesus had been blessed with every "spiritual" blessing (Ephesians 1:3). Evidence exists that we can have every one of these blessings, but to reach out and lay hold on them necessitates some kind of a filling of the Spirit.

Third, the present tense of the verb, "be filled," suggests that God wants us to be filled *continuously*. Without question, therefore, He never intended that believers are to be filled only at certain times.

Fourth, the statement proves that the responsibility for the infilling of the Spirit is ours, not God's responsibility. By contrast, there is never a command in the Scripture for the believer to be continually indwelt or baptized of the Spirit. When we become believers, these are accomplished facts. But in addition, we are commanded to be filled continuously.

Fifth, when we are not filled with the Spirit, the suggestion is that we are breaking the Lord's commands for a selfish lifestyle. The passage reminds us that we must not get drunk on hard liquor and be controlled by it or any other impediment to a godly lifestyle, but rather, the infilling needs to be a primary concern for every believer. To put it in another way, it is just as wrong *not* to be filled with the Spirit as it is to be filled with wine.

Sixth, we must never think of the Spirit like air or water. There is no material connotation with what we are told to do. To be filled means to be "controlled," and just as one can be "filled" and controlled by hard liquor, so in the same way, we are told to be filled or "controlled" by the Holy Spirit.

Purposes and Results of the Infilling of the Holy Spirit. There are quite a few reasons why believers are to be filled with the Holy Spirit.

Power for spiritual ministry. For instance, there is no question that Yohanan the Immerser ministered in the power of the Spirit; even Yeshua commented that he was the greatest of all the prophets.

> But the angel said to him, "Do not be afraid, Zechariah, for your prayer has been heard, and your wife Elizabeth will bear you a son; you will name him Yohanan. Joy and gladness will come to you, and many will rejoice at his birth, for he will be great in the sight of the Lord. He must never drink wine or strong drink, and he will be filled with the Holy Spirit, even before his birth. He will turn many of the people of Israel to the Lord their God. And he will go as forerunner before the Lord in the spirit and power of Elijah, to turn the hearts of the fathers back to their children and the disobedient to the wisdom of the just, to make ready for the Lord a people prepared for him." (Luke 1:13–17)

Strengthening in time of temptation. We note in the accounts of Yeshua's temptation how He was able to answer Satan using the Word. The same Holy Spirit will enable us to put the Word to good use so that we will be strengthened when we are tempted.

> Then Yeshua, full of the Holy Spirit, returned from the Jordan River and was led by the Spirit in the wilderness, where for forty days he endured temptations from the devil. He ate nothing during those days, and when they were completed, he was famished. (Luke 4:1–2)

Bearing witness to the Messiah and leading us in our testimony. In Acts, throughout Kefa's message of explanation, the Holy Spirit illumined the Scripture, enabling people to understand the message concerning Yeshua the Messiah.

> Now when the day of Shavuot had come, they were all together in one place. Suddenly a sound like a violent wind blowing came from heaven and filled the entire house where they were sitting. And tongues spreading out like a fire appeared to them and came to rest on each one of them. All of them were filled with the Holy Spirit, and they began to speak in other languages as the Spirit enabled them. (Acts 2:1–4)

> On the next day, their rulers, elders, and experts in the law came together in Jerusalem. Annas the high priest was there, and Qayafa, Yohanan, Alexander, and others who were members of the high priest's family. After making Kefa and Yohanan stand in their midst, they began to inquire, "By what power or by what name did you do this?" Then Kefa, filled with the Holy Spirit, replied, "Rulers of the people and elders, if we are being examined today for a good deed done to a sick man—by what means this man was healed— . . ." (Acts 4:5–9)

Giving boldness. For those who testify to the Messiah, God effectively removes the fear of man, enabling a person to witness to Him with great power.

> When they were released, Kefa and Yohanan went to their fellow believers and reported everything the high priests and the elders had said to them. . . .
>
> When they had prayed, the place where they were assembled together was shaken, and they were all filled with the Holy Spirit and began to speak the word of God courageously. (Acts 4:23, 31)

Equipping to serve the Lord. In Acts, the seven men who were selected for service were noted to be filled with the Spirit. The Spirit led as they exercised their office as deacons, looking after the poor as a spiritual task, for caring for the needs of those less fortunate is an important ministry.

> Now in those days, when the disciples were growing in number, a complaint arose on the part of the Greek-speaking Jews against the

> native Hebraic Jews, because their widows were being overlooked in the daily distribution of food. So the twelve called the whole group of the disciples together and said, "It is not right for us to neglect the word of God to wait on tables. But carefully select from among you, brothers, seven men who are well-attested, full of the Spirit and of wisdom, whom we may put in charge of this necessary task." (Acts 6:1–3)

We see further instances. For example, the Holy Spirit enabled Sha'ul to proclaim that Yeshua is the Son of God. Where once he had been adamantly opposed to any exaltation of Yeshua to the level of deity, after having been born again, he preached by the power of the Holy Spirit one of the fundamentals of the faith.

> So Ananias departed and entered the house, placed his hands on Sha'ul and said, "Brother Sha'ul, the Lord Yeshua, who appeared to you on the road as you came here, has sent me so that you may see again and be filled with the Holy Spirit." Immediately something like scales fell from his eyes, and he could see again. He got up and was baptized, and after taking some food, his strength returned.
>
> For several days he was with the disciples in Damascus, and immediately he began to proclaim Yeshua in the synagogues, saying, "This man is the Son of God." (Acts 9:17–20)

In the face of suffering and persecution, the Holy Spirit filled the disciples with joy. This was inexplicable from the human point of view, but the Holy Spirit was quite capable in such circumstances.

> So the word of the Lord was spreading through the entire region. But the Jews incited the God-fearing women of high social standing and the prominent men of the city, stirred up persecution against Sha'ul and Bar Navah, and threw them out of their region. So after they shook the dust off their feet in protest against them, they went to Iconium. And the disciples were filled with joy and with the Holy Spirit. (Acts 13:49–52)

The Holy Spirit, when He fills us, enables us to have a song in our hearts and be thankful for whatever comes our way as we seek to serve Him, as Ephesians indicates.

> And do not get drunk with wine, which is debauchery, but be filled by the Spirit, speaking to one another in psalms, hymns, and spiritual songs, singing and making music in your hearts to the Lord, always giving thanks to God the Father for each other in the name of our Lord Yeshua the Messiah, and submitting to one another out of reverence for Messiah. (Ephesians 5:18–21)

We also note that the Holy Spirit enabled Stephen to be filled with courage and even gave him a vision of the Messiah in his hour of death.

> When they heard these things, they became furious and ground their teeth at him. But Stephen, full of the Holy Spirit, looked intently toward heaven and saw the glory of God, and Yeshua standing at the right hand of God. "Look!" he said. "I see the heavens opened, and the Son of Man standing at the right hand of God!" But they covered their ears, shouting out with a loud voice, and rushed at him with one intent. When they had driven him out of the city, they began to stone him, and the witnesses laid their cloaks at the feet of a young man named Sha'ul. (Acts 7:54–58)

Believers today, when faced with death, can also expect the encouragement of the Holy Spirit. Whether we have a vision of the Messiah may or may not be appropriate for the occasion, but we will have all the encouragement necessary to face the ordeal, knowing that our destiny is heaven, in the presence of the Lord.

Conditions for the Infilling of the Holy Spirit. Some of the passages may only be inferences while others may be more direct. The conditions are:

Readiness to be controlled by the Holy Spirit. The infilling of the Spirit means that He will control us. He cannot control us, however, if we insist on controlling our own destiny or gratifying self. In such a case we will not be filled by Him.

> And do not present your members to sin as instruments to be used for unrighteousness, but present yourselves to God as those who are alive from the dead and your members to God as instruments to be used for righteousness. (Romans 6:13)

A thirst for His fullness. If we are not filled with the Spirit after having become a believer, we should ask ourselves if we really thirst for His filling? Do we have the sense that we want as much of God as possible in our lives?

> On the last day of the feast, the greatest day, Yeshua stood up and shouted out, "If anyone is thirsty, let him come to me, and let the one who believes in me drink. Just as the scripture says, 'From within him will flow rivers of living water.'" (Now he said this about the Spirit, whom those who believed in him were going to receive, for the Spirit had not yet been given, because Yeshua was not yet glorified.) (Yohanan 7:37–39)

Readiness to serve and suffer on His behalf. Why do some feel that they will not suffer on His behalf? The infilling was always for the purpose of serving as well as suffering.

It is said of the Messiah:

> Although he was a son, he learned obedience through the things he suffered. (Hebrews 5:8)

The question whether we should we pray for the infilling. There does not seem to be any definite prayer to this effect recorded in Scripture. Yet consider these passages:

> When they heard this, they raised their voices to God with one mind and said, "Master of all, you who made the heaven, the earth, the sea, and everything that is in them, who said by the Holy Spirit through your servant David our forefather,
>
> 'Why do the nations rage,
> and the peoples plot foolish things?

> The kings of the earth stood together,
> and the rulers assembled together,
> against the Lord and against his Messiah.'
>
> "For indeed both Herod and Pontius Pilate, with the Gentiles and the people of Israel, assembled together in this city against your holy servant Yeshua, whom you anointed, to do as much as your power and your plan had decided beforehand would happen. And now, Lord, pay attention to their threats, and grant to your servants to speak your message with great courage, while you extend your hand to heal, and to bring about miraculous signs and wonders through the name of your holy servant Yeshua." When they had prayed, the place where they were assembled together was shaken, and they were all filled with the Holy Spirit and began to speak the word of God courageously. (Acts 4:24–31)

> For this reason I kneel before the Father, from whom every family in heaven and on the earth is named. I pray that according to the wealth of his glory he may grant you to be strengthened with power through his Spirit in the inner person, that Messiah may dwell in your hearts through faith, so that, because you have been rooted and grounded in love, you may be able to comprehend with all the saints what is the breadth and length and height and depth, and thus to know the love of Messiah that surpasses knowledge, so that you may be filled up to all the fullness of God. (Ephesians 3:14–19)

We need not quibble over whether it is necessary to definitely pray for the infilling of the Holy Spirit. It is enough to understand that God is ready to fill us if we desire to serve Him and not seek control over our own will. Actually, He petitions us in order that He might fill us—more often than we seek to be filled with the Holy Spirit.

Questions Concerning the Infilling of the Holy Spirit. Believers sometimes wonder about such questions as the following.

The question of starting out with this fullness. From Acts 2:1–4, it is apparent that believers *do* start with a filling of the Spirit when they accept

Yeshua. The filling at each point in our lives will occur as we understand and appreciate it. As the believer becomes more mature along the way, he or she will have an infilling that will provide for an even greater appreciation for the Lord and His purposes.

The question of losing the infilling. Can a believer lose the infilling of the Holy Spirit? The answer is yes. Once again we emphasize that the infilling and the baptism are not the same. From Acts 4, we note that the disciples had been filled with the Holy Spirit. Why should they be? In their ministry, they needed it in order that they not be tempted by fear. The Holy Spirit gave them courage and boldness.

Conditions whereby the infilling will be minimized. First, because of disobedience, whereby the believer allows self to have the upper hand and therefore excludes what the Holy Spirit wishes. Second, allowing the fear of man to gain the mastery. Third, grieving the Holy Spirit. And fourth, reserving some area of life for self, whereby believers seek to control their own lives.

Nature and causes of experiencing the infilling. We note the remarkable spiritual experiences of men such as Moody, Finney, F. B. Meyer, and R. A. Torrey. These men were greatly used of God. One cannot deny their testimony to the reality to the experience of infilling. However, all such experiences must be interpreted and explained by the Word of God. The nature or causes of infilling, then, are first, because of the new birth itself. Second, it is because of the assurance of salvation whereby the Spirit of God fills us and reminds us that we belong to Him. Third, it can be because of the realization of what we have in the Messiah, whereby

> I can pray this because his divine power has bestowed on us everything necessary for life and godliness through the rich knowledge of the one who called us by his own glory and excellence. (2 Kefa 1:3)

The infilling can also result from the presentation of the body and its members to God:

> Therefore I exhort you, brothers and sisters, by the mercies of God, to present your bodies as a sacrifice—alive, holy, and pleasing to

> God—which is your reasonable service. Do not be conformed to this present world, but be transformed by the renewing of your mind, so that you may test and approve what is the will of God—what is good and well-pleasing and perfect. (Romans 12:1–2)

There are also those occasions where there is a fresh infilling of the Holy Spirit, such as in Acts 4.

Finally, there are those unspeakable experiences that the Lord Himself brings to us when we need Him most.

In conclusion, then, a believer needs to be careful that all such claims to be filled with the Spirit conform with what the Word of God teaches.

Special Topic Four: The Issue of Tongues

Some Biblical Considerations. Note that in Scripture, tongues appear as unusual signs and wonders. They are not always of God. Furthermore, the Messiah warned His disciples that signs would precede the second coming (see Mattai 24:23–24 and 2 Thessalonians).

The only clue as to whether a manifestation of tongues is of God is found in His Word. Satan also produces signs. Deuteronomy 13:1–4 gives the test of false religion, which is twofold: first, does the movement, religion, or person obey the written Word of God? Second, do their teachings harmonize with the great themes of the Bible? As Isaiah proclaimed,

> To the law and to the testimony! If they do not speak according to this word, they have no light of dawn. (Isaiah 8:20 NIV)

The Gift of Tongues. Is there a true gift of tongues? The answer is yes. There is first of all a gift of known tongues. This is the ability to speak languages existing here on earth, as in Acts 2.

Second, there is also a gift of unknown tongues, mentioned in 1 Corinthians 12–14 in the context of spiritual gifts. Note that tongues is the last of all the spiritual gifts listed. It comes at the end of the lists in 1 Corinthians.

Third, the gift of tongues is not intended for all believers. Though some say that believers *must* have the gift of tongues, the following passages indicate otherwise.

> For one person is given through the Spirit the message of wisdom, and another the message of knowledge according to the same Spirit, to another faith by the same Spirit, and to another gifts of healing by the one Spirit, to another performance of miracles, to another prophecy, and to another discernment of spirits, to another different kinds of tongues, and to another the interpretation of tongues. (1 Corinthians 12:8–10)

> Not all are apostles, are they? Not all are prophets, are they? Not all are teachers, are they? Not all perform miracles, do they? Not all have gifts of healing, do they? Not all speak in tongues, do they? Not all interpret, do they? (1 Corinthians 12:29–30)

These gifts are all bestowed as the Holy Spirit wills, not in accordance with an individual's seeking.

> It is one and the same Spirit, distributing as he decides to each person, who produces all these things. (1 Corinthians 12:11)

At the point of salvation, God assigns us a place in His body and our gift. We then seek to discover the gift and use it.

Finally, the gift of tongues is not forbidden, but greater ones are to be desired.

> So then, brothers and sisters, be eager to prophesy, and do not forbid anyone from speaking in tongues. (1 Corinthians 14:39)

The Presence of This Gift in the Church Today. The biblical guidelines for considering the answer to this question are as follows.

First of all, tongues are given for a sign, not to believers but to those who do not believe. In fact, the tongues of the early church were a sign of coming judgment, not spectacular gifts.

> So then, tongues are a sign not for believers but for unbelievers. Prophecy, however, is not for unbelievers but for believers. (1 Corinthians 14:22)

Second, signs were given especially to Jews, who had a right to ask for a sign:

> For Jews demand miraculous signs and Greeks ask for wisdom. (1 Corinthians 1:22)

Third, Scripture lays down rules for the exercise of the gift of tongues.

> If someone speaks in a tongue, it should be two, or at the most three, one after the other, and someone must interpret. But if there is no interpreter, he should be silent in the *qehilah*. Let him speak to himself and to God. (1 Corinthians 14:27–28)

So there should never be more than two or three at most, who speak by turn and in order, and in the presence of someone to interpret. We note in this context that the fruit of the Spirit includes self-control.

Special Topic Five: Possible Sins Against the Holy Spirit

Sins by Unbelievers. Note how in this sequence these sins descend to lower and lower spiritual levels.

Resisting the Holy Spirit.

> You stubborn people, with uncircumcised hearts and ears! You are always resisting the Holy Spirit, like your ancestors did! (Acts 7:51)

This is the first step downward in the experience of unbelievers.

Insulting the Holy Spirit. In one of Hebrews' warning passages to the Jerusalem congregation, we read that those who wish to act like unbelievers can expect a heavy reprimand.

> How much greater punishment do you think that person deserves who has contempt for the Son of God, and profanes the blood of the covenant that made him holy, and insults the Spirit of grace? (Hebrews 10:29)

The danger of treating the ministry of the Holy Spirit in a contemptuous manner can be a real possibility. Unbelievers do this quite often.

Blaspheming against the Holy Spirit.

> And everyone who speaks a word against the Son of Man will be forgiven, but the person who blasphemes against the Holy Spirit will not be forgiven. (Luke 12:10)

The unbeliever can reach the place where he or she does not discern the voice of the Spirit, but actually mistakes it for the voice of Satan.

Sins by Believers. Believers too can sin against the Holy Spirit in a number of ways.

Quenching the Holy Spirit.

> Do not extinguish [NASB: "quench"] the Spirit. (1 Thessalonians 5:19)

A backslidden believer can quench the Spirit, actually suppressing His voice and power. We must never fool ourselves that such behavior is impossible, for Sha'ul warns us,

> Do not lag in zeal, be enthusiastic in spirit, serve the Lord. (Romans 12:11)

Grieving the Holy Spirit.

> And do not grieve the Holy Spirit of God, by whom you were sealed for the day of redemption. (Ephesians 4:30)

A believer can actually do what He hates, sin, and do evil against his or her own person and others in the community of believers.

Lying to the Holy Spirit.

> But Kefa said, "Ananias, why has Satan filled your heart to lie to the Holy Spirit and keep back for yourself part of the proceeds from the sale of the land?" (Acts 5:3)

Can believers actually lie? The conclusion of this account is that the backslidden believer can indeed lie, even to the Holy Spirit. Though it is an abomination, even believers are no exception.

TWELVE

The Doctrine of Man

Some time ago, a popular television presentation featured a roundtable discussion by Hal Lindsey, noted author on biblical prophecy, and an Israeli professor of Jewish Studies. The exchange of views between these two men became a laboratory experiment as to how evangelicals and Jewish people each view the nature of man.

As Lindsey discussed biblical prophecy, he described how God was working in history to ultimately bring about the kingdom of peace as predicted by the prophets in the Hebrew Scriptures. He put great emphasis on the restoration of the people of Israel to their land, after which God would then send His Messiah to rule over Israel and the nations.

The Israeli professor did not for a moment outwardly contradict Lindsey's viewpoint. Rather, he described his life as a young man living in Jerusalem during the 1948–49 War of Independence. He vividly described life under constant bombardment, when basic necessities, including water, were all but cut off. One could not help empathizing with the professor as he expressed the exultation of the people when the Israeli Defense Forces finally broke through the Arab lines, opening a corridor to Jerusalem and bringing food and water to the weary Jewish defendants.

As I reflected on the views of the two men, the differences between evangelicals and Jewish people came into sharp focus. Hal Lindsey was particularly concerned with *the sovereign acts of God*, which will ultimately bring about the worldview as described by the prophets. The Israeli professor, on the other hand, put a far greater emphasis on *the freedom of man* in bringing the kingdom of God.

The two contrasting views also show differences in the area of how man's freedom relates to his fellow man and to society. The Jewish contribution underscores an emphasis on the freedom of man in the "here and now"; man attempts to make this world a better place in which to live. The evangelical view also has implications affecting man's social, cultural, environmental, and political involvement. But for its part, it raises problems concerning the freedom of man, for it recognizes the quirk in man's nature that will not permit him to realize all his goals. As a result, some evangelicals put such an undue stress on the fall of man and his inability to find an atonement based on one's self-effort that they take away the incentive to relate to a "this-world" context.

What we need is to strive for a balance between what Judaism observes concerning the freedom of man, and yet also properly account for the implications of the fall. In that way we can bring an "otherworldly" message to bear on the realities of this world, using basic biblical principles.

The Jewish View of Man

Image of God

In defining the nature of man, the Written Torah declares:

> God created humankind in his own image,
> in the image of God he created them,
> male and female he created them. (Genesis 1:27)

Akiva's comment on this verse is: "Beloved is man for he was created in the image [of God],"[1] while Kohler states, ". . . man has a divine nature, as he was made in the image of God, fashioned after His likeness."[2]

We will not here consider the question of an evolutionary origin of man. However, we note that some Jewish thinkers insist on a theistic evolution whereby God produced Adam and Eve from a higher form of primate. Yet, even with this unusual deflection from Scripture, one writer still asserted, "The idea of evolution does not deliver us from the necessity of postulating

Divine intelligence as the cause of the universe. On the contrary, it intensifies that necessity."[3]

The Meaning of *Image*. Jewish scholars have a variety of opinions regarding the meaning of the word *image*. Most definitions refer to a strong resemblance that is yet "less than" the original. In a much reduced measure, man has those qualities that in God exist in infinite measure. Herberg comments: "The 'image of God' in man establishes an affinity between man and God without in the least obscuring the vast gulf between creature and Creator."[4] Though man is related in physical structure and function to the animal world, yet the image of God makes man unique to the extent that he differs from the animals. The phrase "image of God" can in no way apply to the animal world.

In the *sifrim hisonim*, "the image of God" refers to the gift of immortality that man possesses.[5] While God can think, and be aware of Himself, yet on a more restricted level "man alone among the creatures is capable of sustained thought, creativity, and awareness of God; the light of God is immanent in his spirit (Prov. 20:27)."[6] The same can be true of the other attributes of God. No wonder, then, Jewish scholars echo what the psalmist declared, that man is "only a little lower than God" (Psalm 8:5 NASB; NET and NIV: "than the heavenly beings"; KJV: "than the angels"; Hebrew, *elohim*).[7]

From the Jewish point of view, the most probable explanation is that the "image of God" includes the gift and capacity to reason, which leads to the possibility of making moral choices that carry implications. Gordis has well stated that "This moral freedom is the basis of man's responsibility for his actions without which society cannot exist."[8]

The Biblical Perspective of *Image*. To a great degree, Jewish thinking reflects the biblical view of "the image of God" in man. The Written Torah declares that man is to be distinguished from the animals because of the divine image. It marks the basis for Adam's fellowship with God:

> The LORD God formed out of the ground every living animal of the field and every bird of the air. He brought them to the man to see what he would name them, and whatever the man called each living creature, that was its name. (Genesis 2:19)

Mankind is ranked only a little lower than God Himself (or, than the heavenly beings; see a few paragraphs above).

> Of what importance is the human race, that you should notice them?
> Of what importance is mankind, that you should pay attention to them,
> and make them a little less than the heavenly beings?
> You grant mankind honor and majesty. (Psalm 8:4–5)

Because of the "image," the entire pattern of human life is affected. Man has value in God's sight and he has the right of protection from both animal and fellow man:

> For your lifeblood I will surely exact punishment, from every living creature I will exact punishment. From each person I will exact punishment for the life of the individual since the man was his relative.
> "Whoever sheds human blood,
> by other humans
> must his blood be shed;
> for in God's image
> God has made humankind." (Genesis 9:5–6)

Other biblical implications concerning the image that also correspond to the Jewish understanding is that man has dominion of the earth, that is, naming the animals, reflecting the dominion of God over the entire cosmos:

> So the man named all the animals, the birds of the air, and the living creatures of the field, but for Adam no companion who corresponded to him was found. (Genesis 2:20)

In addition, even as God has the capacity to make choices, so man likewise has the freedom of moral choice:

> Then the LORD God commanded the man, "You may freely eat fruit from every tree of the orchard, but you must not eat from the tree of the knowledge of good and evil, for when you eat from it you will surely die." (Genesis 2:16–17)

Seen in its larger aspect, the image of God means that the complete totality of man's higher powers distinguishes him entirely from the rest of animate creation.

This analysis of the biblical perspective is only exploratory for now, to highlight continuities with the Jewish viewpoint. A more detailed discussion of man from the Written Torah will be found below.

Freedom and Determinism

In philosophy, one of the difficult questions revolves around the relationship of freedom and determinism. One interesting feature of Judaism is how it handles this question of man's free will as contrasted with the sovereignty of God. While philosophers have made many attempts to find a solution to this antimony, in general, religious Judaism never addressed this paradox to any great extent. Generally each area has been considered separately from the other. That is, the ramifications of God's foreseeing has been one question; and the meaning of man's freedom has been another.

Rabbi Akiva boldly asserted that "All is foreseen, but freedom of choice is given."[9] While religious Judaism did not generally play the two factors against each other, there was a strong insistence on the doctrine of man's freedom and responsibility. Perhaps Moses as the teacher in Israel set it forth best of all when he challenged his people with this freedom of choice:

> Look! I have set before you today life and prosperity on the one hand, and death and disaster on the other. (Deuteronomy 30:15)

> Today I invoke heaven and earth as a witness against you that I have set life and death, blessing and curse, before you. Therefore choose life so that you and your descendants may live! (Deuteronomy 30:19)

Adler adds: "In a supreme act of self-limitation the Absolute God gave man freedom of moral choice."[10]

Freedom Is Not Absolute. Judaism has not regarded man's freedom as absolute nor infinite. Jewish tradition says that "Everything is in the hand of heaven except the fear of heaven,"[11] that is, only in the realm of moral decision is man exempt from God's control. Though there are psychological, biological, ecological, economic, and political boundaries that limit man's freedom, yet man is free to express moral choices within each of these areas. Both in the ancient and modern Jewish worlds, man's freedom is an important factor in framing a system of ethics. Man has the best of both worlds; he is earthly, but he also has a dignity like the angels demonstrated by his choice-making. God is to be extolled and glorified in the creation of man.[12]

Man in Relation to Society. Based on this view of man's freedom, Judaism has held that how Jewish people relate with their fellow Jews is of great importance.

Unselfish service. Israel's leaders were meant to lead through unselfish service. It was not appropriate for them to be power happy or morally bereft tyrants. Conduct had to be above reproach or else the sanctity of Torah could be held in question by the community. "If a *ḥaber* is caught in sin, it is a disgrace to him. Why so? Because he mixes purity with impurity. He casts shame upon the Torah which he had held precious . . ."[13]

Forgiving love. Further, correct moral choices epitomize the way of forgiving love. The Torah, Written and Oral, considers the Father's forgiving love incompatible with willful rejection of that love. Such a negative attitude can characterize the person who renders false obedience to God as insincere, or even as rebellious. Prior to the fall of man in the garden, God had provided Adam and Eve with previous descriptive knowledge regarding the tree of the knowledge of good and evil (Genesis 2:17). All our first parents had to do to experience God's love in a deeper way was to choose not to eat. After the fall, with man now in sin (to be be discussed below), in order to experience God's forgiving love, it is necessary to sense the degradation of sin. But Judaism does teach that the right moral choices enable society to see the Father's love.

Responsible leadership. Moral choices also enable one to practice responsible leadership. Through the centuries tradition developed the concept of *mitzvot*, the means for a godly lifestyle that one lived as a demonstration of faith. One does not follow the *mitzvot* as if it is a set of rules that we *must* do. If this becomes the basis for serving God, legalism is just one step away from the injunction: Do! Rather, one needs to live the *mitzvot* as a godly lifestyle, because of our love for the Father. Yes, underneath that love is the ever-present Torah as a constant reminder of our responsibilities, but the glue that gives shape to the *mitzvot* is our love for God.

A work ethic that emphasizes diligence and a high quality of devotion is very much related to and guided by the Scriptures and tradition, and the *mitzvot* therefore finds its application in the total round of life. Through responsible stewardship, the Jewish community, past and present, provides support for houses of worship, courts of justice, school systems, and a highly developed system of social welfare. If one is lazy and wasteful with his own resources, the community has a right to disapprove; such a person cannot be given greater responsibility until he mends his ways.

A faith that works. Consisently, Judaism puts its approval and emphasis on a faith that works. Since man was created in God's image, he is to display through a working faith a decent care and concern for himself, and a love for one's neighbor. The concern and interest as to society is derived from the sanctity of each human life, which in turn goes back to God's unique creation of Adam. This is epitomized in the rabbinic statement, "Let the honour of thy disciple be as dear to thee as thine own and as the honour of thy companion, and the honour of thy companion as the fear of thy teacher, and the fear of thy teacher as the fear of Heaven."[14]

In these and other guidelines, Judaism encourages its adherents to relate to the world by making moral choices compatible and consistent with God's nature reflecting holiness, justice, and righteousness. We have yet to discuss what the Written Torah has to say concerning man's nature and if it is in agreement with the idea that man has complete freedom to make moral choices that will better mankind and society. Man is not so free as he claims to be, but Judaism does have a contribution to make regarding an optimism in what he can accomplish, a topic to which we turn next.

Human Accomplishments. Even those who think only on the horizontal level, in terms of relating to other people and society, can still exhibit an appreciation for good and evil. Most people do not "live in the gutter" and make all the wrong choices possible, and the major reason for not doing so is that we have a moral consciousness—albeit marred—which enables us to have a sense of our rights and dignity. Even apart from a biblical point of view, man can still be regarded as having great worth.

Religious people of any faith, as well as secular people who live on the horizontal level, can make significant contributions for the betterment of the world through literature, by exercising their intellectuality, by producing paintings, sculpture, and music. As one example, it was the political and social forces in the 1700s and early 1800s in Western Europe—which came into being through optimistic humanism and the Enlightenment—which made it possible for the Jewish people to come out of the ghetto and enter into Western society.

Man is a unique creature. Judaism has fostered an optimistic view of man, encouraging him to achieve in every area of life, and teaches that man does not live for himself but in order to glorify God in everything he sets his heart to do.

Believers should not overlook the importance of this viewpoint for their own biblical worldview. Too often, the emphasis of much of biblical preaching has been on the utter sinfulness of man, his depravity, and his inability do anything good. The result of imbibing this emphasis as a steady diet is that believers hesitate, entrapped by a weighty notion of sin, and become paralyzed in trying to serve God and impact society. Judaism offers an optimistic view of man that we as believers can adopt, knowing that with the infilling of the Holy Spirit in our lives, we can have the privilege of redeeming this world, first by reaching people with the redemption in our Messiah, and then by seeking to make changes in every area of society.

The Perspective of the Written Torah and New Covenant Concerning Man

Man's Mental Endowment in the Original Creation

There are two contrasting views that exist today regarding the origin of man. In answer to the question as to who primitive man was, we can consider either that he was a higher form of primate at the beginning of his mental development—the answer of evolution—or that he was a perfect being wholly developed mentally in every way—the point of view of the Torah.

The biblical picture presents man as originally endowed by his Creator with a perfect capacity for reflective and creative intelligence, and yet also capable of further intellectual progress as well as moral and spiritual maturation. Several characteristics demonstrate this capacity:

Invention and Use of Language Symbols.

> So the man named all the animals, the birds of the air, and the living creatures of the field, but for Adam no companion who corresponded to him was found. (Genesis 2:20)

The modern discipline of communications explores how we think, how we use word symbols to reflect thought, and how the receiving person understands what he hears. Because of common grace, all people share this capacity.

Use of Tools. Adam and Eve had the mental capacity to imagine their needs and then develop the tools necessary for the task, skills that were passed on to heir descendants. For example, the Scripture speaks of how Cain's descendants became musicians and developers of metal implements:

> Adah gave birth to Jabal; he was the first of those who live in tents and keep livestock. The name of his brother was Jubal; he was the first of all who play the harp and the flute. Now Zillah also gave birth to Tubal-cain, who heated metal and shaped all kinds of tools made of bronze and iron. The sister of Tubal-cain was Naamah. (Genesis 4:20–22)

Later in the Scripture, we see how these arts were further developed, and they continue to be today.

Ability to Foresee Consequences. They were able to take the consequences of their actions into account ahead of time.

> Then the LORD God commanded the man, "You may freely eat fruit from every tree of the orchard, but you must not eat from the tree of the knowledge of good and evil, for when you eat from it you will surely die." (Genesis 2:16–17)

God gave Adam and Eve a certain amount of descriptive knowledge, including the consequences of an action, to enable them to make correct moral and spiritual choices.

Ability to Contemplate Connections Between Ideas and Reason to Conclusions. An example is the initial presentation of Eve to Adam:

> Then the man said,
> "This one at last is bone of my bones
> and flesh of my flesh;
> this one will be called 'woman,'
> for she was taken out of man."
> That is why a man leaves his father and mother and unites with his wife, and they become a new family. (Genesis 2:23–24)

Appreciation for the Aesthetic.

> The LORD God made all kinds of trees grow from the soil, every tree that was pleasing to look at and good for food. (Now the tree of life and the tree of the knowledge of good and evil were in the middle of the orchard.) (Genesis 2:9)

> When the woman saw that the tree produced fruit that was good for food, was attractive to the eye, and was desirable for making one wise, she took some of its fruit and ate it. She also gave some of it to her husband who was with her, and he ate it. (Genesis 3:6)

Man has an appreciation for art, for music, for sculpture. No two people see every kind of art form in the same way, and therein lies the genius that God has placed in every person.

Treated as Entirely Different from the Animal World.

> So the man named all the animals, the birds of the air, and the living creatures of the field, but for Adam no companion who corresponded to him was found. (Genesis 2:20)

While Adam could name the animals, he found no animal that could commune with him and meet the deepest needs of his heart.

Endowment and the Capacity to Learn Are Two Different Things

In considering the endowment given to Adam and Eve, we note that it is a different thing from the capacity to learn. We can see this in several ways.

A baby who is perfect at birth must nevertheless grow in maturity and in knowledge. It is enough for a baby to be cute and respond to tickling; far more is expected when he or she is twelve years of age. If the child's capacity remained the same as it grows, it would be considered tragic.

Consider also the example of the Messiah Himself:

> And Yeshua increased in wisdom and in stature, and in favor with God and with people. (Luke 2:52)

Even Yeshua needed to grow. This also included maturing in the moral and spiritual areas:

> Although he was a son, he learned obedience through the things he suffered. And by being perfected in this way, he became the source of eternal salvation to all who obey him. (Hebrews 5:8–9)

If the Messiah was to be a perfect redeemer, He needed the experience of growing into spiritual and moral maturity. This maturity was necessary for His human nature, as we have seen in the discussion of the *kenosis*, whereby Messiah emptied Himself so as to be incarnated in mankind.

One must wonder what Adam's and Eve's intellectual, moral, and spiritual progress would have been had they not fallen. This will be discussed below under the topic of man's temptation and God's design for Adam and Eve.

Some Differences Between Man and the Animal World

We made brief reference to the fact that Adam and Eve, as well as all their descendants, were and are different from the animals. We will not expand on this idea. The first few points below may be more open to question now than in the past, because of recent research in the field of animal psychology. Yet the overall point remains.

Self-Consciousness. A man or woman can say, "I am conscious—I am a person." When Descartes said "I think, therefore I am," he was affirming the existence of a distinct and undeniable personality. An animal is conscious, but is it fully self-conscious? If a pig could say "I am a pig," would it cease to be a pig? A parrot repeats sounds; this is not self-consciousness. But when a child first articulates "me," then everyone at home takes note: he or she has become an "I"; he or she has become self-conscious.

Ability to Conceive Concepts. An animal certainly has some kind of perception; it can perceive and remember various articles. But when the animal no longer sees the object, does it carry around in its memory the *idea* of the object? In constrast, man remembers the *idea* of an article.

Use of Language. Words are symbols of concepts or ideas we have in our minds. Man, in contrast to animals, has developed language symbols and can communicate his ideas via symbols that represent these ideas. At times this can occur at a level of great complexity, as in the areas of mathematics, chemistry, or physics. Animals can call for food; they have sharpened senses enabling them to communicate the presence of danger; they can express their likes and dislikes. All this, however, falls short of that with which God has endowed man.

Formation of Judgments. On seeing a gun, a hunting dog can become either excited or fearful, depending on what previous associations it has formed with the gun. But these are learned reactions. Animals can also respond to stimuli. But to form judgments and derive conclusions that lead to other conclusions is man's prerogative.

Creation of Ideas. Man can create new ideas, put them together, and draw conclusions from them, leading in turn to still other new ideas. No animal has used tools or built fires; no animal can reflect and reason, thereby creating new ideas. But man has been endowed with this capacity.

Intuition. With his ability to intuit ideas, man has the ability to sense problems and solutions that relate to space, time, casaulity, all of which are the basic tools of the human mind.

Self-Determination. Animals may have determination—the mule comes to mind!—but they do not lay in their dens making and implementing plans. No mule ever laid in his stall planning to kill his master the next day. In contrast, man can lay plans for good or ill.

Moral Sense. The animal does not exhibit a moral sense. A person can say "I ought" or "I ought not," but no dog has ever returned a stolen bone with a guilty conscience!

Religious Ideas. Man has religious ideas or feelings whereby he can uniquely worship the one true and living God; animals do not exhibit ideas or feelings as to who God is.

Sense of Humor. People have a sense of humor, but do animals? Monkeys can be a delight to watch, but do they laugh at themselves? Man uniquely has such a sense, which reflects a complex use of ideas, remembrance, and application.

What conclusion can one draw from the above considerations? As already noted, in the religious Jewish point of view as well as in the Torah, man is depicted as linked to the animal world below him, but also linked to God above him. He has a body in common with the animals, designed to live in the same environment. But he also has a spirit that enables him to be God-conscious, a factor enabling him to transcend this world.

God's Purpose for Creating Man

This subject was partly treated under Judaism's view of man. Now we will take a closer look at the Torah in order to know God's point of view:

For God's Glory. God did not create man as a machine who could be commanded to love God, or ordered to be thankful. Rather, God created man so that each person on his or her own volition would praise and thank Him. In that way God is glorified, because such a response comes from a uniquely created being.

Thus the prince of the prophets spoke of

> everyone who belongs to me,
> whom I created for my glory,
> whom I formed—yes, whom I made! (Isaiah 43:7)

Note also in this connection:

> You are worthy, our Lord and God,
> to receive glory and honor and power,
> since you created all things,
> and because of your will they existed and were created!
> (Revelation 4:11)

Adam and Eve—and because of common grace, even man since the fall—were created to truly manifest God's glory. Isaiah experienced this same glory firsthand when he saw beyond the earthly temple and heard the voices of the seraphim:

> They called out to one another, "Holy, holy, holy is the LORD who commands armies! His majestic splendor fills the entire earth!" (Isaiah 6:3)

As the temple shook, filling with smoke, and as the prophet recognized his own need for cleansing, the glory of God manifested His true nature.

God's Glory in the Incarnate Messiah. In the incarnation, this same glory of God makes itself felt. As Yohanan declared:

> Now the Word became flesh and took up residence among us. We saw his glory—the glory of the one and only, full of grace and truth, who came from the Father. (Yohanan 1:14)

We may ask, when did this *shaliach*, Yohanan, actually see the Messiah's glory? For as long as Yeshua was in the days of His flesh, it was covered.

At the Mount of Transfiguration, however, he, Yaakov, and Kefa were together with Yeshua. The written record attempts to do justice to what actually happened:

> And he was transfigured before them. His face shone like the sun, and his clothes became white as light. (Mattai 17:2)

The glory of His divine nature that was hidden was allowed to shine through His skin, making it as luminous as the blinding light of the sun. Such a dazzling sight was awesome. Again we note that Adam and Eve, along with their descendants, were created to demonstrate this glory of God, for His image was and is in them.

His glory did not make the Messiah untouchable. As the disciples saw Him, they also saw the Father; the Messiah had a glory even as the Father did. Yeshua's ways of being gracious, acting in truth and love, in His relationship with others—all these were in actuality a manifestation of the Father's glory. Similarly, believers today, and to a certain extent all people, have the opportunity to demonstrate God's glory in tangibly touching the lives of people and society.

God's Glory in the Future. God's glory and graciousness is not confined to this world only. The promise for believers is

> . . . to demonstrate in the coming ages the surpassing wealth of his grace in kindness toward us in Messiah Yeshua. (Ephesians 2:7)

As believers, we will never cease to experience His glory, and more than only *experience* it, each one of us will also *manifest* that glory. For God will never cease to share with us His limitless riches of grace, love, and mercy. The promise to those who belong to Him in such a special way is:

> . . . —if so, then the Lord knows how to rescue the godly from their trials, and to reserve the unrighteous for punishment at the day of judgment, . . . (2 Kefa 2:9)

Man's Original Moral Nature by Creation

Considering again the initial endowment of our first parents, we find a number of interesting observations. From Genesis 2, we learn two things: first, that man must not be regarded as so perfect that he has already attained to moral and spiritual perfection; but on the other hand, neither should man's capacity to learn be regarded as too little to prevent any moral or spiritual progress.

We will now examine what the Word suggests concerning the original nature of Adam and Eve.

Man's Original Moral Nature Positively Good. The high estate of Adam and Eve is suggested, first of all, because they were created in the divine image:

> Then God said, "Let us make humankind in our image, after our likeness, so they may rule over the fish of the sea and the birds of the air, over the cattle, and over all the earth, and over all the creatures that move on the earth." (Genesis 1:26)

We need now to note:

The meaning of the terms. The expression *in our image* is in Hebrew *betsalmenu*, derived from the noun *tselem*. This noun is used for such things as images of tumors (or sores) and golden mice, of molten images, and of painted pictures of men:

> You should make images of the sores and images of the mice that are destroying the land. You should honor the God of Israel. Perhaps he will release his grip on you, your gods, and your land. . . .
>
> They put the ark of the LORD on the cart, along with the chest, the gold mice, and the images of the sores. (1 Samuel 6:5, 11)

> You must drive out all the inhabitants of the land before you. Destroy all their carved images, all their molten images, and demolish their high places. (Numbers 33:52)

> But she increased her prostitution. She saw men carved on the wall, images of the Chaldeans carved in bright red. (Ezekiel 23:14)

Thus, the idea of *tselem* appears to be that of semblance and similarity.

The phrase "in our likeness" is *kedemutenu*. The Hebrew verb *damah* and the related noun *demut*, from which the phrase derives, also carries with it (as does *tselem*) the idea of likeness, similitude, resemblance. Not much difference appears to exist between the two words. Both are used to convey the message that there is a similitude whereby man resembles his Creator in nature.

This image and likeness to God appears to give man his peculiar worth and dignity, in spite of the fact that after the events of Genesis 3, he is a fallen being. One might say that though man has a fallen nature, yet the fingerprints of God are on his soul.

Both a spiritual and a physical nature.

> Do not be afraid of those who kill the body but cannot kill the soul. Instead, fear the one who is able to destroy both soul and body in hell. (Mattai 10:28)

> You will not abandon me to Sheol;
> you will not allow your faithful follower [NIV: "Holy One"]
> to see the Pit. (Psalm 16:10)

David had a hope beyond this life. He would not be abandoned in Sheol, cut adrift. Nor would he, a holy and dedicated servant of God, be allowed to see corruption, as if he were just a "thing" with no hope for a future with God. His *body* did see corruption; but there is more to man than just his body. Note how Kefa took this passage in Psalms and applied it even further to Yeshua:

> David by foreseeing this spoke about the resurrection of the Messiah, that he was neither abandoned to Hades, nor did his body experience decay. (Acts 2:31)

Like David, Yeshua had an indestructible spirit, in this case His divine nature; but in contrast to David, Yeshua's body did not decay, which is to say, it was not in the grave for more than three days.

Spirit, soul, and body.

> Now may the God of peace himself make you completely holy and may your spirit and soul and body be kept entirely blameless at the coming of our Lord Yeshua the Messiah. (1 Thessalonians 5:23)

Does this verse imply that man has three distinct elements in his nature? Theologians are divided over this issue of whether man is a *trichotomy* (a three-part being), or a *dichotomy* (a two-part being, whereby man is comprised of a body and then of an immaterial part, which is his soul and spirit). We will not here pursue this discussion, but the curious reader can refer to other sources.

The "spirit" of man closest in likeness with God. A number of Scriptures point to this truth.

> The human spirit is like the lamp of the LORD,
> searching all his innermost parts. (Proverbs 20:27)[15]

> God is spirit, and the people who worship him must worship in spirit and truth. (Yohanan 4:24)

> The Spirit himself bears witness to our spirit that we are God's children. (Romans 8:16)

> For who among men knows the things of a man except the man's spirit within him? So too, no one knows the things of God except the Spirit of God. (1 Corinthians 2:11)

The soul of man. The Scripture tells us that in the creation of Adam:

> The LORD God formed the man from the soil of the ground and breathed into his nostrils the breath of life, and the man became a living being [or, soul; Hebrew *nefesh*]. (Genesis 2:7)

So, what God breathed into man, the breath of life, is comprised of soul and spirit.[16] But what exactly is the soul, as contrasted from the spirit that is evidently the part of man that makes him God-conscious?

After the death of the body, the soul and spirit return to God's presence, not as a part of God but as a separate entity. For the believer, the day will come when the soul and spirit will be united with a glorified body. Man was created to live in a body made alive by the presence of the soul.

Reproduction of children in man's own "image" and "likeness."

> When Adam had lived 130 years he fathered a son in his own likeness, according to his image, and he named him Seth. (Genesis 5:3)

The ability to do so is God-given. A man and his wife have it in their whole personalities, in the totality of their nature, to give their children this possibility.

This however raises the question as to the origin of the soul and/or spirit. Two major views have been suggested: *creationism*, whereby the parents produce the body while God provides the soul-spirit, or, *traducianism*, according to which the parents have the ability to procreate a total personality, body, soul, and spirit. We will not pursue this discussion any further, but the interested reader can consult other resources.

Pronounced by God as "very good."

> God saw all that he had made—and it was very good! There was evening, and there was morning, the sixth day. (Genesis 1:31)

The Wisdom Literature comments on Adam and Eve in this way:

> This alone have I discovered: God made humankind [Hebrew, *ha-adam*] upright,
> but they have sought many evil schemes. (Ecclesiastes 7:29)

In light of the pronouncement of "very good," we note that God treated man as a fully responsible moral being. A full discussion of this point will take place when considering the doctrine of sin, but we note for now that when God told Adam, and later Eve, not to eat of the tree of the knowledge of good and evil, He fully expected them to exercise their moral prerogative and make the choice to follow God's directives.

The Nature of Man's Original Goodness. Alva McClain's observations are quite helpful:[17]

Moral nature distinguished from moral character. *Nature* reflects an inherent ability, for example, the ability to do what is right; *character* reflects an acquired quality, for example, a good character. But this quality must be *acquired* by experience, that is, through making the right moral choices when tested.

Man did not acquire a holy character in the creation. In creation, man received a moral *nature*, which was holy. But he did not receive a holy *character*. This underscores the first point above: character can only be acquired through testing and immediately following creation, our first parents had not yet undergone any moral testing.

Man acquired a holy moral nature in creation. Through creation, man had the inherent ability to choose what is morally good, but free will unfortunately also allowed for man's *character* to choose what is evil. Some have called this the "damnable feature of the freedom of the will." We will discuss this further below.

While it is premature to discuss the full implications of what believers will experience in the Father's presence one day, we note that Adam began with only a moral nature. The redeemed in the Messiah receive a new holy *nature* through the new birth, and then in this life, go on to develop a holy *character* through a life of moral testing. In eternity, holy people will still be making choices, but the circumstances will be far different than at present. Then, believers will be delivered from the presence of sin and will no longer have to cope with their sin natures.

What then can we conclude concerning the great potential that man had in the beginning? As we will see, Judaism does not hold to the idea that man has a sin nature. Jewish tradition treats man as though he were in the same position as Adam, with the same potential. The exception is that it is recognized that the fall did bring about a curse in that people are affected by physical death. But in Judaism, man has the capacity to make good moral choices in the same way as Adam. He still has the moral nature that Adam had, and life on earth contains opportunities whereby a person can develop his character through testing, just as it was expected of Adam. To some extent, man still has that potential, which Judaism encourages, but as we have already noted, this is an altogether too optimistic view of man. Man also has a fatal flaw, which we will consider in the next chapter on the doctrine of sin.

THIRTEEN

The Doctrine of Sin

We have taken note of the image of God in man; the freedom he possesses to make choices; the primary beliefs that account for Judaism's optimism that man can, in fact, make the right choices. Attention must now be given to the basic reasons why man fails many times to achieve his goals. The procedure will be to first discuss the doctrine of sin within the Jewish understanding, and then proceed to considerations in the Written Torah and New Covenant.

The Rabbinic Perspective Concerning Sin

No Sin Nature in Rabbinic Judaism

The rabbis and rabbinic scholars never teach that man is innately evil. Nor do they accept the concept that man is forever beyond redemption based on self-effort. One of the major watersheds between Judaism and a biblical theology is the idea that man is innately evil; for the rabbis, man can never be regarded as tainted by an "original sin" inherited because Adam and Eve's wrong choice to eat of the tree of the knowledge of good and evil (Genesis 3).

The rabbis assert as part of the daily prayers, "My God, the soul which Thou hast placed in me is pure."[1] In contrast, believers affirm that man has a sin nature from which he cannot escape and that permeates every aspect of his being, thereby preventing him from doing anything good that will significantly aid in his redemption. But the rabbinical response to this affirmation is that "this doctrine represents not only a negation of religion but also a denial of the possibility of ethics."[2] Such a notion, it is said, conceives of man as chained in a prison from where he will never be released. In fact, this picture comes closest to actually describing man's lostness, but we will postpone discussion of the biblical diagnosis until later in this chapter as well as in a later chapter. Suffice it to say for now that Judaism insists that man is free, and that accordingly it is entirely possible for man to redeem himself as well as the society around him.

Selected Modern Jewish Statements on Sin

Judaism certainly has a keen sensitivity to specific acts of sin; there are some one hundred words in the Hebrew Scriptures that define and illustrate evil deeds. Both traditional as well as modern rabbis go to great lengths to show how a person can avoid misdeeds, live righteously, and contribute meaningfully to his or her society.

Friedländer suggested that in order to repent, one must remember what Solomon said about sin:

> For there is not one truly righteous person on the earth
> who continually does good and never sins. (Ecclesiastes 7:20)

and

> The time will come when your people will sin against you (for there is no one who is sinless!) and you will be angry with them and deliver them over to their enemies, who will take them as prisoners to their own land, whether far away or close by. (1 Kings 8:46)

Friedländer also stated that when confession of sin is made, "if it is against God alone that we have sinned, we make silent confession before Him; if we find ourselves guilty of an offence against our fellow-man, we must confess our sin to him."[3]

Solomon Schechter stated that sin is present when one follows his evil inclination (a concept we will discuss) whereby he makes wrong moral choices; in themselves, however, he added, these natural passions are neither good nor bad but "become evil by the improper use man makes of them."[4]

Morris Joseph spoke of sin as that which degrades a person: "It is possible to tell a lie without its entailing any harm save the moral degradation of him who utters it,"[5] and also, "Sin is to be shunned because of the discord it makes between man and God—in other words, because of the degradation in which it involves the sinner; . . ."[6]

Kaufmann Kohler talked about sin as "a straying from the path of God, an offense against the divine order of holiness,"[7] and so sin is therefore an offense against God's holiness and majesty.

Leo Baeck described sin in the sense that "every evil deed is a sin against God and thereby against the element of freedom granted to human life,"[8] where sin is really the failure by man to understand how *God feels about it*.

No matter which Jewish thinker is cited, however, none will admit such a doctrine as "original sin," whereby man is morally depraved. Sin is considered rather to be *acts* of wrongdoing, either against man or God. To admit that somehow man has a *nature* tainted by sin will (according to Jewish thinkers) somehow keep a person from exercising his or her moral choices in a context of following a complete freedom of will.

An Interesting Psychology

***Yetser Hatov* and *Yetser Hara*.** With the development of the Oral Law and later expansions of the *halakhah* (legal traditions), religious Judaism spoke of the presence of two "impulses" or "inclinations" in man: *yetser hatov* (the good inclination), and *yetser hara* (the evil inclination). The word *yetser* appears in a conversation David had with his son Solomon, in which God is described as aware of what is present in every heart. God, it is said, understands every "motive (*yetser*) of one's thoughts" (1 Chronicles 28:9). It was Schechter's opinion that this *yetser* refers to imagination, or the inclination that leads a person to rebellion against God.[9] Quite possibly, the concept can refer to the moral decisions that a person makes in the daily round of life. The evil inclination, and its opposite, were concepts already in place by the end of the first century,[10] and it was thought that the *yetser hara* is present from birth (cf. San.91b) while the *yetser hatov*, the good inclination, begins to function only at the age of *bar mitzvah* (cf. *Avot de Rav Natan* 16:2; *Ecclesiastes Rabba* 4.13.1).

These inclinations must not be understood in the biblical sense of the two natures within the genuine believer, namely, the sin nature (which lies in the very being of a person and which he or she cannot escape) and the new life (which God imparts only through the atonement experience). Judaism in contrast regards man's nature as somehow plastic and with the ability to be molded by the various kinds of moral decisions man makes between the good and evil inclinations in the daily round of life.

***Yetser Hara* and the Biblical Sin Nature.** Several in the Messianic community have maintained that the Jewish concept of *yetser hara* is the same as the biblical idea of the sin nature of man.

In the discussion by Joseph Shulam and Hilary Le Cornu in their very helpful book on Romans, they seem to imply that in Romans 7, an equivalence exists between the *yetser hara* and the sin nature:[11]

> In dying to his evil inclination, a person also dies to the regulations which govern it in the Torah.[12]
>
> He is either "bound," in the "oldness of the letter," to serve his evil inclination ("that by which we were bound"), or he is "freed" from his inclination to serve his Creator.[13]
>
> Before his bar mitzvah he is "free of" (from) the commandments and exempt from their penalties. Once he enters into God's covenant, however, he loses his independence and must either die to sin by putting his evil inclination to death or accept the wages of sin which are death (cf. 6.23).[14]

The Biblical Perspective Concerning Sin

Before we discuss how one attains forgiveness of sin in both Judaism and in the Written Torah and New Covenant, we need to consider sin from a biblical viewpoint. Is man today the same as Adam and Eve, as they came from creation by God's hands? Even though Judaism's optimism concerning man can be a corrective to some preaching in evangelical circles, can it afford to be as optimistic as various Jewish thinkers claim? Only a close look at what happened to Adam and Eve can reveal a dimension to humanity that pursues us to this very day, betraying a troubling quirk in man's nature.

The Moral Testing of Man

The testing of man consisted of two dynamics: First, God had provided an advance descriptive warning to Adam and Eve not to eat of a certain tree in the garden. If they did, they would surely die (Genesis 2:17). Second, Adam and Eve were exposed to temptation by an evil spirit, Satan (Genesis 3:1). We will now explore these two dynamics more fully in accordance with the written text of the Word.

The "Tree of the Knowledge of Good and Evil." In considering the nature of the "tree of the knowledge of good and evil," the context of Genesis 2:17 would demand that God had in mind a literal tree:

> But you must not eat from the tree of the knowledge of good and evil, for when you eat from it you will surely die. (Genesis 2:17)

The language does not suggest something exotic or magical, even though many sagas that trace the origins of the human race contain some story of a tree, a serpent, a garden, etc. The task here is not to explore all these stories and myths but to glean one truth: a common thread appears in all these stories that verifies to some extent the biblical account. In the biblical testimony, it would appear that this particular tree was one of the trees of the garden.

Neither do the Scriptures signify that something is actually present in the fruit itself, so that by eating it, death would ensue. Rather:

> Then the eyes of both of them opened, and they knew they were naked; so they sewed fig leaves together and made coverings for themselves. (Genesis 3:7)

The act of disobedience by both Eve and Adam, and not the fruit itself, was the source of ruin and destruction. The tree was just an ordinary tree with a particular kind of fruit, not necessarily an apple. But the tree was the means that God used to test Adam and Eve in their moral choices.

"Knowledge" of Good and Evil Prior to Eating of the Tree. Another vital question regarding the account is whether the man or the woman had any "knowledge" of good and evil prior to their eating from it. The text does suggest that two kinds of moral knowledge existed. First, there was *descriptive knowledge*, meaning that one hears or reads of certain basic facts that will help him or her avoid making the wrong moral choices. In the case of Adam and Eve, the test was to face up to the moral decision and decide *not* to eat, as God had commanded and desired for their sakes.

Second, there was *experiential knowledge*. As far as this tree was concerned, God's desire was that Adam and Eve choose *not* to eat; in that way, they would learn through experiential knowledge something positive about moral and spiritual choices. But instead, our first parents chose instead to go ahead and eat of that tree, and thus they learned the hard way what it meant to make the wrong moral choice. It also meant that the entire human race suffered as a consequence of this first moral test.

But didn't man have both kinds of knowledge? The answer was, as far as Adam and Eve were concerned, no. They had only *descriptive* knowledge. God told them what to do and what the consequences would be if they did not obey. All our first parents had to do was make the moral decision *not* to eat and their eyes would be opened; then they would be like God, because of their moral choices, but in a positive sense.

The Possibility of Adam and Eve Receiving Experiential Knowledge in a Positive Way. Was it possible for man to receive experiential knowledge if he had *not* sinned? The answer: Of course! If man had made the right decision, which was not to eat, he would have acquired moral and spiritual experiential knowledge, but in a legitimate sense. The ability to live with the advanced descriptive knowledge and make the decision God wanted would have revealed a commendable moral character.

Instead, Adam and Eve entered into the realm of moral experience through the wrong door, and so God commented:

> And the LORD God said, "Now that the man has become like one of us, knowing good and evil, he must not be allowed to stretch out his hand and take also from the tree of life and eat, and live forever." (Genesis 3:22)

"Like one of us"—not that God is a sinner as is man! No, but man did *exercise a moral choice* as God does; unfortunately, it was the wrong choice.

God's Purpose in Testing Man. Several observations can be made:

First, Adam and Eve were created with a holy nature but also with a free will by which to make their choices.

Second, as we saw above, our first parents were tested in order that through the right moral choices, they would have opportunity to develop a holy character. Holiness is achieved through the making of right choices.

Third, this is still God's method today of producing a holy character in believers as they face moral and spiritual testing, either under the best of circumstances, or the most painful of them:

> Now all discipline seems painful at the time, not joyful. But later it produces the fruit of peace and righteousness for those trained by it. (Hebrews 12:11)

> Happy is the one who endures testing, because when he has proven to be genuine, he will receive the crown of life that God promised to those who love him. (Yaakov 1:12)

and

> This brings you great joy, although you may have to suffer for a short time in various trials. Such trials show the proven character of your faith, which is much more valuable than gold—gold that is tested by fire, even though it is passing away—and will bring praise and glory and honor when Yeshua the Messiah is revealed. (1 Kefa 1:6–7)

The lesson we learn when we make wrong moral choices is that no shortcut exists by which we gain the moral character God covets for us. We must make the right choices if we are to mature and develop a holy character. Some ask, could Adam and Eve have resisted Satan successfully, and if so, what would have resulted? What we can say is that they had everything they needed to make the right choice; had they done so, they would have matured and grown. Then the next choice would have been a little easier, good habits would have been established, and most important of all, their holy character would have been confirmed.

Nature of the Temptation

The Identity of the Tempter. In the beginning of the account of Eve's temptation, she is approached by a snake:

> Now the serpent was more shrewd than any of the wild animals that the LORD God had made. He said to the woman, "Is it really true that God said, 'You must not eat from any tree of the orchard'?" (Genesis 3:1)

But nowhere in the Tanach do we find the suggestion that HaSatan (the opposer of God) stood behind the serpent. The first theologizing about this took place in the *sifrim hisonim*.[15] Later on, the rabbinical writings also mention that Satan was the real personality behind this snake. In the New Covenant, a positive identification is made, first by Yeshua as He spoke with some of the religious leaders, identifying Satan as "a murderer from the beginning . . . he is a liar and the father of lies" (Yohanan 8:44), and then by Yohanan who made a positive identification: "So that huge dragon—the ancient serpent, the one called the devil and Satan, who deceives the whole world—was thrown down to the earth, and his angels along with him" (Revelation 12:9). The story is not implausible: Is this some figure who belongs to another world, one we cannot see with the naked eye? But this other nonspatial world is just as real as the one in which we live.

It seems that the naive innocence of the woman is the proof in itself of the validity of the account. Based on the present-day level of communication, experience tells us that snakes do not speak a human language, although it is quite possible some communication did exist in the garden. But Eve had no experience with Satan, much less with such a person using the vocal chords of the snake by which to communicate. But Satan knew how to get Eve's attention, using the snake whose skin was beautiful and who also was crafty.

The Method of the Tempter. The tempter had a well-planned strategy by which he tricked Eve.

Suggesting a doubt. Satan cleverly raised a question as to whether any restriction was placed on any fruit from the trees in the garden:

> Now the serpent was more shrewd than any of the wild animals that the LORD God had made. He said to the woman, "Is it really true that God said, 'You must not eat from any tree of the orchard'?" (Genesis 3:1)

Denying God's truth. Eve responded that they were free to eat of any tree in the garden except one in particular, the tree of the knowledge of good and evil. Then, Satan boldly denied the truth of God:

> The serpent said to the woman, "Surely you will not die." (Genesis 3:4)

Obviously, this statement was a total contradiction to what God had said in His descriptive knowledge (Genesis 2:17—". . . but you must not eat from the tree of the knowledge of good and evil, for when you eat from it you will surely die"). But Satan wanted to plant a seed of doubt in Eve's mind.

Using a half truth. Satan's next tactic was to use a half truth and insinuate something God had not mentioned before, as if He had held out some vital information that should have been shared with Adam and Eve:

> For God knows that when you eat of it your eyes will be opened, and you will be like God, knowing good and evil. (Genesis 3:5 NIV)

Satan was clever; he did not leave his temptation hanging on an outright lie because Eve had already answered him with the truth. But what Satan said in addition was true, although Eve had no knowledge of that. When Satan described what would happen when Adam and Eve would make the choice, he was suggesting they would be exercising their moral choice, and yet, in a way God had not wanted. All Eve knew was that God had not mentioned such a consequence of eating of the tree.

Promising personal benefit from disobedience. Consider again the verse we have just looked at:

> For God knows that when you eat of it your eyes will be opened, and you will be like God, knowing good and evil. (Genesis 3:5 NIV)

God seemingly had not promised such benefits—yet the statement was certainly true. Satan must have had some knowledge of what would happen if Adam and Eve had remained true to the descriptive knowledge God had provided. But now the Enemy wanted to bring ruin on our first parents. Yes, their eyes would be opened, and they would know good and evil as they exercised their moral choice, but the end result would be to bring destruction on the human race. They would learn through experiential knowledge the error of their ways.

One needs to be well aware of how Satan operated then and how he functions in the same way today. All false religions hold out this hope: You will not die; you will be like the gods!

The Avenues of Temptation. The account of the temptation should also make us wary of how Satan uses the various areas of temptation through three major appetites:

> When the woman saw that the tree produced fruit that was good for food, was attractive to the eye, and was desirable for making one wise, she took some of its fruit and ate it. She also gave some of it to her husband who was with her, and he ate it. (Genesis 3:6)

First, Eve saw that the fruit was "good for food," which was an appeal through a *physically felt need*. Second, she also saw that the fruit of this tree was "attractive to the eye," which was certainly a strong appeal to her sense of *a most desirable aesthetic*; the fruit was exquisitely beautiful and the more she looked at it, the more she desired it. Third, Eve saw as well that the fruit appeared "desirable for making one wise," which reflected the appeal that would cater to her felt need for *intellectual stimulation*.

Should we therefore conclude that these three felt needs that every human being has are evil in themselves? Not at all! Under the guidance of the Holy Spirit, each of the three can be put to good use. But when Satan works in these areas, he means us harm as we yield to his will.

These are the three avenues Satan uses, sometimes only one, sometimes a combination of two, and at times, all three. In the temptation of Yeshua, Satan again used all three avenues (Mattai 4:1–10). We are also warned against the misuse by these three avenues, the same ones that Satan had used with Eve:

> . . . because all that is in the world (the desire of the flesh and the desire of the eyes and the arrogance produced by material possessions) is not from the Father, but is from the world. (1 Yohanan 2:16)

In the case of Adam and Eve, their sin came in taking the wrong way to satisfy normal appetites and in forgetting the descriptive knowledge God had given them. Subsequent to the garden experience, Satan uses the same three avenues in most religions of the world in one way or another to attract people to a false worship.

The Fall of Man

Once again, note the Scripture passages involved in this discussion:

> Then the LORD God commanded the man, "You may freely eat fruit from every tree of the orchard, but you must not eat from the tree of the knowledge of good and evil, for when you eat from it you will surely die." (Genesis 2:16–17)

> Now the serpent was more shrewd than any of the wild animals that the LORD God had made. He said to the woman, "Is it really true that God said, 'You must not eat from any tree of the orchard'?" The

> woman said to the serpent, "We may eat of the fruit from the trees of the orchard; but concerning the fruit of the tree that is in the middle of the orchard God said, 'You must not eat from it, and you must not touch it, or else you will die.'" The serpent said to the woman, "Surely you will not die, for God knows that when you eat from it your eyes will open and you will be like divine beings [NIV and NASB: "God"; KJV: "gods"] who know good and evil."
>
> When the woman saw that the tree produced fruit that was good for food, was attractive to the eye, and was desirable for making one wise, she took some of its fruit and ate it. She also gave some of it to her husband who was with her, and he ate it. (Genesis 3:1–6)

Two possible decisions were open to Adam and Eve in the temptation, as we have seen: Either to recognize what God had said in His descriptive knowledge and act on it (Genesis 2:17) so that it would lead to the ultimate good for man; or else to claim that right for *self*, with a result that could only lead to disaster. It had to be one way or another.

Their failure consisted of two acts: First, an act of the will independent of God. Failure derived from an *inward act of the will* independent of God's desires. Such a decision reflected the essence of sin, beginning in the inward parts of a person; and second, also present was the *outward act of disobedience*. Man acted out his decision to sin. He had become like God, entering into the realm of moral experience through his moral decision, and chose by his outward act to eat of the forbidden tree. He used the prerogative of deity, not to follow what God desired but to imagine that he had the right to decide the laws of his own conduct by eating of the fruit of the tree.

Assignment of Responsibility to Both Adam and Eve. The woman was deceived by her own actions, and she led in the transgression. She stepped out of her bounds in her given role as the wife. One could also say that Eve did not have the experience of speaking with the animals as did Adam (although the biblical text is silent on this issue). But Adam did somehow communicate with the animals, though not in the way Eve conversed with the serpent (Satan). She was therefore misled, but she was still responsible for her wrong choice. The man was not *deceived*; he was *persuaded* to follow in the transgression:

> But to Adam he said,
> "Because you obeyed your wife
> and ate from the tree about which I commanded you,
> 'You must not eat from it,'
> cursed is the ground thanks to you;
> in painful toil you will eat of it all the days of your life." (Genesis 3:17)

Sha'ul also commented on what Eve had done and how similar consequences can also happen today:

> But I am afraid that just as the serpent deceived Eve by his treachery, your minds may be led astray from a sincere and pure devotion to Messiah. (2 Corinthians 11:3)

The Problem of How Adam and Eve Could Fall. Many have raised the question as to how Adam and Eve, created innocent and sacred beings, could fall as they did. There is no one complete and satisfactory explanation. One wonders if God could have created Adam and Eve so that it would have been impossible for them to make the wrong choice. But this option removes altogether the possibility of the freedom of the will. Adam and Eve were not computers, programmed to act in a prearranged manner; if such were the case, what would be the point of a moral test so that the first man and woman could develop a moral character through moral testing?

In the very nature of the freedom of the will, man can either make good choices to follow God's directives, or else to go against what God desires. One might say once more: this is the "damnable feature of the free will," where man acts as God and decides to do what (he thinks) is best for him, even if it is contrary to God's wishes. And yet, at the same time, one cannot charge God with evil when Adam and Eve made the wrong moral choices.

The Sin Nature. Ever since the fall, man now has a sin nature (a topic to be discussed below). In the attempt to understand this condition, Yaakov provided some helpful insight:

> Let no one say when he is tempted, "I am tempted by God," for God cannot be tempted by evil, and he himself tempts no one. But each one is tempted when he is lured and enticed by his own desires. Then when desire conceives, it gives birth to sin, and when sin is full grown, it gives birth to death. Do not be led astray, my dear brothers and sisters. All generous giving and every perfect gift is from above, coming down from the Father of lights, with whom there is no variation or the slightest hint of change. (Yaakov 1:13–17)

Several things can be observed. First, in this context, the desire is evil; but desire by itself can be either good or evil. When the natural appetite draws a person out of God's will, then it leads to sin. Second, a person "is lured [NIV: 'dragged away']" instead of controlling what entices him or her. Third, "sin" is the progeny of enticement in control. And fourth, "death" is the progeny of sin.

The Immediate Consequences of the Fall

For the serpent. God declared:

> The LORD God said to the serpent,
> "Because you have done this,
> cursed are you above all the wild beasts
> and all the living creatures of the field!
> On your belly you will crawl
> and dust you will eat all the days of your life." (Genesis 3:14)

In this judgment God issued, we are probably to understand that the serpent and all its offspring would have a different form of movement than what had been the case in the garden. Note also that this change in locomotion does not change in the Messianic kingdom: "a snake's food will be dirt" (Isaiah 65:25).

For the seed of the serpent. Judgment is also passed on the seed of the serpent:

And I will put hostility between you and the woman
and between your offspring and her offspring;
her offspring will attack your head,
and you will attack her offspring's heel. (Genesis 3:15)

This writer takes the judgment of enmity to mean that little love exists between snakes and people. It may be alright to view snakes confined to safe areas in the zoo, but not too many would like to wake one morning and find a snake in his or her bedroom and then proceed to love it as a pet! At this level, this is still a literal interpretation.

It will not be the intent of this writer to enter into a full discussion of this passage. It does, however, end by informing the reader that, ultimately, the symbolic seed of the serpent, Satan (today the leader of all unbelievers), will suffer a fatal blow on the head, while the symbolic seed of the woman (today the head of all believers) will undergo a bruise on the heel, but it will not be fatal. The point is that when the Messiah took the sins of mankind upon Him on the tree, He destroyed the power of Satan "who holds the power of death" (Hebrews 2:14).

For the woman.

To the woman he said,
"I will greatly increase your labor pains;
with pain you will give birth to children.
You will want to control your husband,
but he will dominate you." (Genesis 3:16)

The woman and her offspring will suffer pains in bearing children as well as a new relationship with her husband. The new relationship does *not* mean that the woman is to be degraded or beaten. (Compare the NIV translation, "he will rule over you," rather than NET's "dominate." NASB has, "your desire shall be for your husband.") Rather, she is a valued contributor to the decision making in the home—although after the decision has been agreed on, the husband then takes the responsibility for it. Nor from today's point of view does it mean that the wife cannot work outside of the home to be a teacher, nurse, businesswoman, administrator, and so on. But when she enters the home, a definite headship does exists between her and her husband.

For the man. As far as the man is concerned, the physical environment will now be more hostile and man will be engaged in laborious toil:

> But to Adam he said,
> "Because you obeyed your wife
> and ate from the tree about which I commanded you,
> 'You must not eat from it,'
> cursed is the ground thanks to you;
> in painful toil you will eat of it all the days of your life.
> It will produce thorns and thistles for you,
> but you will eat the grain of the field.
> By the sweat of your brow you will eat food
> until you return to the ground,
> for out of it you were taken;
> for you are dust, and to dust you will return." (Genesis 3:17–19)

But the judgment had far more drastic consequences than weeds growing in the gardens and in the ground of the fields. As a result of God's pronouncement, an entire imbalance in nature has resulted with the presence of diseases that will attack all life, human, animal, and plant, as well as the violence of earthquakes, tornados, typhoons, etc. The genes of all living beings have also been affected, whereby diseases will be passed from generation to the next. All of these defects represent a judgment, known as the "curse on nature"; in other words, everywhere one goes on this earth, the presence of physical evil will be present, and it will not be lifted until the onset of the Messianic kingdom when the Messiah comes to rule on this earth.

For both man and woman. One tragic outcome of disobedience by Adam and Eve was physical death:

> But you must not eat from the tree of the knowledge of good and evil, for when you eat from it you will surely die. (Genesis 2:17)

The message was reinforced in the pronouncement of judgment:

> By the sweat of your brow you will eat food
> until you return to the ground,
> for out of it you were taken;
> for you are dust, and to dust you will return. (Genesis 3:19)

With this, religious Judaism agrees wholeheartedly, asserting that the real consequence of the fall is the presence of physical death among all creatures.

Every time a pet animal dies, we are reminded of the tragic circumstance of the legacy of the fall. Every time a funeral occurs and a loved one is placed in the ground, and tears are shed because of the aching loss of separation, we are to remember the dreadful pronouncement by God on Adam and Eve. Even believers do not escape this time of grief; but for them it is tempered because the separation is only temporary; one day, all believers will be reunited on a more joyous occasion in the presence of God and His Messiah.

A judgment beyond only physical death. Does the biblical text concerning judgment on both the man and woman suggest anything more than just physical death? As we carefully consider the Written Torah, we find more than a hint that the answer is yes. One of the most drastic judgments was the exclusion of both Adam and Eve from the garden and, specifically, preventing them for the possibility in any way of partaking from the tree of life:

> And the LORD God said, "Now that the man has become like one of us, knowing good and evil, he must not be allowed to stretch out his hand and take also from the tree of life and eat, and live forever." (Genesis 3:22)

Without question this word also included Eve as well as Adam.

But what is this tree of life? When considering the fruit of the tree of the knowledge of good and evil, did the fruit in and of itself in some way provide knowledge? We have already given a negative answer.

The same question can be raised with regard to the tree of life. Was it possible that the fruit from this tree, in and of itself, could actually produce life? No doubt God could have provided such food, but we cannot speculate. The point of excluding them from this tree, however, was to make sure that Adam and Eve (and all their descendants, as we shall see) understood that eating of the tree of life in a sinful state, with no possibility of atonement, would be a disaster.

The clue then that Adam and Eve suffered far more than physical death is this: something had happened to man's inner being. A barrier now existed between him and God, as illustrated when Adam and Eve ran away when God called for them in the garden—as their descendants still do:

> Then the man and his wife heard the sound of the LORD God moving about in the orchard at the breezy time of the day, and they hid from the LORD God among the trees of the orchard. (Genesis 3:8)

The point is that our first parents had something drastically wrong with them on the inside; the fall brought about a condition in Adam and Eve called "spiritual death." Note, however, that God's mercy was extended to them by means of excluding them from the tree of life: man must not eat of the tree of life with his changed nature, with the result that he would be immortal in a body already suffering the effects of moral and physical evil. In addition, even though Adam and Even could no longer remain in the garden, God did not abandon them.

Another hint from the text that something more than physical death had occurred is the statement:

> The LORD God made garments from skin for Adam and his wife, and clothed them. (Genesis 3:21)

Some expositors describe how God had to kill animals as sacrifices in order to cover the sin of Adam and Eve, but no case can be made for this concept from the Hebrew word *labash* ("clothed"). This particular word for "covering" has the word picture of adorning, or clothing, oneself with various kinds of beautiful clothes. All that is being said in context is that God took away the flimsy fig leaves and instead gave Adam and Eve proper furs or suitable clothing with which to adorn themselves.

However, the text still leaves us with the question: Where did God obtain these garments of skin, or furs? The only possibility was that God had to take the life of some animal or animals, pointing thereby to the strong hint of the origin of sacrifices to God, and its lessons regarding substitute atonement. While nothing is said explicitly in the text regarding such a suggestion, yet if Abel knew something about sacrifices that had to be offered to God (Genesis 4:4), where had he obtained such information? It could only have been from his father and mother who had some idea already of atonement, or, the necessity for a covering (from the verb *kafar*) for sin. But that would already imply such a necessity for Adam and Eve because of their sin nature.

Much more could be said concerning spiritual death brought about because of the fall, but this information is gleaned from the progressive unfolding of the Scriptures, in the Torah of Moses, the Prophets, the Writings, and finally the New Covenant. We can only conclude regarding the advanced descriptive knowledge provided to Adam and Eve that implied in the warning was a twofold description of what this death was about: *both* physical and spiritual death.

Results of the Fall on the Human Race

There is much controversy as to the consequences of the fall. The best procedure is to allow those Scriptures to speak that point unmistakably to the fact that *something is basically wrong* in man's inner being.

The Teaching of the Tanach on the Sin Nature. While many passages might seem suitable to use to demonstrate the presence of the sin nature in man, Jewish scholars also use these very passages to demonstrate that man has a *yetser hara*, whereby he makes his moral choices but which does not reflect a so-called sin nature.

Unintentional sin. In reply to this viewpoint of Jewish scholars, the first passage for consideration is Moses' statement introducing the sin offering in the Mosaic Covenant:

> Tell the Israelites, "When a person sins by straying unintentionally from any of the LORD's commandments which must not be violated, and violates any one of them— . . ." (Leviticus 4:2)

The word "unintentionally" is in Hebrew *bishgagah*. Moses' choice of this word served as a reminder that this type of sin is not one of *commission*, where a person knows what he must not do. An example of a sin of commission would be when a person steals, knowing that "You shall not steal" (Exodus 20:15). Neither is it an intentional sin of *omission*, where a person knows what he must do but fails to do it, such as described by Yaakov:

> For if someone merely listens to the message and does not live it out, he is like someone who gazes at his own face in a mirror. For he gazes at himself and then goes out and immediately forgets what sort of person he was. (Yaakov 1:23–24)

To sin unintentionally, or in ignorance, points to a quirk in man's nature that is drastically wrong. This cannot be explained away on the basis of the *yetser hara* because unintentional sins show that the person is not even aware of the sin. Can a person sin and not know it? In our quieter moments, we all have to admit that the answer is yes. Many have experienced a moment of horror when someone has confronted us and reminded us of a wrong decision or action we have made whereby we have hurt people—yet we were not even aware of it. Such incidents may happen more than we would care to admit.

Therefore, at the very beginning of describing the sin offering, Moses pointed out that it was for the atonement of the quirk found in every person, a condition in man that can drive him to commit sin where he does not know of it. This condition is known in theological terms as the *sin nature*, the legacy passed down from the fall of Adam and Eve. At the very beginning of our worship of the Lord God, we must be reminded of who we are in our very nature, and seek atonement for it.

Circumcision of the heart. A second passage is the further instruction Moses provides in his call for Israel to walk before their God:

> Now, Israel, what does the LORD your God require of you except to revere him, to obey all his commandments, to love him, to serve him with all your mind and being, and to keep the LORD's commandments

> and statutes that I am giving you today for your own good? (Deuteronomy 10:12–13)

But how was Israel to follow these instructions—especially in view of what had already happened with the first generation that went out of Egypt? Jewish scholars would say that erring people had followed their *yetser hara*, thereby making the wrong moral choices. While these choices were in many cases certainly deplorable, Moses' guidelines for godly living called for a solution to solve an even deeper problem.

Our teacher Moses suggested a drastic action, the only action, that would make it possible to live a godly lifestyle:

> Circumcise your hearts, therefore, and do not be stiff-necked any longer. (Deuteronomy 10:16 NIV)

His mention of the heart shows that man's problem is far more serious than choosing the right inclination. Rather, Moses' challenge was for a complete change in man's nature, a radical alteration in the inner being. In other words, a substitute atonement was necessary to deal with the presence of this sin nature. The heart had to be changed; but this could only be accomplished by other means than by a man's exercise of his *yetser hatov*.

Let us turn to the time of Jeremiah. In his day, the people had all but abandoned the Torah; they had become rebellious before God and His prophet. Had the Lord not intervened on a number of occasions, Jeremiah would have died for the faith. The prophet, using the same words as Moses, also challenged his generation:

> Circumcise yourselves to the LORD, circumcise your hearts, you men of Judah and people of Jerusalem, or my wrath will break out and burn like fire because of the evil you have done—burn with no one to quench it. (Jeremiah 4:4 NIV)

The word "heart," as with Moses, is crucial in understanding what is really wrong with man's nature. This was far more than just a problem with the *yetser hara*.

Jeremiah also makes a profound statement that goes to the very root of the question:

> The human mind is more deceitful than anything else.
> It is incurably bad. Who can understand it? (Jeremiah 17:9)

The word "deceitful" is *aqob*, from the verb *aqeb*, a verb meaning *to be cunning, to take insidious advantage of*. Furthermore, the heart is said to be "beyond cure," *anush* from *nush*, meaning *dangerously sick, incurable*. In other words, nothing can be done by human effort to restore the human heart to what Adam once had before the fall. The heart has been wounded by the sin nature; it is corrupt and depraved. Such a pronouncement is not pleasant to hear; clearly, Jeremiah has gone far beyond the idea of a *yetser hara*. If any change is going to occur, God must accomplish it. He alone can break the chains that hold the heart to its nature that resulted from the fall. This God accomplishes through the principles associated with the sin offering, as we will see under the doctrine of atonement.

Removing the heart of stone. Ezekiel also gives a clue as to what God will yet do to a generation of Israelites who will acknowledge Him:

> I will give you a new heart, and I will put a new spirit within you. I will remove the heart of stone from your body and give you a heart of flesh. I will put my Spirit within you; I will take the initiative and you will obey my statutes and carefully observe my regulations. (Ezekiel 36:26–27)

Ezekiel's analysis of the human heart is that it is stone; that there is something basically and intrinsically wrong with the heart of man. Through the process of rebirth, even in the days of the Tanach, God has preserved a remnant in every generation, those who know they need a change of heart through the work of the Holy Spirit.

The teaching of the Tanach on this subject is epitomized in the statement that it is not merely by choosing what is good, following the *yetser hatov*, that makes a difference in the nature of a person. Rather, he or she needs a radical change of inner being that God alone can provide. This writer would also respectfully suggest that Ezekiel shows that radical change was the only basis by which the people of Judah could find an atonement for their sins. Each one among the remnant of Ezekiel's day had to appropriate this message for himself or herself and ask God for a changed heart.

So central was Ezekiel's message that it became the basis for Sha'ul's theology of sin and justification in the New Covenant, particularly Sha'ul's explanation of what was basically wrong with a human being in sin, and how one can find deliverance from it.

The sin nature carried from generation to generation. One more emphasis from the Tanach that relates directly to this issue is a declaration by David:

> Look, I was guilty of sin from birth,
> a sinner the moment my mother conceived me. (Psalm 51:5)

In confessing his double sin of adultery and murder, in the incident of Bat Sheva and her husband, David was not simply speaking of exercising his *yetser hara*; rather, he stated without any equivocation what is wrong with man's very nature. Yes, he made the decision of wanting Bat Sheva, a terrible choice; but already lurking behind the issue of choice was a fallen nature responsible for his choices. He did not fault his mother; nothing was wrong with her; she did nothing deplorable. Yet through his parents, he received his fallen nature. In other words, one generation passes on this sin nature to the next one; no one is exempt. The only remedy is God's prescribed provision in the sin offering, as already noted.

Many other passages could be explored, but the main ones have been considered. Yes, man has freedom to make choices, and yes, he *can* make good ones. But we are again confronted with the fact that no amount of good choices will satisfy God's requirements of ultimate righteousness. Man has a sin nature for which he is responsible, but only faith in what God has provided will care for it.

The Results of the Fall According to Sha'ul. As this *shaliach* made his pronouncements concerning the fall, he selected Ezekiel as the basis for his theology of sin:

> So then, just as sin entered the world through one man and death through sin, and so death spread to all people because all sinned— . . . (Romans 5:12)

> For just as through the disobedience of the one man many were made sinners, so also through the obedience of one man many will be made righteous. (Romans 5:19)

In the first passage, Sha'ul emphasized how one effect of the fall was spiritual death resulting from man's sin nature, not just from the *yetser hara*. The question can be raised here as to whether Yeshua died to pay the penalty of sin caused by the *yetser hara*, or whether His death was because of our sin nature in order that we can be made righteous.

In the second verse, we all were present in a sense in our first parents, when Adam and Eve made their choices. But Sha'ul was not referring to the choice for and the act of sin, but to the fact that mankind has something far deeper in his or her nature that eventually *leads to* making the wrong choices. People cannot be held directly answerable for their sin nature, but each one is surely responsible for the deeds that come as a result of this nature.

Sha'ul also stated that the fall brought *condemnation* on all men:

> And the gift is not like the one who sinned. For judgment, resulting from the one transgression, led to condemnation, but the gracious gift from the many failures led to justification. (Romans 5:16)

This condemnation came about through the sin of Adam and Eve. But it did not stop just there:

> Consequently, just as condemnation for all people came through one transgression, so too through the one righteous act came righteousness leading to life for all people. (Romans 5:18)

The tragedy of the fall brought a condemnation in which spiritual death was passed on to all men.

We will not note three factors in Sha'ul's theology that we find in Romans 5:12–19. Speaking as a Messianic Jew, he explained what happened to the human race:

Sin by inheritance. We considered above the statement by David describing how the sin nature of his parents was passed on to him. From that pronouncement, we learn that every generation living on this earth carries with it a legacy inherited by the immediately previous generation.

Condemnation by imputation.

Spiritual death is compounded. This issue is compounded because of *inheritance* and *imputation*. The result is clearly seen because of the unity of Adam to the rest of the human race. As we saw, all who follow Adam and Eve are in their image; what affected them also affected the souls and spirits of all who succeeded them. What happened to our first parents brought about spiritual and physical death to all their descendants.

The opposite side of the picture is seen in what the Messiah accomplished through His death. Since He too became a human being through the incarnation, there is a unity of the Messiah and the human race—although He is without sin. Yeshua became the new head of a new body, His own body. There exists now a unity between the Messiah and all believers in this body. Everyone who comes to faith in this Messiah now has an imputed righteousness.

Extent of Sin

Having discussed a number of aspects of the sin nature and the acts that follow from it, we now turn to consider the extent of sin. In considering sin's extent, we will restrict our discussion to only what is relevant regarding the human race. In particular, we will look at passages that point out the ever-present sin nature in man as well as the deeds that follow as a result of that nature.

A Universal Experience. The writers of the Tanach regarded sin as a universal experience among people. A few passages follow:

> The time will come when your people will sin against you (for there is no one who is sinless!) and you will be angry with them and deliver them over to their enemies, who will take them as prisoners to their own land, whether far away or close by. (1 Kings 8:46)

> Who can say, "I have kept my heart clean;
> I am pure from my sin"? (Proverbs 20:9)

> All of us had wandered off like sheep;
> each of us had strayed off on his own path,
> but the LORD caused the sin of all of us to attack him. (Isaiah 53:6)

Most people will acknowledge that they are not perfect and make mistakes. It is easy, however, to point to people who may have committed worse deeds in a effort to consider ourselves better than them. However, Scripture points equally to all people as sinners.

Attested by Yeshua. Our Messiah, the Lord, constantly assumed the sinfulness of all men:

> If you then, although you are evil, know how to give good gifts to your children, how much more will the heavenly Father give the Holy Spirit to those who ask him! (Luke 11:13)

> For this is the way God loved the world: He gave his one and only Son, so that everyone who believes in him will not perish but have eternal life. (Yohanan 3:16)

The passage as recorded by Luke does not need explanation. But what Yeshua said—in one of the most well-known passages of the Scriptures—must be understood in its context from the beginning of the chapter. While Israel's teacher Nicodemus (perhaps Nakdimon ben Gurion, mentioned in the Talmud[16]) may have desired to be in the kingdom, he had to avail himself of the only means for atonement for sin if he wished to truly enjoy God's presence.

The New Covenant and the Issue of Man's Sin. The New Covenant Jewish writers teach clearly that all the world is under sin. Sha'ul pointedly emphasized that this was true of all peoples, both the pagan, cultured Gentile as well as Jewish people. (Note his well-reasoned argument in Romans 1:18–3:20.)

In another telling statement, we read:

> If we say we do not bear the guilt of sin, we are deceiving ourselves and the truth is not in us. . . . If we say we have not sinned, we make him a liar and his word is not in us. (1 Yohanan 1:8, 10)

Even the Best. The writers of the Tanach teach that even the best and most holy of men are guilty of sin. As godly as was Job before the Lord, after his experiences in which he had made some rash statements about God, he said:

> I had heard of you by the hearing of the ear,
> but now my eye has seen you.
> Therefore I despise myself,
> and I repent in dust and ashes! (Job 42:5–6)

The words of Daniel are also instructive:

> I prayed to the LORD my God, confessing in this way: "O Lord, great and awesome God who is faithful to his covenant with those who love him and keep his commandments, we have sinned! We have done what is wrong and wicked; we have rebelled by turning away from your commandments and standards." (Daniel 9:4–5)

One could argue that Daniel himself never sinned in the way his fellow exiles had. But note that as Daniel prayed in intercession, he identified himself wholly with the sins of his exiled people.

Sha'ul also confessed his terrible deeds in persecuting his own people who had become believers in the Yeshua:

> This saying is trustworthy and deserves full acceptance: "Messiah Yeshua came into the world to save sinners"—and I am the worst of them! (1 Timothy 1:15)

The Question Whether Some People Are Without Sin. Some passages in the biblical text *appear* to teach that certain men are not sinful. For example:

> When Yeshua heard this he said, "Those who are healthy don't need a physician, but those who are sick do. Go and learn what this saying means: 'I want mercy and not sacrifice.' For I did not come to call the righteous, but sinners." (Mattai 9:12–13)

The point of the discussion was that some of the leaders had no concern for the needs of the lowliest and most sinful of people, namely, the tax collectors. So as to jar their conscience, Yeshua teased these leaders, saying, "Why, you are healthy, but these sick people need help." Then using a proverb, he reminded them that what was needed from them was mercy, not punctilious worship at the altar. Yeshua never intended to indicate that certain ones are without sin; how else would someone insist that both the neediest as well as those who are whole need help?

Another such passage is:

> Then Kefa started speaking: "I now truly understand that God does not show favoritism in dealing with people, but in every nation the person who fears him and does what is right is welcomed before him." (Acts 10:34–35)

This statement followed on Kefa's visit to the home of Cornelius. Was Cornelius without sin? To the contrary, he would have been the first to admit he was indeed a sinner. Exactly because of his need, he had thrown himself on the mercy of God, leading to his encounter with Kefa. This *shaliach*'s words emphasize that God respects anyone who fears and calls on Him.

Then we have the words of Sha'ul:

> For whenever the Gentiles, who do not have the law, do by nature the things required by the law, these who do not have the law are a law to themselves. (Romans 2:14)

The statement that some Gentiles "do by nature the things required by the law" reflects a common Jewish belief that those without the Law given to Israel are neverthless held under the Noahide laws, first mentioned in the *sifrim hisonim*. These laws were also mentioned briefly by Yaakov at the Jerusalem Council in relation to Gentile believers.

> . . . but that we should write them a letter telling them to abstain from things defiled by idols and from sexual immorality and from what has been strangled and from blood. . . .
>
> . . . that you abstain from meat that has been sacrificed to idols and from blood and from what has been strangled and from sexual immorality. If you keep yourselves from doing these things, you will do well. Farewell. (Acts 15:20, 29)

Seven such laws are enumerated in later Jewish tradition. The point is that even Gentiles were considered without excuse for the deeds of sin they commit. The passage before us does not declare they are without sin but that even Gentiles recognize their needs, realize a moral code, and abide by it.

Finally, Yohanan states:

> Everyone who has been fathered by God does not practice sin, because God's seed resides in him, and thus he is not able to sin, because he has been fathered by God. (1 Yohanan 3:9)

The point is that even a believer who has given up a life of living in *continual* sin recognizes times when he or she commits individual sins; anyone might fail on certain occasions. So, this *shaliach's* prescribed remedy centered on the lessons of the guilt offering as seen in the Messiah's death. He therefore provided instructions on how forgiveness can be attained:

> (My little children, I am writing these things to you so that you may not sin.) But if anyone does sin, we have an advocate with the Father, Yeshua the Messiah the righteous One, and he himself is the atoning sacrifice for our sins, and not only for our sins but also for the whole world. (1 Yohanan 2:1–2)

Sin and guilt offerings will be discussed under the doctrine of atonement.

And Yet, Some People Seem Oblivious of Sin![17]

Consequences of Sin

The consequences of sin's ruination are valuable to note both as a warning to believers, and also as a reminder that God stands ready to provide unbelievers with a new life of fullness and meaning as well as peace of mind and heart. The Messianic Jews who wrote the New Covenant did not mince any words or pictures when describing the horror of sin.

Defilement. David ruefully confessed the horror he went through because of his wrongdoing with Bat Sheva and her husband, Uriah:

> My whole body is sick because of your judgment;
> I am deprived of health because of my sin.
> For my sins overwhelm me;
> like a heavy load, they are too much for me to bear.
> My wounds are infected and starting to smell,
> because of my foolish sins. (Psalm 38:3–5)

This defilement exacted a heavy toll on David. Though God eventually cleansed him, he would never again be the same.

David also admitted how easy it is to become defiled:

> The wicked turn aside from birth;
> liars go astray as soon as they are born. (Psalm 58:3)

While Yeshua, David's greater son, said:

> In the same way, every good tree bears good fruit, but the bad tree bears bad fruit. A good tree is not able to bear bad fruit, nor a bad tree to bear good fruit. (Mattai 7:17–18)

Sha'ul stated as well:

> Therefore, since we have these promises, dear friends, let us cleanse ourselves from everything that could defile the body and the spirit, and thus accomplish holiness out of reverence for God. (2 Corinthians 7:1)

and

> All is pure to those who are pure. But to those who are corrupt and unbelieving, nothing is pure, but both their minds and consciences are corrupted. (Titus 1:15)

Sin, then, defiles and warps our sense of values, and demeans us as human beings.

Disorder. Wrongdoing has a way of twisting an individual's soul as well as creating a complete sense of disorder within a society. Recall how society was made into a hell when the Federal Building was bombed in Oklahoma City, or when terrorists set off bombs in the streets of Tel Aviv.

Isaiah confronted the people of his day with a still-relevant and pointed message:

> Those who call evil good and good evil are as good as dead,
> who turn darkness into light and light into darkness,
> who turn bitter into sweet and sweet into bitter. (Isaiah 5:20)

Sha'ul also vividly pictured the disorder that comes because of drastic wrongdoing between human beings:

> For this reason God gave them over to dishonorable passions. For their women exchanged the natural sexual relations for unnatural ones, and likewise the men also abandoned natural relations with women and were inflamed in their passions for one another. Men committed shameless acts with men and received in themselves the due penalty for their error. (Romans 1:26–27)

He also declared that:

> . . . because the outlook of the flesh is hostile to God, for it does not submit to the law of God, nor is it able to do so. (Romans 8:7)

and,

> The unbeliever does not receive the things of the Spirit of God, for they are foolishness to him. And he cannot understand them, because they are spiritually discerned. (1 Corinthians 2:14)

Concerning the days just before the Messianic kingdom of peace prevails on earth, human and community relationships will become extremely difficult. People will be

> unloving, irreconcilable, slanderers, without self-control, savage, opposed to what is good, . . . (2 Timothy 3:3)

while Yehudah prophesies:

> But these men do not understand the things they slander, and they are being destroyed by the very things that, like irrational animals, they instinctively comprehend. (Yehudah 1:10)

As this age wears on, then, moral and spiritual moorings will be shaken and disorder will ensue.

Paralysis. Again, as this age nears its end, people will follow a righteousness dictated by their own thoughts and feelings. Neither biblical norms nor moral spirituality will be part of their thinking. Society will be paralyzed in doing what God desires because no fear of God will exist.

Sha'ul described exactly what would occur among the majority of the human population:

> They are darkened in their understanding, being alienated from the life of God because of the ignorance that is in them due to the hardness of their hearts. Because they are callous, they have given

themselves over to indecency for the practice of every kind of impurity with greediness. (Ephesians 4:18–19)

He added further concerning the end times:

Now the Spirit explicitly says that in the later times some will desert the faith and occupy themselves with deceiving spirits and demonic teachings, influenced by the hypocrisy of liars whose consciences are seared. (1 Timothy 4:1–2)

Yohanan also echoed such sentiments, describing this paralysis:

Because you say, "I am rich and have acquired great wealth, and need nothing," but do not realize that you are wretched, pitiful, poor, blind, and naked, . . . (Revelation 3:17)

The last passage historically describes a particular local congregation in Laodicea, in what today is Turkey. However, it is possible that the seven churches of Revelation describe specific ages in the history of the church, in which case Laodicea may be a picture of this age as it draws to a close.

Bondage. One of the most deplorable consequences of sin is that evil deeds hold their victims in a dreadful vice. The Wisdom Literature attests to this:

The wicked will be captured by his own iniquities,
and he will be held by the cords of his own sin. (Proverbs 5:22)

In one passage, certain of the religious leaders confidently told Yeshua that they were not in bondage to anyone. Yet in reality, the truth was otherwise:

Then Yeshua said to those Judeans who had believed him, "If you continue to follow my teaching, you are really my disciples and you will know the truth, and the truth will set you free." "We are descendants of Abraham," they replied, "and have never been anyone's

> slaves! How can you say, 'You will become free'?" Yeshua answered them, "I tell you the solemn truth, everyone who practices sin is a slave of sin. The slave does not remain in the family forever, but the son remains forever. So if the son sets you free, you will be really free." (Yohanan 8:31–36)

Yeshua offered them the possibility of true freedom if they would only respond to the truth He affirmed (verse 36, "if the son sets you free, you will be really free"). Only the person who has been delivered from the bondage of sin to serve the Messiah Yeshua knows what it really means to be free.

Sha'ul echoed the same truth that he knew well from his previous experience of trying to serve God in his own way, namely, by harming his kinsmen-believers:

> We know that our old man was crucified with him so that the body of sin would no longer dominate us, so that we would no longer be enslaved to sin. (Romans 6:6)

However, as he attempted to live the life of a believer, he had a fierce struggle with his old nature in the work of sanctification:

> For I delight in the law of God in my inner being. But I see a different law in my members waging war against the law of my mind and making me captive to the law of sin that is in my members. Wretched man that I am! Who will rescue me from this body of death? (Romans 7:22–24)

Only when he finally learned to daily trust the Holy Spirit who lived in him, did he exult in the victory of breaking the bondage. That is when Sha'ul then rose to a crescendo of praise to God.

> What then shall we say about these things? If God is for us, who can be against us? Indeed, he who did not spare his own Son, but gave him up for us all—how will he not also, along with him, freely give us all things? Who will bring any charge against God's elect? It is God

> who justifies. Who is the one who will condemn? Messiah is the one who died (and more than that, he was raised), who is at the right hand of God, and who also is interceding for us. Who will separate us from the love of Messiah? Will trouble, or distress, or persecution, or famine, or nakedness, or danger, or sword? As it is written, "For your sake we encounter death all day long; we were considered as sheep to be slaughtered." No, in all these things we have complete victory through him who loved us! For I am convinced that neither death, nor life, nor angels, nor heavenly rulers, nor things that are present, nor things to come, nor powers, nor height, nor depth, nor anything else in creation will be able to separate us from the love of God in Messiah Yeshua our Lord. (Romans 8:31–39)

Misery. No one who has experienced temptation or succumbing to temptation would ever say that the initial exposure wasn't appealing or enjoyable. The writer to the Hebrews said as much in his description of Moses' experience:

> By faith, when he grew up, Moses refused to be called the son of Pharaoh's daughter, choosing rather to be ill-treated with the people of God than to enjoy sin's fleeting pleasure. (Hebrews 11:24–25)

Yet once one takes the route of sin, sooner or later the aftereffects of misery take the place of pleasure. We see this in passages such as these:

> To the woman he said,
> "I will greatly increase your labor pains;
> with pain you will give birth to children.
> You will want to control your husband,
> but he will dominate you."
> But to Adam he said,
> "Because you obeyed your wife
> and ate from the tree about which I commanded you,
> 'You must not eat from it,'

cursed is the ground thanks to you;
in painful toil you will eat of it all the days of your life."
(Genesis 3:16–17)

The aftermath of Adam and Eve's wrongdoing is that the woman will bring forth children in pain, while the man must struggle with a cursed ground in order to derive a living from it.

There is a way that seems right to a person,
but its end is the way that leads to death.
Even in laughter the heart may ache,
and the end of joy may be grief. (Proverbs 14:12–13)

"But the wicked are like a surging sea
that is unable to be quiet;
its waves toss up mud and sand.
There will be no prosperity," says my God, "for the wicked."
(Isaiah 57:20–21)

Who can begin to empathize with those who have suffered the misery, broken hearts and minds, guilt-ridden souls, pain, and sickness—all because someone wanted to go his or her own way into materialism, or immorality, or abortion, or broken homes, or alcoholism, or drugs. Sin has a price tag that is simply too high, but tragically, people don't see the tag until it is too late.

Guilt. A companion to misery is guilt. Guilt can weigh on a person's soul heavier than a pile of stones. The tendency to deliberately sin can also affect believers. When David, writing as a believer, was forgiven after he had confessed his sin, he stated:

Then I confessed my sin;
I no longer covered up my wrongdoing.
I said, "I will confess my rebellious acts to the LORD."
And then you forgave my sins. (Selah) (Psalm 32:5)

The word for *forgive* here is *nasa'ta*, literally meaning "You have lifted off" the guilt of my sin. God lifted the load of David's guilt from his heart. Unbelievers can testify of the guilt brought on by sin, and nearly every believer knows only too well the experience of being forgiven.

> . . . among whom all of us also formerly lived out our lives in the cravings of our flesh, indulging the desires of the flesh and the mind, and were by nature children of wrath even as the rest . . . (Ephesians 2:3)

Death. We have already seen the consequences of sin as seen in spiritual death. In one statement, Yeshua explained how one can be delivered from it:

> I tell you the solemn truth, the one who hears my message and believes the one who sent me has eternal life and will not be condemned, but has crossed over from death to life. I tell you the solemn truth, a time is coming—and is now here—when the dead will hear the voice of the Son of God, and those who hear will live. (Yohanan 5:24–25)

If, however, one should die in their sins without finding atonement in Yeshua, the consequence is an everlasting death—separation from God—forever. We will consider this further below when discussing what happens when people leave this world, either as a believer or as an unbeliever. Only two passages will be mentioned for now:

> Then Death and Hades were thrown into the lake of fire. This is the second death—the lake of fire. (Revelation 20:14)

> But to the cowards, unbelievers, detestable persons, murderers, the sexually immoral, and those who practice magic spells, idol worshipers, and all those who lie, their place will be in the lake that burns with fire and sulfur. That is the second death. (Revelation 21:8)

While most Jewish scholars and rabbis hold out for a universal repentance, whereby a person can even repent in Gehenna, yet the Scriptures are quite plain that the suffering of unbelievers is for eternity. A few Jewish leaders, however, do agree with this.

Some Problems

Most problems regarding the doctrine of sin fall into two areas. First, there may be a misunderstanding of the sin nature as to what it is and what it is not. Second, there is the question of the extent to which man has fallen into sin. That is, is man always doing what is evil? Can man do anything good for his fellow man? The sections below discuss these issues.

"Totally Depraved"—Seven Misconceptions. The expression "totally depraved" should not be used without adequate explanation. It can be greatly misunderstood and it is therefore perhaps best to drop the phrase altogether and rather explain what is meant in terms of what the Scripture teaches. We will do this by addressing several misconceptions:

Misconception one: the unbeliever has no disposition to do what is right. Sha'ul pointed out that people to whom the Torah was not given were still able to discern what was right and do it:

> For whenever the Gentiles, who do not have the law, do by nature the things required by the law, these who do not have the law are a law to themselves. They show that the work of the law is written in their hearts, as their conscience bears witness and their conflicting thoughts accuse or else defend them. (Romans 2:14–15)

The point is that all men share in a common grace because of their creation in the image of God. Even though that image is marred, yet the fingerprints of God are traceable on the soul of man, no matter how far he has sunk into sin.

Misconception two: the unbeliever can never do anything good.

> Woe to you, experts in the law and you Pharisees, hypocrites! You give a tenth of mint, dill, and cumin, yet you neglect what is more important in the law—justice, mercy, and faithfulness! You should have done these things without neglecting the others. (Mattai 23:23)

A few of the strictest Pharisees gave a tenth of everything they had, down to the lowliest of the spices, namely, mint, dill, and cummin. This they were not required to do. The point is that their lives were exemplary and Yeshua did not condemn them for that; but they should also have paid attention to the issues of justice, mercy, and faithfulness.

A typical newspaper editor can describe problems in his community with pinpoint accuracy, indicating that he possesses a sense of what is just and right. His prescription, however, for rectifying the problems may well leave him far from the Bible moral standard.

Misconception three: the unbeliever commits every form of sin. A little reflection will demonstrate this is simply not true. Compare how the list of sins among the Gentiles who are in gross sin (Romans 1:24–32) differs markedly from the description of cultured Gentiles (Romans 2:1–8):

> Therefore God gave them over in the desires of their hearts to impurity, to dishonor their bodies among themselves. They exchanged the truth of God for a lie and worshiped and served the creation rather than the Creator, who is blessed forever! Amen.
>
> For this reason God gave them over to dishonorable passions. For their women exchanged the natural sexual relations for unnatural ones, and likewise the men also abandoned natural relations with women and were inflamed in their passions for one another. Men committed shameless acts with men and received in themselves the due penalty for their error.
>
> And just as they did not see fit to acknowledge God, God gave them over to a depraved mind, to do what should not be done. They are filled with every kind of unrighteousness, wickedness, covetousness, malice. They are rife with envy, murder, strife, deceit, hostility. They are gossips, slanderers, haters of God, insolent, arrogant, boastful, contrivers of all sorts of evil, disobedient to parents, senseless, covenant-breakers, heartless, ruthless. Although they fully know God's righteous decree that those who practice such things deserve to die, they not only do them but also approve of those who practice them. (Romans 1:24–32)

> Therefore you are without excuse, whoever you are, when you judge someone else. For on whatever grounds you judge another, you condemn yourself, because you who judge practice the same things. Now we know that God's judgment is in accordance with truth against those who practice such things. And do you think, whoever you are, when you judge those who practice such things and yet do them yourself, that you will escape God's judgment? Or do you have contempt for the wealth of his kindness, forbearance, and patience, and yet do not know that God's kindness leads you to repentance? But because of your stubbornness and your unrepentant heart, you are storing up wrath for yourselves in the day of wrath, when God's righteous judgment is revealed! He will reward each one according to his works: eternal life to those who by perseverance in good works seek glory and honor and immortality, but wrath and anger to those who live in selfish ambition and do not obey the truth but follow unrighteousness. (Romans 2:1–8)

And both differ markedly from the list Sha'ul used to describe what Jewish people were doing. The same would be true today as well.

Misconception four: the unbeliever is as bad as he or she can become. Again, a little thought will enable one to realize that such a statement is unfair and illogical. Judges who are not believers in the Messiah Yeshua can make righteous decisions, and sometimes more fair than some believing judges who may be too legalistic!

Misconception five: every unbeliever has made the same progress in sinning. Once more, this accusation will not stand up to careful scrutiny. Some civic leaders have been fair-minded people who have demonstrated a fair degree of righteousness.

Misconception six: when an unbeliever does good, it is for selfish motives. Many generally assume that when an unbeliever does what is right and good, it is for only selfish motives. But it is interesting that Judaism teaches that a person should give as if to God, without asking for anything in return. He understands that he is doing *tsedaka*, or righteousness, for God's sake. To give in a "tit-for-tat" way ("I give to you and so you have to give back to me in kind") is condemned by Jewish leaders.

Yeshua in the New Covenant echoed this same truth:

> Whenever you pray, do not be like the hypocrites, because they love to pray while standing in synagogues and on street corners so that people can see them. Truly I say to you, they have their reward. (Mattai 6:5)

And yet, not everyone followed these instructions, not only to be seen as pious men, or also as people who give far more than what was required, without expecting something in return.

Misconception seven: unbelievers are without the concept of the love of God. Man certainly has a sense of what the love of God means, but *knowing and living it to the full* is another matter because of the sin nature. The unbeliever's sense of God's love can be tainted. Even what sense he or she does have is stained by selfish motives and desires, as the *shaliach* expressed it quite clearly:

> Dear friends, let us love one another, because love is from God, and everyone who loves has been fathered by God and knows God. The person who does not love does not know God, because God is love. (1 Yohanan 4:7–8)

An unsaved person can express a love of God because of the image of God in him or her, which can reflect how God does care. But there is a qualitative difference between the concern demonstrated by the believer and unbeliever.

The fact is that a man or woman can do a great deal of good on the horizontal level—to his family, fellow man, society—through the disciplines of medicine, technology, the law, and government. But none of what unbelievers accomplish can be offered up to God on the vertical plane in exchange for an atonement for sin. This is the real crux of moral depravity: the unbeliever still has a sin nature that is the barrier between him or her and God. Atonement is obtained on the basis of a free gift of

God, but it is supported by what the Messiah has done for us, as we will see below.

The Question of Why God Permitted Sin. This question has baffled the minds of believers down through centuries, and the best theologians have given considerable space to discussing it. Hodge has noted two alternative possibilities:[18]

God unable to prevent sin. In this case, God is a finite being unable to prevent sin in any kind of a world, or at least in a world with free agency. Therefore, the agency for sin must be open.

But this view leaves one cold. However one describes God, can we do without His omnipotence?

A similar view attempts to preserve God's goodness in a case where He is not able to control every instance of sin. Surely, God could work around the effects of sin. This position, however, is a "cop-out" also.

One can only conclude: In explicating our concept of who God is, are we willing to sacrifice His omnipotence merely to preserve His goodness? Is it not possible to find another position that will preserve both ideas?

God did not choose to prevent sin. Some suggest that God did not choose to prevent sin because (1) Sin is a good in itself; or (2) Sin is a necessary way to the greatest good; or (3) Sin can be overruled for the ultimate good; or (4) By permitting sin, less evil will result.

Any of these suggestions must be vehemently denied. It is true that God did permit sin to occur. But in absolutely no way was it for the purpose of the greatest good. Such a view would posit that God is the author of sin, which He is not.

Because free will was given to Adam and Eve, God did not prevent sin. But God must never be charged with sin. Adam did not have to sin; he was given previous descriptive knowledge so that he could make the right choice not to eat. The same is true today for every believer. He or she has all the descriptive knowledge necessary in order to avoid sin and grow morally and spiritually. But in His grace, God gave on the tree where the Messiah died everything necessary for recovery: salvation for the unbeliever, and sanctification for the believer to grow in grace.

FOURTEEN

The Doctrines of Angels, Satan, and Demons

ANGELS

The Existence of Angels

Thirty-four books of the Scripture mention angels—seventeen books of the Tanach and seventeen of the New Covenant. The writers simply assume their existence as they go about teaching about them. The Messiah Yeshua also never questions the existence of angels but assumes that they are real.

The word *angel* occurs about 250 times in the entire Scripture, though if we take into account the other descriptive terms for them, to be discussed below, the number is much greater than that.

The Descriptive Names of Angels

Scripture uses various terms to describe angels.

Messengers. Angels are referred to as *messengers* sent by God in both Hebrew (*malach*; BDB, 521) and in Greek (*angelos*; Abbott-Smith, 4).

Men. Angels can also be referred to as *men*:

> Abraham looked up and saw three men standing across from him. When he saw them he ran from the entrance of the tent to meet them and bowed low to the ground. (Genesis 18:2)

The text initially refers to three men. However, as we read through chapters 18 and 19, it becomes apparent that two of them are angels, who continue their journey to Sodom:

> The two angels came to Sodom in the evening while Lot was sitting in the city's gateway. When Lot saw them, he got up to meet them and bowed down with his face toward the ground. (Genesis 19:1)

Moreover, the third man is referred to as the Lord, understood by some to be the Angel of the Lord:

> When the men got up to leave, they looked out over Sodom. (Now Abraham was walking with them to see them on their way.) Then the LORD said, "Should I hide from Abraham what I am about to do?" (Genesis 18:16–17)

Sons of God. A third designation is *sons of God*:

> Now the day came when the sons of God [also NASB; NIV: "angels"] came to present themselves before the LORD—and Satan also arrived among them. (Job 1:6)[1]

Could these *sons of God* be human beings? Another reference clarifies that the answer is no:

> On what were its bases set,
> or who laid its cornerstone—
> when the morning stars sang in chorus,
> and all the sons of God [also NASB; NIV: "angels"] shouted for joy?
> (Job 38:6–7)

Here, the *sons of God* are shouting for joy at the creation of the earth, before there were any people. Therefore these are nonhumans; they are angels.

Watchers or Sentinels. Angels can also be regarded as *watchers*. This is seen both in the NKJV, which translates the Aramaic literally, as well as in NET's "sentinels." NIV paraphrases as *messenger*. Note that *sentinel* here is paralleled with *holy one*, to be discussed in the next section.

> While I was watching in my mind's visions on my bed,
> a holy sentinel came down from heaven.
> This announcement is by the decree of the sentinels;
> this decision is by the pronouncement of the holy ones,
> so that those who are alive may understand
> that the Most High has authority over human kingdoms,
> and he bestows them on whomever he wishes.
> He establishes over them even the lowliest of human beings.
> As for the king seeing a holy sentinel coming down from heaven . . .
> (Daniel 4:13, 17, 23 [verses 10, 14, 20 MT])

This designation shows that angels function as God's watchmen, reporting back to Him what they have seen of people and events here on earth.

Holy Ones. Angels are also regarded as *holy ones* who respect the sacred presence of God in His temple:

> In the council of the holy ones God is greatly feared; he is more awesome than all who surround him. (Psalm 89:7 NIV; verse 8 MT).

Sons of the Mighty. A sixth designation is *sons of the mighty,* as rendered in ASV, NASB, and NKJV. NIV and NET render as "heavenly beings."

> For who in the skies is comparable to the LORD? Who among the sons of the mighty is like the LORD? (Psalm 89:6 NASB).

The point of this verse is that none of angels can be likened to God.

God's Host. Angels can also be regarded as *God's host*, that is, His army:

> So Jacob went on his way and the angels of God met him. When Jacob saw them, he exclaimed, "This is the camp of God!" So he named that place Mahanaim. (Genesis 32:1–2)

Initially, in verse 1, these beings are called *angels*. However, on seeing them, Jacob designates them specifically as *the camp of God* (KJV: "God's host"), suggesting that God's army was there in order to protect Jacob on his journey back home.

Ministering Spirits. Angels are *ministering spirits* who help believers in their witness, in their service, and when facing danger:

> Are they not all ministering spirits, sent out to serve those who will inherit salvation? (Hebrews 1:14)

Often this angelic service may occur "behind the scenes," without the knowledge of the believer. Some believers, reflecting that they have been spared from a calamity or have been aided in a great work for God, have concluded that there must have been angelic assistance.

Princes. Angels are called *princes*:

> However, the prince of the kingdom of Persia was opposing me for twenty-one days. But Michael, one of the leading princes, came to help me, because I was left there with the kings of Persia. (Daniel 10:13)

Principalities and Powers. Angels are sometimes collectively designated as *principalities and powers* (in some versions) or *rule/rulers and authorities* (in other versions):

> This power he exercised in Messiah when he raised him from the dead and seated him at his right hand in the heavenly realms far above every rule and authority and power and dominion and every name that is named, not only in this age but also in the one to come. (Ephesians 1:20–21)

Sha'ul further tells us that through believers God's wisdom will be made known to these same rulers and authorities:

> The purpose of this enlightenment is that through the *qehilah* the multifaceted wisdom of God should now be disclosed to the rulers and the authorities in the heavenly realms. (Ephesians 3:10)

Angels are designated similarly in these verses as well:

> For our struggle is not against flesh and blood, but against the rulers, against the powers, against the world rulers of this darkness, against the spiritual forces of evil in the heavens. (Ephesians 6:12)

> for all things in heaven and on earth were created by him—all things, whether visible or invisible, whether thrones or dominions, whether principalities or powers—all things were created through him and for him. (Colossians 1:16)

> . . . and you have been filled in him, who is the head over every ruler and authority. (Colossians 2:10)

> Disarming the rulers and authorities, he has made a public disgrace of them, triumphing over them by the tree. (Colossians 2:15)

Personal Names. We assume that every angel has a personal name, though only a few of them are revealed in the Scripture.

One archangel is designated Gabriel, meaning "the mighty one of God":

> Yes, while I was still praying, the man Gabriel, whom I had seen previously in a vision, was approaching me in my state of extreme weariness, around the time of the evening offering. (Daniel 9:21)

A second angel is referred to as Michael, signifying "who is like unto God":

> However, the prince of the kingdom of Persia was opposing me for twenty-one days. But Michael, one of the leading princes, came to help me, because I was left there with the kings of Persia. (Daniel 10:13)

The name of a third is given to us in both Hebrew and Greek, in both cases meaning "destroyer." He is apparently a fallen angel whom Satan uses in his role as "the angel of the Abyss":

They have as king over them the angel of the abyss, whose name in Hebrew is *Abaddon*, and in Greek, *Apollyon*. (Revelation 9:11)

The Origin of Angels

Angels are created beings, as we see in Psalm 148 when the psalmist calls out to the angels along with all creation to praise God:

Praise the LORD!
Praise the LORD from the sky!
Praise him in the heavens!
Praise him, all his angels!
Praise him, all his heavenly assembly!
Praise him, O sun and moon!
Praise him, all you shiny stars!
Praise him, O highest heaven,
and you waters above the sky!
Let them praise the name of the LORD,
for he gave the command and they came into existence.
(Psalm 148:1–5)

Furthermore, consider this verse already cited:

On what were its bases set,
or who laid its cornerstone—
when the morning stars sang in chorus,
and all the sons of God shouted for joy? (Job 38:6–7)

Since the angels are here referred to as the *sons of God*, it appears that each of them is a direct creation of God. And as we have seen, although the specific time of their creation is not indicated in Scripture, these verses show that they were already present when God created the earth.

Characteristics of Angels

Key Marks of Personality and Intelligence. Angels can rejoice, praise, and worship. They speak with one another as well as to God and to human beings.

A Class of Beings Distinct from Humanity. As one example, the writer to the Hebrews describes the ultimate destiny of believers, distinguishing them from the angels who will also be present at that time:

> But you have come to Mount Zion, the city of the living God, the heavenly Jerusalem, and to myriads of angels, to the assembly and congregation of the firstborn, who are enrolled in heaven, and to God, the judge of all, and to the spirits of the righteous, who have been made perfect. (Hebrews 12:22–23)

Do Not End Their Existence. Unlike humans, angels are primarily spiritual beings ("ministering *spirits*"—Hebrews 1:14). While the physical bodies of human beings die, we never note anything similar concerning angels. On the contrary, they are models for what believers will be like in the resurrection:

> But those who are regarded as worthy to share in that age and in the resurrection from the dead neither marry nor are given in marriage. In fact, they can no longer die, because they are equal to angels and are sons of God, since they are sons of the resurrection. (Luke 20:35–36)

Do Not Engage in Sexual Activity. Believers are also compared to the angels in this passage, which is Mark's parallel to the verse just cited from Luke 20:35–36:

> For when they rise from the dead, they neither marry nor are given in marriage, but are like angels in heaven. (Mark 12:25)

The purpose of sex is to bring new persons into existence and to replace those taken by death; but in the case of angels, there is no need for that, since they are directly created and they do not die.

The Physical Appearance of Angels

Always Appear in Human Form. We saw this earlier in the story of Abraham and his three visitors. Recall that two of them were angels, while the third was the Angel of the Lord (understood to be one of the preincarnate appearances of the Messiah). Yet there was nothing unusual about the way they looked:

> Abraham looked up and saw three men standing across from him. When he saw them he ran from the entrance of the tent to meet them and bowed low to the ground. (Genesis 18:2)

Always Appear as Male, Never as Female. We have seen examples of how angels are called "men." Here is another instance:

> While they were perplexed about this, suddenly two men stood beside them in dazzling attire. The women were terribly frightened and bowed their faces to the ground, but the men said to them, "Why do you look for the living among the dead?" (Luke 24:4–5)

Never Depicted with Wings. A possible exception might be the following verse:

> Then I saw another angel flying directly overhead, and he had an eternal gospel to proclaim to those who live on the earth—to every nation, tribe, language, and people. (Revelation 14:6)

Yet there is no place in Scripture where wings are explicitly mentioned. Angels could be capable of flying by some other means.

Always Youthful in Appearance. They do not show any signs of age:

> Then as they went into the tomb, they saw a young man dressed in a white robe sitting on the right side; and they were alarmed. (Mark 16:5)

Sometimes Have a Supernatural Appearance. This is true even though they are clothed in human form. While in the case of Abraham above, there was nothing unusual about the appearance of the three visitors, that is not always the case:

> His appearance was like lightning, and his clothes were white as snow. The guards were shaken and became like dead men because they were so afraid of him. (Mattai 28:3–4)

> After these things I saw another angel, who possessed great authority, coming down out of heaven, and the earth was lit up by his radiance. (Revelation 18:1)

The clothing of these angels is often white and dazzling to the eyes, reflecting their supernatural nature:

> His appearance was like lightning, and his clothes were white as snow. (Mattai 28:3)

> While they were perplexed about this, suddenly two men stood beside them in dazzling attire. (Luke 24:4)

The Character of Angels

Holy.

> For if anyone is ashamed of me and my words in this adulterous and sinful generation, the Son of Man will also be ashamed of him when he comes in the glory of his Father with the holy angels. (Mark 8:38)

Elect.

> Before God and Messiah Yeshua and the elect angels, I solemnly charge you to carry out these commands without prejudice or favoritism of any kind. (1 Timothy 5:21)

Some Have Sinned.

> For if God did not spare the angels who sinned, but threw them into hell and locked them up in chains in utter darkness, to be kept until the judgment, . . . (2 Kefa 2:4)

While Scripture never directly asserts that angels were created holy, we can assume that to be the case by three considerations: First, God is not the author of sin; second, angels are accountable for their sinful actions, indicating that they were originally holy; and third, the statement that angels "sinned" (2 Kefa 2:4, quoted above) also confirms that they were originally holy in character. From this verse we also conclude that there were angels who had *not* sinned; these are the ones designated as *elect* and *holy*.

Unlike Humanity, Have No Bond of Racial Unity. When an angel sins, it is entirely an individual matter. The sin of one angel affects other angels only by way of external influence. When Lucifer rebelled against God, he influenced other angels to followed him.

In contrast, when Adam fell, he involved the entire human race in his sin in a more direct way, because of the bond of racial unity among all people.

The Powers of Angels

Limited Powers. The powers of angels are greater than those of human beings, though they are limited according to God's purposes. Note one such limitation in this verse:

> But as for that day and hour no one knows it—not even the angels in heaven—except the Father alone. (Mattai 24:36)

Their limitations lead angels to exercise caution:

> But even when Michael the archangel was arguing with the devil and debating with him concerning Moses' body, he did not dare to bring a slanderous judgment, but said, "May the Lord rebuke you!" (Yehudah 1:9)

Even angels do not presume to be as bold and arrogant as some people can be!

On the other hand, when it suits the purposes of God, angels can display great powers. Both thoughts are combined in this verse:

Praise the LORD, you angels of his,
you powerful warriors who carry out his decrees
and obey his orders! (Psalm 103:20)

Can Display Great Strength. A clear example is at Yeshua's tomb:

Suddenly there was a severe earthquake, for an angel of the Lord descending from heaven came and rolled away the stone and sat on it. (Mattai 28:2)

Such a stone was extremely heavy, yet it was easy for the angel to roll it away.

Possess an Unusual Degree of Intelligence. In speaking to King David, the wise woman of Tekoa told him:

So your servant said, "May the word of my lord the king be my security, for my lord the king is like the angel of God [NIV: 'an angel of God'] when it comes to deciding between right and wrong! May the Lord your God be with you!" (2 Samuel 14:17)

She repeats the same thought a few verses later:

Your servant Joab did this so as to change this situation. But my lord has wisdom like that of the angel of God [NIV: "an angel of God"], and knows everything that is happening in the land. (2 Samuel 14:20)

Move with Incredible Swiftness. As Daniel was confessing the sins of Israel and praying for the release of the captives from Babylon,

Yes, while I was still praying, the man Gabriel, whom I had seen previously in a vision, was approaching me in my state of extreme weariness, around the time of the evening offering. (Daniel 9:21)

Can Appear Suddenly. Angels have the ability to appear without notice. As we can imagine, this often startles the recipients of their messages! When the shepherds in Luke 2 were on a hillside at night,

> An angel of the Lord appeared to them, and the glory of the Lord shone around them, and they were absolutely terrified. (Luke 2:9)

A further sudden appearance is recounted a few verses later:

> Suddenly a vast, heavenly army appeared with the angel, praising God and saying, . . . (Luke 2:13)

Similarly, when Yeshua was received into heaven following His resurrection, it is said of His disciples that

> As they were still staring into the sky while he was going, suddenly two men in white clothing stood near them. (Acts 1:10)

Can Perform Supernatural Acts. The story of Kefa's release from prison is a well-known example:

> Suddenly an angel of the Lord appeared, and a light shone in the prison cell. He struck Kefa on the side and woke him up, saying, "Get up quickly!" And the chains fell off Kefa's wrists. The angel said to him, "Fasten your belt and put on your sandals." Kefa did so. Then the angel said to him, "Put on your cloak and follow me." Kefa went out and followed him; he did not realize that what was happening through the angel was real, but thought he was seeing a vision. After they had passed the first and second guards, they came to the iron gate leading into the city. It opened for them by itself, and they went outside and walked down one narrow street, when at once the angel left him. (Acts 12:7–10)

In Revelation, angels exercise supernatural control over the natural elements:

> After this I saw four angels standing at the four corners of the earth, holding back the four winds of the earth so no wind could blow on the earth, on the sea, or on any tree. (Revelation 7:1)

> Another angel, who was in charge of the fire, came from the altar and called in a loud voice to the angel who had the sharp sickle, "Use your sharp sickle and gather the clusters of grapes off the vine of the earth, because its grapes are now ripe." (Revelation 14:18)

> Next, the second angel poured out his bowl on the sea and it turned into blood, like that of a corpse, and every living creature that was in the sea died. (Revelation 16:3)

Are Not All Equal in Power. An angel sent by God in response to Daniel's prayer struggles with "the prince of the Persian kingdom" (also an angel; see above under "The Descriptive Names of Angels"). It takes the intervention of a third angel to end the three-week standoff:

> However, the prince of the kingdom of Persia was opposing me for twenty-one days. But Michael, one of the leading princes, came to help me, because I was left there with the kings of Persia. (Daniel 10:13)

Can Perform the Ordinary Functions of Human Beings. In addition to exercising supernatural powers, angels can act as ordinary people do. And so, they speak, they can have their feet washed, and they can eat:

> The two angels came to Sodom in the evening while Lot was sitting in the city's gateway. When Lot saw them, he got up to meet them and bowed down with his face toward the ground.
>
> He said, "Here, my lords, please turn aside to your servant's house. Stay the night and wash your feet. Then you can be on your way early in the morning." "No," they replied, "we'll spend the night in the town square."
>
> But he urged them persistently, so they turned aside with him and entered his house. He prepared a feast for them, including bread baked without yeast, and they ate. (Genesis 19:1–3)

Can Bring Physical Judgment on People. Because the homosexuals of Sodom insisted on having Lot's angelic visitors, we read concerning the angels:

> Then they struck the men who were at the door of the house, from the youngest to the oldest, with blindness. The men outside wore themselves out trying to find the door. (Genesis 19:11)

We need to understand that the angels did this in their commission to serve God; they were not simply inflicting evil on people. Scripture shows that the inhabitants of Sodom had crossed the line of moral depravity. Their "cup of sin" was full, and God had no other recourse but to judge the city. The action of the angels in this passage was preliminary to God's judgment of the entire city.

The Number of Angels

The number of angels is so great that Daniel could only describe them in the following terms:

> While I was watching,
> thrones were set up,
> and the Ancient of Days took his seat.
> His attire was white like snow;
> the hair of his head was like lamb's wool.
> His throne was ablaze with fire
> and its wheels were all aflame.
> A river of fire was streaming forth
> and proceeding from his presence.
> Many thousands were ministering to him;
> Many tens of thousands stood ready to serve him.
> The court convened
> and the books were opened. (Daniel 7:9–10)

It is to be understood that these are angels, standing in God's presence and attending Him.

In the New Covenant, we are given insight into the number of angels in the story of Yeshua's arrest in the garden of Gethsemane:

> Or do you think that I cannot call on my Father, and that he would send me more than twelve legions of angels right now? (Mattai 26:53)

Some scholars have estimated twelve legions to be the equivalent of 72,000. Even that number is only a small portion of the total number of angels.

Further examples are found in Hebrews and in Revelation:

> But you have come to Mount Zion, the city of the living God, the heavenly Jerusalem, and to myriads [NIV: thousands upon thousands] of angels, to the assembly. (Hebrews 12:22)

> Then I looked and heard the voice of many angels in a circle around the throne, as well as the living creatures and the elders. Their number was ten thousand times ten thousand—thousands times thousands— . . . (Revelation 5:11)

While these may seem like exaggerations, the size of the visible universe alone is vast. When we consider that there is also an unseen world, it is no wonder that the creation can accommodate such huge numbers of angels.

The Organization and Rank of Angels

Organized. Scripture gives evidence that both good and evil angels are organized. The psalmist speaks of angels gathered in an "assembly" and a "council":

> O LORD, the heavens praise your amazing deeds,
> as well as your faithfulness in the angelic assembly.
> For who in the skies can compare to the LORD?
> Who is like the LORD among the heavenly beings,
> a God who is honored in the great angelic assembly,
> and more awesome than all who surround him? (Psalm 89:5–7)

Sha'ul's description of our satanic adversaries also reflects the organization of angels. His listing appears to be in ascending order, with "spiritual forces of evil" being the highest level:

> Clothe yourselves with the full armor of God so that you may be able to stand against the schemes of the devil. For our struggle is not against flesh and blood, but against the rulers, against the powers, against the world rulers of this darkness, against the spiritual forces of evil in the heavens. (Ephesians 6:11–12)

This kind of organization is to be expected. Disarray and individualism are useful to neither God nor Satan. Both need their ranks to be ordered and disciplined in order to accomplish their appointed tasks.

Rank of Angels. Within the organized structure of angels, there are differences in rank and position. The Scriptures speak of an "archangel," or "chief angel."

> For the Lord himself will come down from heaven with a shout of command, with the voice of the archangel, and with the trumpet of God, and the dead in Messiah will rise first. (1 Thessalonians 4:16)

Yehudah specifies the archangel Michael:

> But even when Michael the archangel was arguing with the devil and debating with him concerning Moses' body, he did not dare to bring a slanderous judgment, but said, "May the Lord rebuke you!" (Yehudah 1:9)

This same Michael is also referred to as "one of the leading princes":

> However, the prince of the kingdom of Persia was opposing me for twenty-one days. But Michael, one of the leading princes, came to help me, because I was left there with the kings of Persia. (Daniel 10:13)

The two designations of "archangel" and "chief princes" seem to be equivalent. Furthermore, the reference to Michael as *one* of the chief princes suggests that there were other archangels as well.

Some angels seem to be closer to God than do others. Mattai, referring to angels who are assigned to care for children, says that they "see the face" of the Father. This may be a reference to their position.

> See that you do not disdain one of these little ones. For I tell you that their angels in heaven always see the face of my Father in heaven. (Mattai 18:10)

Differences of rank and position are evident among the fallen angels as well. A particular evil angel could therefore be designated as "the prince of Persia":

> He said, "Do you know why I have come to you? Now I am about to return to engage in battle with the prince of Persia. When I go, the prince of Greece is coming." (Daniel 10:20)

The Rank of Angels in Relation to Human Beings.

In the present, occupy a position higher than man. One example is found when Kefa notes that angels are stronger and more powerful than certain "bold and arrogant" men. Above, we saw that angels can display great strength, but here we focus on the contrast with human beings.

> . . . especially those who indulge their fleshly desires and who despise authority. Brazen and insolent, they are not afraid to insult the glorious ones, yet even angels, who are much more powerful, do not bring a slanderous judgment against them before the Lord. (2 Kefa 2:10–11)

In the present, are equal with human beings in service before God. For that reason, an angel refused to allow Yohanan to worship him and called him a "fellow servant":

> I, Yohanan, am the one who heard and saw these things, and when I heard and saw them, I threw myself down to worship at the feet of the angel who was showing them to me. But he said to me, "Do not do

> this! I am a fellow servant with you and with your brothers the prophets, and with those who obey the words of this book. Worship God!" (Revelation 22:8–9)

Nor does Sha'ul permit the worship of angels:

> Let no one who delights in humility and the worship of angels pass judgment on you. That person goes on at great lengths about what he has supposedly seen, but he is puffed up with empty notions by his fleshly mind. (Colossians 2:18)

In the age to come, the position of angels and human beings will be reversed. In the final destiny, the positions will be reversed, as redeemed people will judge angels (which in this verse may refer specifically to fallen angels):

> Do you not know that we will judge angels? Why not ordinary matters! (1 Corinthians 6:3)

Moreover, at that time angels will serve believers:

> Are they not all ministering spirits, sent out to serve those who will inherit salvation? (Hebrews 1:14)

The Rank of Angels in Relation to the Messiah.

In His deity, Yeshua is above the angels. Sha'ul, speaking of Yeshua, says:

> He is the image of the invisible God, the firstborn over all creation, for all things in heaven and on earth were created by him—all things, whether visible or invisible, whether thrones or dominions, whether principalities or powers—all things were created through him and for him. (Colossians 1:15–16)

Angels, then, are among the things Yeshua created.

In His humanity, Yeshua became lower than the angels. However, in the incarnation—when Yeshua took on human nature—He is said to be made a little lower than the angels:

> You made him lower than the angels for a little while. You crowned him with glory and honor. . . .
>
> . . . but we see Yeshua, who was made lower than the angels for a little while, now crowned with glory and honor because he suffered death, so that by God's grace he would experience death on behalf of everyone. (Hebrews 2:7, 9)[2]

In His exaltation, Yeshua once again became higher than the angels. As a result of His redemptive work, the Messiah has now been exalted "to the highest place." Therefore, He has been exalted even above the angels:

> As a result God exalted him
> and gave him the name
> that is above every name,
> so that at the name of Yeshua
> every knee will bow
> —in heaven and on earth and under the earth—
> and every tongue confess
> that Yeshua the Messiah is Lord
> to the glory of God the Father. (Philippians 2:9–11)

Similarly, Kefa says of the Messiah that He is the one

> who went into heaven and is at the right hand of God with angels and authorities and powers subject to him. (1 Kefa 3:22)

Because of our union with Messiah, we will also be higher than the angels. Yeshua is the head of a redeemed humanity. Therefore, because of our union with Him, we too will ultimately be exalted above the angels. It is no wonder that angels take an interest in the work of redemption (an idea we will look at below), for redeemed humanity will ultimately rank even higher than the angels.

The Ministries and Activities of Angels

General.

Praising God. Scripture shows that the angels praise and worship God:

> Praise him, all his angels!
> Praise him, all his heavenly assembly! (Psalm 148:2)

> Acknowledge the LORD, you heavenly beings,
> acknowledge the LORD's majesty and power!
> Acknowledge the majesty of the LORD's reputation!
> Worship the LORD in holy attire! (Psalm 29:1–2)

This praise is accompanied by rejoicing:

> On what were its bases set,
> or who laid its cornerstone—
> when the morning stars sang in chorus,
> and all the sons of God [NIV: "angels"] shouted for joy? (Job 38:6–7)

Have responsibility for divinely assigned tasks.

> Praise the LORD, you angels of his,
> you powerful warriors who carry out his decrees
> and obey his orders! (Psalm 103:20)

Observe events on earth. Angels sometimes appear in the presence of God, the context suggesting that they are spectators of God's plans and purposes. So for instance, we have the story of Job:

> Now the day came when the sons of God [NIV: "angels"] came to present themselves before the LORD—and Satan also arrived among them. . . .
>
> Again the day came when the sons of God [NIV: "angels"] came to present themselves before the LORD, and Satan also arrived among them to present himself before the LORD. (Job 1:6; 2:1)

In reading these verses in context, it seems that the angels observe the interactions between God and Satan and the ensuing events.

Likewise, in the story of Nebuchadnezzar, an angel comes before Daniel to announce the king's future:

> While I was watching in my mind's visions on my bed,
> a holy sentinel came down from heaven. (Daniel 4:13)

The corollary to his announcing what God does among mankind is that He is also observing them.

In the New Covenant, Sha'ul speaks of angels in this context:

> For, I think, God has exhibited us apostles last of all, as men condemned to die, because we have become a spectacle to the world, both to angels and to people. (1 Corinthians 4:9)

Here Sha'ul is not thinking of the humiliation of the *shlichim* but rather quite the opposite: that the angels would observe the triumph of the *shlichim* by the power of God. This would serve as an example to the angels of how redeemed humanity can serve God with honor and distinction.[3]

Communicate to people. In one incident, some Pharisees who are vigorously arguing in support of Sha'ul use this argument:

> There was a great commotion, and some experts in the law from the party of the Pharisees stood up and protested strongly, "We find nothing wrong with this man. What if a spirit or an angel has spoken to him?" (Acts 23:9)

The *spirit* in this passage seems to refers to an angel as well. The Pharisees' argument would not have been unusual; it was a current belief among Jewish people that angels could speak to people, and in fact, the Tanach is replete with examples.

The activities of evil angels. Evil angels—of various ranks (see above)—oppose God's people. Many believers have in fact had the experience of being subjected to spiritual oppression.

> For our struggle is not against flesh and blood, but against the rulers, against the powers, against the world rulers of this darkness, against the spiritual forces of evil in the heavens. (Ephesians 6:12)

For this reason, Sha'ul enjoins believers to put on the full armor of God as protection against the purposes of Satan:

> For this reason, take up the full armor of God so that you may be able to stand your ground on the evil day, and having done everything, to stand. (Ephesians 6:13)

Evil angels oppose not only the people of God but good angels as well:

> However, the prince of the kingdom of Persia was opposing me for twenty-one days. But Michael, one of the leading princes, came to help me, because I was left there with the kings of Persia. (Daniel 10:13)

The final judgment of Satan and his angels shows that the evil angels were carrying out Satan's work. Since those angels did the bidding of Satan, they all share a common destiny:

> So that huge dragon—the ancient serpent, the one called the devil and Satan, who deceives the whole world—was thrown down to the earth, and his angels along with him. (Revelation 12:9)

Ministries in Relation to Yeshua. Angels exercised various ministries in the life of Yeshua.

At His birth. An angel announced Yeshua's upcoming birth to Joseph:

> When he had contemplated this, an angel of the Lord appeared to him in a dream and said, "Joseph, son of David, do not be afraid to take Miriam as your wife, because the child conceived in her is from the Holy Spirit. She will give birth to a son and you will name him Yeshua, because he will save his people from their sins." (Mattai 1:20–21)

After He was born, angels likewise made an announcement to the shepherds:

> But the angel said to them, "Do not be afraid! Listen carefully, for I proclaim to you good news that brings great joy to all the people: Today your Savior is born in the city of David. He is Messiah the Lord. This will be a sign for you: You will find a baby wrapped in strips of cloth and lying in a manger." Suddenly a vast, heavenly army appeared with the angel, praising God and saying,
>
> "Glory to God in the highest,
> and on earth peace among people with whom he is pleased!"
>
> When the angels left them and went back to heaven, the shepherds said to one another, "Let us go over to Bethlehem and see this thing that has taken place, that the Lord has made known to us." (Luke 2:10–15)

Yet a third time, an angel appeared to Joseph to warn him of Herod's plans:

> After they had gone, an angel of the Lord appeared to Joseph in a dream and said, "Get up, take the child and his mother and flee to Egypt, and stay there until I tell you, for Herod is going to look for the child to kill him." (Mattai 2:13)

During His earthly life. Following Satan's temptation of Yeshua in the wilderness, at the beginning of His ministry, angels appeared to Him:

> Then the devil left him, and angels came and began ministering to his needs. (Mattai 4:11)

At the end of Yeshua's ministry, we likewise find an angel ministering to Him as He struggled spiritually in the garden of Gethsemane:

> He went away from them about a stone's throw, knelt down, and prayed, "Father, if you are willing, take this cup away from me. Yet

> not my will but yours be done." Then an angel from heaven appeared to him and strengthened him. (Luke 22:41–43)

And as we have seen, angels stood on call to defend the Messiah Yeshua had He needed them:

> Or do you think that I cannot call on my Father, and that he would send me more than twelve legions of angels right now? (Mattai 26:53)

At the resurrection. Angels are prominent in connection with Yeshua's resurrection. Recall that it was an angel who opened the entrance to the tomb. This same angel announced to the group of women, who had come to anoint His body, that Yeshua was raised from the dead.

> Suddenly there was a severe earthquake, for an angel of the Lord descending from heaven came and rolled away the stone and sat on it. His appearance was like lightning, and his clothes were white as snow. The guards were shaken and became like dead men because they were so afraid of him. But the angel said to the women, "Do not be afraid; I know that you are looking for Yeshua, who was crucified. He is not here, for he has been raised, just as he said. Come and see the place where he was lying." (Mattai 28:2–6)

In relation to the present work of redemption. Angels take a deep interest in the work of redemption. Even before Yeshua came, the Tanach spoke of the gospel. Angels, Kefa tells us, would love to know more about this:

> They were shown that they were serving not themselves but you, in regard to the things now announced to you through those who proclaimed the gospel to you by the Holy Spirit sent from heaven—things angels long to catch a glimpse of. (1 Kefa 1:12)

And when someone responds to the gospel in faith, the angels take notice:

> In the same way, I tell you, there is joy in the presence of God's angels over one sinner who repents. (Luke 15:10)

In relation to Yeshua's second coming. At the ascension of the Messiah, two angels predicted His second coming to the gathered disciples:

> As they were still staring into the sky while he was going, suddenly two men in white clothing stood near them and said, "Men of Galilee, why do you stand here looking up into the sky? This same Yeshua who has been taken up from you into heaven will come back in the same way you saw him go into heaven." (Acts 1:10–11)

When He does return, angels will attend Him:

> When the Son of Man comes in his glory and all the angels with him, then he will sit on his glorious throne. (Mattai 25:31)

The same thought occurs in the context of spiritual priorities and faith:

> For if anyone is ashamed of me and my words in this adulterous and sinful generation, the Son of Man will also be ashamed of him when he comes in the glory of his Father with the holy angels. (Mark 8:38)

Sha'ul echoes the thought that angels will accompany Yeshua on His return:

> For it is right for God to repay with affliction those who afflict you, and to you who are being afflicted to give rest together with us when the Lord Yeshua is revealed from heaven with his mighty angels. (2 Thessalonians 1:6–7)

In connection with the time of the end, angels function as "advance men," preparing the world for God's kingdom as they weed out evil:

> The field is the world and the good seed are the people of the kingdom. The weeds are the people of the evil one, and the enemy who sows them is the devil. The harvest is the end of the age, and the reapers are angels. As the weeds are collected and burned with fire, so it will

be at the end of the age. The Son of Man will send his angels, and they will gather from his kingdom everything that causes sin as well as all lawbreakers. (Mattai 13:38–41)

Angels and the worship of Yeshua. Above, we saw that angels worship God, but here we specifically want to note that angels worship the Messiah Yeshua, who is God in the flesh. This is seen in Hebrews:

> But when he again brings his firstborn into the world, he says, "Let all the angels of God worship him!" (Hebrews 1:6)

It is seen as well as in Revelation:

> Then I looked and heard the voice of many angels in a circle around the throne, as well as the living creatures and the elders.
> Their number was ten thousand times ten thousand—
> thousands times thousands—all of whom were singing
> in a loud voice:
> "Worthy is the lamb who was killed
> to receive power and wealth
> and wisdom and might
> and honor and glory and praise!" (Revelation 5:11–12)

Ministries in Relation to the Affairs of Nations.

Act as messengers in regard to rulers and nations. We see this in the case of the judgment that came on King Nebuchadnezzar:

> This announcement is by the decree of the sentinels;
> this decision is by the pronouncement of the holy ones,
> so that those who are alive may understand
> that the Most High has authority over human kingdoms,
> and he bestows them on whomever he wishes.
> He establishes over them even the lowliest of human beings.
> (Daniel 4:17)

Are guardians over specific nations, and over Israel in particular. The "great prince" Michael protects the people of Israel during the time of distress described in Daniel:

> At that time Michael,
> the great prince who watches over your people,
> will arise.
> There will be a time of distress
> unlike any other from the nation's beginning up to that time.
> But at that time your own people,
> all those whose names are found written in the book,
> will escape. (Daniel 12:1)

Play a part in the fulfillment of God's providential work within human history. Our example comes yet again from the book of Daniel. This time, an angel is said to protect Darius the Mede, the foreign potentate who came to rule over Israel during the return from the Babylonian captivity. The angel is the speaker in this passage:

> However, I will first tell you what is written in a dependable book. (There is no one who strengthens me against these princes, except Michael your prince. . . .
>
> And in the first year of Darius the Mede, I stood to strengthen him and to provide protection for him.) (Daniel 10:21; 11:1)

Ministries in Relation to the People of God. Much angelic activity in the service of believers takes place "behind the scenes." We may be surprised one day to learn just how closely they were involved with our lives!

Serve individual churches. Each of the seven churches mentioned in Revelation 2 and 3 has a specific angel assigned to it. Though their specific tasks are not specified here, each angel receives a written message that concerns their particular church.

> The mystery of the seven stars that you saw in my right hand and the seven golden lampstands is this: The seven stars are the angels of the seven *qehilot*

> and the seven lampstands are the seven *qehilot*. To the angel of the *qehilah* in Ephesus, write the following: This is the solemn pronouncement of the one who has a firm grasp on the seven stars in his right hand—the one who walks among the seven golden lampstands. (Revelation 1:20–2:1)

Observe believers in their worship, work, and suffering. When Sha'ul speaks about the need for a woman to have a head covering, one of his reasons has to do with angels:

> For this reason a woman should have a symbol of authority on her head, because of the angels. (1 Corinthians 11:10)

In the culture of that day, it was necessary for a woman to cover her head. Very likely, this was a sign of respect, not only to the leadership of the congregation but in some way to the angels as well.

A second example comes from Sha'ul's charge to Timothy, which confirms that angels are observers of believers:

> Before God and Messiah Yeshua and the elect angels, I solemnly charge you to carry out these commands without prejudice or favoritism of any kind. (1 Timothy 5:21)

Sha'ul also speaks of angels who observed the sufferings of the *shlichim* as they went about preaching the gospel:

> For, I think, God has exhibited us apostles last of all, as men condemned to die, because we have become a spectacle to the world, both to angels and to people. We are fools for Messiah, but you are wise in Messiah! We are weak, but you are strong! You are distinguished, we are dishonored! To the present hour we are hungry and thirsty, poorly clothed, brutally treated, and without a roof over our heads. We do hard work, toiling with our own hands. When we are verbally abused, we respond with a blessing, when persecuted, we endure, when people lie about us, we answer in a friendly manner. We are the world's dirt and scum, even now. (1 Corinthians 4:9–13)

In spite of their miserable treatment, the *shlichim* offered blessing in return. Angels who observed this marveled at the grace and wisdom of God, who enabled His servants to continue their ministry of outreach.

Play a role in the communication of God's revelation. Angels provided information concerning the Law to Moses, participating in the communication of God's Word:

> Why then was the law given? It was added because of transgressions, until the arrival of the descendant to whom the promise had been made. It was administered through angels by an intermediary. (Galatians 3:19)

We also note that at least some New Covenant revelation came through angels:

> The revelation of Yeshua the Messiah, which God gave him to show his servants what must happen very soon. He made it clear by sending his angel to his servant Yohanan, who then testified to everything that he saw concerning the word of God and the testimony about Yeshua the Messiah. (Revelation 1:1–2)

Are involved in God's answers to prayer. The angel Gabriel, for example, came to Daniel to relate God's response to his prayer:

> Yes, while I was still praying, the man Gabriel, whom I had seen previously in a vision, was approaching me in my state of extreme weariness, around the time of the evening offering. He spoke with me, instructing me as follows: "Daniel, I have now come to impart understanding to you." (Daniel 9:21–22)

Even more dramatic is the incident in Acts 12:

> So Kefa was kept in prison, but those in the *qehilah* were earnestly praying to God for him. On that very night before Herod was going to bring him out for trial, Kefa was sleeping between two soldiers, bound with two

> chains, while guards in front of the door were keeping watch over the prison. Suddenly an angel of the Lord appeared, and a light shone in the prison cell. He struck Kefa on the side and woke him up, saying, "Get up quickly!" And the chains fell off Kefa's wrists. (Acts 12:5–7)

Provide aid in evangelizing. An angel directed Philip to leave an important series of meetings in Samaria, at which many came to the Lord, and to go south:

> Then an angel of the Lord said to Philip, "Get up and go south on the road that goes down from Jerusalem to Gaza." (This is a desert road.) So he got up and went. There he met an Ethiopian eunuch, a court official of Candace, queen of the Ethiopians, who was in charge of all her treasury. He had come to Jerusalem to worship. (Acts 8:26–27)

As we know from the rest of the story, this solitary Ethiopian eunuch was led to faith through Philip, immersed in water, and continued on his way. And who knows how many other Ethiopians he was able to win to the Lord?

On another occasion, angels prepared Cornelius and his family to hear the word of God from Kefa:

> About three o'clock one afternoon he saw clearly in a vision an angel of God who came in and said to him, "Cornelius." Staring at him and becoming greatly afraid, Cornelius replied, "What is it, Lord?" The angel said to him,
>
> "Your prayers and your acts of charity have gone up as a memorial before God. . . .
>
> When the angel who had spoken to him departed, Cornelius called two of his personal servants and a devout soldier from among those who served him. . . .
>
> They said, "Cornelius the centurion, a righteous and God-fearing man, well spoken of by the whole Jewish nation, was directed by a holy angel to summon you to his house and to hear a message from you." (Acts 10:3–4, 7, 22)

Encourage and protect believers in times of danger. The psalmist speaks of angels who guard believers from danger at the command of God:

> For he will order his angels
> to protect you in all you do.
> They will lift you up in their hands,
> so you will not slip and fall on a stone. (Psalm 91:11–12)

Scripture gives specific examples of this angelic ministry. On Sha'ul's wild ship ride in the midst of a frightening storm, it was an angel who encouraged him:

> For last night an angel of the God to whom I belong and whom I serve came to me and said, "Do not be afraid, Sha'ul! You must stand before Caesar, and God has graciously granted you the safety of all who are sailing with you." (Acts 27:23–24)

Earlier on, an angel delivered the apostles from jail, allowing them to continue in their proclamation of the word:

> They laid hands on the apostles and put them in a public jail. But during the night an angel of the Lord opened the doors of the prison, led them out, and said, "Go and stand in the temple courts and proclaim to the people all the words of this life." (Acts 5:18–20)

Similarly, we have already seen how Kefa was delivered from prison by an angel in response to the prayers of God's people:

> So Kefa was kept in prison, but those in the *qehilah* were earnestly praying to God for him. On that very night before Herod was going to bring him out for trial, Kefa was sleeping between two soldiers, bound with two chains, while guards in front of the door were keeping watch over the prison. Suddenly an angel of the Lord appeared, and a light shone in the prison cell. He struck Kefa on the side and woke him up, saying,

> "Get up quickly!" And the chains fell off Kefa's wrists. The angel said to him, "Fasten your belt and put on your sandals." Kefa did so. Then the angel said to him, "Put on your cloak and follow me." Kefa went out and followed him; he did not realize that what was happening through the angel was real, but thought he was seeing a vision. (Acts 12:5–9)

Care for the righteous when death comes. Angels tenderly brought Lazarus to be with Abraham:

> Now the poor man died and was carried by the angels to Abraham's side. The rich man also died and was buried. (Luke 16:22)

Michael the archangel similarly protected the body of Moses. Had Satan gotten ahold of it, he undoubtedly would have turned it into an object of worship, leading many people astray:

> But even when Michael the archangel was arguing with the devil and debating with him concerning Moses' body, he did not dare to bring a slanderous judgment, but said, "May the Lord rebuke you!" (Yehudah 1:9)

Will gather the elect of Israel at the second coming of the Messiah.

> And he will send his angels with a loud trumpet blast, and they will gather his elect from the four winds, from one end of heaven to the other. (Mattai 24:31)

Some interpret this passage to mean that the angels will gather the entire body of the Messiah. However, this event occurs after the tribulation and the distress that will come on Israel at that time (see Mattai 24:29), indicating that the elect in this verse refers to the elect of Israel.

Ministries in Relation to the Unrighteous.

Announce and execute coming judgments. Two angels (called *visitors* in the passage below) arrived in Sodom for the purpose of bringing about its destruction:

> Then the two visitors [NIV: "men"] said to Lot, "Who else do you have here? Do you have any sons-in-law, sons, daughters, or other relatives in the city? Get them out of this place because we are about to destroy it. The outcry against this place is so great before the LORD that he has sent us to destroy it." (Genesis 19:12–13)

At the close of the Scripture, we likewise find angels who execute judgment:

> Then I heard a loud voice from the temple declaring to the seven angels: "Go and pour out on the earth the seven bowls containing God's wrath." (Revelation 16:1)

Then we find an angel who announces the coming judgment at the Battle of Har-Megiddo (Armageddon), at the close of the tribulation period:

> Then I saw one angel standing in the sun, and he shouted in a loud voice to all the birds flying high in the sky:
> "Come, gather around for the great banquet of God,
> to eat your fill of the flesh of kings,
> the flesh of generals,
> the flesh of powerful people,
> the flesh of horses and those who ride them,
> and the flesh of all people, both free and slave,
> and small and great!" (Revelation 19:17–18)

Not only do angels execute judgment on cities and armies but also on individuals:

> Immediately an angel of the Lord struck Herod down because he did not give the glory to God, and he was eaten by worms and died. (Acts 12:23)

Perhaps the ultimate example of angels in connection with God's judgment comes when Satan is bound and imprisoned:

> Then I saw an angel descending from heaven, holding in his hand the key to the abyss and a huge chain. He seized the dragon—the ancient serpent, who is the devil and Satan—and tied him up for a thousand years. The angel then threw him into the abyss and locked and sealed it so that he could not deceive the nations until the one thousand years were finished. (After these things he must be released for a brief period of time.) (Revelation 20:1–3)

Act as harvesters or reapers at the end of the age.

> And the enemy who sows them is the devil. The harvest is the end of the age, and the reapers are angels. As the weeds are collected and burned with fire, so it will be at the end of the age. The Son of Man will send his angels, and they will gather from his kingdom everything that causes sin as well as all lawbreakers. (Mattai 13:39–41)

Angelic Activity on Special Occasions

We have already looked at some of these passages above. At this point we want to draw some of these verses together to show that angelic activity becomes more prominent when God launches new epochs in His program.

At Creation. Angels were present when the world began, rejoicing and praising God:

> Where were you
> when I laid the foundation of the earth?
> Tell me, if you possess understanding!
> Who set its measurements—if you know—
> or who stretched a measuring line across it?
> On what were its bases set,
> or who laid its cornerstone—
> when the morning stars sang in chorus,
> and all the sons of God [NIV: "angels"] shouted for joy? (Job 38:4–7)

At the Giving of the Law. The word of God was spoken by angels and communicated to Moses, and from Moses to the people.

> Why then was the law given? It was added because of transgressions, until the arrival of the descendant to whom the promise had been made. It was administered through angels by an intermediary. (Galatians 3:19)

The book of Hebrews reiterates this idea in connection with the binding nature of the Law:

> For if the message spoken through angels proved to be so firm that every violation or disobedience received its just penalty, how will we escape if we neglect such a great salvation? It was first communicated through the Lord and was confirmed to us by those who heard him. (Hebrews 2:2–3)

At the Events Surrounding the Ministry of Yeshua. We previously observed passages showing the presence of angels at the announcement of Yeshua's birth and in the protection of Yeshua's family. We also noted the presence of angels in the book of Acts, that is, in the early days of the body of Messiah. At that time they both aided believers and rendered judgment against others, for example, King Herod. Finally, we saw that angels will be present at the second coming of the Messiah when He gathers the believers.

Where Angels Reside

The angels designated as "holy" serve on earth, but have their abode in heaven. So, for example, we find phrases to that effect in verses such as these:

> Suddenly there was a severe earthquake, for an angel of the Lord descending from heaven came and rolled away the stone and sat on it. (Mattai 28:2)

> For when they rise from the dead, they neither marry nor are given in marriage, but are like angels in heaven. (Mark 12:25)

> When the angels left them and went back to heaven, the shepherds said to one another, "Let us go over to Bethlehem and see this thing that has taken place, that the Lord has made known to us." (Luke 2:15)

Some fallen angels are likewise in heavenly places, if we understand "the rulers and the authorities in the heavenly realms" to refer to evil angels:

> The purpose of this enlightenment is that through the *qehilah* the multifaceted wisdom of God should now be disclosed to the rulers and the authorities in the heavenly realms. This was according to the eternal purpose that he accomplished in Messiah Yeshua our Lord. (Ephesians 3:10–11)

Other evil angels are on earth, doing the bidding of Satan. The four angels mentioned in Revelation are an example:

> . . . saying to the sixth angel, the one holding the trumpet, "Set free the four angels who are bound at the great river Euphrates!" Then the four angels who had been prepared for this hour, day, month, and year were set free to kill a third of humanity. (Revelation 9:14–15)

And some of the evil angels are already in the abyss, particularly the one known as the "angel of the abyss":

> They have as king over them the angel of the abyss, whose name in Hebrew is *Abaddon*, and in Greek, *Apollyon*. (Revelation 9:11)

Judgment and Punishment of Evil Angels

Some of the evil angels are already suffering punishment even before their final judgment. Kefa and Yehudah refer to such angels:

> For if God did not spare the angels who sinned, but threw them into hell and locked them up in chains in utter darkness, to be kept until the judgment, . . . (2 Kefa 2:4)

> You also know that the angels who did not keep within their proper domain but abandoned their own place of residence, he has kept in eternal chains in utter darkness, locked up for the judgment of the great Day. (Yehudah 1:6)

When these angels are brought into judgment as Kefa and Yehudah state, their judges will be the believers in the body of Messiah. They will sit with the Messiah to render their judgment:

> Do you not know that we will judge angels? Why not ordinary matters! (1 Corinthians 6:3)

At that time the evil angels will be committed to their place of final punishment:

> Then he will say to those on his left, "Depart from me, you accursed, into the eternal fire that has been prepared for the devil and his angels!" (Mattai 25:41)

While it may sound strange for angels to end up in such a place, we must realize that they have freedom of will much as do people. And they too can exercise that freedom by making wrong choices that lead to their ultimate judgment.

Satan

A Key Passage: A Portrait of Satan

We now turn to consider Lucifer, the primary archangel, who after his fall became the archenemy of God, called HaSatan ("the opposer"). By way of introduction, let us look at Isaiah 14:1–20, a key passage concerning Satan. As we read it, however, we may wonder: who is Isaiah addressing? Is it the literal king of Babylon, or is it Satan as the one standing behind this despot? We will take a look at this passage before going on to consider the actual doctrine of Satan.

Here is the passage in full, with verse numbers indicated for the following discussion:

> [1] The LORD will certainly have compassion on Jacob; he will again choose Israel as his special people and restore them to their land. Resident foreigners will join them and unite with the family of Jacob. [2] Nations will take them and bring them back to their own place. Then the family of Jacob will make foreigners their servants as they settle in the LORD's land. They will make their captors captives and rule over the ones who oppressed them. [3] When the LORD gives you relief from your suffering and anxiety, and from the hard labor which you were made to perform, [4] you will taunt the king of Babylon with these words:
> "Look how the oppressor has met his end!
> Hostility has ceased!
> [5] The LORD has broken the club of the wicked,
> the scepter of rulers.
> [6] It furiously struck down nations
> with unceasing blows.
> It angrily ruled over nations,
> oppressing them without restraint.
> [7] The whole earth rests and is quiet;
> they break into song.
> [8] The evergreens also rejoice over your demise,
> as do the cedars of Lebanon, singing,
> 'Since you fell asleep,
> no woodsman comes up to chop us down!'
> [9] Sheol below is stirred up about you,
> ready to meet you when you arrive.
> It rouses the spirits of the dead for you,
> all the former leaders of the earth;
> it makes all the former kings of the nations
> rise from their thrones.
> [10] All of them respond to you, saying:
> 'You too have become weak like us!

You have become just like us!
[11] Your splendor has been brought down to Sheol,
as well as the sound of your stringed instruments.
You lie on a bed of maggots,
with a blanket of worms over you.
[12] Look how you have fallen from the sky,
O shining one, son of the dawn!
You have been cut down to the ground,
O conqueror of the nations!
[13] You said to yourself,
'I will climb up to the sky.
Above the stars of El
I will set up my throne.
I will rule on the mountain of assembly
on the remote slopes of Zaphon.
[14] I will climb up to the tops of the clouds;
I will make myself like the Most High!'
[15] But you were brought down to Sheol,
to the remote slopes of the pit.
[16] Those who see you stare at you,
they look at you carefully, thinking:
'Is this the man who shook the earth,
the one who made kingdoms tremble?
[17] Is this the one who made the world like a desert,
who ruined its cities,
and refused to free his prisoners so they could return home?'
[18] As for all the kings of the nations,
all of them lie down in splendor,
each in his own tomb.
[19] But you have been thrown out of your grave
like a shoot that is thrown away.
You lie among the slain,
among those who have been slashed by the sword,
among those headed for the stones of the pit,

as if you were a mangled corpse.
[20]You will not be buried with them,
because you destroyed your land
and killed your people.
The offspring of the wicked
will never be mentioned again." (Isaiah 14:1–20)

The View of Edward J. Young. The scholar Edward J. Young has advanced one possible interpretation. He suggests that the Babylonian king—the "shining one" or "morning star" (NIV) of verse 12, in imagery perhaps borrowed from the terminology used of an ancient god—attempted to reach for the heavens and become like God, reigning above the stars. Says Young:

> How could the Babylonian spirit ever plan such a thing? The answer is that Babylon had sought to render void the work of God. God's plan was to bring salvation to the world through the coming of a Saviour. Babylon had set herself in opposition to God; she would thwart His plans by means of self-exaltation against the true God. We are not to understand any of the individual Babylonian kings as specifically ever having uttered precisely these words, but what they express is rather the intention of the Babylonian power or spirit.[4]

So Young interprets this passage as referring in general to the spirit of the Babylonian kings who sought to oppose God.

The View of Alva MacLain. Another possibility is that of Alva MacLain, who suggests that Isaiah is referring to a *particular* Babylonian king who will one day reign over the final Babylon. MacLain thereby connects the Isaiah passage with Revelation 17. He also suggests, however, that Isaiah 14:12–15 refers to Satan himself, by whose power this future "Babylonian" king will arise.

The View of This Writer. My own view is that the prophet Isaiah is speaking of the Babylonian king who would conquer Judah in 586 B.C.E., initiating the Babylonian captivity and ending the First Temple and Commonwealth. The language of Isaiah 14:4–11 suggests the arrogance of the

Babylonian king, yet as we continue to verses 12–15, Isaiah appears to be addressing *someone else*. Then beginning with Isaiah 14:16, the prophet again takes up the word concerning the king of Babylon.

The idea that the prophet is addressing a spirit *behind* the king finds support from a passage we have already encountered in Daniel:

> However, the prince of the kingdom of Persia was opposing me for twenty-one days. But Michael, one of the leading princes, came to help me, because I was left there with the kings of Persia. (Daniel 10:13)

The angel who speaks with Daniel is referring to a certain spirit of Satan that stands behind the earthly king of Persia. At the same time, other spirits—from God rather than from Satan—also stand behind rulers, who are then pulled from one side to another as they make decisions.

Though he himself does not hold to the view of this writer, Young points out that regarding Isaiah 14:12, "Tertullian, Gregory the Great, and others have referred this verse to the fall of Satan, . . ."[5] Indeed, the context of Isaiah 14:12–15 suggests that Satan attempted to be like God, intending to depose Him from His throne, but was himself knocked out of his high position and sent to Sheol. Though Satan at present is not confined to Sheol, we have in Isaiah a picture of how God one day—after He has used him for His own purposes—will put him away forever.

Three arguments can be advanced in favor of this view:

First, verses 4–11 seem to be a description of the king of Babylon who came in pomp and power to conquer Judah in 586 B.C.E. Yet these verses also depict that his power is not total and that he himself will one day be conquered.

Second, from other passages in Scripture, we learn that Satan can influence living creatures, human or otherwise. Sometimes we see that Satan himself is addressed through the person or animal that he is using. In the examples below, we see Satan being addressed through the serpent, through Kefa, and in reference to Yehudah:

> The LORD God said to the serpent,
> "Because you have done this,

> cursed are you above all the wild beasts
> and all the living creatures of the field!
> On your belly you will crawl
> and dust you will eat all the days of your life.
> And I will put hostility between you and the woman
> and between your offspring and her offspring;
> her offspring will attack your head,
> and you will attack her offspring's heel." (Genesis 3:14–15)

> So Kefa took him aside and began to rebuke him: "God forbid, Lord! This must not happen to you!" But he turned and said to Kefa, "Get behind me, Satan! You are a stumbling block to me, because you are not setting your mind on God's interests, but on man's." (Mattai 16:22–23)

> Yeshua replied, "Didn't I choose you, the twelve, and yet one of you is the devil?" (Yohanan 6:70)[6]

The third argument is that Scripture elsewhere uses the device of beginning a passage with a description of a historical person, then envisioning someone else who stands behind that individual. We find this in Ezekiel 28. Verses 1–10 concern the historic king of Tyre:

> The word of the LORD came to me: "Son of man, say to the prince of Tyre, 'This is what the sovereign LORD says:
> "'Your heart is proud and you said, "I am a god;
> I sit in the seat of gods, in the heart of the seas"—
> yet you are a man and not a god,
> though you think you are godlike.
> Look, you are wiser than Daniel;
> no secret is hidden from you.
> By your wisdom and understanding you have gained wealth for yourself;
> you have amassed gold and silver in your treasuries.
> By your great skill in trade you have increased your wealth,
> and your heart is proud because of your wealth.

"'Therefore this is what the sovereign Lord says:
Because you think you are godlike,
I am about to bring foreigners against you, the most terrifying of nations.
They will draw their swords against the grandeur made by your wisdom, and they will defile your splendor.
They will bring you down to the pit, and you will die violently in the heart of the seas.
Will you still say, "I am a god," before the one who kills you–
though you are a man and not a god—
when you are in the power of those who wound you?
You will die the death of the uncircumcised by the hand of foreigners;
for I have spoken, declares the sovereign LORD.'" (Ezekiel 28:1–10)

But once we pass to verses 11–16, the description moves far beyond what could apply to the king of Tyre, for it was only Satan himself who had access to the garden of Eden:

The word of the LORD came to me: "Son of man, sing a lament for the king of Tyre, and say to him, 'This is what the sovereign LORD says:
"'You were the sealer of perfection,
full of wisdom, and perfect in beauty.
You were in Eden, the garden of God.
Every precious stone was your covering,
the ruby, topaz, and emerald,
the chrysolite, onyx, and jasper,
the sapphire, turquoise, and beryl;
your settings and mounts were made of gold.
On the day you were created they were prepared.
I placed you there with an anointed guardian cherub;
you were on the holy mountain of God;
you walked about amidst fiery stones.
You were blameless in your behavior from the day you were created,
until sin was discovered in you.

> In the abundance of your trade you were filled with violence,
> and you sinned;
> so I defiled you and banished you from the mountain of God—
> the guardian cherub expelled you from the midst of the stones of fire.
> (Ezekiel 28:11–16)

Finally, in verses 17–19, the subject is again the historic king of Tyre where he is again addressed as in verses 1–10:

> Your heart was proud because of your beauty;
> you corrupted your wisdom on account of your splendor.
> I threw you down to the ground;
> I placed you before kings, that they might see you.
> By the multitude of your iniquities, through the sinfulness of your trade,
> you desecrated your sanctuaries.
> So I drew fire out from within you; it consumed you,
> and I turned you to ashes on the earth
> before the eyes of all who saw you.
> All who know you among the peoples are shocked at you;
> you have become terrified and will be no more. (Ezekiel 28:17–19)

Existence, Personality, and Nature of Satan

Existence. Satan is mentioned in seven books of the Tanach (Genesis, 1 Chronicles, Job, Psalms, Isaiah, Ezekiel, and Zechariah) as well as by every writer of the New Covenant. Yeshua Himself refers to Satan as a distinct personality, as seen in twenty-five out of twenty-nine passages in the gospels in which Yeshua speaks.

Personality. Personal pronouns are used when referring to Satan, showing that he has personality as a distinct individual. Furthermore, Satan has all the marks of personality. One such mark is the power of speech:

> The LORD said to Satan, "Where have you come from?" And Satan answered the LORD, "From roving about on the earth, and from walking back and forth across it." . . .

> Then Satan answered the LORD, "Is it for nothing that Job fears God? Have you not made a hedge around him and his household and all that he has on every side? You have blessed the work of his hands, and his livestock have increased in the land. But extend your hand and strike everything he has, and he will no doubt curse you to your face!" (Job 1:7, 9–11)

> And the LORD said to Satan, "Where do you come from?" Satan answered the LORD, "From roving about on the earth, and from walking back and forth across it." . . .
>
> But Satan answered the LORD, "Skin for skin! Indeed, a man will give up all that he has to save his life!" (Job 2:2, 4)

> The tempter came and said to him, "If you are the Son of God, command these stones to become bread." . . .
>
> . . . and said to him, "If you are the Son of God, throw yourself down. For it is written, 'He will command his angels concerning you' and 'with their hands they will lift you up, so that you will not strike your foot against a stone.'" . . .
>
> And he said to him, "I will give you all these things if you throw yourself to the ground and worship me." (Mattai 4:3, 6, 9)

A second mark of personality is the ability to express the purposes of one's will:

> You said to yourself,
> "I will climb up to the sky.
> Above the stars of El
> I will set up my throne.
> I will rule on the mountain of assembly
> on the remote slopes of Zaphon.
> I will climb up to the tops of the clouds;
> I will make myself like the Most High!" (Isaiah 14:13–14)

A third mark is the ability to engage in reflective thought, in the example below, "treachery":

> But I am afraid that just as the serpent deceived Eve by his treachery [NIV: "cunning"], your minds may be led astray from a sincere and pure devotion to Messiah. (2 Corinthians 11:3)

A fourth mark is to be treated as morally responsible. It is evident that this is true of Satan, since there will be a final judgment when he will be put into the eternal fire:

> Then he will say to those on his left, "Depart from me, you accursed, into the eternal fire that has been prepared for the devil and his angels!" (Mattai 25:41)

Nature.
Created without sin.

> You were blameless in your behavior from the day you were created, until sin was discovered in you. (Ezekiel 28:15)

Primarily a spiritual being. This is true even though he can manifest himself in physical ways:

> Clothe yourselves with the full armor of God so that you may be able to stand against the schemes of the devil. For our struggle is not against flesh and blood, but against the rulers, against the powers, against the world rulers of this darkness, against the spiritual forces of evil in the heavens. (Ephesians 6:11–12)

Higher in rank than any other angelic being. His high status is suggested by the reference to him as a cherub in Ezekiel.

> I placed you there with an anointed guardian cherub;
> you were on the holy mountain of God;
> you walked about amidst fiery stones. (Ezekiel 28:14)

NIV especially suggests this high rank with its different translation, "You were anointed as a guardian cherub . . ."

And his status as higher than any other angel is confirmed when Michael the archangel refuses to dispute with him but leaves the rebuke to the Lord:

> Yet these men, as a result of their dreams, defile the flesh, reject authority, and insult the glorious ones. But even when Michael the archangel was arguing with the devil and debating with him concerning Moses' body, he did not dare to bring a slanderous judgment, but said, "May the Lord rebuke you!" (Yehudah 1:8–9)

Though Michael is an archangel, Satan before his fall was the chief archangel, Lucifer. Therefore, he was actually the highest among all the angelic beings.

The Descriptive Names of Satan

A number of terms are used to describe Satan. The most well-known, of course, are *Satan* ("Opposer"), occuring fifty-three times in the NIV, and the *Devil* ("Slanderer"), occuring thirty-three times. But many other descriptive epithets are also given to Satan. We can only see a sampling of the verses in which they are used:

The Evil One.

> . . . and in all of this, by taking up the shield of faith with which you can extinguish all the flaming arrows of the evil one. (Ephesians 6:16)

The Dragon.

> Then war broke out in heaven: Michael and his angels fought against the dragon, and the dragon and his angels fought back. (Revelation 12:7)

The Tempter.

The tempter came and said to him, "If you are the Son of God, command these stones to become bread." (Mattai 4:3)

The Accuser.

Then I heard a loud voice in heaven saying,
"The salvation and the power and the kingdom of our God,
and the ruling authority of his Messiah, have now come,
because the accuser of our brothers and sisters,
the one who accuses them day and night before our God,
has been thrown down. (Revelation 12:10)

The Serpent. Note that three other epithets are used as well in this verse:

So that huge dragon—the ancient serpent, the one called the devil and Satan, who deceives the whole world—was thrown down to the earth, and his angels along with him. (Revelation 12:9)

In addition to these single-word terms, various phrases are used in describing Satan:

Beelzebub, the Ruler of Demons.

But when the Pharisees heard this they said, "He does not cast out demons except by the power of Beelzebul, the ruler of demons!" (Mattai 12:24)

The Ruler of This World.

Now is the judgment of this world; now the ruler of this world will be driven out. (Yohanan 12:31)

The God of This Age.

. . . among whom the god of this age has blinded the minds of those who do not believe so they would not see the light of the glorious gospel of Messiah, who is the image of God. (2 Corinthians 4:4)

The Ruler of the Kingdom of the Air/The Ruler of the Spirit That Is Now Energizing the Sons of Disobedience.

> . . . in which you formerly lived according to this world's present path, according to the ruler of the kingdom of the air, the ruler of the spirit that is now energizing the sons of disobedience, . . . (Ephesians 2:2)

The Spirit of the World.

> Now we have not received the spirit of the world, but the Spirit who is from God, so that we may know the things that are freely given to us by God. (1 Corinthians 2:12)

The One Who Is in the World.

> You are from God, little children, and have conquered them, because the one who is in you is greater than the one who is in the world. (1 Yohanan 4:4)

At the Arrest of Yeshua, Satan's Activity Is Also Described as "The Power of Darkness."

> Day after day when I was with you in the temple courts, you did not arrest me. But this is your hour, and that of the power of darkness! (Luke 22:53)

Compare NIV's rendition of the final phrase as "when darkness reigns."

Satan's Original State

Scripture provides several vivid descriptions of Satan's pristine moral character, before he fell. Such descriptions make the most sense if he was the chief archangel and even "next in line" to God Himself.

Isaiah refers to Satan as the "shining one" ("morning star" or "Lucifer" in some translations).

Look how you have fallen from the sky,
O shining one, son of the dawn!
You have been cut down to the ground,
O conqueror of the nations! (Isaiah 14:12)

However, the fullest descriptions of his original state appears in Ezekiel:

Son of man, sing a lament for the king of Tyre, and say to him, "This is what the sovereign LORD says:
'You were the sealer of perfection,
full of wisdom, and perfect in beauty.
I placed you there with an anointed guardian cherub;
you were on the holy mountain of God;
you walked about amidst fiery stones.
You were blameless in your behavior from the day you were created,
until sin was discovered in you.'" (Ezekiel 28:12, 14–15)

In the New Testament, the phrase "in the heavens" may point to Satan's original estate:

For our struggle is not against flesh and blood, but against the rulers, against the powers, against the world rulers of this darkness, against the spiritual forces of evil in the heavens. (Ephesians 6:12)

The Fall of Satan and Its Results

Satan's fall was caused by pride. Five times he uses the word *I* in declaring his ambition to depose God:

You said to yourself,
"*I* will climb up to the sky.
Above the stars of El
I will set up my throne.
I will rule on the mountain of assembly
on the remote slopes of Zaphon.

> *I* will climb up to the tops of the clouds;
> *I* will make myself like the Most High!"
> (Isaiah 14:13–14, emphasis added)

This unbridled hubris was in complete opposition to God's design. Though Satan had the freedom of will to make such a choice, once he did, there was no turning back. Without repentance, he has become the archenemy of God and continues to this day to oppose God's will.

The fall of Satan marks the entrance of sin into the universe, together with all of its disorders. Yeshua characterized Satan in this way:

> You people are from your father the devil, and you want to do what your father desires. He was a murderer from the beginning, and does not uphold the truth, because there is no truth in him. Whenever he lies, he speaks according to his own nature, because he is a liar and the father of lies. (Yohanan 8:44)

Satan's disorder then entered into the world of humanity with the fall of Adam and Eve, as well as into the natural world with its physical evils.

As a result of his fall, Satan became not only the enemy of God but also the adversary of the people of God. He is the one responsible for sowing weeds among the wheat:

> But while everyone was sleeping, an enemy came and sowed weeds among the wheat and went away. (Mattai 13:25)

In the parable, this is likened to sowing evil and destruction among people who themselves in turn become God's enemies. At the end of the age, evil will be rooted out (see Mattai 13:41). But until then, Scripture warns us about Satan's present activity and what our response should be:

> Be sober and alert. Your enemy the devil, *like a roaring lion*, is on the prowl looking for someone to devour. Resist him, strong in your faith, because you know that your brothers and sisters throughout the

world are enduring the same kinds of suffering.
(1 Kefa 5:8–9, emphasis added)

The Present Position and Powers of Satan

Controls Fallen Angels and Demons. Satan is described as "the prince of demons":

> But when the Pharisees heard this they said, "He does not cast out demons except by the power of Beelzebul, the ruler of demons!" (Mattai 12:24)

As such, he rules over a demonic kingdom comprising many fallen angelic followers. For that reason, in the final judgment both Satan *and* his angels are judged, as Yeshua indicated:

> Then he will say to those on his left, "Depart from me, you accursed, into the eternal fire that has been prepared for the devil and his angels!" (Mattai 25:41)

Controls the Present World System. Satan exercises control over all aspects of the present world system:

> We know that we are from God, and the whole world lies in the power of the evil one. (1 Yohanan 5:19)

For this reason he is also called "the ruler of this world":

> Now is the judgment of this world; now the ruler of this world will be driven out. (Yohanan 12:31)

Political control. We already saw this aspect in relation to powers that stand behind the nations.

Ecclesiastical control over the religions of the world. Sha'ul reminds his audience about Satan in these words:

> . . . among whom the god of this age has blinded the minds of those who do not believe so they would not see the light of the glorious gospel of Messiah, who is the image of God. (2 Corinthians 4:4)

Deception is also involved in this area of Satan's control:

> For such people are false apostles, deceitful workers, disguising themselves as apostles of Messiah. And no wonder, for even Satan disguises himself as an angel of light. Therefore it is not surprising his servants also disguise themselves as servants of righteousness, whose end will correspond to their actions. (2 Corinthians 11:13–15)

Working through religious systems, Satan can cause harm and suffering to believers:

> I know the distress you are suffering and your poverty (but you are rich). I also know the slander against you by those who call themselves Jews and really are not, but are a synagogue of Satan. (Revelation 2:9)[7]

In one instance, even members of a local congregation had fallen under the influence of Satan:

> I know where you live—where Satan's throne is. Yet you continue to cling to my name and you have not denied your faith in me, even in the days of Antipas, my faithful witness, who was killed in your city where Satan lives. (Revelation 2:13)

This serves as a warning to be always on guard against Satan's wiles, for even the very elect can be deceived at times:

> For false messiahs and false prophets will appear and perform great signs and wonders to deceive, if possible, even the elect. (Mattai 24:24)

Spiritual control. Yeshua characterized some of the leaders as followers of the "father of lies," because they would not hear what the Messiah had to say.

> You people are from your father the devil, and you want to do what your father desires. He was a murderer from the beginning, and does not uphold the truth, because there is no truth in him. Whenever he lies, he speaks according to his own nature, because he is a liar and the father of lies. (Yohanan 8:44)

Satan's Powers. It must be understood that Satan's powers are exercised only by the permission of God.

Uses the forces of nature. Satan brought misfortune on Job's family by means of a lightning storm (burning up Job's sheep and servants), followed by a strong desert wind (collapsing his house and killing Job's children):

> While this one was still speaking, another messenger arrived and said, "The fire of God has fallen from heaven and has burned up the sheep and the servants—it has consumed them! And I—only I alone—escaped to tell you!"
>
> While this one was still speaking another messenger arrived and said, "The Chaldeans formed three bands and made a raid on the camels and carried them all away, and they killed the servants with the sword! And I—only I alone—escaped to tell you!"
>
> While this one was still speaking another messenger arrived and said, "Your sons and your daughters were eating and drinking wine in their oldest brother's house, and suddenly a great wind swept across the wilderness and struck the four corners of the house, and it fell on the young people, and they died! And I—only I alone—escaped to tell you!" (Job 1:16–19)

Has great supernatural powers. All Satan's supernatural powers operate within the permissive will of God.

Sometimes we see a very specific instance, as when Satan speaks through animals such as the serpent to communicate to people:

> Now the serpent was more shrewd than any of the wild animals that the LORD God had made. He said to the woman, "Is it really true that God said, 'You must not eat from any tree of the orchard'?" (Genesis 3:1)

We are also told in general terms that Satan's working is supernatural. Regarding the future anti-Messiah:

> The arrival of the lawless one will be by Satan's working with all kinds of miracles and signs and false wonders. (2 Thessalonians 2:9)

Can influence people. This includes believers, too, if they open themselves to Satan's suggestions. An example is the story of Ananias and Sapphira, two believers in the early church:

> But Kefa said, "Ananias, why has Satan filled your heart to lie to the Holy Spirit and keep back for yourself part of the proceeds from the sale of the land?" (Acts 5:3)

One curious passage that may fall into this category concerns a situation in the Corinthian church. Here, Sha'ul instructs the congregation to hand over an errant believer to Satan:

> Turn this man over to Satan for the destruction of the flesh, so that his spirit may be saved in the day of the Lord. (1 Corinthians 5:5)

It is unclear exactly what this entails. One possibility is that Satan will drive this believer even further into sin, so that his conscience will so to speak "work overtime," causing him a great deal of discomfort (and leading to his repentance). Another possibility is that it refers to the expulsion of the believer from the congregation so that he can no longer enjoy its fellowship; at that point his conscience would accuse him of all the wrong he had committed. In both interpretations, the result would be similar to what David experienced when he described his remorse and repentance after his affair with Bat Sheva (see Psalm 51).

Can cause physical disease. We have the example of a woman who is described in these terms:

> And a woman was there who had been disabled by a spirit for eighteen years. She was bent over and could not straighten herself up completely. . . .
>
> . . . "Then shouldn't this woman, a daughter of Abraham whom Satan bound for eighteen long years, be released from this imprisonment on the Sabbath day?" (Luke 13:11, 16)

Yeshua's ministry of healing is likewise described this way in one passage:

> . . . with respect to Yeshua from Nazareth, that God anointed him with the Holy Spirit and with power. He went around doing good and healing all who were oppressed by the devil, because God was with him. (Acts 10:38)

Sha'ul also described how Satan, by God's permission, had tormented him with an illness:

> even because of the extraordinary character of the revelations. Therefore, so that I would not become arrogant, a thorn in the flesh was given to me, a messenger of Satan to trouble me—so that I would not become arrogant. (2 Corinthians 12:7)

Whatever the nature of the illness that troubled him, Sha'ul believed that this physical affliction was permitted by God in order to keep him humble before God.

Can take possession of people. We have one specific instance of this, when Satan entered Yehudah, setting him on his task of betraying his master, Yeshua.

> Then Satan entered Yehudah, the one called Iscariot, who was one of the twelve. (Luke 22:3)

We must recognize, however, that Satan's entrance into the inner being of any person does not need to go unopposed. Anyone, including unbelievers, can resist the entrance of demonic powers. Certainly Yehudah could have done so because of all that he had experienced after walking with Yeshua for some three and a half years.

Can inflict death. Notice the description of Satan according to the writer to the Hebrews:

> Therefore, since the children share in flesh and blood, he likewise shared in their humanity, so that through death he could destroy the one who holds the power of death (that is, the devil), and set free those who were held in slavery all their lives by their fear of death. (Hebrews 2:14–15)

As we have noted several times, this does not mean that Satan holds this power in and of himself. Rather, it is only by God's permission, and even then, it is with certain limits as determined by God. Satan does not have any *independent* authority to take people's lives. Though he is capable of doing such a thing, it is always within the permissive will of God.

Satan's Tactics and Strategies.

In relation to God. One of Satan's tactics, permitted by God Himself, is to *slander God and make Him out to be a liar*. This was the method Satan used when he "made his case" to Eve for disobeying God by eating the fruit of the tree of the knowledge of good and evil.

> The serpent said to the woman, "Surely you will not die, for God knows that when you eat from it your eyes will open and you will be like divine beings who know good and evil." (Genesis 3:4–5)

This contradicted God's earlier word:

> But you must not eat from the tree of the knowledge of good and evil, for when you eat from it you will surely die. (Genesis 2:17)

We might say that Satan's tactic at this point was to tell a half-lie, or give a half-truth. God's ultimate purpose for Adam and Eve was indeed that they should be and act like Him, knowing good and evil—but through being obedient to Him, including obeying His prohibition. In the end, through their own mistakes, Adam and Eve learned that the primary activity of Satan is to oppose God and His truth.

Another of Satan's tactics is to *directly oppose the work of God*. When Yeshua went into the desert to fast and pray, Satan came along to tempt him. Note that with each of Satan's three different temptations, Yeshua's method was to use the Word of God in deflecting them.

Satan also *counterfeits God and His work*. He can make himself out to be an angel of light, apparently doing what is right and making choices that appear to be godly—but that however in the long run are contrary to God's will. Satan's kingdom workers follow in his footsteps by making themselves also to be angels of light. In such a way people, including believers, are led astray.

> And no wonder, for even Satan disguises himself as an angel of light. Therefore it is not surprising his servants also disguise themselves as servants of righteousness, whose end will correspond to their actions. (2 Corinthians 11:14–15)

In the final opposition to God's purposes, Satan will aid and abet the "man of sin,"[8] complete with deception and counterfeit activities:

> The arrival of the lawless one will be by Satan's working with all kinds of miracles and signs and false wonders, and with every kind of evil deception directed against those who are perishing, because they found no place in their hearts for the truth so as to be saved. (2 Thessalonians 2:9–10)

And if people do not wish to follow God, He will permit them to believe such lies:

> Consequently God sends on them a deluding influence so that they will believe what is false. (2 Thessalonians 2:11)

In relation to the nations. Satan's deception extends to the nations of the world. After the final battle at Har Megiddo (Armageddon) where the nations will fight against the people of Israel and against the Messiah:

> The angel then threw him [Satan] into the abyss and locked and sealed it so that he could not deceive the nations until the one thousand years were finished. (After these things he must be released for a brief period of time.) (Revelation 20:3)

In relation to the people of God. Satan *accuses and slanders God's people*. He is called "the accuser of our brothers":

> Then I heard a loud voice in heaven saying,
> "The salvation and the power
> and the kingdom of our God,
> and the ruling authority of his Messiah,
> have now come,
> because the accuser of our brothers and sisters,
> the one who accuses them day and night before our God,
> has been thrown down." (Revelation 12:10)

Recall the story of Job; even after God had declared Job to be morally upright, Satan continued to accuse him:

> So the LORD said to Satan, "Have you considered my servant Job? There is no one like him on the earth, a pure and upright man, one who fears God and turns away from evil."
>
> Then Satan answered the LORD, "Is it for nothing that Job fears God? Have you not made a hedge around him and his household and all that he has on every side? You have blessed the work of his hands, and his livestock have increased in the land. But extend your hand and strike everything he has, and he will no doubt curse you to your face!" (Job 1:8–11)

Satan *tempts people*. The classic example is in the garden of Eden, where he tempted Eve to doubt, disbelieve, and finally disobey God's instructions, and furthermore to involve Adam in disobedience as well:

> Now the serpent was more shrewd than any of the wild animals that the LORD God had made. He said to the woman, "Is it really true that God said, 'You must not eat from any tree of the orchard'?" The woman said to the serpent, "We may eat of the fruit from the trees of the orchard; but concerning the fruit of the tree that is in the middle of the orchard God said, 'You must not eat from it, and you must not touch it, or else you will die.'" The serpent said to the woman, "Surely you will not die, for God knows that when you eat from it your eyes will open and you will be like divine beings [NIV: "like God"] who know good and evil." (Genesis 3:1–5)

Another tactic is for Satan to *cause confusion and misunderstanding among believers*. The parable of the wheat and the tares suggests that Satan accomplishes this by means of working through unbelievers:

> He presented them with another parable: "The kingdom of heaven is like a person who sowed good seed in his field. But while everyone was sleeping, an enemy came and sowed weeds among the wheat and went away. When the plants sprouted and bore grain, then the weeds also appeared. So the slaves of the owner came and said to him, 'Sir, didn't you sow good seed in your field? Then where did the weeds come from?' He said, 'An enemy has done this.' So the slaves replied, 'Do you want us to go and gather them?'" . . .
>
> "The field is the world and the good seed are the people of the kingdom. The weeds are the people of the evil one." (Mattai 13:24–28, 38)

However, note that Satan even worked through Kefa to reject the Messiah's message of His suffering, death, and resurrection:

> From that time on Yeshua began to show his disciples that he must go to Jerusalem and suffer many things at the hands of the elders, chief priests,

> and experts in the law, and be killed, and on the third day be raised. So Kefa took him aside and began to rebuke him: "God forbid, Lord! This must not happen to you!" But he turned and said to Kefa, "Get behind me, Satan! You are a stumbling block to me, because you are not setting your mind on God's interests, but on man's." (Mattai 16:21–23)

In regard to this, we saw in the chapter on Yeshua's death that among the Jewish people of that day, there was no concept of a Messiah who would suffer and die for sin. But why not? We must recognize that *Satan stood behind this misinterpretation of Scripture*, so as to engender confusion concerning the reason for Messiah's coming.

In handling these temptations, believers need to be constantly on guard each day of their lives in order to have victory over the spirit world. In the well-known passage on spiritual warfare, Sha'ul advises believers to:

> Clothe yourselves with the full armor of God so that you may be able to stand against the schemes of the devil. (Ephesians 6:11)

In this way we can be victorious and sidestep what Satan throws at us.

Sha'ul also advised the Corinthian believers to be on guard against the wiles of Satan. In one particular case, the believers were under some great external pressure; due to their social circumstances, they could not live together as man and wife. The *shaliach* instructed them in this way:

> Do not deprive each other, except by mutual agreement for a specified time, so that you may devote yourselves to prayer. Then resume your relationship, so that Satan may not tempt you because of your lack of self-control. (1 Corinthians 7:5)

Indeed, one of Satan's strongest delusions is in tempting believers to sexual immorality. Nothing hinders God's work more than when a believer lapses into sexual sin, bringing disrepute to his or her congregation.

Finally, note that Satan can also incite unbelievers to *persecute believers because of their faith and testimony*:

> Do not be afraid of the things you are about to suffer. The devil is about to have some of you thrown into prison so you may be tested, and you will experience suffering for ten days. Remain faithful even to the point of death, and I will give you the crown that is life itself. (Revelation 2:10)

We therefore need to be on guard against any temptation to be unfaithful under persecution.

In relation to unbelievers. Satan will always be active in *opposing the progress of gospel proclamation.* As the Word is proclaimed so that it may enter the hearts of the listeners, Satan is also busy:

> Those along the path are the ones who have heard; then the devil comes and takes away the word from their hearts, so that they may not believe and be saved. (Luke 8:12)

Scripture gives a specific instance of this: as the Word was being proclaimed on the island of Cyprus, Satan used a sorcerer named Elymas to oppose Sha'ul and Bar Navah. Satan's intention was that the proconsul would not accept the Lord:

> But the magician Elymas (for that is the way his name is translated) opposed them, trying to turn the proconsul away from the faith. But Sha'ul (also known as Paul), filled with the Holy Spirit, stared straight at him and said, "You who are full of all deceit and all wrongdoing, you son of the devil, you enemy of all righteousness—will you not stop making crooked the straight paths of the Lord?" (Acts 13:8–10)

Satan in fact *blinds the minds of unbelievers* to the good news concerning the Messiah:

> . . . among whom the god of this age has blinded the minds of those who do not believe so they would not see the light of the glorious gospel of Messiah, who is the image of God. (2 Corinthians 4:4)

Above, we saw that Satan tempted the believers Ananias and Saphira to lie (Act 5:3). He likewise tempts unbelievers to lie and even to murder. Cain killed his own brother because he "was of the evil one":

> . . . not like Cain who was of the evil one and brutally murdered his brother. And why did he murder him? Because his deeds were evil, but his brother's were righteous. (1 Yohanan 3:12)

When Satan incites people to crimes and immorality, his purpose is always to defeat the work of God. As his very name means *Opposer*, he will do everything in his power to stand against God and defeat Him. Satan's ultimate object is not so much to set up a kingdom of crime and immorality as much as to have a kingdom of his own that can endure *apart from God.*

Satan and the Redemptive Work of the Messiah

Satan's Final Defeat. Recall the return of the seventy-two disciples when with joy they announced that the demons had submitted to them through the name of Yeshua. The Messiah responded in this way:

> Then the seventy-two returned with joy, saying, "Lord, even the demons submit to us in your name!" So he said to them, "I saw Satan fall like lightning from heaven." (Luke 10:17–18)

In the ministry of Yeshua and His disciples, and in His power over the demonic world, we see God's approval of His redemptive work as well as His ultimate defeat of Satan.

Yeshua's Intercession as a Bulwark Against Satan. Yeshua's ministry of intercession is based on His redemptive work. When Satan demanded to "sift" Kefa for his lack of moral backbone in denying Yeshua, Yeshua's encouragement to Kefa was to speak of prayer:

> Shimon, Shimon, pay attention! Satan has demanded to have you all, to sift you like wheat, but I have prayed for you, Shimon, that your faith may not fail. When you have turned back, strengthen your brothers. (Luke 22:31–32)

Never discount the power of intercession in achieving victory over demonic spirits and Satan's power. It is a very effective weapon!

Satan Already Judged. Because of the Messiah's sacrificial death on the tree, Satan has been judged. This theme is reiterated in several passages:

> Now is the judgment of this world; now the ruler of this world will be driven out. (Yohanan 12:31)

> I will not speak with you much longer, for the ruler of this world is coming. He has no power over me, but I am doing just what the Father commanded me, so that the world may know that I love the Father. Get up, let us go from here. (Yohanan 14:30–31)

> . . . and concerning judgment, because the ruler of this world has been condemned. (Yohanan 16:11)

> Therefore, since the children share in flesh and blood, he likewise shared in their humanity, so that through death he could destroy the one who holds the power of death (that is, the devil). (Hebrews 2:14)

The Final Victory of Believers over Satan. This will happen in the great cosmic battle that will some day take place between Michael and his angels on one side, and Satan and his forces on the other. Satan with his armies will ultimately be cast down to the earth, never again to return to the heavenly realms.

In this battle, the believers who stand firm overcome Satan in this way:

> But they overcame him
> by the blood of the Lamb
> and by the word of their testimony,
> and they did not love their lives so much that they were afraid to die.
> (Revelation 12:11)

Three means of victory are mentioned here: "by the blood of the Lamb," "by the word of their testimony," and the fact that "they did not love their lives so much that they were afraid to die."

These three means for victory over the powers of darkness apply today as well. Tremendous power can be unleashed because of the blood of the Lamb. And since *blood* and *life* are synonymous, therefore it is through the victorious life of the Messiah that we are conquerers in the spiritual warfare that we face.

The Limitations of Satan

It is worthwhile repeating what we have stated several times: Satan's power is limited. One of his limitations is that he is a finite being; he does not have unlimited power as does God. Though he is called "the god of this age " (2 Corinthians 4:4 NET and NIV; NASB: "god of this world"), that does not mean that he has a title to this world. At any time God can interpose His will and overcome Satan's deeds.

Furthermore, people—even unbelievers—can resist Satan's purposes. In particular, believers can resist him through the power of the Holy Spirit resident within them.

And finally, we need to recognize that God exercises ultimate control. While Satan can inflict illness and affect the physical world, it is always within the purposes of God and by His express permission.

Satan's Final Destiny

Surely Satan knows that he is doomed, because he knows what the Word of God says concerning his ultimate destruction. Nevertheless, that knowledge does not stop him from trying, even as Hitler imagined that by offering up his armies on the altar of sacrifice, he could somehow stave off defeat by the Russians.

Nevertheless, his ultimate defeat is assured. The Scripture portrays his final destiny in terms of the following. We have seen these verses above, but it will be helpful to draw them together here as we contemplate the final judgment of Satan:

> Then he will say to those on his left, "Depart from me, you accursed, into the eternal fire that has been prepared for the devil and his angels!" (Mattai 25:41)

> Then war broke out in heaven: Michael and his angels fought against the dragon, and the dragon and his angels fought back. But the dragon was not strong enough to prevail, so there was no longer any place left in heaven for him and his angels. So that huge dragon—the ancient serpent, the one called the devil and Satan, who deceives the whole world—was thrown down to the earth, and his angels along with him. (Revelation 12:7–9)

> Then I saw an angel descending from heaven, holding in his hand the key to the abyss and a huge chain. He seized the dragon—the ancient serpent, who is the devil and Satan—and tied him up for a thousand years. The angel then threw him into the abyss and locked and sealed it so that he could not deceive the nations until the one thousand years were finished. (After these things he must be released for a brief period of time.) (Revelation 20:1–3)

> Now when the thousand years are finished, Satan will be released from his prison and will go out to deceive the nations at the four corners of the earth, Gog and Magog, to bring them together for the battle. They are as numerous as the grains of sand in the sea. They went up on the broad plain of the earth and encircled the camp of the saints and the beloved city, but fire came down from heaven and devoured them completely. And the devil who deceived them was thrown into the lake of fire and sulfur, where the beast and the false prophet are too, and they will be tormented there day and night forever and ever. (Revelation 20:7–10)

Believers and Satan Today

How then should believers think about Satan in their daily lives? One thing to note is that we should *never speak of Satan contemptuously*. The archangel Michael did not accuse Satan but instead left it to the Lord to rebuke him. We too should always be careful in speaking about Satan.

> Yet these men, as a result of their dreams, defile the flesh, reject authority, and insult the glorious ones. But even when Michael the

> archangel was arguing with the devil and debating with him concerning Moses' body, he did not dare to bring a slanderous judgment, but said, "May the Lord rebuke you!" (Yehudah 1:8–9)

In addition, we can *recognize that God does use Satan in various ways among believers*. In the incident with Kefa already mentioned, Satan was involved in God's providential work of "sifting":

> Shimon, Shimon, pay attention! Satan has demanded to have you all, to sift you like wheat. (Luke 22:31)

God can also use Satan for discipline among believers, as when God used him to prevent Sha'ul from becoming conceited:

> . . . even because of the extraordinary character of the revelations. Therefore, so that I would not become arrogant, a thorn in the flesh was given to me, a messenger of Satan to trouble me—so that I would not become arrogant. (2 Corinthians 12:7)

We also need to remember that deliverance from Satan's power often comes *through intercessory prayer and through vigilance*:

> And do not lead us into temptation, but deliver us from the evil one. (Mattai 6:13)

> Be sober and alert. Your enemy the devil, like a roaring lion, is on the prowl looking for someone to devour. Resist him, strong in your faith, because you know that your brothers and sisters throughout the world are enduring the same kinds of suffering. (1 Kefa 5:8–9)

As part of our vigilance, we are not to give Satan any place in our lives whatsoever:

> Do not give the devil an opportunity. (Ephesians 4:27)

To that end, we must *put on the entire armor of God*:

> Clothe yourselves with the full armor of God so that you may be able to stand against the schemes of the devil. For our struggle is not against flesh and blood, but against the rulers, against the powers, against the world rulers of this darkness, against the spiritual forces of evil in the heavens. For this reason, take up the full armor of God so that you may be able to stand your ground on the evil day, and having done everything, to stand. Stand firm therefore, by fastening the belt of truth around your waist, by putting on the breastplate of righteousness, by fitting your feet with the preparation that comes from the good news of peace, and in all of this, by taking up the shield of faith with which you can extinguish all the flaming arrows of the evil one. And take the helmet of salvation and the sword of the Spirit, which is the word of God. With every prayer and petition, pray at all times in the Spirit, and to this end be alert, with all perseverance and requests for all the saints. (Ephesians 6:11–18)

Even as we saw that believers in the tribulation period will overcome Satan through the "blood of the Messiah," "the word of their testimony," as well as not loving "their lives so much that they were afraid to die," so in the same ways we too will know what victory really means:

> But they overcame him
> by the blood of the Lamb
> and by the word of their testimony,
> and they did not love their lives so much
> that they were afraid to die. (Revelation 12:11)

Always, we need to recognize the necessity for God's help, remembering that He is faithful in giving us strength and protection:

> But the Lord is faithful, and he will strengthen you and protect you from the evil one. (2 Thessalonians 3:3)

He is a defeated foe; he has already been judged by the sacrificial death of the Messiah; therefore we should not fear him.

For all these reasons, we should really not give Satan too large a place in our thinking or conversation. There is enough to think about concerning ministry and the tremendous possibilities we have in that area. That is what should consume most of our thoughts and energy.

So what *does* belong to Satan? Nothing! Though we sometimes think of someone "selling his soul to the devil," in reality it is not his soul to sell. God created the souls and spirits of humanity. In the end, God will judge the souls and spirits of unbelievers and consign them to a lost eternity in the lake of fire. And there, Satan will be only one prisoner among many. He will not even have charge of the final place of misery and suffering by unbelievers.

Demons

Both the Tanach and the New Covenant teach the existence of personal beings called demons, evil spirits, familiar spirits, or unclean spirits. The majority of references are in the New Covenant, particularly in the Synoptic Gospels (Mattai, Mark, and Luke). Yohanan has only three such references, all of them accusations against the Messiah.

Yeshua never questioned the belief in the existence of demons. In the gospel accounts of His ministry, a large amount of material is devoted to deliverance from demonic possession and from the resultant evil. All attempts to demonstrate that Yeshua only "accommodated" His teaching to the so-called superstitions of His day have failed.

Note that Scripture demonstrates great reserve when describing demons and their activities. None of the exaggerated and morbid notions found in medieval Christian literature or in modern accounts of "witchcraft" are to be found in the Scriptures. Rather, they consist of very careful documentation, substantiated by eyewitnesses, with no bizarre embellishments.

The Nature and Character of Demons

Spirits Who Exhibit Characteristics of Personality. Demons have the ability to reason. The demons who inhabited two men in the region of the Kinneret (Sea of Galilee) reasoned with Yeshua in making their request:

> Then the demons begged him, "If you drive us out, send us into the herd of pigs." (Mattai 8:31)

The capacity for reason—along with the ability to persuade—is also indicated in this example:

> When an unclean spirit goes out of a person, it passes through waterless places looking for rest but does not find it. Then it says, "I will return to the home I left." When it returns, it finds the house empty, swept clean, and put in order. Then it goes and brings with it seven other spirits more evil than itself, and they go in and live there, so the last state of that person is worse than the first. It will be that way for this evil generation as well! (Mattai 12:43–45)

A third instance show that demons recognized who Yeshua was:

> Leave us alone, Yeshua the Nazarene! Have you come to destroy us? I know who you are—the Holy One of God! (Mark 1:24)

As one last example, the Scripture notes how demons believe that God exists, for they fear and respect Him:

> You believe that God is one; well and good. Even the demons believe that—and tremble with fear. (Yaakov 2:19)

These and similar passages demonstrate that demons are personal beings with the capacity to reason, retain knowledge, and think through to logical conclusions. They exhibit clear-cut marks of personality.

Different Beings than Angels. The names for angels and for demonic spirits are never used interchangeably. Each one serves a master, the one on the good side of the unseen world and the other on the evil side of the unseen world. As we will see, angels and demons are two different orders of beings with different objectives, serving under two contrasting leaders.

Not the Spirits of Dead People Brought Back to Life. The spirits of human beings pass at death into another realm, one of either rest or of torment. One thing is clear: they never return to the world of living humankind. A study of the encounter between Abraham and the rich man demonstrates that there is a great chasm between those souls already at rest and those in torment:

> Besides all this, a great chasm has been fixed between us, so that those who want to cross over from here to you cannot do so, and no one can cross from there to us. (Luke 16:26)

On only a few very special occasions have good men been brought back to earth by God for a specific purpose. In the well-known story of the transfiguration, Moses and Elijah conversed with the Messiah for a brief time, when His glory was revealed, shining through His humanity.

> Six days later Yeshua took with him Kefa, Yaakov, and Yohanan and led them alone up a high mountain privately. And he was transfigured before them, and his clothes became radiantly white, more so than any launderer in the world could bleach them. Then Elijah appeared before them along with Moses, and they were talking with Yeshua. So Kefa said to Yeshua, "Rabbi, it is good for us to be here. Let us make three shelters—one for you, one for Moses, and one for Elijah." (For they were afraid, and he did not know what to say.) (Mark 9:2–6)

The situation concerning the after-death appearance of Samuel to Sha'ul (1 Samuel 28) will be taken up below.

Desire to Reside in a Body. In some of the descriptions concerning demons, we see an almost desperate desire to reside in a body, though Scripture is silent on the underlying reason for this. The following passage is a case in point: knowing they were to be cast out by Yeshua, the demons desired to be sent into other physical bodies, in this case, the bodies of pigs:

> When he came to the other side, to the region of the Gadarenes, two demon-possessed men coming from the tombs met him. They were extremely violent, so that no one was able to pass by that way. They cried out, "Son of God, leave us alone! Have you come here to torment us before the time?" A large herd of pigs was feeding some distance from them. Then the demons begged him, "If you drive us out, send us into the herd of pigs." (Mattai 8:28–31)

Demons seem to become greatly distressed when they are cast out of people, and so they constantly look for other bodies to inhabit.

Always Described as Evil. The Bible never speaks of a "good demon" but rather uses the terminology of "evil" and "unclean." In one instance, a demon was so evil that only through effectual intercessory prayer could it be driven out:

> A member of the crowd said to him, "Teacher, I brought you my son, who is possessed by a spirit that makes him mute. Whenever it seizes him, it throws him down, and he foams at the mouth, grinds his teeth, and becomes rigid. I asked your disciples to cast it out, but they were not able to do so." . . .
>
> He told them, "This kind can come out only by prayer." (Mark 9:17–18, 29)

Evil spirits are also described as deceitful. Furthermore, such demons work through their followers, described here as having the "hypocrisy of liars":

> Now the Spirit explicitly says that in the later times some will desert the faith and occupy themselves with deceiving spirits and demonic teachings, influenced by the hypocrisy of liars whose consciences are seared. (1 Timothy 4:1–2)

The Powers and Activities of Demons

Trouble Human Beings. A good example is the story of the spirit that tormented Sha'ul. The only relief came when David played on his harp:

> Now the Spirit of the LORD had turned away from Saul, and an evil spirit from the LORD tormented him. Then Saul's servants said to him, "Look, an evil spirit from God is tormenting you!" . . .
>
> So whenever the spirit from God would come upon Saul, David would take his lyre and play it. This would bring relief to Saul and make him feel better. Then the evil spirit would leave him alone. (1 Samuel 16:14–15, 23)

Though there are questions that surround the nature of this demonic torment, one possibility is that Sha'ul, realizing that there would be a change in leadership, became depressed and then opened himself up to demonic influence.

Take Possession of People. The result of such possession is physical infirmity, disease, and mental disorder. In one case, the demons caused their victims to lose all social contact with the world around them:

> When he came to the other side, to the region of the Gadarenes, two demon-possessed men coming from the tombs met him. They were extremely violent, so that no one was able to pass by that way. (Mattai 8:28)

Mark appears to elaborate the situation of one of the men:

> So they came to the other side of the lake, to the region of the Gerasenes. Just as Yeshua was getting out of the boat, a man with an unclean spirit came from the tombs and met him. He lived among the tombs, and no one could bind him anymore, not even with a chain. For his hands and feet had often been bound with chains and shackles, but he had torn the chains apart and broken the shackles in pieces. No one was strong enough to subdue him. Each night and every day among the tombs and in the mountains, he would cry out and cut himself with stones. (Mark 5:1–5)

In another instance, demons caused seizures and accidents:

> When they came to the crowd, a man came to him, knelt before him, and said, "Lord, have mercy on my son, because he has seizures and suffers terribly, for he often falls into the fire and into the water. I brought him to your disciples, but they were not able to heal him." Yeshua answered, "You unbelieving and perverse generation! How much longer must I be with you? How much longer must I endure you? Bring him here to me." Then Yeshua rebuked the demon and it came out of him, and the boy was healed from that moment. (Mattai 17:14–18)

The exact nature of demonic control is not clear; all we can say is that the presence of the demons is real and their damage to their victim is serious. By way of contrast, consider the change in this man after the demons had left him for a herd of pigs:

> They came to Yeshua and saw the demon-possessed man sitting there, clothed and in his right mind—the one who had the "Legion"—and they were afraid. (Mark 5:15)

Communicate with the World Around Them. To accomplish this, demonic spirits often speak through the vocal apparatus of their hosts. Notice how in the following passage, the demon works through the slave girl to speak out loudly:

> Now as we were going to the place of prayer, a slave girl met us who had a spirit that enabled her to foretell the future by supernatural means. She brought her owners a great profit by fortune-telling. She followed behind Sha'ul and us and kept crying out, "These men are servants of the Most High God, who are proclaiming to you the way of salvation." She continued to do this for many days. But Sha'ul became greatly annoyed, and turned and said to the spirit, "I command you in the name of Yeshua the Messiah to come out of her!" And it came out of her at once. (Acts 16:16–18)

It was no good testimony to have such commendation come from a source like this! And so Sha'ul commanded the spirit to come out of her, which however made her of no use to her employers. And since they had lost their financial investment in the girl as a fortune-teller, they had Sha'ul and his companion Silas arrested! (See Acts 16:19 through the end of the chapter for the full account.)

Instigate Factionalism and Disorder Among God's People. Yaakov may have had this in mind when he wrote:

> But if you have bitter jealousy and selfishness in your hearts, do not boast and tell lies against the truth. Such wisdom does not come from above but is earthly, natural, demonic. (Yaakov 3:14–15)

When believers fail to stay close to the Lord and neglect putting on the full armor of God, they can open themselves up to demonic activity. This in turn can lead to friction and division among God's people within a local assembly.

Increase Their Activity as We Come to the End of the Age. We can expect that there will be special demonic activity as the second coming of the Messiah approaches. In light of that coming event, demons will seem to "work overtime."

> Now the Spirit explicitly says that in the later times some will desert the faith and occupy themselves with deceiving spirits and demonic teachings, influenced by the hypocrisy of liars whose consciences are seared. They will prohibit marriage and require abstinence from foods that God created to be received with thanksgiving by those who believe and know the truth. (1 Timothy 4:1–3)

This phenomenon is particularly observable in the book of Revelation, in these passages pertaining to the end times preceding the coming of Messiah:

> The rest of humanity, who had not been killed by these plagues, did not repent of the works of their hands, so that they did not stop worshiping demons and idols made of gold, silver, bronze, stone, and wood—idols that cannot see or hear or walk about. (Revelation 9:20)

> The second beast [the religious anti-Messiah or false prophet] was empowered to give life to the image of the first beast so that it could speak, and could cause all those who did not worship the image of the beast to be killed. (Revelation 13:15)

> Then I saw three unclean spirits that looked like frogs coming out of the mouth of the dragon, out of the mouth of the beast, and out of the mouth of the false prophet. For they are the spirits of the demons performing signs who go out to the kings of the earth to bring them together for the battle that will take place on the great day of God, the All-powerful. (Revelation 16:13–14)

> He shouted with a powerful voice:
> "Fallen, fallen, is Babylon the great!
> She has become a lair for demons,
> a haunt for every unclean spirit,
> a haunt for every unclean bird,
> a haunt for every unclean and detested beast." (Revelation 18:2)

The demonic activity at the end of the age will be fearsome, possibly because the demons will know that the time is short and judgment imminent.

Demon Possession

Basic Characteristic.

Differences Between the Tanach and the New Covenant. There are some differences between the Tanach and New Covenant regarding demon possession. Within the Mosaic Covenant, any person having a "familiar spirit" was held responsible and was subject to the penalty of death by stoning.

> A man or woman who has in them a spirit of the dead or a familiar spirit must be put to death. They must pelt them with stones; their blood guilt is on themselves. (Leviticus 20:27)

We should understand these situations to be occasions when people *actively sought* the presence of demons so as to use their powers over other people.

As part of the whole practice of pagan worship, it was condemned by the Mosaic Covenant because it acknowledged a god other than the God of Israel.

In the New Covenant, however, people "possessed by demons" were treated with compassion by the Messiah Yeshua and were healed from the disease and paralysis that often came as a result:

> So a report about him spread throughout Syria. People brought to him all who suffered with various illnesses and afflictions, those who had seizures, paralytics, and those possessed by demons, and he healed them. (Mattai 4:24)

By contrast with the Tanach, the New Covenant emphasizes situations in which people *do not want* the presence of demons but have been *overpowered* by them to the point that the demons have taken up residence in their hosts. Disease and other serious health problems ensue. Yeshua's ministry therefore included healing people from the demonic influences, which was done by casting out the demons.

The distinction between the cases in the Tanach and those in the New Covenant seems to lie in what the person wanted—on their attitude toward the dark side of the unseen world. Did someone actively cultivate the presence of demons, using their powers and extending the dominion of the demons? Or was it a case where people were unwillingly possessed by demons and as a result became ill? This is the essence of the difference.

Possession by more than one demon. We also encounter situations where someone is possessed by many demons and therefore appears to have a split personality because of the variety of demons manifesting themselves. We noted the case of the man from whom an evil spirit had gone out. Though he had put his moral house in order, he was still not a believer. As a result, he ended up possessed by eight spirits:

> When an unclean spirit goes out of a person, it passes through waterless places looking for rest but does not find it. Then it says, "I will return to the home I left." When it returns, it finds the house empty, swept clean, and put in order. Then it goes and brings with it

> seven other spirits more evil than itself, and they go in and live there, so the last state of that person is worse than the first. It will be that way for this evil generation as well! (Mattai 12:43–45)

A particularly notable case is that of Miriam Magdalene, out of whom seven demons had been cast:

> . . . and also some women who had been healed of evil spirits and disabilities: Miriam (called Magdalene), from whom seven demons had gone out, . . . (Luke 8:2)

Recall also the situation where a man was indwelt by "a legion" of spirits, the term *legion* signifying "many":

> Yeshua asked him, "What is your name?" And he said, "My name is Legion, for we are many." (Mark 5:9)

Some have suggested that a *legion* could be as many as two thousand spirits!

Close pyschological identification with their human victims. When we read that a man in the synagogue "with an unclean spirit" suddenly "cried out," this implies that the spirit within the man, using the vocal apparatus of its host, was the one who actually did the shouting. Note too that the demon asked Yeshua what He wanted to do with *them*, that is, with the demon. Furthermore, the demon stated that he knew exactly who Yeshua was:

> Just then there was a man in their synagogue with an unclean spirit, and he cried out, "Leave us alone, Yeshua the Nazarene! Have you come to destroy us? I know who you are—the Holy One of God!" But Yeshua rebuked him: "Silence! Come out of him!" After throwing him into convulsions, the unclean spirit cried out with a loud voice and came out of him. (Mark 1:23–26)

But the host himself—the man attending the synagogue service—had no idea as to the true identity of Yeshua; rather, it was the demon who knew.

Nor did the man seem to recognize the presence of the demon. There is a distinction between their personalities, yet the same time the demon and its host are very closely identified.

Another instance occurs in the incident we have already looked at, when a "legion" of demons spoke through their host to request that they be sent into the nearby herd of pigs.

Can control the actions of their victims. In the following passage, we note that not only did the demon speak through its host, but that it also physically acted, either directly by itself or else through the possessed man:

> But the evil spirit replied to them, "I know about Yeshua and I am acquainted with Sha'ul, but who are you?" Then the man who was possessed by the evil spirit jumped on them and beat them all into submission. He prevailed against them so that they fled from that house naked and wounded. (Acts 19:15–16)

We have seen another example of this:

> For his hands and feet had often been bound with chains and shackles, but he had torn the chains apart and broken the shackles in pieces. No one was strong enough to subdue him. (Mark 5:4)

Demon possession as a cause of disease, infirmity, and mental and nervous disorders. As we have seen, the people indwelt by demons often suffer adverse consequences. Certainly not all mental disorders are due to the presence of demons, as modern medicine has shown. But this does not mean that demons cannot produce this effect as well. The same man we met in Mark 5:4 (see preceding paragraph) was healed of the consequences of having been possessed:

> They came to Yeshua and saw the demon-possessed man sitting there, clothed and in his right mind—the one who had the "Legion"—and they were afraid. . . .
>
> But Yeshua did not permit him to do so. Instead, he said to him,

> "Go to your home and to your people and tell them what the Lord has done for you, that he had mercy on you." (Mark 5:15, 19)

Note that when Yeshua healed those possessed by demons, relief was often accompanied by convulsions and the complete prostration of the host:

> It shrieked, threw him into terrible convulsions, and came out. The boy looked so much like a corpse that many said, "He is dead!" (Mark 9:26)

Demons, it seems, only come out reluctantly from their victims, demonstrating once again that they desperately want to reside in a physical body.

Demon Possession and Physical Disease. We have touched on this topic already, and now we want to look at it more closely.

Demon possession is clearly distinguished by both the Messiah Yeshua and by the New Covenant writers from nondemonic physical disease. Consider these verses:

> When it was evening, many demon-possessed people were brought to him. He drove out the spirits with a word, and healed all who were sick. (Mattai 8:16)

> Yeshua called his twelve disciples and gave them authority over unclean spirits so they could cast them out and heal every kind of disease and sickness. (Mattai 10:1)

> When it was evening, after sunset, they brought to him all who were sick and demon-possessed. The whole town gathered by the door. So he healed many who were sick with various diseases and drove out many demons. But he would not permit the demons to speak, because they knew him. (Mark 1:32–34)

> They cast out many demons and anointed many sick people with oil and healed them. (Mark 6:13)

These passages all suggest a clear distinction between demon possession and illness. It would seem, then, that demon possession does not *necessarily* mean that physical disease follows as a result.

On the other hand, demon possession *can* bring attendant physical disease, as we see here:

> When they came to the crowd, a man came to him, knelt before him, and said, "Lord, have mercy on my son, because he has seizures and suffers terribly, for he often falls into the fire and into the water. I brought him to your disciples, but they were not able to heal him." Yeshua answered, "You unbelieving and perverse generation! How much longer must I be with you? How much longer must I endure you? Bring him here to me." Then Yeshua rebuked the demon and it came out of him, and the boy was healed from that moment. (Mattai 17:14–18)

In such cases, when the host is relieved of his affliction, the Scripture says he is "healed," or "cured":

> Then they brought to him a demon-possessed man who was blind and mute. Yeshua healed him so that he could speak and see. (Mattai 12:22)

> At that very time Yeshua cured many people of diseases, sicknesses, and evil spirits, and granted sight to many who were blind. (Luke 7:21)

In these instances there *does* seem to be a connection: for instance, when Yeshua had driven out the demon, the man was no longer mute and blind.

Note that no matter what the situation, demon possession is never considered merely as a disease. Demon possession and its physical effects are, however, both dealt with at the same time.

Finally, it is possible that in some instances, there was an interplay between the demons and their hosts so that the latter also recognized that the one who actually healed them was none other than the Messiah Himself. In such cases, the healed individuals afterward became followers of Yeshua, as we sometimes see in the gospel accounts.

The Casting out of Demons. In the Scripture, demons are "cast out" or "driven out" either by the Messiah Himself or else by His followers who were given authority and power to do so "in the name of the Messiah." Casting out demons in Messiah's name seems to have always been necessary because Yeshua the Messiah was always the ultimate authority demons recognized.

The power to drive out demons in Yeshua's name was apparently not restricted to the apostolic band. Note this occasion:

> Yohanan said to him, "Teacher, we saw someone casting out demons in your name, and we tried to stop him because he was not following us." But Yeshua said, "Do not stop him, because no one who does a miracle in my name will be able soon afterward to say anything bad about me." (Mark 9:38–39)

Though authority was given by the Messiah to those who drove out the demons, in special cases, intercessory prayer was an absolute necessity:

> Then, after he went into the house, his disciples asked him privately, "Why couldn't we cast it out?" He told them, "This kind can come out only by prayer." (Mark 9:28–29)

The Demons and Yeshua

Knew Who Yeshua Was and Acknowledged His Deity.

> Demons also came out of many, crying out, "You are the Son of God!" But he rebuked them, and would not allow them to speak, because they knew that he was the Messiah. (Luke 4:41)

Fearful of Yeshua. They were afraid of Yeshua because of His power, realizing that their final doom was already sealed:

> They cried out, "Son of God, leave us alone! Have you come here to torment us before the time?" (Mattai 8:29)

> When he saw Yeshua from a distance, he ran and bowed down before him. Then he cried out with a loud voice, "Leave me alone, Yeshua, Son of the Most High God! I implore you by God—do not torment me!" (Mark 5:6–7)

> And they began to beg him not to order them to depart into the abyss. (Luke 8:31)

This implies that the demons understood there to be an appointed time for their judgment. In each case, the demons were particularly afraid because they knew what was in store for them.

Forbidden to Testify to the Messiah.

> And whenever the unclean spirits saw him, they fell down before him and cried out, "You are the Son of God." But he sternly ordered them not to make him known. (Mark 3:11–12)

The same thing is implied in the story we have already seen concerning the fortune-telling slave girl:

> Now as we were going to the place of prayer, a slave girl met us who had a spirit that enabled her to foretell the future by supernatural means. She brought her owners a great profit by fortune-telling. She followed behind Sha'ul and us and kept crying out, "These men are servants of the Most High God, who are proclaiming to you the way of salvation." She continued to do this for many days. But Sha'ul became greatly annoyed, and turned and said to the spirit, "I command you in the name of Yeshua the Messiah to come out of her!" And it came out of her at once. (Acts 16:16–18)

Sha'ul did not want testimony that he was a *shaliach* of the Messiah to come from a questionable source. An effective confession must come as a result of a holy life. Demonic testimony to the Messiah would be useless or worse in the ears of Messiah's enemies.

Demons, Idolatry, and Pagan Religions

When someone trafficked with "familiar spirits" or the "unclean spirits," Scripture generally associated the practice with idolatry and the horrible rites of pagan religions. A godly king like Josiah saw to it that the nation was rid of such practices:

> Josiah also got rid of the ritual pits used to conjure up spirits, the magicians, personal idols, disgusting images, and all the detestable idols that had appeared in the land of Judah and in Jerusalem. In this way he carried out the terms of the law recorded on the scroll that Hilkiah the priest had discovered in the Lord's temple. (2 Kings 23:24)

By contrast, the evil king Manasseh, though son of the godly Hezekiah, did the opposite:

> In the two courtyards of the LORD'S temple he built altars for all the stars in the sky. He passed his sons through the fire in the Valley of Ben-hinnom and practiced divination, omen reading, and sorcery. He set up a ritual pit to conjure up underworld spirits and appointed magicians to supervise it. He did a great amount of evil in the sight of the LORD and angered him. He put an idolatrous image he had made in God's temple, about which God had said to David and to his son Solomon, "This temple in Jerusalem, which I have chosen out of all the tribes of Israel, will be my permanent home." (2 Chronicles 33:5–7)

As a result, God judged Manasseh, for he led the nation astray when the people also became involved with the "familiar spirits."

This truth is found not only in the Tanach but is also echoed by the New Covenant writers, particularly by Sha'ul, who often found himself in sharp opposition to pagan religions. Sha'ul was well acquainted with the connection between idolatry and demonism in the cities of the Roman Empire.

Note how Sha'ul makes the connection in 1 Corinthians, warning them not to become participants with demons:

> So then, my dear friends, flee from idolatry. . . .
>
> Am I saying that idols or food sacrificed to them amount to anything? No, I mean that what the pagans sacrifice is to demons and not to God. I do not want you to be partners with demons. You cannot drink the cup of the Lord and the cup of demons. You cannot take part in the table of the Lord and the table of demons. (1 Corinthians 10:14, 19–21)

Sha'ul clearly distinguishes unbelievers, who are said to worship the demons, and believers, who are to honor and worship God and the Lord Messiah.

Believers Today and Demonic Presence

The Reality of Demonic Activity. We might first ask, does the kind of demonic activity we have described exist today in the West? There is no doubt that it does, but it takes place under more subtle and less violent forms. When we step out to the non-Western mission fields, however, we also encounter demonic activity as it appears in New Covenant forms. Some may dismiss that, refusing to believe that such demonic activity actually takes place. But any seasoned missionary can give testimony to encounters he or she has had with the evil side of the unseen world. Therefore every believer needs to recognize demonic activity as a real phenomenon, and thankfully most do.

Demonic Activity to Be Avoided. This is true of both believers and unbelievers. The Tanach provided sound, sane advice when God said to the people of Israel:

> The person who turns to the spirits of the dead and familiar spirits to commit prostitution by going after them, I will set my face against that person and cut him off from the midst of his people. (Leviticus 20:6)

That is one of the best pieces of advice anyone could follow. Demonism is not an area in which to meddle. While this writer does not believe in demon *possession* of believers, there can certainly be demon *oppression*, particularly if a new believer has come from a background in the occult and has dabbled with this side of the unseen world. God provided these instructions for the good of His people, and both believers and unbelievers need to take heed.

The story of Sha'ul and the woman of Endor is instructive. The entire story can be found in 1 Samuel 28. Near the end of his life, he had gone to inquire as to a word from the Lord by asking a medium to call up Samuel. It is not clear as to whether this was the real Samuel or something concocted by the medium. The important point is that Scripture tells us that Sha'ul died because he was unfaithful to God:

> So Sha'ul died because he was unfaithful to the LORD and did not obey the LORD's instructions; he even tried to conjure up underworld spirits. He did not seek the LORD's guidance, so the LORD killed him and transferred the kingdom to David son of Jesse. (1 Chronicles 10:13–14)

Moreover, there is a special danger in leaving the "soul house" empty, particularly if the person is an unbeliever. Recall the spirit who departed from a particular host but came back with seven even more wicked ones.

> Then it says, "I will return to the home I left." When it returns, it finds the house empty, swept clean, and put in order. Then it goes and brings with it seven other spirits more evil than itself, and they go in and live there, so the last state of that person is worse than the first. It will be that way for this evil generation as well! (Mattai 12:44–45)

The reality is that if an unbeliever does not stand firm against the entry of a spirit, he then becomes a victim and will fall prey to possession. This would not be true of believers, although even in that case, if he or she had been involved with the occult to any extent prior to making a decision for faith, then he or she needs to be careful that the demonic oppression does not continue. The only way to have victory and to make demonic oppression cease is for a believer to stand firm, put on the entire armor of God, and with the power of the Word, plead the blood of the Messiah.

The Need to Evaluation Demonic Activity. Believers need to be careful in making judgments concerning demon possession. It would be very difficult to dogmatically assert that a particular person is a willing host to a demon. Especially if the person is physically afflicted, one may mistakenly assign the illness to the presence of demons when in reality it is caused by other factors. The only infallible test of possession is if, in a counseling situation, the demon responds to the counselor according to the principles laid down in the New Covenant.

In the days of the New Covenant, the confession of demons regarding the person of Yeshua was no doubt often prompted by fear of His immediate presence. This was true in the case of the fortune-telling slave girl whom we have looked at. When demons did confess Yeshua during His time here on earth, it was for the purpose of bringing His work and ministry into disrepute, thereby giving the Pharisees the opportunity to say that the Messiah Yeshua was in league with the Devil. As "seducing spirits" they took whatever attitude they felt would injure the work of the Messiah when He was here.

Ever since Yeshua's ascension, demons may have changed their tactic to that of denial of Messiah Yeshua. Probably they are following Satan in attempting to deceive people with false religion, attracting them in that way to the worship of Satan. Nevertheless, should a demon ever confess the Messiah as the Son of God, 1 Yohanan 4:1–4 offers us one way to see if his confession is real:

> Dear friends, do not believe every spirit, but test the spirits to determine if they are from God, because many false prophets have gone out into the world. By this you know the Spirit of God: Every spirit that confesses Yeshua as the Messiah who has come in the flesh is from God, but every spirit that does not confess Yeshua is not from God, and this is the spirit of the anti-Messiah, which you have heard is coming, and now is already in the world.
>
> You are from God, little children, and have conquered them, because the one who is in you is greater than the one who is in the world. (1 Yohanan 4:1–4)

FIFTEEN

A Biblical Ecclesiology With an Adaptation for Messianic Congregations

THE *QEHILAH* AS AN INSTITUTION

Definition and Description

The Words *Qahal, Qehilah, Ekklesia*. The Hebrew verb *qahal* means *to call together*, and the noun *qehilah* describes the assembly that has been called together. Compare Deuteronomy 33:4 where the *assembly* (Hebrew, *qehilah*) refers to Jacob's descendants as a special called-out body:

> Moses delivered to us a law,
> an inheritance for the assembly of Jacob. (Deuteronomy 33:4)

The Greek *ekklesia* in the New Covenant has the same meaning, referring to a new body of believers, namely, those who believe in Yeshua as Messiah.

The Universal Body.

Its nature as a mystical body and an organism. The universal body is an organism, not an organization:

> For in one Spirit we were all baptized into one body. Whether Jews or Greeks or slaves or free, we were all made to drink of the one Spirit. (1 Corinthians 12:13)

Yeshua the Messiah, the Lord, is the head of this body.

Its origin. This body is comprised of Jews and Gentiles, called out from their respective peoples, and had its beginning with the *Shavuot* (Pentecost) recorded in Acts 2, when this body originated.

Its members. All believers since that *Shavuot* are a part of an ever-growing body to the present day. This is now a new community of believers, existing alongside the community of Israel. We could very well say that most of the body of Messiah is already at home with the Lord.

Its special relationship to the Messiah. The universal *qehilah* is considered a bride in an endearing relationship to an espoused husband, the Messiah, in much the same way as Israel was married to her husband, the Lord, at Sinai. Consider these verses:

> For I am jealous for you with godly jealousy, because I promised you in marriage to one husband, to present you as a pure virgin to Messiah. (2 Corinthians 11:2)

> Wives, submit to your husbands as to the Lord, because the husband is the head of the wife as also Messiah is the head of the *qehilah*—he himself being the savior of the body. . . .
>
> For no one has ever hated his own body but he feeds it and takes care of it, just as Messiah also does the *qehilah*, for we are members of his body. For this reason a man will leave his father and mother and will be joined to his wife, and the two will become one flesh. This mystery is great—but I am actually speaking with reference to Messiah and the *qehilah*. (Ephesians 5:22–23, 29–32)

Its triumphant destiny. This universal *qehilah* of Jewish and Gentile believers will one day be presented to the Messiah in glorified bodies at the great "catching away," as described by Sha'ul:

> For the Lord himself will come down from heaven with a shout of command, with the voice of the archangel, and with the trumpet of God, and the dead in Messiah will rise first. (1 Thessalonians 4:16)

Those who have already fallen asleep in the Messiah will have their souls and spirits united with a glorified body and then be resurrected.

After this,

> Then we who are alive, who are left, will be suddenly caught up together with them in the clouds to meet the Lord in the air. And so we will always be with the Lord. (1 Thessalonians 4:17)

Those alive and present at His coming will not die but will also receive a glorified body. Then the entire triumphant body will be caught up to be presented to the Messiah. Following that, each will receive or else suffer the loss of the reward for deeds performed while on earth:

> If what someone has built survives, he will receive a reward. If someone's work is burned up, he will suffer loss. He himself will be saved, but only as through fire. (1 Corinthians 3:14–15)

Finally, we will enjoy the presence of the Messiah at the great wedding of the Lamb:

> Let us rejoice and exult
> and give him glory,
> because the wedding celebration of the Lamb has come,
> and his bride has made herself ready. (Revelation 19:7)

The Local Body. While the universal body is an organism, the local body is an organization.

In Israel. Sha'ul referred to local congregations that were already present by about 50 C.E.

> But I was personally unknown to the *qehilot* of Judea that are in Messiah. (Galatians 1:22)

Congregations in Judea and the Galilee persisted until the 500s, as we know from extant records. The number of congregations of Jewish believers began to decrease in the late 500s because of the powerful pressure on them to conform to the Hellenized church's lifestyle and expressions of belief. With the subsequent Arab invasion, the total area became Arabized, and what Jewish believers were left in the land were assimilated as "Christians" into the church. No longer was there found the distinctive presence of Jewish believers in the homeland. (See Yitzchak ben Zvi's writings on this subject; he was the second president of Israel and quite an authority of what happened to these Jewish believers. He stated that many of the current Arab Christians are in reality descendants of these early Jewish believers!)

Moving to the modern period, few believers were in Israel in 1948. After that date the number of Messianic congregations in Israel grew very slowly until the 1980s, when they began to grow more rapidly. By 1993, some thirty-two such congregations existed.

Sha'ul's work. Sha'ul's ministry was to establish churches wherever he went:

> He passed through Syria and Cilicia, strengthening the *qehilot*. (Acts 15:41)

He refers to these local congregations in his letters:

> . . . to the *qehilah* of God that is in Corinth, to those who are sanctified in Messiah Yeshua, and called to be saints, with all those in every place who call on the name of our Lord Yeshua the Messiah, their Lord and ours. (1 Corinthians 1:2)

> . . . and all the brothers with me, to the *qehilot* of Galatia. (Galatians 1:2)

> From Sha'ul and Timothy, slaves of Messiah Yeshua, to all the saints in Messiah Yeshua who are in Philippi, with the overseers and deacons. (Philippians 1:1)

> From Sha'ul and Silvanus and Timothy, to the *qehilah* of the Thessalonians in God the Father and the Lord Yeshua the Messiah. Grace and peace to you! (1 Thessalonians 1:1)

Appropriate terminology. The Hebrew word in Israel used for a congregation is *qehilah*. This writer thinks that this is the more appropiate word to use, whether in Israel or elsewhere, rather than *synagogue*. As words appear in common usage, the term *synagogue* is usually applied to Traditional or Conservative places of worship. We should not confuse terms that relate to where various Jewish people worship. Messianic Jews have specific distinctives and we do not need to feel that we are losing our identity just because we do not use the usual ethnocentric vocabulary. We can develop our own way of referring to matters of belief and practice, as we will see below.

The congregation's own preference of identification can come in the terms attached to *qehilah*: *Qehilat B'nai Yeshua* (Congregation of the Sons of Yeshua), or *Qehilat 'Edut* (or, *'Adat*) *Yeshua* (Congregation of the Testimony of Yeshua), to name just two designations. A great variety of such names exists today.

God's Intentions for a New Community

No teaching concerning the *qehilah* can be derived from the Tanach. Rather, the prophets prophesied concerning the Messianic kingdom over which the Messiah would preside. Israel will be at the head of the nations; the Messiah will sit on the throne of David in Jerusalem, the city of the great King, and govern the nations.

Theoretically, when Yeshua came to Israel, He presented Himself to the people, and then to the Sanhedrin, waiting for them to respond to Him. Had they done so, accepting Him as their king, the Romans would have put Him to death anyway, for they would have never acknowledged Him as their king. Subsequently He would have been resurrected and begun the kingdom. The fact that the Sanhedrin did *not* accept Him was the sign that the kingdom could not begin *in its fullness*. How could it, if the leadership of the nation would not accept their rightful king?

The *Qehilah* Intimated in Yeshua's Teaching

> And I tell you that you are Kefa, and on this rock I will build my *qehilah*, and the gates of Hades will not overpower it. (Mattai 16:18)

Yeshua made reference to the *qehilah*, but nothing further was said because it would all depend on how Israel would respond to the Messiah.

The *Qehilah*, a Provision by God in Light of His Knowledge of Israel's Response. In God's omniscience, He knew how Israel would respond to Yeshua the Messiah. He, therefore, made provision for the *qehilah*, or church, which is an institution similar to the family and the state. Membership in the *qehilah* is neither hereditary nor compulsory (see below concerning entrance into the *qehilah*).

A Last Offer to Israel. At the Spirit's leading, Kefa made a last offer to Israel of the Messiah and the fullness of the kingdom in its spiritual and material blessings. If only the people and leadership would humble themselves, repent, and turn to God:

> Therefore repent and turn back so that your sins may be wiped out, so that times of refreshing may come from the presence of the Lord, and so that he may send the Messiah appointed for you—that is, Yeshua. (Acts 3:19–20)

For that reason, nothing too much is said about the new community of the *qehilah* until after Acts 3:20.

The Founding of *Qehilot*. Two commissions were enacted for the founding of *qehilot*. First, Kefa with his colleagues and followers had God's sanction to preach to Jewish people, discipling them and founding congregations among them. This work continued until the Arab conquest of the Middle East in the 600s C.E. Second, Sha'ul was commissioned by God to work among the Gentiles. Both commissions are mentioned in this passage:

> On the contrary, when they saw that I was entrusted with the gospel to the uncircumcised just as Kefa was to the circumcised (for he who

> empowered Kefa for his apostleship to the circumcised also empowered me for my apostleship to the Gentiles) and when Yaakov, Kefa, and Yohanan, who had a reputation as pillars, recognized the grace that had been given to me, they gave to Bar Navah and me the right hand of fellowship, agreeing that we would go to the Gentiles and they to the circumcised. (Galatians 2:7–9)

Sha'ul founded various local congregations, as we noted above. However, he also was always interested in reaching his own kinsmen:

> I ask then, they did not stumble into an irrevocable fall, did they? Absolutely not! But by their transgression salvation has come to the Gentiles, to make Israel jealous. Now if their transgression means riches for the world and their defeat means riches for the Gentiles, how much more will their full restoration bring? (Romans 11:11–12)

As a result, in many of Sha'ul's congregations, both Jewish and Gentile believers could be found. These congregations had a good understanding of the Jewish backgrounds of their faith, as, for example, the Corinthians and their knowledge of the practices of the Passover:

> Clean out the old yeast so that you may be a new batch of dough—you are, in fact, without yeast. For Messiah, our Passover lamb, has been sacrificed. So then, let us celebrate the festival, not with the old yeast, the yeast of vice and evil, but with the bread without yeast, the bread of sincerity and truth. (1 Corinthians 5:7–8)

We can also say that these congregations were providentially structured. Once the Second Temple was lost, and especially after the second revolt against Rome in 132–135 C.E., Jewish people fled Judea and ended up in cities where congregations of Jewish and Gentile believers could be a cogent witness to those who were undoubtedly looking for answers to life's problems in trying times.

The Kingdom Did Begin, but Not in Its Fullness. What was promised by Jeremiah in chapter 31 of his prophecy did come to fruition at that first-century *Shavuot*. But, without Yeshua reigning as King in Jerusalem, only the totality of spiritual blessings were possible. The totality of *all* blessings, *spiritual and physical,* will not be fulfilled until the day when Israel will call for their king and accept Him as their redeemer. God had only promised to provide for our spiritual needs within the body of Messiah:

> And my God will supply your every need according to his glorious riches in Messiah Yeshua. (Philippians 4:19)

If material blessings do in fact accrue, abound, they are by God's grace.

LEADERSHIP OF THE *QEHILAH*

Kinds of Leaders

Elders. The Hebrew terms are *zaken* (sing.) and *zeqenim* (pl.). One of Sha'ul's tasks was to appoint elders in every congregation he founded. He always looked for men who could take spiritual and moral responsibility, so as to conserve the work that was started and then lead people on to maturity.

Overseers. The terms are *episkopes* (Greek) and *manhig* (the Hebrew equivalent in the Hebrew New Testament, modern translation)

> This saying is trustworthy: "If someone aspires to the office of overseer [*episkopes*], he desires a good work." (1 Timothy 3:1)

According to the NIV Study Bible,

> In the Greek culture the word was used of a presiding official in a civic or religious organization. Here it refers to a man who oversees a local congregation. The equivalent word from the Jewish background of Christianity is "elder." The terms "overseer" and "elder" are used interchangeably in Acts 20:17, 28; Tit. 1:5–7; 1 Pet. 5:1–2.[1]

The function of the overseer can be easily defined (see below), but it is much more difficult to find the right word by which to address this official in a Messianic congregation. Possible choices include:

Elder, zaken. The Greek equivalent is *presbuteros*, as found in 1 Kefa 5:1:

> So as your fellow elder and a witness of Messiah's sufferings and as one who shares in the glory that will be revealed, I urge the elders among you: . . . (1 Kefa 5:1)

Shepherd (or pastor). This implies someone who, as the KVJ renders it, "feeds God's flock," as we see in 1 Kefa 5:2:

> Give a shepherd's care to God's flock among you, exercising oversight not merely as a duty but willingly under God's direction, not for shameful profit but eagerly. (1 Kefa 5:2)

Manhig. This Hebrew term, referred to above, derives from *to drive* or *to guide*, but it is not used in Israel.

Mashgiah. This Hebrew word comes from *to look at, over* (see 1 Kefa 5:2 about "oversight" or "overseers"). It is a more acceptable word than *manhig* in Israel, but it is hardly ever used as a title of such a person.

Congregational Leader. This is the term that the *Jewish New Testament* uses but it is more or less simply a definition of the office.

Rav, Rabbi. This term of address also has its problems. In ordinary usage, the word is applied to a person who has gone through a specific kind of education and training and serves as the religious leader of a Jewish place of worship, Traditional, Conservative, or Reform. There are Messianic leaders who apply these terms to people who have gone through only a minimum of training, or even of a spiritual leader who has merely started a congregation. This writer only raises the note of caution that we need to accurately reflect our position as Messianic Jews. Having said all what we have concerning the terminology of address, the use of a specific term of address that will satisfy every Messianic Jewish person still eludes us.

Deacons, Servants. The *designation* of the office is found in 1 Timothy 3:8–13 while the *function* of these servants is described in Acts 6:1–6.

> Deacons likewise must be dignified, not two-faced, not given to excessive drinking, not greedy for gain, holding to the mystery of the faith with a clear conscience. And these also must be tested first and then let them serve as deacons if they are found blameless. Likewise also their wives must be dignified, not slanderous, temperate, faithful in every respect. Deacons must be husbands of one wife and good managers of their children and their own households. For those who have served well as deacons gain a good standing for themselves and great boldness in the faith that is in Messiah Yeshua. (1 Timothy 3:8–13)

> Now in those days, when the disciples were growing in number, a complaint arose on the part of the Greek-speaking Jews against the native Hebraic Jews, because their widows were being overlooked in the daily distribution of food. So the twelve called the whole group of the disciples together and said, "It is not right for us to neglect the word of God to wait on tables. But carefully select from among you, brothers, seven men who are well-attested, full of the Spirit and of wisdom, whom we may put in charge of this necessary task. But we will devote ourselves to prayer and to the ministry of the word." The proposal pleased the entire group, so they chose Stephen, a man full of faith and of the Holy Spirit, with Philip, Prochorus, Nicanor, Timon, Parmenas, and Nicolas, a Gentile convert to Judaism from Antioch. They stood these men before the apostles, who prayed and placed their hands on them. (Acts 6:1–6)

What should be the term of address? Once again it is far easier to describe the function of the person occupying this office than to have a formal term by which to address him. The term in the Scripture is:

Deacon. The common term for this office derives from the Greek term *diakonos*.

Shammash, shammashim *(pl.)*. This is how the *Jewish New Testament* renders the term.

We note that a term for this congregational office might not be as necessary as it is for the congregation's spiritual leader.

Qualifications of Leaders

Elder, Overseer. A number of qualifications are indicated for an elder in these passages:

> This saying is trustworthy: "If someone aspires to the office of overseer, he desires a good work." The overseer then must be above reproach, the husband of one wife, temperate, self-controlled, respectable, hospitable, an able teacher, not a drunkard, not violent, but gentle, not contentious, free from the love of money. He must manage his own household well and keep his children in control without losing his dignity. But if someone does not know how to manage his own household, how will he care for the *qehilah* of God? He must not be a recent convert or he may become arrogant and fall into the punishment that the devil will exact. And he must be well thought of by those outside the faith, so that he may not fall into disgrace and be caught by the devil's trap. (1 Timothy 3:1–7)

> The reason I left you in Crete was to set in order the remaining matters and to appoint elders in every town, as I directed you. An elder must be blameless, the husband of one wife, with faithful children who cannot be charged with dissipation or rebellion. For the overseer must be blameless as one entrusted with God's work, not arrogant, not prone to anger, not a drunkard, not violent, not greedy for gain. Instead he must be hospitable, devoted to what is good, sensible, upright, devout, and self-controlled. He must hold firmly to the faithful message as it has been taught, so that he will be able to give exhortation in such healthy teaching and correct those who speak against it. (Titus 1:5–9)

Great care should be taken in selecting elders in accordance with the guidelines Sha'ul enumerates. Failure to do so has resulted in serious consequences for the *qehilah*. Spiritual leaders should never be placed in office based on a popularity contest; rather, the local congregation is a theocracy in microcosm, and the men selected to the office of elder are in reality servants of the Lord to guide God's people. In fact, no person should be placed in the *office* of elder if he is not already doing the *ministry* of an elder.

Illustrations of the function of the elder appear in Acts 20:

> From Miletus he sent a message to Ephesus, telling the elders of the *qehilah* to come to him. . . .
>
> For I did not hold back from announcing to you the whole purpose of God. Watch out for yourselves and for all the flock of which the Holy Spirit has made you overseers, to shepherd the *qehilah* of God that he obtained with the blood of his own Son. I know that after I am gone fierce wolves will come in among you, not sparing the flock. Even from among your own group men will arise, teaching perversions of the truth to draw the disciples away after them. Therefore be alert, remembering that night and day for three years I did not stop warning each one of you with tears. (Acts 20:17, 27–31)

Deacons, *Shammashim*. The qualifications for the *shammash* are listed in 1 Timothy 3:8–13, found above. What was said concerning elders also applies to the person who desires to serve as a *shammash*. The training ground for elders can often begin for those who are serving as the *shammashim*.

An excellent illustration of a godly *shammash* is Stephen who was humble enough to wait on tables to serve less fortunate brothers and sisters. But he also was a man of God, filled with Torah and the Spirit, and bold to the point of confronting the Sanhedrin for their failure to recognize in Yeshua Israel's Messiah. For that effort, he forfeited his life:

> They continued to stone Stephen while he prayed, "Lord Yeshua, receive my spirit!" Then he fell to his knees and cried out with a loud voice, "Lord, do not hold this sin against them!" When he had said this, he died. And Saul agreed completely with killing him.
>
> Now on that day a great persecution began against the *qehilah* in Jerusalem, and all except the apostles were forced to scatter throughout the regions of Judea and Samaria. (Acts 7:59–8:1)

Functions of Leaders

Kinds of Functions of Ministry. Various offices[2] still in existence in Sha'ul's day are mentioned in Ephesians:

> It was he who gave some as apostles, some as prophets, some as evangelists, and some as pastors and teachers, . . . (Ephesians 4:11)

Apostles. This office has been defined in a restricted sense to refer to those Yeshua called to serve with Him and who fellowshipped with Him after His resurrection. One of their tasks was to be God's spokesmen in a special way. God's desire was that the apostles receive and transmit an inerrant record to all who would come after them. The special aspect of this office ceased with the death of those who were designated apostles.

However, a wider usage of the term does exist among some brethren. It is possible to apply the term *apostle* as meaning *shaliach* (in Hebrew) and *apostolos* (in Greek), as a "sent one," with a special task for ministry.

New Testament prophets. There was a reason for the office of New Covenant prophets. Through them, oral revelation provided guidance for believers, as for instance when Agabus warned Sha'ul in an oral prophetic word:

> While we remained there for a number of days, a prophet named Agabus came down from Judea. (Acts 21:10)

And of course, Sha'ul, Kefa, Yohanan, and others were given revelation that was then inscripturated. Note that the Torah test as to the validity of a prophet's message applied to them, as it still does to any prophet to this day. They had to be 100 percent accurate in their short-range prophecies—short-range meaning from days, weeks, months, up to a year:

> The LORD your God will raise up for you a prophet like me from among you—from your fellow Israelites; you must listen to him. This accords with what happened at Horeb in the day of the assembly. You asked the LORD your God: "Please do not make us hear the voice of the LORD our God any more or see this great fire any more lest we

> die." The LORD then said to me, "What they have said is good. I will raise up a prophet like you for them from among their fellow Israelites. I will put my words in his mouth and he will speak to them whatever I command. I will personally hold responsible anyone who then pays no attention to the words that prophet speaks in my name.
>
> "But if any prophet presumes to speak anything in my name that I have not authorized him to speak, or speaks in the name of other gods, that prophet must die. Now if you say to yourselves, 'How can we tell that a message is not from the LORD?'—whenever a prophet speaks in my name and the prediction is not fulfilled, then I have not spoken it; the prophet has presumed to speak it, so you need not fear him." (Deuteronomy 18:15–22)

Based on this short-range test, their long-range prophecies in the New Testament Scriptures can be held as valid, some of which will not be fulfilled until beyond our own day.

Some, however, feel that the Torah test is too stringent, especially since the completion of the New Covenant. In a number of publications,[3] Wayne Grudem asserted the possibility of the "gift of prophecy." Grudem's view is that it is possible for believers today to be specially enlightened by the Holy Spirit, for example, to pray for fellow believers in crises; at a later date, knowledge comes to light that, indeed, the needs were real and the knowledge communicated by the Holy Spirit was correct. Therefore, this kind of "prophecy" is legitimate.

Obviously, there is going to be disagreement among believers if indeed this is or is not legitimate prophecy. Some will question if we have sufficient control on what can be called prophecy. We will not attempt to solve this question at this point, but have only mentioned it to point out differences of opinions among our brethren on this issue.

Evangelists.

> On the next day we left and came to Caesarea, and entered the house of Philip the evangelist, who was one of the seven, and stayed with him. (Acts 21:8)

To these servants is committed the gift of evangelism so that in their preaching, many respond and become believers.

Pastors, poimenas (Greek), or shepherds. This office has already been mentioned and is equivalent to that of the elder. One of the functions of the elders is to feed the flock of God:

> Give a shepherd's care to God's flock among you, exercising oversight not merely as a duty but willingly under God's direction, not for shameful profit but eagerly. (1 Kefa 5:2)

In the early *qehilot*, there was a rulership by elders whereby each elder had a different gift. One would preach, another would teach, another would evangelize, and so on. In time, as the congregations became larger and more established, the leading elder became the pastor as the term is understood today. In the Messianic congregation today, for the most part, we have returned to a large extent to what was originally a rulership by elders, in which one of the elders serves as the congregation leader.

Teachers. Some leaders have the gift of teaching.

Note that it is quite possible that one person can have two or more gifts.

Purpose of Ministry

> . . . to equip the saints for the work of ministry, that is, to build up the body of Messiah. (Ephesians 4:12)

The function of every leader is that of enabling believers to also serve God and build up the body of Messiah.

Result of Ministry

> . . . until we all attain to the unity of the faith and of the knowledge of the Son of God—a mature person, attaining to the measure of Messiah's full stature. (Ephesians 4:13)

This verse depicts the goal of the leaders' service. In fact, elders should so do their work that they will establish other elders who can continue the ministry. In the long run, some of the elders should be encouraged to go forth and plant new congregations.

Establishing Congregations and Training Leaders

The Founding of Congregations. Congregations are formed in many ways:

Through various societies. A society involved in reaching Jewish people has workers at various stations around a given country. Each one in his own way gathers around him those he leads to faith in the Messiah and then sets out to disciple them. The group keeps growing and the worker keeps on discipling new believers. At some time, however, the leader must look for potential elders and start to train them to take over the task of exercising leadership as Sha'ul instructed Timothy:

> And entrust what you heard me say in the presence of many others as witnesses to faithful people who will be competent to teach others as well. (2 Timothy 2:2)

Then, when leaders are in place, along with the possibility of a specially trained congregational leader, the new congregation can go independent of the society.

Through individuals. An individual, with varying amounts of training, can be led of the Lord to gather believers around him and disciple them. It is highly desirable, however, that such a person will look for the fellowship, counsel, and support of an existing congregation. But the process is still the same; that person too must go through the process of finding those with leadership potential and then train them as elders.

Outreach to the Jewish community. To reach Jewish people with the message of life and love of Yeshua is commendable. God has always blessed a legitimate outreach and He always will prepare hearts where the seed of the Word of God can take root and work in a person to lead him to faith in Yeshua. To then lead such a person into fellowship with other believers in a Messianic congregation is the normal scheme of things.

However, no missionary or congregation planter should envision building a congregation by taking Jewish believers out of the existing Gentile Christian congregations. Obviously, there are times when Jewish believers from such congregations might want to visit and take part in special holiday observances or other occasions. But we need to maintain an integrity in our ministry of building Messianic congregations that precludes enticing our brethren from their freedom of choice of remaining in established congregations.

A Scriptural Mandate to Develop Potential Leaders.

Sha'ul's directive to Timothy.

> So you, my child, be strong in the grace that is in Messiah Yeshua. And entrust what you heard me say in the presence of many others as witnesses to faithful people who will be competent to teach others as well. (2 Timothy 2:1–2)

Note carefully the instructions given to Timothy concerning training those who will in time be able to train others. The congregation leader must always be on the lookout for potential leaders and seek to lead them on for the exercise of their gifts.

An example of failure. After thirty years, there were in those in the Jerusalem congregation who barely demonstrated real growth:

> On this topic we have much to say and it is difficult to explain, since you have become sluggish in hearing. For though you should in fact be teachers by this time, you need someone to teach you the beginning elements of God's utterances. You have gone back to needing milk, not solid food. For everyone who lives on milk is inexperienced in the message of righteousness, because he is an infant. (Hebrews 5:11–13)

The writer says that these people should have been teachers, they had the capacity for it, but they did not avail themselves of the possibilities. Such situations are tragic.

***Training in the local* qehilah.** The local *qehilah* is the place where believers are challenged for service and trained in their use of their gifts:

> Now there are different gifts, but the same Spirit. And there are different ministries, but the same Lord. And there are different results, but the same God who produces all of them in everyone. (1 Corinthians 12:4–6)

Leaders and people in a *qehilah* need to be imaginative with the ways in which each can serve and how to develop the potential at its disposal.

Respect. There needs to be obedience within the fellowship as well as respect for the elders and their ministry:

> Now we ask you, brothers and sisters, to acknowledge those who labor among you and preside over you in the Lord and admonish you, and to esteem them most highly in love because of their work. Be at peace among yourselves. And we urge you, brothers and sisters, admonish the undisciplined, comfort the discouraged, help the weak, be patient toward all. (1 Thessalonians 5:12–14)

> Remember your leaders, who spoke God's message to you; reflect on the outcome of their lives and imitate their faith. (Hebrews 13:7)

Existing Training. Some of the larger individual congregations have schools that fulfill the function of training leaders. But, in addition, the Union of Messianic Jewish Congregations has established a Yeshiva program consisting of a good number of courses, taught as modules for several days, in both a winter and summer program, wherein the student independently completes the work of reading assigned texts, writing a paper, and taking an exam. After completing a required number of courses, the student is ordained as a "rabbi" (possibly, however, some other more contemporary term needs to be used). The international group has some similar training while the Fellowship of Messianic Congregations already has leaders who are seminary trained. These leaders should in turn train those with potential gifts for use in the congregation.

Overcoming Difficulties. The Yeshiva program is good for training potential leaders to be elders in a congregation. Nevertheless, there are two shortcomings:

The congregation leader is the sole leader. A few instances do exist when, as a congregation grows, the one leader continues to make the basic decisions, and does not look for or seek to train potential leaders for that congregation. If he remains the sole leader, then we must affirm he is not serving in a biblically prescribed manner. The congregation then revolves around that leader and this can become an unhealthy situation. As already indicated, potential leadership must be trained; the congregation leader should, as much as possible, work toward a plurality of leadership and to make sure that there can be an ongoing leadership should anything happen to him as the primary elder.

The training of young people for leadership. The Messianic congregation movement began, for the most part, some twenty years ago. By this time, there should be the selection of young people for education and training to be the future leadership of these congregations. Some congregations have performed an excellent job in training young people to take responsible positions in the congregations and who can also be congregation planters.

But we do need the possibility for our young people coming out of high schools to have a well-integrated undergraduate education that will also include Jewish and pastoral studies. Since 1923, the Moody Bible Institute has had an evangelism track in Jewish studies and the program has been constantly upgraded to where a B.A. in Jewish and Modern Israel Studies is offered. Today, however, there is now in place a second track in the undergraduate school of a combination of Jewish and pastoral studies, combined with general education, biblical, and theological studies. This can be the start for educating young people, and the congregations themselves can be the context for actual hands-on training by well-established congregation leaders. At least, this can be a start for preparing the next generation of leadership for the various Messianic congregation groups. Graduate or seminary training is a further possibility. Education and training remains a high area of concern that needs to be addressed.

The Reward for Faithful Leaders

> Believers who make up the congregations are the crown of the leaders:
> For who is our hope or joy or crown to boast of before our Lord Yeshua at his coming? Is it not of course you? For you are our glory and joy! (1 Thessalonians 2:19–20)

Examples in the Local *Qehilah* at Philippi. Think of the original believers at Philippi:

Lydia.

> On the Sabbath day we went outside the city gate to the side of the river, where we thought there would be a place of prayer, and we sat down and began to speak to the women who had assembled there. A woman named Lydia, a dealer in purple cloth from the city of Thyatira, a God-fearing woman, listened to us. The Lord opened her heart to respond to what Sha'ul was saying. (Acts 16:13–14)

Lydia's household.

> After she and her household were baptized, she urged us, "If you consider me to be a believer in the Lord, come and stay in my house." And she persuaded us. (Acts 16:15)

Possessed slave girl.

> She continued to do this for many days. But Sha'ul became greatly annoyed, and turned and said to the spirit, "I command you in the name of Yeshua the Messiah to come out of her!" And it came out of her at once. (Acts 16:18)

Jailer.

> Then he brought them outside and asked, "Sirs, what must I do to be saved?" (Acts 16:30)

Jailer's household.

> The jailer brought them into his house and set food before them, and he rejoiced greatly that he had come to believe in God, together with his entire household. (Acts 16:34)

People Who Are Reached by the Efforts of the Congregations' Leaders Are Regarded as Their Crowns.

> Then when the Chief Shepherd appears, you will receive the crown of glory that never fades away. (1 Kefa 5:4)

Accountability of Leaders

Each believer will be examined at the judgment seat of Messiah:

> Therefore, each of us will give an account of himself to God. (Romans 14:12)

At the same time, the elders somehow are also present to verify testimony, whether for gain or loss of reward. The issue of entrance into heaven is not germane to this judgment, but what is evident is that elders either can commend the believer or have to ruefully confess that a believer has not reached out for the opportunities to serve the living God:

> Obey your leaders and submit to them, for they keep watch over your souls and will give an account for their work. Let them do this with joy and not with complaints, for this would be no advantage for you. (Hebrews 13:17)

Experience of Individual Believers in the *Qehilah*

Entrance into the *Qehilah*

Through the New Birth.

> Yeshua replied, "I tell you the solemn truth, unless a person is born from above, he cannot see the kingdom of God." Nicodemus said to him, "How can a man be born when he is old? He cannot enter his mother's womb and be born a second time, can he?"
>
> Yeshua answered, "I tell you the solemn truth, unless a person is born

of water and spirit, he cannot enter the kingdom of God. What is born of the flesh is flesh, and what is born of the Spirit is spirit." (Yohanan 3:3–6)

Involved in the new birth is:

Regeneration.

A woman named Lydia, a dealer in purple cloth from the city of Thyatira, a God-fearing woman, listened to us. The Lord opened her heart to respond to what Sha'ul was saying. (Acts 16:14)

This is a special work of God that changes the individual whereby the Spirit of God moves into the believer to take His residence and seal him or her:

And when you heard the word of truth (the gospel of your salvation)—when you believed in Messiah—you were marked with the seal of the promised Holy Spirit, who is the down payment of our inheritance, until the redemption of God's own possession, to the praise of his glory. (Ephesians 1:13–14)

Repentance.

Kefa said to them, "Repent, and each one of you be baptized in the name of Yeshua the Messiah for the forgiveness of your sins, and you will receive the gift of the Holy Spirit." (Acts 2:38)

The word for repentance (Hebrew, *teshuvah*) comes from the verb *shuv,* meaning to turn around. This consists of a mental turnaround whereby, before coming to faith, the person is set against Messiah, but after coming to faith the believer has turned around to face the Messiah with a different frame of mind.

Immersion into the universal body of Messiah.

For just as the body is one and yet has many members, and all the members of the body—though many—are one body, so too is Messiah. For in one Spirit we were all baptized into one body. Whether Jews

> or Greeks or slaves or free, we were all made to drink of the one Spirit. (1 Corinthians 12:12–13)

The term *baptize* or *immerse* still remains to be discussed, but when a person has an atonement for sin, he or she belongs to a different order because the believer is now in an unbroken relationship with the Messiah.

Accompanying signs?

> And tongues spreading out like a fire appeared to them and came to rest on each one of them. (Acts 2:3)

> Kefa said to them, "Repent, and each one of you be baptized in the name of Yeshua the Messiah for the forgiveness of your sins, and you will receive the gift of the Holy Spirit." (Acts 2:38)

> While Kefa was still speaking these words, the Holy Spirit fell on all those who heard the message. The circumcised believers who had accompanied Kefa were greatly astonished that the gift of the Holy Spirit had been poured out even on the Gentiles. (Acts 10:44–45)

Signs were present with the early formation of the body of Messiah to demonstrate the validity of Yeshua's identity and of the acknowledgment that a new community was now being brought into existence. Jewish believers experienced these signs (the passages quoted above from Acts 2) and Gentile believers did later on (Acts 10).

The Local *Qehilah* and Immersion. One of the ordinances of the *qehilah* is immersion. The term *ordinance* is a theological designation and it is difficult to find a Hebrew equivalent. Perhaps the closest would be *tsav*, from the verb *tsavah*, meaning charge, or command. *Tsav* can mean precept and it could be a good word to use. However, with no agreement on terminology, it is best to continue using the word *ordinance*.

A* mikveh *experience? In ordinary usage, the *mikveh* is used by the woman for purification on a monthly basis. Furthermore, in the traditional setting, when a Gentile becomes a Jew, he goes through a series of teaching sessions, then is questioned by a number of rabbis concerning whether his change is genuine, followed by the final step of immersion in the *mikveh*. When the temple was still in existence, the priests went into the *mikveh* to cleanse themselves for service at the altar.

Because of this all-inclusive usage of the term *mikveh*, many Jewish believers in Messianic congregations, in North America and Israel, rather than describing immersion as "the *mikveh* experience," have instead opted for the use of *tevilah*, from *taval*, with the basic idea of "to dip so as to cover" to describe immersion (as is done in the *Hebrew New Testament, New Translation*). *Tevilah* can be done in a *mikveh* or at any other suitable place. *Tevilah* is the preferred word, therefore, for immersion.

Immersion, *tevilah*, should be done publicly, and where the person is immersed, there he or she will share publicly the change that took place on becoming a believer.

Commanded by Messiah.

> Therefore go and make disciples of all nations, baptizing them in the name of the Father and the Son and the Holy Spirit, teaching them to obey everything I have commanded you. And remember, I am with you always, to the end of the age. (Mattai 28:19–20)

> He said to them, "Go into all the world and preach the gospel to every creature. The one who believes and is baptized will be saved, but the one who does not believe will be condemned." (Mark 16:15–16)[4]

Note the order: first, we disciple and preach. After the people receive the message and become believers, then immersion follows. A biblical immersion takes place after one comes to faith.

Practiced by the early believers. Immersion accompanied the preaching of Kefa to Jewish people (but keep in mind the order noted above of preaching first, then immersion):

> So those who accepted his message were baptized, and that day about three thousand people were added. (Acts 2:41)

Likewise as Sha'ul preached to both Jews and Gentiles:

> They replied, "Believe in the Lord Yeshua and you will be saved, you and your household." Then they spoke the word of the Lord to him, along with all those who were in his house. At that hour of the night he took them and washed their wounds; then he and all his family were baptized right away. (Acts 16:31–33)

However, Sha'ul himself only immersed a few so as to start a congregation; he then left it to the ordained elders to administer the ordinance further:

> Is Messiah divided? Sha'ul wasn't crucified for you, was he? Or were you in fact baptized in the name of Sha'ul? I thank God that I did not baptize any of you except Crispus and Gaius, so that no one can say that you were baptized in my name! (I also baptized the household of Stephanus. Otherwise, I do not remember whether I baptized anyone else.) For Messiah did not send me to baptize, but to preach the gospel—and not with clever speech, so that the tree of Messiah would not become useless. (1 Corinthians 1:13–17)

> Crispus, the president of the synagogue, believed in the Lord together with his entire household, and many of the Corinthians who heard about it believed and were baptized. (Acts 18:8)

An aggadah *(homily) of Sha'ul: Romans 6:1–5.*

> What shall we say then? Are we to remain in sin so that grace may increase? Absolutely not! How can we who died to sin still live in it? Or do you not know that as many as were baptized into Messiah Yeshua were baptized into his death? Therefore we have been buried with him through baptism into death, in order that just as Messiah was raised from the dead through the glory of the Father, so we too may live a new life.
>
> For if we have become united with him in the likeness of his death, we will certainly also be united in the likeness of his resurrection. (Romans 6:1–5)

The *aggadah* declares the Messiah's death, burial, and resurrection. Sha'ul also sets forth our death to the life of sin, emphasizing our burial in the likeness of His death, as well as our walk of a new life in the likeness of His resurrection.

God-Designed Experiences and Worship in the *Qehilah*

> They were devoting themselves to the apostles' teaching and to fellowship, to the breaking of bread and to prayer. (Acts 2:42)

In this verse we find each of the components that follow. We will examine in turn fellowship, worship, prayer, preaching and teaching, and the Lord's Supper.

Fellowship.

Common meeting ground. The *qehilah* is a cross section of society. Brothers and sisters in the Messiah have a fellowship that many times is closer than with unsaved members of earthly families.

Encouragement. We are social beings and need to derive help, comfort, and support from one another:

> . . . not abandoning our own meetings, as some are in the habit of doing, but encouraging each other, and even more so because you see the day drawing near. (Hebrews 10:25)

> Therefore encourage one another and build up each other, just as you are in fact doing. (1 Thessalonians 5:11)

> But exhort one another each day, as long as it is called "Today," that none of you may become hardened by sin's deception. (Hebrews 3:13)

By such fellowship and encouragement, we can create ideals for ourselves, provide motives for service, and direct our energies for ministry.

Worship.

Oneness (Unity). Sha'ul had declared of His body:

> For he [Yeshua] is our peace, the one who made both groups into one and who destroyed the middle wall of partition, the hostility. (Ephesians 2:14)

This is a theological pronouncement that the body of Messiah is one. All of us, no matter what our backgrounds might be, are all one in a spiritual organism. But does this mean that the various ethnocentricities that make the body cease to exist as a result of the oneness? Not at all!

Variations in worship. We have a multiplicity of congregations that have various possibility for styles of worship, depending, for example, on ethnicity such as black, Hispanic, Korean, Thai, Chinese, and so on. Not all worship in the same way, but what they do, as evangelical congregations, is to proclaim their faith in their cultural context.

Variations in ministry focus. Not only does worship differ, but the specific focus of ministry does likewise. One congregation emphasizes music, another youth, another work with adults to reach families, etc. Every congregation must realize, says George Barna, that

> . . . *a church cannot be all things to all people.* When Paul wrote that he became "all things to all men" (1 Cor. 9:22, *NIV*), he was stressing the importance of contextualizing his message and ministry. He was not, as some church leaders suggest, pushing every single congregation to try to satisfy each need of every individual who comes into contact with that church . . .
>
> . . . the successful churches resisted that impulse to be the answer to everyone's every problem by focusing on their vision for ministry, by reaffirming their commitment to quality, and by recognizing their limitations.[5]

A biblically-designed focus. The ministry of Kefa and Yaakov was in the land of Israel where the congregations reflected more of the Jewish cultural pattern. Sha'ul's ministry consisted of planting congregations among Gentile believers and they assumed a specific cultural pattern.

Messianic focus in worship. For the very reason Barna advances,

Messianic congregations are designed with one purpose in mind: to be a witness to Jewish people and seek to reach them by bringing them into an environment that will relate to religious-cultural needs. Messianic congregations do not consist of Jewish believers entirely; the mix is usually a 70/30 or a 60/40 and occasionally an almost even mix where the majority is Jewish. The point is that Gentile believers desire the Messianic worship pattern, as a way by which they can worship, but also for the possibility of bringing their unsaved Jewish friends.

What should the structure of Messianic worship be? That will depend largely on what the leadership desires: Messianic liturgy (in varying amounts), Messianic music, the reading from the Torah scroll if this is desired, and so on. Should there be an *Oneg Shabbat* on Friday evenings, a *Shabbat* service, or should the congregation meet on Sunday morning? Such choices must be left largely to the leadership and those whom they will reach, whether identified as religious Jews, secularized Jews, and so on. But the focus is that Messianic Jewish congregations have a specific purpose in mind and they and their leaders should not be faulted for trying to be true to their convictions for ministry focus.

Will some Gentile believers feel that this raises the "middle wall of partition"? There is no doubt that some will raise this issue. But as already pointed out, oneness in the body of Messiah does not preclude the possibility of the desire of various ethnocentric groups of people to be true to their identity, including Messianic Jews. Many Anglos will not want to worship in an African-American congregation and the same would be true of those in the latter ethnic group who would not be at home in Anglo congregations.

Again, the elders in Messianic congregations do have the right to focus on that which will best reflect theology and lifestyle to reach Jewish people. If Gentile believers do not like this emphasis, they should be reminded that they have a right to find a congregation where they can best serve God in a context where they will be confirmed in their spirit.

Prayer. There is definitely a place for both private and corporate prayer. We see private prayer in this passage:

> But whenever you pray, go into your room, close the door, and pray to your Father in secret. And your Father, who sees in secret, will reward you. (Mattai 6:6)

People should be encouraged to do so, preferably at a set time and at a set place.

In addition, there is also a definite place for corporate prayer by the congregation:

> When they had prayed, the place where they were assembled together was shaken, and they were all filled with the Holy Spirit and began to speak the word of God courageously. (Acts 4:31)

> When Kefa realized this, he went to the house of Miriam, the mother of Yohanan Mark, where many people had gathered together and were praying. (Acts 12:12)

> While they were serving the Lord and fasting, the Holy Spirit said, "Set apart for me Bar Navah and Sha'ul for the work to which I have called them." Then, after they had fasted and prayed and placed their hands on them, they sent them off. (Acts 13:2–3)

> Now as we were going to the place of prayer, a slave girl met us who had a spirit that enabled her to foretell the future by supernatural means. She brought her owners a great profit by fortune-telling. (Acts 16:16)

Sometimes this corporate prayer will take place within the course of the liturgy, or at some place in the course of the service. Elders need to plan for this experience so that it can be accomplished.

The people of a congregation must learn by personal experience to pray publicly, to be bold in prayer, and to see God's answers to prayer.

Preaching and Teaching Doctrine. If Messianic congregations are going to remain a viable and potent force, it will only be as leaders and members are grounded in the Torah and New Covenant, and specifically in doctrine. The Word must be preached and taught. While there is a place for liturgy, it can never take the place of knowing and being captured by the Word, and then being led forth to serve the living Messiah.

To build up the believers.

> . . . to equip the saints for the work of ministry, that is, to build up the body of Messiah, until we all attain to the unity of the faith and of the knowledge of the Son of God—a mature person, attaining to the measure of Messiah's full stature. (Ephesians 4:12–13)

Doctrine is of extreme importance. Sha'ul made a practice in his letters to first teach doctrine and then relate it to practice. The flow is always from orthodoxy to orthopraxy:

> Every scripture is inspired by God and useful for teaching, for reproof, for correction, and for training in righteousness. (2 Timothy 3:16)

> Make every effort to present yourself before God as a proven worker who does not need to be ashamed, teaching the message of truth accurately. (2 Timothy 2:15)

Note also the structure of the book of Romans: doctrine in chapters 1–11; followed by practice in chapters 12–16.

A believer practices what he or she believes, not vice versa. We need a biblical ideology to guide our thinking and actions.

The Lord's Supper: A Second Ordinance.

Term. A few Messianic congregations have employed the term *yizkor*, or memorial, from 1 Corinthians 11:24–25:

> And after he had given thanks he broke it and said, "This is my body, which is for you. Do this in remembrance of me." In the same way, he also took the cup after supper, saying, "This cup is the new covenant in my blood. Do this, every time you drink it, in remembrance of me." (1 Corinthians 11:24–25)

The *Hebrew New Testament, New Translation*, employs *yizkor* for remembrance. However, *yizkor* also refers to that part of the Yom Kippur (Day of Atonement) services when one prays for one's departed loved ones. If children are present, bearing the same names of the ones for whom prayer is being made, they must exit the service at that point. Because of this connotation of *yizkor*, many have felt it best not to apply this term for the ordinance.

The term used in Israel is *Se'udat HaAdon*, literally "Lord's Supper," reflecting the terminology of 1 Corinthians 11:20:

> Now when you come together at the same place, you are not really eating the Lord's Supper. (1 Corinthians 11:20)

The word *se'udah* derives from *sa'ad,* to support, or to *refresh with a meal*:

> . . . as well as wine that makes people feel so good,
> and so they can have oil to make their faces shine,
> as well as food that sustains [Hebrew, *yis'ad*, from *sa'ad*] people's lives.
> (Psalm 104:15)

> He woke up early in the morning on the fifth day so he could leave, but the girl's father said, "Get some energy [NIV: "Refresh yourself," Hebrew: *s'ad*, from *sa'ad*]. Wait until later in the day to leave!" So they ate a meal together. (Judges 19:8)

This is the word used for the third Shabbat meal, *se'udah shlishah,* taken late in the afternoon before *Shabbat* ends. Such a designation certainly captures the idea of the Lord's Supper.

In the United States, some use the phrase *Seder HaMashiah* for the Lord's Supper, but the use of the word *seder* suggests *pesach*. Although the Lord's Supper comes from the *pesach*, at the Lord's Supper we do not sit to observe the entire *pesach*. We only observe what the Messiah instituted in a special emphasis on the bread and cup.

Instituted by Messiah. The *Se'udat HaAdon* was instituted by the Messiah at the close of His last *pesach* so as to convey the lessons of His ministry, His death, resurrection, and to show that He offers eternal life because of His special redemptive ministry through His death:

> Then he took bread, and after giving thanks he broke it and gave it to them, saying, "This is my body which is given for you. Do this in remembrance of me." (Luke 22:19)

An obligation. The observance of the Lord's Supper is an obligation on every believer in his or her local *qehilah*:

> In the same way, he also took the cup after supper, saying, "This cup is the new covenant in my blood. Do this, every time you drink it, in remembrance of me." For every time you eat this bread and drink the cup, you proclaim the Lord's death until he comes. (1 Corinthians 11:25–26)

Note the emphasis on the cup, "Do this, every time you drink it, in remembrance of me." The imperative likewise exists with the taking of the bread.

A unique practice. In the beginning, believers first enjoyed a fellowship meal or love feast, and then the elements of the Lord's Supper were taken. Later, Sha'ul forbade the abuse of the fellowship meal and stopped the participation in it by the members:

> Now when you come together at the same place, you are not really eating the Lord's Supper. For when it is time to eat, everyone proceeds with his own supper. One is hungry and another becomes drunk. Do you not have houses so that you can eat and drink? Or are you trying to show contempt for the *qehilah* of God by shaming those who have nothing? What should I say to you? Should I praise you? I will not praise you for this! (1 Corinthians 11:20–22)

The practice by congregations as to when the bread and cup are taken will vary. In congregations that incorporate more of the Jewish practice, a good time would be after the reading of the Torah when, as everyone comes forward, the elders can then serve the bread and cup. Each congregation needs to find the most appropriate time to serve the elements.

A type study. There is a divine tie between the thanksgiving offering in the sacrificial system (Leviticus 3; 7:29–34) and the Lord's Supper. Each in a sense is the table of the Lord; believers of long ago rejoiced in what the Lord had done for them through His blessings. Likewise, believers today can sit at the Lord's Supper and thank HaShem for His blessings in providing Yeshua as our personal redeemer and for all the rest of His abundance, as we see in Acts:

> Every day they continued to gather together by common consent in the temple courts, breaking bread from house to house, sharing their food with glad and humble hearts. (Acts 2:46)

RESPONSIBILITIES OF THE *QEHILAH*[6]

To Bear Witness to the Truth

The *qehilah* witnesses to the reality of redemption and to a biblical ethic and a prophetic morality, all in the context of the total needs of society.

> . . . in case I am delayed, to let you know how people ought to conduct themselves in the household of God, because it is the *qehilah* of the living God, the support and bulwark of the truth. (1 Timothy 3:15)

> For I did not hold back from announcing to you the whole purpose of God. Watch out for yourselves and for all the flock of which the Holy Spirit has made you overseers, to shepherd the *qehilah* of God that he obtained with the blood of his own Son. (Acts 20:27–28)

To Challenge and Equip for Evangelism

> Then Yeshua came up and said to them, "All authority in heaven and on earth has been given to me. Therefore go and make disciples of all nations, baptizing them in the name of the Father and the Son and the Holy Spirit, teaching them to obey everything I have commanded you. And remember, I am with you always, to the end of the age." (Mattai 28:18–20)

> But you will receive power when the Holy Spirit has come upon you, and you will be my witnesses in Jerusalem, and in all Judea and Samaria, and to the farthest parts of the earth. (Acts 1:8)

Note the progression on the book of Acts: Jerusalem and Judea in chapters 1–7, Samaria in chapters 8–9, and the "ends of the earth" in chapters 10 on. We also see examples of contextualization according to the culture or background of the people.

Kefa and the Circumcision.

> On the contrary, when they saw that I was entrusted with the gospel to the uncircumcised just as Kefa was to the circumcised (for he who empowered Kefa for his apostleship to the circumcised also empowered me for my apostleship to the Gentiles) and when Yaakov, Kefa, and Yohanan, who had a reputation as pillars, recognized the grace that had been given to me, they gave to Bar Navah and me the right hand of fellowship, agreeing that we would go to the Gentiles and they to the circumcised. (Galatians 2:7–9)

We see various examples of Jewish people coming to faith.

> So those who accepted his message were baptized, and that day about three thousand people were added. (Acts 2:41)

> But many of those who had listened to the message believed, and the number of the men came to about five thousand. (Acts 4:4)

> The word of God continued to spread, the number of disciples in Jerusalem increased greatly, and a large group of priests became obedient to the faith. (Acts 6:7)

> But I was personally unknown to the *qehilot* of Judea that are in Messiah. (Galatians 1:22)

Sha'ul and the Uncircumcision. See Galatians 2:7–9 immediately above, and also:

> Now there were these prophets and teachers in the *qehilah* at Antioch: Bar Navah, Simeon called Niger, Lucius the Cyrenian, Manaen (a close friend of Herod the tetrarch from childhood) and Sha'ul. While they were serving the Lord and fasting, the Holy Spirit said, "Set apart for me Bar Navah and Sha'ul for the work to which I have called them." Then, after they had fasted and prayed and placed their hands on them, they sent them off.
>
> So Bar Navah and Sha'ul, sent out by the Holy Spirit, went down to Seleucia, and from there they sailed to Cyprus. (Acts 13:1–4)

Similarly, we find examples of Gentiles coming to faith.

> When they arrived and gathered the *qehilah* together, they reported all the things God had done with them, and that he had opened a door of faith for the Gentiles. (Acts 14:27)

> The whole group kept quiet and listened to Bar Navah and Sha'ul while they explained all the miraculous signs and wonders God had done among the Gentiles through them. (Acts 15:12)

Ensuing Changes in Lifestyle and Community.
Jerusalem.

> They were devoting themselves to the apostles' teaching and to fellowship, to the breaking of bread and to prayer. Reverential awe came over everyone, and many wonders and miraculous signs came about by the apostles. All who believed were together and held everything in common, and they began selling their property and possessions and distributing the proceeds to everyone, as anyone had need. Every day they continued to gather together by common consent in the temple courts, breaking bread from house to house,

sharing their food with glad and humble hearts, praising God and having the good will of all the people. And the Lord was adding to their number every day those who were being saved. (Acts 2:42–47)

Ephesus.

Large numbers of those who had practiced magic collected their books and burned them up in the presence of everyone. When the value of the books was added up, it was found to total fifty thousand silver coins. . . .

"And you see and hear that this Sha'ul has persuaded and turned away a large crowd, not only in Ephesus but in practically all of the province of Asia, by saying that gods made by hands are not gods at all. There is danger not only that this business of ours will come into disrepute, but also that the temple of the great goddess Artemis will be regarded as nothing, and she whom all the province of Asia and the world worship will suffer the loss of her greatness."

When they heard this they became enraged and began to shout, "Great is Artemis of the Ephesians!" The city was filled with the uproar, and the crowd rushed to the theater together, dragging with them Gaius and Aristarchus, the Macedonians who were Sha'ul's traveling companions. (Acts 19:19, 26–29)

Thessalonica.

For people everywhere report how you welcomed us and how you turned to God from idols to serve the living and true God and to wait for his Son from heaven, whom he raised from the dead, Yeshua our deliverer from the coming wrath. (1 Thessalonians 1:9–10)

We observe this in modern communities as well. The *qehilah* has always made an impact on the communities where it exists, and when revived, it has always changed societies. In England, we can think of the Wesleyan revival in the 1700s and the changes in the whole of society in the 1800s. Of course, one major impact has been the beginning of the modern missionary movement. In Africa and Asia, we can cite the growth of the church in Indonesia and Bangladesh as examples. In Israel, too, there has been a growing movement of Israelis to faith in Yeshua.

To Discipline

For Private Offenses.

> So then, if you bring your gift to the altar and there remember that your brother has something against you, . . . (Mattai 5:23)

> If your brother sins, go and show him his fault when the two of you are alone. If he listens to you, you have regained your brother. But if he does not listen, take one or two others with you, so that at the testimony of two or three witnesses every matter may be established. If he refuses to listen to them, tell it to the *qehilah*. If he refuses to listen to the *qehilah*, treat him like a Gentile or a tax collector. (Mattai 18:15–17)

For Public Offenses, Which Incriminate the Whole Congregation.

> For even though I am absent physically, I am present in spirit. And I have already judged the one who did this, just as though I were present. When you gather together in the name of our Lord Yeshua, and I am with you in spirit, along with the power of our Lord Yeshua, turn this man over to Satan for the destruction of the flesh, so that his spirit may be saved in the day of the Lord. (1 Corinthians 5:3–5)

Note also that once forgiveness is extended, the sin is then forgotten!

> But we command you, brothers and sisters, in the name of our Lord Yeshua the Messiah, to keep away from any brother who lives an undisciplined life and not according to the tradition they received from us. (2 Thessalonians 3:6)

To Be Administered with Great Care. Discipline must be coupled with counsel:

> Brothers and sisters, if a person is discovered in some sin, you who are spiritual restore such a person in a spirit of gentleness. Pay close attention to yourselves, so that you are not tempted too. (Galatians 6:1)

There must be patient reclamation, done with great care:

> And have mercy on those who waver; save others by snatching them out of the fire; have mercy on others, coupled with a fear of God, hating even the clothes stained by the flesh. (Yehudah 1:22–23)

To Be Shared by All the Leaders.

Relation of Local *Qehilot* to One Another

Equality Among Congregations

No one congregation controls another.

Fellowship and Cooperation Between Congregations

No one congregation can ignore the existence of the other. They must be mindful of the mutual furtherance of each other's welfare.

Consultation Among Congregations

There should be constant discussion on advancing the witness in evangelism and congregation planting. Likewise, there should be mutual interaction concerning the identity of believers with Israel in general and believers in particular. Advice should be both sought and taken, led by the Spirit of God.

The Breaking of Fellowship

Fellowship can be broken when a congregation departs from the basis of the Word of God, or departs from sound practices or a godly lifestyle. Here is where spiritually strong congregations need to extend a helping hand to those in need.

A Final Word

There is no perfect congregation to be found. Congregations as well as the individuals within them are at varying levels of maturity. However, we must always be zealous for the good name of our congregation; for example, we must learn how to "put out a fire" among fellow believers, rather than feeding it. Above all, the *qehilah* is meant to bring eternal glory to God.

> Now to him who by the power that is working within us is able to do far beyond all that we ask or think, to him be the glory in the *qehilah* and in Messiah Yeshua to all generations, forever and ever. Amen. (Ephesians 3:20–21)

NOTES

Introduction

[1] [See "Biography of Louis Goldberg" below.—Ed.]

Chapter 1

[1] BDB, s.v. "יָרָה."

[2] Ibid., s.v. "תּוֹרָה." Other definitions given by BDB are *direction* and *law*.

[3] Harry A. Cohen, *A Basic Jewish Encyclopedia: Jewish Teachings and Practices Listed and Interpreted in Order of Their Importance Today* (Hartford: Hartmore House, 1965), 28.

[4] Hans-Helmut Esser, "Law," in *New International Dictionary of New Testament Theology* (Grand Rapids: Zondervan, 1979), 2:438.

[5] This constitution should not be confused with the Abrahamic Covenant, which guarantees the right of existence to Israel (Abraham to Isaac and then to Jacob and to his children) as long as there is a history of the human race (Genesis 17:7). Because this covenant is unconditional in its nature, it can convey such a promise to a particular people.

[6] John Calvin, *Institutes of the Christian Religion*, trans. Henry Beveridge, 2.7 (Grand Rapids: Eerdmans, 1957), 299–313. [Calvin speaks of a threefold use of the moral law, which he distinguishes from the ceremonial law.—Ed.]

[7] ["Leviticus revealed to Israel the holiness of God (19:2). All the other characteristics of God, such as His righteousness, truthfulness, faithfulness, mercy and love, are closely related to His holiness, and holiness may be considered the very essence of God" (Louis Goldberg, *Leviticus: A Study Guide Commentary* [Grand Rapids: Zondervan, 1980], 11).—Ed.]

[8] ["God never demanded that people follow these commandments in a legalistic sense; to do so only warps the concept God had in mind for a new life within a covenant relationship. His primary design was that people should first be born again and then the Decalogue can serve as a guide by which to live a holy life and serve others" (Louis Goldberg, *Deuteronomy: Bible Study Commentary* [Grand Rapids:

Lamplighter Books, 1986], 55).—Ed.]

[9] [For details, see Goldberg, *Leviticus*, ch. 1–2.—Ed.]

[10] [See Louis Goldberg, *Our Jewish Friends* (Chicago: Moody, 1977), 13–17, 78–79.—Ed.]

[11] [Ibid.—Ed.]

[12] In the second major division of the Hebrew Bible, the earlier prophetic books in the Hebrew Bible consist of Joshua, Judges, 1 and 2 Samuel, and 1 and 2 Kings. The later prophetic books are those of Isaiah, Jeremiah, Ezekiel, and the Minor Prophets.

[13] In 175–180 C.E., Celsus made critical assessments of Israel as a people: 1) he thought of them as descendants of the Egyptians; 2) he asserted that the God of the Old Testament was an overworked deity, tired out after a so-called six-day creation. For a reply to Celsus, see Edward J. Young, "Celsus and the Old Testament," *Westminster Theological Journal* 6:2 (May 1944): 166–97. Origen had in 248 C.E. attacked Celsus's statements in *Contra Celsus*. In the latter 200s, Porphyry wrote *Against the Christians* and in his 12th book attacked Daniel as a bona-fide prophet. Porphyry asserted that Daniel did not write in the sixth century B.C.E., attributing the book to a second century B.C.E. author and questioning the ability to prophesy the future. Porphyry also denied Mosaic authorship for the first five books. For a reply regarding the denial of Daniel as a prophet, see Edward J. Young, "Porphyry and His Criticism of Daniel," in *The Prophecy of Daniel: A Commentary* (Grand Rapids: Eerdmans, 1949), 317–20.

[14] Called by some scholars Jamnia or Jabneh.

[15] See Jacob Neusner, *A Life of Rabban Yohanan ben Zakkai, Ca. 1–80 C.E.* (Leiden: E. J. Brill, 1962), 142–44. Yohanan understood ". . . that through *hesed* the Jews might make atonement, and that the sacrifices now demanded of them were love and mercy," acts of compassion he derived from Hosea 6:8.

[16] A few attempts have been made to rebuild the temple as a so-called third one.

[17] William Reed Newell, *Hebrews, Verse by Verse* (Chicago: Moody, 1947), 262–63.

[18] Lewis Sperry Chafer, *Systematic Theology* (Dallas: Dallas Seminary Press, 1948), 7:225.

[19] Werner Elert, *Law and Gospel*, trans. Edward H. Schroeder (Philadelphia: Fortress Press, 1967), 38, citing "Gustav Kawerau in his article on the Antinomian Controversies in the *Realenzyklopaedie für die Protestantische Theologie und Kirche*, Vol. I (3rd ed.: Leipzig, 1896), p. 588." See Elert's discussion on these sentences that, though attributed to Luther, Elert argues actually come from Melanchthon.

[20] [In this verse, "tree" is the translation of the NET, rather than being our editorial substitution for the word "cross."—Ed.]

[21] [For detailed discussion, see Goldberg, *Leviticus*, 26–34.—Ed.]

[22] Yaakov is possibly making a hurried reference to the Noahide Laws.

[23] The Theodosian Code, finally formulated under Emperor Theodosius II "marks a serious deterioration in the position of the Jews. His first law, of May 408, is directed against the feast of Purim, since it was believed that the Jews then burned images of the cross. . . . in 438 an important statute was issued in which the Jews were defined as 'enemies of the Roman laws and of the supreme majesty' . . . The civil inferiority of the Jews and discrimination against them were thus legally sanctioned." (Alfredo Mordechai Rabello, "Theodosius II," *Encyclopedia Judaica* 15:1101–2.)

Chapter 2

[1] Jacob Joshua Ross, "Revelation, in Talmudic Literature," *Encyclopedia Judaica* 14:119.

[2] Kaufmann Kohler, *Jewish Theology Systematically and Historically Considered* (New York: Macmillan, 1918), 35, n. 1.

[3] Ibid., 34.

[4] Kaufmann Kohler, "Revelation," *Jewish Encyclopedia* 10:396.

[5] Ibid.

[6] Ibid.

[7] Kohler, *Jewish Theology*, 35.

[8] Ibid.

[9] Edward Lipinski, "Revelation," *Encyclopedia Judaica* 14:118.

[10] For one writer's views, see Isidore Fishman, *Introduction to Judaism*, rev. ed. (London: Jewish Chronicle Publications, 1973), 15–16.

[11] Kohler, *Jewish Theology*, 36–37.

[12] A curse had been placed on the line of Solomon (Jeremiah 22:28, 30) so that while Yeshua could receive the physical regal blessings of the line of Solomon through Yosef, he could however not be biologically related to Yosef. So, the link is established through his mother, Miriam, back to this brother of Solomon, Nathan, to David.

[13] Sha'ul could have had Greek classical training in Tarsus where he grew up, studying the Greek language, the poets, and philosophers, etc. The portions he cited are, first, one by Epimenides in his *Cretica,* "For in thee we live and move and have our being" (ca. 600 B.C.E.), while the second is by Aratus, from his *Phaenomena*, "for we are also his offspring" (ca. 315–240 B.C.E.). See Richard N. Longenecker, "Acts," in *The Expositor's Bible Commentary*, ed. Frank E. Gabelein (Grand Rapids: Zondervan, 1981), 9: 476. While the pagan poets used the words to extol Zeus, Sha'ul applied the message to the one God of the universe, leaving no question as to whom he was referring.

[14] P. E. Hughes, "Grace," in *Evangelical Dictionary of Theology*, ed. Walter A. Elwell (Grand

Rapids: Baker, 1984), 479–82, esp. 479–80. Jewish people also have a keen sense of morality because of the Ten Words, amplified in the case of the more Conservative and Orthodox views of man's evil and good inclinations. But generally, all people have a sense of good and evil, whereby one has a responsibility to God his Maker.

[15] Abraham Cohen, *Everyman's Talmud: The Major Teachings of the Rabbinic Sages* (New York: Schocken Books, 1995, orig. 1949), 368. [The actual quote from Cohen is, "The following have no share in the World to Come; He who says that the doctrine of the Resurrection is not deducible from the Torah, who maintains that the Torah does not come from Heaven, and the epicurean."—Ed.]

[16] b. *Sanhedrin* 99a (Soncino Talmud, *Nezikin* III, 672).

[17] Ross, "Revelation, in Talmudic Literature," 120.

[18] Samson Raphael Hirsch, *Judaism Eternal: Selected Essays from the Writings of Rabbi Samson Raphael Hirsch*, trans. I. Grunfeld (London: Soncino, 1956), 2: 216.

[19] Solomon Schechter, *Some Aspects of Rabbinic Theology* (New York: Macmillan, 1923), 127.

[20] [NET has "like a lion they pin my hands and feet."—Ed.]

[21] [NET: "All of us had wandered off like sheep; / each of us had strayed off on his own path, / but the LORD caused the sin of all of us to attack him." By Yeshua's day the Targum Isaiah interpreted this passage to describe the suffering of the nation Israel. The Targums will be discussed in a later chapter.—Ed.]

[22] In biblical Hebrew, two major prefixed and suffixed forms of the verbs designate either completed or incompleted action, which can be past, present, or future. Since the verbs themselves do not specify past, present, or future tenses, these are implied from the context. See Jacob Weingreen, *A Practical Grammar for Classical Hebrew* (Oxford: Clarendon Press, 1948), 99ff.

[23] The First Temple was lost in 586 B.C.E., but the altar of burnt offering was placed in service by Judean returnees and the foundations of the Second Temple were laid in 536 B.C.E. (Ezra 3:2, 10). The Second Temple was not finally completed until 516 B.C.E., some seventy years after the loss of the First Temple.

[24] The rabbis must have struggled with how to explain Isaiah 53: was this the death of the Messiah or the suffering of the nation? In the end, as we see in the Targum of Isaiah 53, the verses concerning suffering are relegated to the nation while verses speaking of exaltation are referred to the Messiah's experience when the kingdom of peace is established on earth.

[25] It is not our purpose to enter into a discussion as to which materials served as the prototypes or bases for the first gospels. Should the reader be interested in this highly technical discussion, he or she can consult the available New Testament introductions.

[26] [NET has "divine secret" in place of "mystery" in this verse.—Ed.]

[27] Such an offer did not eliminate the necessity for His death. If the Sanhedrin had accepted the Messiah as Israel's rightful king, the Romans would have certainly

killed Yeshua because they would never have tolerated any rival king to their Caesar, nor accept a kingdom that the God of Israel had envisioned. Yeshua would have been buried by the Romans but He would have been raised up again on the third day to wreak vengeance on the Roman authority. Eventually, in short order, the kingdom and its fullness of spiritual and material blessings could have been established 2,000 years ago. See Louis Goldberg, *Turbulence over the Middle East: Israel and the Nations in Confrontation and the Coming Kingdom of Peace on Earth* (Neptune: Loizeaux Brothers, 1982). Such a scenario did not happen, of course, and the Sanhedrin made their final negative decision regarding Yeshua's claims. It was left to Sha'ul to explain the mystery of the body of the Messiah.

[28] Kohler, "Revelation," 396.

[29] See Kaufmann Kohler's discussion in "Inspiration," *Jewish Encyclopedia* 6:607–9.

[30] Ross, "Revelation, in Talmudic Literature," 121. BB 15a = *Baba Bathra* 15a.

[31] For this idea, see *Exodus Rabbah* 47:9 (Soncino Midrash Rabbah III, 545).

[32] See Kohler's discussion, "Inspiration," 608.

[33] In fact, the very word "they were carried along" (2 Kefa 1:21) is the same word used to describe how the wind of the storm caught the ship on which Sha'ul and other prisoners sailed: "we were driven along," Acts 27:15, implying that no one could control it. This could serve to picture how the writers were under the strong guidance of the Holy Spirit; while they were free to choose the sources and even the words, yet the final record is what God intended.

[34] *Exodus Rabbah* 5:9 (Soncino Midrash Rabbah III, 87)

[35] The use of *HaShem, The Name*, avoids the direct use of the name of God, and recognizes the lofty holiness of God. He Himself spoke to Moses concerning His name in a special sense (Exodus 3:15) and the name of Yeshua is similarly referred to in verses such as Acts 9:15, 27.

[36] Schechter, *Some Aspects*, 118.

[37] The debate is found in b. *Baba Metzia* 59b (Soncino Talmud, *Nezekin* I, 353).

[38] [However, compare Bruce K. Waltke and M. O'Connor, *An Introduction to Biblical Hebrew Syntax* (Winona Lake, IN: Eisenbrauns, 1990), 571: "No differentiation is possible between the regular and long (ָה-) forms of the imperative, since they occur in similar contexts."—Ed.]

[39] A rival school, Bet Midrash Shammai, was established concurrently, and often the two schools were in conflict with each other over interpretation of the Torah. Shammai represented one end of the *Parushim* or Pharisaic schools, taking the Scriptures literally and at times taking a legalistic position. Hillel was the moderate, standing between Shammai and the other end of the *Parushim* who were more mystical in their beliefs.

[40] Judah Goldin, trans., *The Fathers According to Rabbi Nathan*, Yale Judaica Series 10

(New Haven: Yale University Press, 1955), ch. 37, 154.

[41] Louis Jacobs, "Hermeneutics," *Encyclopedia Judaica* 8:367.

[42] Ibid., 367–70.

[43] The seven rules are listed with some observations by Benjamin Bernfeld, "Hermeneutics, Talmudic," *Universal Jewish Encyclopedia* 5:324.

[44] Ibid.

[45] [NET: "Abram believed the LORD, and the LORD considered his response of faith as proof of genuine loyalty."—Ed.]

[46] [NET: "How blessed is the one whose wrongdoing the LORD does not punish, in whose spirit there is no deceit."—Ed.]

Chapter 3

[1] Schechter, *Some Aspects*, 126.

[2] We might observe, however, tongue in cheek, that some evangelicals use the writings of their denominations' founders, or the works of the Reformers, as a kind of evangelical oral law to interpret the Word for today! Sometimes this use of what the Reformers taught takes on almost a kind of authoritative tradition within the church.

[3] b. *Arakin* 15b (Soncino Talmud, *Kodashim* III, 89).

[4] b. *Rosh HaShanah* 31b (Soncino Talmud, *Moed* IV, 152).

[5] b. *Baba Bathra* 15b (Soncino Talmud, *Nezekin* II, 76). The Soncino edition reads "splinter from between your teeth," relying (according to the Soncino footnote) on the text of *'En Yakob*, though the Talmud text says "eyes.").

[6] b. *Baba Metzia* 49a (Soncino Talmud, *Nezikin* I, 291). – lit. "that your 'yes' should be just and your 'no' should be just!"

[7] b. *Berachot* 10a (Soncino Talmud, *Zera'im*, 51).

[8] m. *Pesahim* 10:8 (Danby, 151).

[9] For example, John Fischer and David Bronstein, *Siddur for Messianic Jews* (Palm Harbor, FL: Menorah Press, 1988). Other Messianic *siddurim* are also used among the congregations as well. Some also use the traditional Jewish *siddur* of the synagogue, drawing on those portions appropriate to the service.

[10] Many Messianic congregations opt to meet on *Shabbat* morning, while others prefer to worship on Sunday morning. But certainly a freedom of choice exists that enables the particular congregation to minister to the specific needs of the local Jewish community, whether Traditional or Reform. See further in the chapter on ecclesiology.

[11] [LG's statement here implies not that the Mishnah was written earlier than the New Covenant writings but that common oral material was available to be utilized by Sha'ul and also later by the compilers of the Mishnah.—Ed.]

[12] *m. Avot* 1:2 (Danby, 446).

[13] Goldin, *Fathers*, ch. 4, 34.

[14] Neusner, *Yohanan ben Zakkai*, 144.

[15] See H. H. Ben-Sasson, "The Middle Ages," in *A History of the Jewish People*, ed. H. H. Ben-Sasson (Cambridge: Harvard University Press, 1976), 488.

[16] Certainly, "convert" does not have the idea of changing one's religion from Judaism to Christianity as it was understood in Christendom after the 400s and 500s. The word itself means *turn around*, that is, turn from one's *sins* to face *God* and receive a new life. In Yohanan's case, it means that Judeans were "turning" from their sins to face the coming kingdom over which the Messiah would preside.

[17] *b. Sanhedrin* 98b (Soncino Talmud, *Nezikin* III, 667).

[18] Samuel Tobias Lachs, *A Rabbinic Commentary on the New Testament: The Gospels of Matthew, Mark and Luke* (Hoboken: KTAV; New York: Anti-Defamation League of B'nai B'rith, 1987), 74.

[19] [NET: "the oppressed will possess the land..."—Ed.]

[20] See C. G. Montefiore, *Rabbinic Literature and Gospel Teachings* (1930; repr., New York: KTAV, 1970), 17–23.

[21] Reuven Hammer, trans., *Sifre: A Tannaitic Commentary on the Book of Deuteronomy,* Yale Judaica Series 24 (New Haven: Yale University Press, 1986), Piska 96, 144.

[22] Some examples appear in the Targum Isaiah: the Scripture "I will hide my eyes" (Isaiah 1:15) is understood in the Targum as "I take up the face of my Shekhinah from you"; 2) when Isaiah said, "my eyes have seen the King, the Lord Almighty" (Isaiah 6:5), the Targum renders it as, "my eyes have seen the glory of the Shekinah" (see *The Isaiah Targum: Introduction, Translation, Apparatus and Notes*, trans. Bruce D. Chilton, The Aramaic Bible, vol. 11 (Wilmington, DE: Michael Glazier, 1987), 3, 14.

[23] See *Leviticus Rabbah* 9:9 (Soncino Midrash Rabbah IV, 115–20). Even though this statement appears much later in written form, at about 750 C.E., yet the sentiments of the statement were already a part of the thinking of the rabbis.

[24] James H. Charlesworth, ed., *The Old Testament Pseudepigrapha* (Garden City, NY: Doubleday, 1983–1985), 1:180.

[25] Regarding Isaiah, "And they seized Isaiah the son of Amoz and sawed him in half with a wood saw," *Martyrdom and Ascension of Isaiah* 5:11, in Charlesworth, *The Old Testament Pseudepigripha* (1985), 2:164. Judean rebels, refusing to listen to Jeremiah's warning against going to Egypt, traveled there anyway, forcing the prophet to go with them (see Jeremiah 43). He is buried there in an unmarked grave.

[26] *m. Avot* 4:10 (Danby, 454).

[27] *b. Shabbat* 88b (Soncino Talmud, *Mo'ed* I, 419).

[28] Isidore Epstein, *The Faith of Judaism: An Interpretation for Our Times* (New York: Soncino

Press, 1954), 84, who cites Saadya in this note: "*Emunot we-Deot, Introduction*, Slucki ed. p. 13; Rosenblatt, E.T. [English translation], p. 32."

[29] Epstein, *Faith of Judaism*, 87–88.

[30] Moses Maimonides, *The Guide for the Perplexed*, trans. Shlomo Pines (Chicago: University of Chicago Press, 1963), book I, ch. 31, 65–67.

[31] Ibid., book II, ch. 25, 327–30.

[32] This discussion will be taken up in greater detail in a later chapter.

[33] This removal of anything that smacks of humanity in referring to God is an important emphasis to be discussed in later chapters, inasmuch as it has a direct bearing on a person's relationship with the Lord.

[34] See Louis Goldberg, "Some Observations Concerning the Attributes of God in Jewish Philosophy" (M.A. thesis, Roosevelt University, 1975).

[35] Isidore Epstein, *Judaism: A Historical Presentation*, 3rd ed. (Baltimore: Penguin Books, 1964), 214.

[36] Moses Mendelssohn, *Jerusalem: A Treatise on Ecclesiastical Authority and Judaism*, trans. M. Samuels (n.p.: Longman, Orme, Brown and Longmans, 1838), 89ff.

[37] Epstein, *Faith of Judaism*, 89–90.

[38] Hirsch, *Judaism Eternal*, 2:231–32.

[39] [NET: "Then you must recall the LORD's instructions and the prophetic testimony of what would happen. Certainly they say such things because their minds are spiritually darkened."—Ed.]

Chapter 4

[1] R. Schippers, "Fullness," in *New International Dictionary of New Testament Theology* (Grand Rapids: Zondervan, 1975), 1:733, 735.

[2] Ulrich Luz, *Matthew 1–7, A Commentary*, trans. Wilhelm C. Linss (Minneapolis: Augsburg Press, 1989), 260–61.

[3] Ibid., 261–64.

[4] As for example, Commandment 6, murder (Mattai 5:21–22); Commandment 7, adultery (Mattai 5:27–28); divorce, as a corollary of Commandment 7 (Mattai 5:31–32); and fulfillment of vows, or promises, where one does not lie, Commandment 9 (Mattai 5:33–37).

[5] G. Campbell Morgan, *The Gospel According to Matthew* (Westwood, NJ: Revell, 1929), 58.

[6] [NET has "the faithfulness of Jesus Christ" in place of NIV's "faith in Jesus Christ." This reflects scholarly differences over the best translation.—Ed.]

[7] See below on Psalm 103:12.

[8] David H. Stern, *Messianic Jewish Manifesto* (Jerusalem: Jewish New Testament Publications, 1988), 127–28.

[9] [NET has "Christ's faithfulness" in place of NIV's "faith in Christ."—Ed.]
[10] [NIV: "thoroughly trained in the law of our fathers"—Ed.]
[11] [NET: "cleanse your heart"—Ed.]
[12] [NET has a long circumlocution by way of paraphrase: "Just as ritual circumcision cuts away the foreskin as an external symbol of dedicated covenant commitment, you must genuinely dedicate yourselves to the LORD and get rid of everything that hinders your commitment to me"—Ed.]
[13] [NET has "Non-christians" in place of NIV "pagans"—Ed.]
[14] C. E. B. Cranfield, *A Critical and Exegetical Commentary on the Epistle to the Romans*, International Critical Commentary (Edinburgh: T & T Clark, 1975–79), 2:853.
[15] [NET in fact translates as "God-fearing proselytes."—Ed.]
[16] David H. Stern, trans., *Jewish New Testament* (Jerusalem; Clarksville, MD: Jewish New Testament Publications, 1989).

Chapter 5

[1] As cited in Wayne Grudem, *Systematic Theology: An Introduction to Biblical Doctrine* (Leicester: Inter-Varsity Press; Grand Rapids: Zondervan, 1994), 1169.
[2] Philip Schaff, *History of the Christian Church* (1884–91; repr., Grand Rapids: Eerdmans, 1955–58), 3:319.
[3] As we have seen elsewhere, there is freedom of choice in practice as long as a biblical base for the gospel is upheld.
[4] Bellarmino Bagatti, *The Church from the Circumcision: History and Archaeology of the Judaeo-Christians* (Jerusalem: Franciscan Printing Press, 1971), 93. Bagatti also points out that eighteen Jewish bishops were present in the land of Israel of which the Gentile Bishops had no knowledge. Had they been present at the Council of Nicea, one can only wonder if some freedom of choice could have been allowed the Jewish brethren, as long as they adhered to a sound interpretation of the Word.
[5] [NET: "Both dreams of Pharaoh have the same meaning."—Ed.]
[6] [NET: "they become a new family," paraphrasing; cf. more literal NIV "they will become one flesh"—Ed.]
[7] M. Rosenbaum and A. M. Silbermann, trans., *Pentateuch with Targum Onkelos, Haphtaroth, and Rashi's Commentary* (London: Shapiro, Vallentine, 1930), 2:126.
[8] *b. Sanhedrin* 38b (Soncino Talmud, *Nezikin* III, 245–46).
[9] Ibid., 246, n. 6.
[10] The de-anthropomorphization of God was an exercise engaged in by the religious leaders in Israel from 400 B.C.E. onward. So as to protect the holiness of God whereby Israel would realize that He is not like the gods of the nations, the leaders began to develop an entire vocabulary in speaking of God. There was liberal use of terms such as *memra*, *shekinah*, *power* used when referring to the "bodily parts"

of God. There was an avoidance also of certain expressions, whereby for instance one could not say "God sees," "God hears" but rather, "it was seen before Him," "it was heard before Him." The result was that by the first century C.E., a great chasm existed in the thinking of the people of Israel regarding God; while He is personal, He is in heaven while man is on earth; so that this emphasis on His holiness made Him appear to be far removed from any person.

[11] See Gershom Scholem, "Metatron," *Encyclopedia Judaica* 11:1443–46.

[12] Burton L. Visotzky, trans., *The Midrash on Proverbs*, Yale Judaica Series 27 (New Haven: Yale University Press, 1992), 117–18.

[13] See A. J. Rosenberg, ed., *Proverbs: A New English Translation. Translation of Text, Rashi and Commentary* (New York: Judaica Press, 1988), 188–89.

[14] Robert Girdlestone, *Synonyms of the Old Testament: Their Bearing on Christian Faith and Practice* (London: Longmans, Green, 1871), 36.

[15] Goldberg, "Some Observations Concerning the Attributes of God."

[16] Epstein, *Judaism: A Historical Presentation*, 212.

[17] By no means was this assessment an easy statement, as we will explore further below. No such concept existed in Jewish thought at the end of the Second Temple period, nor does it exist today.

[18] [NIV's translation of the *Shema* matches the phraseology in use by Jewish people today. Cf. NET's "Listen, Israel, the Lord our God, the Lord is one."—Ed.]

Chapter 6

[1] See Augustus Hopkins Strong, *Systematic Theology* (1907; repr., Old Tappan, NJ: Revell, 1954), 251-52.

[2] See William G. Moorehead, "The Moral Glory of Jesus Christ, a Proof of Inspiration," in *The Fundamentals: A Testimony to the Truth*, vol. 2, ed. R. A. Torrey, A. C. Dixon et al. (1917; repr., Grand Rapids: Baker, 1988), 2:61–79.

[3] [In v. 3 NET has "all the families of the earth will bless one another."—Ed.]

[4] In passing we should note that God says that He performed all this, not because Israel was the greatest of all nations, for they were the least of all peoples, but rather because of His promises to the patriarchs and His faithfulness in keeping His covenant of love with those who love Him and keep His commands (Deuteronomy 7:7–9).

[5] [KJV: "inhabiteth eternity"; NET: "rules forever"; NIV: "lives forever."—Ed.]

[6] [NET has "placed ignorance in the human heart"—but the Hebrew is *olam*, the usual word for eternal, eternity. "Ignorance" traces back to a different but similar word. Most commentators interpret as "eternity" or a variation of that.—Ed.]

[7] Strong, *Systematic Theology*, 248.

[8] [Here reference was made to Strong, 272; Strong comments on this point in the last paragraph on that page.—Ed.]

[9] [NET: "the person of integrity will live because of his faithfulness."—Ed.]

[10] See further in G. R. Lewis, "God, Attributes of," in *Evangelical Dictionary of Theology*, 451–59, esp. 454–55.

[11] [NET has "totally reliable" for NIV's "true."—Ed.]

[12] [NET has "faithful God" for NIV's "God of truth."—Ed.]

[13] [See note 12.—Ed.]

[14] [See note 12.—Ed.]

[15] BDB, s.v. "אָמַן."

[16] [See note 12.—Ed.]

[17] Lewis, "God, Attributes of," 497.

[18] Alva McClain, unpublished theological classroom notes.

[19] BDB, s.v. "צדק," and subentries.

[20] G. Abbott-Smith, *A Manual Greek Lexicon of the New Testament*, 3rd ed. (Edinburgh: T. & T. Clark, 1937), 116. [For a more recent lexicon, see Frederick William Danker, ed., *A Greek-English Lexicon of the New Testament and Other Early Christian Literature*, 3rd ed. (Chicago: University of Chicago Press, 2001).—Ed.]

[21] Ibid.

[22] [NIV is used here because it translates the Hebrew as "righteous," where NET generally has "just."—Ed.]

[23] [NIV and NET both translate as "true pasture."—Ed.]

[24] [NET has "faithfulness of Yeshua" or similar expressions for NIV's "faith in Yeshua." The difference reflects how best to render the underlying Greek phrase. Most commentators understand it as does NIV. Both concepts, in different words, occur throughout the New Testament: Yeshua is faithful in obedience to the Father and in other ways; and we also have to have faith in Him.—Ed.]

[25] [See note 24.—Ed.]

[26] BDB, s.v. "אָמַן."

Chapter 7

[1] The Second Commonwealth covered the period from the end of the Babylonian exile until the loss of the Second Temple in 70 C.E. The building of traditional interpretation of the Scriptures began with the religious leaders soon after the death of Ezra, i.e., ca. 400 B.C.E. Traditional rabbinical authorities would insist that the Oral Law was given at Mount Sinai along with the Tanach, the Written Law, a view that is challenged by the best of Jewish historical criticism.

[2] In succession, the religious leaders represented various periods of Jewish history, the *soferim* of 400–200 B.C.E., the *hasidim*, from about 200–128 B.C.E., and then the *parushim* (Pharisees) from 128 B.C.E.–70 C.E. After that period, the leaders were the *tannaim* who guided the nation until 200 C.E. All had their part in the

development of the Targumim, and possibly also, the development of the Sabbath Torah readings as well as the corresponding *haftorah*, or prophetic portion. The Targumic translation of the books of Moses, known as the Targum Onkelos, is a good translation into Aramaic, but the work on the Prophets, Targum Yonatan, oscillates between that of a translation and a paraphrase.

[3] Marcus Jastrow, *A Dictionary of the Targumim, the Talmud Babli and Yerushalmi, and the Midrashic Literature* (New York: G. P. Putnam's Sons, 1903), 2:775.

[4] As cited in *The Targum Onqelos to Exodus*, The Aramaic Bible 7, trans. Bernard Grossfeld (Wilmington, DE: Michael Glazier, 1988), 45. Various font styles and typographical marks used in The Aramaic Bible series have been simplified in these and following quotes.

[5] Kaufmann Kohler, "Memra," *Jewish Encyclopedia* 8:465, citing the Targum Yerushalmi. Scholars have identified several Targumim for the Torah or Pentateuch: 1) Onkelos, 2) Palestinian Targum, and 3) the Yerushalmi, probably an offshoot of the Palestinian Targum.

[6] Grossfeld, *Targum Onqelos to Exodus*, 94.

[7] As cited in *The Targum Onqelos to Deuteronomy*, The Aramaic Bible 9, trans. Bernard Grossfeld (Wilmington, DE: Michael Glazier, 1988), 20.

[8] As cited in Chilton, *Isaiah Targum*, 89.

[9] Kohler, "Memra," 465.

[10] Chilton, *Isaiah Targum*, see Isaiah 45:12, p. 90.

[11] Kohler, "Memra," 465.

[12] Chilton, *Isaiah Targum*, 127.

[13] George Foot Moore, *Judaism in the First Centuries of the Christian Era: The Age of the Tannaim* (1927–30; repr., New York: Schocken Books, 1971), 1: 419.

[14] Ibid.

[15] H. A. Wolfson, *Philo: Foundations of Religious Philosophy in Judaism, Christianity, and Islam* (Cambridge: Harvard University Press, 1948), 1:287.

[16] Onkelos was reputed to be the editor, that is, the one to begin the process of putting the Targum of the five books of Moses into writing, which until then had been carried orally.

[17] Martin McNamara, *Targum and Testament: Aramaic Paraphrases of the Hebrew Bible: A Light on the New Testament* (Grand Rapids: Eerdmans, 1972), 103–4. The author provides a citation from the Neofiti manuscript (Palestinian Targum) describing the work of creation: "The earth was void and empty and darkness was spread over the face of the abyss. *And the Word* [*Memra*] *of the Lord was the light and it shone* . . .; and he called it the first night." "If the Word of the Lord shone at creation," McNamara comments, "this can only be because it was the light. . . . This is precisely what John in his Prologue says of the Logos. 'In the beginning was the Word . . . and the

Word was God. In him was light and the light shines in darkness' (John 1:1–3). And like the targumist, John is speaking of the activity of the Logos at creation. He was then light, and this light still shines in Christ."

[18] Reider suggests the usual later understanding of Jewish people on the Wisdom passage, "Hence, Gregg concludes, it is plain that the writer had no intention of hypostatizing the Logos, but had in mind only the customary Jewish periphrasis for the Lord, *i.e.*, the *memra* of Yahweh, meaning the Divine Being in self-manifestation." Joseph Reider, *The Book of Wisdom: An English Translation with Introduction and Commentary* (n.p.: Dropsie College for Hebrew and Cognate Learning; New York: Harper and Brothers, 1957), 210.

[19] Again, a reference to a council under the recognized leadership of Yohanan ben Zakkai, which met in the village of Yavneh, not far from the Tel Aviv of today, from about 70–90 C.E., for the purpose of restructuring Judaism without the temple worship.

[20] Louis Ginzberg, "Anthropomorphism and Anthropopathism," *Jewish Encyclopedia* 1:623, citing Z. Frankel, *Vorstudien zu der Septuaginta*, 1841, 174–79. By "mainstream" Judaism this writer refers to the traditional Judaism that produced the literature that became the norm for Jewish thought, i.e., the Judaism of the *Tannaim* and their predecessors. [The actual quote in Ginzberg: "Frankel, in his 'Vorstudien,' was the first to deny that any traces of Greek influence can be discovered in the Septuagint; and Freudenthal has fully demonstrated the correctness of this assertion."—Ed.]

[21] See Louis Jacobs, *A Jewish Theology* (New York: Behrman House, 1973), 141–46.

[22] See William Wrede, *The Messianic Secret*, trans. J. C. G. Greig (1901; repr., Greenwood, SC: Attic Press, 1971).

[23] David Flusser, "Two Notes on the Midrash on 2 Sam. vii," in *Israel Exploration Journal* 9 (1959): 107–9.

[24] Ibid., 107.

[25] When comparing all the parallel accounts of this incident, it appears that the girl was at the point of death but had not as yet died when her father went looking for Yeshua. He must have surmised that by the time he actually spoke with the Messiah, she would already have been dead.

[26] [For relevant statements in the Mishnah, see *m. Shevuoth* 4:3, 13 (Danby, 414–15).—Ed.]

[27] *b. Sanhedrin* 38b (Soncino Talmud, *Nezekin* III, 245).

[28] Jean Daniélou, *The Theology of Jewish Christianity*, trans. John A. Baker (London: Darton, Longman & Todd; Philadelphia: Westminster Press, 1964), 149.

[29] Ibid., 164–65. [The Greek font in Daniélou has been rendered in transliteration in these quotes in this note and the preceding one.—Ed.]

[30] Ibid., 166–72.

Chapter 8

[1] [LG used the edition of J. F. Stenning, *The Targum of Isaiah* (London: Oxford University Press, 1949). The Stenning edition was not available to me. In its place, the version used here and in subsequent references to the Isaiah Targum is from Chilton, *Isaiah Targum*.—Ed.]

[2] [Chilton, *Isaiah Targum*, 103–5. Since Chilton adheres to the RSV, that version is used for the biblical text in this chart.—Ed.]

[3] Ibid., note the paraphrase of Isaiah 52:13 and 53:10.

[4] Ibid., note Isaiah 53:5–6, 9–12.

[5] Beginning in the Middle Ages, many Jewish religious leaders applied the idea of the Suffering Servant to Israel even though ancient Jewish interpreters never suggested this concept. For a further discussion on this drastic change and opposition to it, see David Baron, *The Servant of Jehovah: The Sufferings of the Messiah and the Glory That Should Follow; An Exposition of Isaiah Chapter 53* (London: Morgan and Scott, 1922).

[6] The concept of two Messiahs, Messiah ben Yosef and Messiah ben David, will be discussed at the end of this chapter.

[7] Chilton, *Isaiah Targum*, see Isaiah 53:4, 7, 12, pp. 104–5.

[8] Ibid., see Isaiah 53:12, p. 105.

[9] Could this already be a reference to the Messiah ben Yosef? A good part of the Targum of Isaiah already existed by Yeshua's day, though not committed to writing until about 200 C.E. and so by this date there could have been opportunity to make reference to ben Yosef.

[10] [Cited passages are taken from Charlesworth, *The Old Testament Pseudepigrapha*, vol. 1, except *Psalms of Solomon*, which is from vol. 2. Dates of composition are those given in those volumes.—Ed.]

[11] [See Charlesworth, *The Old Testament Pseudepigrapha*, 1:354–61.—Ed.]

[12] Louis Goldberg, "Reader Response: The Dead Sea Scrolls—Again" [editorial], *Moody Student* (February 20, 1992): 6.

[13] *m. Pesahim* 10 (Danby, 150–51).

[14] At that point in the history of the *pesach*, no special plate with three *matzot* was present on the table as it is today at the seder; neither is there any mention of it in the *seder* of Mishnah *Pesahim* or in the Gemara commentary. The question remains: When was this plate of three *matzot* added to the seder? This writer has contacted sources in the United States as well as in Israel, with no response in answer to the question, except from Safrai. Rashi is the first Jewish writer who mentions this plate, which only compounds the mystery.

[15] [Note that some place this writing less than thirty years after. Scholars vary on the issue of dating the gospels.—Ed.]

[16] *m.Yoma* (Danby, 162–72).

[17] *m.Yoma* 6:6 (Danby, 170). The idea was that since this goat carried the sins of the nation, to make sure that it would not wander back into the city.

[18] *m.Yoma* 6:2 (Danby, 169).

[19] Moore, *Judaism*, 1:503, citing *Avot de Rav Natan* 4, 5.

[20] Because of the strong reaction on the part of the rabbis of this period, we infer that the Messianic Jews must have carried on a vital witness, continuing through the 300s. See Bagatti, *Church from the Circumcision*, for a number of examples.

[21] The council also developed a way of ferreting out all apostates from the synagogues, including Messianic Jews. They did this by inserting into the *Shemoneh Esre*, the Eighteen Benedictions, a malediction known as *Birkat HaMinim*: "I thank God I am not a *min*." While the word can include a reference to all apostates, the directive by the council became a way to stop Jewish believers in Yeshua from any fellowship with Jewish people, in the synagogue as well as in any other gathering. See the discussion by Jacob Jocz, *The Jewish People and Jesus Christ: The Relationship Between Church and Synagogue*, 3rd ed. (Grand Rapids: Baker, 1979), "The Minim," 174–90.

[22] *b. Rosh HaShanah* 18a (Soncino Talmud, *Moed*, IV, 71).

[23] Goldin, *Fathers*, ch. 4, 32.

[24] Moore, *Judaism*, 2:370.

[25] Ibid.

[26] *b. Baba Bathra* 123b (Soncino Talmud, *Nezikin* II, 512).

[27] *b. Sukkah* 52a (Soncino Talmud, *Mo'ed* III, see 247).

[28] Moore, *Judaism*, 2: 371.

Chapter 9

[1] V. L. Walter, "Arianism," in *Evangelical Dictionary of Theology*, 74.

[2] [NIV gives the usual rendering; NET has "Extraordinary Strategist" in place of "Wonderful Counsellor."—Ed.]

[3] [The original source of this quote was unavailable to me.—Ed.]

[4] See H. E. Dana and Julius R. Mantey, *A Manual Grammar of the Greek New Testament* (New York: Macmillan, 1957, orig. 1927), 139–40. [". . .without the article *theos* signifies divine essence, while with the article divine personality is chiefly in view." Transliteration has been substituted for Greek font in this quote.—Ed.]

[5] [NET: "I am present at the very beginning and at the very end."—Ed.]

[6] [In place of "her offspring," NIV reads, "he will crush your head, and you will strike his heel."—Ed.]

[7] [NET has "young woman" instead of "virgin." The Hebrew word *almah* essentially

signifies a young woman of marriageable age; by implication she would be a virgin.—Ed.]

[8] The mention of Joseph in Luke 3:24 refers to another person in the line; the name Joseph was quite a common one in first-century Jewish society.

[9] [NIV: "Beyond all question, the mystery of godliness is great."—Ed.

[10] Louis Berkhof, *Systematic Theology*, 4th ed. (1941; repr., Grand Rapids: Eerdmans, 1984), 321.

[11] For elaboration, see Strong, *Systematic Theology*, 701–4.

[12] [NET: "God publicly displayed him at his death as the mercy seat accessible through faith."—Ed.]

[13] For elaboration, see John F. Walvood, *Jesus Christ Our Lord* (Chicago: Moody, 1969), 192–200.

[14] [LG did not expand this section. For studies of the historicity of the resurrection, see, e.g., Frank Morrison, *Who Moved the Stone?* (Grand Rapids: Zondervan, 1987); Lee Strobel, *The Case for Easter: A Journalist Investigates the Evidence for the Resurrection* (Grand Rapids: Zondervan, 2003); Gary R. Habermas and Michael R. Licona, *The Case for the Resurrection of Jesus* (Grand Rapids: Kregel, 2004).—Ed.]

Chapter 10

[1] Not too many writers have provided a definitive work on the Spirit's work in the Old Testament. For that reason, an entire conference of the Evangelical Theological Society was given over to a consideration of "The Holy Spirit—His Presence, Ministry, and Gifts" during November 20–22, 1996 in Jackson, Mississippi. The opening paper at the plenary session ("Empowered by the Spirit of God: The Holy Spirit in the Historiographic Writings of the Old Testament," by Daniel I. Block, then professor at Southern Baptist Theological Seminary, now as of 2008 at Wheaton College), set the tone with the recurring observation, "Why isn't more said of the work of the Spirit in the Old Testament?"

[2] On that verb, see BDB, s.v. "שָׁכֵן, שָׁכַן".

[3] Alan Unterman, "Shekhinah," *Encyclopedia Judaica*, 14:1349–50.

[4] J. B. Payne, "Shekinah," in *Evangelical Dictionary of Theology* (Grand Rapids: Baker, 1984), 1010–11.

[5] Unterman, "Shekhinah," 1350.

[6] BDB, s.v. "I. צָלַח" where the verb suggests "rush," and in a cognate language, "cleave, penetrate."

[7] C. F. Keil and F. Delitzsch, *Commentary on the Old Testament*, vol. 1, *Pentateuch*, "The First Book of Moses," trans. James Martin (repr., Grand Rapids: Eerdmans, 1951), 350.

[8] Gleason L. Archer Jr., "Daniel," in *The Expositor's Bible Commentary*, ed. Frank E.

Gabelein (Grand Rapids: Zondervan, 1981), 7: 60–61.

[9] Charles Caldwell Ryrie, *The Holy Spirit* (Chicago: Moody, 1965), 42.

[10] BDB, s.v. "רוּחַ." The translation depends on the context. Sometimes, as in BDB's examples, if the word *spirit* is understood, it can also be rendered as *temper*, *disposition*, *courage*, *anger*, *prophetic spirit*, etc.

[11] [This quote is said to come from page 21 of a work by W. T. Connor with no title cited. Possibly his *Christian Doctrine* (Nashville: Broadman, 1949).—Ed.]

[12] G. W. H. Lampe, "Holy Spirit," in *The Interpreter's Dictionary of the Bible*, ed. George Arthur Buttrick (New York; Nashville: Abingdon, 1962), 2: 626–27.

[13] [The Hebrew word for "spirit" (*ruach*) also can mean "wind"; so the NET, "a wind came into me." Here we give the NIV, which follows LG's understanding. In the NET notes, it is pointed out that there are many instances where the word clearly refers to God's Spirit: in the phrase "the Spirit of the LORD," and so on.—Ed.]

[14] W. O. E. Oesterley and Theodore H. Robinson, *An Introduction to the Books of the Old Testament* (London: Society for Promoting Christian Knowledge, 1937), 397.

[15] R. B. Y. Scott, *The Relevance of the Prophets* (New York: Macmillan, 1953), 46.

[16] See Sigmund Mowinckel, "'The Spirit' and the 'Word' in the Pre-exilic Reforming Prophets," *Journal of Biblical Literature* 53:3 (October 1934): 199–227.

[17] Hobart E. Freeman, *An Introduction to the Old Testament Prophets* (Chicago: Moody, 1968), 58.

[18] The Haftorah passage for this particular *Shabbat* must have been Isaiah 61:1–9 in Yeshua's day, but this passage does not appear in the current Haftorah readings as a part of the *Shabbat* Pareshah. Instead, the passage picks up with Isaiah 61:10, no doubt one of those actions taken to minimize the claims of the Messiah Yeshua.

[19] [NET: "until new life is poured out on us." The Hebrew is *ruach*.—Ed.]

[20] Goldberg, *Leviticus*, 26–33.

[21] J. A. Thompson, *Deuteronomy: An Introduction and Commentary*, Tyndale Old Testament Commentaries (London: Inter-Varsity Press, 1974), 149.

[22] C. F. Keil and F. Delitzsch, *Commentary on the Old Testament*, vol. 8, *Jeremiah, Lamentations* [Part One], trans. David Patrick (repr., Grand Rapids: Eerdmans, 1950), 104.

[23] A. B. Davidson, *The Theology of the Old Testament* (1904; repr., Edinburgh: T. & T. Clark, 1952), 216.

[24] Ibid.

[25] See Walter Kaiser, "The Holy Spirit in the Old Testament," in *Pentecostalism in Context: Essays in Honor of William C. Menzies*, ed. Wonsuk Ma and Robert P. Menzies, *Journal of Pentecostal Theology*, Supplement Series, vol. 11 (Sheffield: Sheffield Academic Press, 1997), 38.

[26] George T. Montague, *The Holy Spirit: Growth of a Biblical Tradition* (New York: Paulist Press, 1976), 46–47.

[27] Kaiser, "Holy Spirit in the Old Testament," 45–46.

Chapter 11

[1] [NET: "your life-giving breath" in place of NIV "your Spirit."—Ed.]

[2] [NET: "a mere word from his mouth"; NIV is more literal.—Ed."

[3] [The pronouns in these passages are also plural. It is not clear what LG had in mind in referring them to the individual believer.—Ed.]

Chapter 12

[1] *m. Avot* 3:15 (Danby, 452).

[2] Kohler, *Jewish Theology*, 206.

[3] Morris Joseph, *Judaism as Creed and Life*, 6th ed. (New York: Bloch Publishing, 1929), 54.

[4] Will Herberg, *Judaism and Modern Man: An Interpretation of Jewish Religion* (New York: Harper Torchbooks, 1951), 72.

[5] *Wisdom of Solomon* 2:23: "for God created man for incorruption, and made him in the image of his own eternity," in the edition of Bruce M. Metzger, ed., *The Oxford Annotated Apocrypha* (New York: Oxford University Press, 1977), 104.

[6] Israel Adler, "Man, the Nature of, in the Bible," in *Encyclopedia Judaica* 11:844.

[7] [Hebrews 2:7, quoting this verse, has "angels."—Ed.]

[8] Robert Gordis, "A Basis for Morals: Ethics in a Technological Age," *Judaism* 25:1 (winter 1976): 20–43; this quote is on p. 33.

[9] *m. Avot* 3:16 (Danby, 452).

[10] Adler, "Man, the Nature of," 844.

[11] *b. Berakhot* 33b (Soncino Talmud, *Zera'im*, 210).

[12] *Genesis Rabbah* 5:1 (Soncino Midrash Rabbah I, 34–35): "Said the Holy One, blessed be He: 'If these which have neither mouth or speech praise Me, how much more [will I be praised] when man is created!'"

[13] Visotzky, *Midrash on Proverbs*, ch. 6, 40. The term *ḥaber* refers to a fellow sage or rabbi.

[14] *m. Avot* 4:12 (Danby, 454).

[15] [Compare NIV: "The lamp of the LORD searches the spirit of a man."—Ed.]

[16] [Here LG may be thinking of the fact that this verse uses the two Hebrew words *ruach* and *nefesh*, often translated respectively as "spirit" and "soul."—Ed.]

[17] Alva McClain, unpublished theological classroom notes.

Chapter 13

[1] *b. Berachot* 60b (Soncino Talmud, *Zera'im*, 378).

[2] Trude Weiss-Rosmarin, *Judaism and Christianity: The Differences* (1943; repr., New

York: Jonathan David, 1972), 48.

[3] Michael Friedländer, *The Jewish Religion* (London: Kegan Paul, Trench, Trübner, 1891), 407.

[4] Schechter, *Some Aspects*, 267.

[5] Joseph, *Judaism as Creed and Life*, 117.

[6] Ibid., 140.

[7] Kohler, *Jewish Theology*, 238.

[8] Leo Baeck, *The Essence of Judaism*, trans. Irving Howe (1948; repr., New York: Schocken Books, 1970), 133. [The quote in LG's manuscript reads, "Every act of the evildoer is a sin against God and the divine, against the true freedom in the life of men"—perhaps from a different translation?—Ed.]

[9] Schechter, *Some Aspects*, 243. [The actual quote is, "1 Chron. 28 9 and 29 18 . . . are generally understood to mean simply imagination, or desire, whatever the nature of this desire may be, good or evil."—Ed.]

[10] See ibid., 242–43.

[11] Joseph Shulam with Hilary Le Cornu, *A Commentary on the Jewish Roots of Romans* (Baltimore: Messianic Jewish Publishers, 1997), and see the references in the following notes.

[12] Ibid., 239, on v. 4.

[13] Ibid., 241, on v. 6.

[14] Ibid., 245, on v. 9.

[15] *Wisdom of Solomon* 2:24: "but through the devil's envy death entered the world, and those who belong to his party experience it," in Metzger, *Oxford Annotated Apocrypha*, 104.

[16] [See for instance, *b. Gittin* 56a; *b. Ta'anit* 19b–20a.—Ed.]

[17] [Here reference was made to refer to Strong, *Systematic Theology*, 577–82 and 650–52.—Ed.]

[18] Archibald Alexander Hodge, *Outlines of Theology* (London: Thomas Nelson, 1879), 319, citing "Prof. Haven of Chicago."

Chapter 14

[1] The NET and NASB reflect the literal Hebrew phrase used.

[2] [This is a quote from Psalm 8:5 (verse 6 in MT). LG notes that in the original psalm, the wording is "a little lower than God" (although NIV has "heavenly beings"). Hebrews applies the original psalm not only to mankind but particularly to Yeshua, so that in the incarnation, Yeshua was both lower than God and lower than the angels. For more details, consult the commentaries on Hebrews.—Ed.]

[3] [LG differs from the usual interpretation of the passage, which understands the procession to be a procession of slaves slated to die in the arena, hence the idea of

humiliation; note the phrase "like men condemned to die."—Ed.]

[4] Edward J. Young, *The Book of Isaiah: A Commentary* (1965; repr., Grand Rapids: Eerdmans, 1996), 1:442. For more details on the evidence for this position, see Young's footnotes.

[5] Ibid., 441.

[6] [Compare Yohanan 13:27: "As soon as Yehudah took the bread, Satan entered into him."—Ed.]

[7] [This verse is often taken as evidence for anti-Semtism in the NT. LG would surely have wanted to argue against that viewpoint.—Ed.]

[8] 2 Thessalonians 2:3 in NKJV. NIV: "man of lawlessness."

Chapter 15

[1] *The NIV Study Bible* (Grand Rapids: Zondervan, 1985), note for 1 Timothy 3:1, p. 1838.

[2] [The present discussion merges the ideas of "gift" and "office." For example, *pastor* is, strictly speaking, a gift and not an office (Ephesians 4:11), and is to be distinguished from *elder*. I wish to thank the late Harold Hoehner for pointing this out.—Ed.]

[3] Wayne Grudem, "Why Christians Can Still Prophesy," *Christianity Today* (September 16, 1988): 29–35. He expanded on this idea in *The Gift of Prophecy in the New Covenant and Today*, rev. ed. (Wheaton: Crossway, 2000).

[4] [Mark 16 is not generally considered by modern scholars to be part of the original text, but it is included in printed Bibles, usually with a footnote, for otherwise the gospel appears to lack an ending.—Ed.]

[5] George Barna, *User Friendly Churches: What Christians Need to Know About the Churches People Love to Go To* (Ventura, CA: Regal Books, 1991), 50–51.

[6] [Here LG had a note: "This author ran out of time to comment more succinctly on the outline. I only provide it for referencing as to what I shall expand on at a later time. The questions raised regarding Messianic Congregations were largely covered in what I have discussed above."—Ed.]

BIBLIOGRAPHY

Abbott-Smith, G. *A Manual Greek Lexicon of the New Testament*. 3rd ed. Edinburgh: T. & T. Clark, 1937.

Adler, Israel. "Man, the Nature of, in the Bible." *Encyclopedia Judaica* 11:844.

Archer, Gleason. "Daniel." *The Expositor's Bible Commentary*, edited by Frank E. Gabelein, 7:3–157. Grand Rapids: Zondervan, 1985.

Baeck, Leo. *The Essence of Judaism*. Translated by Irving Howe. 1948. Reprint. New York: Schocken Books, 1970.

Bagatti, Bellarmino. *The Church from the Circumcision: History and Archaeology of the Judaeo-Christians*. Jerusalem: Franciscan Printing Press, 1971.

Barna, George. *User Friendly Churches: What Christians Need to Know About the Churches People Love to Go To*. Ventura, CA: Regal Books, 1991.

Baron, David. *The Servant of Jehovah: The Sufferings of the Messiah and the Glory That Should Follow; An Exposition of Isaiah Chapter 53*. London: Morgan and Scott, 1922.

BDB = Brown, Francis, S. R. Driver, and Charles A. Briggs. *A Hebrew and English Lexicon of the Old Testament*. Oxford: Clarendon Press, 1907.

Ben-Sasson, H. H. "The Middle Ages." In *A History of the Jewish People*, ed. H. H. Ben-Sasson. Cambridge: Harvard University Press, 1976.

Berkhof, Louis. *Systematic Theology*. 4th ed. 1941. Reprint. Grand Rapids: Eerdmans, 1984.

Bernfeld, Bernjamin. "Hermeneutics." *Universal Jewish Encyclopedia* 5:324.

Calvin, John. *Institutes of the Christian Religion*. Translated by Henry Beveridge. Grand Rapids: Eerdmans, 1957.

Chafer, Lewis Sperry. *Systematic Theology*. Dallas: Dallas Seminary Press, 1948.

Charlesworth, James, ed. *The Old Testament Pseudepigrapha*. 2 vol. Garden City, NY: Doubleday, 1983–1985.

Chilton, Bruce D., trans. *The Isaiah Targum: Introduction, Translation, Apparatus and Notes*. The Aramaic Bible. Vol. 11. Wilmington, DE: Michael Glazier, 1987.

Cohen, Abraham. *Everyman's Talmud: The Major Teachings of the Rabbinic Sages*. New York: Schocken Books, 1949.

Cohen, Harry A. *A Basic Jewish Encyclopedia: Jewish Teachings and Practices Listed and Interpreted in Order of Their Importance Today*. Hartford, CT: Hartmore House, 1965.

Cranfield, C. E. B. *A Critical and Exegetical Commentary on the Epistle to the Romans*. 2 vol. International Critical Commentary. Edinburgh: T & T Clark, 1975–79.

Dana, H. E., and Julius R. Mantey. *A Manual Grammar of the Greek New Testament*. New York: Macmillan, 1927.

Danby, Herbert, trans. *The Mishnah: Translated from the Hebrew, with Introduction and Brief Explanatory Notes*. London: Oxford University Press, 1933.

Daniélou, Jean. *The Theology of Jewish Christianity*. Translated by John A. Baker. London: Darton, Longman & Todd; Philadelphia: Westminster Press, 1964.

Davidson, A. B. *The Theology of the Old Testament*. 1904. Reprint. Edinburgh: T. & T. Clark, 1952.

Elert, Werner. *Law and Gospel*. Translated by Edward H. Schroeder. Philadelphia: Fortress Press, 1967.

Epstein, Isidore. *The Faith of Judaism: An Interpretation for Our Times*. New York: Soncino Press, 1954.

———. *Judaism: A Historical Presentation*. 3rd ed. Baltimore: Penguin Books, 1964.

Esser, Hans-Helmut. "Law." In *New International Dictionary of New Testament Theology*. 2:436–56. Grand Rapids: Zondervan, 1976.

Fischer, John, and David Bronstein. *Siddur for Messianic Jews*. Palm Harbor, FL: Menorah Press, 1988.

Fishman, Isidore. *Introduction to Judaism*. Rev. ed. London: Jewish Chronicle Publications, 1973.

Flusser, David. "Two Notes on the Midrash on 2 Sam. vii." *Israel Exploration Journal* 9 (1959):107–9.

Freeman, Hobart. *Introduction to the Old Testament Prophets*. Chicago: Moody, 1968.

Friedländer, Michael. *The Jewish Religion*. London: Kegan Paul, Trench, Trübner, 1891.

Ginzberg, Louis. "Anthropomorphism and Anthropopathism." *Jewish Encyclopedia* 1:621–625.

Girdlestone, Robert. *Synonyms of the Old Testament: Their Bearing on Christian Faith and Practice*. London: Longmans, Green, 1871.

Goldberg, Louis. *Deuteronomy: Bible Study Commentary*. Grand Rapids: Lamplighter Books, 1986.

———. *Leviticus: A Study Guide Commentary*. Grand Rapids: Zondervan, 1980.

———. *Our Jewish Friends*. Chicago: Moody, 1977.

———. "Reader Response: The Dead Sea Scrolls—Again" [editorial], *Moody Student* (February 20, 1992): 6.

———. "Some Observations Concerning the Attributes of God in Jewish Philosophy." M.A. thesis, Roosevelt University, 1975.

———. *Turbulence over the Middle East: Israel and the Nations in Confrontation and the Coming Kingdom of Peace on Earth*. Neptune, NJ: Loizeaux Brothers, 1982.

Goldin, Judah, trans. *The Fathers According to Rabbi Nathan*. Yale Judaica Series 10. New Haven: Yale University Press, 1955.

Gordis, Robert. "A Basis for Morals: Ethics in a Technological Age." *Judaism* 25:1 (winter 1976):20–43.

Grossfeld, Bernard, trans. *The Targum Onqelos to Deuteronomy*. The Aramaic Bible. Vol. 9. Wilmington, DE: Michael Glazier, 1988.

———. *The Targum Onqelos to Exodus*. The Aramaic Bible. Vol. 7. Wilmington, DE: Michael Glazier, 1988.

Grudem, Wayne. *The Gift of Prophecy in the New Testament Today*. Rev. ed. Wheaton: Crossway, 2000.

———. *Systematic Theology: An Introduction to Biblical Doctrine*. Leicester: Inter-Varsity Press; Grand Rapids: Zondervan, 1994.

———. "Why Christians Can Still Prophesy." *Christianity Today* (September 16, 1988):29–35.

Hammer, Reuven, trans. *Sifre: A Tannaitic Commentary on the Book of Deuteronomy.* Yale Judaica Series 24. New Haven: Yale University Press, 1986.

Herberg, Will. *Judaism and Modern Man: An Interpretation of Jewish Religion*. New York: Harper Torchbooks, 1951.

Hirsch, Samson Raphael. *Judaism Eternal: Selected Essays from the Writings of Rabbi Samson Raphael Hirsch*. Translated by I. Grunfeld. 2 vol. London: Soncino, 1956.

Hodge, Archibald Alexander. *Outlines of Theology*. London: Thomas Nelson, 1879.

Hughes, P. E. "Grace." In *Evangelical Dictionary of Theology,* edited by Walter A. Elwell, 479–82. Grand Rapids: Baker, 1984.

Jacobs, Louis. "Hermeneutics." *Encyclopedia Judaica* 8:567.

———. *A Jewish Theology*. New York: Behrman House, 1973.

Jastrow, Marcus. *A Dictionary of the Targumim, the Talmud Babli and Yerushalmi, and the Midrashic Literature*. 2 vols. New York: G. P. Putnam's Sons, 1903.

Jocz, Jacob. *The Jewish People and Jesus Christ: The Relationship Between Church and Synagogue*. 3rd ed. Grand Rapids: Baker, 1979.

Joseph, Morris. *Judaism as Creed and Life*. 6th ed. New York: Bloch Publishing, 1929.

Kaiser, Walter. "The Holy Spirit in the Old Testament." In *Pentecostalism in Context: Essays in Honor of William W. Menzies*, edited by Wonsuk Ma and Robert P. Menzies. Sheffield: *Journal of Pentecostal Theology*, Supplement Series 11 (December 1997):38–47.

Keil, C. F., and F. Delitzsch. *Biblical Commentary on the Old Testament*. Translated by James Martin. 10 vols. Reprint. Grand Rapids: Eerdmans, 1951.

Kohler, Kaufmann. "Inspiration." *Jewish Encyclopedia*, 6:608.

———. *Jewish Theology Systematically and Historically Considered*. New York: Macmillan, 1918.

———. "Memra." *Jewish Encyclopedia*, 8:465.

———. "Revelation." *Jewish Encyclopedia*, 10:396.

Lachs, Samuel T. *A Rabbinic Commentary on the New Testament: The Gospels of Matthew, Mark and Luke.* Hoboken, NJ: KTAV; New York: Anti-Defamation League of B'nai B'rith, 1987.

Lampe, G. W. H. "Holy Spirit." In *The Interpreter's Dictionary of the Bible*, edited by George Arthur Buttrick. 2:626–39. Nashville: Abingdon, 1962.

Lewis, G. R. "God, Attributes of." In *Evangelical Dictionary of Theology*, edited by Walter L. Elwell, 451–59. Grand Rapids: Baker, 1984.

Lipinski, Edward. "Revelation." *Encyclopedia Judaica* 14:118.

Longnecker, Richard N. "Acts." In *The Expositor's Bible Commentary,* edited by Frank E. Gabelein. 9:207–573. Grand Rapids: Zondervan, 1981.

Luz, Ulrich. *Matthew 1–7, A Commentary*. Translated by Wilhelm C. Linss. Minneapolis: Augsburg Press, 1989.

Maimonides, Moses. *The Guide for the Perplexed*. Translated by Shlomo Pines. Chicago: University of Chicago Press, 1963.

McClain, Alva. Unpublished class notes on biblical theology. N.p., n.d.

McNamara, Martin. *Targum and Testament: Aramaic Paraphrases of the Hebrew Bible: A Light on the New Testament*. Grand Rapids: Eerdmans, 1972.

Mendelssohn, Moses. *Jerusalem: A Treatise on Ecclesiastical Authority and Judaism*. Translated by M. Samuel. London: Longman, Orme Brown and Longmans, 1838.

Metzger, Bruce M., ed. *The Oxford Annotated Apocrypha*. New York: Oxford University Press, 1977.

Montague, George T. *The Holy Spirit: Growth of a Biblical Tradition*. New York: Paulist Press, 1976.

Montefiore, C. G. *Rabbinic Literature and Gospel Teachings*. 1930. Reprint. New York: KTAV, 1970.

Moore, G. F. *Judaism in the First Centuries of the Christian Era: The Age of the Tannaim*. 2 vol. 1927–30. Reprint. New York: Schocken Books, 1971.

Moorehead, William G. "The Moral Glory of Jesus Christ, a Proof of Inspiration." In *The Fundamentals: A Testimony to the Truth*, edited by R. A. Torrey, A. C. Dixon et al. 2: 61–79. 1917. Reprint. Grand Rapids: Baker, 1988.

Morgan, G. Campbell. *The Gospel According to Matthew*. Westwood, NJ: Revell, 1929.

Mowinckel, Sigmund. "'The Spirit' and the 'Word' in the Pre-exilic Reforming Prophets." *Journal of Biblical Literature* 53:3 (October 1934):199–227.

Neusner, Jacob. *A Life of Rabban Yohanan ben Zakkai, Ca. 1–80* C.E. Leiden: E. J. Brill, 1962.

Newell, William Reed. *Hebrews, Verse by Verse*. Chicago: Moody, 1947.

The NIV Study Bible. Grand Rapids: Zondervan, 1985.

Oesterley, W. O. E., and Theodore H. Robinson. *An Introduction to the Books of the Old Testament*. London: S.P.C.K., 1937.

Payne, J. B. "Shekinah." In *Evangelical Dictionary of Theology*, edited by Walter A. Elwell, 1010–11. Grand Rapids: Baker, 1984.

Rabello, Alfredo Mordechai. "Theodosius II." *Encyclopedia Judaica* 15:1101–2.

Reider, Joseph. *The Book of Wisdom: An English Translation with Introduction and Commentary*. N.p.: Dropsie College for Hebrew and Cognate Learning; New York: Harper and Brothers, 1957.

Rosenbaum, M., and A. M. Silbermann, trans. *Pentateuch with Targum Onkelos, Haphtaroth, and Rashi's Commentary*. London: Shapiro, Vallentine, 1930.

Rosenberg, A. J., ed. *Proverbs: A New English Translation. Translation of Text, Rashi and Commentary*. New York: Judaica Press, 1988.

Ross, Jacob Joshua. "Revelation, in Talmudic Literature." *Encyclopedia Judaica* 14:119–22.

Ryrie, Charles Caldwell. *The Holy Spirit*. Chicago: Moody, 1965.

Schaff, Philip. *History of the Christian Church*. 8 vols. 1884–91. Reprint. Grand Rapids: Eerdmans, 1955–58.

Schechter, Solomon. *Some Aspects of Rabbinic Theology*. New York: Macmillan, 1923.

Schippers, R. "Fullness." In *New International Dictionary of New Testament Theology*. 1:735–41. Grand Rapids: Zondervan, 1975.

Scholem, Gershom. "Metatron." *Encyclopedia Judaica* 11:1443–6.

Scott, R. B. Y. *The Relevance of the Prophets*. New York: Macmillan, 1953.

Shulam, Joseph with Hilary Le Cornu. *A Commentary on the Jewish Roots of Romans*. Baltimore: Messianic Jewish Publishers, 1997.

Soncino Midrash Rabbah = *Midrash Rabbah*. Edited by H. Freedman and Maurice Simon. London: Soncino Press, 1983.

Soncino Talmud = *The Babylonian Talmud*. Edited by I. Epstein. London: Soncino Press, 1935–48.

Stenning, J. F. *The Targum of Isaiah*. London: Oxford University Press, 1949.

Stern, David H., trans. *Jewish New Testament*. Jerusalem; Clarksville, MD: Jewish New Testament Publications, 1989.

———. *Messianic Jewish Manifesto*. Clarksville, MD: Jewish New Testament Publications, 1991.

Strong, Augustus Hopkins. *Systematic Theology*. 1907. Reprint. Old Tappan, NJ: Revell, 1954.

Thompson, J. A. *Deuteronomy: An Introduction and Commentary*. Tyndale Old Testament Commentaries. London: Inter-Varsity Press, 1974.

Unterman, Alan. "Shekhinah" [first part]. *Encyclopedia Judaica* 14:1349–52.

Visotzky, Burton L., trans. *The Midrash on Proverbs*. Yale Judaica Series 27. New Haven: Yale University Press, 1992.

Walter, V. L. "Arianism." In *Evangelical Dictionary of Theology*, edited by Walter A. Elwell, 74–75. Grand Rapids: Baker, 1984.

Walvoord, John F. *Jesus Christ Our Lord*. Chicago: Moody, 1969.

Weingreen, Jacob. *A Practical Grammar for Classical Hebrew*. Oxford: Clarendon Press, 1948.

Weiss-Rosmarin, Trude. *Judaism and Christianity: The Differences*. 1943. Reprint. New York: Jonathan David, 1972.

Wolfson, H. A. *Philo: Foundations of Religious Philosophy in Judaism, Christianity, and Islam*. 2 vol. Cambridge: Harvard University Press, 1948.

Wrede, William. *The Messianic Secret*. Translated by J. C. G. Greig. 1901. Reprint. Greenwood, SC: Attic Press, 1971.

Young, Edward J. *The Book of Isaiah: A Commentary*. 3 vol. 1965. Reprint. Grand Rapids: Eerdmans, 1996.

———. "Celsus and the Old Testament." *Westminster Theological Journal* 6:2 (May 1944):166–97.

———. *The Prophecy of Daniel: A Commentary*. Grand Rapids: Eerdmans, 1949.

INDEX

Bold text indicates the main treatment of a topic.